English Constitutional Documents

English Constitutional Documents

1307–1485

Edited by

ELEANOR C. LODGE

C.B.E., M.A., D.Litt., Litt.D.

*Honorary Fellow, and sometime Principal of Westfield
College, University of London; Honorary Fellow of
Lady Margaret Hall, Oxford*

and

GLADYS A. THORNTON

B.A., Ph.D.

*Lecturer in History at Westfield College,
University of London*

CAMBRIDGE

AT THE UNIVERSITY PRESS

1935

CAMBRIDGE
UNIVERSITY PRESS

University Printing House, Cambridge CB2 8BS, United Kingdom

Cambridge University Press is part of the University of Cambridge.

It furthers the University's mission by disseminating knowledge in the pursuit of
education, learning and research at the highest international levels of excellence.

www.cambridge.org
Information on this title: www.cambridge.org/9781107536746

© Cambridge University Press 1935

First published 1935
First paperback edition 2015

A catalogue record for this publication is available from the British Library

ISBN 978-1-107-53674-6 Paperback

PREFACE

Bishop Stubbs published his first edition of the *Select Charters* in 1870, and though it has since that time been revised and enlarged by Professor H. W. C. Davis in 1913, the original plan of the work has not been changed. The Bishop was content to conclude his book with the reign of Edward I because as he says in the Introduction "the machinery is now completed, the people are at full growth. The system is raw and untrained and awkward, but it is complete". Since he wrote these words much has been done by scholars in the constitutional field, especially on the history of parliament and council, and the reign of Edward I seems perhaps less of a landmark than it once did; whilst the study of administrative history, little understood in the past, has now come to be regarded as of paramount importance. Teachers of English History of the fourteenth and fifteenth centuries have long felt the need of some book in which their pupils could find original documents for the period between the *Select Charters* and J. R. Tanner's *Tudor Constitutional Documents*; for though many such documents are actually in print, they are either in large collections not always accessible, or scattered in the footnotes of volumes which few undergraduates are able to possess. It is hoped, therefore, that this book may meet a real need, and enable students to make themselves familiar with some of the chief authorities of this period, as well as to read a number of records hitherto unpublished. Each section is headed by a brief introduction to explain the main points which are illustrated in the documents, and it is hoped that the short bibliographies may indicate lines of further study. The documents themselves, however, have been left in chronological order rather than divided according to subjects within each section, in order to give readers the opportunity of sorting their own illustrations.

Our thanks are due to the following for their kind permission to print copyright material. To the Controller of His Majesty's Stationery Office, for extracts from *Statutes of the Realm*; *Rotuli Parliamentorum*; *Parliamentary Writs*; *Proceedings and Ordinances of the Privy Council*, ed. N. H. Nicolas; *Abbreviatio Placitorum*; *Proceedings in Chancery in the Reign of Queen Elizabeth*; *Rotulorum Originalium in Curia Scaccarii Abbreviatio*; *The Red Book of the Exchequer*, ed. H. Hall; *Ancient Kalendars and Inventories of the . . . Exchequer*; *Report on the Public Records*, 1800; *Chronicles of the Reigns of Edward I and II*, vol. II, ed. W. Stubbs; *Adae Murimuth continuatio chronicarum*, ed. E. M. Thompson; *Johannis de Trokelowe . . . Chronica et Annales*, ed. H. T. Riley; *Chronicon Angliae*, ed. E. M. Thompson; *Henrici Knighton . . . Chronicon*, ed. J. R. Lumby; *Wars of the English in France during the Reign of Henry VI*, ed. J. Stevenson; *The Black Book of the Admiralty*, ed. T. Twiss; *Munimenta Gildhallae Londoniensis, Liber Albus*, ed. H. T. Riley. To the Council of the Selden Society, for extracts from *Select Passages from Bracton and Azo*, ed. F. W. Maitland; *Select Cases from the Coroners' Rolls*, ed. C. Gross; *Select Cases in Chancery*, ed. W. P. Baildon; *Select Pleas of the Forest*, ed. G. J. Turner; *The Eyre of Kent*, ed. F. W. Maitland, L. W. V. Harcourt and W. C. Bolland; *Select Cases before the King's Council*, ed. I. S. Leadam and J. F. Baldwin. To the Council of the Canterbury and York Society, for an extract from *Registrum Ade de Orleton*, ed. A. T. Bannister. To Messrs C. G. Crump and C. Johnson, and the editor and publishers of the *English Historical Review*, for an extract from vol. XXVII (1912) of the review. To the Council of the Royal Historical Society, for extracts from Warkworth's *Chronicle*, ed. J. O. Halliwell; and *The Stonor Letters and Papers*, ed. C. J. Kingsford. To the Society of Antiquaries of London, for extracts from *Ordinances and regulations of the King's Household*, 1787–90. To the Surtees Society, for an extract from *Testamenta Eboracensia*, Part I. To the Corporation of Bristol, for extracts from *The Little Red Book of Bristol*, ed. F. B. Bickley. To the Bristol Record Society, for extracts from *Bristol Charters*, ed. N. D. Harding. To the

Corporation of Leicester and the Syndics of the Cambridge University Press, for extracts from *Records of the Borough of Leicester*, ed. M. Bateson. To the Corporation of Norwich, for extracts from *Records of the City of Norwich*, ed. W. Hudson and J. C. Tingey. To the Oxford Historical Society, for an extract from *Munimenta Civitatis Oxonie*, ed. H. E. Salter. To the Corporation of Reading, for extracts from *The Diary of the Corporation of Reading*, ed. J. M. Guilding. To the Southampton Record Society, for extracts from *The Charters of the Borough of Southampton*, ed. H. W. Gidden, *The Black Book of Southampton*, ed. A. B. Wallis Chapman, and *The Oak Book of Southampton*, ed. P. Studer. To the Manchester University Press, for an extract from *The Anonimalle Chronicle*, ed. V. H. Galbraith. To the Clarendon Press, for extracts from Fortescue's *Governance of England*, ed. C. Plummer; and for an extract from *Royal Letters addressed to...Oxford*, ed. O. Ogle. Finally to the Corporation of London, for permission to print extracts from the Letter Books at the Records Office, Guildhall.

We wish to thank several friends who have advised us on various points. Above all we are grateful to Mr Gaillard Lapsley, of Trinity College, Cambridge, for the interest which he has taken in our project, and for the valuable criticism and help which he has given us.

E. C. L.
G. A. T.

January 1935

CONTENTS

PART II

THE CHURCH

PART III

LOCAL GOVERNMENT

CONTENTS

LIST OF DOCUMENTS

Part I. CENTRAL GOVERNMENT

Chapter I. THE CROWN

CHAPTER III. THE HOUSEHOLD: WARDROBE
AND CHAMBER

CHAPTER IV. PARLIAMENT

CHAPTER V. THE CHANCERY

CHAPTER VI. THE SEALS

CHAPTER VII. THE EXCHEQUER

CHAPTER VIII. JUSTICE

(1) THE COURTS OF COMMON LAW

(2) THE EYRE AND ITINERANT JUSTICES

(3) THE PREROGATIVE COURTS

(a) *The marshalsea*

(b) *Court of the constable and marshal*

Part II. THE CHURCH

Part III. LOCAL GOVERNMENT

Chapter I. THE JUSTICES OF THE PEACE

CHAPTER VII. THE TOWNS

Bristol

Leicester

London

ABBREVIATIONS

A.P.C. *Proceedings and ordinances of the privy council*, ed. Nicolas. London, 1834–7.

E.H.R. *English Historical Review.*

Foedera. Rymer, T., *Foedera, conventiones, litterae, etc.* London, 1706.

Holdsworth, *History of English law.* Holdsworth, W. S., *A history of English law*, 3rd edition. London, 1922.

P.R.O. Public Record Office.

Rot. Parl. Rotuli Parliamentorum. London, 1783.

S.R. Statutes of the realm. London, 1810–28.

S.S. Selden Society.

Stubbs, *C.H.* Stubbs, W., *The constitutional history of England*, Library edition. Oxford, 1880.

Stubbs, *S.C.* Stubbs, W., *Select charters*, 9th edition revised, by H. W. C. Davis. Oxford, 1913.

Tout, *Chapters.* Tout, T. F., *Chapters in the administrative history of medieval England.* Manchester, 1920–30.

Tout, *Edward II.* Tout, T. F., *The place of the reign of Edward II in English history.* Manchester, 1914.

Trans. R.H.S. Transactions of the Royal Historical Society.

Except for the extension of abbreviations, the exact spelling and punctuation of the documents have been retained as in the printed text and MS. source.

PART I

CENTRAL GOVERNMENT

CHAPTER I

THE CROWN

INTRODUCTION

In the history of the crown and the royal prerogative the later middle ages are of great interest and significance. The period saw the deposition of two kings who were in the rightful line of succession; of the three dynasties inaugurated after Richard II's downfall the Lancastrian had no direct hereditary claim, while the short-lived legitimist Yorkist rule was succeeded by the Tudor *régime*, and, as Fuller declared, Henry VII's claim by descent "was but the back door to the crown".

When we recall the history of kingship before 1307 two developments are noticeable. In the first place the crown had greatly increased its powers during the medieval period, for to the personal rights of the Anglo-Saxon monarchy had been added the tenurial privileges of a feudal king, and in consequence of the reforms of Henry II the notion of the crown as fountain of justice had been developed and exemplified. The crown had indeed the inestimable advantage of a long-established tradition and a vast reserve of hitherto undefined powers. The royal resources were at first considerable, for in addition to the demesne lands and judicial dues the king had, for example, the right of prisage, which was specially important with the increase of trade, of preemption, of purveyance, which included the custom of demanding men and supplies for war (6), and of patronage and appointments; some of the royal powers came to be delegated, as to the chancellor or justices, but in theory final decision lay with the king.

On the other hand, at no time after the Norman Conquest was the crown entirely free from some moral and practical limitation. In the feudal state the relation between king and tenants in chief was admittedly contractual; they were bound by feudal law to give him advice and he was expected to seek it, though no given vassal had a right to be summoned to his court. There was in fact a generally recognised theory that the king was subject to the law. Magna Carta, essentially a feudal document, exemplifies the king's subjection to the law expressed in the coronation oath which is itself older than feudalism. In Bracton's view the king could not go beyond the law, because of the very nature of his office, and if he had no peer it was only in his position as representative of God and as administrator of the law. In the later thirteenth century some held a more extreme view, that the king had associates, *comites*, in government, and that his *curia* was superior to him. This theory can be traced in the Song of Lewes; it is to be found in an early addition to Bracton;[1] it is given in the so-called "Fleta"; and it is expressed in syllogistic form by a justice, possibly John of Longueville, in a commentary on the same addition to Bracton(2).[2] Yet this more extreme theory was not widely accepted, and in actual practice the judges were usually unwilling to give an opinion against the crown. In a famous case in 1292(1) when the magnates were protesting that it was not their custom to take oath, the judges declared that the king's prerogative set him above the law, *pro communi utilitate*. It is clear that, whatever the theory, the problem of how to enforce the law against the king was not to be easily solved.

The history of the prerogative in the late medieval period is intimately bound up both with the development of the household and of parliament. It was natural that the crown should rely increasingly on household officials, and under Henry III and still more under Edward I the activities of the wardrobe were much extended. The distinction between royal and public interests, however, was by no means clear, and the household was inevitably drawn into political conflict. Both Edward II and his son went even further in using wardrobe and chamber in such a way as to challenge, at least for a time, the chancery and exchequer. This policy failed, but when the household was subordinated to the other departments, its officials continued to transact much administrative work and to provide an efficient "civil service".[3] As for the relation between crown and parliament, the crown had the advantage of deciding on the time of summons and the duration of parliament itself. It will be seen, however, that in matters of

[1] G. E. Woodbine, *Bracton de legibus et consuetudinibus Angliae*, 1, 332–3. Yale University Press, 1915.

[2] Cf. J. C. Davies, *The baronial opposition to Edward II*, p. 16.

[3] See below, Household section, pp. 94 ff.

legislation and the control of revenue royal rights were challenged and considerably defined, while limitations were set to royal purveyance (13) and to demands for military service (10, 11).[1]

The struggle between crown and baronage which had been approaching during the thirteenth century was by no means continuous, for the king and magnates were still very largely interdependent: in Edward I's reign, however, the baronial opposition was becoming more definitely political, especially after 1297, and the events at the turn of the century go far to explain the attitude of the barons at the beginning of the next reign. In February, 1308, a new form of coronation oath was used by Edward II (3);[2] the first three clauses seem to go back to the threefold promise made by the Anglo-Saxon and Norman kings; in the fourth clause there was a new departure, the king promising to keep the laws which the commonalty of the realm shall have chosen.[3] Stubbs considered that the oath in its new form was intended to replace the coronation charter, the last having been granted by Henry II.[4] In May, 1308, Edward had to consent to the banishment of Gaveston, and the struggle between king and barons which followed is of the utmost importance in the history of the prerogative. The barons were unconsciously arriving at a theory that the person and office of a king were not necessarily one, and that a king who debased his office might be rightfully resisted. Their view, however, was by no means consistent; it was clearly enunciated in the 1308 declaration about Gaveston (4), but in the charges against the Despensers in 1321–2 the barons were blaming individuals for an action which they had themselves committed as a body earlier (7).[5]

A policy of reform was initiated, the articles of Stamford were drawn up in 1309, and by accepting them Edward obtained Gaveston's recall. The articles were soon evaded, however, while Gaveston once again completely alienated the magnates, and in order to prevent further delay twenty-one ordainers (eight earls, six barons and seven bishops) were chosen in 1310 to draw up a programme of reform. They produced preliminary articles in August, and in the next year a full list of ordinances was presented

[1] See below, Parliament section, pp. 122–3.
[2] See paper by B. Wilkinson in *Essays in honour of James Tait.*
[3] C. H. McIlwain, *Growth of political theory in the west* (1932), p. 196, accepts Brady's view that this clause refers to existing custom and not, as Prynne argued, to future legislation.
[4] Stubbs, *C.H.* II, 344.
[5] J. C. Davies, *op. cit.* pp. 24–5, and cf. his whole introductory chapter.

to the king(5). He was able, however, to avoid many of the limitations imposed, for the opposition was by no means united; the political situation varied very considerably between 1311 and 1322, when the royal policy triumphed, and the last years of the reign saw Edward independent. His deposition in 1327 can mainly be accounted for by the fact that the magnates were united in their opposition to Despenser, who had roused their animosity by his activities in the Welsh march,[1] and their support was cleverly utilised in the political intrigue of Queen Isabella and Mortimer.

The chief interest in the deposition is in the legality which was observed throughout.[2] There is no reference to the proceedings in the rolls of parliament, and possibly no official record was drafted. In October, 1326, the young Edward had been proclaimed guardian of the realm(8), but writs were sent out in Edward II's name until January 21, 1327, the parliament which met on January 7 being summoned in this way. The chief difficulty confronting parliament was the absence of the king. On January 13, when London had already shown its loyalty to the queen, a number of prelates, magnates, lower clergy, knights and burgesses took their oath outside parliament in her support. Most probably on the same day Edward II was deposed in parliament. A representative deputation waited on him at Kenilworth on January 20, obtained his abdication, and on the next day allegiance and homage were renounced in the name of the whole realm, as reported in parliament three days later(9). The deposition, and the proclamation of Edward III in parliament, had not served to make him king, and he was not legally recognised until his father's abdication had been accepted by the representative committee of estates.

During Edward III's reign there was more sympathy between crown and magnates, partly due to the French war and to the king's activities. In the political crises of the reign, and especially after 1340–1, the king was able to avoid the main issues, but before the end of the reign it is seen that a stage had been reached; a procedure had been evolved whereby proceedings could be taken against royal officials, who were no longer saved by royal prerogative.[3] At this time the form and procedure of parliament

---

[1] Tout, *Edward II*, pp. 136–43, 153–6.

[2] See paper by M. V. Clarke, in *Essays in honour of James Tait*, whose account is followed here.

[3] Cf. the survey given by Miss Clarke of the main tendencies at this time, in *Oxford essays...presented to H. E. Salter*, especially pp. 166–74.

were developing, and it is not surprising that when Richard II was faced by baronial opposition parliament itself became the scene of combat. Richard inherited not only the acute economic problems of his predecessor but the immediate troubles already brewing among the political factions of his grandfather's court. After the death of his mother in 1385 and the departure of John of Gaunt for Spain in the next year, Richard's government was open to the attack of magnates who could certainly rely on a general feeling of discontent. The leaders of the opposition, to be known later as the lords appellant, were more capable than the ordainers had been, and they represented wide interests; Henry of Derby, for example, stood for the Lancastrian house, the adherence of the Duke of Gloucester, Richard's uncle, was significant, and there was considerable ecclesiastical support. At first the king would not meet the parliamentary attack of 1386(15), and refused to dismiss his officials. Gloucester and Arundel, sent to confer with Richard at Eltham, then invoked alleged statutes regulating the relation of crown and parliament and authorising the deposition of a king under certain circumstances. The king thereupon gave way in so far that he agreed to attend the parliament and to allow a change of ministers, but he was unable to save his chancellor Suffolk from impeachment, and a commission was set up to inquire into the abuses of government. Before the close of the session Richard made his protest in very definite phrase(16).

During the next months he toured the country in a desperate attempt to obtain adherents; he consulted sheriffs on the possibility of influencing the elections to parliament, and he further secured an opinion from five of his judges on the recent commission(17). The magnates, however, were determined to resist and finally Richard yielded, only to see his followers accused of treason in the Merciless Parliament of 1388. At the same time a declaration of the supremacy of the law of parliament was a noteworthy reply to the king's claim for the royal prerogative.[1] In view of the severity of the acts of this parliament it is all the more remarkable that Richard, on assuming the government in 1389, was so restrained and apparently unrevengeful.

When the blow fell on the lords appellant in 1397 it is interesting that Richard in his turn used parliament as a convenient weapon of attack. In the next session at Shrewsbury in 1398 he was given grants for life, and a parliamentary commission was set up, at first with limited powers, though these may have been

[1] See Parliament section, pp. 156–7.

extended.[1] After these successes the deposition of Richard was as sudden as his own *coup d'état*. A most interesting article has recently shed new light on the details of his renunciation, and has suggested that the evidence of the official parliamentary roll is most probably unreliable.[2]

The so-called constitutionalism of the Lancastrians is partly bound up with the prevalent ideas of Richard II's absolutism. If the sequence of events in 1399 is examined there seems little to justify the claim of Stubbs that the new accession was a "solemn national act". Henry of Lancaster was leader of a faction and he was singularly fortunate in the weakness of possible rivals and in the turn of events. On August 19, when Richard surrendered, writs were sent out in his name to summon a parliament to Westminster. His abdication was obtained on September 29 (cf. 19); on the next day, in an assembly of lords spiritual and temporal and of other people,[3] the abdication was accepted, a long list of charges against him was read(20), and a commission was set up to depose him(21). Henry then challenged the realm, basing his claim to the throne on hereditary descent(22). On the next day William Thirning addressed Richard in an interesting speech, distinguishing the estates from parliament(23), and re-nounced homage on behalf of the realm. Meanwhile writs had been issued in Henry's name and parliament met on October 6 as the first of the new reign, Arundel explaining in his speech as chancellor the theory of the cession of the crown following on the abdication and deposition of Richard(24, cf. 29). It was later definitely stated that Henry IV had royal power as great as that of his predecessors(25).

During the three Lancastrian reigns it is difficult to see that the theory of the prerogative was weakened,[4] in spite of the development of conciliar government and of aggressive demands of the commons. Certain of the royal powers might be limited in practice, as seen, for example, in a judicial opinion that letters patent might not override a statute(26). In fact there was an ever widening gulf between the theory and practice of kingship, as seen

[1] J. G. Edwards, "The parliamentary committee of 1398", *E.H.R.* xl, 1925. See below, p. 158.

[2] M. V. Clarke and V. H. Galbraith, "The deposition of Richard II", in the *Bulletin of the John Rylands Library*, 1930. Cf. G. Lapsley, "The parliamentary title of Henry IV", *E.H.R.* xlix, July, October, 1934.

[3] Mr Lapsley argues that this assembly is a convention and not a parliament.

[4] Cf. T. F. T. Plucknett, "The Lancastrian Constitution," in *Tudor Studies* (ed. R. W. Seton-Watson), 1924.

especially in Henry VI's reign, under whose personal rule the crown was much discredited. In consequence the factions of magnates became more dangerous, and the civil wars of York and Lancaster followed. The claims of Richard of York to the throne were at first evaded, then a compromise was reached by which the duke was to be considered as heir to Henry VI(28). York and many of his adherents fell in battle in the same year, but by 1461 Edward of York with the help of Warwick had made good his claim to succeed, on the plea that his was the right by legitimate descent and that the Lancastrian kings had usurped the throne. A party of nobles saluted Edward as king, the Londoners acclaimed him, and parliamentary recognition of his title followed. The Yorkist kings managed to maintain a stronger personal rule than that of Henry VI, and although social disorders were too great for them to effect many necessary reforms, yet it is true to say that the interlude of Yorkist rule made Tudor reorganisation more quickly possible.

The works of Sir John Fortescue, lord chief justice and loyal adviser to Henry VI until 1471, when he was pardoned by Edward IV to whom his later writing was addressed, are the most interesting of this period. In his *De natura legis naturae* (1461–3) and further in the *De laudibus legum Angliae* (1468–70)(30), and the *Governance of England* (1471–6)(31) he claimed England as a *dominium politicum et regale*, as contrasted with the absolutism of France, a *dominium regale*. In the *De laudibus* he exhorted the young prince Edward, son of Henry VI, to adhere to the rule of law, whereby the king was morally bound. Thus at the end of the period as at the beginning we find the insistence on the strength of law as opposed to unbridled prerogative, a contrast which was to be of fundamental importance in a later age.

We have lastly to notice the history of the law of treason during this period. Its origin can be traced in Alfred's law,[1] and it developed naturally with the increasing powers of kingship. In the early fourteenth century a crime was treated as treason if it could be shown, even constructively, to involve an offence against the crown. Following on a petition of the commons against the vagueness and danger of such constructions, in 1352 treason was defined by statute(12) as compassing the death of the king, the queen and their heir, of violating the wife or eldest unmarried daughter of the king, of levying war against the king in his realm,

[1] Stubbs, *S.C.* p. 70.

8 CENTRAL GOVERNMENT

or adhering to his enemies in the land, etc.[1] The judges were
forbidden to go beyond this and directed to refer cases of con-
structive treason to parliament, which was extending the law in
1382 to include beginning a riot or rumour against the king(14).
In 1388 the magnates insisted that it was the right of parliament
and not of the judges to decide on the legality of the appeal of
treason brought against the King's friends.[2] In 1398 Richard II
secured an act of parliament making treasonable any reversal
of its statutes; and in the same session the definition of treason
was extended to include conspiracy to depose a king(18). Under
Henry IV the recent acts of treason were repealed, and in
Henry VI's reign the extensions of the law of treason were
unimportant, only referring to escape from prison(27), arson, and
the treatment of the English on the Welsh border. Apart from
the statutory legislation, the main interest in the fifteenth century
is in the judicial interpretation of treason, and it has been shown
that there were several cases during the century wherein the
judges of the common law considered that words constituted high
treason, and offenders were put to death as traitors.[3]

[1] Miss Clarke in *Trans. R.H.S.* xiv, 1931, 80 ff., considers that this statute
was due rather to political agitation than to commons' petitions, and that both
king and magnates benefited by this narrow interpretation of treason.
[2] Stubbs, *C.H.* iii, 559.
[3] Cf. article by I. D. Thornley, *E.H.R.* xxxii, 1917.

BIBLIOGRAPHY

1. ORIGINAL SOURCES

FORTESCUE, SIR JOHN. *De laudibus legum Angliae*, ed. F. Gregor. Cin-
cinnati, 1874.
—— *De natura legis naturae*, ed. Lord Clermont. London, 1864.
—— *The governance of England*, ed. C. Plummer. Oxford, 1885.
Rotuli parliamentorum, 6 vols. 1278–1503. London, 1783.
RYMER, T. *Foedera, conventiones, litterae, etc.* London, 1706.
Statutes of the realm, vols. i, ii, Ed. I—Hen. VII. London, 1810–28.

2. SECONDARY AUTHORITIES

BLOCH, M. *Les rois thaumaturges*. Strasbourg and Paris, 1924.
DAVIES, J. C. *The baronial opposition to Edward II*. Cambridge, 1918.
PICKTHORN, K. *Early Tudor government. Henry VII*. Cambridge, 1934.
STUBBS, W. *The constitutional history of England*, vols. ii, iii. Oxford, 1880.
TAYLOR, A. *The glory of regality*. London, 1820.
TOUT, T. F. *The place of the reign of Edward II in English history*. Man-
chester, 1914.

3. ARTICLES AND ESSAYS

CLARKE, M. V. "The origin of impeachment", *Oxford essays in medieval history presented to H. E. Salter*. Oxford, 1934.
—— "Committees of estates and the deposition of Edward II", *Essays in honour of James Tait*. Manchester, 1933.
—— "Forfeitures and treason in 1388", *Trans. R.H.S.* 4th series, XIV, 1931.
CLARKE, M. V. and GALBRAITH, V. H. "The deposition of Richard II", *Bulletin of the John Rylands Library*. Manchester, 1930.
LAPSLEY, G. "The parliamentary title of Henry IV", *E.H.R.* XLIX, July, October, 1934.
SKEEL, C. A. J. "The influence of the writings of Sir John Fortescue", *Trans. R.H.S.* 3rd series, X, 1916.
THORNLEY, I. D. "Treason by words in the fifteenth century", *E.H.R.* XXXII, 1917.
WILKINSON, B. "The coronation oath of Edward II", *Essays in honour of James Tait*. Manchester, 1933.

(1) *Royal prerogative and the law; ruling of the judges in the case between Humphrey de Bohun and Gilbert de Clare* 1292

......

Et quia Dominus Rex per literas suas patentes mandavit Justiciariis suis hic, quod...voluit...per ipsos Justiciarios quod inde rei veritas inquireretur, per sacramentum tam Magnatum quam aliorum proborum et legalium hominum, de partibus Wallie, et Comitatuum Gloucestrie et Herefordie,...Ita quod nulli parceretur in hac parte, eo quod res ista Dominum Regem et Coronam et dignitatem suam tangit;...

Dictum est, ex parte Domini Regis, Johanni de Hasting, et omnibus aliis Magnatibus supranominatis, quod pro statu et jure Regis,...apponant manum ad librum ad faciendum id quod eis ex parte Domini Regis injungetur.

Qui omnes unanimiter responderunt quod inauditum est quod ipsi vel eorum antecessores hactenus in hujusmodi casu ad prestandum sacramentum aliquod coacti fuerunt.

Dicunt etiam quod nuncquam consimile mandatum regium venit in partibus istis, nisi tantum quod res tangentes Marchiam istam deducte fuissent secundum usus et consuetudines partium istarum.

Et licet prefatis Johanni et aliis Magnatibus expositum fuisset quod nullus in hac parte potest habere Marchiam Domini Regis qui, pro communi utilitate, per prerogativam suam in multis casibus est supra leges et consuetudines in regno suo usitatas, ac pluries eisdem Magnatibus ex parte ipsius Regis, conjunctim et separatim, libroque eis porrecto, injunctum est, quod faciant sacramentum, Responderunt demum omnes singillatim, quod nichil inde facerent sine consideratione parium suorum.

. . . . . .

Rot. Parl. i, 71.

(2) *A justice of assize writing on the theory of kingship*
Temp. Edward I or Edward II

Rex ideo sibi associat comites, barones et milites et alios ministros ut sint participes honoris et oneris, quia per se non sufficit sibi ipsi ad regendum populum. Rex enim dicitur a regendo. et qui regere debet praecipere oportet et non praecipi, quia aliter sequeretur quod non esset regens et gubernatus [gubernans] set potius rectus et gubernatus. quod quidem non est verum, et satis hoc probatur in littera. quia parem non habet nec superiorem. set hoc videtur instantiam recipere, quia comites dicuntur socii regis. et sic arguo: Qui habet socium habet magistrum: rex habet socium, scilicet comitem, ergo rex habet magistrum. et ultra: Qui habet magistrum habet superiorem: rex habet magistrum, ergo rex habet superiorem.

Select passages from. . .Bracton and Azo (S.S.) p. 125, notes attributed to John of Longueville, a justice of assize, oyer and terminer and gaol delivery.

(3) *The coronation oath* 1308

Et fuerunt verba Regis in Coronatione prædicta sub Juramento præstita, ut patet in Cedula annexa.

Petitio. Sire, volez vous graunter, e garder, et, par vostre Serment, confirmer au Poeple d'Engleterre les Leys, et les Custumes, a eux grauntees par les auntienes Rois, voz Predecessours droitures et devotz a Dieu; et nomement les Lois, les Custumes, et les Franchises, grauntez au Clergie, e au Poeple, par le Glorieus Roi Seint Edward, vostre Predecessour?

Responsio. Jeo les grante et promette.

   Sire, garderez vous a Dieu, et Seint Eglise, et au Clerge, et au Poeple Paes, et acord en Dieu entierment, solonc vostre Poer?

   Jeo les garderai.

   Sire, freez vous faire, en touz voz Jugements, ove droit Justice et discretion, en misericorde et verite, a vostre Poer?

   Jeo le frai.

Sire, graunte vous a tenir et garder les Loys, et les Custumes droitureles, les quiels la Communaute de vostre Roiaume aura esleu, et les defendrez et afforterez, al honur de Dieu, a vostre Poer?

Jeo les graunte et promette.

Foedera, III, 63.

(4) *Declaration of the magnates, distinguishing between the crown and the person of the king* 1308

Anno Domini MCCCVIII, et regni regis Edwardi post conquæstum secundi primo, in parliamento in quindena Paschæ Londoniis edito, ipse rex ad pacem regni confirmandam consensit quod magnates Angliæ consulerent et diffinirent super statu domini Petri de Gavastone supradicti; unde omnes et singuli tam de consilio regis quam magnatum terræ, ratiocinantes et deliberantes, in hac forma finaliter proponebant; "homagium et sacramentum ligiantiæ potius sunt et vehementius ligant ratione coronæ quam personæ regis, quod inde liquet quia, antequam status coronæ descendatur, nulla ligiancia respicit personam nec debetur; unde, si rex aliquo casu erga statum coronæ rationabiliter non se gerit, ligii sui per sacramentum factum coronæ regem reducere et coronæ statum emendare juste obligantur, alioquin sacramentum præstitum violatur. Præterea quærendum est quomodo in tali casu rex reducendus est, an per formam legis vel asperitatis; per sectam legis dirigi non potest eo quod judices non habentur nisi per regem, in quo casu, si regia voluntas rationi dissonaret nihil aliud eveniret nisi error fortius confirmatus. Quocirca propter sacramentum observandum, quando rex errorem corrigere vel amovere non curat, quod coronæ dampnosum et populo nocivum est, judicatum est quod error per asperitatem amoveatur, eo quod per sacramentum præstitum se obligavit regere populum, et ligii sui populum protegere secundum legem cum regis auxilio sunt astricti".

Item quantum ad personam domini Petri de Gavastone, in eodem parliamento fuit ostensum...quod dominus Petrus coronam exheredavit, et suo incitamento regem a concilio procerum regni sui amovit,...; propositum fuit insuper per commune consilium quod...comites præfatum Petrum,...convictum et dampnatum pronuntiarent,...; et dominus rex consensit et scripto roboravit, quod dictus Petrus...ab Anglia corporaliter recederet, nunquam ad eandem ex quavis causa, sub pœna quæ competit, reversurus;...

Gesta Edwardi de Carnarvan, auctore canonico Bridlingtoniensi (R.S.) 1883, pp. 33-4.

(5) *The ordinances* 1311

A touz ceux as queux cestes Lettres vendrount, Saluz. Sachez qe come le seszisme jour de Marz, l'an de nostre Regne tierce, a l'honour de Dieu, et pur le bien de Nos et de nostre Roiaume, eussoms graunte de nostre fraunche volunte par Noz Lettres overtes as Prelatz, Countes, et Barons, et Communes de dit Roiaume, q'il puissent eslire certeines persones des Prelatz, Countes, et Barons,...et eussoms auxint graunte par meismes les Lettres a ceux qi deussent estre esluz,...plein poer de ordiner l'estat de nostre Hostiel et de nostre Roiaume desus ditz,...Et come l'onurable Piere en Dieu Robert, par la grace de Dieu Ercevesqe de Cauntirbirs, Primat de tote Engleterre, Evesqes, Countes, et Barouns a ceo esluz...eient ordeine sur les dites choses en la fourme qe se ensuit:...

1. *De Franchise de Seinte Eglise.*
   En primes Nous ordenoms, Qe les ordenaunces avaunt faites par Nous et monstreez au Roi soient tenuz et gardees, les queux sont prescheinement souz escrites. En primes ordeine est, Qe Seinte Esglise eit totes ses fraunchises, si avaunt come ele deit avoir.

2. *De la pees le Roi garder*...

3. *De Douns faitz par le Roi sanz assent des Ordenours*...

4. *Des Custumes liverer a l'Escheqier.*
   Derechief ordeine est, Qe les Coustumes du Roiaume soient gardees et receuz par gentz du Roiaume meismes et noun pas par aliens, et qe les issuz et les profitz de meismes les Coustumes ...entierment viegnent a l'Escheqier le Roi, et par le Tresorer et les Chaumberleins soient livereez pur l'oustiel le Roi maintenier,...issint qe le Roi puisse vivre du soen, saunz prises faire autres qe auntienes dues et acoustumeez, et totes autres ceissent.

5. *De Marchantz Aliens arestoir*...

6. *De la Graunde Chartre tenir*...

7. *De Douns le Roi repeller*...

8. *De totes maners issues du Roialme liverer a l'Escheqier.*
   Por ceo qe autre foiz fut ordeinee qe les Coustumes du Roiaume fuissent receuz et gardees par gentz du Roiaume et noun pas par

aliens, et qe les issues et les profitz de meismes les Coustumes...
entierment venissent a l'Escheqier...Dount Nous ordeinoms, Que
les dites Coustumes, ensemblement ove totes les issues du Roiaume
come avant est dit, soient receuz et gardez par gentz du Roiaume,
et liverez a l'Escheqier en la fourme susdite.

9. *Qe le Roi ne aile hors du Roiaume.*

Pur ceo qe le Roi ne doit emprendre fait de guerre countre
nuly, ne alier hors de son Roiaume, saunz comun assent de son
Barnage, pur moultz des perils qe purrount avenir a lui et a son
Roiaume, Nous ordeinoms, Que le Roi desoremes ne aile hors de
son Roiaume, n'enprenge countre nuly fait de guerre, saunz commun assent de son Barnage, et ceo en Parlement. Et si autrement
le face, et si sur cele emprise face somoundre son servise, soit la
somonse pur nule, et sil aviegne qe le Roi empreigne fait de
guerre countre nuly, ou aille hors de terre, par assent de son dit
Barnage et bosoigne q'il mette Gardein en son Roiaume, dunt le
mette par commun assent de son Barnage, et ceo en Parlement.

10. *Qe totes prises cessent.*

...Nous ordeinoms, Qe totes prises ceissent desoremes, sauves
les prises antienes droitureles et dues au Roi et as autres as queux
eles sont dues de droit...

11. *De noveles Custumes et maletoutes oustez.*

...Nous ordeinoms, Que totes maneres des coustumes et mal-
toutes leveez puis le Coronement le Roi Edward fiz le Roi Henri,
soient entierment oustees, et de tot esteintz pur touzjours, nient
contre esteaunte la Chartre qe le dit Roi Edward fist as Marchauntz aliens, pur ceo qe ele fut faite contre la Graunde Chartre,
et encontre la fraunchise de la Citee de Loundres, et saunz assent
del Barnage. Et si nuly, de quele Condicion q'il soit, rien preigne
ou leve outre les aunciennes coustumes dues et droitureles, ou
desturbance face, par quei les Marchauntz ne puissent de leur
biens faire leur volunte, et de ceo soient atteintz, soient agardez
as pleintifs lur damages, eauntz regard al purchace, a la suite, as
custages et pertes que il averount eu, et a l'offense de la Grande
Chartre,...Sauve neqedent au Roi les coustumes de leyne, peaux,
et de cuirs,...Et desoremes viegnent, demoergent, et ailent les
Estraunges Marchauntz solunc les aunciennes Coustumes, et solunc
ce qe auncienement soleint faire.

12. *De damages aver en l'attach sur la prohibition.*

13. *De mal Conseilliers le Roi ouster.*

Et pur ceo qe le Roi ad este malguiee et consaillez par mauveis

Counseilliers, come est susdite, Nous ordeinoms, Qe touz les mauveis Conseilliers soient oustez et remuez de tout, issint qe eux ne autres tieux ne soient mes pres de luy, ne en office le Roi retenuz, et qe autres Gentz covenables soient mis en lur lieux. Et en meisme la manere soit fait des menengs et des gentz de office qui sont en l'oustiel le Roi qui ne sont pas covenables.

14. *De Officiers et Ministres le Roi faire.*

Et pur ceo qe moultz des maus sont avenuz par tieux Conseillers et tieux Ministres, Nous ordeinoms, Qe le Roi face Chauncellier, chief Justice de l'un Bank et de l'autre, Tresorer, Chauncellier et chief Baron de l'Escheqiere, Seneschal de son houstiel, Gardeyn de la Garderobe, et Countrerollour, et un Clerk covenable pur garder son Prive Seal, un chief Gardein de ses Forestes decea Trente, et un autre dela Trente, Et ausi un Eschetour decea Trente, et un autre dela, chief Clerk le Roi en le commun Bank, par le conseil et l'assent de son Barnage, et ceo en Parlement. Et s'il aviegne par ascune aventure q'il convient mettre ascun des ditz Ministres avant ceo qe Parlement soit, dunqe le Roi y mette par le bon conseil q'il avera pres de li, desqes au Parlement. Et issint soit fait desoremes des tieux Ministres quaunt mestier serra.

15. *Del Gardein de Cink Portz . . .*

16. *De Ministres faire en terres foreines . . .*

17. *De Viscontes faire en Countez.*

Estre ceo Nous ordeinoms, Que Viscountes soient desormes mis par le Chauncellier, et Tresorer, et les autres du Conseil qui serront presentz: Et si Chauncellier ne soit present, soient mis par le Tresorer et Barons de l'Escheqier, et par les Justices du Bank, et qe tieux soient mis et faitz qi soient covenables et suffissantz, et qi eient terres et tenementz dount il puissent respoundre au Roi et au Poeple de lour faitz, et qe nuls autres qe tieux ne soient mis, et qe eux eient Commission desouz le Graunt Seal.

18. *De Gardeins de Forestes . . .*

19. *Des enditementz de la Foreste . . .*

20. *De Pieres de Gavaston . . .*

21. *De Emeri Friscombaud . . .*

22. *De Monsire Henri de Beaumont . . .*

23. *De la Dame de Vescy . . .*

24. *De acquitances en l'Escheqier.*

25. *De plez tenir en l'Escheqier.*

Pur ceo qe comunes Marchauntz et autres plusours du poeple sont receuz de pleder a l'Escheqier plez de dette et de trespas, par la reson q'il sont avouez par les ministres de la dite place plus avaunt qe estre ne deveroient, dount les acountes et les autres choses tochauntes le Roi sont le plus delaiez, . . . Nous ordeinoms, qe desormes ne soient tenuz plez en la dite place de l'Eschequier forsqe les plez tochauntz le Roi et ses ministres, qi sont responsables en l'Escheqier par la reson de leur offices, et les ministres de meisme la place et leur mesnengs et lour servauntz qi tout le plus sont demorauntz ovesqes eux en les lieux ou l'Escheqier demoert. Et si nul soit receu par avouerie de la dite place de pledier en le dit Escheqier encountre la fourme susdite, eient les empledez leur recoverier en Parlement.

26. *De plez tenir en la Mareschaucie.*

Ensement, pur ceo qe le poeple se sent moult grevez qe Seneschaux et Mareschaux tiegnent moltz des plez qi a leur office ne appendent, et auxi de ceo qe eux ne voillent receivre attournez auxi bien pur les defendauntz come pur les pleintifs, Nous ordeinoms, qe desormes reteinent attournez ausi bien pur les defendantz come pur les pleintifs, et qe il ne tiegnent plez de fraunc tenement, ne de dette, ne de covenaunt, ne de contract, ne nul commun plai des gentz du poeple, fors taunt soulement de trespas de l'houstiel, et autres trespas faitz dedeinz la Verge, et de contractes et de covenauntz qe ascun de l'houstiel le Roi avera fait as autres de meisme l'oustiel, et en meisme l'oustiel et ne my aillours. Et qe nul plai de trespas ne pledent autre qe ne soit attache par eux avaunt qe le Roi isse hors de la Verge ou le trespas serra fait, et les plederont hastivement de jour en jour issint qe il soient parpledez et terminez avaunt ceo qe le Roi isse hors de les bounndes de cele Verge ou le trespas fut fait. Et si par cas dedenz les bounndes de cele verge ne poent estre terminez, ceissent tieux plez devant le Seneschal, et se purchacent les pleintifs par la commune lei, ne desoremes ne preigne le Seneschal conissaunce de dettes, ne d'autres choses . . .

Et si le Seneschal et Mareschaux rien facent contre cest ordeinement, soit lour fait tenuz pur nul, et qe ceux qi se sentiront grevez contre la dite ordeinaunce eient Bref en Chauncellerie pledable en Baunk le Roi, et recoverent leur damages vers eux qi tiegnent le plai . . .

27. *De office de Coroner faire deinz la Verge.*

Et pur ceo qe avant ces heures moltz des felonies faites dedenz la Verge ount este despunies, pur ceo qe les Coroners du pais ne se sont pas entremys d'enquere de tieu manere des felonies dedenz la Verge mes le Coroner del houstiel le Roi, de quei issue n'ad my este faite en due manere, ne les felons mys en Exigendes, ne utlagez, ne rien de tieu felonie presentee en Eire, qe est a graunt damage le Roi...Nous ordenoms, qe desoremes en cas de mort de homme ou office de Coroner appent, et les vewes des corps mortz et as enquestes de ceo faire soient maundez les Corouners du pais ou des fraunchises par la ou les mortz serront trovez qi ensemblement ove le Coroner de l'houstiel face l'office qi append, et le mette en son roulle...

28. *De les chartres le Roi de sa pees...*

29. *De Parlementz tenir de an en an.*

Pur ceo qe moultes Gentz sont delaiez en la court le Roi de leur demaunde, par taunt qe la partie allegge qe les demaundauntz ne devient estre respounduz saunz le Roi, et auxint moltz de gentz grevez par les ministres le Roi encountre droiture, des queles grevaunces homme ne purra avoir recoverier sanz commune Parlement, Nous ordenoms, Qe le Roi tiegne Parlement une foiz par an, ou deux foiz si mestier soit, et ceo en lieu covenable. Et qe en meismes les Parlementz soient les pledz qe sont en la dite fourme deslaiez et les pledz la ou les justices sont en diverses opinions, recordez et terminez. Et en meisme la manere soient les billes terminez qe liverez serront en Parlement, si avant come lei et reson le demaunde.

31. *De touz estatuz garder...*

32. *Qe lei de terre ne soit delaee par lettres du Prive Seal.*

Por ceo qe la lei de la terre et commune droit ount este sovent delaiez par lettres issuz desouz le Prive Seal le Roi, a graunt grevaunce du poeple, Nous ordenoms, Qe desoremes la lei de la terre ne commune droit ne soient deslaiez ne desturbez par lettres du dit Seal. Et si rien soit fait en nule des places de la Court nostre Seignur le Roi, ou aillours, par tieles lettres issues desouz le Prive Seal encountre droiture ou lei de terre, rien ne vaille et pur nient soit tenuz.

33. *De l'estatut de marchantz...*
......

38. *De la Graunt Chartre et la Chartre de la Foreste.*

39. *De serment de Ministres.*

Ensement Nous ordeinoms, Qe Chauncellier, Tresorer, Chiefs Justices de l'un Baunk et de l'autre, Chauncellier de l'Escheqier, Tresorer de la Garderobe, Seneschal de L'oustiel le Roi, toutes Justices, Viscountes, Eschetours, Conestables, Enquerours a queu chose qe ceo soit, et touz autres Baillifs et Ministres le Roi, soient jureez a toutes les foiz q'il receivent leur baillies et offices, de garder et tenier toutes les Ordenaunces faites par les Prelatz, Countes, et Barons a ceo esleuz et assignez, et chescune d'eles, saunz venir countre nul point d'eles.

40. *De Gentz assigner en Parlementz.*

Ensement Nous ordeinoms Qe en chescun Parlement soient assignez un Evesqe, deux Countes, et deux Barons, de oier et terminer totes les Pleintes de ceux qi pleindre se vodrount des ministres le Roi, queux qil soient, qi serrount countrevenuz les Ordenaunces susdites. Et si les ditz Evesqe, Countes, et Barons, ne puissent touz entendre ou soient desturbez de oier et terminer les dites pleintes, adunqe le facent trois ou deux de eux, et ceux qi serront trovez countrevenuz encountre les dites Ordenaunces soient puniz devers le Roi et devers les Pleintifs, par la descretion des ditz assignez.

41. *De ces Ordinaunces publier.*

Ensement Nous ordenoms, Qe les Ordenances susdites soient maintenues et gardees en touz leur pointz, et qe nostre Seignur le Roi les face mettre desouz son Graunt Seal et envoier en chescun Counte D'engleterre a publier, tenir, et fermement garder, ausi bien deinz fraunchises come dehors. Et en meisme la manere soit maunde au Gardein de Cink Portz q'il parmie tote sa Baillie les face publier, tenier, et garder, en la fourme avauntdite.

Nous meismes celes Ordeinaunces a Nous monstrees, et le Lundy prechein devant la Feste de Seint Michel drein passe publiez, agreoms, acceptoms, et affermoms, et voloms et grauntoms, pur Nous, et pur Nos heires, Qe toutes les dites Ordenaunces, et chescune d'eles, faites solunc la fourme de Noz Lettres avantdites, soient publiez par tout nostre Roiaume, et desoremes fermement gardez et tenuz. En tesmoignaunce de queux choses, Nous avoms fait faire cestes Nos Lettres Patentes, donez a Loundres le quint jour de Octobre, l'an de nostre Regne quint.

In Dorso. Memorandum quod in Parliamento tento apud Eboracum anno xv° Edwardi II. Ordinationes suprascripte revocantur et adnullantur, ut patet in magno Rotulo Statutorum,...

Rot. Parl. I, 281–6.

(6) *A military levy* 1316

Acordee est et assentu par nostre Seignur le Roi et Prelatz, Countes, et Barons, et autres de la communalte, qe Baneretz ou autres suffisauntz gentz soient assignez qi eient poer de nostre Seignur le Roi de lever le commun del poeple del Counte dEverwyk si les enemis dEscoce veignent en la terre dEngleterre..., e qe ceux assignez eient desouz eux en chescun wapentache un chevaler ou un serjaunt suffisaunt de lever le pople de le dit wapentache, e qe celui chevaler ou serjant eit desouz li le plus avise home de chescun paroche, pur fere lever le dit pople en la forme avantdite, et qe le dit poeple seit mis as armes, chescun solonc son estat, si qe chescun home defensable del commune eit aketon bacinet et launce, ou au meins aketon sil seit de nule value, ou rien eit de quoi, issint qe quant homme orra novels de la venue des enemis en Engleterre, les ditz assignez facent lever le poeple daler ove le Roi...Cest a savoir touz entre les deux ages de cesze et seisant aunz, qi sont defensables, et qe ceux qi serront assignez en les paroches, soient entendantz a ceux qi serront assignez en les wapentaches, e eux, et les assignez en les wapentaches, soient entendauntz a ceux qi serront assignez en le counte. Et acorde est qe ceux qi serront trovez rebels sil eient biens et chateux terres et tenementz, leur biens...soient pris en la mein le Roi et detenu tanqe ordine seit par le Roi, et par les Prelatz Countes et Barons et les graunz qi serront pres du Roi, certeine peine countre tieux rebells, et de ceux qi ne ount pas terres...leur biens et chateux soient...detenu,...et de ceux qi ne averont terres ne tenementz biens ne chateux, leur corps seient pris et mis a la prisone...

Parliamentary Writs, II, ii, 479.

(7) *Charges against the Despensers* 1321

Exilium Hugonis le Despenser, patris et filii.

Al Honur de Dieu et de Seinte Esglise et de nostre Seignur le Roi...lui mustrent prelatz, Countes, Barouns, et les autres piers de la terre, et Commune du Roialme, countre Sir Hugh le Despenser le fitz et Sir Hugh le Despenser le piere; qe come le dit Sir Hugh le fitz, a parlement a Everwyk, fust nome...destre en loffice de Chaumbreleyn nostre Seignur le Roi...; a queu parlement fust auxint assentu qe certeins prelatz, e autres grauntz du Roialme, demurreient pres du Roi par sesouns del an pur mieux conseiller nostre Seignur le Roi, santz queux nul grosse bosoigne ne se deveroit faire, le dit Sir Hugh le fitz, attret a lui Sir Hugh son pere,...e entre eux deux acrochaunt a eux real poer sur le Roi, ses Ministres, et le guiement de son Roialme, a deshonur du Roi, enblemissement de la corone et destruccion du roialme,...et fesoient les malveistees southescrites, en cumpassaunt de esloigner le quoer nostre Seignur le Roi des piers de la terre, pur avoir entre eux deux soul governement du Roialme.

En primes qe Sir Hugh le Despenser le fitz fust corouce devers le Roi, et sur ceo curouce fist une bille, sur la quele bille il voleit aver en alliaunce de sire Johan Giffard...et dautres, de aver mene le Roi par asparte a faire sa volunte, issi qe en lui ne remist mie qil ne le eust fait. La tenur de la bille sensuist southescrit. Homage et serment de ligeaunce est plus par resoun de la Corone qe par resoun de la persone le Roi, et plus se lye a la Corone qe a la persone; et ceo piert qe avant qe lestat de la corone soit descendu, nule ligeaunce est a la persone regardaunte; dount si le Roi par cas ne se meigne par resoun, en dreit de la Corone, les liges sont liez par serment fait a la Corone de remenir le Roi et lestat de la Corone par reson, et autrement ne serroit point le serment tenuz. Ore fait a demaunder coment lem deit mener le Roi, ou par sute de lei, ou par asparte; par sute de ley ne lui poet homme pas redrescer, car il naveroit pas Juges, si ceo ne soit depar le Roi, en quieu cas si la volentie le Roi ne soit acordaunte a resoun, si naveroit il forsqe errour meintenu et conferme; dount il covient pur le serment sauver, qe quant le Roi ne voet chose redrescer, ne oster qest pur le commun poeple malveise et damagouse et pur la Corone, ajuger est qe la chose soit oste par asprete, qil est lie par son serment de governer le poeple et ses liges, et ses liges sont lyes de governer en eide de lui et en defaute de lui.

S.R. I, 181–2.

(8) *Edward, Duke of Aquitaine, proclaimed guardian of the realm* 1326

De Recessu Regis a Regno, et Filio Custode constituto; ac de Reditu Regis, et Magno Sigillo eidem Filio et Reginæ commisso.

Memorandum quod, vicesimo sexto die Octobris, Anno Regni Regis Edwardi vicesimo,

Ipso Rege a Regno suo Angliæ, cum Hugone le Despenser Juniore, et Magistro Roberto de Baldok, Inimicis Isabellæ Reginæ Angliæ,...et Edwardi,...Ducis Aquitaniæ,...notorie Inimicis recedente, eodem Regno suo sine Regimine dimisso,

Venerabiles Patres, A. Dubliniensis Archiepiscopus,...Et alii Barones et Milites, tunc apud Bristoll existentes, in præsentia dictæ Dominæ Reginæ, et dicti Ducis, de assensu totius Communitatis dicti Regni,...eundem Ducem in Custodem dicti Regni unanimiter elegerunt; sic quod idem Dux et Custos, Nomine et Jure ipsius Domini Regis,...dictum Regnum regeret et gubernaret:

......

Postmodum vero, vicesimo die Novembris proximo sequente, captis Inimicis prædictis, et dicto Domino Rege in dictum Regnum suum revertente, iidem, Domina Regina et Dux, Prælatique et Proceres prædicti, de assensu Communitatis prædictæ, tunc apud Herefordiam existentes,...Dominum Herefordensem Episcopum ad ipsum Dominum Regem in Nuncium miserunt; supplicando eidem Domino Regi, ut ipse præcipere vellet quod de Magno Sigillo suo, penes dictum Dominum Regem tunc existente, fierent ea, quæ pro Pace, in eodem Regno conservanda et Justitia exhibenda, essent facienda.

......

Et idem Dominus Rex, auditis sic sibi expositis, habita inde aliquali deliberatione penes se, respondebat quod placuit sibi mittere dictum Magnum Sigillum suum præfatis Consorti suæ et Filio;...et idem Dominus Rex dictum Magnum Sigillum liberari fecit Domino Willielmo le Blount Militi, deferendum,... ad prædictos, Reginam et Ducem,...

......

Die vero Dominica proximo sequente,...apud Cirencestriam, in Camera ipsius Dominæ Reginæ, infra Abbatiam, ibidem iidem, Regina et Dux, existentes, dictum Magnum Sigillum,...tradiderunt, ex parte dicti Domini Regis, præfato Domino Norwicensi Episcopo, et præceperunt sibi quod illud...inde faceret quod ad officium Custodis dicti Magni Sigilli pertineret...

Foedera, IV, 237–8.

(9) *Announcement of Edward II's abdication* 1327

De Pace Regis proclamanda.

Memorandum quod dictus Dominus Edwardus, vicesimo quarto die Januarii,...Anno Domini Millesimo, Trescentesimo, Vicesimo sexto, fecit pacem suam in Civitate Londoniæ proclamari, et publicari per verba, quæ sequuntur;

Pur ceo que Sire Edward, n'adgairs Roi d'Engleterre, de sa bone volunte, et de commun conseil et assent des Prelatz, Countes et Barons, et autres Nobles, et tote la Communalte du Roialme, s'en est ouste del Governement du Roialme, et ad grante, et veut que le Governement du dit Roialme deveigne a Sire Edward, son Fiutz eyne, et Heir, et q'il governe Regne, et soit Roi Corone,
Par qai touz les Grantz ount fait Homage,
Nous crioms et publioms la Pees nostre dit Seignur Sire Edward, le Fiutz, et comandoms, et defendoms, de par lui, fermement a touz, et a chescun, sur peigne et paril de desheritance, et departe de Vie et de Membre, que nul n'enfreigne la Pees nostre dit Seignur le Roi;
Kar il est, et serra prest, a touz, et a chescun, del dit Roialme, en totes choses, et countre touz, auxi bien as Petitz, come Grantz, a faire Droiture.
Et, si nul eit Rien a demandre vers autre, le demande par Voi de action, sanz force mettre, ou autre violence.

Foedera, IV, 243.

(10) *Military service defined* 1327

Item le Roi voet qe desormes nul soit charge de soi armer autrement qil ne soleit entemps de ses auncestres Roys Dengleterre; Et qe nuls soient destreintz daler hors de lour Countez, si noun par cause de necessite de sodeyne venue des estraunges enemys en Roialme; et adonqes soit fait come ad este fait avant ces houres pur defens du Roialme.

S.R. I, 255, 1 Ed. III, s. 2, c. 5.

(11) *No finding of men of arms but by tenure or grant in parliament* 1352

Auxint acorde est et assentu, qe nul homme soit arte de trover gentz darmes, hobellers narchers autres qe ceux qi tiegnent par tiele service, sil ne soit de commune assent et grant fait en parlement.

S.R. I, 321, 25 Ed. III, s. 5, c. 8.

(12) *Statute of treasons* 1352

Auxint purceo qe diverses opinions ount este einz ces heures qeu cas, quant il avient doit estre dit treson, et en quel cas noun, le Roi a la requeste des Seignurs et de la Commune, ad fait declarissement qi ensuit, Cest assavoir; quant homme fait compasser ou ymaginer la mort nostre Seignur le Roi, ma dame sa compaigne, ou de lour fitz primer et heir; ou si homme violast la compaigne le Roi, ou leisnesce fille le Roi nient marie, ou la compaigne leisne fitz et heir du Roi; et si homme leve de guerre contre nostre dit Seignur le Roi en son Roialme, ou soit adherant as enemys nostre Seignur le Roi en le Roialme, donant a eux eid ou confort en son Roialme ou par aillours, et de ceo provablement soit atteint de overt faite par gentz de lour condicion: et si homme contreface les grant ou prive sealx le Roi, ou sa monoie, et si homme apport faus monoie en ceste Roialme contrefaite a la monoie Dengleterre,...sachant la monoie estre faus, pur marchander, ou paiement faire en deceit nostre dit Seignur le Roi et son poeple; et si homme tuast Chanceller, Tresorer, ou Justice nostre Seignur le Roi del un Baunk ou del autre, Justice en Eir et des assises et toutes autres Justices assignez a oier et terminer esteiantz en lours places en fesantz lours offices: et fait a entendre qen les cases suisnomez doit estre ajugge treson qi sestent a nostre Seignur le Roi et a sa roial majeste; et de tiele manere de treson la forfaiture des eschetes appartient a nostre Seignur le Roi...; et ovesqe ceo il yad autre manere de treson, cest assavoir quant un servant tue son meistre, une femme qi tue son baron, quant homme seculer ou de religion tue son Prelat...; et tiele manere de treson donn forfaiture des eschetes a chescun Seignur de son fee propre: et pur ceo qe plusurs autres cases de semblable treson purront escheer en temps a venir, queux homme ne purra penser ne declarer en present, assentu est qe si autre cas supposee treson... aviegne de novel devant ascunes Justices, demoerge la Justice saunz aler au juggement de treson, tanqe par devant nostre Seignur le Roi en son parlement soit le cas monstree et desclarre le quel ceo doit estre ajugge treson ou autre felonie...

S.R. i, 319, 25 Ed. III, s. 5, c. 2.

(13) *Regulation of purveyance* 1362

Item pur la grevouse pleinte qad este fait des Purveours des vitailles del Hostel le Roi, la Roigne, et lour eisne filz, et des dautres Seignurs et Dames du realme, le Roi de sa propre volente, sanz mocion des grauntz ou communes, ad grante...qe desore nul homme du dit Realme eit prise, fors soulement lui mesmes et la Roigne sa compaigne: et outre,...est ordeigne...qe sur tieux purveances desore affaire pur les hosteulx le Roi et la

Roigne soit prest paiement fait en poigne, cestassavoir le pris pur
quel autiels vitailles sont venduz communement, en marchees
environ: et qe le heignous noun de purveour soit chaunge et nome
Achatour; et si le chatour ne purra bonement acorder ove le
vendour, de ce qe il enbusoignera, adonqes les prises...soient
faites par veue...des Seignurs, ou lour baillifs, Conestables et
quatre prodeshommes de chescune ville,...; et qe le noumbre des
achatours soit amenuse en taunt come homme purra bonement;
et qe tieux soient achatours qi soient sufficiantz de responde au
Roi et au poeple, et qe nul de eux eit depute; et qe les commissions soient ensealees du grant seal, et chescun demy an
restitutz en la Chancellerie et autres de novel faites,...et qe
mesmes les commissions soient faites sur la fin du dit parlement,...
et si nul achatour, apres les novelles commissions faites, face
ascunes prises...en autre manere qe nest compris en lour dites
commissions, eit punissement de vie et de membre; come en
autres estatutz est ordene des Purveours...

S.R. i, 371, 36 Ed. III, s. 2.

(14) *Extension of the law of treason* 1381

...Et le Roi defende estroitement a toutes maneres des gentz, sur
peine de quanqe ils purront forfaire devers lui en corps et en
biens, qe nully desore face ne recomence par voie quelconqe
celles riot et rumour nautres semblables. Et si nully le face et ce
provez duement soit fait de luy come de Traitre au Roi et a son
dit Roialme.

S.R. ii, 20, 5 Ric. II, s. 1, c. 6.

(15) *Parliamentary opposition to Richard II* 1386

"Domine Rex, proceres et domini atque totus populus communitatis parliamenti vestri cum humillima subjectione se com-
mendant excellentissimo patrocinio regalis dignitatis vestræ,
cupientes prosperum iter invincibilis honoris vestri contra inimicorum potentiam, et validissimum vinculum pacis et dilectionis
cordis vestri erga subditos vestros in augmentum commodi vestri
erga deum et salutem animæ vestræ, et ad inedicibilem conso-
lationem totius populi vestri quem regitis. Ex quorum parte
haec vobis intimamus, quod ex antiquo statuto habemus et consuetudine laudabili et approbata...quod rex noster convocare
potest dominos et proceres regni atque communes semel in anno

ad parliamentum suum tanquam ad summam curiam totius regni...

Dicunt etiam quod habent ex antiquo statuto quod si rex a parliamento suo se alienaverit sua sponte, non aliqua infirmitate aut aliqua alia de causa necessitatis, sed per immoderatam voluntatem proterve se subtraxerit per absentiam temporis xl. dierum tanquam de vexatione populi sui et gravibus expensis eorum non curans, extunc licitum omnibus et singulis eorum absque domigerio regis redire ad propria et unicuique eorum in patriam suam remeare. Et jam vos ex longiori tempore absentastis, et qua de causa nesciunt, venire renuistis.

[Richard's reply is then given, and a further remonstrance from parliament.]

Sed et unum aliud de nuncio nostro superest nobis ex parte populi vestri vobis intimare. Habent enim ex antiquo statuto et de facto non longe retroactis temporibus experienter, quod dolendum est, habito, si rex ex maligno consilio quocunque vel inepta contumacia aut contemptu seu proterva voluntate singulari aut quovis modo irregulari se alienaverit a populo suo, nec voluerit per jura regni et statuta ac laudabiles ordinationes cum salubri consilio dominorum et procerum regni gubernari...sed capitose in suis insanis consiliis propriam voluntatem suam singularem proterve exercere, extunc licitum est eis cum communi assensu et consensu populi regni ipsum regem de regali solio abrogare, et propinquiorem aliquem de stirpe regia loco ejus in regni solio sublimare. Quæ forte dissensio aut error gravis ne in populo oriatur, et populus regni novo aliquo dissidio dolendo, et inimicis regni placibili, in diebus vestris per insanum consilium ministrorum vestrorum subruatur, regnumque Angliæ tam honorificum et in toto orbe terrarum præ cæteris regnis tempore patris vestri hactenus in militia nominatissimum, nunc vero diebus vestris per divisionem malæ gubernationis impropriose desoletur, regnique tanti damno titulus pro debili gubernatione sub perpetua memoria personæ vestræ scandalosæ quam regni vestri atque populi, et animum ab inepto consilio revocetis et eos qui vobis talia suggerent nec solum non audiatis sed etiam de consilio vestro penitus amoveatis; nam in eventu vario parum aut nihil vobis prodesse poterunt in effectu.

His et aliis talibus loquelis rex ab ira semotus animum de melancholia revocavit, sicque pacificatus promisit se venire ad parliamentum post triduum et eorum petitioni cum maturitate se libenter adquiescere velle. Venit igitur rex ad parliamentum ut

promisit, et tunc dominus Johannes de Fortham episcopus Dunelmensis amotus est de officio thesaurariæ et episcopus Herfordensis
factus est thesaurarius. Dominus Mychael de Pole comes de
Southfolke depositus est cum ingenti rubore de officio cancellariæ...

Chronicon Henrici Knighton (R.S.) (1895), ii, 216–20.

(16) *Royal protest at the close of parliament* 1386

Fait a remembrer, qe le Roi en plein Parlement, devant le fyn
d'icell, fist overte Protestation par sa bouche demesne, Qe pur
riens q'estoit fait en le dit Parlement il ne vorroit qe prejudice
avendroit a luy ne a sa Corone; einz qe sa Prerogatif, et les
Libertees de sa dite Corone feussent sauvez et gardez.

Rot. Parl. iii, 224 (35).

(17) *Declaration of the judges on the king's prerogative* 1387

Memorandum, quod vicesimo quinto die mensis Augusti, anno
regni Regis Ricardi secundi undecimo, apud Castrum Notyng-
hamie, coram dicto Domino nostro Rege, Robertus Tresilian
Capitalis Justiciarius, et Robertus Bealknap Capitalis Justiciarius
de Communi Banco Domini nostri Regis predicti, et Johannes
Holt, Rogerus Fulthorp, et Willelmus Burgh, Milites, Justiciarii
Socii predicti Roberti Bealknap, ac Johannes Loketon Serviens
dicti Domini Regis ad Legem, in presentia Dominorum et
aliorum Testium subscriptorum personaliter existentes, per dictum
Dominum nostrum Regem requisiti in fide et ligeantia quibus
eidem domino nostro Regi firmiter sunt astricti, quod ad certas
Questiones inferius designatas, et coram eis recitatas, fideliter
responderent, et super eis secundum discretionem suam legem
dicerent.

Inprimis, querebatur ab eis, An illa nova Statutum, et Ordinatio,
atque Commissio, facta et edita in ultimo Parliamento apud
Westmonasterium celebrato, derogant Regalie et Prerogative dicti
Domini nostri Regis? Ad quam quidem Questionem unanimiter
responderunt, Quod derogant, presertim eo quod fuerant contra
voluntates Regis.

Item, querebatur ab eis, Qualiter illi qui Statutum, Ordinacionem, et Commissionem predicta fieri procurarunt sunt
puniendi? Ad istam Questionem unanimiter responderunt, Quod

pena capitali, scilicet mortis, puniri merentur, nisi Rex in ea parte voluerit eis gratiam indulgere.

......

Item querebatur ab eis, Qualem Penam merentur illi qui compulerunt sive artarunt Regem ad consentiendum confectioni dictorum Statuti, Ordinacionis, et Commissionis? Ad quam quidem Questionem unanimiter responderunt, Quod sunt ut Proditores merito puniendi.

......

Item querebatur ab eis, Numquid Rex quandocumque sibi placuerit poterit dissolvere Parliamentum, et suis Dominis et Communibus precipere quod ab inde recedant, An non? Ad quam quidem Questionem unanimiter responderunt, Quod potest. Et si quis extunc contra voluntatem Regis procedat ut in Parliamento, tanquam Proditor puniendus existit.

Item quesitum erat ab eis, Ex quo Rex potest quandocumque sibi placuerit removere quoscumque Officiarios et Justiciarios suos et ipsos pro delictis eorum justificare et punire, Numquid Domini et Communes possint absque voluntate Regis Officiarios et Justiciarios ipsos impetere super delictis eorum in Parliamento, An non? Ad istam Questionem unanimiter responderunt, Quod non possunt. Et si quis in contrarium fecerit, est ut Proditor puniendus.

......

In quorum omnium testimonium Justiciarii et Serviens predicti sigilla sua presentibus apposuerunt. Hiis Testibus...

Rot. Parl. III, 233.

(18) *Extension of the law of treason* 1398

Item ordeine est...qe chescun qi compasse...la mort du Roy ou de luy deposier ou desuis rendre son homage liege, ou celluy qi leve le poeple et chivache encontre le Roy afaire de guerre deinz son roialme et de ceo soit duement atteint et adjuggez en parlement soit adjuggez come traitour de haute traison encontre la Corone, et forface de luy et ses heirs qiconqes toutz sez terres tenementz possessions et libertees...queux il ad ou ascun autre ad a son oeps, ou avoit le jour de traison perpetrez,...Et qe cest estatut se extende et teigne lieu sibien as ceux qi sont adjuggez ou atteintz pur ascun des quatre pointz des ditz traisons en cest parlement, come de touz ceux qi serront adjuggez ou atteintz en parlement en temps advenir des ascuns des quatre pointz de traisons susditz. Et nest pas lentencion du Roy ne de les seignurs ne assent des Communes avantditz qe si ascun tiele qi forface en manere susdice soit enfeoffez en ascuny terre tenement ou possession a autry oeps qe ceo soit compris en celle forfaiture.

Item le Roy de lassent susdit ad ordeigne...qe si ascun...pursue procure ou conseille de repeller...ascuns des juggementz renduz devers ascuns...estatuz ou ordenances faitz en mesme le parlement ou ascune parcelle dicelles en ascune manere, et ceo duement provee en parlement, qil soit adjugge et eit execucion come traitour au Roy et a Roialme. A queles ordenance et estatut bien et loialment tenir et garder les seignurs du roialme sibien espirituels come temporels sount jurrez et sermentz devant le Roy come piert en le Rolle de parlement.

S.R. II, 98, 21 Ric. II, cc. 3, 4. (In 1399 all treason legislation enacted since 1352 was repealed, *S.R.* II, 114, 1 Hen. IV, c. 10.)

(19) *Commission set up to accept Richard II's abdication* 1399

Memorandum, Quod die Lune in festo Sancti Michaelis Archangeli, anno regni Regis Ricardi Secundi vicesimo tertio, Domini Spirituales et Temporales, et alie persone notabiles [16 *names follow*], de quorundam Dominorum Spiritualium et Temporalium, ac Justiciariorum, et aliorum tam in Jure Civili et Canonico quam in Regni Legibus peritorum, apud Westmonasterium in loco consueto Consilii congregatorum, assensu et avisamento, ad Actum subscriptum primitus deputati, ad presentiam dicti Regis Ricardi, ...circiter nonam pulsationem horilogii accesserunt. Et recitato coram eodem Rege per...Comitem Northumbreland, vice omnium predictorum...Qualiter idem Rex alias apud Conewey in North Wallia in sua libertate existens, promisit...se velle cedere et renunciare Corone Anglie et Francie et sue Regie Magestati,... Idem Rex...dixit, Se velle cum effectu perficere quod prius in ea parte promisit. Desideravit tamen habere colloquium cum Henrico Duce Lancastrie, et prefato Archiepiscopo, consanguineis suis, antequam promissum suum hujusmodi adimpleret. Petivit tamen copiam Cessionis per eum faciende sibi tradi, ut super illa posset interim deliberare: qua quidem copia sibi tradita dicti Domini et alii ad sua hospitia redierunt. Postea eodem die post prandium,...idem Dux Lancastrie, Domini et Persone superius nominati, ac etiam dictus Archiepiscopus Cantuariensis, venerunt ad presentiam dicti Regis in Turri predicta,...Et postquam idem Rex cum dictis Duce et Archiepiscopo...colloquium habebat ad

partem, vultu hillari hinc inde inter eos exhibito prout circum-
stantibus videbatur, tandem dictus Rex,...dixit publice coram
illis, Quod paratus erat ad renunciandum et cedendum secundum
Promissionem per eum ut premittitur factam. Sicque incontinenti,
licet potuisset ut sibi dicebatur ab aliis Cessionem et Renuncia-
tionem, in quadam Cedula pergameni redactam, per aliquem
Deputatum organum vocis sue fecisse pro labore tam prolixo
lecture vitando, Idem tamen Rex gratanter, ut apparuit, ac
hillari vultu, Cedulam illam in manu sua tenens dixit semetipsum
velle legere, et distincte perlegit eandem; necnon absolvit ligeos
suos, renunciavit, et cessit, juravit, et alia dixit et protulit in
legendo, et se subscripsit manu sua propria, prout plenius continetur in dicta Cedula, Cujus tenor sequitur, in hec verba:
[*Richard's formal abdication then follows.*]

Rot. Parl. iii, 416.

(20) *Charges brought against Richard II*[1] 1399

Item, in Parliamento ultimo celebrato apud Salopiam, idem Rex
proponens opprimere Populum suum, procuravit subtiliter et
fecit concedi, quod Potestas Parliamenti de consensu omnium
Statuum Regni sui remaneret apud quasdam certas Personas, ad
terminandas, dissoluto Parliamento, certas Petitiones in eodem
Parliamento porrectas protunc minime expeditas. Cujus concessionis colore Persone sic deputate processerunt ad alia genera-
liter Parliamentum illud tangentia; et hoc de voluntate Regis: in
derogationem Status Parliamenti, et in magnum incomodum
totius Regni, et perniciosum exemplum. Et ut super factis eorum
hujusmodi aliquem colorem et auctoritatem viderentur habere,
Rex fecit Rotulos Parliamenti pro voto suo mutari et deleri,
contra effectum concessionis predicte.

Item, idem Rex nolens justas Leges et Consuetudines Regni
sui servare seu protegere, set secundum sue arbitrium Voluntatis
facere quicquid desideriis ejus occurrerit, quandoque et fre-
quentius quando sibi expositi [*sic*] et declarati fuerant Leges Regni
sui per Justiciarios et alios de Consilio suo, et secundum Leges illas
petentibus justiciam exhiberet; Dixit expresse, vultu austero et
protervo, quod Leges sue erant in ore suo, et aliquotiens in
pectore suo: Et quod ipse solus posset mutare et condere Leges

[1] See Stubbs, *C.H.* ii, 550–2, for an analysis of the charges; and cf. article by
Clarke and Galbraith, "The deposition of Richard II."

Regni sui. Et opinione illa seductus, quam-pluribus de ligeis suis Justiciam fieri non permisit, set per minas et terrores quam-plures a prosecutione communis Justicie cessare coegit.

Item, licet Terre et Tenementa, Bona et Catalla cujuscumque Liberi hominis, per Leges Regni ab omnibus retroactis temporibus usitatas, capi non debeant nisi fuerint forisfacta; nichilominus dictus Rex proponens et satagens Leges hujusmodi enervare, in presentia quam-plurimum Dominorum et aliorum de Communi-tate Regni frequenter dixit et affirmavit, Quod Vita cujuscumque ligei sui, ac ipsius Terre, Tenementa, Bona et Catalla sunt sua ad voluntatem suam, absque aliqua forisfactura: Quod est omnino contra Leges et Consuetudines Regni sui supradicti.

Item, quamvis Populus Regni Anglie vigore Ligeantie sue satis plene Regi suo teneatur et astringatur, ipseque Rex Populum suum si quovis modo deliquerit per Leges et Consuetudines Regni corrigere valeat et punire; Tamen dictus Rex cupiens subpeditare ac nimis opprimere Populum suum, ut liberius exequi et sequi valeret sue inepte et illicite voluntatis arbitrium, per suas Literas ad omnes Comitatus Regni sui directas induxit etiam et mandavit, ut ligei sui quicumque tam Spirituales quam Temporales certa Juramenta prestarent in genere que eis fuerant nimium odiosa, queque verisimiliter causare possent destructionem finalem Populi sui; et quod sub literis et sigillis eorum Juramenta hujusmodi roborarent. Cui quidem mandato Regio Populus Regni sui paruit et obedivit, ne ipsius indignationem incurreret aut offen-sam, ac etiam metu mortis.

Rot. Parl. III, 418 (25); 419 (33); 420 (43); 421 (45).

(21) *Commission appointed to depose the king* 1399

Et quoniam videbatur omnibus Statibus illis, superinde singil-latim ac etiam communiter interrogatis, quod ille Cause Crimi-num et Defectuum erant satis sufficientes et notorie ad deponen-dum eundem Regem,... Unde Status et Communitates predicti certos Commissarios, videlicet Episcopum Assavensem, Abbatem Glastonie, Comitem Gloucestrie, Dominum de Berkeleye, Thomam Erpyngham et Thomam Grey, Milites, et Willielmum Thirnyng, Justiciarium, unanimiter et concorditer constituerunt et deputarunt publice tunc ibidem, ad ferendum sententiam Depositionis hujusmodi, et ad deponendum eundem Ricardum Regem ab omni Dignitate, Magestate, et Honore Regiis,... prout in consimilibus casibus de antiqua consuetudine dicti Regni fuerat observatum. Et mox iidem Commissarii...ante dictam Sedem Regalem pro Tribunali sedentes,...eandem Sententiam de ipsorum Commissariorum voluntate et mandato legi et recitari fecerunt, in hec verba:

In Dei nomine Amen. Nos Johannes Episcopus Assavensis, Johannes Abbas Glastonie [etc.], per Pares et Proceres Regni Anglie Spirituales et Temporales, et ejusdem Regni Communitates omnes Status ejusdem Regni representantes, Commissarii ad infra scripta specialiter deputati, pro Tribunali sedentes, attentis Perjuriis multiplicibus, ac Crudelitate, aliisque quampluribus Criminibus dicti Ricardi, circa Regimen suum in Regnis et Dominio...commissis...; necnon Concessione predicti Ricardi recognoscentis et reputantis, ac veraciter ex certa scientia sua indicantis, se fuisse et esse insufficientem penitus et inutilem ad Regimen et Gubernationem Regnorum et Dominii predictorum..., ac propter sua demerita notoria non inmerito deponendum, per ipsum Ricardum prius emissa, ac de voluntate et mandato suis coram dictis Statibus publicata, eisque notificata...in vulgari,...ipsum Ricardum ex habundanti, et ad cautelam ad Regimen et Gubernationem dictorum Regnorum ac Dominii, Juriumque...fuisse et esse inutilem, inhabilem, insufficientem penitus, et indignum; ac propter premissa, et eorum pretextu, ab omni Dignitate et Honore Regiis,...merito deponendum Pronunciamus, Decernimus et Declaramus,...Dominis Archiepiscopis, Episcopis, et Prelatis, Ducibus, Marchionibus, Comitibus, Baronibus, Militibus, Vassallis, et Valvassoribus, ac ceteris Hominibus dictorum Regnorum et Dominii, ac aliorum Locorum ad dicta Regna et Dominium spectantium, Subditis ac ligeis suis quibuscumque, Inhibentes expresse, ne quisquam ipsorum de cetero prefato Ricardo, tanquam Regi vel Domino Regnorum aut Dominii predictorum, pareat quomodolibet vel intendat.

Rot. Parl. III, 422 (51, 52).

(22) *Claim of Henry of Lancaster to the throne* 1399

...Et confestim, ut constabat ex premissis, et eorum occasione Regnum Anglie cum pertinentiis suis vacare, prefatus Henricus Dux Lancastrie de loco suo surgens, et stans adeo erectus quod satis intueri posset a Populo, et muniens se humiliter signo Crucis in fronte et in pectore suo, Christi nomine primitus invocato, dictum Regnum Anglie, sic ut premittitur vacans, una cum

Corona ac omnibus membris et pertinentiis suis, vendicavit in lingua materna, sub hac forma verborum:

In the name of Fadir, Son, and Holy Gost, I Henry of Lancastre chalenge yis Rewme of Yngland and the Corone with all ye membres and ye appurtenances, als I yt am difendit be right lyne of the Blode comyng fro the gude lorde Kyng Henry therde, and thorghe yat ryght yat God of his grace hath sent me, with helpe of my Kyn and of my Frendes to recover it: the whiche Rewme was in poynt to be undone for defaut of Governance and undoyng of the gode Lawes.

Post quam quidem vendicationem et clameum, tam Domini Spirituales quam Temporales, et omnes Status ibidem presentes, singillatim et comuniter interrogati, Quid de illa vendicatione et clameo sentiebant? iidem Status, cum toto Populo, absque quacumque difficultate vel mora ut Dux prefatus super eos regnaret unanimiter consenserunt...

Rot. Parl. III, 422–3 (53, 54).

(23) *Speech of William Thirning to Richard II* 1399

Les Paroles qe William Thirnyng parla a Monsire Richard nadgairs Roy d'Engleterre, a le Toure de Loundres, en sa Chambre, le Mesqerdy prochein apres le fest de Seint Michell l'Archaunchell', s'ensuent:

Sire, it is wele knowe to zowe, that ther was a Parlement somond of all the States of the Reaume for to be at Westmynstre, and to begynne on the Teusday in the morne of the fest of Seint Michell the Archaungell that was zesterday, by cause of the whiche sommons all the States of this Londe were ther gadyrd, the whiche States hole made thes same Persones that ben comen here to zowe nowe her Procuratours, and gafen hem full auctorite and power, and charged hem, for to say the wordes that we sall say to zowe in her name and on thair behalve; that is to wytten, the Bysshop of Seint Assa for Ersbisshoppes and Bysshoppes; the Abbot of Glastenbury for Abbotes and Priours, and all other men of holy Chirche Seculers and Rewelers; the Erle of Gloucestre for Dukes and Erles; the Lord of Berkeley for Barones and Banerettes; Sir Thomas Irpyngham, Chaumberleyn, for all the Bachilers and Commons of this Lond be southe; Sire Thomas Grey for all the Bachilers and Commons by north; and my felawe Johan Markham and me, for to come wyth hem for all thes States. And so, Sire, thes wordes and the doyng that we sall say to zowe is not onlych our wordes bot the wordes and the doynges of all the States of this lond and our charge and in her name...

And we,...zeld zowe uppe, for all the States and Poeple forsayd, Homage liege and Feaute, and all Ligeance, and all other bondes, charges, and services that longe ther to. And that non of all thes States and Poeple fro this tyme forward ne bere zowe feyth, ne do zowe obeisance os to thar Kyng.

Rot. Parl. III, 424 (59).

(24) *Declaration of Archbishop Arundel at the opening of parliament* 1399

Au Parlement somons et tenuz a Westmonstier par le Roy Henry le Quart,...le vime jour d'Octobre, l'an du regne...primer;... Thomas d'Arundell Ercevesqe de Canterbirs reherceant, Coment, le Maresdy darrein passez, qe feust lendemain de Seint Michel et le jour de Seint Jerome le Doctour, a quel jour le Roy Richard... avoit somonez son Parlement d'y estre tenuz; quele sommons ne feust du null force n'effect, a cause de l'acceptacion de la Renunciacion fait par le dit Roy Richard, et de la Deposition de mesme le Roy Richard qe feust fait le Maresdy suis dit, come par le Record et Proces ent faitz et enrollez en cest Rolle du Parlement piert pluis au plein;...monstra et declara...Qe cest honorable Roialme d'Engleterre, q'est la pluis habundant Angle de Richesse parmy tout le monde, avoit estee par longe temps mesnez, reulez, et governez par Enfantz, et conseil des Vefves; par ont mesme le Roialme feust en point de perdition,...s'il ne feusse qe Dieu tout-puissant de sa grand grace et mercy avoit mys un Homme sachant et discret pur Governance de mesme le Roialme, lequele par l'eide de Dieu voet estre governez...par les Sages et Aunciens de son Roialme,...

Rot. Parl. III, 415 (1, 2).

(25) *The commons and the royal prerogative* 1399

Item, come al request Richard darrein Roy d'Engleterre en un Parlement tenuz a Wyncestre, les Communes du dit Parlement luy graunteront, q'il serreit en auxi bon Libertee come sez progenitours devant luy furent: Pur quele Graunte le dit Roy disoit q'il purroit tourner les Leyes a sa voluntee, et les fist tourner encountre son serment,...Et ore en cest present Parlement les Communes d'icell, de lour bon gree et voluntee, confiantz en les

nobeley, haut discretion, et graciouse governance le Roy nostre
Seignur, luy ount grauntez, Q'ils voillent, q'il soit en auxi
graunde Libertee Roial come ses nobles progenitours furent devant luy: Sur quoy, mesme nostre Seignur, de grace Roial et
tendre conscience, ad graunte en pleyn Parlement, Qe il n'est
pas son entente ne voluntee pur tourner les Leyes, Estatutz, ne
bones Usages, ne pur prendre autre avantage par le dit Graunte,
mes pur garder les anciens Leyes et Estatuz...et faire droit a touz
gentz, en mercy et veritee, solonc son serment.

Responsio. Le Roy le voet.

Rot. Parl. III, 434 (108).

(26) *Year Book case: letters patent against a
statute disallowed* 1409

Un qui fuit utlage en breve de Dette, et eyt son Charter de
pardon, et sur ceo eyt sue un *Scire facias*, mist avant un Protection
quia profecturus est en le company Thome fits du Roy en Ireland.
Skrene. Le protection est purchase pendant le breve, et par le
statute de an 13 R. 2. cap. 16. tiel protection ne serra my allow,
sinon que il alera ove le Roy mesme, ou en voyage Royal, ou en
message le Roy, et le defendant est en nul de ceux cases, par
quoi, etc. *Tildesley.* Voyage Royal ne puit estre, sinon que il
avera ascun hoste d'estre amesne par le terre vers Ireland.
Tirwit. J'ay regard le statute de cest matter, et a ma entent si
cest protection serra allow, le statute ne servera de riens, et il
covient que il serve a ascun purpose, et come ad estre touche, cest
aler en Ireland, ne puit estre dit voyage Royal, sans l'amesne d'un
hoste, come Thomas le Duke de Glouc' fist un foits en France, et
auxint monsire Robert Knowles, et ceux voiages fuerent adjudge
Royals, pur ce que ils alerent come le Lieutenant le Roy ove lour
host...*Hankford* a *Horton.* Veies que vous voile faire, pur ce que
nostre mastre et nous sumus avises que le protection ne serra my
allow, etc.

Year Book (1679 edition), 11 Hen. IV, Mich. term, pl. 17. (We
are indebted to Dr S. B. Chrimes for this reference, and similarly
for document 29 below.)

(27) *Extension of the law of treason* 1423

...Ordeinez est...par auctorite dicest present parlement par
estatut, qe si ascune persone soit endite appelle ou pris pur suspecion de graunt traison come avant est dit et soit commys et

detenuz en prisone du Roy pur celle cause et eschape voluntere-
ment hors du dit prisone, qe tiel eschape soit adjugge et declare
traison si tiel persone ent soit duement atteint solonc le ley de
ceste terre:...et teignent cest ordinance...effect del xx jour
Doctobre darrein passe tanqe au parlement proscheinement
avenir.

S.R. II, 226, 2 Hen. VI, c. 21.

(28) *The title of the Duke of York* 1460

...Wheruppon, on the morn the xviii day of October,...the
forseid Lordes sent for the Kyngs Justices into the Parlement
Chambre, to have their avis and Counsell in this behalf, and
there delyvered to theym the writyng of the cleyme of the seid
Duc, and in the Kyngs name gave theym straitely in commaundement, sadly to take avisament therin, and to serche and fynde all
such objections as myght be leyde ayenst the same, in fortefying
of the Kynges right.

Wherunto the same Justices, the Monday, the xx day of
Octobre then next ensuyng, for their answere...seiden, that they
were the Kyngs Justices, and have to determyne such maters as
com before theym in the lawe, betwene partie and partie, and in
such maters as been betwene partie and partie they may not be of
Counseill; and sith this mater was betwene the Kyng and the
seid Duc of York as two parties, and also it hath not be accustumed
to calle the Justices to Counseill in such maters, and in especiall
the mater was so high, and touched the Kyngs high estate and
regalie, which is above the lawe and passed ther lernyng, wherfore
they durst not enter into eny communication therof, for it per-
teyned to the Lordes of the Kyngs blode, and th'apparage of this
his lond, to...medle in such maters; and therfore they humble
bysought all the Lordes, to have theym utterly excused...

And then the seid Lordes,...sent for all the Kyngs Sergeauntes
and Attourney, and gave theym straight commaundement in the
Kyngs name, that they sadly and avisely shuld serche and seke
all such thinges as myght be best and strengest to be alegged for
the Kynges availe...

Wherunto the seid Sergeaunts and Attourney...answered and
seiden...sith that the seid matier was soo high that it passed the
lernyng of the Justices, it must nedes excede their lernyng, and
also they durst not entre eny communication in that matier...

...And than it was agreed by all the Lordes, that every Lord shuld have his fredome to sey what he wuld sey, withoute eny reportyng or magre to be had for his seiyng. And theruppon...it was concluded, that thes maters and articles hereunder writen, shuld be alegged and objecte ayenst the seid clayme and title of the seid Duc.

First, it is thought that the Lordes of this lond must nedes calle to their remembrauncez, the grete Othes the which they have made to the Kyng oure Soverayn Lord,...

Item, it is thought also, that it is to be called to remembraunce, the grete and notable Acts of Parlements,...the which Acts be sufficient and resonable to be leyde ageyn the title of the seid Duc of York: The which Acts been of moche more auctorite than eny Cronycle, and also of auctorite to defete eny manere title made to eny persone.

Item, it is thought that ther is to be leyde ageyn the seid title, dyvers entayles made to the heires males as for the Corone of Englond,...

Item, it is thought yf the seid Duc shuld make eny title...by the lyne of Sir Leonell, that the same Duc shuld bere the armes of the same Leonell, and not the armes of Edmund Langley, late Duc of York.

Item, it is to be allegged ageyn the title of the seid Duc, that the tyme that Kyng Herry the fourth toke uppon hym the Corone of Englond, he seid he entred and toke uppon hym the Corone, as right enheriter to Kyng Herry the third, and not as a Conquerour.

[*The Duke of York then made answer, and there was further
discussion among the lords, who consulted the king.*]

Concordia facta inter Regem et prefatum Ducem.

...To the which Richard Duc of York, as son to Anne, doughter to Rogier Mortymer Erle of Marche, son and heire to the said Phelippe, doughter and heire to the said Leonell, the third goten son of the seid Kyng Edward the third, the right, title, dignite roiall and estate, of the Corones of the Reaumes of Englond and of Fraunce, and of the Lordship...of Irelond, of right...belongeth, afore eny issue of the seid John of Gaunt, the fourth goten son of the same Kyng Edward.

The said Title natheles natwithstandyng,...the seid Richard Duc of York, tenderly desiryng the wele, rest and prosperite of this lande,...; and consideryng the possession of the seid Kyng Herry the sixt,...is content,...that he be had, reputed and taken, Kyng of Englond and of Fraunce, with the Roiall estate, dignitee and preemynence belongyng therto, and Lord of Irelond, duryng his lyf naturall; and for that tyme, the said Duc withoute hurte or prejudice of his said right and title, shall take, wurship and honour hym for his Soverayn Lord.

Rot. Parl. v, 376–8.

(29) *Year Book case*: *the outlawry of John Paston*: *discussion if officials retain office under a new king*: *opinion that parliament is dissolved by the king's death* 1465

Edwardus dei gratia Rex Angliæ et Franciæ, Quia in recordo et processu ac etiam in promulgacione utlagariæ in Johannem Paston Seniorem in Comitatu Suffolk, Gentleman,...error intervenit manifestus ad grave dampnum ipsius Johannis, sicut per inspectionem recordi et processus prædictorum, etc. Et le breve fuit ouster accordant al comen course del forme del breve d'error, etc. Et en maner touts Justices disoient que est estrange breve,... car par cel brief n'appiert le quel il soit utlage al suit del party, ou al suit del Roy, ou a quel suit, ou a quel chose, et poit estre que il est utlage de felony, ou de det, trespas, ou accompt, ou pur fine al Roy sur condempnation, et issint le breve n'est certeine, et les Juistices ne ont...power certein sur quel matter ou recorde d'utlagary ils duissent proceder reverser le utlagary,...[*Reference was then made to some of the Masters of Chancery*]. Et les Justices desiront les Masters avantdit de aler en le Chancery, et a commoner ove lour compaignions, issint que nous averomus certein conusance de le course en cest case etc., et les Masters aleront lour voye, etc. *Markham.* Le Chief Justice dit, que si le course soit tiel que le brief d'error est general, donques *Paston* ad fait bien, et si le course soit auter, donques n'est bien fait, etc. Mes les Justices fuerent accordes que *Supersedeas* especial issera al Viscont, *quod caperet securitatem de J. Paston pro Rege, quod non elongabit bona sua, quousque discussum fuerit*, etc. et que l'Escheator ou Viscont ne seisera les biens de John Paston, tanque discusse soit pur le Roy ou pur John Paston, issint que si le utlagary soit reverse, il avera ses biens en peace, et si les utlages ne soient reverse, donques le Roy avera les biens sur le forfaiture de utlagary,...

Et puis par avis de touts les Justices, Sir John Paston, avoit tiel *Supersedeas* especial come le comen cours est a faire, etc. *Yelverton.* Avant a ce que est dit que les coroners avantdit ne fuerent novelment eslues en temps le Roy que ore est, issint que ils ne sont coroners a Roy,...semble que ils sont, car le coroner n'ad commission sicome auter minister ad, ou come auter Judge ad, mes par brief le Roy, il est eslue, quel eleccion certifie en le Chancery, est act de record et judicial act, en quel case al meins judicial acts fait en temps le Roy que fuit, sont affirmes par le Roy et tout son councel, et par nostre ley, issint que les coroners avantdit sont uncore coroners...*Choke.* Ils fuerent un foits eslues, quel est certifie de record en le Chancery par comen entent,...et issint ils sont coroners uncore,...tanque auter election soit fait par le commandement le Roy par breve ou commission, issint que ils soyent discharge et removes par auctoritie et par le precept le Roy, et issint le power de les coroners avantdit uncore demurrust en force, pur ascun chose que est dit etc. *Catesby.* Sir ce n'est judicial act le election des coroners a tiel entent que coroners eslues en temps le Roy que fuit, pur sever et estre coroners al Roy que ore est, sont pluis que Chyvalers des Counties eslues en temps le Roy que fuit a un temps de son Parliament, quel election est certifie al Chancery ou al clerc del Parliament, et est record sicome auters elections des burges des villes eslues en les cities ou villes sont certifie, etc. et quel Parliament le Roy que fuit par son demis par case est discontinue, et le Roy que ore est sumone novel Parliament, et direct briefs a chescun Countie de Engleterre par son esluer novel Chivalers etc. si tiel election par case fait en un County ou auter, uncore les Chivalers que fuerent en le darrein Parliament devant, ne serront my Chivalers en ce novel Parliament, car lour power est determine quant cel Parliament est discontinue ou determine, et issint est de Parliament nostre Seignior le Roy que ore est, si ce Parliament soit dissolve et puis novel Parliament sommone, les eisne Chivalers del eisne Parliament ne serront my Chivalers del novel Parliament, sinon que novel election et novel act soit pur eux etc. *Sothill.* Le Atturney le Roy, si les verdours del forest soient eslues par breve de Roy en temps le Roy que fuit, etc. ore mesme verdours et le officers de forest estoient en temps le Roy que ore est, sinon que auter novel election soit fait par breve ou precept le Roy, etc. *Catesby et Pigot,* et auters, tout est un case et equedubium, etc.

Year Book (1680 edition), 4 Ed. IV, Hilary term, pl. 4.

(30) *Sir John Fortescue: "De laudibus legum Angliae" (written* 1468–70)

Chapter IX. *Rex politice dominans non potest mutare leges regni sui*
Secundum vero, Princeps, quod tu formidas, consimili nec majori opera elidetur. Dubitas nempe, an Anglorum legum vel Civilium studio te conferas, dum Civiles supra humanas cunctas leges alias,

fama per orbem extollat gloriosa. Non te conturbet, Fili Regis, hec mentis evagatio: Nam non potest Rex Anglie ad libitum suum leges mutare regni sui, principatu namque nedum regali, sed et politico, ipse suo populo dominatur. Si regali tantum ipse pre-esset eis, leges regni sui mutare ille posset, tallagia quoque et cetera onera eis imponere ipsis inconsultis, quale dominium de-notant leges Civiles, cum dicant "Quod Principi placuit, legis habet vigorem." Sed longe aliter potest rex politice imperans genti sue, quia nec leges ipse sine subditorum assensu mutare poterit, nec subjectum populum renitentem onerare imposicioni-bus peregrinis, quare populus ejus libere fruetur bonis suis, legibus quas cupit regulatus, nec per regem suum, aut quemvis alium depilatur; consimiliter tamen plaudit populus, sub rege regaliter tantum principante, dummodo in tirannidem ipse non labatur. De quali rege dicit Philosophus III. Politicorum, quod "melius est civitatem regi viro optimo, quam lege optima". Sed quia non semper contingit presidentem populo hujusmodi esse virum, Sanctus Thomas in libro quem regi Cypri scripsit, de Regimine Principum, optare censetur, regnum sic institui, ut rex non libere valeat populum suum tirannide gubernare, quod solum fit, dum potestas regia lege politica cohibetur:...

Chapter X. *Interrogacio Principis*

Tunc Princeps illico sic ait. Unde hoc, Cancellarie, quod rex unus plebem suam regaliter tantum regere valeat, et regi alteri potestas hujusmodi denegetur? Equalis fastigii cum sint reges ambo, cur in potestate sint ipsi dispares nequeo non admirari.

Chapter XI. *Renuncio ad alias tractata*

Cancellarius. Non minoris esse potestatis regem politice imper-antem, quam qui ut vult regaliter regit populum suum, in supra-dicto Opusculo sufficienter est ostensum; diverse tamen autori-tatis eos esse in subditos suos ibidem aut jam nullatenus denegavi; cujus diversitatis causam, ut potero, tibi pandam.

Chapter XII. *Qualiter regna tantum regaliter regulata primitus inchoata sunt*

Homines quondam potencia prepollentes, avidi dignitatis et glorie, vicinas sepe gentes sibi viribus subjugarunt, ac ipsis servire, obtemperare quoque jussionibus suis compulerunt, quas jussiones extunc leges hominibus illis esse ipsi sancierunt. Quarum per-pecione diutina, subjectus sic populus, dum per subjicientes a ceterorum injuriis defendebatur, in subjiciencium dominium con-senserunt: opportunius esse arbitrantes, se unius subdi imperio,

quo erga alios defenderentur, quam omnium eos infestare volencium oppressionibus exponi. Sic que regna quedam inchoata
sunt, et subjicientes illi, dum subjectum populum sic rexerunt, a
regendo sibi nomen *regis* usurparunt, eorum quoque dominatus
tantum regalis dictus est. Sic Nembroth primus sibi regnum
comparavit, tamen non *rex* ipse, sed "robustus venator coram
Domino" Sacris Literis appellatus est:...

Chapter XIII. *Qualiter regna politice regulata primitus inceperunt*

Sanctus Augustinus in Libro XIX. de Civitate Dei, Cap. XXIII.
dixit quod "populus est cetus hominum, juris consensu et utilitatis
communione sociatus". Nec tamen populus hujusmodi dum
acephalus, id est sine capite est, corpus vocari meretur. Quia ut in
naturalibus capite detruncato, residuum non corpus, sed truncum
appellamus; sic et in politicis, sine capite communitas nullatenus
corporatur. Quo primo politicorum dixit Philosophus, quod
"quandocunque ex pluribus constituitur unum inter illa, unum
erit regens, et alia erunt recta". Quare populum, se in regnum
aliudve corpus politicum erigere volentem, semper oportet unum
preficere tocius corporis illius regitivum, quem per analogiam in
regnis, a regendo *regem* nominare solitum est....Et sicut in naturali
corpore, ut dixit Philosophus, cor est primum vivens, habens in se
sanguinem, quem emittit in omnia ejus membra, unde illa vege-
tantur et vivunt; sic in corpore politico, intencio populi primum
vivens est, habens in se sanguinem, viz. provisionem politicam
utilitati populi illius, quam in caput et in omnia membra ejusdem
corporis ipsa transmittit, quo corpus illud alitur et vegetatur.
Lex vero, sub qua cetus hominum populus efficitur, nervorum
corporis phisici tenet racionem; quia sicut per nervos compago
corporis solidatur, sic per legem, que a *ligando* dicitur, corpus
hujusmodi misticum ligatur, et servatur in unum, et ejusdem
corporis membra ac ossa, que veritatis qua communitas illa sus-
tentatur soliditatem denotant, per legem, ut corpus naturale per
nervos propria retinent jura. Et ut non potest caput corporis
phisici nervos suos commutare, neque membris suis proprias vires,
et propria sanguinis alimenta denegare, nec rex, qui caput corporis politici est, mutare potest leges corporis illius, nec ejusdem
populi substantias proprias subtrahere, reclamantibus eis aut
invitis. Habes ex hoc jam, Princeps, institutionis regni politici
formam, ex qua metiri poteris potestatem, quam rex ejus in leges
ipsius aut subditos valeat exercere. Ad tutelam namque legis
subditorum, ac eorum corporum et bonorum Rex hujusmodi
erectus est, et hanc potestatem a populo effluxam ipse habet, quo

ei non licet potestate alia suo populo dominari. Quare ut postu-
lationi tue, qua certiorari cupis, unde hoc provenit quod potes-
tates regum tam diversimode variantur, succinctius satisfaciam.
Firme conjector, quod diversitates institucionum dignitatum
illarum, quas propalavi, predictam discrepanciam solummodo
operantur, prout racionis discursu tu ex premissis poteris ex-
haurire. Sic namque regnum Anglie, quod ex Bruti comitiva
Trojanorum, quam ex Italie et Grecorum finibus perduxit, in
dominium politicum et regale prorupit: sic et Scotia, que ei quondam ut ducatus obedivit, in regnum crevit politicum et regale...

Chapter XIV. *Princeps hic succincte epilogat quod Cancellarius
diffuse antea declaravit*

Cui Princeps; Effugasti, Cancellarie, declarationis tue lumine
tenebras quibus obducta erat acies mentis mee, quo clarissime
jam conspicio, quod non alio pacto gens aliqua, proprio arbitrio,
unquam se in regnum corporavit, nisi ut per hoc se et sua quorum
dispendia formidabant, tucius quam antea possiderent; quasi pro-
posito gens hujusmodi fraudaretur, si exinde facultates eorum
eripere possit rex suus, quod antea facere ulli hominum non lice-
bat. Et adhuc gravius multo populus talis lederetur, si deinde
peregrinis legibus, ipsis forsan exosis, regerentur. Et maxime, si
legibus illis eorum minoraretur substancia, pro cujus vitanda
jactura, ut pro suorum tutela corporum, ipsi se regis imperio
arbitrio proprio submiserunt, non potuit revera potestas hujusmodi ab ipsis erupisse; et tamen si non ab ipsis, rex hujusmodi
super ipsos nullam obtineret potestatem. E regione, aliter esse
concipio de regno, quod regis solum autoritate et potencia in-
corporatum est; quia non alio pacto gens talis ei subjecta est, nisi
ut ejus legibus, que sunt illius voluntatis placitati, gens ipsa, que
eodem placito regnum ejus effecta est, obtemperaret et regeretur.
Neque, Cancellarie, a mea hucusque memoria elapsum est, quod
alias in tractatu de Natura Legis Nature, horum duorum regum
equalem esse potentiam doctis racionibus ostendisti, dum potestas
qua eorum alter perperam agere liber est, libertate hujusmodi non
augetur; ut posse languescere morive, potentia non est, sed
propter privationem in adjecto, impotentia potius denominandum
est. Quia, ut dicit Boecius, "Potencia non est nisi ad bonum";
quo posse male agere, ut potest rex regaliter regnans liberius
quam rex politice dominans populo suo, potius ejus potestatem
minuit, quam augmentat...

Fortescue, *De laudibus legum Angliae* (ed. Gregor), pp. 232–8.

(31) *Sir John Fortescue on "The Governance of*
England" (written 1471–6)

Chapter I. *The deference bi twene dominium regale*
and dominium politicum et regale

Ther bith ij kyndes off kyngdomes, of the wich that on is a lordship callid in laten *dominium regale*, and that other is callid *dominium*
politicum et regale. And thai diuersen in that the first kynge mey
rule his peple bi suche lawes as he makyth hym self. And therfore
he mey sett vppon thaim tayles and other imposicions, such as he
wol hym self, withowt thair assent. The secounde kynge may not
rule his peple bi other lawes than such as thai assenten unto.
And therfore he mey sett vpon thaim non imposicions withowt
thair owne assent. This diuersite is wel taught bi Seynt Thomas,
in his boke wich he wrote *ad regem Cipri de regemine principum*. But
yet it is more openly tredid in a boke callid *compendium moralis*
philosophie—and sumwhat bi Giles in his boke *de regimine principum*.
The childeryn of Israell, as saith Seynt Thomas, aftir that God
hade chosen thaim *in populum peculiarem et regnum sacerdotale*, were
ruled bi hym vndir Juges *regaliter et police*, in to the tyme that
thai desired to haue a kynge, as tho hade al the gentiles, wich we
cal peynymes, that hade no kynge but a man that reigned vppon
thaim *regaliter tantum*. With wich desire God was gretly offendyd,
as wele for thair folie, as for thair vnkyndnes;...Wereby it mey
appere that in tho dayis *regimen politicum et regale* was distyngued
a regemine tantum regale; and that it was bettir to the peple to be
ruled politekely and roialy than to be ruled only roialy. Seynt
Thomas also in his said boke prasith *dominium politicum et regale*,
bi cause the prince that reigneth bi such lordshippe mey not frely
falle into tyrannye, as mey the prince that reigneth *regaliter*
tantum. And yet thai both bith egall in estate and in poiar, as it
mey lightly be shewed and provid by infallyble reason.

Chapter II. *Whi oon king regneth regaliter, and another*
politice et regaliter

Hit mey peraventur be mervellid be some men, whi on reaume
is a lordeshippe only roialle, and the prince therof rulith it bi his
lawe callid *Jus regale*; and a nother kyngdome is a lordshippe
roiall and politike, and the prince therof rulith hit bi a lawe
callid *Jus polliticum et regale*; sithin thes ij princes bith of egal
estate. To this doute it mey be answerde in this maner. The first
institucion of thes ij realmes vppon the incorperacion of thaim is

cause of this diuersite. Whan Nembroth be myght for his owne glorie made and incorperate the first realme, and subdued it to hymself bi tyrannye, he wolde not have it gouernyd bi any oþer rule or lawe, but bi his owne wille; bi wich and for the accomplisshment þerof he made it. And therfore though he hade thus made hym a realme, holy scripture disdeyned to call hym a kynge, *quia rex dicitur a regendo*; wich thynge he did not, but oppressyd the peple bi myght, and therfore he was a tirraunt and callid *primus tirrannorum.* But holy write callith hym *robustus venator coram Domino*...Aftir hym Belus that was first callid a kynge, aftir hym is sone Ninus, and aftir hym other paynemes, þat bi ensample of Nembroth made hem realmes, wolde not haue thaim ruled bi oþer lawes then be ther owne wylles. Wich lawes ben right gode vndir gode princes, and thair kyngdomes bethe than most resembled to the kyngdome of God,...Wherfore mony cristen princes vsen the same lawe; and therfore it is that þe lawes seyn, *quod principi placuit, legis habet vigorem.* And thus I suppose first be gan in Realmes *dominium tantum regale.* But aftirwarde, whan mankynde was more mansuete, and bettir disposid to vertu, grete comunaltes, as was the felowshippe that came in to this lande with Brute, willynge to be vnite and made a body pollitike callid a reawme, hauynge an hed to gouerne it;—as aftir the saynge of the philosopher, euery comunalte vnyed of mony parties must nedis haue an hed;—than they chese the same Brute to be þer hed and kynge. And thai and he...ordenyd the same reaume to be ruled and justified by suche lawes as thai all wolde assent vnto; wich lawe therfore is called *polliticum*, and bi cause it is ministrid bi a kynge, it is callid *regale. Policia dicitur a* poles, *quod est plures, et* ycos, *scientia; quo regimen politicum dicitur* regimen plurium scientia siue consilio ministratum. The kynge of Scottis reignith vppon is peple bi this lawe, videlicet, *regemine politico et regali.* And as Diodorus Siculus saith in is boke *de priscis historiis,* the reawme of Egipte is ruled bi the same lawe, and therfore the kynge therof chaungith not his lawes withowt the assent of his peple...Now as me semyth it is shewid openly ynough, whi on kynge reignith vpon is peple *dominio tantum regali,* and that other reignith *dominio politico et regali;* ffor that on kyngdome be ganne of and bi the might of the prince, and that oþer be ganne bi the desire and institucion of the peple of the same prince.

Fortescue, *Governance of England* (ed. Plummer), pp. 109–13.

CHAPTER II

THE COUNCIL

INTRODUCTION

By the end of the thirteenth century the process of dismemberment of the *curia regis*, which had begun with the emergence of the exchequer in the twelfth century, was further advanced. First the financial, then the judicial and executive business of government, necessitated the formation of a specialised department. After 1272 the chancery was at last distinct from the household as a public department, and the courts of common law were becoming separate. The main interest of the history of the central government is in the development of the council as a consultative and advisory body, yet retaining a residue of all the powers of the *curia regis*. In the council the king had supreme authority, whether in matters of justice or general administration, and from the council other departments were controlled. The chief problems connected with the council in the fourteenth and fifteenth centuries are twofold; first, concerning its personnel—including the difference between the council in parliament, great council, and continual council; and secondly, the significance of the struggle between king and barons, in which parliament was later involved, for the control of the composition and powers of the council.

In earlier times the council consisted of those whom the king wished to be summoned, normally the great officers, members of the royal household, and sometimes barons. From Henry II's time the baronial element was less often included, and in the thirteenth century the barons were actively claiming their right to give counsel to the king. In the critical years after 1258 an attempt was made to set up a continual council to be resident with the king; in that year the magnates had succeeded in nominating great officials such as chancellor, treasurer and justiciar, but the reason for their ultimate failure is to be found in their neglect of the royal household. Actually the king was left with a vast sphere of control, since the officials of the wardrobe carried on a large part of the routine of government; in Edward I's reign the wardrobe was to be specially developed and was to take its place with chancery and exchequer as a great department.[1]

At the end of Henry III's reign an important step in conciliar development was taken; in 1271 the council was sworn, apparently a voluntary move on the part of the king instead of under baronial pressure as before,[2] and after Edward I's accession it was usual for the small advisory council to be thus sworn. The numbers of this council might vary, but for the regular administrative business it normally consisted of great officials, such as the chancellor and treasurer, of officials of the household such as the chamberlain, steward and keeper of the wardrobe, and of judges. At the same time the magnates might be specially summoned by writ to a council, and further, Edward I was developing the practice of summoning by writ under the great seal representatives of the shires and boroughs to his council, probably for administrative as well as for financial purposes. It is true in one sense that there was only one council with equal and unlimited powers, whether a small body of councillors meeting regularly, or an enlarged council including magnates, or the council with representatives meeting as parliament;[3] but during the fourteenth century there is greater distinction, and a threefold development can be traced.

1. Gradually the council came to be separate from parliament.[4] At first during Edward I's reign and in the next half century the king's council in parliament had real control, and during this time the main work of parliament was judicial. The council in parliament originated statutes, and at first the local representatives of county and borough had little share in the government; after their dismissal the council remained, transacting all important business. But this initiative was not left unchallenged; the council came to be the object of political attack which eventually weakened its authority in parliament. A great development was also taking place in parliament itself; two houses were emerging and the commons were beginning to cooperate in parliamentary business. Legislation by common petition was becoming more important than individual petition, and the legislative work of parliament was increasing, though throughout the medieval period its judicial character was never lost. The judges, for example, after Edward III's reign sat in parliament as advisors only,[5]

---

[1] See below, pp. 93–4.
[2] Baldwin, *King's council*, pp. 30–7.
[3] *Ibid.* pp. 67–8.
[4] See Parliament section, p. 122.
[5] Baldwin, *op. cit.* pp. 76–7.

though the commons might petition for their presence(14). As a result of these developments the council and parliament were separating, though very gradually. In 1383 a distinction was made between petitions which could only be treated in parliament, and those which could only be dealt with by the council;[1] the distinction is most clearly seen in the rivalry of the lords in parliament with the council concerning jurisdiction. By the fifteenth century the term "council in parliament" might be used, but it meant the magnates in parliament, later to be known as the house of lords; and it was in the upper house that judicial authority was retained, as in the case of impeachments.

2. In the history of the great council there are problems not all of which have been solved. Especially in Edward III's reign there was a close similarity between the personnel of the great council, to which magnates, clergy and local representatives might be summoned, and of parliament; at least eight great councils can be traced between 1327 and 1353 to which the commons were more or less regularly summoned, and it has been suggested that an attempt was being made to deal with the increasing administrative work by means of afforced councils independent of the judicial tribunal of parliament.[2] By 1353, however, such a policy was failing; after this time, while great councils might still be summoned by writ of privy seal, their records were not entered in the rolls of parliament,[3] and little is known in detail about their activities.[4] In the early fifteenth century contemporaries were distinguishing between the different aspects of the council(28,35);[5] the great council dealt with important business under Henry V and his son, as at the time of a political crisis,[6] and one of its duties was to deliberate on the advisability of summoning a parliament(34). Most probably it declined as the magnates themselves lost influence and it is rarely mentioned in later records.[7]

3. The history of the continual council is more straightforward. It was essential to have a small regular council for effective administration, and the main interest here is to trace out the

[1] Baldwin, *op. cit.* p. 334.
[2] H. G. Richardson and G. Sayles, "The parliaments of Edward III", in *Bulletin of the Institute of Historical Research*, VIII, no. 23, pp. 65–77.
[3] Baldwin, *op. cit.* pp. 257 ff.
[4] Cf. Tout, *Chapters*, III, 336 n. 5, 470–3.
[5] Baldwin, *op. cit.* pp. 107–8.
[6] *Ibid.* pp. 192, 200, 203; and cf. article by T. F. T. Plucknett, *Trans. R.H.S.* 1918, pp. 165 ff.
[7] Cf. *Documents illustrating Henry VII's reign* (ed. A. F. Pollard), II, 46.

struggles for control of this council. From Edward I's reign the officials of the household had had an especially prominent part in the sworn council; and one great aim of the baronial opposition to Edward II was to reinforce the council by fit men who should control the king.[1] They would have set up a responsible council to act with the king, but no attempt was made to prescribe the exact form of election, on which point the projects of 1258–9 had failed. The baronial council of 1316 with Lancaster at its head (2) was a failure, as were later councils, such as that of 1318 (4). The magnates were on the whole incapable of maintaining a consistently strong policy, whereas the king's household was sufficiently well organised and staffed to enable him to evade many of the baronial demands, except for a short period after the battle of Bannockburn. The more moderate government after 1318 gave him fuller scope, and in 1322 the Lancastrian forces were defeated and the Despensers restored. The end of the reign is remarkable in that, among the officials who now controlled the government, there were some leaders with a clearly defined policy which effected a reform of the whole administration and gave it a structure which was to outlast the medieval period.[2]

Edward III, after the short-lived rule of Isabella and Mortimer, at first cooperated with the magnates, but later began to evade their control, relying on the officials of his household as Edward II had done, and his military needs at the outbreak of the Hundred Years' War led him to extend this policy. By the Walton ordinance of 1338 he had arranged for a dual council control, subordinating the council in England to that in France,[3] but Archbishop Stratford gained the upper hand for the magnates in September, 1339, and was perforce recognised by Edward as chief councillor and was again made chancellor. In the parliament of March, 1340, grants were made to the king only when he consented to certain petitions, and the triumph of the aristocratic party was for the moment complete. When the king realised that his renewed demands for supplies for his campaign were meeting with little response, in November, 1340, he returned to England in a fury, dismissed a great number of officials (5), and precipitated a parliamentary crisis which was fought on old and new issues.[4] The bitter public attack made by the king upon the archbishop had little result, nor did Edward reap much advantage from his interference with local

[1] See Crown section, pp. 3–4.
[2] See below, pp. 95–6.   [3] Tout, *Chapters*, III, 80 ff.
[4] Cf. article by G. Lapsley, *E.H.R.* 1915.

officials or his attempt to institute a general eyre. A compromise was finally reached, whereby magnates and officials were to share the duties of the council, and in the following years there was peaceful administration while the French war proved successful for English arms. New appointments were made later,[1] but it is doubtful if any ministry could have given satisfaction in the troublous time especially after 1371 (cf. 10), which saw the failure of the war, financial difficulties, corruption at home, and a degenerate court. The stage was set for that most spectacular of medieval parliaments, the Good Parliament of 1376, which produced an unprecedented number of petitions,[2] including one that the council should be afforced with worthy men. Nine councillors were appointed and sworn(11), and an attack upon the king's favourites was successfully carried out in the form of an impeachment, but the king avoided the real issue by leaving the great officials uncontrolled. During Edward's last illness John of Gaunt restored the fortunes of the court party, and disregarded the petitions of the last parliament; he in turn lost much authority before the end of the reign as the result of aristocratic opposition.

The first years of Richard II's reign saw a notable development in the continual council.[3] In 1377 twelve councillors were appointed by the magnates(12), while a salaried council of nine was chosen in the October parliament to carry on the government with the cooperation of the great officials(13), who were to be appointed by the magnates in parliament(15). A third council was similarly appointed in November, 1378, but the administration was not a success; the council disappointed the commons by demanding extra supplies, and in 1380 it was petitioned in parliament that the council should be removed, leaving only the five chief officials to be chosen(17). Instead of government by council, parliament now tried the plan of setting up a commission for the reform of the household. This had been attempted in 1379, and there were similar commissions in 1380(17) and in the next year(18), when the administration had to face a rapidly increasing economic crisis and a widespread peasant revolt. The commissions had little result; during the next years Richard was building up a court party, and in his turn was relying on tried officials of the household. In 1385 he refused to nominate his council in parliament,

[1] Tout, *Chapters*, III, 270–5.
[2] See Parliament section, p. 150.
[3] Cf. article by N. B. Lewis, *E.H.R.* 1926, correcting Baldwin's reference to the council in 1377, *op. cit.* pp. 120–2.

and this, with other causes, gave rise to the baronial attack in
1386. In the end the king was forced to dismiss his ministers,
Pole was impeached, and a commission of magnates and knights
was set up to act as a council(19). Little is known of the work of
the commission, but the triumph of the opposition is seen in the
Merciless Parliament of 1388. Once again a council was appointed in parliament, and in it the Lords Appellant predominated.
It ruled for a year; then Richard declared himself of age,
but in so doing he did not dismiss the council, or suspend its
members, but ˙chose rather to introduce gradually some of his
own officials and favourites. The magnates tended to absent themselves, salaries were no longer given, and during the years that
followed there was apparent peace, though with some signs of
future trouble, as seen in Richard's quarrel with London in
1392[1] (p. 398).

In spite of the apparent absolutism of the last years, Richard II's
reign is of the greatest importance in the history of the council.
First, we have much clearer knowledge of the continual council.
Only a small number attended its regular meetings, and these
were mainly the chief officials. From 1390 there are records of
proceedings of the council, at first incomplete, but throwing much
light on its proceedings.[2] As shown in the ordinance of that
year(20), the work was mainly administrative and judicial matters
were to go where possible to the courts of common law and the
chancery; the king was bound to take advice from the councillors
in matters of grants and appointments, and the procedure of the
council was regulated.[3] It is true that this ordinance was later
ignored, but it is valuable in the revelation which it gives of
conciliar development. The administrative council was now
clearly distinct from parliament and from the chancery.

Secondly, it is seen that in all the political crises of the reign the
commons in parliament were trying to take a part in the control
of the executive, as in the appointment of ministers, and of the
council.[4] Too much must not be made of this change, since the
influence of the magnates was clearly most important and decisive.
The weakness of parliament itself is shown in the events after
1397(cf. 22), and when Richard was accused in 1399 of having
used favourites as councillors, this was only a sign of the baronial
hatred of the administration of the household.

[1] See above, Crown section, pp. 5–6.
[2] *Proceedings and ordinances of the privy council* (ed. Nicolas).
[3] Tout, *Chapters*, III, 465 ff.   [4] See below, Parliament section, p. 124.

The defeat of Richard's plans in 1398–9, indeed, laid the foundations for the strong control of an aristocratic council, which was of supreme importance in Lancastrian politics. Until the end of Henry VI's minority the continual council, which might at times be afforced by additional magnates, really monopolised the government, though its inefficiency was often the ground for complaint, as in 1404. The king was asked in the same year to nominate his councillors in public (25), and in 1406 the council was forced to take oath before the commons, who, in the second session, drew up thirty-one articles of reform for the council (27). Attacks were also still levelled against the royal household, especially in Henry IV's reign (24, 26). Nevertheless, it was impracticable for the council to be changed at every succeeding parliament, and, after the first years of Henry IV's reign, the council was more permanent and was closely influenced by the magnates, though the official element was never absent. The authority of Prince Henry then secured for a time a united council under the influence of Beaufort, bishop of Winchester, though his policy was again reversed before 1413. In the next reign the council was predominantly aristocratic, but the lords were engrossed in the French war, and business was transacted by the great officials with little outside interference. In both these reigns, indeed, the magnates performed their duties very indifferently, and the routine work fell upon the chancellor, treasurer and keeper of the privy seal.

During the minority of Henry VI the lords in parliament again showed their power. A salaried aristocratic council was chosen, with extensive powers (29), and few of the prerogative rights were left to the Duke of Bedford as Protector, or to Humphrey, Duke of Gloucester acting in his brother's absence. The councillors actually made their own conditions upon taking office, and although in 1423 the list of their names was read publicly, there was no question of appointment in parliament; salaries were granted on a regular scale, with deductions for absence. Additional rules for business were drawn up in 1423 (30, 31) and extended in 1429.[1] The council gained further influence when Gloucester quarrelled with Beaufort after 1425; and when Bedford died ten years later there was no really responsible leader. Yet while the council had sovereign powers, it failed woefully to fulfil its functions; its judicial work was not carried out, and in administration it was hopelessly ineffective, and, still worse, corrupt. The furious

[1] Stubbs, *C.H.* III, 105 ff., 269 ff.

quarrels of the factions of Gloucester and Beaufort added to the misfortunes of such a rule.

Henry VI came of age in 1437; he assumed the prerogative powers, including the right of patronage, so that service in the council had not the same attraction for the magnates; but it was his misfortune to be blamed for the maladministration which seems to have been increasing (cf. 36).[1] Gloucester and Beaufort both died in 1447, and the royal favourite, the Duke of Suffolk, was disinclined to use the council, which in consequence began to lose its coherence. In the same way, the Duke of Somerset, who came into favour after Suffolk's death in 1451, disliked conciliar government and dispensed with it whenever possible. The Duke of York, who was coming to the fore as leader of the opposition, on the other hand used a council of his own supporters in 1454 when he acted as regent (38), which ceased in the next year when Henry recovered and restored Somerset to power. A second protectorate from 1455 to 1456 similarly failed. The council, thus rent by party feuds, had become corrupt and useless, and the evils of the central government had their counterpart in local troubles and disorders even before the outbreak of civil war.

Of the Yorkist council little is known. There are no registers of the council from 1460 to 1540, and contemporary documents are singularly silent on council affairs for this period. It would seem that Edward IV nominated his council and that the official element was strong at the expense of the baronial. He doubtless retained control in his own hands, even of judicial business (40), in which the council was more active after 1468, though here the chancery had made great headway.[2] Fortescue, writing during the reign, outlined a plan for a reformed council free from the undue influence of magnates and dependent solely upon the king (42); and it is possible that his writings had some effect later.[3]

The work of the council during these two centuries was very varied. In the judicial sphere procedure had been gradually defined. From early times the council had received and acted upon petitions, and appeals multiplied when the courts of common law were themselves developing. At first petitions were normally addressed to the king and his council (9), and only gradually to the chancellor alone.[2] If parliament was sitting petitions were

---

[1] Baldwin, *op. cit.* pp. 184 ff.; and cf. Plucknett, *op. cit.* pp. 181 ff.
[2] See below, p. 184.
[3] Cf. Baldwin, *op. cit.* pp. 419–35, on the Yorkist council.

dealt with there, but between sessions the council had considerable work. Further, it had its recognised jurisdiction over cases that could not be dealt with in the courts of common law, such as those concerning alien merchants, or maritime law. As compared with the procedure of the courts of common law that of the council was simple and speedy; a case was begun by bill or petition, the parties and witnesses could be examined on oath, no jury was needed.[1] The council had further adopted certain of the writs of chancery, notably *quibusdam certis de causis* and *sub pœna*; it had, in fact, more effective means of enforcing its decisions than had the courts of common law, and in the rivalry which perforce resulted, the commons in parliament championed the common law, opposing the issue of the newer writs. The opposition to the council is to be seen also in frequent petitions during the fourteenth century, which led to statutory limitation of conciliar jurisdiction, as in 1331, and 1352(8). These and later statutes did not succeed in altering the procedure of the council, but its jurisdiction was definitely limited in that it could not deal with cases concerning freehold; this included cases of treason, since the penalty here involved was death and the forfeiture of freehold, and it came to be assumed that the council could give only minor punishments, with the result that the courts of common law were left to deal with the most serious crimes. The council, however, still had wide if ill-defined powers of jurisdiction, which were increased in the Lancastrian period. Then during and after the civil wars its own weakness must have limited the number of petitions with which it had to deal.

The council had in addition a vast field of administration, the variety of which can be seen from the records of its proceedings. It possessed all the powers of government, and in theory it always retained the right to advise the king and to consent to many of his actions. The councillor's oath shows clearly the position of its members; the oath as taken in the fourteenth and fifteenth centuries(1, 33) differs very little from that in 1257, save that justices were no longer included.[2] Further, the king could legislate in council by ordinance.

With its increasing business, the organisation of the council was developed. Already in the mid-fourteenth century it was occupying special buildings of the star chamber instead of using the

[1] Cf. Baldwin, *op. cit.* pp. 296 ff., 529 ff., giving an example of the inquisitorial procedure of the council.

[2] *Ibid.* pp. 345–54.

exchequer or other places as before.[1] In this century there were clerks of the council,[2] and in Richard II's reign John Prophet seems to have been a very energetic holder of this office. His promotions are typical: he was clerk of the council, then secondary clerk of the privy seal, in 1402 king's secretary, and four years later keeper of the privy seal.[3] In 1422 the office of clerk of the council was specially mentioned with a salary of forty marks, while the clerk of the parliament received forty pounds. The office of privy seal had come to be specially associated with the council, and by Richard II's reign was engrossing all the official secretarial work that did not need the formality of the great seal.[4] While the privy seal was thus becoming a public office, much of the king's own correspondence was being carried on under the signet, in the keeping of the secretary, who in his turn was to become the most important council official, though not until Tudor times.

BIBLIOGRAPHY

1. ORIGINAL SOURCES

LEADAM, I. S. and BALDWIN, J. F. (eds.). *Select cases before the king's council,* S.S. vol. XXXV. 1918.

Proceedings and ordinances of the privy council, vols. I–VI, 1386–1461, ed. Sir N. H. Nicolas. London, 1834–7.

Rotuli parliamentorum. London, 1783.

RYMER, T. *Foedera, etc.* London, 1706.

Statutes of the realm. London, 1810–28.

2. SECONDARY AUTHORITIES

BALDWIN, J. F. *The king's council in England during the middle ages.* Oxford, 1913.

PALGRAVE, SIR F. *An essay upon the original authority of the king's council.* London, 1834.

PICKTHORN, K. *Early Tudor government. Henry VII.* Cambridge, 1934.

STUBBS, W. *The constitutional history of England,* vols. II, III. Oxford, 1880.

TOUT, T. F. *Chapters in the administrative history of medieval England,* vols. II–V. Manchester, 1920–30.

[1] Baldwin, *op. cit.* pp. 354 ff.   [2] *Ibid.* p. 363.
[3] *Ibid.* pp. 364–5; and Tout, *Chapters,* III, 466–7; v, 52.
[4] See below, pp. 209–10.

3. ARTICLES

LAPSLEY, G. "Archbishop Stratford and the parliamentary crisis of 1341", *E.H.R.* xxx, 1915.

LEWIS, N. B. "The 'Continual Council' in the early years of Richard II, 1377–80", *E.H.R.* xli, 1926.

PLUCKNETT, T. F. T. "The place of the council in the fifteenth century", *Trans. R.H.S.* 4th series, i, 1918.

WILKINSON, B. "The protest of the Earls of Arundel and Surrey in the crisis of 1341", *E.H.R.* xlvi, 1931.

(1) *The councillor's oath* 1307

Celui qe serra jurrez du Consail le Roy soit chargez des points cy desouz escritz. Et sil deyve estre Justice, soit chargez du darein point.

Que bien et loiaument conseillerez le Roy selonc vostre sen et vostre poair.

Que bien et loiaument son conseil celerez.

Et que vous ne encuserez autre de chose qil dirra au Conseil.

Et qe vostre poyne, aide, et consail a tot vostre poair dorrez et mettrez as droitures le Roi, et de la Corone garder, meintenir, sauver, et repeler, par la ou vous purrez sanz tort faire.

Et la ou vous saverez les choses de la Corone et le droitz le Roy concellez, ou a tort alienez, ou soustrez, qe vous le frez saver au Roi.

Et qe la Corone acrestrez a votre poair, et en loais manere.

Et qe vous ne serrez en lieu ne Consail ou le Roy se decreste de chose qe a la Corone appent, si ce ne soit chose qe vous coviegne faire.

Et qe vous ne lerrez pur nulli, pur amour, ne pur haour, pur bon gre ne pur maveis gre, qe vous ne facez faire a chescun, de quel estat ou condicion quil soit, droiture et reson solonc vostre poair et a vostre escient, et qe nulli rien ne prendrez pur tort fair, ne droit ne delaer. Et qe en Jugement et a droiture faire la ou vous serrez assignez vous n'espernirez nulli pur hautesce, pur poverte, ne pur richesce, qe droit ne soit fait.

Et si vous eiez fait alliance a Seigneurage, ou a autre, par quoi vous ne peussez cestes choses faire ou tenir sanz tele alliance effreindre, qe vous le dirrez, ou frez saver au Roi.

Et qe desoremes alliance de serment ne frez a nulli sanz conge du Roy.

Et qe rien ne prendrez de doun de nulli pur pled ne pur autre chose qil eit a faire devant vous, si ce ne soit manger et bevire a la jornee.

Rot. Parl. I, 218–19. This oath is printed in Baldwin's *King's council*, pp. 347–8, from the Close Roll, and he compares it with the oath of 1257, *ibid.* pp. 346–7, and that of 1341, *ibid.* pp. 351–2.

(2) *Proceedings at the parliament of Lincoln* 1316

Die Martis proxima ante Carniprivium in parliamento Domini Regis Edwardi filii Regis Edwardi anno regni sui nono apud Lincolniam in presencia Domini Regis et Prelatorum ac Procerum et aliorum pro parliamento illo ibidem existencium, Dominus Johannes Norwicensis Episcopus, de mandato Domini Regis recitavit causam quare Dominus Rex parliamentum illud fecerat summoneri, et alia negocia Dominum Regem tangencia, ut in alio rotulo continetur et ulterius locutus fuit Thome Comiti Lancastrie ex parte Domini Regis aliqua verba ad amovendum quandam dubietacionem quam dicebatur ipsum Comitem habuisse de dicto Domino Rege, intimando sibi quod Dominus Rex erga ipsum et alios Proceres regni sui gerebat sinceram et integram voluntatem, ipsosque veluti homines suos fideles et ligios tenebat in speciali benivolencia regia ut decebat; et quod Dominus Rex voluit quod idem Comes esset de consilio Domini Regis capitalis, Rogando eundem Comitem ex parte Domini Regis et Prelatorum ac Procerum regni ibidem existencium, quod ipse vellet illud effectualiter assumere, et in negociis Domini Regis et regni prout tenebatur apponere consilium et auxilium oportuna, et dictus Comes inde regracians Domino Regi humiliter supplicavit quod ipse posset deliberare, et postea respondere.

Parliamentary Writs, II, ii, 157.

(3) *Summons to a council* 1317

Edward par la grace de Dieu Roy Dengleterre, etc., al honorable piere en Dieu, Adam par la meisme grace Evesqe de Hereford, saluz. Por acunes grosses et chargeauntes busoignes tochauntes nous de lestat de notre Roiaume dunt nous voloms avoir conseil et avisement de vous, vous maundoms et chargeoms en la foi, et en la ligeaunce que vous nous devez, que veues cestes lettres totes autres choses lessees, giegnez [*sic*] a nous a Loundres, a tote la haste que vous unques porrez. Et ceo en nule manere ne lessez. Et par vos lettres et par le portur de cestes nous remandez a queu jour vous y serrez. Done sous notre prive seal a Waltham, le xvj jour Doctobre, le an de notre Regne xj.

Registrum Ade de Orleton, Episcopi Herefordensis, Cant. and York Soc. p. 50.

(4) *Appointment of the council* 1318

Fait a remembrer, qe come nadgaires certeins Prelatz, Countes, et Barouns, de la volunte nostre Seignur le Roy et assent des plusours Grantz du Roialme, et autres du Conseil le Roi, lors esteauntz a Norhampton, fuissent alez devers le Counte de Lancastre, de parler et treter ovesqes lui sur le profit et l'onur nostre Seignur le Roi et de son Roialme, et en la parlaunce et tretiz entre les ditz Prelatz, Countes et Barouns, et le dit Counte de Lancastre, parle et trete fust, qe Evesqes, Countes, et Barouns, fuissent demorauntz devers nostre Seignur le Roi por lui consellier es bosoignes qi si touchierent tauntqe en son prochein Parlement...

...qe les Evesqes de Norwicz, Cicestre, Ely, Salesbury, Seint David, Kardoil, Hereford, et Wirecestre, les Countes de Pembrok, Richemund, Hereford, et Arundell, Sire Hugh de Courteny, Sire Roger de Mortimer, Sire Johan de Segrave, Sire Johan de Grey, et un des Banretz le Counte de Lancastre q'il vodra nomer, por un quartier demoergent pres de nostre Seignur le Roi tauntqe a prochein Parlement, issint qe deux des Evesqes, un des Countes, un des Barounz, et un des Banretz, le dit Counte de Lancastre au meines demoergent pres du Roi adesseement; et qe tutes choses qe a charger facent qe se porrount et deverount faire sans Parlement se facent por lour assent, et si outrement soient fait soit tenuz por nient, et adresce en Parlement par agard des Piers, et totes choses covenables soient redresseez par eux. Et au Parlement soient esluz de eux et des autres qi devient demorer pres de nostre Seignur le Roi par quartiers solonc ce q'il serount esluz et assigne en Parlement a faire et conseiller nostre Seignur le Roi en la forme avauntdit...

Rot. Parl. I, 453-4 (29).

(5) *Edward III's return from France* 1340

...Postea vero, cum omnes Anglici qui cum rege in Gandavo fuerunt crederent ipsum regem Angliæ festa Natalis Domini celebraturum ibidem, idem dominus rex cum paucis, scilicet viij. de suis, fingens se velle spatiari, equitavit secrete, nullis quasi familiaribus præmunitis, venit ad Selondiam, ubi posuit se in mari...et in nocte sancti Andreæ, circa gallicantum, turrim Londoniarum per aquam intravit...Et statim in gallicantu misit pro cancellario, thesaurario, et aliis justiciariis tunc præsentibus Londoniis. Et statim episcopum Cicestrensem ab officio cancellariæ amovit, et episcopum Coventriensem ab officio thesaurariæ...

[*Judges, merchants, chancery clerks, etc., were imprisoned.*]

Item, in isto adventu regis fuit Johannes archiepiscopus per Willelmum Killesby verbotenus apud Gildehalle Londoniarum, et postea per literas regis, de ingratitudine et aliis publice diffamatus...

Et cito, post hujusmodi adventum suum amovit rex omnes vicecomites et alios ministros in suis publicis officiis constitutos,...et fecit quendam militem cancellarium Angliæ, videlicet dominum Robertum le Bourser et alium thesaurarium...et consilio juvenum utebatur, spreto consilio seniorum...

Adae Murimuth, *Continuatio Chronicarum* (R.S.), pp. 116-18.

(6) *Petition concerning the appointment of ministers* 1341

Item, pur ce qe moltz des Malx sont avenuz par malveis Conseillers et Ministres, prient les Grantz et la Commune, q'il pleise ordeigner, par avis des Prelatz, Countes, et Barouns, Qe le Roi face Chaunceller, chief Justice de l'un Baunk et de l'autre, Tresorer, Chaunceller, et chief Baron de l'Escheqer, Seneschall de son Houstel, Gardeyn de la Garderobe, et Contreroullour, et un Clerk covenable pur garder son Prive Seal, chief Clerks le Roi en le commune Baunk, et ce en Parlement. Et issint soit fait desoremes de tieux Ministres quant miester serra, lesqueux soient jurez devant les Pieres en Parlement de garder les Leies, come desus est dit; Et ce selonc les Ordenances devant ces heures sur ce faites.

Rot. Parl. II, 128 (15).

(7) *Restriction on aliens* 1346

Item, Soit defendu par tut, qe nul Alien envoi Lettres outre meer, ne resceive Lettres qi vendront d'illoeqes, saunz ce q'il les monstre au Chanceller, ou a autre Grant et prive du Conseil, ou au meyns as chiefs Gardeyns des Portz, ou a lour Lieutenantz, pur monstrer outre au dit Conseil; sur peyne de quant q'il purra forfaire devers

le Roi. Et endroit de ceste matire est plus pleinement acordez
par les respons des Petitions donez par les Communes.
Rot. Parl. II, 163 (47).

(8) *Limitation of conciliar jurisdiction* 1352

Estre ceo, come contenu soit en la grant Chartre des franchises
Dengleterre qe nul soit pris ne emprisone, ne ouste de son frank
tenement ne de ses franchises ne de ses franches custumes, sil ne
soit par lei de la terre; Acorde est,...qe nul desore soit pris par
peticion ou suggestion faite a nostre Seignur le Roi ou a son
conseill, sil ne soit par enditement ou presentement des bones et
loialx du visnee ou tiele fait se face, et en due manere, ou proces
fait sur brief original a la commune lei; ne qe nul soit ouste de ses
franchises ne de son franktenement sil ne soit mesne duement en
respons, et forjugge dyceles par voie de lei; et si rien soit fait al
encontre soit redresse et tenue pur nul.

S.R. I, 321, 25 Ed. III, s. 5, c. 4. (There are similar laws in 1331
(*S.R.* I, 267), in 1354 (*S.R.* I, 345) and in 1368 (*S.R.* I, 388), etc.)

(9) *Case before the council. Lombards v. the Mercers' Company* 1359

A. [*Details are given of the misdemeanours of the Mercers and their servants.*]
......
Item qe pleise a nostre tresredoute seignur le Roi e son conseil
de faire venir deuant sa persone propre les Mestres e les plus
grantz del mestier e de prendre de eux sibone e sufficiante seurtee
qe james ils ne facent a nous nul mal ne vileinie ne soeffrent estre
a nous fait par lour assent en manere come desus est dit, ou
autrement ne purrons viure ne demourer en pees e meement si
nostre seignur le Roi soit hors Dengleterre.

Les noms des Mercers de Londres:
> Johan Bernes, visconte de Londres
> Simon Worstede Alderman
> William Todenham
> Johan Worstede
> Alein Euerard
> Johan de Stapele
> Wauter Berneye
> Johan Wychyngham

Thomas Starkol
Johan Redyng
Adam Euerard (nichil habet ubi potest premuniri)
Wauter Bret
Nichol Bedyngton (mortuus est)
Johan Elesdon
Nichol Plunket
Henri Coue
William Coue

B. [*Writ of praemunire.*]
......

Edwardus [etc.], . . . vicecomitibus London, salutem. Quibusdam certis de causis tibi precipimus firmiter injungentes quod premunire faciatis Henricum Coue, [22 *names follow*] quod quilibet eorum sub pena Centum librarum in propria persona sua sit coram consilio nostro apud Westmonasterium hac instanti die Martis ad loquendum cum eodem consilio super hiis que eis tunc ibidem exponentur ex parte nostra et ad faciendum ulterius et recipiendum quod per dictum consilium ordinari contigerit in premissis. Et hoc sub incumbenti periculo nullatenus omittatis. Et habeatis ibi nomina illorum per quos eos premunire feceritis et hoc breve. Teste me ipso apud Westmonasterium viij die Julii anno regni nostri Anglie tricesimo tercio, regni vero nostri Francie vicesimo.

per consilium.   Burstall.

Endorsed: Virtute istius brevis premunire fecimus Henricum Coue [18 *others*] infrascriptos quod sint coram vobis ad diem et locum in brevi contentos ad faciendum quod interius precipitur sub pena in brevi contenta per Johannem Penne et Johannem Broun.

Adam Euerard infrascriptus nichil habet in balliva nostra ubi potest premuniri.

Nicholaus Bedyngton infrascriptus mortuus est. Ideo de eo nichil fecimus.

C. Responsio Johannis Bures et Johannis de Byernes, vicecomitum.
Manucaptores Willelmi de Wodeford:
[6 *names*]
Manucaptores Nicholai de Sharpenham, Mercer:
[4 *names*] de Comitatu Surrie.
Manucaptores Thome Euerard de London, Mercer:
[5 *names*] de London.

Manucaptores Thome de Maldone:
   [6 *names*] de London.
Manucaptores Ade de Wroxham:
   [7 *names*] de London.

D. Alanus Euerard et alii manuceperunt Thomam Euerard Adam Wroxham et Henricum Forester.

Willelmus Weld et alii manuceperunt Henricum Coue.

Henricus Coue et alii manuceperunt Willelmum Coue.

Alanus Euerard et alii manuceperunt Willelmum Wodeford.

Johannes de Wychyngham et alii manuceperunt Thomam de Maldone.

Ista cedula scripta fuit in consilio juxta informacionem datam per quosdam Merceros Londinienses tunc ibidem existentes, pro eo quod rotulus de manucapcionibus predictis non fuit ibi presens.

Select cases before the king's council (S.S.), pp. 42–7.

(10) *Petition of the commons for a lay ministry* 1371

Et pur ce qe en cest present Parlement fu monstre a nostre Seignur le Roi par touz les Contes, Barons, et Communes d'Engleterre, qe la Government du Roialme ad longement este faite par Gentz de Seinte Esglise, queux ne sont mye justiciables en touz cas, par ount grantz Meschiefs et Damages sont ent avenuz en temps passe, et plus purront escheir en temps a venir, en desheritesoun de la Coroune, et grant prejudice du dit Roialme, par diverses causes qe l'en purroit declarer, Qe plese a nostre dit Seignur le Roi, qe Lays Gentz de mesme le Roialme, sufficeauns et ables de estat a ce esluz, et nulles autres persones soient desoreenavant faitz Chanceller, Tresorier, Clerk du Prive Seal, Barouns de l'Escheqer, Chamberleyns de l'Escheqer, Countrerollour, et touz autres grantz Officers et Governours du dit Roialme; Et qe ceste chose soit ore en tiel manere establi en la fourme suisdite, qe par nulle voie ore soit defait, ne riens faite au contrarie en nul temps a vener. Sauvant toutdys al Roi nostre Seignur le Election et le Remuer de tieux Officers, mais qe toutes voies ils soient Gentz Lays tieux come desus est dit.

Responsio. Le Roi ordeinera sur ceo point sicome lui semblera meltz, par avis de son bon Conseil.

Rot. Parl. ii, 304 (15). (One writer thinks that this was the work of great council *or* parliament (Tout, *Chapters*, iii, 268, n. 4), but

Richardson and Sayles (article in *Bulletin*, VIII, no. 23, p. 67) take this as a regular parliament, held at Westminster, February, and hold that the Winchester assembly in June was a great council.)

(11) The "Good Parliament". Nomination of the council 1376

Le secunde iour apres, le duk et les autres seignours del parlement envoierent certeins seignours al roy pur luy nuncier la parlauns de les communes et assent de les seignours pur luy conseiler de wayver ceux qe furount pres de luy queux ne furount poynt bones ne profitablez et ouster ceux qe furount de soun conseil et dame Alice Perrers toute outrement, notifiauntz a luy de lour affers coment ils avoient faitz en desceyt de luy et qil vodroit prendre a luy tiels conselours queux vodroient loialment et profitablement luy governer et ordiner pur soun estate et pur le roialme et nyent doner foy et credence as mawez conselours et male fesours. Et le roy benygnement dist a les seignours qil vodroit volunters fair ceo qe serroit profit al roialme; et les seignours luy amercierent, empriaunt a soun tressexcellent seignourye qil vodroit eslire trois evesqes, trois countz et trois barouns come avaunt est dite, pur estre de soun conseil, qare ceo appent a luy de eslire et nyent as autres del parlement. Et le roy respondist pacientement qil ferroit volunters par lour avyse et bone ordinaunce. Et si enterparlerent quels purrount estre; et eliserount lercevesque de Caunterbury, le evesqe de Loundres, le evesqe de Wyncestre, les countz de Arundell', del Marche et de Stafford, le seignour de Percy, monsire Guy de Brian et monsire Roger Bewchampe. Et quaunt ceo fuist fait, il maunda pur le duk de Loncastre et soun frere le count de Caumbrige, et pur les ix seignours avauntditz et quaunt ils furount a luy venuz, comenceront a moustrer lour conseil del ordinaunce avaunt ordine et parle en parlement. Adonqes le roy pria a les ditz ix seignours qils voilloient estre entendaunt a luy et a soun conseil et ordiner pur luy et pur le roialme et redresser les trespas queux ount este faitz et usez avaunt ces houres. Et les seignours benygnement graunterent de fair soun pleser en quauntqe qils purrount et furount iurrez destre loialles al roy et loialment governer luy et le roialme a lour poair.

En mesme le tenps furount oustez de conseil le roy le seignur de Latymer, monsire Johan de Neville et monsire Richard de Stafford et dame Alice Perrers; et le roy mesmes fist serement avaunt les seignours qe iames apres la dite Alice de vendrast en soun compaigny; et fuist ordine par comune assent qe les ix seignours avauntditz deveroient demurrer en Loundres, ou pres le roy ou qil fuist, issint qils purrount toutz iours estre prestez de luy conseiler quaunt tenps serroit; et adonqes departirent et repaierent a Loundres a le parlement; et le duk de Loncastre nyent paie mes malement greve et anoie de ceo qil ne fuist my eslew destre une de les conseilers.

The anonimalle chronicle (ed. V. H. Galbraith), pp. 91–2.

(12) *The council of twelve, appointed in July* 1377.
De Conciliariis Regis constitutis

Le Roy a touz ceux, qi cestes Lettres verront, Salutz.
Come n'adgairs,

De l'assent des Prelatz, Ducs, Contes, Barons, et autres, esteantz delez nous en nostre Conseil, tenuz a Westmonstier, lendemain de nostre Coronement,

Eussiens ordenez que, par nous et eux, Dousze Persones (c'estassavoir) Deux Evesqes, Deux Contes, Deux Barons, Deux Baneretz, et Quatre Bachilers, serroient Esleuz noz Conseillers sur noz Bosoignes, touchantz l'Estat, Honour, et Profit de nous Roialmes, Seignuries, et Terres, en eide noz Chanceller et Tresorer,

Et que meismes les Conseillers, ensi a Eslire, apres ces q'ils serroient Esleuz, averoient noz Lettres Patentz a Faire et Excercer les dites Choses,

Et que les ditz Chanceller et Tresorer mettroient duement en Execucion les choses, que par eux, et par les ditz Esleuz, ou par la Greindre Partie d'iceux, serroient ordenees,

Seur quoi feurent Esleuz, par nous et par les Prelatz et Seigneurs susditz, Les Honorables Piers en Dieu,

> William Evesque de Londres,
> Et Rauf Evesque de Saresbirs:
> Noz cheres et foialx Cosyns,
> Esmon Conte de la Marche,
> Et Richard Conte d'Arundel:
> Et, Noz cheres et foialz,
> William Sire Latymer,
> Et Johan Sire de Cobeham,
> Barons: Roger de Beauchamp,
> Et Richard de Stafford,
> Baneretz: Et Johan Knyvet,
> Rauf de Ferreres,
> Johan Devereux,
> et Hugh de Segrave, Bachilers;

Les queux feurent jurez, en nostre presence, noz Conseillers, a Faire et Excercer les dites Choses, en la forme avantdite, tantcome nous plerroit,

......

Pur ce que, a cause de certeins Grosses et Chargeantz Bosoignes, touchantes la Salvacion et necessaire Defense de nostre Roialme d'Engleterre, que demandent grande effusion de Despenses, nous avons bosoigne en present de certeines Sommes de Deniers,

Nous constituons et Assignons, par ses presentz, les ditz Esleuz noz Conseillers, et Sys de eux, ensemblement ovesque les Chanceller et Tresorer avantditz, a faire, en nome de nous, Chevances de queconqes Sommes de Deniers, a nostre oeps, par voie d'Apprest, Engagement...la meilloure q'ils purront ou verront meltz, et de queconqes Persones que faire se purra: Et si averons Ferm et Aggreable quanque ensi par les ditz Esleuz, ensemblement ovesque les Chanceller et Tresorer avantditz, ou par la Greindre Partie d'iceux, serra fait en nostre noun, comme dessus, es choses susdites et en chescune d'icelles, et le volons estre fermement Gardez.

En Tesmoignance de quele chose nous avons fait faire cestes noz Lettres Patentes a durer a nostre volente.

Done a nostre Paleys de Westmonstier le xx. Jour de Juyl.
Per Billam ipsius Regis de Signeto.

Foedera, VII, 161–2. (Cf. article in *E.H.R.* 1926, showing that Baldwin in *King's council*, pp. 120 ff., confused the two councils appointed in July and October, 1377.)

(13)   *The council of nine, appointed in October* 1377

Quant a la primere Requeste qe les dites Communes monstrent a nostre Seignur le Roy et as Seignurs du Parlement,...qe le Conseill nostre dit Seignur le Roy fust enlargez par le nombre de oept suffisantz persones de diverses estatz et degrees, pur estre continuelment residentz du Conseil avec les Officers dessus ditz sur les busoignes du Roi...

Nostre Seignur le Roy entendant la dite Requeste estre honurables...l'ad ottroiez, purveuz toutes voies qe Chanceller, Tresorer, Gardein du Prive Seal, Justices de l'un Bank et de l'autre, et touz les autres Officers du Roi, purront faire et esploiter les busoignes qi touchent lours Offices sanz la presence de tieux Conseillers. Et nostre Seignur le Roy, pur certains causes qi luy moevent a present, par l'advis des Seignurs de Parlement y voet

avoir ceste present anee tant soulement neof persones ses tieux
Conseillers, et les ad fait eslire en dit Parlement; C'est assavoir,
les Evesqes de Londres, de Kardoill, et de Salesbirs; les Contes
de la March, et de Stafford; Messires Richard de Stafford, et
Henry le Scrop, Baneretz; et Messires Johan Deverose, et Hugh
Segrave, Bachilers. Et est ordenez, qe les ditz neof Conseillers
issint esluz, et auxint les oept Conseillers qe pur le temps serront,
ne demurront en dit Office fors qe soulement un an entier. Et
celle an fini ne deveront mye celles mesmes persones estre reesluz a celle office par deux ans proscheins ensuantz.

Rot. Parl. III, 6 (21 and 22). (Cf. Parliament section, doc. 32.)

(14) *Petition of the commons for judges to advise the council* 1377

Item, soit requys qe la Graunte Chartre soit confermez, et fortement tenuz en touz pointz; et qe touz les pointz de ycelles soient
un jour luz en cest present Parlement devant les Prelats, Seignurs,
et toute la Baronage, et Commune; et si aucun point soit obscure,
qe elle point eu pointz y purront estre declarrez,...par ceux qi
serront ordenez d'estre de le Continuel Conseil, ensemble ovesqe
l'advys des toutz les Justices et Serjantz, et des autres tielx qe
ceux de Conseil veullient a eux appeller quant ils verront temps et
heure deinz le terme avant dit: Eiant regarde a la grante nobley
et la sage descression q'estoit en le Roialme quant la dite Grande
Chartre estoit ordene et establiz. Et qe ceux pointz declarrez et
amendez par le dit Conseil, et des autres avant nommez, puissent
estre monstrez as Seignurs et Communes au prochein Parlement,
et adonqes estre encresceez et affermez pur Estatut s'il semble a
eux q'il soit a faire; eiant regarde coment le Roi est chargee a son
Coronement de tenir et garder la dite Chartre en touz ses pointz.
Responsio. La dite Chartre si ad este lue en ce Parlement devant
les Seignurs et Communes, et le Roi voet qe ce soit tenuz et fermement gardez.

Rot. Parl. III, 15 (iii).

(15) *The appointment of ministers* 1377

Item ils prient, pur ceo qe moultz des Malx et Damages sont
avenuz par tieux Conseillers et tieux Ministres avant nommez, si
bien au Roy come al Roialme; qe plese ore a sa Hautesse, par
advys de touz les Seignurs du Parlement, qe tan qe il soit au plein
age a conustre les bons et les malx, granter qe touz les Conseillers

et Officers apres escriptz puissent estre faitz et purveieuz par Parlement; C'est assavoir, Chanceller, Haut Tresorier, Chief Justices de l'un Bank et de l'autre, et Chief Baron de l'Escheqier, Seneschal, et Tresorier de son Hostiel, Chief Chaumberlein, Clerc de Prive Seal, un Chief Gardein de ses Forestes decea Trent, et un autre dela. Et s'il aviegne par aucune aventure, qe y covient a mettre aucuns des ditz Ministres par entre un Parlement et autre, q'en tiel cas y plese au Roy nostre dit Seignur granter, qe tiel Ministre puisse estre mys par son Grant Conseil, tan qe le Parlement proschein ensuant.

Responsio. Quant a cest Article, il est assentuz, qe tant come nostre Seignur le Roi soit issint de tendre age, qe les ditz Conseillers, et aussint les Chanceller, Tresorier, Seneschal de son Hostiel, et Chaumberlein, soient esluz par les Seignurs en Parlement: Salvez toutdys l'estat et l'eritage du Conte d'Oxenford del dit Office de Chaumberlin. Mais s'il avenist issint qe aucun de eux morust, ou feust par cause resonable remuez, entre Parlement et Parlement, adonqes le Roi par l'advys des Seignurs de son Continuel Conseil les ferra en le moiene temps. Et quant as autres Officers dessus nomez, le Roy les ferra par l'assent des Seignurs du son dit Conseil.

Rot. Parl. III, 16 (50). (A similar request was made in 1386, *Rot. Parl.* III, 221 (20).)

(16) *Penalties for maintenance* 1377

Item ordeigne est et establi et le Roi nostre seignur defend estroitement qe nul Conseiler Officer ou servant nautre ovesqe lui nascun autre persone du Roialme Dengleterre de quel estate ou condicion qils soient, nenpreignent desore ou susteignent ascun querell par mayntenance en pais ou aillours, sur grevouse peyne; cest assavoir les ditz Conseillers et grantz Officers du Roi sur peyne qe serra ordeigne par le Roi mesmes del avys des seignurs de Roialme; et les autres meyndres Officers et servantz le Roi, sibien en lescheqer et en toutes sez autres Courtes et places come de sa propre meignee, sur peyne de perder lour offices et services et destre emprisonez, et dilloqes estre reintz a la volunte le Roi,...et toutz autres persones parmy le Roialme, sur la dite peyne denprisonement, et destre reintz come les autres desusditz.

S.R. II, 2, 1 Ric. II, c. 4.

(17) *Demands of the commons for reform* 1380

Item les Communes, apres q'ils furent advisez de lour dite Charge, retournerent en Parlement en presence de nostre Seignur le Roi: et Monsire Johan de Gildesburgh, Chivaler, q'estoit eslit par la Commune d'avoir pur eulx les paroles, faisant sa protestation...
Dist, qe lour sembloit a la dite Commune, qe si lour Seignur lige eust este bien et resonablement governez en ses Despenses par dedeinz le Roialme et autrement, il n'eust ore busoigne de lour aide...Em priantz, qe les Prelatz, et autres Seignurs du Continuel Conseil, q'ont longement travaillez en dit affaire, feussent oultreement deschargez,...et qe nuls tielx Conseillers soient pluis retenuz devers le Roi; aiant regard, qe nostre Seignur le Roi si est ore de bone discretion et de bele stature; aiant regard de son age,...Em priantz oultre, qe en ce Parlement soient esluz et choises les Cynk principalx Officers, des pluis suffisantz deinz le Roialme, qi soient tretables, et qi mieltz scievent et purront faire lours Offices: C'est assavoir, Chanceller, Tresorer, Gardein du Prive Seal, Chief Chamberlein, et Seneschal de l'Hostiel le Roi...
Et auxint em priantz, pur remeder le defaute del dit Governail, si nul y soit en celle partie, qe une suffisante Commission et general feusse fait, a mieltz qe l'on le sauroit deviser, a certains Prelatz, Seignurs, et autres des pluis suffisantz, loialx, et sages del Roialme d'Engleterre, de surveer diligeaument, et examiner en toutes les Courtes et Places du Roi, si bien en son Hostiel mesmes come aillours, l'estat del dit Hostiel, et les Despenses et Resceites quelconqes faitz par quelconqes ses Ministres en quelconqes Offices del Roialme...

[*Details of the commission follow.*]

Rot. Parl. III, 73 (11, 12, 13).

(18) *Petitions of the commons for reform* 1381

17. Item les Communes avaunt dites retournerent autre foitz en Parlement,...en disantz, Qe sur les Charges a eux donez ils avoient diligeaument communez avec les Prelats et Seignurs a eux sur ce donez, et lour sembloit purvoir, qe si la governance du Roialme ne soit en brief temps amendez, mesme le Roialme serra oultrement perduz et destruit...Qar voirs est, qe y a tielles defautes en dit Governaille, quoi entour la persone le Roi, et en son Hostell, et pur outrageouses nombre des Familiers esteantz en dit Hostiel; et quoy en ses Courtes, si bien c'est assavoir en la Chancellerie, Bank le Roi, Commune Bank, et l'Escheqier; et par

grevouses oppressions en pays par la outrageouse multitude bra-
ceours des quereles, et maintenours, qi sont come Rois en pays,...

18. Et est assavoir, qe puis apres quant le Roi nostre Seignur
avec les Seignurs du Roialme et son Conseil s'avoit fait adviser
sur cestes Requestes...il voloit...qe certains Prelats, Seignurs,
et autres, furent assignez pur survere et examiner en Prive Conseil
si bien l'Estat et Governaill de la Persone nostre dit Seignur, come
de son dit Hostiel,...

Et furent esluz a ce faire en dit Hostiel, les Seignurs dessouz
escritz, c'est assavoir le Duc de Lancastre, le Eslit de Canterbirs,
l'Ercevesqe d'Everwyk, les Evesqes de Wyncestre, Ely, Excestre,
et Roucestre; le Conts d'Arondell, Warrwyk, Stafford, Suffolk, et
Salesbirs; le Sire de la Zouche, le Sire de Nevill, le Sire de Grey
de Ruthin, le Sire Fitz-Wauter; Monsire Richard le Scrop,
Monsire Guy de Brian, et autres. Et sur celle Charge seierent en
Prive Conseil plusours jours, sanz rienz faire de autre chose en
Parlement. Et fait a remembrer, qe le Confessour nostre dit
Seignur le Roi fust chargez en presence du Roi et des Seignurs,
q'il soi abstiegnast de venir ou demurer en l'Ostiel du Roi, sinoun
tant seulement a les quatre principalx Festes de l'An;...

   [*The commons then brought general complaints against the
      Household, Chancery, Exchequer, and the justices, etc.*]
......

28. Et fait a remembrer, quant mesmes les articles estoient lues
en dit Parlement si fuist assentuz, qe si bien les Clercs de la
Chancellerie de les deux principalx Degrees, et les Justices, et
Sergeantz, Barons, et grantz Officers de l'Escheqier, tres-touz, et
auxint certaines persones des melliours Apprentices de la Loi,
serront chargez par lour ligeances et serementz, chescune degree
par soy, de lour adviser diligealment de les abusions,...qe furent
faites et usez en lours Places, et en les Courtes du Roi, et auxint en
les Courtes d'autres Seignurs parmy le Roialme;...

29. Et puis apres quant ils s'avoient advis de lours charges et
appointes, les meschiefs et remedies, les ditz degres singulerement
firent report devant les Seignurs et Communes a diverses journees,
aucuns en escrit, et aucuns par bouche, de ce qe lour ent sembloit
par leur charge a remedier, dont en partie remede est purveuz en
cest Parlement, si bien c'est assavoir de ceulx de l'Escheqier, come
de les Marchandies. Et de la Chancellerie, si defaute y serra
trovez en lour governaill, le Chanceller ad dit q'il le fra amender
a tout son poair, et sanz delay.

Rot. Parl. III, 100–3.

(19) *Appointment of a commission* 1386

[*Details of grants to the king.*]

Et outre ce, les ditz Seigneurs et Communes ount grantez, par les ditz enchesons, un autre demy Disme, et demy Quinszisme, a lever de les leys gentz...sur certein condition; C'est assavoir, qe si les suis ditz Grantz, sanz la dite darrein demy Disme et demy Quinszisme, ovesqe autres bens le Roi, purroient suffire pur les Charges et Defenses du Roialme par un an prochein a venir, par la diligence et bone ordenance de les honorables Peres en Dieu William Ercevesqe de Canterbirs, Alexsander Ercevesqe d'Everwyk; et les uncles le Roi, Esmon Duk d'Everwyk, Thomas Duc de Gloucestre; et les honorables Peres en Dieu William Evesqe de Wyncestre, Thomas Evesqe d'Exestre; et Nichol Abbe de Waltham; Richard Count d'Arundell, Johan Sire de Cobeham, Richard le Scrop, Chivaler, et Johan Deveros, Chivaler; et trois Officers le Roi, c'est assavoir, Chaunceller, Tresorer, et Gardein du Prive Seal, ordeinez et assignez par nostre Seigneur le Roi, par sa Commission enseale souz son Grant Seal, de son auctorite roial,...et par avis des Prelatz, Seigneurs, et Communes en cest present Parlement; en eide de bone Governance du Roialme, et bone et due execution des Leys, et en Relevement de l'estat du Roi et de son poeple en temps a venir; d'estre del continuel Conseill de nostre dit Seigneur le Roi;...

Rot. Parl. III, 221 (18).

(20) *Minutes of the council* 1390

Lordenance faite sur le gouvernement a tenir par le Consail du Roi.

Premierement que les seignurs du consail se taillent estre au consail parentre oyt et noef de la clokke au plustard.

Item que les busoignes du Roi et du roiaume soient examinez premierement devant toutes autres quant les greindres du consail ct autres officers serrount presentz.

Item que les busoignes touchantes la comune ley soient envoiez pur estre determinez devant les justices.

Item que les busoignes touchantes loffice du Chanceller soient envoiez pur estre determinez devant lui en la chauncellerie.

Item que les busoignes touchantes loffice du Tresorer soient envoiez pur estre determinez devant lui en lescheqer.

Item que toutes autres matires que ne purront estre exploitez

saunz especiale grace et coungie du Roi soient exposer a lui pur
ent avoir son avys et voluntee.

Item que nul doun ou graunt que purra tournir a disencrees
du profit du Roi passe saunz avys du consail et lassent des Ducs
de Guyene et Deverwyk de Gloucestre et du Chanceller ou deux
de eux.

Item que toutes autres busoignes mandez au consail pur avoir
lour avys et autres du grant charge soient determinez par ceux
du consail qi serront presentz ovec les officers.

Item que toutes autres billes du poeple du meindre charge
soient examinez et exploitez devant le Gardein du prive seal et
autres du consail qi serrount presentz pur le temps.

Item que les ordenances touchantes les offices a doner par le
Roi faites autrefoiz par assent de lui et de son consail soient tenuz
et gardez.

Item que nuls seneschalx ne justices soient desore enavant
ordenez a terme de vie.

Item que les bachilers esteauntz du consail du Roi eient gages
resonables pur le temps quils serront travaillantz entour mesme le
consail.

Item que les seignurs esteauntz de mesme le consail eient regard
pur lour travaux et coustages par avys du Roi et de son counsail.

Item puisque une matire soit attamez en le conseil quils ne
passent a nulle autre matire tanque respounse soit done a la
matire premierement attamee.

Le oytisme jour de Marz lan etc. treszisme ceste ordenaunce
estoit faite a Westmonstier en presence du Roi esteantz illoeqes
le Duc de Guyene le Duc Deverwik le Comte de Saresbirs le
Comte de Northumbreland le Comte de Huntyndon, le Chanceller
le Tresorer le Prive Seal le Seneschall Lovell Stury et Dalingrugg.

A.P.C. i, 18 a–b.

(21) *Appeal of the sheriff of Devon to the council* 1392

A l'Ercevesqe D'everwyk Chanceller d'Engleterre et as autres
seigneurs de conseil notre seignur le Roy supplie William Cormy-
nowe nadgairs viscont de Deveneshire que come notre seignur le
Roy a la supplication del commune de son roialme ad grante en
darrein parlement que son conseil eit poaire et autorite de faire
grace a viscontz chargez de outrageouses et importables fermes de
lour contees que ne poent duement estre levez de temps en temps
selonc lour discretion sanz poursuyt faire a Roy mesmes que
pleise faire grace a dit suppliant ore charge en son accompt en

l'Escheqer de outrageouse et importable ferme de dit contee que
ne poet estre duement levez de lx li. ou autrement anientez pour
touz jours pour Dieu et en oevere de charite...
[*Dors.*] Le secunde jour de May l'an etc. xvme le Conseil estoit
assentuz que le suppliant eu pardon de quarante liveres.

A.P.C. I, 40.

(22) *Royal answer to the petition for household reform* 1397
Item, Vendredy en la Feste de la Chandellure, le Roy fit venir
a lui a Westmonstier, apres manger, en le dit Parlement, les
Seignurs Espirituels et Temporels, et leur monstra, coment il avoit
entendu, q'ils feurent le Joedy devant ovek les Communes, et qe
les Communes leur monstrerent et toucherent certeins diverses
matiers, desqueles il sembla a Roy q'acunes feurent encontre sa
Regalie et Estat, et sa Roiale Libertee; comandant a le Chanceller pur lui dire et monstrer les matiers sus dites. Sur quoy
mesme le Chanceller, du comandement du Roy, lui fit relation de
mesmes les matiers, q'estoisent en quatres pointz...
Item le quart article estoit, qe le grant et excessive Charge de
l'Hostel du Roy serroit amendez et amenusez; C'est assaver de la
multitude d'Evesqes...et aussi de pluseurs Dames et leur meignee
qi demuront en l'Ostel du Roy, et sont a ses Costages,...
Item al quart article, touchant le Charge de l'Hostiel le Roy,
et la demuree d'Evesqes et Dames en sa compaignie, Le Roy prist
grandement a grief et offense, de ce qe les Communes qi sont ses
lieges deussent mesprendre ou presumer sur eux ascune ordenance
ou governance de la person de Roy, ou de son Hostiel, ou d'ascuns
persones d'Estat q'il plerroit avoir en sa compaignie. Et sembloit
a Roy, qe les Communes firent en ce grant offense et encontre sa
Regalie, et sa Roiale Mageste, et la Liberte de lui et de ses honorables progenitours, queles il est tenuz et voet maintenir et sustenir par l'eide de Dieu. Par quoy le Roy comanda les ditz
Seignurs Espirituels et Temporels, q'ils deussent le Samady matin
ensuiant monstrer et declarer as ditz Communes pleinement la
volunte du Roy sur celle maticre. Et outre, le Roy entendant
coment les ditz Communes feurent moez et enformez par un
Bille baillee a eux pur parler et monstrer la dit darrein article, si
comanda a le Duc de Guyen et de Lancaster pur charger Monsire
Johan Bussy Parlour pur les Communes, sur sa ligeance de
counter et dire a lui le Noun de cellui qi bailla as ditz Communes
la dite Bille.

Rot. Parl. III, 338–9 (13, 14, 15).

(23) *Summons to a council* 1401

Reverentz peres en Dieu [et noz tresbien amez]. Nous vous salvoms tressouvent en vous signifiant que pour certeines charge-antes matires touchantes nous et nostre roiaume nous avons ordennez de conseiller sibien ovec le tresreverent pere en Dieu et nostre trescher cousin Lercevesque de Canterbirs et toutz les autres prelatz come ovec toutz les countes et barons de nostre roiaume les quelx nous voloms par celle cause que soient devers nous a nostre paloys de Westmonstier lendemain de Lassumpcion de nostre Dame prouchein veignant. Vueillans aussi que y soient a celle mesmes jour de chescun countee de nostre roiaume oyt sept sys cynk ou quatre des plus souffisant et discretz chevalers selon la quantite du countee et le nombre des chevalers en icel demourantz par manere et selon ce que nostre trescher escuier Johan Durward a qi de ce parle avoms vous en scait reporter plus au plain. Si voloms nous pour ce et vous mandoms que sibien as ditz prelatz countes et barons come as tielx chevalers des contees come desus vous facez sur estre faites noz lettres desoubz nostre prive seel en due forme et icelles noz lettres faces en nous facez signifier en toute haste possible dez nomes de ceulx as quelx icelles noz lettres sont adressees come nous nous fioms de vous. Done soubz nostre signet a la Priorie de Selborne le xx. jour de Juyl.

A.P.C. I, 155.

(24) *Household reform* 1404

Item, mesme le Samady, les ditz Communes prierent a nostre dit Seignur le Roy, q'en l'ordinance a faire en l'Ostell mesme nostre Seignur le Roy, y serroient nomez et faites persones honestes et vertuouses, et bien renomez, desqueux notice se purra faire as ditz Seignurs et Communes en cest Parlement, et qe tiel ordinance se serroit qi purroit estre plaisant a Dieux, et honour et profit pur l'estat du Roy et de son Roialme.

Rot. Parl. III, 525 (19).

Item fait a remembrer, qe le primer jour de Marce, accordez estoit par le Roy et les Seignurs Espirituelx et Temporelx en Parlement, qe certeines fermes, revenues, issues, profitz, et emolu-mentz contenuz en l'enroullement des Lettres patentes deins escriptz, demoergent et soient emploiez pur et sur les Despenses de l'Oustiel du Roy. La note desquelles Lettres patentes feust lue devant les Seignurs en Parlement, et puis liverez au Chanceller, d'ent faire Lettres patentes dessoutz le grand Seal du Roy, solonc lour dite accorde, come par l'enroullement d'icelles icy proscheinement ensuantz y purra pluis pleinement apparoir.

Rex, etc. Omnibus ad quos, etc. salutem; Sciatis, quod Nos, de avisamento,...Dominorum tam Spiritualium quam Temporalium in presenti Parliamento nostro Nobis assistentium, Volumus, Concedimus et Ordinamus, quod omnia et singula firme, revenciones, exitus, proficua, et emolumenta quecumque, tam per manus Vicecomitum Comitatuum, Civitatum, Villarum, et Burgorum, quam Ballivorum Libertatum Regni nostri Anglie, levabilia,...usque ad Summam Duorum Millium librarum per annum: quodque omnia exitus et proficua parve Custume nostre...usque ad summam Mille et trescentarum librarum per annum...Ac quod omnia exitus et proficua Hanaperii Cancellarie nostre usque ad summam Duorum Millium librarum per annum: [*other details follow of the sources of income*]...super expensis Hospicii nostri, bene, fideliter, et integre, in partem solutionis earundem expensarum exnunc persolvendarum, integre remaneant, et applicentur, ac ante omnes alias concessiones...super eisdem firmis...Thesaurarius Hospicii nostri predicti...per manus illorum per quos levabuntur,...per Indenturam inter ipsum Thesaurarium et ipsos de quibus hujusmodi summas sic recipiet,...

Proviso semper, quod Domini et Magnates, ac alii quicumque, qui super hujusmodi revencionibus, custumis...per Nos vel progenitores seu predecessores nostros, aliquas annuitates...optinent, de eisdem annuitatibus...plene et fideliter persolvantur, juxta tenorem Cartarum et Litterarum patentium eis in hac parte confectarum, presentibus voluntate, concessione et ordinatione non obstantibus, quodque de residuo dictorum exituum...ultra summas per Nos tenore presentium pro Expensis predictis in forma predicta assignatas...pro Camera et Garderoba nostris assignatas, omnes et singuli ligei nostri, qui inde annuitates ad terminum vite optinent, fideliter persolvantur. Volentes et concedentes, quod nunc Thesaurarius noster Hospicii nostri, ac alii Thesaurarii ejusdem Hospicii pro tempore existentes, de omni eo quod sic recipient per hujusmodi Indenturam, in Compotis suis ad Scaccarium nostrum de tempore in tempus onerentur; quodque iidem Thesaurarii per eorum Sacramenta de omni eo quod vigore presentium non recipient ad idem Scaccarium absque difficultate...de tempore in tempus exonerentur in Compotis suis supradictis. Volentes insuper,...quod si alique Littere patentes exnunc alicui persone...per nos in contrarium, ex inadver-

tencia, vel quovis alio modo, fieri contigerit, quod eedem Littere
...nullius sint effectus, vigoris vel virtutis; nec quod Thesaurarius
et Barones Scaccarii nostri pro tempore existentes aliquam de eis
allocationem in Scaccario predicto faciant, nec facere teneantur
quovis modo. In cujus rei etc. per biennium duraturum. Teste
Rege apud Westmonasterium primo die Martii.

Per ipsum Regem et Consilium suum in Parliamento.

Rot. Parl. III, 528 (32). (The total sum to be devoted to the household was £12,100; cf. Stubbs, *C.H.* III, 46–7.)

(25) *The names of the council published in parliament* 1404

Item, aufyn qe bone et jouste governance et remede se facent des
pleuseurs Compleintz, Grevances, et Meschiefs monstrez au Roy
nostre Seignur en cest Parlement, mesme nostre Seignur le Roy,
a la reverence de Dieux, et a les grantes instances et especiales
requestes a luy faitz diverses foitz en cest Parlement par les Communes de son Roialme, pur ease et confort de tout son Roialme,
ad ordeignez certeins Seignurs et autres south-escriptz d'estre de
son grant et continuel Conseil; c'est assavoir,

> L'Ercevesqe de Canterbirs,
> L'Evesqe de Nicole, Chanceller d'Engleterre,
> L'Evesqe de Roucestre,
> L'Evesqe de Wircestre,
> L'Evesqe de Bathe,
> L'Evesqe de Bangore;
> Le Duc d'Everwyk;
> Le Cont de Somerset,
> Le Cont de Westmerland;
> Le Sire de Roos, Tresorer d'Engleterre,
> Le Gardein du Prive Seal,
> Le Sire de Berkeley,
> Le Sire de Wilughby,
> Le Sire de Furnyvall,
> Le Sire de Lovell;
> Monsire Piers Courteney,
> Monsire Hugh Waterton,
> Monsire Johan Cheyne,
> Monsire Arnald Sauvage,
> Johan Northbury,
> Johan Doreward,
> Johan Curson.

Rot. Parl. III, 530 (37).

(26) *Minutes of the council and household reform* 1406

Le viij jour de Decembre lan etc. viij^e apres noone sassemblerent en consail a Westmonstier mon redoubte seignur le Prince et messeignurs Lercevesqe de Cantirbirs Levesqe de Duresme, Chanceller le Duc Deverwyk le Conte de Somerset le Tresourer les Seneschall Chamberlein et Tresorer del houstiel la ou ils firent appointer certains ordenances.

Et primerement touchant la bone gouvernance del houstiel nostre seignur le Roy, il semble au dit consail molt expedient qe bons et loiaux officers soient faitz et ordenez en dit hostell et par especial qe y soit un bon contreroullour et a ce feurent nommez Monsire Thomas Bromflet et Monsire Arnaut Savage desqueux soit lun contreroullour sil plest au Roy. Et porce qe au dit consail nestoit avisez de la nominacion dautres suffissantz persones a estre constitutz en autres offices deinz le dit houstel selonc ce qe busoigne serra, il feut dit et parle as ditz Seneschall et Tresorer de eux aviser daucuns tieux sufficeantes persones et pur lour noms demonstrer a nostre dit seignur le Roy et son dit consail.

Item qe provision soit faite daucune somme covenable pur les expenses de mesme loustiel encountre la feste de Noel prochein venant.

Item il semble busoignable qe le dit feste finiz il plese a nostre dit seignur le Roy soy treher a aucun lieu covenable ou par avis et deliberacion [de lui et] de son conseil et ses officers puisse estre ordenee moderate governance deinz le dit houstel tiele qe puisse estre desore enavant continuee au plesir de Dieu et du poeple.

A.P.C. I, 295.

(27) *Articles of reform* 1406

(66) Item, mesme le jour [*December* 22], le dit Monsire Johan Tibetot myst avaunt en Parlement une Rolle, contenant plusours diverses Articles faitz par advys et assent du Roy et des Seignurs et Communes suis ditz, et pria, qe mesmes les Articles purront estre enactez et entrez de record en Rolle de Parlement. Au quele prier fuist responduz, Le Roy le voet, sauvant toutesfoitz a luy son Estat et Prerogative de son Corone.—Et outre ceo pria le dit Monsire Johan, en noun des ditz Communes, qe toutes les Seignurs de Conseil soient jurrez devaunt le Roy et toutes les Estates de Parlement, Q'ils garderont toutes les Articles contenuz en le dit rolle. A quoy l'Ercevesqe de Canterbirs pur luy mesmes, et les autres Seignurs du Conseil pur eux mesmes, fierent

Protestation severalment, Q'ils ne vorroient en nulle manere en-prendre celle charge sur eux, si ne soit qe le Roy de ses propre volunte et motion leur vorroit charger en especial de ceo faire... Et sur ce le Roy de ses volunte et mocion propre comanda les ditz Seignurs du Conseil de ce faire;...Sur quoy mesmes les Seignurs du Conseil illoeqes presentz,...furent jurrez et serementez several-ment sur les seintz Evangelx, de garder et observer bien,...les Articles contenuz en le dit Rolle,...

...[le Roy] chargea le Clerc du Parlement d'entrer les Articles suis ditz de record en Rolle de Parlement. Desqueux Articles les tenures s'ensuent.

I. Primerment, purtant q'il ad pleu a nostre tres soverain Seignur le Roy, d'eslier et nommer sez Conseillers et Officers plesantz a Dieu, et agreables a son poeple, es queux il se voet bien affier, pur luy conseiller et estre de son Conseil continuel tan q'al proschein Parlement, et a resonable nombre dez queux ascuns puissent continuelment demurrer entour sa Persone Roial; et qe ascuns de eux du dit Conseil q'ensy demureront entour sa Persone facent report de la volunte de nostre dit Seignur le Roy de temps en temps a les autres du dit Conseil, des matiers q'appar-teignent au Conseil, et nemy autres;...

V. Item, qe please a nostre dit Seignur le Roy doner en charge a ses dites Conseillers, d'avoir plein conisance et notice de l'estate et governance de ses tres honurables Hostiell, Chambre, et Garderobe,...et pur y ordeiner le meulx q'ils purront pur le profit nostre dit Seignur le Roy,...

VIII. Item,...si please a mesme nostre Seignur le Roy considerer la sage Governance d'autres Princes Cristiens bien governez; et soi en confourmant a tiel Governance, luy pleise assigner deux jours le semaine pur la receptione des tielx Petitions; c'est assaver, le Mesqerdy, et Venderdy, et qe de ce soit fait intimation as toutes les Estates du Roialme en cest present Parlement, aufin qe les ditz autres jours de la semayne nostre dit Seignur le Roy se puisse le meulx desporter, sanz estre distourbez par tielx suytes; et qe, les jours de la reception de tielx Petitions, soient entour nostre dit Seignur le Roy ceux du dit Conseil assignez d'estre entour sa persone...

X. Item, qe pleise a nostre dit Seignur le Roy commaunder ceux de soun Conseil, q'ils ne traient devaunt eux, pur y estre deter-minez, aucunes matiers ne querelles determinables a la commune Ley, si ce ne soit pur cause resonable, et par advys des Justices.

XXIV. Item, soient toutes ceux du Grand Counseil du Roy, et

auxi les Chiefs Officers, c'est assavoir, Chaunceller, Tresorer d'Engleterre, Seneschall, Chamberlein, Gardein de Prive Seal, Tresorer et Countrollour d'Ostiel le Roy, assurez et jurrez en cest present Parlement,...

XXXI. Item, ordeine soit et assentuz, qe toutes les suis ditz Articles, et les contenuz en ycelles, en la fourme et par manere come ils sount declarez, estoisent et teignent lour force et effect, de commencement de cest present Parlement jusqes au fin du proschein Parlement tant soulement.

Rot. Parl. III, 585–9. (There were similar articles of reform in 1409–10 (*Rot. Parl.* III, 623 ff.) when the commons were also wanting to know the names of councillors, etc. (*Rot. Parl.* III, 632).)

(28) *Statement of the Duke of Bedford* 1414

Le declaracyon fait par Monsire Johan Duc de Bedford gardeyn del est march et capitayn de Berwyk al Henry le quynt lan secund du son reigne.

Plese au Roy nostre soverain seignur destre remembrez coment en temps du tresnoble Roy vostre piere qe Dieu pur sa grande mercie assoille estoit bien souvent foitz sibien en plusours et diverses parlementz come en grandes conseils et especialment pardevant le conseil assigne pur la governance du roialme monstrez et declarez depar Monsire Johan vostre treshumble frere conestable Dengleterre et gardein del estmarche vers Escoce la grant mischief lors esteant en la dite marche pur defaute de bonne governance et especialment de les matiers contenuz en les articles dessoubz escriptz....

A.P.C. II, 136.

(29) *Powers of the council* 1422

26. Fait assavoir, qe apres ceo qe le Roi nostre soverain Seignur, de l'assent et advis de les Seignurs Espirituelx et Temporelx, estcantz en ccstc Parlement, et auxi de la Commune d'Engleterre, assemblez en la mesme, avoit ordeinez et constitut le puissant Prince Humfrey Duc de Gloucestre son Uncle, Protectour et Defensour de les Roialme et Esglise d'Engleterre, et son Principal Conseillour, en l'absence de l'excellent Prince Johan Duc de Bedeford, Uncle auxi a nostre dit soverain Seignur,...a la requeste de la dite Commune furent, par l'advis et assent de tres toutz les Seignurs avantditz, nomez et eslutz certeins persones

d'estate si bien Espirituelx come Temporelx, pur Conseillers assistentz a la governance, les nons des queux persones escriptz en une petit Cedule lueez overtement en ceste Parlement cy ensuent.

Le Duc de Gloucestre;
L'Ercevesqe de Canterbirs;
L'Evesqe de Loundres,
L'Evesqe de Wyncestre,
L'Evesqe de Norwice,
L'Evesqe de Worcestre.
Le Duc d'Excetre;
Le Count de la March,
Le Count de Warrewyk,
Le Count Mareschall,
Le Count de Northumbreland,
Le Count de Westmerland;
Le Sire Fitz Hugh;
Monsire Rauf Crumbwell,
Monsire Wauter Hungerford,
Monsire Johan Tiptoft,
Monsire Wauter Beauchamp.

27. Et fait auxi assavoir, qe mesmes les persones issint nomez et eslutz Conseillers assistentz, puis cell nomination et election, condescenderent emprendre tiele assistence a la governance, en manere et fourme contenuz en une Cedule de papire escript en Englois, contenaunt si bien toutz lours nons,...de la quell Cedule le tenure cy ensuit.

28. The which Lordis abovesaid ben condescended to take it up on hem in the manere and fourme that sueth. First, for asmuche as execution of lawe, and kepyng of Pees, stant miche in Justice of Pees, Shirrefs, and Eschetours, the profits of the Kyng, and the revenuz of the Roialme ben greetly encresced, or anientisched by Coustumers, Countroullours, Poisours, Sercheours, and all suche other Officers. Therfore the same Lordes wol and desireth, that suche Officers, and all othre, be maad by advys and denomination of the said Lordes, saved alweys and reserved to my Lordes of Bedford, and of Gloucestre, all that longeth unto hem by a special Act maad in Parlement; and to the Busschop of Wynchestre that, that he hath graunted hym by oure souverein Lord that last was, of whois soule God have mercy, and by auctorite of Parlement confermed.

29. Item, that all maner Wardes, Mariages, Fermes, and other

casueltees that longeth to the Coroune, whan thei falle, be leeten, sold, and disposed by the said Lordis of the Counseill, and that indifferently atte the derrest, with oute favour...

30. Item, that if eny thyng shold be enact doon by Counseill, that six, or foure at the lest, withoute officers of the said Counseill, be present; and in all grete maters that shall passe by Counseill, that all be present, or ellys the more partye; and yf it be suche matere that the Kyng hath been accustumed to be conseilled of, that than the said Lordes procede not ther ynne withoute th'advise of my Lordys of Bedford, or of Gloucestre.

31. Item, for asmiche as the two Chaumberlains of th'Escheqer, ben ordenned of old tyme to countrolle the receptes and the paiements in eny maner wyse maad; The Lordys desireth, that the Tresourer of England beyng for the tyme, and either of the Chamburlains, have a keye of that that shold come in to the receit, and that they be sworne to fore my Lord of Gloucetre, and all the Lordis of the Counseill, that for no frendship they schul make no Man privee, but the Lordis of the Counseill, what the Kyng hath withynne his Tresour.

32. Item, that the Clerc of the Counseill be charged and sworn to treuly enacte, and write daylich, the names of all the Lordis that shul be present fro tyme to tyme, to see what, howe, and by whom, eny thyng passeth....

Rot. Parl. IV, 175–6.

(30) *Ordinances for the council* 1423

17. Thise ben certein Provisions for the good of the gouvernance of this Land, that the Lordes which ben of the K. Counsaill desireth:

Frost, that my Lord of Gloucestre, ne noon other Man of the Counsaill, in no suyte that shal be maad unto hem, shal no favour graunte, nethir in Billes of right, ne of office, ne of benefice, that loongeth to the Counsaill, but oonly to ansuere that the Bille shal be seen by all the Counsaill, and the Partie suying so to have ansuere.

Item, that alle the Billes that shul be putt unto the Counsail, shuld be onys in the Weke att the lest, that is to seie on the Wednesday, redd byfore ye Counsaill, and yere ansueres endoced by the same Counsaill. And on the Friday next folwyng, declared to the partie suyng.

Item, that alle the Billes that comprehende materes terminable atte the Commune Lawe, that semeth noght fenyd, be remitted there to be determined; but if so be that ye discrecion of the Counsaill feele to greet myght on that oo syde, and unmyght oo that othir.

. . . . . .

Item, that in alle suytes that shuld be maad to the Counsaill, in materes whois determination loongeth unto the Counsail, but if it so be that they touche the weell of the K. oure soverein Lord, or of his Reaume, hastily to be sped, elleys that they be nought enact doon by the Counsaill oo lesse than to the nombre of vi, or foure atte the lest of the Counsaill, and the Officers that ben present be of oon assent, and atte alle tymes the names of th' assenteurs to be wryten of thar owen hand, in the same Bille.

Item, for as miche as it is to greet a shame, that in to straunge Countrees oure soverein Lord shal write his Letters by th' advyse of his Counsail, for such materes and persones as the Counsail writeth in his name, and singuler persons of the Counsail to write the contrarie; that it be ordenned, that no Man of the Counsaill presume to do it, on peyne of shame and reproef.

Item, that the Clerc of the Counsail be sworn, that every day that the Counseill sitteth on ony Billes bitwyx partie and partie, that he shall, as fer as he can, aspye which is the porest Suyturs Bille, and that first to be redd and answered, and the Kinges Sergeant to be sworne trewly and plainly, to yeve the poor Man that for suche is accept to the Counsail, assistense and trewe Counsaill in his matere so to be suyd, wyth oute eny good takyng of hym, on peyne of discharge of ther Office.

Item, for asmuch that it is likly that many materes shull be treted afore the Counsaill, the whiche toucheth the Kinges prerogatif and freehold, o that o partie and othir of his sougets, o that othir, in the whiche materes the Counsaill is not lerned to kepe the Kynges ryghts, and the parties both, withouthe th'advise of the Kynges Justices, whiche be lerned both in his prerogatifs, and his commune lawe. That in alle suche materes his Juges be called therto, and their advise, with yair namys also, to be entred of record, what and howe thei determyne and advise therinne.

Rot. Parl. IV, 201. (Cf. IV, 343-4 for 1429 ordinances.)

(31) *Arrangements for sealing documents* 1423

vᵒ. die Februarii anno primo apud Westmonasterium presentibus dominis Ducibus Gloucestrie et Exonie Archiepiscopo Cantuariense Wyntoniense et Wigorniense Episcopis Comitibus Marchie

Cromwell Tiptoft et Hungerford Cancellario Thesaurario et
Custode privati sigilli concordatum et concessum erat quod quo-
cienscumqe et quandocumqe dominus Thesaurarius Anglie qui
nunc est nominabit aut presentabit per billam aut billas sub
signeto suo personam vel personas assignatas vel assignandas
officio vel officiis infra regnum Anglie cui vel quibus Thesaurarius
Anglie pro tempore existens per billam aut billas sub signeto suo
solebat nominare personam aut personas Cancellario Anglie pro
tempore existenti ad habendas super eisdem litteras Regis patentes
de dicto officio aut officiis Cancellarii Anglie qui nunc est...Idem
Cancellarius faciet de tempore in tempus persone aut personis...
litteras Regis patentes in forma debita.

A.P.C. III, 24.

(32) *Judicial work of the council* 1425

Ordinez est et assentuz en cest present Parlement, de l'advis des
Seignurs Espirituelx et Temporelx, et de l'assent des Communes
en icell Parlement esteantz; qe toutz les Petitions baillez en
mesme le Parlement par les ditz Communes, pur especialx et
privatz persones, et nient responduz, soient commis au Counseill
du Roi par auctorite suisdite, d'oier toutz les matires comprisez
deinz mesmes les Petitions, et icelles determiner solonc lour discretions, et bone foy et conscience.

Rot. Parl. IV, 301 (21).

(33) *The councillor's oath* 1425

Ye shall as fer furth as your connyng and discretion suffiseth,
trewely, justely and evenly, Counsaille and advyse the Kyng in
alle matiers to be comoned, treted and demened in the Kyng's
Counsaille, or by You as the Kynges Counsailler, and generally
in all thinges that may be to the Kynges worship, proufit and
behove, and to the gode of his Reaumes, Lordeships and Subgittz,
withouten parcialtee or acceptacion of persons, not levyng or
eschewing so to do for affection, love, mede, doubte or drede, of
eny persone or persones. And ye shall kepe secrete the Kynges
Counsaill, and alle that shall be comuned by way of Counsaille
in the same, withouten that ye shall common it, publish it, or
discover it by worde, wryting, or in eny wyse, to eny persone oute
of the same Counsaille, or to any of the same Counsaille, yf it
touch hym, or yf he be partie thereto. And that ye shall no yift,
mede nor gode, ne promisse of goode, by you nor by meen persone,

receyve nor admytt, for promotion, favouryng, nor for declaryng, lettyng or hinderyng, of eny matiere or thing to be treted or do in the seid Counsaille. Ye shall also with all your might and poair, help, strength and assiste, unto the Kynges said Counsaille, duryng the Kyngs tendre age, in all that shall be thoght unto the same Counsaille for the universale gode of the Kynge and of his Land, and for the Pees, Rest and Tranquillitee of the same; and withstonde any persone or persones, of what condition, estate or degree that thei be of, that wold by way of feet or ellus, attempte or entende unto the contrarie.

And generally ye shall observe, kepe and do, alle that a gode and trewe Counsailler oweth for to doo unto his Souveraine Lorde.

Rot. Parl. v, 407. (Cf. Baldwin, *King's council*, p. 353.)

(34) *Work of the great council* 1430

Sexto die Octobris anno ix°. apud Westmonasterium in magno consilio Regis convocato, concordatum est, quod auctoritate regia convocaretur parliamentum apud Westmonasterium die Veneris proximo ante festum Sancti Hillarii tunc proximum futurum celebrandum, dummodo domini de consilio Regis circa latus suum in regno Francie concenserint in id idem. Subsequenter vero xxvij° die mensis Novembris anno predicto delate erant littere Regis in filacio in officio privati sigilli remanentes ad consilium existens eodem die in camera stellata Westmonasterii, quibus lectis, concordatum fuit denuo, quod Custos privati sigilli faceret warantum Domino Cancellario ad scribendum modo et forma consuetis pro convocacione dicti parliamenti...

A.P.C. iv, 67.

(35) *Protest of Humphrey, Duke of Gloucester, against the liberation of the Duke of Orleans* 1440
. . . . . .
Thees ben in partie the pointes and articles the whiche I, Humfrey duc of Gloucestre...wolde yeve in writing,...unto youre hignesse, advertising youre excellence of such thinges in partie as have be doen and used in youre tendre age, into derrogacion of your noble estate, and hurte of bothe your royaumes...

First, the cardinal the bisshop of Winchestre toke upon him the state of cardinal, which was nayed and denyed hym by the kyng of moost blessed memory, my lord your fadre...How be it that

my saide lord, youre fadre, wolde have agreed hym to have had
certaine clerks of this lande cardinals, they having noo bisshop-
riches in Englande; yeet his entent was never to do so greet
derrogacion to the chirche of Caunterbury to make hem that were
his suffrigans to sitte above thair ordinarie and metropolitan; but
the cause was that, in general counsailles and in alle maters that
might concerne the wele of hym and of his royaume, he shulde
have promoters of his nacione, as alle other Cristen kynges had,
in the courte of Rome, and not to abide in this lande as eny part
of youre counsaille, as be alle other lords spirituell and temporell
at the parlements and greet counsailles, whan youre liste is to
calle hem. And therfore, thogh it like you to do hym that
worship to sette hym in youre prive counsaille, where that you
list, yeet in youre parlements, where every lord spirituell and
temporel have thair place, hym aught to occupie his place but as
bisshop.

*Letters and Papers illustrative of the wars of the English in France
during the reign of Henry VI* (ed. J. Stevenson), R.S. vol. II, pt. II
(1864), pp. 441–2.

(36) *Minutes of the council c.* 1440–3

. . . . . .

Furst of any lorde of his Counsaill or othir or any man aboute
his persone...and be immediat labor or to the Kyng for þexpedi-
cion of any bille for an othir persone, that he subscribe himselfe
in the said bille, so that it may be knowen at all tymes by whoos
meanes and labour everi bille is, and if he þat sueth the bille
canne nat write him selfe, that thanne summe man for him that
canne write, write the said suters name upon the said bille to
thintente abovesaid.

Item that all billes so subscribed and receyved by the Kyng be
delivered to such persone or persones as it shall plese his highnesse
to assigne and depute therto, and þat the saide persone or
persones visite and see þe continue of every bille.

Item if thar be billes of justice and conteyne matere of commune
lawe that they whitoute any more advertyse the Kinges good
grace þerof to þentent þat it may like þe Kyng yf it plese him to
commaunde þeime to be sent to his Counsail þat þei may by
þadvis of his said Counsail be remitted to þe commune lawe...

Item if þe matier conteined in the said billes be matere of
grace, thanne the saide persone or persones shall clerely and
trewely put shortly in writing on the bakside of the saide billes

what by whome and howe many thinges been asked þerinne and subscribe the saide writinges with his owne hande, so þat his highnesse may verily undrestande what is desired and why, and so to use his grace or noo or commaunde it to be sent to his Counsaill to have their advis as it shall please him. And yf it please his highnesse to shewe his grace and graunte the bille or part þerof, the saide persone...with his owne hande shall write upon the said bille forthwith...in what manere and fourme it hath pleased the Kyng to shewe his grace,...with þe day and place where the saide bille or part þerof is graunted and in whoos presence and specially in the presence of what lord or lordes as is þere at þat tyme if any be, thanne the Kinges goodenesse if it please him to put þerto his hande and signe þe bille immediatly after þe saide writinges or commaunde his chambrelain to subscribe it or take it to his secretary commaundyng him þerwith, so þat fro þat tyme þat it be in manere and fourme abovesaide signed noo man shall mowe adde þerto or mynussh.

Item þat in all lettres by the which the King graunteth and yeveth any thinge to any persone this clause be put inne, provided alway þat the Kyng hath not graunted the thinges asked to any othir persone afore that tyme.

Item that the warrantes to þe signet and also the copies of all that shall passe the signet, be it lettres missives or oþir, be truely and redily kept to þentent that as ofte as the Kinge wol commaunde it may be seen what þinges be passed him and also þat no thinge be writen contrary to þat þat passeth before.

Item þat for asmuch as it is like that suche thinge as passeth the handes of many persones shal the more redily and sadely passe and any hurte that shulde elles mowe growe to þe King or to prejudice of any othir persone the more to be eschewed, it is þought þat all billes whanne the King of his goode grace hath graunted þeim, be delivered to his secretary and lettres to be conceyved upon theim directed undre the signet to the Keper of the prive seal, and from þens under the prive seel to the Chaunceller of Englande.

Item that the Keper of the prive seal what tyme he receyveth lettres under the signet shall if it be thought to him þat the matere conteyned in the same be of greet charge, have recours to þe lordes of the Counsaill and open to þeim the matere, to þentente þat if it be thought necessarie to theim the King be advertised þerof or it passe.

Item if þadvisamentes beforesaide pleese þe King and be

acceptable to his highnesse, þat the persone or persones abovesaide
deputed and ordeyned to visette billes be sworn in fourme þat
foloweth.

Ye shall swere þat as ferforth as in you shall be, ye aswell in
visityng and overseeing as in writing and subscribing of billes,
the articles abovesaide and everiche of þeim that touche ye shall
trewely justely and faithfully observe and kepe withoute any
parcialtee or accepcion of persone or persones, not leving nor
eschewing so to doo for affeccion love mede doubte or drede of
any persone or persones, and þat ye shall noo yifte mede goode ne
promisse of gode by you nor by noone meane persone receyve nor
admitte for promocion favoring nor for declaringe speding letting
or hindering of any bille to be graunted by the King or to be
laide aparte.
. . . . . .

A.P.C. VI, 316–19.

(37) *A case before the council* 1441

Also þere as Will Flete for certain causes in his bille put unto þe
Kyng hath complained upon Ryman, as in þe said bille is con-
tained mor at large. The which Ryman by force and vertue of
þe Kinges commandement in þis behalfe maad hath appered and
is now in persone before þe Kynges counsail for to her what
shold be said unto him on þis behalf. For as moche as þe said
counsail is now in departing and þat þe heryng ánd dissecucion
of þe said bille and complainte wolde axe. . .a tract of tyme with
meur advis and deliberacion. It is gyve. . .þe said Ryman in
commandement to apper before þe Kyng and his counsail in
xvᵃ Hillarij next comyng upon peine comprised in þe writ of
proclamacion by vertue of þe which he cam in þis behalf and
appered.

A.P.C. V, 172.

(38) *Arrangements for a council* 1454

Instruction yeven by the Duk of York, the Kynges Lieutenaunt
of his Parlement, and othir Lordes Spirituell and Temporell of
the said Parlement, to the right reverent Fadres in God the
Bishops of Wynchestre, Ely and Chestre; th'Erles of Warrewyk,
Oxenford and Shrovesbury; the Viscountes Beaumont and
Bourghchier; the Lordes Priour of Seint John's, Faucomberge,
Duddeley, and Stourton jointely: The whiche Credence they shall

opene, if they fynde the Kynges disposition suche, that he shall mowe and will attende to the heryng and understondyng therof, and ellys they shall opene but oonly the furst and second Articles. ...[*article* 5]

Item, they shall remembre that it pleased the Kynges Highnesse in this his Parlement at Redyng, to commaunde to be openned to the Communes of this Lande, his gracious entent to ordeigne and stablishe a discrete and a sadde Counsaill, the whiche was to the seid Communes a grete rejoysing and comfort, insomoche that nowe late by the mouth of there Speker, among othir thynges at too tymes hath be made requestes to the seid Lieutenaunt and Lordes, that the seid Communes myght understonde and have knowelege, of effectuell procedyng to the stablishyng of the said Counsaill, wherfor certaine Lordes and persones be named under the Kynges correction, to take uppon theym the seid charge; and they shall mowe declare what persones be soo named, and understande whethir the Kynges good grace be content with the seid persones, or whethir he will chaunge or sette asyde eny of theym, to th'entent that his will may be observed and kept.

Rot. Parl. v, 240–1 (31).

(39) *Relation between king and councillors* 1455

The xxii[ti] day of Novembre, the yere of oure seid Soverayne Lord xxxiiii[ti], the moost Cristen Prince the Kyng oure moost drad Soverayne Lord, at his Paleys of Westminster, remembryng that to the politique governaunce and restfull reule of this his Realme, apperteneth grete diligence and actuell laboure, the which is to his moost noble persone full tedious and grete to suffre and bere. Also that every Prince must of verray necessitee have Counsaillers to helpe hym in his charges, to whome he muste trust and leene; for thees causes and other such as moeve his high wisedome, consideryng that God hath endued such as been of his Counsaill with grete wisdome, cunnyng and experience,...ordeyned and graunted, that his Counsaill shuld provyde, commyne, ordeyne, spede and conclude, all such matiers as touche and concerne the good and politique rule and governaunce of this his land, and lawes therof, and directe thayme as it shal be thought to theire wisdomes and discretions behovefull and expedient: soo alwaye that in all such matiers as touchen the honour, wurship and suertee of his moost noble persone, they shall late his Highnes have knowelech what direction they take in theym: desiryng his said Counsaill hertely, for the wele and ease of his said persone, and kepyng and beryng up his Roiall astate, to take this his wille and ordenaunce upon thaym. The which Lordes protestyng, that the high prerogative, preemynence and auctorite of his Mageste Roiall, and also the soverauntee of thaym and all this lande, is and alwey mot reste...in his moost excellent persone, offre thayme of humble obeissaunce, to put thaym in as grete diligence and devoir, to doo all that that mowe preferre or avaunce the said high prerogatyve...and also to the politique reule and gover-naunce of his lande, and the good publique, reste and tranquillite of his subgettes, as ever did eny Counsaillers or subgettes to theire moost drad Soverayne Lord, and therunto at all tymes to be redy, not sparyng therfore at eny tyme that it shall nede, to putte theire bodyes in jeopardie.

Rot. Parl. v, 289–90 (41).

(40) *Case before the council. Tenants v. Waynflete* 1462
R.E.[1] By the kyng.

Trusty and welbeloued. Howe it be that upon the complaintes made by the tenantes of the Reuerent fadre in God, the Bishop of Wynchestre, and in especiall of the lordship of Estmeone in our countee of Hampshire in our last parlement, the matiers con-cernyng the said complaintes were rypely examyned, and either partie herd, as ferre as they or any of thaym coude shewe or allegge for himself. And finally by the consideracion of the grete proves shewed on the behalf of the said Reuerent fadre in God, and noon resonable matier shewed by the partie contrarie that sholde or might exclude hym of his right demaunded of his said tenantes, it was aduised and understande that the said tenantes sholde and ought to paye theire rentes and doo and continue their suetes,...as they had doon in tyme passed, as more atte large is conteygned in an acte therupon made: yit that notwith-standyng the said tenantes have not only not doo nor observed the said advisement; but also in the monethe of Maye last passed complayned unto us of certaine of their neighbours emprisoned by the said Reuerent fadre. Whereupon we willed thaim to retorne and to sende ayen this fest of Witsontide ii or iii of euery hundred of the said lordship, and also charged the said Reuerent fader to send hider by the same tyme a discrete and a sadde personne or personnes fully instruct of his entent in all thinges concernyng the

[1] The sign manual of Edward IV.

variaunce betwix him and his said tenauntes, to thentent that we thaym herde and understande might by thauis of our counsaill take suche direction therein as shuld be to the pleasire of God and ease, rest and pees of either partie. And notwithstandyng that, accordyng to our said commaundement, both the counsaill of the said Reuerent fader in God were here redy for that cause, and also, as we understande, a greet compaignye of the said tenantes, yit the said tenantes, for what cause we wote not, sodeinly departed hens, the said matier not herde nor examined, in their owen defaute, to our grete mervayllyng, and also hurt and tediouse vexacion of the said Reuerent fadre in God, and also to his grete charges and expenses. Wherefore we wol and charge you that ye, going to suche places in the said lordship as shal be thought to your discrecion moost expedient, declare and notifie on oure behalfe to alle the said tenantes the premisses, willing and chargyng thaym and eche of thaym that,...they paye their rentes, doo and contynue their seutes, seruices, werkes and custumes, as they aught and haue be accustumed to doo in tyme passed, soo that in their defaute we be noo more vexed nor troubled in that partie,...

And ouer this wol and charge you that ye assiste...the seid Reuerent fadre in alle thinges belongyng to your office accordyng to the duetee therof...Yeven etc. at our Castell of Leycester the ixth day of Juyn the secunde yere of our reigne.

To our trusty and welbeloued The Shirrief of our countee of Hampshire.

[*Endorsed*:] The iiide daye of Juyll' the seconde yere of the reigne of our souuerain and liege lord King Edward the fourthe in the sterred Chambre at Westminster, the same our souuerain and liege lord by thauis of his counsaill commaunded his Chaunceller of England to doo make writtes under the greet seal directed to the shirrief of our countee of Suthampton, and to suche other as shal be thought expedient, commaundyng by the same to make proclamacion as it is remembred in this minute within writen signed with the kynges owen hande, ther beyng present the lordes Tharchebisshop of Caunterbury, the Bisshopes of Excestre, Chaunceller of England, and Norwich, Therles of Worcestre, tresorer of England, and Kent, The prior of Saint Johns, The lord Dacre, The keper of the kinges priue seal, The Dean of Saint Severyngs, John Saye, etc.   [*Signed*:] T. Kent.

Select cases before the king's council (S.S.), pp. 114–15.

(41) *Complaints against the king's rule* 1469

The duc of Clarance, th'archebisshoppe of Yorke, and th'erle of Warwyk.

Right trusty and welbelovid, we grete you welle. And welle ye witte that the Kyng oure soveregne lordys true subgettes of diverse partyes of this his realme of Engelond have delivered to us certeyn billis of Articles, whiche we suppose that ye have in thoos parties, rememberynge in the same the disceyvabille covetous rule and gydynge of certeyne ceducious persones; that is to say, the Lord Ryvers, the Duchesse of Bedford his wyf,...and other of theyre myschevous rule opinion and assent, wheche have caused oure seid sovereyn Lord and his seid realme to falle in grete poverte of myserie,...The seid trewe subgettis with pitevous lamentacion callyng uppon us and other lordes to be meanes to oure seid sovereyne Lord for a remedy and reformacion; werfore we, thenkyng the peticioun comprised in the seid articles reson-abyll and profitable for the honoure and profite of oure seid sovereyn Lord and the comune welle of alle this his realme... desiryng and pray you to dispose and arredie you to accom-payneye us thedir, with as many persones defensabyly arrayede as y can make, lettyng you wete that by Goddis grace we en-tende to be at Caunterbury uppon Sonday next comyng. Wretyn undre oure signettis and signe manuell the xijth day of Juyll, A^o 1469.

In three the next articles undrewretin are comprisid and specified the occasions and verry causes of the grete inconveniencis and mischeves that fall in this lond in the dayes of Kyng Edward the ij^{de}, Kyng Ric' the ij^{de}, and Kyng Henry the vj^{te}, to the distruccion of them, And to the gret hurt and empoverysshyng of this lond.

First, where the seid Kynges estraingid the gret lordis of thayre blood from thaire secrete Councelle, And not avised by them; And takyng abowte them other not of thaire blood, and enclynyng only to theire counselle, rule and advise, the wheche persones take not respect ne consideracion to the wele of the seid princes, ne to the comonwele of this lond, but only to theire singuler lucour and enrichyng of themself and theire bloode, as welle in theire greet possessions as in goodis; by the wheche the seid princes were so enpoverysshed that they hadde not sufficient of lyvelode ne of goodis, wherby they myght kepe and mayntene theire honorable estate and ordinarie charges withynne this realme.
......

Document printed in the notes to *Warkworth's chronicle* (Camden Series), 1839, pp. 46–7.

(42) *Sir John Fortescue on " The Governance of England" (written* 1471–6)

How the kynges counsell mey be chosen and estableshed.

The kyngis counsell was wonned to be chosen off grete princes, and off the gretteste lordes off þe lande, both spirituelles and temporellis, and also off oþer men that were in grete auctorite and offices. Wich lordes and officers had nere hande also mony maters off thair owne to be treded in the counsell, as hade þe kynge. Wherthrough, whan thai come to gedre, thai were so occupied with thair owne maters, and with the maters off thair kynne, seruantes, and tenantes, þat thai entendet but litle, and oþer while no thynge, to þe kynges maters...And what lower man was þer sytinge in þat counsell, þat durste say ayen the openyon off any off the grete lordis? And whi myght not then men make be meanes off corrupcion somme off the seruantes and counsellers off somme off the lordes to moue the lordes to parciallite, and to make hem also ffauorable and parcial as were the same seruantes, or the parties þat so moved hem? Then couude no mater treted in the counsell be kept prive...

Wich thynges considered, and also mony oþer wech shall be shewid hereaftir, hit is thought gode, that þe kynge had a counsell chosen and estableshed in the fourme that ffolowith, or in some oþer ffourme like þerto. Ffirst, þat ther were chosen xij spirituell men, and xij temporell men, off þe wysest and best disposed men þat can be ffounde in all the parties off this lande; and that thai be sworne to counsell the kynge aftir a ffourme to be devysed ffor þer owthe. And in especiall, þat thai shall take no ffee, nor clothynge, nor no rewardes off any man, except only off þe kynge; like as þe Justices off þe kynges benche, and off þe Common place be sworne, when thai take ther offices. And þat thes xxiiij. be alway counsellers, but yff þer be any defaute ffounde in hem, or þat hit lyst the kynge, be the advise off þe more parte off hem, chaunge any off hem. And þat euery yere be chosen be þe kynge iiij. lordes spirituell, and iiij. lordes temporall, to be ffor þat yere off þe same counsell, in like ffourme as þe said xxiiij^tl shall be. And that thai all haue an hed, or a cheeff to rule þe counsell, on off þe said xxiiij^tl, and chosen be the kynge, havynge is office at the kynges pleasur; wich mey thanne be callid, *Capitalis consiliarius.* It shall not be necessarie, þat the xij spirituell men off this covnsell, haue so gret wages as the xij temporall men; be cause thai shull not nede to kepe an houshold in thair contray, while

thai ben absent, as the temporell men moste nedes doo ffor thair
wyffes and childeren. . . The said viij^{te} lordes also, wich be reason
off þer baronyes and estates bith to þe kyng, *consiliari nati*, and
þerfore awghton to counsell hym at all tymes when he woll, nede
not to haue gret wages ffor thair attendance to is covnsell, wich
shall last ffor a yere. . . And thoughe þat wages off the said
xxiiij^{ti} counsellers seme a newe and a grete charge to þe kynge,
yet when hit is considered, how gret wages the grete lordes and
other men, wych were off the kynges counsell in tymes passede,
toke ffor thair attendance therto, wich maner off counsell was
nothynge so behouefull to the kyng and to his reaume as this will
be, wich wages shall than forthwarde cesse; þe wages off þe
xxiiij^{ti} counsellours shall apere no gret charge to the kynge. . . And
if the same wagis be thought to grete charge vnto þe kyng, þe
forsaid counsellours mowe be in lesse nowmbre, as to be xvj
counsellours off privatis personis, with ij lordes spirituell, and ij
lordes temporell; so as then thai be in all but xx^{ti} persones. Thies
counsellors mowe contenually, at soche owres as shal be asseigned
to thaym, comune and delibre vppon the materis of defeculte
that ffallen to the kynge; and then vppon the materes off þe
pollycye off þe reaume; as how þe goyng owt off þe money may
be restrayned, how bullyon mey be brought in to þe lande, how
also plate, juelles, and mony late borne owt, mey be geytun ageyn;
off wich right wyse men mowe sone fynde the meanes. . . How
owre nauy mey be mayntened and augmented, . . . How also þe
lawes mey be amendet in suche thynges as thay neden reformacion
in; wher through þe parlementes shall mowe do more gode in a
moneth to þe mendynge off the lawe, then thai shall mowe do
in a yere, yff þe amendynge þeroff be not debatyd and be such
counsell ryped to thair handes. Þer mey be off this covnsell, when
thai liste come þerto, or þat thai be desired be þe said counsellours, þe grete officers off þe lande, as Chaunceler, tresourer
and prive seell; off wich þe chaunceler, when he is present, mey
be presydent, and haue þe supreme rule off all þe counsell.
Also the Juges, the Barones off þe exchequier, þe clerke off the
rolles, and suche lordes as þe forsaid counsellours woll desire to
be with thaym for materes off gret deficulte, mey be off this
counsell when thai be so desyred, and ellis not. All oþer materes
wich shall conserne this counsell, as when a Counsellour dyeth,
how a new counsellour shall be chosen, how mony owres off the
day this counsell shall sytt, when thai shall haue any vacasion,
how longe any off hem mey be absent, and how he shall haue his

leue, with all oþer artycles necessarye ffor the demeynynge and rule off this counsell, mowe be conseyued be layser, and putt in a boke, and that boke kept in this counsell as a registir or a ordinarye, howe thai shall doo in euery thynge.

Sir John Fortescue, *The Governance of England*, edition by C. Plummer (1885), pp. 145–9.

(43) *Case before the council. Whele v. Fortescue* 1482

In the sterre chambre at Westminster the secunde daye of Maye the xxij yere of the reigne of our soueraigne lord the king Edwarde the iiijth present my lordes Tharchebisshop of York Chaunceller of England the Bisshoppes of Lincoln priue Seal Worcestre Norwich Durham and Landaff Therle Ryvers the lordes Dudley Ferres Beauchamp Sirs Thomas Borough William Parre Thomas Vaghan and Thomas Greye knightis in full and plenary counsaill was openly radde the Jugement and decree made by my lordis of our said soueraignes lordes counsaill afore that tyme for the partie of Richard Whele otherwise called Richard Pierson decreed . . . ayenst John Fortescue squier in maner and fourme and under the thenure that foloweth. In the matier of question . . . betwix John Fortescue squier and Richard Whele otherwise called Pierson of that the said John Fortescue alleggith and seith that the said Richard is a Scotte borne and of thalligiance of the King of Scottis and for such oon hath take hym and is in possession as his prisoner the said Richard evidently proving the contrarie and that he is an Englissheman boren and noo Scotte as in the writinges of the said Fortescue for his partie and also of . . . Richard for his defence it is conteigned all at large whiche matier longe hath hanged in the kinges counsaill undecided. Therfore the xxi^{tl} daye of Nouembre the xxi^{tl} yere of the reigne of our soueraigne lord the King Edwarde the iiijth in the sterre Chambre at Westminster afore the lordes of the Kinges Counsaill the said writinges for either partie with all such evidences and proves by auctorite examined and by grete deliberacion seen and understanded. And after either of the said parties bothe in thaire owne persone as by thair counsaill at diuers tymes diligently herde in all that they coude or wolde allege and saie in that behalf it appered to the lordes of the said counsaill that the said Richard Whele . . . is and was an Englissheman borne and noo Scotte and that he was borne in the towne of Newcastell upon Tyne and therefore it is considered adiuged and decreed by the same lordes the same

Richard so to be holden...as the kinges ligeman to be demeaned
and entreated in all places and noon otherwise...
and the said John Fortescue to be putte and so was putte to per-
petuell silence of further besynes sute or vexacion of the said
Richard for the cause aboue pretended in tyme to come in any
manerwise; than present my lordes tharchebisshop of Yorke
Chaunceller of England and Bisshoppis of Lincoln priue seall,
Bathe, Worcestre and Durham, Maisters Gunthorp, Cook, the
popis collectour, the lordis Haward, Sir Thomas Vaghan and Sir
Richard Harecourt Knightes and Thomas Thwaytes, etc.

[*Signed*:] Langport.

Datum etc. apud Westmonasterium, xxvi^{to} die Junii anno etc.
xxij.

Select cases before the king's council (S.S.), pp. 117–18.

CHAPTER III

THE HOUSEHOLD: WARDROBE AND CHAMBER

INTRODUCTION

At the end of the Anglo-Saxon period the king's household was the centre of government. It included the royal servants, some of whom, like the chancellor and chamberlain, were becoming important officials, and others with duties of great dignity and tradition, such as the steward, marshal and butler. No distinction was at first made between public and private business and the members of the household were in a position to advise the crown. The central administration of the household lay with the chamber, originally the king's bedroom for the safe storing of the royal clothes and valuables, and the increased royal business after the Norman conquest naturally devolved on the chamber, which had to increase its staff, especially to deal with financial affairs. Some differentiation, however, was inevitable; and in Henry I's reign the exchequer developed as a specialised financial department, though still intimately connected with the *curia*.[1]

The chamber, which had thus lost much power, was further weakened by the emergence of its own offshoot, the wardrobe, and after the first years of Henry III the chamber practically disappears from the records for about a century. Its place was taken by the wardrobe, which in origin had been the closet adjoining the king's bedchamber, for the storage of royal valuables and apparel. Early in Henry III's reign the wardrobe came to monopolise the administrative work hitherto in the hands of the chamber, whose staff it took over; and after 1230 it had possession of the small royal seal as distinct from the great seal of chancery.[2]

In the years after 1232 Henry III seems to have tried to establish his own control over the administration; he appointed inferior men to take charge of the chancery and exchequer, and the office of justiciar fell into abeyance. Royal policy was determined without the advice of the magnates, and the work of administration fell mainly into the hands of the officials of the

[1] See below, pp. 226–7.   [2] See below, p. 208.

wardrobe, while the exchequer, reformed by Peter of Rivaux, and the chancery cooperated. Henry's policy thus aimed at a complete centralisation, but he was not sufficiently strong to carry out the responsibilities involved. He alienated the old baronage by his rewards to foreign favourites, and still further by his unstatesmanlike policy at home and abroad. The crisis came in 1258 after several forewarnings. In that year the barons demanded a share in the administration; they attempted to obtain control of the annual appointments of the great officials, chancellor, treasurer and the restored justiciar, they inaugurated a much-needed reform of local government, and they hoped to secure their authority by a complicated scheme of conciliar government.[1] Yet there was little change in the detailed organisation of exchequer and chancery, and no serious attempt was made to reform the household after the first outcry against aliens. Already in 1261 Henry was able to replace some of the baronial nominees with his own officials, and although after the battle of Lewes in 1264 more drastic changes were made in the appointment of higher officials, yet after 1265 the household was again entirely under royal control.[2]

Edward I was to realise even more fully the value of a well-organised household in close cooperation with the great departments, and early in his reign an important document known as the household ordinance of 1279 was drawn up,[3] which gives in detail the names and duties of the chief officials of the household. The keeper of the wardrobe was responsible for all accounts, and in his position seemed likely to rival the treasurer himself; under him was the controller who had a counter-roll for accounts, and also had charge of the privy seal. All arrangements connected with the moving of the household on the royal progresses were in charge of the usher, and the document goes into the greatest detail likewise for the less important aspects of organisation. Before 1307, indeed, the wardrobe possessed a highly complex financial system, and though it had to account to the exchequer for its expenditure, it was in many ways independent. In the administrative activities, too, it was rivalling the chancery, and its privy seal was being used more prominently, at a time when the

[1] See Stubbs, *S.C.* pp. 369 ff.
[2] On this period cf. E. F. Jacob, *Studies in the period of baronial reform and rebellion* (*Oxford studies in social and legal history*, 1925); and R. F. Treharne, *The baronial plan of reform, 1258–63* (1932).
[3] Tout, *Chapters*, II, 27 ff., 158–63. Cf. article by B. Wilkinson, *History* (1927).

great seal kept by the chancellor was being reserved for public affairs. The wardrobe's best opportunity for development was in wartime when the king was in financial difficulties; this is seen both in Edward I's reign and later, and it explains the differentiation within the wardrobe itself which was taking place. The great wardrobe, an offshoot of the wardrobe, from Henry III's time had come to have control of the purchase of bulky commodities for the household, and it had its own keeper, as seen in the 1279 ordinance.[1] Yet another offshoot, the privy wardrobe, was emerging in the early fourteenth century, though its importance dates from the French war: it was stationed at the Tower, and its main purpose was for the supply of military provisions.[2]

Of the troubles at the end of Edward I's reign it has been said that they are "of special moment because they allowed the wardrobe to assume the greatest share it ever took in the direction of the policy and finance of the English state".[3] From this time, indeed, the departments of the household were to play an important part in the political contest for power between king and barons, since the household offered the best opportunity for royal rule independent of the great departments. The barons had shown their opposition to Edward I's centralisation by the *Articuli super artas* of 1305.[4] These articles were not carried out, but they are a fitting prelude to the baronial efforts in the next reign to restrain royal powers and prerogative. The baronial programme in opposition to Edward II can be seen in the ordinances of 1311, of which some of the most important clauses referred to the household.[5] An attempt was made to check the development of the wardrobe by ordering that it should have no sources of supply independent of the exchequer. There was to be a clerk for the keeping of the privy seal; and the judicial powers of steward and marshal were carefully defined. Some of the baronial demands were not new; some were to be reiterated again and again during the century, as in the case of jurisdiction of the household; but they illustrate the struggle between king and barons which was at once personal and selfish, yet with fundamental issues involved.

Edward II at first evaded the baronial demands, then had to submit in 1314; but by relying on his household he was able even then to maintain some form of independence. The administrative

---

[1] Tout, *Chapters*, IV, 349 ff.
[2] *Ibid.* IV, 439 ff.
[3] *Ibid.* II, 122.
[4] *Ibid.* II, 153–4.
[5] See above, Crown section, pp. 12–17.

departments went on steadily in spite of political crises (cf. 2), and most significant is the revival of the chamber, which was not bound to account to the exchequer nor necessarily dependent on it for supply. Early in the reign a considerable estate was allotted to the chamber from the forfeited lands of Walter Langton and the Templars, and in spite of the 1311 ordinances it received further grants (1). The barons, who had insisted on making appointments in the wardrobe, for some reason ignored the chamber, though in 1318 the choice of Despenser as chamberlain was recognised in parliament. Especially after 1314 the chamber, with its capable staff of officials, increased enormously in power, and the association of a new secret seal with its administration extended its influence over much secretarial business.[1]

In view of this independent development of the chamber, the administrative reforms which were carried out especially by the younger Despenser, Baldock, and Stapeldon after 1318 are all the more remarkable, for by these reforms the prerogative departments, including the rehabilitated chamber, were brought into line with the general administration. By the ordinance of York in 1318 the household was treated as one unit, each of its parts having a detailed and carefully balanced organisation (3).[2] Its jurisdiction was defined, and the office of privy seal was finally set up, with a keeper and four clerks, practically independent of the household.[3] A later ordinance for household reform in 1323 was most probably inspired by the exchequer, since its main object was to secure punctual and regular accounting there by the wardrobe.[4] Most significant, however, is the way in which the chamber was subordinated to the exchequer. In July, 1322, the lands reserved to the chamber were transferred to the treasurer and his officials (4–6), although just before this time the estate had been much increased. The chamber continued to be very active in administration during the rest of the reign, but this was in matters of its own concern.[5]

The exchequer, which was thus restored to a position of complete authority among the departments, was itself reformed in 1323, when, owing to the energies of the treasurer Stapeldon, the Cowick ordinance was issued, regulating its judicial as well as its financial powers.[6] This was followed by a supplementary

[1] Tout, *Chapters*, II, 314 ff.
[2] Document in Tout, *Edward II*, pp. 270–314; cf. *Chapters*, II, 245 ff.
[3] See below, p. 214.   [4] Tout, *Edward II*, pp. 314–18; *Chapters*, II, 260–3.
[5] *Ibid.* II, 340 ff.   [6] See below, pp. 227–8.

ordinance in the next year(7), and a third in 1326, when Archbishop Melton was treasurer. These ordinances, between 1318 and 1326, were of such permanent importance that we can say that they formulated the relationship between the departments of the court, household and state for the rest of the medieval period. After 1327, although the king might revive temporarily a household department, as Edward III did the chamber, yet the exchequer maintained its ultimate control.

This is seen particularly well during the first stages of the Hundred Years' War, when Edward III looked to his household to obtain extra supplies. During these years we can trace a two-fold development, first in the renewed activity of the wardrobe and its offshoots, and secondly in the temporary re-establishment of the chamber as an independent department for the king's personal affairs. The rapid development of the great and privy wardrobes was naturally hastened by the demands of war, and the wardrobe of the household was left free for administrative work. In 1338 and 1340 the king took the wardrobe abroad with him and stationed it at Antwerp (cf. 8). Edward was in dire straits for money, and the wardrobe had to negotiate for loans from the Italian bankers, many of whom were later ruined, and from merchant houses such as that of the Poles. The difficulties occasioned by this administrative dualism accounted very largely for the political crisis of 1340–1.[1] It is significant that with such increased powers, the wardrobe had still to account to the exchequer, and the same is true of its offshoots: since 1323 the great wardrobe had been separated from the wardrobe and except for a short period from 1351 to 1360, it accounted to the treasurer;[2] the privy wardrobe was also mainly dependent upon the exchequer, to which it rendered its accounts.[3]

Edward III had begun to reserve lands for the chamber as early as 1333, and its estate increased rapidly;[4] after 1349, for example, all escheated lands were to be assigned directly to the chamber, instead of being controlled by escheators for the exchequer. More chamber officials were appointed to cope with its greater responsibilities and their status was improved. A special seal, known as the Griffin, was used for the administration of the estate between 1335 and 1354, and during that time it superseded the secret seal for the business of the chamber(cf. 11).[5] The exchequer

---

[1] See above, pp. 46–7.
[2] Tout, *Chapters*, IV, 430 ff.
[3] *Ibid.* IV, 466.   [4] *Ibid.* IV, 238 ff.   [5] *Ibid.* V, 181–92.

was far less ready than the chancery to accept this "sub-depart-
mental seal" as Professor Tout described it, and the consequent
rivalry between exchequer and chamber must have created much
confusion at a time when every available resource was needed for
war. The attempt, however, to re-establish an independent chamber
was short-lived. As early as 1349 it was seen that its activities
would have to be restricted (9, 10), although it was not until 1356
that the lands reserved to the chamber were transferred to the
exchequer (12). In future the chamber was dependent upon a
fixed income from the treasury, although this *certum* varied in
amount at different times. It is not known when the secret seal was
taken from the custody of the receiver of the chamber, but by
Richard II's reign a signet had replaced the secret seal, and was
soon to have an organised office.[1]

It is natural that, although the reforms of the preceding reign
were in effect maintained, Edward III's use of his household
should have been looked on with much suspicion by the commons in parliament. Constant petitions were being made against
the extension of the jurisdiction of steward and marshal,[2] and
a general reform was being demanded, especially after 1377.
Nevertheless in actual fact the wardrobe and chamber were fast
becoming stabilised, and declining in political importance. The
wardrobe, for example, tended to have permanent quarters, while
the king moved round with a small court, as in Richard II's time.
After the middle of the fourteenth century, indeed, there is little
of constitutional importance in the history of the household
departments. As Professor Tout wrote, "The administrative
history of the fifteenth century has still to be written, but it is
doubtful whether it will disclose tendencies different from those
which we have endeavoured to study in the thirteenth and
fourteenth centuries".[3] It is true that attempts were made later
to reform the household and to define its income, as in 1404, but
in the succeeding period it is increasingly clear that the council,
and not the household, was to be the centre of political
conflicts.[4]

At one time in the fifteenth century, when Henry V was preparing
for his campaigns, it was seen that the household could still be

[1] See below, p. 210.
  See below, section on Justice, p. 283.
[3] Tout, *Chapters*, IV, 67.
[4] See above, pp. 49–50. The references to the household after 1356 are to be
found in the Council section.

used for military purposes, but this was only temporary.[1] By the end of the century, while the judicial work of the chancery had enormously increased, other state departments such as the exchequer and office of privy seal had become rigid and formalised, and the household had come to have domestic rather than public interests. In the early sixteenth century the chamber was to be revived for financial purposes,[2] but it was the secretary in charge of the signet who was able to carry on an increasingly vigorous administrative policy, and it is in the evolution of that office that we can best see the transition from medieval to modern administration.[3]

BIBLIOGRAPHY

1. ORIGINAL SOURCES

P.R.O. Exchequer accounts.
—— Memoranda rolls, K.R., L.T.R.
—— Pipe roll.
HALL, H. (ed.). *Red book of the exchequer*, pt. III, R.S. London, 1896.

2. SECONDARY AUTHORITIES

BALDWIN, J. F. *The king's council in England during the middle ages.* Oxford, 1913.
DAVIES, J. C. *The baronial opposition to Edward II.* Cambridge, 1918.
TOUT, T. F. *Chapters in the administrative history of medieval England.* Manchester, 1920–30.
—— *The place of the reign of Edward II in English history.* Manchester, 1914.

3. ARTICLES

STEEL, A. "Some aspects of English finance in the fourteenth century", *History*, XII, Jan. 1928.
WILKINSON, B. "The household ordinance of 1279 (historical revision)", *History*, XII, April, 1927.

---

[1] Tout, *Chapters*, IV, 225.
[2] Cf. A. P. Newton, "Tudor reforms in the royal household", in *Tudor studies* (ed. R. W. Seton-Watson), and article on "The king's chamber under the early Tudors", *E.H.R.* XXXII, 1917.
[3] See below, p. 211.

(1) *Issues from lands reserved to the chamber* 1314

Edward par la grace de dieu etc. au lieu tenant du Tresorer et as Barons de nostre Eschekier, Salutz. Nous vous mandoms qe de laconte qe nostre bien amez Alexandre de Compton nous deit du temps quil estoit nostre gardeyn daucuns manoirs et terres iadis des Templers es Contez de Leycestre et de Warrewyk rien ne vous mellez car nous voloms quil nous rende mesme laconte en nostre Chambre et nemye aillours. Done souz nostre priue seal a Nicol le xx iour Daveril lan de nostre regne septisme.

Baronibus pro Alexandro de Compton.

Memoranda roll, K.R. no. 87, m. 27. (Cf. A. M. Leys, "The forfeiture of the lands of the Templars in England", in *Oxford Essays...presented to H. E. Salter*, 1934, pp. 157–60.)

(2) *Wardrobe accounts* 1314–15

Contra rotulus expensarum garderobe per Robertum de Wodehous de tempore Willelmi de Melton, custodis garderobe, videlicet a primo die Decembris, anno viij° vsque vij diem Julij anno eodem finiente. de prima parte compoti eiusdem W.[1]

Contra rotulus de anno ix°

f. 1 d.

Summa totalis expensarum hospicij domini Regis Edwardi filij Regis Edwardi in denariis inter octauum diem Julij anno regni sui nono incipiente et vltimum diem Januarii anno eodem, prout patet per rotulum expensarum hospicij eiusdem.

f. 3.

v mill'. ix^cxxxvj li. x s. viij d.

Titulus de Elemosina Regis Edwardi...data in denariis a festo translacionis Sancti Thome Martiris, videlicet viij die Julij, anno regni sui nono incipiente, vsque ad vltimum

f. 3 d.

---

[1] This account book gives the details of wardrobe administration for a few months after December 1, 1314, as drawn up in the counter roll of Robert de Wodehouse, controller of the wardrobe. The full accounts of William Melton, keeper of the wardrobe from December 1, 1314 to February 1, 1316, were later enrolled in the pipe roll of 14 Edward II. At this time the baronial ordinances were being partly enforced, as the income of the wardrobe was derived almost entirely from the exchequer, but its expenditure was still considerable and a rigid economy had not been effected. Cf. Tout, *Chapters*, II, 237–8.

diem Januarij anno eodem. tempore Willelmi de Melton
tunc custodis Garderobe Regis predicti, et Roberti de. . .
Wodehous, tunc contrarotulatoris eiusdem garderobe.
Et est summa totalis istius tituli de Elemosina, vt patet in
fine eiusdem,
$$\text{c } \overset{\text{xx}}{\text{iiij}} \text{ xiiij li. xj s. xj d.}$$

f. 4. [e.g.] Fratri Roberto de Sancto Albano et socio suo, fratribus
Quidam de ordine Sancti Augustini, nunciantibus domino Regi
fratres de concessionem missarum per fratres eiusdem ordinis in
Ordine capitulo suo generali nuper apud Huntyngdon celebrato
Sancti factam, videlicet, quod in qualibet domo dicti ordinis tam
Augustini. infra Angliam quam Hiberniam cotidie vnus frater
diuina celebraret pro anima domini Petri de Gauaston
quondam Comitis Cornubie defuncti, per vnum annum
plenarie completum de dono et elemosina Regis per
manus fratris Willelmi de Armeston socij sui apud Alwal-
ton xxij° die Octobris,
$$\text{xiij s. iiij d.}$$

f. 5 d. Johanni de Twykinham pauperi clerico Regis studenti
Expense Oxoniensi, de dono et elemosina Regis pro communis et
Johannis de aliis necessariis suis inter primum diem Decembris anno
Twykinam, viij° et vltimum diem Julij, . . . per manus domini Hugonis
scolarii de Lenninstre custodis garderobe domini Edwardi filij
Oxoniensis. Regis, Comitis Cestrie, liberantis ei denaria per precep-
tum ipsius domini Regis,
$$\text{xl s. iiij d.}$$

f. 9 d. Titulus de necessariis diuersis emptis et prouisis pro
domino Rege Edwardo. . . et familia sua, equis emptis ad
opus dicti Regis missis et expensis nunciorum solempnium
missorum vsque curiam Romanam et alibi. . ., victualibus emptis pro municionibus villarum et castrorum
suorum in marchia Scocie, vadiis quorundam qui non
sunt in rotulo marescalcie vna cum calciamentis diuersorum valletorum et garcionum de hospicio Regis a festo
Translacionis Sancti Thome Martiris, etc. . .
Summa totalis tituli neccessariorum,
$$\text{m}^\text{l}\ \text{m}^\text{l}\ \text{m}^\text{l}\ \text{m}^\text{l}\ \text{Dxliiij li. xij s. ob.}$$

[Details of sheriffs' accounts for food.]

f. 22. Summa totalis tituli de victualibus,
$$\overset{\text{xx}}{\text{Dccc iiij}} \text{ vij li. xiiij s. j d.}$$

[*The wages of carpenters, archers, etc.*] f. 27.

Summa totalis tituli qui non sunt, cxlvj li. xv s. x d. ob. f. 28.

Summa totalis istius tituli de calciamentis, f. 31 d.

xliij li. xiij s. iiij d.

Summa totalis titulorum neccessariorum victualium qui
non sunt, et calciamentorum coniuncta,

v mill. Dcxxij li. v s. iiij d.

Titulus de donis datis in denariis per dictum Regem... f. 39 d.
Et est summa totalis istius tituli...

iij mill. xviij li. xiiij s. viij d.

Titulus de denariis liberatis diuersis militibus de hospicio f. 53 d.
Regis Edwardi...nomine annui feodi eorundem...
Et est summa totalis istius tituli... $\overset{xx}{c}$ iiij xvj li. xiij s. iiij d.

Titulus de vadiis diuersorum Banerettorum militum et f. 59 d.
aliorum in guerra scocie...
Et est summa totalis istius tituli... ix m^l ix^c lviij li. j d.

Domino Adomaro de Valencia comiti Pembroke, assig- f. 60. [e.g.]
nato per Regem et consilium suum ad morandum cum
equis et armis suis in partibus Noui Castri super Tynam et
alibi in marchia Scocie prout melius et comodius viderit
expedire pro saluacione et defensione parcium earundem
tanquam capitaneus et custos marchie predicte, et
habenti in comitiua sua centum homines ad arma in
seruicio Regis,...
Summa, m^l m^l Dccc $\overset{xx}{iiij}$ viij li. xij s. ij d.

Titulus de vadiis Balistariorum seruiencium Regis ad f. 65.
arma...
Et est summa totalis... $\overset{xx}{iiij}$ xiij li. xij s. iiij d.

Vicesimo sexto die Decembris admissus fuit Bernardus f. 65 d.
Remundi de porta ad vadia et robas domini nostri Regis
tanquam seruiens ad arma de hospicio ipsius domini
Regis nunciante Oliuero de Burdegala ex parte domini
Regis.

[e.g.]   Remundo Prouost pro vadiis suis ab viij die Julij…vsque
R. Prouost.   vltimum diem Januarij…vtroque computato per ccviij
dies de quibus fuit presens in Curia per cxxvij dies percipiens per diem viij d. quia sine equo…et extra curia…
in negociis domini Regis vicissim per iiij j dies percipiens
per diem xij d. per compotum secum factum apud Westmonasterium vltimo die Junij…

                                                  viij li. vs. viij d.

f. 67 d.   Titulus de denariis liberatis diuersis nautis morantibus
super mare ad frenandum maliciam scocorum inimi-
corum Regis pro vadiis suis…
Et est summa totalis…   Dcccxl li. xiij s. vj d.

[e.g.]   Henrico de Horseye magistro Nauis Regis vocate la
H. de   Cristofre de Jernemuth, pro vadiis suis vnius consta-
Horseye.   bularii et lxviij sociorum suorum nautarum eiusdem nauis
a xv⁰ die Augusti…vsque xiij diem Octobris…vtroque
computato per lx dies predicto Henrico percipiente per
diem vj d. constabulario vj d. et quolibet aliorum nautarum predictorum per diem iij d. per compotum factum
apud Jernemuth xix die Decembris   liiij li.

f. 73 d.   Titulus de nautis et cokynis domini Regis Edwardi…
missis diuersimode in nunciis Regis.
Et est summa totalis…   xlvij li. vij s. j d.

f. 81 d.   Titulus de vadiis et expensis diuersorum falconariorum
falconum venatorum et canum Regis…
Et est summa totalis…   clxix li. ix s. xj d.

f. 85 d.   Titulus de denariis liberatis pro Robis Militum, clericorum et aliorum diuersorum de hospicio Regis…
Et est summa totalis…   Dcxxvij li.

[*There is very great detail concerning the liveries of
all officials.*]

f. 98 d.   Titulus de…ciphis, firmaculis…et aliis iocalibus diuersis emptis et alio modo in garderoba prouenientibus et
datis diuersis per dominum Regem…
Et est summa totalis…   cccxxxiiij li. xviij s. xj d.

Titulus de empcionibus vinorum pro expensis hospicii f. 104.
domini Regis...
Et est summa totalis...   m^l clxli. xiijs. ixd.

Summa omnium titulorum istius libri vsque hic,   f. 104 d.

xxij mill. cclxiiijli. xxijd.

[*Diverse payments, no title.*]   f. 108.
                                                            [e.g.]

Domino Radulpho de Stokes, clerico magne garderobe,

Summa totalis istius tituli...
                              xx mill. cc iiij ijli. xixs. vijd.

Summa totalis omnium titulorum istius libri   f. 119.

xlij m^l Dxlvijli. xvijd.

Summa totalis omnium titulorum predictorum cum
summa expensarum hospicij annotata in principio istius
libri coniuncta,
                              xlviij mill. cccc iiij iijli. xijs. jd.

Debita que debentur diuersis creditoribus inter primum f. 122.
diem Decembris anno viij° et vltimum diem Januarii anno
nono, videlicet de tempore Willelmi de Melton, custodis
garderobe Regis.   Contra rotulus.

Summa totalis omnium summarum particularum istius f. 136.
quaterne,   vj m^l Dxiiijli. xiiij s. jd.
Exchequer account, 376/7.

(3) *Preamble to the household ordinance of York* 1318

Pour ceo qe lez officers del lostiell nostre seignur le Roi
ount estez toutz iours en arere, en [et] noun certein de ceo
qils deueront faire et prendre du Roi, par reason de lour
officez, par quoy due examinement dez ditz officers ne
poiat estre fait, ne lez officers chargez si come estre
deuoient, a grand damage et dishonour du Roi et en
desarament de soun hostiell; et Nostre dit seignur le Roi,
eiant regard al estat de son dit hostell meyns bien garde,

et a sez chosez en autre manere despenduez qi estre ne
duissent; si comanda a monsire Berthelmeu de Badelesmere, Seneschall de soun hostiell, monsire Hugh le
Despenser, chamberleyn, Sire Roger de Northborough,
Tresorer, et a Sire Gilbert de Wyggetone, contreroullour
de sa Garderobe, qe eux ordinassent sur la remedie, lez
queux par vertue du dit comaundement ount ordeigne
lez chosez souzescritz en amendement dez defautez desusditz: lez quelez ordinauncez furont leuez et assentuez
deuaunt le Roi et en presence larceuesqe de Deuerwik,
leuesqe Dely, Chaunceller Dengleterre, leuesqe de North-
wich, et leuesqe de Sarum, monsire Henry de Scrope, et
monsire Henry Spigurnell, Justicez, qi sensuit:...

Additional MS. 32097, f. 46 d. (Printed in Tout,
Edward II, p. 270.)

(4) *Auditors of chamber accounts, and the exchequer* 1322

Baronibus
pro Rege. Rex thesaurario et Baronibus suis de scaccario, salutem.
Cum mandauimus custodibus terrarum et tenementorum
que fuerunt inimicorum et rebellium nostrorum et aliorum in diuersis Comitatibus regni nostri in manu nostra
existencium, quod ipsi de exitibus aliquorum terrarum
tenementorum predictorum de quibus hactenus nobis
responsum fuit in cameram nostram exnunc nobis re-
sponderi faciant ad scaccarium nostrum et receptoribus
exituum terrarum et tenementorum illorum ac auditoribus compotorum Balliuorum ministrorum et aliorum receptorum in terris et tenementis illis, quod dicti custodes
receptores et auditores super custodia terrarum et tenementorum predictorum et receptorem exituum eorundem
nec non et dictis compotis audiendis aliqua faciant que
pro nostro comodo videntur facienda, et quod vos distincte et aperte certificent prout in transcriptis breuium
nostrorum, dictis custodibus, receptoribus et auditoribus
inde directorum, que quidem transcripta vobis mittimus
presentibus interclusa potestes (*sic*) videre plenius con-
tineri. Vobis mandamus quod, inspectis transcriptis predictis, certificaciones quas predicti custodes, receptores
et auditores vobis fecerint de premissis, recipiatis, et
excusationes inde vlterius faciatis prout pro comodo foro

(*sic*) videritis faciendum. Teste me ipso, apud Eboracum, xxiiij° die Julii, anno nostro xvj°...

Memoranda roll, L.T.R. 15 Ed. II, m. 63. (Cf. Tout, *Chapters*, II, 341 n. 3.)

(5) *The exchequer to receive the issues of chamber lands* 1322

Thesaurario per regem. Edward par la grace de Dieu, etc. al honurable piere en Dieu W. per la meisme grace Esvesqe de Dexcestre, nostre tresorer, salutz. Nous vous feissoms sauer qe nostre entencion est qe les issues de totes les terres et tenemens des forfaitz, auxi bien de ceux qe sount lesses come dautres, veignent entierement a nostre escheqier desore. Donee south nostre priue seal a Thresk, le xxvme jour de Juyl, lan de regne xvj^me.

Memoranda roll, L.T.R. 15 Ed. II, m. 63. (Printed in Tout, *Chapters*, II, 342 n. 1.)

(6) *Receivers of lands to account to the exchequer* 1322

Rex Nicholao de la Bech, salutem. Licet nuper vobis commisissemus custodiam omnium terrarum et tenementorum bonorum et catallorum Ricardi de Waleys in Comitatibus Essex' Hertford' et Middlesex', ac eciam omnium terrarum Comitis Hereford in eodem Comitatu Essex' certis de causis in manu nostra existentium, simul cum omnibus bonis et catallis eorundem custodiendis quamdiu nobis placuerit Ita quod de exitibus earundem terrarum et tenementorum et de bonis et catallis illis responderetis in cameram nostram, volentes nichilominus quod inde respondeatur ad scaccarium nostrum, vobis firmiter iniungendo mandamus quod considerato quanta necessitas sit ad presens quod pecuniam habeamus in promptu non modicam ad expensas hospicij nostri et ad stipendia et vadia quibusdam nobilibus et aliis hominibus ad arma, necnon aliis tam equitibus quam peditibus armatis et peditibus aliis in progressu nostro contra inimicos nostros de Scocia fauente domino deuincendos in multitudine grandi nobis cum existentibus persoluenda, omnes denarios quos habetis de custodia antedicta et quos estis recepturi de die in diem quo celerius poteritis

habeatis ad scaccarium nostrum apud Eboracum, Thesaurario et camerariis nostris de eodem scaccario liber-
andos. Et habeatis in crastino Sancti Michelis proximo
futuro ibidem hoc breue simul cum omnibus denariis
quos prius de custodia predicta non solueritis. Teste, W.
Exoniense Episcopo, Thesaurario nostro, apud Eboracum, xxv die Julij, anno regni nostri sexto decimo, per
breue de magno sigillo directum Thesaurario et Baronibus, et breue de priuato sigillo directum Thesaurario.

Memoranda roll, L.T.R. 15 Ed. II, m. 90.

(7) *Exchequer ordinance; clauses concerning household reform* 1324

Dominus Rex mandavit hic breve suum de Magno
Sigillo suo quod est inter Communia de anno xvij°
in hæc verba:

Edwardus,...Thesaurario et Baronibus suis de Scaccario salutem. Quandam ordinationem per nos et consilium nostrum factam, de compotis in dicto Scaccario
nostro recipiendis observandam, vobis mittimus sub pede
sigilli nostri, mandantes quod ordinationem illam exnunc
in omnibus observetis. Et hoc nullatenus omittatis. Teste
me ipso apud Westmonasterium, vj die Maij, anno regni
nostri septimo (*sic*). Per ipsum Regem.

Tenor ordinationis prædictæ sequitur in forma
subscripta.

Por ce qe le Gardeyn de la Garderobe de notre houstiel
ad este chargez de plusours acountes foreins des queux il
ne poet avoir conoissaunce, ne trier les defautes si nules y
fuissent, et ad auxi este chargez des plusours receites de
grant summe des deniers, qi ne sount pas venuz en sa
main, dachatz et des liverees faites par autres qe par lui,
et des plusours autres choses chargeantes et noun covenables parquoi lacounte ad este tant delayez et arreri qe
hom ne poet aver conissaunce de les parceles ne venir a
bon issue, a grant damage de nous. Si avons sur ce ordine
remedie par le counseil pres de nous en la forme qensuyt.
[*The ordinance then states how the Keeper of the Wardrobe, the
Clerk of the Great Wardrobe, the King's Butler, should receive
the monies for their offices. Purveyors and others should account
to the Exchequer.*]

vj.   Qe le Clerk del Hanaper en la Chauncellerie acounte al Escheqier.

Item nous voloms qe le Clerk del Hanaper de notre Grant Seal rende son acounte a notre Escheqier, et face sovent veuwe dacounte, au meyns par quart del an, et paie les deners a la resceite de notre Escheqier, et preigne illoeques taille qi alloue lui soit sur son final acounte.

. . . . . .

xiij.   Qe clerk soit assigne en lEscheqier a receivre les Estretes de la Marchaucie et du Marchee.

Item nous voloms qe par le Tresorier et Barons de notre Escheqier soit un clerk de la place assigne, ou autre qi peusse entendre a receivre les estretes et les endentures qe le seneschal de nostre hostiel et notre clerk des mesures enverront illoeques, et les certifications et les endentures des gentz des villes tochauntz la purveaunce de noz vyns, et auxi remembrer les deners qi serront paiez pur grant messagerie outre mier et les deners qi serront liverez au grant garderobe et au Botiller, issint qe home puisse aver prestement a charger chescun selonc son estat, quant il vendront al acounte, et a reveyvre les endentures du grant garderober, et qe celui soit sur lacounte de lui et des autres pur charger chescun selonc les dites certifications,...et a resceivre les certifications qi se fount par le gardeyn de notre Garderobe des aprestz qi sount en certeyn apres le jour de payement passe, si nules y soient, ovesques toutes autres remembraunces qi soleient touchier lacounte de notre garderobe qi se deyve ore faire en lEscheqier.

xiiij.   Des jours donez au gardein de la garderobe et a grant garderober et a Botiller dacounter.

Item, pur ce qe lan del acounte de notre garderobe finisse a la feste de la Translacion Seynt Thomas, si voloms qe le gardeyn de notre Garderobe eit jour de arraier son acounte de ceu temps tantque a la quinzeyne de Seynt Michel prochein suyant, et le grant garderober et le Botiller tanque lendemeyn de Seint Michel, issint qil soient prestement al Escheqier a les jours avant ditz a

rendre lour acountes saunz nule manere de delai, et
issint de an en an saunz plus long delai avoir.

Explicit.

Red book of the exchequer, pt. III, pp. 908–28.

(8) *Wardrobe accounts*[1] 1338–40

p. 5. Hunc librum liberauit hic Willelmus de Northwell nuper
custos Garderobe Regis, xiiij° die Maij anno xv° Regis
Edwardi tercii a conquestu.

p. 7. Incipit Recepta denariorum primo, videlicet:

[*The amounts received from the Exchequer are given for
each term with much detail.* e.g.]

p. 35. Secunda pars Recepte scaccarij de termino Michelis de
anno xvj° tempore Willelmi de Cusaunce, thesaurarii.

...tercio die Decembris, per vnam talliam liberatam
Johanni de Coggeshale vicecomiti Essex pro tot denariis
ab eo receptis pro expensis hospicii Regis per litteram
custodis, xxjli. xiijs. jd.

Eodem die per vnam talliam liberatam Johanni de Den-
ton maiori ville Noui castri super Tynam, et Escaetori
Regis, pro expensis hospicii per litteram eiusdem custodis, cxs. iiijd.

vij die Decembris per manus Griffun de camera in partem
solucionis xli. sibi debitarum per billam, xls.

Eodem die per manus magistri Johannis de Mildenhale
in persolucionem tot denariorum sibi debitorum per
billam, iiijli. vs.

Eodem die per manus proprias in precio x duodenarum
pergamenti. precium duodene ijs. super officio garderobe,
xx s. ...

[1] William Norwell was keeper of the wardrobe from July 12, 1338
to May 27, 1340, during the period of Edward III's campaigns in
the Netherlands, and his account was made on May 14, 1341. The
exchequer supplied less than half of the income of the wardrobe
during the two years, for the wardrobe was negotiating loans and
receiving money direct from the Antwerp staple. Already before this
time the expenditure was being divided into *expensa hospicii* and
expensa forinseca; and during the first stages of the war, while the
expensa hospicii increased considerably as a result of the royal journeys,
the *expensa forinseca* advanced by leaps and bounds. The debts that
resulted were due directly to the extraordinary war administration.
Cf. Tout, *Chapters*, IV, 98, 102–6; III, 91–2.

viij die Decembris per manus Willelmi de Cusaunce
clerici recepte denariorum in partem solucionis Dcliiij li.
iiij s. vj d. debitorum Willelmo filio Johannis Muchet et
Willelmo Talmach pro lano ab eis empto ad opus Regis,
xx li...
Eodem die [14 December] per manus Abbatis de Aber-
coneway, collectoris decime triennalis in diocese Assau'
per litteram custodis lxxix s. vj d...

Summa huius pagine,   Dclviij li. xxij d. ob.

Summa totalis Recepte per Willelmum de Northwell, p. 39.
custodem garderobe ad Receptam scaccarii,

$\overset{xx}{\text{iiij}}$ vj m^l Dlxxvj li. iiij s. vj d. q.

Recepta de scaccario compotorum.   p. 41.
Summa,   xxj m^l Dcccxxx li. ix s. q.

[*Details are given of the customs; of the payment of the subsidy
in the port of London; and similarly for Hull, Boston, Lynn,
Ipswich, Yarmouth, Newcastle, York.*]

Recepta forinseca.   p. 54.
De Bonefacio et Thoma de Peruchia et aliis sociis suis [e.g.]
mercatoribus de societate de Peruchie
Summa, [*including other foreign merchants*]

viij m^l Dc $\overset{xx}{\text{iiij}}$ xij li. xiij s. iij d.

De Roberto Houel, clerico mercati et coronatore hospicii [e.g.]
domini Regis de exitibus eiusdem mercati in vna particula, xiij li. xj s. vij d. ob. Et in alia particula, lix s. j d.

xvj li. x s. viij d. ob.

De Johanne de Grymesby clerico marescalcie Regis in
precio cxxij equorum carectariorum...per ipsum Johannem receptorum tam de diuersis vicecomitibus quam
Abbatibus et Prioribus Anglie, et postea per eundem
Johannem venditorum ad diuersa precia in partibus
Brabancie, sicut patet per particulas de vendicione eorundem equorum...
lxx li. x s. ix d.

De domino Johanne Giffard, custode hospicii Sancti
Leonardi Eboraci, pro fine facto pro duabus cartis
Regis habendis.   xl marce.

De Johanne Bottourt de fine pro terris suis in custodia Regis ratione minoris etatis sue existentibus habendis apud Walton', anno xij°

cc marce.

p. 73. Expense hospicij Regis Edwardi tercij post conquestum a xij die Julij anno xij° vsque xxvij diem Maij anno regni sui Anglie xiiij° et ffrancie primo, tempore Northwell.

[e.g.]
Die Vene-
ris xvij die
Julij.
Portus
aque de
Swyn.

Dispensaria, xxj s. x d. ob. Butillaria, vij li. iij s. Garde-roba, xlvij s. v d. ob. Coquina, ciiij s. iij d. Scutillaria, xx s. Salsaria, ij s. j d. Aula nichil. Camera nichil. Stabulum xj li. vij s. iiij d. Vadia, cvj s. j d. Elemosina, iiij s. Summa,   xxxiij li. xvj s. j d.

Die Sab-
bati,
xviij die
Julij.

Dispensaria, xxj s. x d. ob. Butillaria, vij li. iij s. Garde-roba, lxv s. ij d. q. Coquina, cxv s. j d. Scutillaria, xj s. j d. Salsaria, ij s. iiij d. Aula, nichil. Camera, nichil. Stabulum, xj li. vij s. iiij d. Vadia, cvj s. j d. Elemosina, iiij s. Summa,   xxxiiij li. xv s. xj d. ob. q.

Summa expensarum istius septimane, [July 12–18]

cclviij li. vij s. vij d. ob.

Die Domi-
nica, xix
die Julij.
Ernemuth.

Dispensaria, xxij s. viij d. ob. Butillaria, viij li. iij s. Garderoba, xxv s. xj d. Coquina, vij li. ix s. v d. ob. Scutillaria, xj s. iij d. Salsaria, ij s. vj d. Aula, nichil. Camera, nichil. Stabulum, xj li. vij s. iiij d. Vadia, cvj s. j d. Elemosina, iiij s. Summa,   xxxv li. xij s. iij d.

Die Lune,
xx die
Julij.

[Similar details]

Summa,   xxxiiij li. ij s. xj d. ob.

Die Mar-
tis, xxj die
Julij.
Andewer-
pia.

[Similar details]

Summa,   xxxiij li. xvij s. vj d. ob. q.

Die
Mercurii,
xxij die
Julij.

[Similar details]

Summa,   xlviij li. viij d. ob. q.

Die Jovis,
xxiij die
Julij.

Dispensaria, xxxij s. vj d. ob. Butillaria, iiij li. xvj s. x d. Garderoba, xxxix s. vj d. ob. Coquina, viij li. xix s. ij d. Scutillaria, xlvj s. ix d. ob. Salsaria, iiij s. v d. Aula, vj s. ij d. Camera, xxiij d. Stabulum, x li. xiij s. xj d. ob. q. Vadia, vs. iij d. Elemosina, iiij s. Summa,   xxxj li. x s. vij d. q.

Dispensaria, xxv s. ixd. q. Butillaria, lviijs. iiijd. Gar- Die Veneris, xxiiij die Julij.
deroba, xlviijs. ob. Coquina, cxviijs. ij d. Scutillaria,
xiiijs. ixd. Salsaria, ijs. viijd. ob. Aula, ijs. Camera,
xiiijd. Stabulum, xli. viijs. vijd. q. Vadia, vs. iijd.
Elemosina, iiijs.
Summa,   xxiiijli. viijs. ixd. ob.

Dispensaria, xxix s. vijd. Butillaria, lxxix s. Garderoba, Die Sabbati, xxv die Julij.
ixli. vijs. Coquina, vjli. xxd. Scutillaria, xxvs. xjd.
Salsaria, iiijs. jd. ob. Aula, vs. ijd. Camera, xiiijs.
Stabulum, xli. viijs. vijd. q. Vadia, vs. iij d. Elemosina,
iiijs.
Summa,   xxxiiijli. iiijs. iijd. ob. q.

Summa expensarum istius septimane,
                          ccxljli. xvijs. ijd. ob.

Summa totalis expensarum hospicij Regis a xij die Julij p. 171.
anno regni sui xij, vsque xxvij diem maij anno regni
sui xiiij vtroque die computato per vj^c iiij^{xx} vj dies quia
annus bisextilis fuit annus quartusdecimus,
                          xxiij m^l Dccxlvjli. xxd. ob.

Incipiunt particule expensarum forinsecarum factarum p. 173.
in garderoba domini Edwardi...inter xj diem Julij anno
regni sui Anglie xij, et xxviij diem Maij anno regni sui
Anglie xiiij et Francie primo.
ut in elemosinis, necessariis, Donis, Nunciis, ffeodis, robis,
restauro equorum, vadijs hominum ad arma, sagittario-
rum et Nautarum et passagio equorum.
Elemosina.
Summa totalis huius tituli de elemosina,   p. 177.
                          ccccxxxixli. xxijd.
Incipiunt necessaria.   p. 178.
Summa totalis huius tituli de Necessariis,   p. 194.
                  xxiij mill. Dc iiij^{xx} xjli. xvijs. vjd. ob.
Titulus donorum.   p. 196.

Dona data diuersis per Regem infra tempus huius compoti.
Summa totalis...   xxxiiij m^l clxxvjli. iiijs. ijd. p. 217.

p. 218. Incipiunt nuncii.
[e.g.]   Willelmo de Skelton deferenti litteras Regis sub signo
domino Archiepiscopo Cantuariensi, pro expensis suis,
apud Walton, per manus proprias xiij die Julij anno
xij°, ijs. j d. Johanni de Dunstaple deferenti litteras Regis
sub priuato sigillo et litteras Comitis Derb' Balliuis de
Dunwich' et Kirkelee, pro expensis suis, xvij die Julij,
ijs. iiij d.

p. 240. Summa totalis...   cccvj li. xix d.

p. 241. Incipiunt feoda militum.
$$\overset{xx}{}$$
Summa totalis...   m^l ccc iiij x li.

p. 243. Incipiunt robe et calciatura.
$$\overset{xx}{}$$
p. 247. Summa totalis...   m^l m^l iiij ij li. xv s. iiij d.

p. 249. Incipiunt restaurum equorum.
         [*No final total is given, but each page is totalled.*]

p. 261. Incipiunt vadia hominum ad arma.
p. 282. Summa totalis,...
$$\overset{xx}{}$$
         iiij xiij m^l Dccccxvj li. xvij s. iiij d.

p. 283. Incipiunt vadia sagittariorum.
         Summa totalis...   xxvij m^l ccccxiiij li. xiij d.

p. 288. Incipiunt vadia nautarum.
$$\overset{xx}{}$$
p. 304. Summa totalis...   m^l m^l m^l m^l Dcc iiij xvij li. xj s. vj d.

p. 305. Incipit passagium equorum magnatum et aliorum de
partibus transmarinis versus Angliam apud Sclus men-
sibus Januarii et ffebruarii anno xiij° finiente et xiiij°
incipiente.
p. 310. Summa totalis...   m^l Dxl li. vj s. viij d.

p. 311. Recepta Jocalium et liberacio eorundem.
Jocalia, vessellamenta et alia subscripta recepta de
domino Edmundo de la Beche nuper custode garderobe
per indenturam datam apud Walton' xij die Julij anno
regni Regis supradicti xij, videlicet...

p. 314   Jocalia et vestimenta inuenta in garderoba xij° die Julij
anno xij° quo die Willelmus de Northwell suscepit
officium dicte garderobe que jocalia et vestimenta fuerunt
de diuersis Abbaciis et prioratibus de quibus Edmundus
de la Beche qui tunc dimisit dictum officium noluit se
intromittere nec certificare quorum fuerunt...

Jocalia vessellamenta et alia recepta de domino Roberto p. 315.
de Wodehous, thesaurario et camerariis de scaccario per
indenturam datam xv die Maii, anno xij°

......

Lane regis recepte per custodem garderobe de Gerardo p. 324.
Boueuseigne et sociis suis, mercatoribus de societate
Bardorum...
Titulus de prestitis factis diuersis infra tempus huius p. 327.
compoti.
Domino Johanni Darcy filio Johannis Darcy de pre- p. 333.
stitis per manus Edmundi de la Beche... [e.g.]
Summa totalis... cxvj m¹ Dcccxlvijli. x s. vijd. q. p. 360.
Miscellaneous book of the exchequer, no. 203.

(9) *Accounts of the receiver of the chamber as submitted
to the exchequer*[1] 1345–9

Compotus Roberti de Burton clerici, Receptoris denariorum de camera Regis de quibusdam receptis et solucionibus suis diuersis hominibus tam in cismarinis quam transmarinis partibus factis per breue Regis de priuato sigillo
directum Thesaurario et Baronibus datum die Sancti
Georgij, scilicet xxiij° die Aprilis anno xxiij°...In quo
continetur quod prefatus Robertus nuper de precepto
Regis et per litteras ipsius Regis de waranto fecit diuersas
soluciones Waltero de Wetewang nuper custodi Garderobe Regis et plurimis hominibus aliis de quibus ipse
Robertus penes se recepit diuersas indenturas memoranda billas et acquietancia testificantes easdem soluciones
de tempore quo Rex erat in guerra sua in dictis partibus
transmarinis per quod breue Rex mandat prefatis
Thesaurario et Baronibus quod ipsi sine dilatione ad opus
compoti eiusdem Roberti capiendum procedant et visis

[1] Robert Burton succeeded Thomas Hatfield as receiver of the
chamber from December, 1344 until September, 1348, and his account
was enrolled in the pipe roll, 194/43. At the very moment when the
chamber seemed in a position of supreme control, the process of
subordinating it to the exchequer was begun in 1348–9. Henry
Greystock, the last chief steward of the chamber and in office from
May 1349 until 1356, was mainly responsible for the transference,
which was not completed until 1356. Cf. Tout, *Chapters*, IV, 255–8,
288 ff.

indenturis...eidem Roberto super dictum compotum suum omnes soluciones per ipsum iuxta tenorem et effectum dictarum litterarum Regis factas debito modo faciant allocare, videlicet, de predictis receptis et solucionibus suis factis per diuersas vices et tempora diuersa inter xviij die ffebruarii anno xix° et predictum xxiij die Aprilis anno xxiij° sic infra continetur.

Recepta.
[e.g.] Summa,   xxxviij mill. cccclxviij li. viij s. vj d.

Idem recepit compotum de Dc iiij xvj li. ix s. x d. receptis de priore de Wymundham, Johanne de Burnham et Thoma Gannok de denariis Regis de nona garba vellerum et agnorum in Comitatu Norff'...et de finibus eorundem Prioris Johannis et Thome oneratis super ipsum Robertum ad Receptam scaccarij, de prestito super officio suo primo die Marcij anno xix°...

Et de xxvj s. viij d. receptis de Thesaurario et Camerariis ad Receptam predictam per manus Roberti Balistarii de London' operantis balistas ad opus Regis xviij° die Augusti dicto anno xix° super vadiis ipsius Roberti Balistarii...

Et de m^l m^l c iiij li. receptis de eisdem Thesaurario et camerariis ad eandem Receptam eodem x° die Aprilis super expensis dicte Camere Regis sicut continetur ibidem...

Soluciones.
[e.g.] Idem compotus liberatur Bartholomeo de Burgherssh de dono Regis in recompensacionem certarum solucionum et expensarum per ipsum Bartholomeum super expedicione grossorum negociorum Regem tangencium de precepto ipsius Regis factarum Dc iiij xvj li. ix s. x d. per breue Regis sub sigillo Griffon datum xxj° die ffebruarii anno xix°. In quo continetur quod certis de causis camere sue reseruauit D iiij xiij li. iij s. ij d. de quadam summa m^l cclx li. iij s. ij d. Regi de nona garba vellerum et agnorum nuper Regi in Comitatu Norff' concessa per priorem de Wymundham, Johannem de Burnham et Thomam atte Gannok deputatum Johannis Cailly nuper collectores eiusdem none detente. et eciam lxx li. de fine per dictum Johannem de Burnham et xxxiij li. vj s. viij d. de fine per dictum Thomam coram Johanne de Sharde-

lowe et sociis suis assignatis ad inquirendum de diuersis
transgressionibus in Comitatu predicto pro detencione
denariorum predictorum factis...
Summa,   m^l m^l D̄cccc iiij̄ li. ix s. x d.

Et Johanni Marreys valleto camere Regis in denariis sibi   Prestita.
liberatis ad eandem Receptam de prestito xxij° die   [e.g.]
ffebruarii dicto anno xxj° super vadiis suis vnde prefatus
Receptor similiter oneratur supra infra summam Recepte, xiijs. iiijd. per idem breue.
Summa,   xxxvj mill. D̄ccxvli. xjs. viijd. ob.

Summa totalis solucionum et prestitorum,

              xxxix mill. D̄c iiij̄ xvj li. xviijd. ob.

......

Pipe roll, no. 194/43.

(10) *Subordination of the chamber to the*
exchequer begun 1349

Rex Thesaurario Baronibus de scaccario et camerariis   De memor-
suis salutem. Cum vt accepimus dilectus clericus noster   andis
Nicholaus de Bokelond auditor compotorum camere   compotos
nostre reseruatorum extentas terrarum rotulos com-   Regis tan-
potorum et percellas compotorum indenturas com-   thesaurario
missiones literas de Waranto tallias et alia memoranda   Baronibus
compota predicta tangencia ab anno regni nostri Anglie   rariis Regis
nono vsque diem confeccionis presencium habuerit in   liberandis.
custodia, Nos volentes tam pro nostra quam ipsius
Nicholai indempnitate in hac parte de securiori custodia
memorandorum predictorum prouidere, vobis mandamus
quod omnia extentas rotulos...et alia memoranda quecumque cameram nostram predictam tangencia et in
custodia ipsius Nicholai vt premittitur existencia et que
vobis per ipsum Nicholaum liberari mandauimus ab
eodem Nicholao per indenturam inde inter vos et ipsum
Nicholaum modo debito conficiendam cuius quidem indenture vnam partem penes vos remanendam sigillo
eiusdem Nicholai et alteram partem penes dictum
Nicholaum similiter remanendam sigillo dicti scaccarij
volumus consignari recipiatis et ea in cistis duabus

seruris firmatis quarum vna clauis penes vos et alia penes
auditores compotorum dicte camere nostre qui pro tempore erunt pro inspeccione rotulorum et memorandorum
predictorum...remaneant, necnon cistas predictas cum
omnibus rotulis et memorandis illis in quadam noua
camera infra palacium nostrum Westmonasterij pro
audicione et reddicione compotorum dicte camere nostre
ordinata poni faciatis. Et volumus quod omnes extente
terrarum rotuli compotorum...et omnia alia memoranda
predicta in scaccario nostro existencia tam pro tempore
preterito quam futuro [teneatis]. Volumus eciam quod
auditores compotorum dicte camere nostre qui sunt vel
qui pro tempore erunt exnunc de anno in annum omnia
compota coram ipsis audita...et omnia alia memoranda
compota illa tangencia vobis liberent ad ea custodiri
facienda in forma supradicta. Ita quod ijdem auditores
post liberacionem memorandorum huiusmodi ac eorum
heredes et executores inde erga nos exonerati sint et
quieti. Teste Rege apud Westmonasterium quarto die
Octobris.   per literam sub sigillo vocato Griffon.
Close roll, 22 Ed. III, pt. II, m. 15.

(11) *Royal mandates to the chamber*[1]
1349

(1) Edwardus...Senescallo et Receptoribus terrarum et
tenementorum camere nostre reseruatorum necnon auditoribus compotorum terrarum et tenementorum eorundem, salutem. Volentes cercis de causis cerciorari si
nobis de illa annua firma quam dilectus et fidelis noster
Rogerus filius et heres Edmundi de Mortuo mari nobis
pro custodia castri de Radnore (?) et commoti de War-
threnoun ac villarum de Knyghton et Prestmede ac can-
tredi et terre de Kery in Wallia ac manerii de Pembrugg
cum pertinentiis reddere tenebatur nobis in dicta camera
nostra per ipsum Rogerum plenarie sit satisfactum. Vobis
mandamus quod scrutatis rotulis et memorandis recepte
dicte camere nostre premissa tangentibus nos de eo quod
inde inueneritis reddatis in Cancellaria nostra sub sigillo

---

[1] These mandates show the normal form of royal letters to the
chamber, addressed to the steward and auditors, for its administration. Cf. Tout, *Chapters*, IV, 270 and n.

nostro vocato Griffoun distincte et aperte sine dilatione cerciores hoc breue nobis remittentes. Teste me ipso apud Wodestok tercio die maij anno regni nostri Anglie vicesimo tercio regni vero nostri ffrancie decimo.

Exchequer account, 391/8, m. 31. (Some of these places can be found in *Cal. Inquisitions post mortem*, vol. x, Ed. III, pp. 255–6, in an inquisition on the lands of Joan, wife of Roger Mortimer, 1356.)

1353

(2) Edwardus...dilecto clerico suo Henrico de Greystok, Senescallo camere nostre, ac auditoribus compotorum eiusdem camere, salutem. Cum Johannes de Molyns chiualer de eo quod ipse certa bona et catalla in quodam mesuagio vocato Filettes iuxta Henle in Comitatu Oxonie et alibi...inuenta postquam nos eadem bona et catalla ...in manum nostram capi fecimus in nostri contemptum cepit et occupauit, coram nobis nuper impetitus se gratie nostre submiserit, et nos volentes eidem Johanni gratiam in hac parte facere specialem, pardonauimus ei contemptum predictum necnon omnimoda fines exitus amerciamenta et alia quecumque que ad nos pertinent... volentes et concedentes pro nobis et heredibus nostris quod prefatus Johannes et heredes sui tam de bonis et catallis predictis quam de contemptu finibus...et aliis predictis erga nos et heredes nostros quieti sint...vobis mandamus quod predictum Johannem tam de bonis et catallis predictis quam de finibus...erga nos ad dictam cameram exonerari et quietum esse facietis...

Teste me ipso apud Wyndesore vij die Januarii anno regni nostri Anglie vicesimo sexto regni vero nostri ffrancie tercio decimo. per litteram de secreto sigillo. Burstall.

Exchequer account, 391/8, m. 8.

(12) *Chamber lands restored to the exchequer* 1356

Pro rege. Rex Thesaurario et Baronibus suis de scaccario, salutem. Quia volumus quod omnia terre et tenementa et alie res quecumque, ante hec tempora camere nostre reseruata, exceptis terris et tenementis Isabelle, einicie filie nostre, ad terminum vite sue habendis, per nos datis et concessis, scaccario predicto reiungantur, et quod

omnia compota eandem cameram tangencia, que non
dum sunt reddita nec determinata, in scaccario predicto
audiantur et terminentur, et quod omnes pecuniarum
summe in dictam cameram nobis debite ad opus nostrum
in eodem scaccario leuentur, et per breue nostrum mandauimus senescallo et auditoribus compotorum camere
nostre predicte quod omnes rotulos compotorum et alia
memoranda cameram predictam tangencia que in custodia sua existunt, ac nomina illorum qui compota et
arreragia, siue alia debita in cameram predictam reddere
seu soluere tenentur, vobis liberent ad execucionem inde
in scaccario predicto faciendam, vobis mandamus quod
rotulos et memoranda predicta a prefatis senescallo et
auditoribus recipiatis, et execucionem vlterius inde fieri
faciatis, prout de iure fuerit faciendum: volumus enim
quod compota in camera predicta reddita et alia negocia
ibidem determinata in suo robore permaneant et effectu.
Teste me ipso, apud Westmonasterium, xx⁰ die Januarii
anno regni nostri Anglie vicesimo nono, regni vero nostri
Francie, sextodecimo.

Memoranda roll, K.R. 132, writs, Hilary term. (Printed
in Tout, *Chapters*, IV, 305 n.)

CHAPTER IV

PARLIAMENT

INTRODUCTION

By the beginning of Edward II's reign the practice of holding a parliament at frequent intervals was already established, but the nature of its later development was far from certain. After 1311 the commons were always present in parliament, with the exception of the Hilary parliament, 1320, and that held at midsummer, 1325; but, although the commons were coming to be more of a political force, their presence did not in any way affect the functions of parliament. "Parliaments are of one kind only and the essence of them is the dispensation of justice";[1] the king and some of the magnates could deal with petitions(3), and with general business, *en pleyn parlement*(7).[2] There was no rule as to which of the tenants-in-chief were to be summoned to parliament, and the number of lords receiving writs of summons varied from year to year. The value of such meetings, however, was becoming recognised, and repeated claims for annual parliaments followed the demand made by the lords ordainers in 1311(29, 34).[3] There was also no rule as to how parliaments should sit. The division into two houses had not yet been made, and there was no certainty that knights and burgesses would join to form the commons. It seemed indeed more likely that members would fall into groups according to their different interests, and this was exemplified by the assessment of taxation, which might be granted in varying amounts from lords, clergy, knights and townsmen. Another possibility was that the knights would draw nearer to the lords than to the burgesses, and in that case three groups might have developed as they did in the French states-general(8). The one certain element in the early parliament was the council. "A

[1] H. G. Richardson and G. Sayles, *Bulletin of the Institute of Historical Research*, VI, no. 17, p. 78.
[2] A. F. Pollard, *The evolution of parliament*, p. 33, considers that this means in open rather than in full parliament.
[3] See Crown section, p. 16.

parliament is at first no more than the counsellors of the king
sitting in a particular kind of session called a parliament."[1] A
parliament could be held if only the council was present, as was
the case for a short time in 1341(12). In consequence it is not
easy to distinguish between representative great councils which
were fairly frequent between 1327 and 1353(9, 21),[2] and parliaments in which the king sat in his council(1). This close connection
between council and parliament influenced the nature of parliamentary business and accounted for the importance of the official
element in parliament. The king's ministers and chief justices
might sit as members, even when they were neither qualified by
rank nor elected as representatives.

The fourteenth and fifteenth centuries witnessed the gradual
development of parliament into its modern form and to something of its modern functions.

There is evidence that the two houses were separating. The
upper house became a definite body, though it was not called the
house of lords until the sixteenth century. Certain families came
to receive writs of summons as a matter of course, although at first
the practice seems to have been attached to the estate rather than
to the person. From the middle of Edward III's reign the normal
number to whom writs were sent was about fifty, and the same
names constantly recurred. In 1387 Richard II introduced the
grant of barony by letters patent conferring hereditary dignity,
and by degrees the writ of summons to parliament accompanied
the hereditary title. Theoretically the prelates also sat as barons;
certain abbots and priors claimed exemption from attendance on
the plea that they were not tenants-in-chief (p. 186), and in 1388
the archbishop of Canterbury claimed for the prelates the status
of peers.[3] It would seem, however, that some prelates summoned
to parliament held by frankalmoign alone, and that "the selection
of the narrow ecclesiastical 'peerage' of the later Middle Ages
was not...effected on any consistent principle".[4] Peers were drawn
together by definite privileges, such as the right of personal access
to the king, and they were gradually asserting the principle that
no peer could be judged on a capital charge save by his
peers(13, 41, 61).

[1] Pollard, *op. cit.* p. 279; and cf. p. 58.   [2] See Council section, p. 45.
[3] Pike, *A constitutional history of the house of lords*, pp. 160–1. See Church
section (18).
[4] H. M. Chew, *The English ecclesiastical tenants-in-chief and knight service* (Oxford,
1932), p. 175.

Meanwhile the knights and burgesses were tending to unite, at first rather by the command of the king than by community of interests, but by degrees the commons as such emerged and acted as a body(8, cf. 17). Professor Pollard would date the germ of this unity as early as 1325 with the beginning of the commons' petitions(5).[1] Some recent writers consider that petitions presented in the name of the commonalty might represent the views of magnates or other influential people, but not necessarily of the knights and burgesses, still less of the nation as a whole.[2] In any case the practice of commons' petitions as contrasted with individual petitions came to be a recognised part of parliamentary business, and such petitions had eventually their special procedure, as they went straight to the council through the clerk of parliament, instead of going to the auditors and triers as did the other petitions(2, 12).[3] This growing unity was typified by the appearance of a speaker who represented the commons and was ultimately elected by them(16, 31, 35). Knights and burgesses came to sit apart from the lords of parliament and to have a special meeting place of their own(23, 27). This separation into two houses, so marked a feature of the English parliament, was a development of Edward III's reign and had become the regular practice by the time of the parliament of 1376(29). This so-called "Good Parliament" forms to some extent a landmark in parliamentary growth, despite the repeal of all its measures before the end of the reign. For some time, however, the old division of interests between knights and burgesses was not wholly overcome, but showed itself from time to time in varying money grants, and in an occasional desire for separate discussions.

Another change which came about gradually and without any obvious cause was the withdrawal of the clerical proctors from parliament, thus enabling the spiritual lords to draw close to the temporal lords, instead of forming a group apart with their own clergy. By the reign of Edward III the clergy were regularly granting their taxes in convocation; but the bishops and the chief abbots remained with the temporal lords, and claimed to exercise full judicial authority with them. This their spiritual character rendered impossible when it came to a judgment involving the penalty of death.[4]

[1] Pollard, *op. cit.* pp. 118 ff.
[2] Richardson and Sayles, *Bulletin*, IX, no. 25, pp. 9–11.
[3] Cf. Richardson and Sayles, in *E.H.R.* 1932, pp. 195 ff., 379 ff.
[4] On this subject see the section on the Church.

During the fourteenth century came also the gradual separation of council from parliament, which Pike suggests was accomplished in the reign of Richard II,[1] although the connection was not completely severed, for we still hear of the council in parliament (59), as later in Tudor times. The continual council was meanwhile becoming a separate administrative body, over which parliament was trying to obtain some control.

As the form of parliament became established, so also its powers grew, and especially interesting is the development of the commons, strengthened as they were by the vigorous knights of the shire. Maitland speaks of the five functions of parliament in the early fourteenth century: the discussion of affairs of state, legislation, taxation or supply, the audience of petitions, and above all the determination of causes criminal and civil.[2] The judicial aspect of parliament was at first its marked characteristic (cf. 6), and the one which was chiefly recognised and valued at the time. The legislative and administrative work of parliament did indeed increase at the expense of the judicial, especially when petitions were limited and when the equitable jurisdiction of chancery was attracting suitors, yet parliament never lost its judicial character. This is seen in the development of impeachment. At first it was uncertain if peers would sit in judgment on those who were not themselves peers (6), but it came to be understood that a commoner could not be tried by the lords except on the accusation of the commons.[3] Impeachment by the commons and trial by the lords came to be the regular means of bringing an unpopular minister or royal favourite to judgment (29, 40). As a political weapon it was less used in the fifteenth century, and the impeachment of Suffolk in 1450 failed (63). In its stead there was resort to sentence by attainder, a definite legislative act requiring the assent of the commons, lords and crown (64, 65, 73).

The granting of taxes came to be more and more in the hands of parliament, and in the reign of Edward III new statutes were passed, which decreed parliamentary control for any taxes which were not expressly mentioned in the *Confirmatio cartarum* of 1297. Not only was a parliamentary grant becoming necessary for all taxation (10, 11, 24, 26, 37, 74), but the making of such a grant

---

[1] Pike, *op. cit.* pp. 280, 321.

[2] F. W. Maitland, *Memoranda de parliamento*, R.S. p. xlviii.

[3] Pollard, *op. cit.* pp. 97, 112. See paper by M. V. Clarke, *Oxford Essays...presented to H. E. Salter*, showing that the procedure by indictment, instead of by petition, of the commons, was established in the Good Parliament, 1376.

became increasingly the duty of the commons, who passed it with
the consent of the lords(50). The voting of taxation was not
enough, however, to secure to parliament the real control of
finance; and so the grant often came to be accompanied by definite
conditions, and to be made for definite purposes(15, 28, 33, 38).
The appropriation of supplies(45), followed gradually by the
audit of accounts(14, 30, 36, 60), gave to parliament some real
control of money matters, and the eventual postponement of the
grant till the end of the session meant that the redress of grievances must precede supply, and thus much increased the power
of the representative body to enforce its wishes(44, 72).

The business of legislation was not at first exclusively in the
hands of parliament. Laws might still be passed with the consent of the group immediately concerned, and an ordinance of
king and council was little if at all distinguishable from a statute
of parliament. It is true that a clause in the repeal of the Ordinances (1322) provided that no legislation should be valid without
the assent of the king, lords and "the commonalty of the
realm"(4); but the main purpose here was to revoke the ordinances
of 1311, and otherwise the situation was left as before that date.[1]
Quite soon, however, the share of parliament in legislation
became active, for laws were often made in consequence of
petitions(9, 18, 29), and after a time an ordinance to become permanent required the recognition of parliament(20, 22), and could
only thus be converted into a statute. This distinction was being
made during the fourteenth century, and at the end of the century
an attempt was made to treat the statutes, as edited by the judges,
as permanent; in the next century, while the statute roll continued, the terms statute, act and ordinance were being used
more freely.[2] The original method of obtaining legislation was by
petition; at first these were from individuals; then from about
1327 to 1423 there was also the comprehensive commons'
petition, a collection of several petitions to the king, each needing
a separate answer which, being sent in the name of the commons,
was more likely to secure an immediate hearing. Sometimes
individuals or groups had their petitions sponsored by the commons, so that the commons' petition did not necessarily represent
the especial interests of the local representatives: but while it is
difficult to claim direct initiative for the commons, at least their

---

[1] Cf. G. Lapsley's article, *E.H.R.* 1913, and also Richardson and Sayles,
Bulletin, VI, no. 17, p. 76 and n.
[2] See H. L. Gray, *The influence of the commons on early legislation*, chap. XI.

cooperation came to be indispensable for legislation(53). The passage from petition to statute was a doubtful one, full of pitfalls, and petitions might be mutilated or worded in such a way as to fail in securing the desired end. The first step, therefore, towards control was to prevent any change in the wording of petitions(19), and after 1423, when commons' petitions or bills were produced separately, the main difficulty concerned the royal answer or amendment;[1] the procedure by passage of a bill from one house to the other became usual for public as well as private bills(55, 67).

As parliament developed it became more prominent in political matters, and the commons began to play an increasingly active part, though it is clear that they could still be much influenced by king or magnates(42). Especially from Richard II's reign efforts to influence the executive showed the increasing ambition of the representative body.[2] Impeachments were a means of punishing unpopular ministers(29, 40, 63), and they were followed by attempts at controlling the actual choice of ministers and councillors(32, 49, 68). Commissions were first appointed in parliament for definite business and for limited periods; then members were added to the king's council; and eventually owing to the weakness of the Lancastrian title, parliament secured a voice in the membership of the council and the names of councillors were read in parliament. This did not continue even to the close of the Lancastrian period, but it was an important precedent for parliament to have recorded and the lines were laid for future progress.

This growth in power began to make membership of parliament a more important matter than it had been in the past. It has been proved by Miss McKisack that attendance of burgesses was much more regular, and the value of representation far earlier recognised than was at one time thought;[3] but it was only by degrees that the duty of attendance became converted into a privilege. The effort to secure fair election began when king and magnates were contriving through the sheriffs to influence the return of mem-

---

[1] Gray, *op. cit.* pp. 46–7. Professor Gray has examined the original parliamentary records of the fourteenth and fifteenth centuries, and considers that statutes were sometimes based on commons' petitions in the fourteenth century, and consistently under Henry IV and Henry V, but that in the later fifteenth century king and lords interfered with commons' bills. Nevertheless it is difficult to assume direct initiative for the commons.

[2] See Council section, pp. 47 ff.

[3] M. McKisack, *The parliamentary representation of the English boroughs*, especially chap. IV. See also the articles on knights of the shire in *E.H.R.* 1919, 1932, 1933; and the paper by J. G. Edwards in *Essays presented to T. F. Tout*.

bers(46, 51). The demands for residence and for the return of belted knights showed the desire for representatives who could not easily be coerced(52), and the qualification of iorty shilling freehold for electors may have been intended to secure similar independence on the part of those who chose the members(56). The method of indenture and the heavy penalties imposed on sheriffs who were found conducting elections unfairly all point to the aim of averting the danger of a packed parliament(48, 62).

The position of a member was also a privileged one. Wages were still necessary to secure attendance(54, 57), but there were certain advantages, such as freedom from arrest both for members and their servants, which showed the importance attached to the representatives and their work(47, 58, 71). Although freedom of speech was not yet secured as a right(69), there was a growing sense that all matters came under parliamentary purview, and that the king and his household were fair subjects for discussion and criticism(43, 69).

In the later fifteenth century there was a significant change in the frequency of parliaments. There had been regular assemblies under Henry IV and his son, but during the personal rule of Henry VI the intervals between parliaments became longer, while Edward IV had only seven parliaments, Richard III one, and Henry VII seven. It would seem that parliament became less important as the influence of the magnates grew weaker. Nevertheless, by the end of the medieval period parliament had become a real force in the country and had acquired certain definite powers which were not to be lost in the next century.

BIBLIOGRAPHY

I. ORIGINAL SOURCES

Parliamentary writs, 2 vols. Edward I, Edward II, ed. F. Palgrave. London, 1830–4.

PRYNNE, W. *Brief register...of...parliamentary writs*, 4 pts. London, 1659–64.

Reports from the lords' committees...touching the dignity of a peer, 5 vols. London, 1820–9.

Rotuli parliamentorum. London, 1783.

Statutes of the realm. London, 1810–28.

2. SECONDARY AUTHORITIES

GRAY, H. L. *The influence of the commons on early legislation* (*Harvard historical studies*, vol. XXXIV). 1932.

McILWAIN, C. H. *The high court of parliament and its supremacy.* New Haven, 1910.

McKISACK, M. *The parliamentary representation of the English boroughs during the middle ages.* Oxford, 1932.

MAITLAND, F. W. *Records of the parliament at Westminster* (1305). *Memoranda de parliamento*, R.S. London, 1893.

PICKTHORN, K. *Early Tudor government, Henry VII.* Cambridge, 1934.

PIKE, L. O. *A constitutional history of the house of lords.* London, 1894.

POLLARD, A. F. *The evolution of parliament*, 2nd edition. London, 1926.

STUBBS, W. *The constitutional history of England.* Oxford, 1880.

3. ARTICLES AND ESSAYS

CLARKE, M. V. "The origin of impeachment", *Oxford essays in medieval history presented to H. E. Salter.* Oxford, 1934.

EDWARDS, J. G. "The personnel of the commons in parliament under Edward I and Edward II", *Essays...presented to T. F. Tout.* Manchester, 1925.

—— "The parliamentary committee of 1398", *E.H.R.* XL, 1925.

LAPSLEY, G. "The commons and the statute of York", *E.H.R.* XXVIII, 1913.

—— "Knights of the shire in the parliaments of Edward II", *E.H.R.* XXXIV, 1919.

LATHAM, L. C. "Collection of the wages of the knights of the shire in the fourteenth and fifteenth centuries", *E.H.R.* XLVIII, 1933.

LEWIS, N. B. "Re-election to parliament in the reign of Richard II", *E.H.R.* XLVIII, 1933.

LOWRY, E. CLARK. "Clerical proctors in parliament and knights of the shire, 1280–1374", *E.H.R.* XLVIII, 1933.

NEALE, J. E. "The commons' privilege of free speech in parliament", *Tudor studies* (ed. R. W. Seton-Watson). London, 1924.

RICHARDSON, H. G. and SAYLES, G. "The king's ministers in parliament", *E.H.R.* XLVI, XLVII, 1931, 1932.

—— —— "The early records of the English parliaments", *Bulletin of the Institute of Historical Research*, vols. V, VI, nos. 15, 17.

—— —— "The parliaments of Edward III", *Bulletin*, vols. VIII, IX, nos. 23, 25.

ROUND, J. H. "Barons and peers", *E.H.R.* XXXIII, 1918.

WEDGWOOD, J. C. "John of Gaunt and the packing of parliament", *E.H.R.* XLV, 1930.

WOOD-LEGH, K. L. "The knights' attendance in the parliaments of Edward III", *E.H.R.* XLVII, 1932.

(1) *Council and parliament* 1315

Responsiones facte coram Rege et Magno Consilio, in Parliamento ipsius Regis quod summonitum fuit apud Westmonasterium in octabis Sancti Hillarii anno etc. viii.

A nostre Seignur le Roi et a son Consail prie David Count d'Asceles remedi de son heritage, le quel fust done durant les Ordinaunces, c'est a savoir le xv jour de July l'an quint, encontre les Ordinaunces. Et dount le dist Count prie a nostre Seignur le Roi et a son Consail, qe mesme le doun soit par le dites Ordinaunces repelle, et a luy rendu, desicome il est de tuttes ses terres en Escoce, pur l'amur nostre Seignur le Roi, pur luy et pur ses heires forsjugez a touzjours taunt come en eux est.

Responsio. Responsum est per Consilium: Ceste Petition fu lue par comandement de nostre Seignur le Roi en pleyn Parlement, devant Prelatz, Countes, Barons, et touz autres: Et respondu par assent e acord de touz en la manere suzescrist...

Rot. Parl. i, 294 (28).

(2) *Receivers and triers of petitions* 1316

Eodem die concordatum fuit, quod Petitiones reciperentur et expedirentur, prout ad alia Parliamenta prius fieri consuevit, et quod reciperentur usque in crastinum Purificationis beate Marie tunc proximo futurum, et eodem crastino. Et nominati fuerunt pro Petitionibus Angliam tangentibus recipiendis Robertus de Askeby, Clericus de Cancellaria, et Adam de Lymbergh, unus Rememoratorum de Scaccario; et pro Petitionibus Vasconiam, Walliam, Hiberniam, et Scotiam tangentibus, Magister Edwardus de Londoniis, Clericus de dicta Cancellaria, et Magister Willelmus de Maldon', unus Camerariorum Domini Regis de Scaccario suo; et inde Proclamatio facta fuit. Post hec injunctum fuit predictis Cancellario et Thesaurario et Justiciariis de utroque Banco, quod ipsi negotia coram eis in placeis suis pendentia, que extra Parliamentum non possent terminari, sub compendio in scriptis redigi facerent, et ea in dicto Parliamento referrent, ita quod ibi eisdem fieret quod deberet.

Die Jovis sequenti concordatum fuit quod super Petitionibus procederetur usque adventum prefati Comitis Lancastrie et aliorum Procerum sic absentium, et nominati fuerunt pro Petitionibus Angliam tangentibus audiendis et expediendis Johannes

Norwicencis, Johannes Cicestrensis, et Rogerus Sarum, Episcopi: Edwardus Deyncourt, Philippus de Kyme, Johannes de Insula, unus Baronum de Scaccario, Henricus L'escrop, unus Justiciariorum de Banco, et Robertus de Bardelby, Clericus de Cancellaria: Et pro Petitionibus Vasconie, et Insularum, Henricus Wyntoniensis, Walterus Exoniensis, et Johannes Bathoniensis et Wellensis, Episcopi; Willelmus Inge... [4 *others*] Clerici: Et pro Petitionibus Wallie, Hibernie, et Scotie, Radulphus filius Willelmi, Magister Willelmus de Birston, Archidiaconus Gloucestrie, Magistri Johannes Walewayn, Escaetor citra Trentam, Johannes Bush [2 *others*] Clerici, ac Johannes de Mutford, unus Justiciariorum ad Assisas.

Rot. Parl. 1, 350.

(3) *The magnates in parliament* 1320

Parliamentum apud Westmonasterium convocatum die Lune in Octabis Sancti Michelis anno regni Regis Edwardi filii Regis Edwardi quartodecimo.

Inprimis Dominus Rex eodem die Lune, assidentibus sibi W. Archiepiscopo Cantuariense, J. Norwicense Episcopo, Cancellario Anglie, W. Exoniense Episcopo, Thesaurario ipsius Domini Regis, ac S. Londoniense, J. Eliense, et W. Coventrense et Lychfeldense, Episcopis, Adomaro de Valencia Comite Pembroch, Edmundo de Woodstok fratris ipsius Domini Regis, ac quibusdam aliis Magnatibus et Proceribus Regni sui, ordinavit de modo recipiendi et expediendi Peticiones porrigendas in eodem Parliamento. Et in presencia eorundem Prelatorum, Magnatum, Procerum, et aliorum, idem Dominus Rex ordinavit et precepit quod Adam de Lymbergh, et Willelmus de Herlaston, Clerici reciperent omnes Peticiones Anglie et Wallen' liberandas in eodem Parliamento:...

Consideracio Domini Edwardi filii Regis Edwardi in pleno Parliamento suo apud Westmonasterium in octabis Sancti Michelis anno Regni sui xiii° convocato,...

Rot. Parl. 1, 365.

(4) *Revocation of the ordinances* 1322

[*Recital of the ordinances of* 5 *Edward II.*]

Les queles ordenances le dit nostre Seignur le Roi, a son parlement a Everwyk a treis semeignes de Pask, Lan de son regne quinzisme, par Prelatz, Countes, et Barons, entre queux furent touz le plus

des ditz ordenours qi adoncs furent en vie, et par le Commun du
Roialme...fist rehercer et examiner: Et pur ceo qe par cel
examinement trove feust en dit parlement, qe par les choses
issint ordenees le poair real nostre dit Seignur le Roi feust re-
streynt, en plusors choses, countre devoir, en blemissement de
sa seignurie reale, et encountre lestat de la Coronne;...acorde
est...au dit parlement par nostre Seignur le Roi, et par les
ditz Prelatz, Countes, et Barons, et tote la Commune du Roialme,
...qe totes les choses par les ditz ordenours ordenees, et contenues en les dites ordenaunces, desoremes pur le temps avenir
cessent,...Les estatutz et establissementz faitz duement par nostre
Seignur le Roi, et ses auncestres, avaunt les dites ordenances,
demorauntz en lour force: et qe desore james en nul temps, nule
manere des ordenaunces, ne purveaunces faites par les Suggetz
nostre Seignur le Roi, ou de ses Heirs, par quele poair ou commission qe ceo soit, sur le poair real de nostre Seignur le Roi, ou
de ses Heirs, ou countre lestat nostre dit Seignur le Roi, ou de ses
Heirs, ou countre lestat de la Coronne, soient nulles et de nule
manere de value ne de force; Mes les choses qi serrount a establir,
pur lestat de nostre Seignur le Roi, et de ses Heirs, et pur lestat
du roialme et du poeple, soient tretes...en parlementz, par nostre
Seignur le Roi, et par lassent des Prelatz, Countes et Barouns, et
la communalte du roialme; auxint come ad este acustume cea
enarere.

S.R. I, 189, 15 Ed. II.

(5) *Petitions in parliament* 1325

A nostre Seignur le Roy monstrent ses liges gentz, qe come eaux
et lour Auncestres eient donnez plusours taillages as Auncestres
nostre Seignur le Roi pur avoir la Chartre de la Foreste, laquele
Chartre nous avoms de nostre Seignur le Roy qe ore est conferme,
pur le nostre a lui largement donant. Puis venent les Ministres
de la Foreste decea Trente et dela, et ount repris en Foreste Viles,
terres, et boys auxi enticrment come unqes feurent, encontre la
forme de la dite Chartre, a grant damage de son poeple, et fount
abatre fosses, et destourbent lour gaignages, et pernent de eaux
grevouses et soveneres redemptions, a grant destruction du poeple,
de quai eux prient pur Dieu et l'alme son Piere remedie.
......
   Auxint prient les dites gentz pur tote la Commune, qe come
diverses terres ore sont devenuz en la meyn le Roi par forfeiture

de ses Rebeaux, lesqueux ils purpristrent par force de Seignurie et par disseisine faite as divers gentz dont plusours enquestes sount returnez en Chauncellerie et nul issue de lay est fait, au grant arrerissement du poeple...par ount ils prient a sa Seignurie, qe de teles Terres Manoirs, Villes, Rentes, Baillies de fee, et franchises ensi seisiz en la meyn le Roi, il voille comaundre issue de lai selonc ceo q'ils purrent monstrer par enquestes ou par Chartres de ses progenitours, ou de lui meismes, q'ils eient reson des tiels terres avoir...

Rot. Parl. 1, 430 (1), (4).

(6) *Justice in parliament* 1330

Judicium Rogeri de Mortuomari

Ces sont les Tresons...faites par Roger de Mortymer,...Item, Le dit Roger en deceyvante manere fist les Chivalers des Countez grantier, au dit Parlement de Winchestre, au Roi de chescune Ville d'Engleterre qi respount par Quatre et le Provost en Eyre, un homme d'armes a lur custages en sa Guerre de Gascoigne par un an; laquele charge le dit Roger avoit compasse a tourner en aucun autre profist pur lui et autres de sa covyne, en destruction du poeple...

Dont le dit nostre Seignur le Roi si vous charge, Countes et Barouns, les Pieres de son Roialme, qe desicome cestes choses touchant principaument a lui, a vous, et a tut le poeple de son Roialme, qe vous facez au dit Roger droit et loial Jugement come affiert a un tiel d'aver, qi de totes les coupes susescrites si est veritablement coupable, a ce q'il entent, et qe les dites choses sont notoires et conues pur veritables a vous et a tut le poeple du Roialme. Lesqueux Countes, Barouns, et Peres, les articles par eux examinez, reviendrent devant le Roi en mesme le Parlement, et disoient tres touz par un des Peres, qe totes les choses contenues es ditz Articles feurent notoires et conues a eux et au poeple; et nomement l'Article tochant la mort Sire Edward, Piere nostre Seignur le Roi qi ore est. Pur quoi les ditz Countes, Barouns, et Pieres, come Juges du Parlement, par Assent du Roi en mesme le Parlement, agarderent et ajugerent, Que le dit Roger, come Treitur et Enemy du Roi et du Roialme, feust treyne et pendu. Et sur ce estoit comande a Counte Mareschal a faire l'Execution du dit Jugement...

Judicium Simonis de Bereford.

Item, en mesme le Parlement, si chargea nostre Seignur le Roi

les ditz Countes, Barouns, et Pieres, a doner droit et loial Jugement, come affiert, a Simon de Bereford, Chivaler, qi estoit aidant
et conseilant au dit Roger de Mortymer en totes les Tresons,
Felonies, et Malveistes, pur lesqueles le avantdit Roger issint fust
agarde et juge a la mort, come conue chose et notoire est as ditz
Peres, a ce qe le Roi entent. Lesqueux Countes, Barouns, et
Peres revyndrent devant nostre Seignur le Roi en mesme le
Parlement, et disoient touz come d'une voice, qe l'avantdit Simon
ne feust pas lur Pere, par qoi eux ne furent pas tenuz a jugger lui
come Pere de la terre: Mes pur ce qe notoire chose est et conue a
touz, qe l'avantdit Simon estoit aidant et conseillant au dit Roger
en totes les Tresons, Felonies, et Malveistes susditz, lesqueles
choses sont en purpris de Roial Poer, murdre de Seignur lige, et
destruction du Sank real; et q'il estoit auxint coupable d'autres
diverses Felonies et Roberies, et principal Meyntenour de Rob-
beours et Felonns; si agarderent et ajuggerent les ditz Countes,
Baronns, et Peres come Juges du Parlement, par assent du Roi en
mesme le Parlement, Qe le dit Simon, come Treitre et Enemy du
Roi et du Roialme, feust treyne et pendu...

Rot. Parl. II, 52–3.

(7) *The magnates in parliament* 1332

Ces sont les Remembraunces du Parlement somons a Westmonstier le Lundi prechein apres la Feste de Seint Gregoir...

A queu jour de Lundi, si furent les deus Articles precheins suantz
luez devant nostre Seignur le Roi, et touz les Prelatz et autres
Grantz adonqes au dit Parlement venuz...Et pur ce qe l'Ercevesqe
de Canterbirs, et plusours autres Grantz...n'estoient adonqes
venuz si n'y avoit il plus fait a la journe...

Et puis en pleyn Parlement si feust pronuncie par le dit
Ercevesqe en fourme de predication, en la presence nostre Seignur
le Roi et des touz les Prelatz et autres Grantz, la cause pur quele
le Parlement estoit somons;...et sur ce demanda il de par nostre
Seignur le Roi les consealx et avis des Prelatz, Countes, Barouns,
et de touz les autres Grantz en pleyn Parlement...

Fait auxint a remembrer qe le Samedi prechein apres le primer
jour du Parlement avoient les Chivalers des Countes, Citeins, et
Burgeys au dit Parlement somons, et auxint la Clergie, conge
d'aler vers lur pays, issint qe les Prelatz, Countes, Barouns, et
Gentz du Conseil le Roi, y demorassent...

Item, Mesme le jour de Lundi [apres le dit Samedi] si feust

reherce par le dit Monsire Geffrei [le Scrop'] en pleyn Parlement, coment sur aucunes Debatz muez par entre Monsire Johan de Grey de Rotherfeld et Monsire William la Zouche de Assheby, feust defendu a l'une part et l'autre au darrein Parlement, qe nul ne feist a autre mal...

Rot. Parl. II, 64 (1), (4); 65 (11), (12).

(8) *The method of meeting* 1332

A queu jour de Joedi euent trete et deliberacioun, c'est assaver les ditz Prelatz par eux mesmes, et les ditz Countes, Barouns, et autres Grantz par eux mesmes, et auxint les Chivalers des Countes par eux mesmes, si respondirent, q'ils avoient grant consideracion as noveles qe de jour en autre viendrent des parties d'Escoce...
Et conseillerent pur le mielz, qe nostre Seignur le Roi demorast en Engleterre, et se treissist devers les parties de North, et q'il eust ovesqe lui sages Gentz et forcibles pur sauvation du dit Roialme et de son poeple,...
Et pur ce qe nostre Seignur le Roi ne puist cestes choses perfaire sanz ce q'il soit aide de son Poeple, si ount les ditz Prelatz, Countes, Barouns, et autres Grantz, et les Chivalers des Countes, et tote la Commune de lur franche volunte, pur perfaire les susdites choses, et issint qe nostre Seignur le Roi vive de soen, et paye pur ses despenses, et ne greve poynt son poeple par outraiouses prises n'en autre manere, grante a nostre dit Seignur le Roi le Quinzisme deiner, a lever de la Communalte, et le Disme dener a lever des Citez, Burghs, et les Demeyns le Roi...

Rot. Parl. II, 66 (3).

(9) *Petition to the council* 1337

A nostre Seignour le Roy et a son Conseil monstre Richard de Bettoyne de Loundres, qe come au Coronement nostre Seignour le Roy qi ore est, il adonqe Meire de Londres fesoit l'office de Botiller, ove ccc e lx Vadletz vestutz d'une sute, chescun portant en sa mayn un coupe blanche d'argent, come autres Meirs de Londres ount faitz as Coronementz des progenitours nostre Seigneur le Roy, dont memorie ne court, et le fee qi appendoit a cel jorne, c'est asavoir un Coupe d'or ove la covercle, et un Ewer d'or enamaille, lui fust livere, par assent du Counte de Lancastre et d'autres Grantz qu'adonqes y furent du Conseil nostre Seigneur le Roy, par la mayn Sire Robert de Wodehouse; et ore vient en

estreite as Viscountes de Londres hors del Chekker, de faire lever
des Biens et Chateux du dit Richard iiii ix li. xii s. vi d. pur le fee
avantdit, dont il prie qe remedie lui soit ordeyne...

Responsio. Soit mande as Tresorer et Barons de l'Escheker q'ils
serchent les Roules et Remembranz de l'Escheker touchantz la
dite bosoigne, s'ils treffent qe les Meirs de Londres en temps des
Coronomentz de progenitours le Roy ount en tieu fee aloue a
l'Escheker, qe adonqes facent alouer au dit Richard meisme le
fee, et facent surser de la demaunde q'ils lui font pur meisme le
fee.

Rot. Parl. II, 96 (2).

(10) *Taxation in parliament* 1339

A queu jour fu monstre as Communes la cause de la Somons du
dit Parlement: C'est assavoir, de doner bon et greable Respons
sur la promesse q'il firent au Parlement darrein passez, d'un
covenable Eide faire a nostre Seignur le Roi, pur la grante et
chargeaunte Necessite q'il ad pur l'espoit de ses grosses busoignes
par dela et par decea; Et pur la salvation du Roialme et de eux
meismes; Et auxint de la Meer, de la Marche d'Escoce, de Gascoigne, et des Isles. Et fu dit a eux, qe si la manere d'aider qe
autre foitz fu monstrez et touchez a eux par les Grauntz en
chargeaunce manere ne lour pleust, q'il s'acordassent a ascune
certeine et covenable manere d'Aide faire, par laquel nostre
Seignur le Roi purra meuther et plus covenablement estre eidez,
et le menu Poeple meyns grevez. Sur quele demonstraunce il
respoundrent, q'il voleint parler ensemble et treter sur cest
bosoigne; Et qe, od l'eide de Dieu, ils durroient tieu response qe
ce serroit a la pleisance de lour lige Seignur, et de tut son Conseil.
Sur quel bosoigne ceux de la Commune demorerent de lour
respons doner tan qe a Samady le xix jour de Feverer.

A queu jour ils offrerent d'aidir a nostre Seignur le Roi en
ceste Necessite de xxx M. Saks de Leyne, souz certeynes Condicions comprises es Endentures sur ceo faites, et enseales souz
les Seax des Prelatz et autres Grauntz: Qe en cas qe les Con-
diciounes ne feussent acompliez il ne serront pas tenuz de faire
l'aide, Et pur ceo qe les choses contenuz en cestes Endentures
toucherent si pres l'estat de nostre Seignur le Roi, si fu il avis au
dit Counseil, q'il covendroit qe nostre Seignur le Roi et son
Secrez Counseil pres de lui ent feusent avises. Par qoi acordez

fust et assentuz, d'envoier a nostre Seignur le Roi les dites
Endentures, od l'avis de son Counseil par decea, au fyn q'il ent
purroit comander sa volente. Et fait a remembrer, qe a meisme
le jour les Countes et Barouns esteantz en dit Parlement granterent, pur eux et pur lour Piers de la terre qi tiegnent par Baronie,
la disme garbe, la disme tuzon, le disme aignel, de totes lour
demeignes terres.

Rot. Parl. II, 107 (6), (7).

(11) *Grants in parliament* 1340

(1) *Grant of a subsidy of the ninth lamb, etc.: burgesses inferior to knights*

A quele requeste les ditz Prelatz, Countes, et Barons pur eux
et pur touz lour Tenantz, et les Chivalers de Conteez pur eux
et pur les Communes de la terre, eant regard as Meschiefs et
Perils d'une part, en cas qe l'Aide fausiste, qe Dieux defende;
et a l'honur, profit, et quiete d'autre parte qe purront avenir
od l'eid de Dieu, au dit nostre Seignur le Roi...meismes cestui
Lundy graunteront au nostre Seignur le Roi par les causes susditz l'Eide souzescrit; C'est assavoir, la Neofisme garbe, la Neofisme toison, et la Neofisme aignel de totes lour garbes, toisons,
et aigneux, a prendre des adonqes par deux aunz proscheinement
suantz. Et les Citeyns et Burgeis du Roialme la verrai Neofisme
de touz lour Biens; et Marchaundz qi demorent poynt en Citees
n'en Burghs, et autres gentz qi demorent en Forestes et Gasteyns,
et qi ne vivent poynt de lour gaignerie ou de lour estore de
Berbitz, la Quinzisme de touz lour biens solonc la verroi value.
Souz la Condition, qe nostre Seignur le Roi de sa bone grace
eant a graunt Charge et Subsides dont ils ont este chargez einz
ces heures, et a ce Graunt q'il ount fait a ore qe lour semble mout
chargeant, lour ottrei les Petitions queles ils mistront devant lui
et devant son Counsail, et lesqueles sont continuez desouz, et
commencent ceste fourme: "Cestes sont les Petitions, etc."

Rot. Parl. II, 112 (6). (Cf. *S.R.* I, 288.)

(2) *Grant of a subsidy on wool, woolfells, etc. exported*

Et coment qe les communes du Roialme prierent au Roi, qil
vousist par assent du parlement granter et establir, qe jammes ne
feust pris plus de custume dun sak de leine, qe un demy mark,
ne de plum, esteym, quirs ne pealx lanutz, forsqe launciene
custume nepurquant le Roi pria as Prelatz, Contes, Barons, et as

toux les communes qe pur grosses busoignes qil avoit ore entre meins, come ils bien savoient, qils lui vousissent grantier ascun eide, sur les leines, quirs, pealx lanutz, et autres marchandises a durer un piece; sur quoi, eu deliberacion, les ditz Prelatz Contes Barons et communes de son roialme, lui ont grante quarante souldz, a prendre de chescun sak de leine, et quarante souldz de chescun trois Centz pealx lanutz, et de chescun last de quirs quarant soldz, et dautres marchandises a la ferant, qi passeront outre meer; et a comencier a la feste du Pasche en lan du regne le Roi qorest quatorzisme, et a durer tanqe a la feste de Pentecost preschein seuant et de cel fest de Pentecost preschein seuant en un an. Et pur cel grant, le Roi par assent des Prelatz Contes Barons et touz autres assemblez a son parlement, si ad grante, qe de la feste de Pentecost qi vient en un an, lui ne ses heirs nene demanderont,...plus de custume de un sak de leine, de null engleys, forsqe un demy marc de custume tantsoulement; et sur pealx, et quirs launcien custume;...Et a cest establissement leal- ment tenir et garder, si ad le Roi premys en la presence des Prelatz, Contes, Barons, et autres en son plein parlement, sanz plus de charge mettre, ou asseer, sur la coustume forsqe en manere come est susdit. Et en mesme la manere les Prelatz, Contes, Barons, ont lealment premys tant come en eux est, qils procure- ront le Roi, tant come ils pount, a le tenir; et qe en null manere, ils ne assenteront au contraire, si ce ne soit par assent des Prelatz, Contes, Barons et communes de son roialme, et ce en plein parlement...

S.R. I, 289, 14 Ed. III, s. I, c. 21.

(3) *The above subsidy not to be a precedent*

Edward...a touz ceux as queux cestes lettres vendront, salutz. Sachiez qe come Prelatz, Contes, Barons, et communes de nostre roialme Dengleterre...nous aient grantez de lour bone gree et de bone volente...la noefisme garbe le noefisme tuyson et le noefisme aignel a prendre par deux annz prescheins avenir...et les Citeyns des Citeez, et Burgeys de Burghs, la verroi noefisme de toutz lour biens, et les marchantz foreyns et autres...le quinzisme de lour biens loialment a la value: Nous...voilloms et grantoms pur nous et pur noz heirs...qe ce grant qi est si chargeant ne soit autrefoitz trette en ensaumple, ne ne chete a eux en prejudice en temps avenir; ne qe eux soient desore chargiez ne grevez de commune eide faire, ou charge sustenir, si ce ne soit par commune assent des Prelatz, Countes, Barouns, et autres grantz et communes de nostre dit Roialme Dengleterre, et ce en parlement; et qe touz les profitz sourdantz du dit eide, et des gardes, mariages, Custumes, Eschetes...soient mys et despenduz sur la meintenance de la sauve garde de nostre dit Roialme Dengleterre, et de nos guerres Descoce, France, et Gascoigne...

S.R. 1, 289, 14 Ed. III, s. 2, c. 1.

(12) *Council acting as parliament: appointment of receivers and triers of petitions* 1341

Le Parlement tenuz a Westmonstier le Lundy en la Quinzeyne de Pasche,...

En primes, Acordez est qe Sire Thomas de Drayton' soit Clerk du Parlement.

Item, Acordez est par nostre Seignur le Roi et ceux de son Conseil qe adonqes estoient venuz, qe une Proclamation se face, qe nul homme porte Armes, en la manere qe soleit estre fait as autres Parlementz: Laquele Proclamation fu fait meisme le jour, en la fourme qi s'ensuyt...

Item, Une Crie fu fait, qe chescun qi voudra mettre Petition a nostre Seignur le Roi et a son Conseil les mette entre cy et Samady preschein a venir le jour compris deinz la Crie.

Et serront assignez de resceivre les Petitions d'Engleterre les souzescritz, c'est assavoir,

> S. Thomas de Evesham,
> S. Johan de Wodehous, } Clerks de la Chauncellerie.
> S. Edmond de Grymesby,

Et pur les Petitions de Gascoigne, Gales, Irlande, Escoce, et des Isles,

> S. Johan de Marton,
> S. Elys de Grymesby, } Clerks de la Chauncellerie.
> S. Robert de Kellesey,

Et pur oier les Petitions d'Engleterre, sont assignez,

> L'Evesqe de Duresme,
> L'Evesqe de Sarum,
> Le Counte de Northampton,
> Le Counte d'Arundell, } associez a eux Chaunceller
> Le Seignur de Wake, } et Tresorer quant miester
> Monsire Thomas de Berkele, } serra.
> Monsire Robert de Sadyngton,
> Monsire William Scot,
> S. Thomas de Heppescotes,

Item, pur oier les Petitions de Gascoigne, Gales, Irland, d'Escoce et des Isles, sont assignez,

L'Evesqe de Ely,
L'Evesqe de Hereford,
Le Counte de Huntyngdon,
Le Counte de Devenshire,
Monsire Johan de Cherleton,
Monsire Roger Hillary,
Monsire Robert de Scardeburgh
S. Roger de Bankewell,

associez a eux les Chaunceler et Tresorer quant mester serra.

Item, est acordez, pur ce qe les Prelatz, Countes, Barons, et autres Grantz, ne sont pas pleynement venuz yce Lundy le primer jour du Parlement, de continuer le Parlement tan qe a lendemeigne; c'est assaver, le Mardy preschein apres la quinzeyne.

Item, Le Mardy est fait une continuance tan qe a Meskerdy par meisme la cause, et de Meskerdy tan qe au Joedy.

Et fait a remembrer, qe le Joedy susdit furent purposees les Causes du dit Parlement, en presence des Prelatz et autres Grantz souz-escritz; C'est assaver, des Evesqes de Wyncestre, Duresme, d'Ely, Cestre, Excestre, Hereford, Seint Davy, Baa, Sarum; Monsire Robert d'Artoys; des Countes de Northampton, d'Arundell, de Huntyngdon, de Pembrogge, d'Anegos, d'Oxenford, de Devenshire, de Sarum, et de Suffolk; Et des Seignurs de Percy, de Wake, Monsire Hugh le Despenser, Monsire Nichol de Cantelou, le Seignur de Segrave; et Justices, et d'autres du Conseil, en la manere qi s'ensuit:...

Rot. Parl. II, 126 (1), (3), (4).

(13) *Trial of peers* 1341

...Et pur ce qe, entre autres choses contenues en la Prier des Grantz est fait mention, Qe les Piers de la terre, Officers ne autres, ne serront tenuz de respondre de trespas qe lour est surmys par le Roi, fors qe en Parlement: queu choses, fust avys au Roi, qe ce serroit inconvenient, et contre son estat: Si prierent les ditz Grantz au Roi, q'il voloit assentir, qe quatre Evesqes, quatre Countes, et quatre Barons, ensemblement ove ascuns Sages de la Leye, fussent esluz, de trier en queu cas les ditz Piers serroient tenuz de respondre en Parlement, et nulle parte aillours, et en quel cas ne my; et de reporter lour avys a lui. Et furent esluz a ceste chose faire, les Evesqes de Excestre, Cicestre, Baa, Loundres; les Countes d'Arundel, Sarum, Huntyngdon, et Suffolk; les

Seignurs de Wake, Percy; Monsire Rauf de Nevill, et Monsire Rauf Basset de Drayton. Lesqueux douze reporterent lour avys en pleyn Parlement, le Lundy preschein suant, en une cedule, dont la copie s'ensuit, en ceste forme.

Honorable Seignur, a la reverence de Vous semble d'un assent as Prelatz, Countes, et Barouns, qe les Piers de la terre ne deivent estre aresnez, ne menez en Juggement sinoun en Parlement, et par lour Piers. Et sur ce ad este de novel ascun debat, si ascun des Piers, soit ou eit este Chaunceller, Tresorer, ou autre Officer quecunqe, deive ennoier celle Franchise, auxi bien par cause de lour office come en autre manere. Est avis as Pieres de la terre, qe touz les Piers de la terre, Officer ou autre, par cause de lour office des choses touchantes lour office, ne par nul autre cause, ne deivent estre menez en Juggement, ne perdre lour temporaltez, terres, tenementz, biens, ne chatelx; n'estre arestuz ne emprisonez, outlagez, ne forsjuggez, ne ne deivent respoundre, n'estre juggez, fors qe en pleyn Parlement, et devant les Piers ou le Roi se fait partie. Salvees a nostre Seignur le Roi les Leies dreiturelement usees par du processe; et salve la suite de partie...

...Et puis pria l'Ercevesqe au Roi, q'il pleust a sa Seignurie, qe desicome il est diffamez notoirement par tut le Roialme et aillours, q'il puisse estre aresnez en pleyn Parlement devant les Pieres, et illoeqes respoundre, issint q'il soit overtement tenuz pur tiel come il est. Queu chose le Roi ottreia...

Rot. Parl. II, 127 (6), (7), (8).

(14) *Commons' petition for audit of accounts* 1341

Item, prient les Grantz et la Commune de la terre, et pur commune profit de lui et de eux, Qe soient certeynes gentz deputez par Commission d'oier les acompts des touz ceux q'ont resceu les Leynes nostre dit Seignur, ou autres Eides a lui grantez; et auxint de ceux q'ont resceuz et despenduz ses deniers auxi bien par dela la meer come par decea puis le comencement de sa guerre tan qe a ore; et qe Roulles et autres Remembrances, Obligations, et autres choses faites par dela soient liverez en la Chauncellerie, d'estre enroullez et mys en remembrance, sicome homme soleit faire einz ces heures.

Rot. Parl. II, 128 (12).

Respons as Communes.

· · · · · ·

Item, Quant al seconde article, C'est assavoir, d'acomptes oier de eux q'ont resceu les Leynes le Roi, et autres Eides, etc. Il plest au Roi qe la chose se face par bones Gentz a ce deputer, issint qe le Tresorer et le Chief Baron y soient ajointz: Et soit fait de ce come autre foitz fust ordeigne; et soient esluz les Seignurs en ce Parlement. Et auxint qe touz Roules, Remembrances, et Obligations faitz dela le meer soient liverez a la Chuncellerie.

Rot. Parl. II, 130 (38).

(15) *Royal reply to petitions in statute form, in return for a grant* 1341

Et fait a remembrer, Qe sur les Respons susdites, auxi bien a les Requestes des Grantz come de ceux de la Commune et de la Clergie, feurent faitz les Estatuz souzescritz par les ditz Grauntz et Communes, et monstrez a nostre Seignur le Roi; Ensemblement od ascunes Condicions qe les Grantz et la Commune demanderent du Roi, pur le Grant q'ils ferroient a lui de xxx M. saks de Leyne, en recompensation de la Neofisme garbe, aignel, et toison, de l'an second. Lesqueux Estatutz et Conditions puis furent lieues devant le Roi. Et le Chaunceller, Tresorer, et ascuns Justices de l'un Baunk et de l'autre, et le Seneschal de l'Houstiel le Roi, et le Chaumberleyn, et ascuns autres feurent jurez sur la Croice de Cantirbirs, de les tenir et garder si avant come a eux attient. Mes les ditz Chaunceller, Tresorer, et ascuns des Justices, firent lour protestation, q'ils ne assentirent a la fesance ne a la forme des ditz Estatutz, ne qe eux ne les purroient garder, en cas qe meismes les Estatutz fussent contraires a les Leies et Usages du Roialme, lesqueux ils feurent serementez de garder. Et puis feurent meismes les Estatutz et Condicions ensealez du Grant Seal le Roi, et liverez as Grantz, et as Chivalers du Countee; lesqueux Estatutz et Condicions, ensemblement od l'avis des Grantz et autres en sur ascuns pointz contenuz en les Commissions faites as Grantz, d'enquer des Oppressions, Extorsions, Grevances, et Excesses faitz par Ministres le Roi et autres, en divers Counteez, sont plus pleynement contenuz au dos de cesti Roulle.

Rot. Parl. II, 131 (42).

Conditions: . . . Definition of statutes

Item, Qe les Petitions par les Grantz et la Commune monstrez soient affermees, selonc ce q'ils sont grauntees par le Roi; C'est assavoir, les pointz a durer par Estatut, et les autres par Chartre

ou Patent, et liverez as Chivalers des Counteez sanz rien paier.
Et qe pleise a nostre Seignur le Roi de perfournir la Grace quele
il ad promys as Grauntz, endroit des Attachez et Emprisonez ore
en cel Parlement. Et ceux qi ont fait Fyns, estoysent a lour Fyns,
ou a la Comune Lei a lour chois.

Rot. Parl. II, 133 (61). (Cf. article by G. Lapsley, in *E.H.R.* 1915,
for this and preceding documents. Edward III later evaded some
of the statutes. See Council section, pp. 46–7.)

(16) *Representative of the commons (later speaker)* 1343

A queu jour les ditz Prelatz et Grantz assemblez en la Chaumbre
Blanch, responderent, Qe lour fust avys qe les dites Trewes
estoient honurables et profitables a nostre Seignur le Roi, et a
touz les soens;...
Et puis vindrent les Chivalers des Counteez et les Communes, et
responderent par Monsire William Trussell en la dite Chaumbre
Blanche, qi en presence de nostre Seignur le Roi, et des ditz
Prelatz et Grantz purposa pur les Chivalers et Communes, Q'ils
se sont pleynement assentuz et acordez a les dites Trewes tenir,
aufyn qe bone et honurable Pees se preigne...

Rot. Parl. II, 136 (9). (Cf. H. G. Richardson and G. Sayles,
E.H.R. 1932, p. 395; they consider that Trussel was neither a
knight nor a burgess, but in the king's service.)

(17) *The commons consulted on peace and war, but ask to be excused* 1348

...A queu jour furent les Causes du Parlement purposez par
Monsire William de Thorp, en la presence nostre Seignur le Roi,
et des Prelatz, Contes, Barons, et Communes du Roialme illoeqes
assemblez;...l'une cause, de la Guerre quele nostre Seignur le
Roi ad empris contre son Adversair de France par commune
assent de touz les Grantz et Communes de sa terre susdite, en
diverses Parlementz qi ont estez cea en arere, come sovent foitz
ad este rehercez, coment ent serra fait au temps de la Trewe qi
ore est serra finie. L'autre cause, de la Pees d'Engleterre, coment
et en quele manere ele se purra meutz garder. Et sur ce fut coman-
dez as Chivalers des Countees, et autres des Communes, q'ils se
deveroient trere ensemble, et ce q'ils ent sentiroient le deveroient
monstrer au Roi et as Grantz de son Conseil. Lesqueux Chivalers
et autres des Communes eu ent avisement par quatre jours, au

drein respoundirent a l'article touchant la Guerre en la manere qi s'ensuyt:

Tresredotez Seignur, Quant a vostre Guerre et l'arrai d'icelle, nous sumes si mesconissantz et simples qe nous ne savons ne poons ent conseiller: De quei nous prions a vostre graciouse Seignurie nous avoir de l'ordenance pur escusez, et qe Vous pleise, par avis des Grantz et Sages de vostre Conseil ordener sur cel point ceo qe moutz Vous semblera pur honur et profit de Vous et de vostre Roialme. Et ceo qe serra ensi ordenez par assent et acorde de Vous et des Grantz susditz, nous nous assentons bien, et le tendrons ferme et estable...

Rot. Parl. II, 164–5 (4), (5).

(18) *The commons ask for petitions to be answered in parliament* 1348

Et prie la Commune, qe totes les Petitions suantz, monstreez par la Commune pur commune profit et pur amendement avoir des Meschiefs, soient responduz et endossez en Parlement devant la Commune; issint qe ils puissent savoir l'Endossementz, et ent avoir remedie solonc l'Ordenaunce du Parlement.

Rot. Parl. II, 165 (8).

(19) *The commons ask for petitions not to be altered* 1348

Item prie la Commune, qe les Petitions liverees en le drein Parlement par la dite Commune, et par nostre dit Seignur le Roi, Prelatz, et Grantz de la terre pleinement respondues et grantees, soient tenues; et qe par nulle Bille liveree en ce Parlement en noun de Commune ou de autri ne soient les Respons avant grantez changez: Qar la Commune ne avowe nulle tiele Bille, si ascune y soit liveree en Parlement de faire le contraire.

Responsio. Autre foitz le Roi, par avis des Prelatz et Grantz de la terre, fist respondre a les Petitions des Communes touchantes la Lei de la terre, Qe les Leis eues et usees en temps passez, ne le Proces d'icelle usez cea en arere, ne se purront changer saunz ent faire novel Estatut: A queu chose faire le Roi ne poait adonqes, ne unqore poet entendre, par certeines causes. Mes a plus tost q'il purra entendre, il prendra les Grantz et les Sages de son Conseil par devers lui, et ordeignera sur cels articles et autres touchantz Amendement de Lei, par lour avis et conseilx, en manere qe reson et equite serront faites as touz ses Liges et Suggitz et a chescun de eux.

Rot. Parl. ii, 203 (30).

(20) *Ordinance and statute* 1351

Come nadgairs contre la Malice des Servauntz queux furent preceouse, et nient voillantz servire apres la Pestilence...nostre Seignur le Roi eust ordeigne par assent des Prelatz, Nobles, et autres de son Conseil, qe tiels maners des Servantz, si bien hommes come femmes fuissent tenuz de servir, resceivantz Salaries et Gages acustumes es lieus ou ils deveront servir,...

Et ja, par tant qe done est entendre a nostre dit Seignur le Roi en cest present Parlement par la Petition de la Commune, Qe les ditz Servantz, nient eaunt regard a la dite ordinance,...Dont il estoit prie par mesme la Commune de remedie. Par quei en mesme le Parlement, par assent des Prelatz, Countes, Barons, et autres Grauntz, et de la dite Commune illoeqes assemblez, pur refreindre la Malice des ditz Servantz sont ordeignez et establis les choses subscrites,...

Rot. Parl. ii, 233 (47).

(21) *A great council* 1353

Rotulus Ordinationum apud Westmonasterium in Magno Consilio ibidem summonito...

Au Lundy prochein apres la Feste de Seint Matheu l'Apostle,... si feust un Grant Conseil somons a Westmonstier...Au queu Vendredy, assemblez en la Chaumbre Blaunche nostre Seignur le Roi, Prelatz, Ducs, Countes, Barons, et les Communes, feust monstre par Monsire William de Shareshull, Chief Justice le Roi, la Cause de somons du dit Conseil,...nostre Seignur le Roi par assent des ascuns Prelatz et Grantz de meisme son Roialme, pur l'encres et relevement de son poeple, ad ordine qe l'Estaple des Leines, Peaux lanutz, Quirs, et Plom, soit tenue en son Roialme d'Engleterre, et en ses terres de Gales et d'Irland, en certeins lieux. Et de l'assent et avisement des ditz Prelatz et Grantz ad ordine pur la Maintenance et bon Governement de meisme l'Estaple ascuns pointz, queux il fist overtement lire devant les Prelatz, Grantz, et Communes, d'avoir lour assent. Et aussint qe s'ils veissent riens a adjouster ou d'amenuser, q'ils le deussent monstrer en escript. Et sur ceo les Communes demanderent

Copie des ditz pointz; quele Copie lour feust baillie; C'est
assavoir, une as Chivalers des Countees, et une autre as Citezeins
et Burgeis...

Rot. Parl. II, 246 (2).

(22) *Ordinance and statute* 1353

Item, Pur ceo qe plusours Articles tochantz l'Estat le Roi, et
commune Profit de son Roialme sont acordez et assentuz par lui,
les Prelatz, Grantz, et Communes de sa terre, a ce Conseil ore
tenu; Prie la dite Commune, qe les Articles susditz soient a preschein Parlement recitez, et entrez en Roule de mesme ce Parlement; a tiel entent, qe les Ordinances et Acortes faites en Conseils
ne soient de Recorde, come s'ils fuissent faitz par commune
Parlement.

Responsio. Quant al disme Article, il plest au Roi, Qe totes les
Ordinances faites de l'Estaple soient publiez et criez en chescun
Countee d'Engleterre, et en chescun lieu ou les Estaples sont,
aufyn q'ils soient fermement tenues: Et a preschein Parlement,
pur greindre fermete, eles serront rehercez et mys en Roule du
Parlement.

......
Et si prierent les dites Communes en cest Parlement, qe les
Ordinances de l'Estaple, et totes les autres Ordinances faites au
darrein Conseil tenuz a Westmonstier le Lundy preschein apres la
Feste de Seint Matheu l'Apostle darrein passez, queles ils avoient
veu ove bone deliberation et avisement, et queles lour semblerent
bones et profitables pur nostre Seignur le Roi et tut son poeple,
soient affermez en cest Parlement, et tenuz pur Estatut a durer
pur touz jours. A quele priere le Roi et touz les Grantz s'acordent
unement...

Rot. Parl. II, 253 (42); 257 (16).

(23) *The method of meeting; gradual separation* 1366

Et ceste chose faite, feust commande as Grantz et Communes q'ils
se departisont, et q'ils y feussent lendemain, c'est assaver les
Prelatz et Grantz en la Chambre Blanche, et les Communes en
la Chambre de Peinte. Au quele lendemain nostre Seignur le Roi,
les Prelatz, Ducs, Countes, Barons, en mesme la Chambre Blanche
esteantz, les Chivalers des Countees, Citeins et Burgeis demurantz
en la Chambre de Peinte, Feust monstre a eux par le Chanceller,

coment ils avoient entenduz les Causes du Sommons du Parlement
en general, mes la volunte le Roi fust qe les Causes feussent
monstrez a eux en especial. Lour disoit, Coment le Roi avoit
entendu qe le Pape, par force d'un fait quel il dit qe le Roi Johan
fesoit au Pape, de lui faire Homage pur le Roialme d'Engleterre
et la Terre d'Irlande, et qe par cause du dit Homage q'il lui
deveroit paier chescun an perpetuelment Mill' Marcs, est en
volunte de faire Proces devers le Roi et son Roialme pur le dit
Service et Cens recoverir. De qoi le Roi pria as ditz Prelatz,
Ducs, Countes, et Barons lour avys et bon conseil, et ce q'il en
ferroit en cas qe le Pape vorroit proceder devers lui ou son dit
Roialme par celle cause. Et les Prelatz requeroient au Roi q'ils se
purroient sur ce par eux soul aviser, et respondre lendemain.
Queux Prelatz le dit lendemain adeprimes par eux mesmes, et
puis les autres Ducs, Countes, Barons, et Grantz respondirent, et
disoient, Qe le dit Roi Johan ne nul autre purra mettre lui ne
son Roialme ne son Poeple en tiele subjection, saunz Assent et
accorde de eux. Et les Communes sur ce demandez et avisez,
respondirent en mesme la manere. Sur qoi feust ordeine et
assentu par commune Assent en manere q'ensuit:...

Rot. Parl. ii, 289 (7). (Cf. Church section, no. 13.)

(24) *No imposition upon wools without assent of parliament* 1371

Item est accorde et establi qe nul imposicion ou charge soit mys
sur les leines pealx lanuz ou quirs, autre qe la custume et subside
grantez au Roi nulle part saunz assent du parlement, et si nul
soit mys soit repelle et tenuz pur nul.

S.R. i, 393, 45 Ed. III, c. 4.

(25) *No lawyer or sheriff to sit in parliament* 1372

Les Petitions queles les Communes avoient mis en Parlement, et
les Respons sur eles donez, furont luez, et auxi une Ordenance
faite en mesme le Parlement, en manere q'ensuyt; Purce qe
Gentz de Ley qi pursuent diverses busoignes en les Courts le Roi
pur singulers persones ove queux ils sont, procurent et font mettre
plusours Petitions en Parlementz en noun des Communes, qe
rien lour touche mes soulement les singulers persones ove queux
ils sont demorez: Auxint Viscontz, qi sont communes Ministres
au Poeple, et deivent demurer sur lour office pur droit faire a
checuny, sont nomez et ont este devant ces heures et retournez en

Parlementz Chivalers des Countees par mesmes les Viscontz; est accorde et assentu en cest Parlement, Qe desormes null Homme de Ley pursuant busoignes en la Court le Roi, ne Viscont pur le temps q'il est Viscont, soient retournez ne acceptez Chivalers des Countees, ne qe ces qi sont Gentz de Ley et Viscontz ore retournez en Parlement eient gages. Mes voet le Roi, qe Chivalers et Serjantz des meulz vanes du paies soient retournez desore Chivalers en Parlementz, et q'ils soient esluz en plein Countee.

Rot. Parl. II, 310 (13). (Cf. Gray, *op. cit.* p. 344; and Richardson and Sayles in *Bulletin*, IX, no. 25, p. 12.)

(26) *Grant of tonnage and poundage* 1372

Et apres ce conge done as Chivalers des Countees a departir et de suer lour Briefs pur lour Despenses. Et issint departirent ils.

Mes comande feust as Citezeins et Burgois q'estoient venuz au dit Parlement, q'ils demurassent par ascuns causes: queux Citezeins et Burgois mesme le jour apres assemblez devant le Prince et autres Prelatz et Grantz en une Chambre pres la Blanche Chambre, feust monstre a eux, Coment l'an passe estoit grante par un certein terme pur le sauf et seure conduement des Niefs et Merchandises venantz en ceste terre par meer, et passant d'ycelle, un Subside, C'est assavoir, de chescun Tonell de Vyn venant en ceste terre deus soldz; et de chescun livre de qeconqe Merchandie qe ce feust venant ou passant vi d. quel terme est ja passe. Qe ils voloient avoir consideration as perils et meschiefs qi poent avenir a lour Niefs et Merchandises par les Enemys sur la meer, granter un autiel Subside, a durer par un an, pur les causes suisdites. Quel Subside ils granteront au Roi a prendre et lever en manere come estoit pris et leve l'an darein passe. Et issint departiront.

Rot. Parl. II, 310 (14), (15).

(27) *Deliberation of lords and commons* 1373

Au quel jour, vindront ascons des Communes en noun de touz en mesme la Chambre Blanche, et prierent as Seignurs illeoqes esteantz, q'ils purroient avoir ascons Evesqes, Contes, et Barons, ove queux ils purroient treter, parler, et debatre pur le meulz faire issue et exploit sur la matire qe lour estoit enjoynt: et demanderont les Evesqes de Londres, de Wyncestre, et de Baa et Welles; et les Counts d'Arundell, March, et Salesbirs; Monsire

Guy Brian, et Monsire Henry le Scrop; queux estoit accorde d'aler
a les Communes et treter ovesqes eux sur les dites pointz et
causes en la Chambre le Chamberlein. Et issint en deliberation
entre les ditz Grantz et Communes sur les causes avant nomez tan
qe Mardy en la Veille de Seint Andreu.

Rot. Parl. ii, 316 (5).

(28) *Grant of tonnage and poundage with conditions* 1373

La Fourme et Manere du Grant fait au Roi en cest Parlement.
Les Seignurs et Communes d'Engleterre ont grante a nostre
Seignur le Roi a cest present Parlement la Quinszime en aunciene
manere, leve par deux anz proscheins a vener, en manere q'en-
sust; a paier as Festes de la Purification et Pentecost prochein a
veners, par owels portions, le primer an. Et le second an, a paier
as mesmes les Festes, en cas qe les Guerres du Roi et de sa Corone
dure si longement. Et ensement graunte est de chescune livre de
Merchandises passantz la meer hors du Roialme sys deniers, hors
pris Leins, Pealx lanutz, Quires, et Vyn; et des Merchandises
venantz par dela la Meer sys deniers del livre, en manere susdite.
Et deux souldz de chescun Tonel de Vyn a prendre mesmes les
deux anz; C'est assavoir, le primer an sanz condition, Et le
second an sur la condition susdite, si la Guerre dure. Et auxint
graunte est les Subsidies des Leins, a prendre en l'an prochein
venant apres la Fest de Seint Michell prochein a venir, sanz
condition. Et le second an apres sur la condition susdite,
sanz ascune autre charge ou imposition sur le Poeple d'Engleterre
durantz les deux anz avant ditz. Et si les Guerres cessont en le
second an, touz les Grauntz et Charges avant nomez soient
annullez...Et qe nulles Chivalers des Countees, ne Esquiers,
Citezeins, ne Burgeys, queux sont retournez pur cest present
Parlement, ne soient Coillours de ceste Charge durantz les anz
avant ditz.

Rot. Parl. ii, 317 (12).

(29) *The "Good Parliament"* 1376

2. A quel lendemain s'assemblerent les Prelatz, Duc, Conts,
Barons, et les autres Grantz et Communes, Justices, Sergeantz de
Ley, et autres en la Chambre de Peintee; et illoeqes devant le Roy
meismes, et touz les autres, Monsire Johan Knyvet, Chivaler,
Chanceller d'Engleterre, par commandement du Roy fist pro-

nunciation des Causes de la Sommonce de ce present Parlement:...

3. Et partant lour priast meisme le Chanceller de par le Roi, q'ils se ent aviserent diligeaument. C'est assavoir, les Prelatz et Seignurs par eux meismes, et les Communes par eux meismes, et ent durroient lour bone Responce a pluis tost q'ils purroient bonement, pur pluis hastive esploit de Parlement. Et sur ce y feurent assignez certains Prelatz et Seignurs d'estre Triours, et certains Clercs d'estre Resceivours, de Billes de Parlement, desqueux les Nouns ensuent, et y feurent luez devaunt le Roi mesmes par la forme qi s'ensuit:

8. Item puis apres les ditz Prelatz, Seignurs et Communes assemblez en Parlement, fust dit a les ditz Communes de par le Roy, q'ils se retraiassent par soi a lour aunciene Place en la Maison du Chapitre de l'Abbe de Westmonstier, et y tretassent et conseillassent entre eux meismes,...et les Prelatz et Seignurs y ferroient semblable tretee de lour part:...Et issint se departirent les Communes a lour dit place...

Attempt to control the executive

10. Item, les Communes considerantz les Meschiefs de la terre, monstrent au Roi et as Seignurs du Parlement, qe serroit honur al Roy, et profit a toute la terre...Par quoi ils prient, qe le Conseil nostre Seignur le Roy soit enforcez de Seignurs de la terre, Prelatz, et autres, a demurrer continuelment tan qe al nombre de dys ou xii selonc la volunte du Roi; par manere tielle, qe nulle groos Bosoigne y passe ou soit delivers sanz l'assent et advis de touz: et autres meyndres Bosoignes par l'advis et assent de sys ou quatre au meyns, selonc ce qe le cas requert. Issint au meins, qe six ou quatre des tielx Conseillers soient continuelment residentz du Conseil le Roi. Et nostre Seignur le Roy entendant la dite requeste estre honurables et bien profitables a luy et a tout son Roialme, l'ad ottroie. Purveuz toutes voies, qe Chanceller, Tresorer, et Gardein de Prive Seal, et touz autres Officers du Roi, purront faire...les busoigncs qi touchent lour offices, sanz la presence des ditz Conseilles,...Et est ordenez...qe meismes les Conseillers q'ore sont assignez,...soient sermentz de garder ceste Ordenance, et de faire droit a chescuny selonc lour poairs...

Finance

15. Et puis apres les ditz Communes vindrent en Parlement, y faisantz protestation overtement, q'ils furent de auxi bone volente

et ferme purpos d'aider a lour noble Seignur lige ove Corps et Biens, et quan qe q'ils aveient, come unqes y furent nulles autres en aucun temps passe, et toutdys serroient a tout lour poair. Mais ils y distrent, qe leur semblait pur chose veritable, qe si lour dit Seignur lige eust euz toutdys entour luy des loialx Conseillers, et bons Officers, meisme nostre Seignur le Roy eust este bien rychez de Tresor, et partant n'eust mye grantment bosoigne de charger sa Commune par voie de Subside, ou de talliage, n'autrement; aiant consideration as grandes sommes d'or q'ont este apportez deinz le Roialme des Ranceons des Roys de France et d'Escoce, et d'autres Prisoners et pays, q'amonte a une tresgrande somme...

16. Et puis apres, meismes les Communes se firent pleindre en Parlement par especial des persones desouz-escritz, affermantz plusours desceites et autres malx estre faitz al Roy et a son Roialme par la manere qi s'ensuit:

Impeachments

17. Primerement, Richard Lyons, Marchant de Londres, estoit empeschez et accusez par les dites Communes de plusours disceites, extorsions, et autres malx faitz par luy au Roy nostre Seignur, et a son Poeple, si bien du temps q'il ad este repeirant a la maison et al Conseil du Roy, come autrement du temps q'il estoit Fermer des Subsides et Custumes le Roi...

20. Item, William Sire de Latymer estoit empeschez et accusez par clamour des ditz Communes, de diverses disceites, extorsions, grevances, et autres malx faitz par luy et autres des soens et de sa covyne, du temps q'il ad demurrez devers le Roy nostre Seignur, si bien en Bretaigne quant il y estoit en office ovesqe le Roi, come autrement en Engleterre, du temps q'il ad este Chamberleyn et du Prive Conseil meisme nostre Seignur le Roi.

29. Et sur ce le dit Seignur de Latymer trovast en Parlement certains Prelatz, Seignurs, et autres, ses mainpernours durant le Parlement, de avoir son Corps devant le Roy et les Seignurs a respondre pluis avant a les articles dont il estoit issint arettez, souz certaine paine et forme comprises en une cedule annexe a ycestes. Et par celle mainprise le Mareschal d'Engleterre luy lessast aler a large &c.

31. Item, William Elys de Grant Jernemuth est empeschez et accusez en ceste presente Parlement, en diverses maneres...

34. Item, Johan Seignur de Nevill estoit semblablement empeschez, de ce qe tant come il estoit Officer nostre Seignur le Roy et de son Prive Conseil, il avoit achatez diverses Tailles

d'assignementz faitz par nostre Seignur le Roy a diverses gentz de son Roialme, as queux il estoit Dettour, et ent avoit le dit Seignur entier paiement et due allouance en l'Escheqer, les parties de rienz ou poy ent serviz;...

A Quoy le dit Seignur de Nevill, present en Parlement, respoignant y dist, qe voirs estoit qe la Dame de Ravensholm luy devoit nadgaires une certaine somme de deniers,...Et sur ce les Communes prierent juggement envers le dit Seignur de Nevill, et q'il fust oustez de tout Office entour le Roy...

45. Item, fust fait en ce present Parlement une certaine Ordenance des Femmes pursuantz busoignes es Courtz nostre Seignur le Roi, en la forme qi s'ensuit: Por ce qe pleinte est faite au Roy, qe aucuns Femmes ont pursuys en les Courtz du Roi diverses Busoignes et Quereles par voie de maintenance, et pur lower et part avoir; quele chose desplest au Roi, et le Roi defende qe desormes nulle Femme le face, et par especial Alice Perers, sur peine de quan qe la dite Alice purra forfaire, et d'estre bannitz hors du Roialme.

47. Item, Adam de Bury, Citezein de Londres, estoit empeschez par le clamour des Communes en ce Parlement, de plusours desceites et autres malx faitz au Roy et a son Poeple, du temps q'il ad este Mair de Caleys, et Capitain de Balyngeham, et autrement, come pluis au plain appiert en une grant Bille baille en Parlement de darrain jour de cest Parlement a Eltham. Et sur ce le dit Adam estoit envoiez pur venir a respondre en Parlement, et ne vint mye, ne ne poait mye estre trovez: par ont y estoit agardez, qe touz ses Biens et Chateux fuissent mys en arest. Et issint fust fait par Briefs envoiez a les Viscontz de Londres et de Kent; et la dite Bille est en le filace, avec especiales Petitions de Parlement.

Recognition of Richard's title

50. Item, les dites Communes prierent humblement a nostre Seignur le Roy en dit Parlement, qe pleust a lour dit Seignur le Roi en grande Confort de tout le Roialme faire venir avant en Parlement luy nobles Enfantz Richard de Burdeux, filz et heir Monsire Edward nadgairs eisnez Filz du dit nostre Seignur le Roi et Prince de Gales, qi Dieux assoille, issint qe les Seignurs et Communes du Roialme y purreient veer et honurer le dit Richard come verrai Heir apparant du Roialme. Quelle requeste fust ottroiez, et issint y vynt le dit Richard devant touz les Prelatz, Seignurs, et Communes en Parlement le Mesquardy lendeman Saint Johan,...

Petitions of the commons

Cy apres s'ensuont les Petitions baillees avant en escrit au Parlement par les Communes, avec les Responces faites a ycelles Petitions en mesme le Parlement.

e.g. No. i. De les Grant Chartre et Chartre de la Forest.
No. ii. Empanellement des Jurrours.
No. viii. De la Franchise des Citees et Burghs.
No. xviii. De Hundredz lessez a ferme par Seignurs.
No. xxiii. Qe Viscontz ne soient a terme de vie.
No. xli. De Seneschal et Mareschal de l'Hostel le Roi.
No. xliv. Bille encontre le Pape et les Cardynaux.
No. li. Bille encontre le Pape.
No. lvii. Bille des Laboriers.

Request for annual parliaments and free elections

186. Item, prie la Commune, qe pleise establier par Estatut en cest present Parlement, qe chescun an soit tenuz un Parlement, de faire corrections en Roialme des Erroures et Fauxtees, si nuls y soient trovez. Et qe les Chivalers des Countees pur celles Parlementz soient esluz par commune Election de les meillours Gentz des ditz Countees: Et nemye certifiez par le Viscont soul saunz due election, sur certeine peyne. Et en mesme le manere soient les Viscontz des Countees du Roialme d'an en an esluz, et nemye faitz par brocage en la Courte du Roi come ils soleient faire, pur leur singuler profit, et par procurement des Meyntenours du pays, pur sustener leur fausetees et malices, et leur fauxes quereles, come ils ont fait communement avant ces hures, en destruction du poeple.
Responsio. Endroit du Parlement chescun an, il y a ent Estatutz et Ordenances faitz, lesqueux soient duement gardez et tenuz.

Et quant as Viscontes, il y a une Bille responduz. Et quant a l'article de l'Election des Chivalers qi vendront a Parlement, le Roi voet q'ils soient esluz par commune assent de tout le Contee.

Et sur ce mesmes les Communes y baillerent avant en Parlement une grande Rolle, ou une grande Cedule, et une autre Bille annexez a mesme le Rolle, contenantes entour xli articles. Mais une article y estoit cancellez et denygrez par manere come ce est: Ore empriantz humblement au Roi lour Seignur lige, et as continuels Conseillers ordenez entour le Roy, qe de toutz celles articles comprises en ditz Roulle, Cedule et Bille, queux sont en filace avec autres Billes de cest Parlement, fust bone execution et due justice fait pur profit du Roi nostre Seignur, et de tout le Roialme d'Engleterre. Et sur ce apres y fust dit par le Chanceller d'Engleterre de par le Roi, as Chivalers des ditz Contees, et Citezeins, et Burgeoys, illeoqes presentz, Q'ils feissent pursuyte pur les Briefs pur lour Gages de Parlement, par manere accustumez. Et tantost apres se leverent les Prelatz et Seignurs, et pristrent lour congie del Roi nostre Seignur dessus dit: et issint se departist ce present Parlement al dit lieu de Eltham, mesme le Parlement continuez devant de jour en autre puis le comencement d'ycelle tan qe a ce present Joefdy, qi fust le sisme jour de Juyl, l'an present, mesme cest Parlement durant en tout x sesmaynes et pluis...

Rot. Parl. II, 321–60.

(30) *Grant of a poll tax and demand for treasurers for the tax* 1377

Les nobles Seignurs et Communes assembles en cest Parlement... ont grantez a nostre dit Seignur le Roy, en maintenance de ses dites Guerres, Quatre Deniers, a prendre des Biens de chescune persone de meisme le Roialme, si bien Masles come Femmeles, outre l'age de xiiii ans. Exceptes tant soulement verrois Mendinantz sanz fraude. Em priantz moelt humblement a lour dit Seignur lige, qe luy pleust lour avoir pur excusez de ce q'ils ne luy poaient ore granter greignour Subside:...

Et auxint y prierent les dites Communes, qe pleust a nostre Seignur le Roy de nomer deux Contes, et deux Barons, de tieux qe luy mieltz sembleroit, qe serroient Gardeins et Tresoriers si bien de ceste Subside ore grante, et del Subside qe le Clergie d'Engleterre q'est encores a granter al Roy nostre Seignur, come del Subside des Leyns, Quirs, et Pealx lanutz grantez en derrain Parlement: Et qe ceux quatre Countes et Barons y feussent jurrez en lour presence, qe quan qe fust par eux resceuz des ditz Subsides serroit entierment expenduz sur mesmes les Guerres, et en nul autre oeps; Et qe le Haut Tresorier d'Engleterre n'ent prenoit rienz, ne ne se medleroit en aucune manere.

Rot. Parl. II, 364 (19, 20).

(31) *First mention of a speaker of the commons by name* 1377

Fait a remembrer, qe le dit derrain jour de ce Parlement, apres ce qe les dites Communes Petitions y furont luez avec lour Responces faites, come desus est dit, Monsire Thomas de Hungerford, Chivaler, qi avoit les paroles pur les Communes d'Engleterre en cest Parlement, y dist devant les Prelatz, Seignurs et Communes, les paroles qi s'ensuent:...

Rot. Parl. ii, 374 (87).

(32) *Attempts to control the executive*[1] 1377

Et puis apres les Communes y vindrent en Parlement devant le Roi, et illoeqes Monsire Peres de la Mare, Chivaler, q'avoit les paroles de par la Commune, faisant sa Protestation, qe ce q'il y avoit a dire nel' dirroit del soen propre moevement, einz del mocion, assent, et voluntee expres de toute la Commune illoeqes esteante...

Et pur ce qe nostre Seignur le Roi, qi Dieu salve, si est a present innocent et de tendre age, la dite Commune, pur amendement des Meschiefs avaunt ditz et autres, et pur salvation du Roialme qi maintenant est en grant peril, et pluis qe unqes n'estoit devant, priont au Roi nostre Seignur et as Seignurs du Parlement des trois choses en especial:

Primerement, qe lour pleust ordeiner et lour nomer ore en ce present Parlement oept suffisantz persones de diverses estatz, d'estre continuelment residentz du Conseil sur les busoignes du Roy et del Roialme avec les Officers du Roi, des tieux persones qi mieltz scievent et pluis diligeaument vorront et purront travailler sur l'amendement des Meschiefs avant ditz, et le bone Governement et Salvation del dit Roialme; issint qe la Commune purra estre clerement acertee des nouns d'yceux Conseillers, qi serroient Expendours et Ordeinours de ce q'ils verront granter pur les Guerres, et partant avoir la greindre corage de faire a nostre Seignur le Roy ce q'ils ont de luy en charge, come dessus est dit.

Rot. Parl. iii, 5 (15), (17), (18).

(33) *Attempts to control finance* 1377

Item, les Seignurs et Communes du Roialme d'Engleterre apperceivantz clerement le grant Peril du Roialme, q'est en point d'estre perduz, si Dieu n'y mette remede le pluis en haste, par my les grandes Guerres...Et partant en aide de les Despenses qe l'en faut mettre entour la governance de la Guerre du Roialme, en resistence de tantz des Enemys, et en socour et rescous del Roialme avant dit, a l'aide nostre Seignur ils grantent ore de lour

---

[1] On the whole question of the control of parliament over the executive see the section on the Council.

liberale volentee a mesme nostre Seignur le Roi deux Quinszimes
par dehors Citees et Burghs, et deux Dismes deinz mesmes les
Citees et Burghs a lever de lour Biens, si bien c'est assavoir des
Seignurs des Villes come des Religious, pur leurs Biens provenantz de lours Terres et Tenementz purchacez ou appropriez
puis l'an vintisme le Roi E. filz le Roi Henry, et d'autres seculers
gentz quelconqes, nully esperniant en celle partie, par entre cy et
la Chandeleure proschein venant, par autielles sommes de deniers
et nemye greignours ne meindres come ont este acustumez estre
levez des Villes parmy le Roialme quant tielles Dismes et Quins-
zismes ont este grantez, a une foitz ou a diverses foitz pur deux
ans. Em priantz humblement a lour Seignur lige, et les autres
Seignurs du Parlement, qe si bien de ceux Deniers, come des
Deniers de les Dismes ore a granters par la Clergie d'Engleterre,
et auxint de les Deniers provenantes de les Subsides de Leynes,
feussent certains persones suffisantz assignez de par le Roi d'estre
Tresoriers ou Gardeins, au tiel effect qe celles Deniers feussent
tout entierment appliez a les Despenses de la Guerre, et nemye
autre part par aucune voie. Et fait a remembrer, qe celle Requeste
lour estoit ottroiez par le Roi, salvant au Roi entierment la sue
anciene Custume de demi marc des Denszeins, et dis soldz des
Foreins, due de chescun saak de Leyne a passer hors du Roialme
etc. Et sur ce nostre Seignur le Roi fist assigner William Walworth,
et Johan Philypot, Marchantz de Londres, d'estre Gardeins des
dites sommes, a l'oeps avant dit, et de faire loial accompte de lours
Resceites et Issues par manere come serroit ordene par nostre
Seignur le Roy et son dit Grant Conseil en resonable manere. Et
sur ce, par comandement nostre dit Seignur le Roi, les ditz William,
et Johan, pristrent lour charge, et a ce faire loialment furent ils
sermentez et jurrez devant le Roy mesmes en plein Parlement.
Sauvez toutes foitz au Roi, q'il soit repaiez primerement de la
somme par luy chevee et paiee a ceste darreine viage sur la Meer,
q'amonte pluis qe a xv mill' Livrs d'esterlings, dont le Roi est
encores Dettour as Creditours.

Rot. Parl. iii, 7 (27).

(34) *Petition for annual parliaments* 1377

Item, pur ce qe mayntz gentz sont delaiez en la Court du Roi
de lour Demandes, partaunt qe ascun foitz la partie allegge qe les
Demaundantz ne doyvent estre responduz sanz le Roi, et ascun
foitz la partie Pleintif allegge en mesme la manere, et auxint

moult des gentz grevez par les Ministres du Roi, encountre
droiture: desqueux grevances homme ne purra avoir recoverir
sanz commune Parlement; Qe plese a nostre dit Seignur de tenir
Parlement un foitz par an au meynz, et ceo en lieu covenable:
Et q'en mesmes les Parlementz soient les Plees qi sont en la dite
forme delaiez, et les Plees la ou les Justices sont en diverses
opinions recordez et terminez: Et q'en mesme la manere purrent
les Billes estre terminez qe serront liverez en Parlement si avaunt
come raison et Ley demaunde.

Responsio. Quant a ceo qe Parlement serroit tenuz chescun an,
soient les Estatutz ent faitz tenuz et gardez; mais quant al lieu
ou le Parlement se tendra, le Roi ent ferra sa volentee. Et quant
as Plees desquelles les Justices serroient en diverses opinions,
il y a Estatutz ent faitz, queux le Roi voet qe soient gardez et
fermement tenuz.

Rot. Parl. III, 23 (95).

(35) *The speaker of the commons* 1378

Et puis apres les Communes y revindrent devant le Roi, les Prelatz et Seignurs en Parlement, et illoeqes Monsire James de
Pekeryng, Chivaler, q'avoit les paroles de par la Commune,
faisant sa Protestation si bien pur lui mesmes come pur toute la
Commune d'Engleterre illoeqes assemble: Et primerement pur
la dite Commune, qe si par cas il y deist chose qi purroit soner en
prejudice,...de nostre Seignur le Roi ou de sa Coroune, ou en
amenusement de l'honour et l'estat des grantz Seignurs du
Roialme, qe ce ne feust acceptez par le Roi et les Seignurs, einz
tenuz pur nul, et come rienz n'ent eust este dit: desicome la
Commune n'est en autre volentee, mais souvrainement desirent
l'oneur et l'estat de nostre Seignur le Roi...
Et pur sa propre persone demesne, faisant sa Protestation, qe si
pur meins bone discretion, ou en autre manere, il y deist chose qi
ne fust del commune assent de ses compaignons, ou par cas
forvoiast de rienz en ses paroles, q'il feust par eulx susportez et
amendez, ore devant lour departir, ou en apres quant lour pleust.

Rot. Parl. III, 34 (16).

(36) *Control of taxation; accounts to be submitted to parliament* 1379

Et pur estre pleinement appris de la veritee des ditz necessaires
Despenses faitz et a faire, les Tresoriers de la dice Guerre serront
prestz et apparaillez, a quelle heure qe vous plest, de vous

monstrer clerement en escrit lours Resceites et Despenses faitz puis le dit darrein Parlement, et les sommes dues, avec les autres necessaires Despenses dessus ditz a mettre si bien sur la March' de Caleys, come a Chirburgh', Brest, la March' d'Escoce, Irlande, et aillours...

Rot. Parl. III, 56 (7).

Ces sont les Nouns des Prelatz et Seignurs assignez pur examiner l'estat du Roi, a la requeste des Communes; c'est assavoir, L'Ercevesqe de Canterbirs, l'Evesqe de Londres, l'Evesqe de Roucestre, le Conte de la Marche, le Conte de Warrwyk, le Conte de Stafford, le Sire de Latymer, Monsire Guy de Brien, ou Monsire Johan de Cobham, et Monsire Roger de Beauchamp. Primerement d'examiner les Revenues provenantz del Subside des Leynes rescuz puis la Feste de Seint Michel darrein, et qe vraisemblablement ent sont a resceivre, tan qe al Feste de Seint Michel proschein. Item, de veoir si bien touz les Revenues du Roialme resceuz depuis le dit temps, come les Revenues des Priours Aliens, et de l'auncien maltolt des Leynes, des voidances des Evesqes, Abbeis, et des autres profitz quelconqes, et queux vraisemblablement ent purront estre resceuz et levez, tan qe al dit Feste de Seint Michel, si bien par les mains des Tresorers de la Guerre come en le Resceite, et del Hanaper de la Chauncellerie, et es autres places nostre Seignur le Roi qeconqes...

Rot. Parl. III, 57 (12).

(37) *A poll tax* 1380

En primes, les Seignurs et Communes si sont assentuz, qe y serra donez pur les Necessitees suis dites, de chescune Laie persone du Roialme deinz Franchise et dehors, si bien des madles come des females, de quiel estat ou condicion q'ils soient, qi sont passez l'age de xv ans, Trois Grotes, forspris les verrois Mendinantz qi ne serront de riens chargez. Sauvant toutes foitz, qe la levee se face en ordeinance et en forme, qe chescune Laye persone soit chargez owelment selonc son afferant, et en manere q'ensuyt: C'est assavoir, qe a la Somme totale acomptez en chescune Ville les suffisantz selonc lour afferant eident les meindres; Issint qe les pluis suffisantz ne paient oultre la somme de LX Grotes pur lui et pur sa femme, et nule persone meins q'un Grot pur lui et pur sa femme: Et qe nule persone soit chargez de paier forsqe par la ou la demoere de lui et de sa femme et ses enfantz en sont ou en lieu ou il demoert en service. Et qe touz Artificers, Laborers, Servantz, et autres Laies, si bien des Servantz demurrantz ove Prelatz et Seignurs Temporelx qeconqes, Abbees, Priours Collegieles, Clercz de la Chancellerie, et en le Commune Bank, Bank le Roi, Escheqier, Receite, et ove touz autres Officers, Chivalers, Esquiers, Marchantz, Citeins, Burgeis, et ove toutes autres persones, qe chescun de eux soit assis et taillez selonc l'afferant de son estat, et en la fourme suis dite...

Rot. Parl. III, 90 (15).

(38) *Grant of taxation with conditions* 1383

Les Communes d'Engleterre assemblez en ce present Parlement, ovesqe l'assent des Seignurs pur diverses perils considerez avenir a la Roialme...grauntent a nostre Seignur le Roi, en defense du Roialme, et pur eschuir les perils semblables avenir des toutz partz tant par Terre come par Mier, sur condicions q'ensuent, la Moitee d'un Quinzisme q'est acustumez entre les laies d'estre levez quant un tiel Grant est grantez, pur estre paiez et mys en execution la ou pluis y bosoigne, et selonc qe le temps demande,... purveuz qe toutz les Deniers qi purront sourdre du dit Subside soient duement levez, et loialment controllez sanz estre lessez a ferme, mes entierment liverez a les Admiralx ore nomez,...Protestant outre, qe l'un Moitee ne l'autre n'est nostre entent a graunter sanz les conditions ensuantz: Primerement, qe l'estat de Clergie emportent et grauntent a leur afferant si bien pur la salvacion de eux come de nous, as mesmes les jours et termes come devant est dit. Auxint, qe toutz maners des gentz Layes d'estat d'avoir, de quielconqe degree qe ceo soit, en soient contributoires ovesqe les povres sanz nully espernir...

Rot. Parl. III, 151 (13).

(39) *The "Merciless Parliament"; declaration* *on the laws of parliament* 1388

A quel temps les Justices et Sergeantz, et autres Sages du Ley de Roialme, et auxint les Sages de la Ley Civill, feuront chargez de par le Roi nostre dit Seignur de doner loial conseill as Seignurs du Parlement de duement proceder en la cause de l'Appell sus dit. Lesqueux Justices,...pristront ent deliberation, et responderont as ditz Seignurs du Parlement, Q'ils avoient veue et bien entendu le tenour du dit Appell, et disoient qe mesme l'Appell ne feust pas fait ne afferme solonc l'ordre qe l'une Ley ou l'autre requiert. Sur quoy les ditz Seignurs du Parlement pristront ent deliberation et avisement, et par assent du Roi...et de lour commune acorde estoit declare, Qe en si haute Crime come est pretendu en cest Appell, qi touche la persone du Roi...et l'estat de tout son Roialme, perpetre par persones qi sont Peeres du Roialme, ovesqe autres, la Cause ne serra aillours deduc q'en Parlement, ne par autre Ley qe Ley et Cours du Parlement, Et q'il appartient as Seignurs du Parlement et a lour Fraunchise et Libertee d'aun-cien Custume du Parlement, d'estre Juges en tieux cas, et de tieux cas ajugger par assent du Roi. Et qe ensi serra fait en cest cas par agarde du Parlement, pur ce qe le Roialme d'Engleterre n'estoit devant ces heures, ne a l'entent du Roi nostre dit Seignur et Seignurs du Parlement unqes ne serra, reule ne governe par la Ley Civill: Et auxint lour entent n'est pas de reuler ou governer si haute Cause come cest Appell est, qi ne serra aillours trie ne termine q'en Parlement, come dit est, par cours, processe, et ordre use en ascune Court ou Place plus bas deinz mesme le Roialme; queux Courtes et Places ne sont qe Executours d'aun-ciens Leys et Custumes du Roialme et Ordinances et Establise-mentz de Parlement. Et feust avis au mesmes les Seignurs du Parlement, par assent du Roi...qe cest Appell feust fait et afferme bien et assetz deuement, et le processe d'ycell bone et effectuel solonc les Leys et Cours du Parlement, et pur tiel l'agar-deront et ajuggeront.

Rot. Parl. III, 236. (Cf. Crown section, p. 5.)

(40) *Impeachments* 1388

Item, le Lundy, le seconde jour du Moys de Marcz prochein ensuant, Sire Robert Bealknap nadgairs Chief Justice de Com-mune Bank, Sire Roger Fulthorp, Sire John Holt, et Sire William Burgh, nadgairs ses compaignons Justices de mesme le Bank, Sire John Cary nadgairs Chief Baron de l'Escheker, et John Lokton nadgairs Sergeant le Roi a la Ley, feuront amesnez en mesme le Parlement al request del Commune du dit Parlement, et la par touz les Communes illeoqes assemblez pur touz les Countees, Citees, et Burghs d'Engleterre, feuront accusez et empeschez, de ceo qe la ou les ditz Appellez, convictz de Treson, et ajuggez come devant est dit, par lour Roial poair q'ils avoient a eux acroche...

Rot. Parl. III, 238.

(41) *Privilege of peers* 1388

En ycest Parlement, toutz les Seignurs si bien Espiritels come Temporels alors presentz clamerent come lour Libertee et Franchise, qe les grosses matires moevez en cest Parlement, et a movers en autres Parlementz en temps a venir, tochantz Pieres de la Terre, serroient demesnez, ajuggez, et discus par le cours de Parlement, et nemye par la Loy Civile, ne par la Commune Ley de la Terre, usez en autres plus bas Courtes du Roialme: quell claym, liberte, et franchise le Roy lour benignement alloua et ottroia en plein Parlement.

Rot. Parl. III, 244 (7).

(42) *A committee to represent parliament* 1398

Item, mesme le Joefdy, les Communes prierent au Roy, qe come ils aient devers eux diverses Petitions, si bien pur especials persones come autres, nient luez ne responduz, et auxi pleuseurs autres matiers et choses aient estee moevez en presence du Roy, lesqueux pur briefte du temps ne purront bonement estre terminez a present; Qe plerroit au Roy commettre plein poair as certeines Seignurs, et autres persones queux luy plerra, d'examiner, respondre, et terminer les ditz Petitions, et les matiers et choses suis ditz, et toutes les dependences d'icelles. A quel prier le Roy s'assenti. Et sur ceo, par auctorite et assent du Parlement, ad ordine et assigne Johan Duc de Lancastre, Esmon Duc d'Everwyk, Edward Duc d'Aumarle, Thomas Duc de Surrey, Johan Duc d'Excestre, Johan Marquys de Dorset, Roger Cont del Marche, Johan Cont de Sarum, Henri Cont de Northumbreland, Thomas Cont de Gloucestre, Thomas Cont de Wircestre, et Thomas Cont de Wilts', ou sys de eux; Johan Bussy, Henri Grene, Johan Russell, Richard Chelmeswyk, Robert Teye, et Johan Golafre, Chivalers venantz pur le Parlement ou trois de eux, de examiner, respondre, et pleinement terminer, si bien toutz les ditz Petitions, et les matiers comprisez en ycelles, come toutes autres matiers et choses moevez en presence du Roy, et toutes les dependences d'icelles nient determinez, solonc ceo qe meulx lour semblera par lour bon advys et discretion en celle partie, par auctorite du Parlement suis dit.

Grants to the king for life

Item, mesme le jour, les Communes du Roialme, par assent des Seignurs Espirituels et Temporels, granterent au Roy la Subside des Leyns, Quirs, et Peaux lanutz a terme de sa vie, et une Quinszisme, et Disme, et une dimy-Quinszisme et dimy-Disme, en la manere et forme ensuantz:

Rot. Parl. III, 368 (74, 75).

(43) *Reversal of judgment on Haxey* 1399

Item, come al Parlement tenuz a Westmonstier le jour de Seint Vyncent, l'an le Roy Richard vyntisme, pur honour et profit du dit Roy et de tout le Roialme, Thomas Haxey, Clerc, bailla une Bille as Communes du dit Parlement; pur quele Bille, de volunte du dit Roy, le dit Thomas estoit adjuges Traitour, et forfaita tout ceo q'il avoit, encontre droit et la course quel avoit este use devant en Parlement, en anientisment des Custumes de lez Communes. Qe plese a nostre tres gracious Seignur le Roy en cest present Parlement ycell Jugement casser, et adnuller, come erronous; et restituer mesme celui Thomas entierment a ses degree, estate, biens, et chateux, fermes, annuites, pensions, terres, tenementz, rentz, office, advowesons, et possessions quielconqes, ove leurs appurtenantz, et q'il purra entrer en les avant ditz fermes,...et possessions, et eux tenir come il les tenoit le jour del fesance du dit Bille:...

Responsio. Le Roy voet, de l'advis et assent des toutz le Seignurs Espirituelx et Temporelx, qe le Juggement rendu vers Thomas Haxey, Clerc, en Parlement tenuz a Westmonstier l'an xxme luy nadgairs Roy Richard, soit de tout cassez,...et tenuz de nul force n'effect; et qe le dit Thomas soit restitut a ses Noun et Fame, et fait et tenuz persone hable en manere come il feust devant le dit Juggement ensi rendu: Come en le Record ent fait et enrollez par devant en cest Rolle de Parlement y piert plus au pleyn.

Rot. Parl. III, 434 (104). (Cf. J. E. Neale, in *Tudor Studies*, p. 259, and Tout, *Chapters*, IV, 17 ff.)

(44) *Demand for redress of grievances before supply* 1401

Item, mesme la Samady, les ditz Communes monstrerent a nostre dit Seignur le Roy, qe come es pluseurs Parlementz devant ces heures leur communes Petitions n'ont estee responduz devant q'ils avoient fait leur Grante d'ascun aide ou Subside a nostre Seignur le Roy; Et sur ceo prierent a mesme nostre Seignur le Roi, qe pur grande ease et confort des ditz Communes y pleust a nostre Seignur le Roy de grantir as mesmes les Communes, q'ils puissent avoir conisance des Responses de leur dites Petitions devant ascune tiele Grante ensy a faire. A quoy leur feust responduz, Qe de ceste matire le Roy vorroit communer ovesqe les Seignurs du Parlement, et sur ceo faire ceo qe meulx luy verroit a faire par advys des ditz Seignurs. Et puis apres, c'est assavoir le darrein jour de Parlement, leur feust responduz Qe celle manere de fait n'ad este veue ne use en nul temps de ses progenitours ou predecessours, q'ils aueroient ascun Respons de leur Petitions, ou conisance d'icelle, devant q'ils avoient monstrez et faitz toutz leur autres bosoignes du Parlement, soit il d'ascune Grante a faire, ou autrement. Et partant le Roy ne vorroit ascunement chaunger les bones Custumes et Usages faitz et usez d'auncien temps.

Rot. Parl. III, 458 (23).

(45) *Appropriation of supplies* 1404

Item, Samady le primere jour de Marce, en presence du Roy et des Seignurs en Parlement, l'Ercevesqe de Canterbirs, par commandement du Roy, monstra as ditz Seignurs l'entention mesme nostre Seignur le Roy touchant sa Governance...Et feust outre la volentee mesme nostre Seignur le Roy, qe de le Grante a faire par les Seignurs et Communes ore en cest present Parlement pur les Guerres, et pur la Defense du Roialme, q'y serroient ordeignez par advys des ditz Seignurs et Communes certeins Tresorers de mesme le Grant, aufyn qe la Monoie ent provenant serroit mys sur les Guerres, et en null autre oeps...Et puis apres, par commandement du Roy, et par advys des ditz Seignurs, mesmes les matires feurent monstrez et declarrez par le dit Ercevesqe as ditz Communes en lour Maison d'assemble pur le Parlement deinz l'Abbee de Westmonstier, et ils s'agreroient bien d'icelles, come le dit Ercevesqe ent fist report de par les ditz Communes a mesme nostre Seignur le Roy et a les Seignurs avant ditz.

Rot. Parl. III, 528 (33).

(46) *Attempt to control elections. Thomas Thorpe's case* 1404

Item, por ce qe le Brief de Somons de Parlement retourne par le Viscont de Roteland ne feust pas sufficientement ne duement retournee, come les ditz Communes avoient entenduz, mesmes les Communes prierent a nostre Seignur le Roy et as Seignurs en Parlement, qe celle matire purra estre duement examinee en Parlement: Et q'en cas qe defaut y serra trovez en celle matire qe tiel punissement ent serroit fait, qe purroit tournir en Ensample as

autres de trespasser autre foitz en tiel manere. Sur qoy nostre
dit Seignur le Roy en plein Parlement comanda as Seignurs du
Parlement d'examiner la dite matire, et d'ent faire come mieltz
leur sembleroit par leur discretions. Et sur ce les ditz Seignurs
firent venir devant eux en Parlement, si bien le dit Viscont,
come William Ondeby qi feust retourne par le dit Viscont pur un
des Chivalers du dit Countee, et Thomas de Thorp...Et mesmes
les parties duement examinez,...agardez est par mesmes les
Seignurs, qe por ce qe le dit Viscont n'ad fait sufficientement son
Retourne du dit Brief, q'il amende mesme le Retourne, et q'il
retourne le dit Thomas...come il feust eslu en le dit Countee pur
le Parlement. Et outre ceo, qe le dit Viscont pur cel defaut soit
dischargiez de son Office, et q'il soit commys a la prisone de
Flete, et q'il face fyn et raunceon a la volentee du Roy.

Rot. Parl. III, 530 (38).

(47) *Privilege of members; freedom from arrest.*
Richard Cheddre's case 1404

Item priont les Communes, qe come toutz les Seignurs, Chivalers,
Citezeins, et Burgeis, ove lour servantz venantz a Parlement par
Brief le Roy, en venant, demurant, et retournant, ils sont soutz
vostre protection Roialle, et plusours meschiefs et diseases sovent
aveignont as ditz Seignurs, Chivalers, Citeins, Burgeys, et lour
servantz meynales, en temps avan dit, come par murdre, maheymes, et bateries par gentz gisantz en agaite, ou autrement, dount
due remedie n'est unqore purveu; et nomment en especial en cest
present Parlement de le orrible baterie et mal-fait q'est fait a
Richard Cheddre, Esquier, qi fuist venuz a ycest present Parlement ovesqe Sire Thomas Brook, Chivaler, un des Chivalers pur
le Counte de Somerset et meynall' ove luy, par Johan Salage,
autrement appelle Savage, dount l'avant dit Richard Cheddre
est emblemiz et mahemiz, et tout sur le peril de mort: Qe pleise
ordeiner remedie sur ceste matire, suffisant remedie,...ensi qe le
punissement de luy purra doner ensample et terrour a autres
d'ensi malefaire en temps a venir; C'est assaver, qe si ascune tue
ou murdre ascun q'est venuz ency soutz vostre protection al
Parlement, q'il soit ajugge Treson, et si ascun maheyme ou
disfigure ascun tiel ensi venuz south protection, q'il perde sa
mayn...

Responsio. Pur ceo qe le fait feust fait deinz le temps de cest
Parlement, soit fait proclamation la ou le dit fait se fist, qe Johan

Sallage deinz escript appierge, et soi rende en Bank le Roy deinz un quarter d'un an apres la proclamation faite. Et s'il ne le face, soit le dit Johan atteint de le fait suis dit, et paie au partie endamagee ses damages, au double, a taxer par discretion des Juges...

Rot. Parl. III, 542 (78).

(48) *Elections by indenture* 1406

Item nostre seignur le Roy al grevouse compleint de sa Commune del non dewe eleccion des Chivalers des Countees pur le parlement, queux aucune foitz sont faitz de affeccion des Viscountz, et autrement encountre la forme des briefs as ditz Viscountz directe, a grand esclaundre des Countees et retardacion des busoignes del Communalte du dit Countee; nostre soverein seignur le Roy vuillant a ceo purveier de remedie, de lassent des seignurs espirituelx et temporelx et de tout la Commune en cest present parlement, ad ordeignez et establiz qe desore enavant les eleccions des tielx Chivalers soient faitz en la forme qenseute. Cestassavoir qe al proschein Countee a tenir apres la livere du brief du parlement, proclamacion soit fait en plein Countee de le jour et lieu de parlement, et qe toutz ceux qi illeoqes sont presentz, sibien suturez duement somoines pur cele cause, come autres, attendent la eleccion de lours Chivalers pur le parlement; et adonqes en plein Counte aillent al eleccion liberalment et endifferentement non obstant aucune prier ou comaundement au contrarie; et apres qils soient esluz, soient les persones esluz presentz ou absentz, soient lour nouns escriptz en endenture dessoutz les sealx de toutz ceux qi eux eslisent et tacchez au dit brief du parlement; quele endenture issint ensealez et tacchez soit tenuz pur retourne du dit brief qant as Chivalers des Countees...

S.R. II, 156, 7 Hen. IV, c. 15.

(49) *Control of the executive* 1406

Item, lundy le xxiiij jour de May, les Comunes vindrent devaunt le Roy et les Seignurs en Parlement, et illeoqes le dit Monsire Johan rehercea, Coment, samady darrein passe, le Roy s'agrea et desira la bone Governance, et pur execution et esploit d'icell il avoit esluz l'Ercevesqe de Cantirbirs, et autres Seignurs, pur estre de soun Counseil; et pria le dit Monsire Johan, qe les Comunes purroient avoir conussance si mesmes les Seignurs vouldroient

prendre sur eux d'estre du dit Counseil, ou noun. A quoy le dit
Ercevesqe respondy, si bien pur luy mesmes come pur les autres
Seignurs esluz du dit Counseil, qe si sufficiantie de Biens purroit
estre trovez sur quel bone Governance purra estre fait, ils vouldroient prendre sur eux d'estre du dit Counseil, et sur ce faire lour
poaire et diligence pur profit du Roy et de Roiaume; et autrement nemye.

Rot. Parl. III, 573 (32).

(50) *The commons claim the right to initiate money bills* 1407

Item, Vendredy le second jour Decembre, qe feust le darrein jour
de Parlement, les Communes viendrent devaunt le Roy et les
Seignurs en Parlement, et illeosqes par mandement du Roy une
cedule de Indempnitee sur certein altercation moeve par entre
les Seignurs et les Communes feust lue; et sur ce commande feust
par mesme nostre Seignur le Roy, qe mesme la cedule soit entrez
de record en Rolle de Parlement; de quele cedule le tenure
s'enseute.—Fait a remembrer, qe le Lundy le xxi jour de Novembre, le Roy...esteant en la Chaumbre du Counseil deinz l'Abbacie
de Gloucestre, y esteantz en sa presence les Seignurs Espirituelx
et Temporelx a cest present Parlement assemblez, communez
estoit entre eux de l'estate du Roialme,...Et sur ce des suis ditz
Seignurs demandez feust par voie de question, Quele Aide purroit suffisre et serroit busoignable en ce cas? A laquell demande et
question feust par mesmes les Seignurs severalement responduz,
Qe consideree la Necessite du Roy d'une parte, et la Poverte
de soun poeple d'autre parte, meindre Aide suffisre ne purroit,
qe d'avoir une Disme et demy des Citees et Burghs, et une
Quinzisme et demy des autres laies gentz. Et outre, de graunter
prorogation du Subsidie des Lains, Quirs, et Pealx lanutz, et de
Trois souldz de Tonell, et Dusze deniers de la Livre,...Sur quoy,
par commaundement du Roy nostre dit Seignur, feust envoiez au
Commune de cest present Parlement, de faire venir devaunt
mesme nostre Seignur le Roy, et les ditz Seignurs ascune certein
noumbre des persones de leur compaignie, pur oier et reporter a
lour compaignons ce q'ils aueroient en commandement de nostre
Seignur le Roy suis dit. Et sur ce les ditz Communes envoierent a
la presence du Roy nostre dit Seignur, et des ditz Seignurs, dusze
de lour compaignons; as queux, par commandement de mesme
celuy nostre Seignur le Roy feust declare Question suis dite, et la
Responce des suis ditz Seignurs a ycelle severalement donee.

11-2

Quele Responce la volunte d'icelui nostre Seignur le Roy estoit q'ils ferroient reporter a les autres de lour compaignons; aufin q'ils soy vorroient prendre le pluis pres pur lour conformer a l'entent des Seignurs avaunt ditz. Quele Report ensi fait as ditz Communes, ils ent furent grandement destourbez, en disant et affermant ce estre en grant prejudice et derogation de lour Libertees; Et depuis qe nostre dit Seignur le Roy ce avoit entenduz, nient veullant qe riens soit fait a present, n'en temps advener, qi tournir purroit ascunement encontre la Libertee de l'Estate, pur quelle ils sont venuz au Parlement, n'encountre les Libertees de les Seignurs suis ditz, voet, et graunte, et declare, de l'advis et assent de mesmes les Seignurs, en la manere q'enseute. C'est assaver, qe bien lise as Seignurs, de comuner entre eux ensemble en cest present Parlement, et en chescun autre en temps advener, en Absence du Roy, de l'estate du Roialme, et de le remedie a ce busoignable. Et qe par semblable manere bien lise as Communes, de lour part, de comuner ensemble de l'estate et remedie suis ditz. Purveux toutesfoitz, qe les Seignurs de lour part, ne les Communes de la leur, ne facent ascun report a nostre dit Seignur le Roy d'ascun Grant par les Communes grantez, et par les Seignurs assentuz, ne de les communications du dit Graunt, avaunt ce qe mesmes les Seignurs et Communes soient d'un assent et d'un accord en celle partie, et adonqes en manere et forme come il est accustumez, c'est assaver par bouche de Purparlour de la dite Commune pur le temps esteant, aufin qe mesmes les Seignurs et Communes avoir puissent lour gree de nostre dit Seignur le Roy...

Rot. Parl. III, 611 (21).

(51) *Penalties for the non-observance of the statute regulating elections* (1406) 1410

Primerement come en le parlement tenuz a Westmonstier lan du Regne nostre dit seignur le Roy seoptisme ordennez fuit et establiez par estatut, en conservacion de les franchises et libertees del eleccion des Chivalers de Countees usez parmy le Roialme certeine forme et manere de la eleccion de tielx Chivalers... Ordeigne est et establie qe les Justices as Assises prendre aient poair denquer en lours sessions des assises de tielx retournes faitz, et si par enquest et due examinacion trovee soit devant mesmes les Justices qe ascun tiel Viscont ait fait ou face enapres ascun retorne encontre la tenure du dit estatut qe mesme le Viscont encorge la peyne de C livres, a paiers a nostre dit seignur le Roy. Et outre ceo qe les Chivalers des Countees ensi nient duement retornez perdent lour gages du parlement dancien temps acustumez.

S.R. II, 162, 11 Hen. IV, c. 1.

(52) *Electors and elected to be resident* 1413

Nostre seignur le Roy a son parlement tenuz a Westmonstier a les trois semaignes de Pasche lan de son regne primere...ad ordeignez et establiz...

Primerement qe les estatuts faitz de la eleccion des Chivalers des Countees pur venir au parlement soient tenuz et gardez en toutz pointz; adjoustant a ycelles qe les Chivalers des Countees qe desores serrount esluz en chescun Countee ne soient esluz sils ne soient receauntz deinz les Countees ou ils serrount issint esluz le jour de la date du brief de somons de parlement; et qe les Chivalers et Esquiers et autres qi serrount eslisours des tielx Chivalers des Countees soient auxi receauntz deins mesmes les Countees en manere et fourme come dessus est dit. Et outre ceo ordeignez est et establiz qe les Citeins et Burgeises des Citees et Burghs soient esluz hommes Citeins et Burgeises receauntz demurrauntz et enfraunchises en mesmes les Cites et Burghs et nulles autres en nulle manere.

S.R. II, 170, 1 Hen. V, c. 1.

(53) *Assent of the commons to legislation* 1414

Item fait a remembrer, Qe les Communes baillerent a Roi nostre Seignur tres soverain en cest present Parlement une Petition, dont le tenure ensuyt de mote a mote.

Oure soverain Lord, youre humble and trewe lieges that ben come for the Commune of youre lond bysechyn on to youre rizt riztwesnesse, That so as hit hath evere be thair liberte and fredom, that thar sholde no Statut no Lawe be made oflasse than they yaf therto their assent: Consideringe that the Commune of youre lond, the whiche that is, and evere hath be, a membre of youre Parlement, ben as well Assentirs as Peticioners, that fro this tyme foreward, by compleynte of the Commune of eny myschief axkynge remedie by mouthe of their Speker for the Commune, other ellys by Petition writen, that ther never be no Lawe made theruppon, and engrosed as Statut and Lawe, nother by addicions nother by diminucions, by no maner of terme ne termes, the whiche that sholde chaunge the sentence, and the entente axked by the Speker mouthe, or the Petitions biforesaid...withoute assent of the forsaid Commune. Consideringe oure soverain Lord, that it is not in no wyse the entente of youre Communes, zif hit be so that they axke you by spekyng, or by writyng, too thynges or three, or as manye as theym lust: But that evere it stande in the fredom of your hie Regalie, to graunte whiche of thoo that you luste, and to werune the remanent.

Responsio. Þe Kyng of his grace especial graunteþ þat fro hens forþ no þyng be enacted to þe Peticions of his Comune, þat be contrarie of hir askyng, wharby þey shuld be bounde wiþoute their assent. Savyng alwey to our liege Lord his real Prerogatif, to graunte and denye what him lust of þeir Petitions...

Rot. Parl. IV, 22 (22).

(54) *Wages of knights of the shire* 1414

Item supplient les gentils et autres gentz qi teignent lour Terres par les services de chivaler deins le Gyldable en le Countee de Kent; Que come les gages du Chivalers qi veignent as Parlementz pur le dit Countee, ne sont pas levables de autres gentz deins le dit Countee, solonc la custume illoeqes de tout temps dount memorie ne court use, sinoun de ceux qi teignont lour Terres deins le dit Countee par les services de Chivaler, si bien deins fraunchise come dehors. Et ore tarde les Viscountes du dit Countee facent lever les ditz gages de Chivalers, tant soulement de ceux qi teignont lour Terres par les services de Chivalers deins le dit Gyldable en le dit Countee...Que pleise a nostre Seignur le Roi ordeiner, qe les ditz gages du Chivalers soient desore en avaunt levez par les Viscountes du dit Countee, generalment de toutz ceux qi teignent lour Terres par les services de Chivaler, si bien deins fraunchise come dehors, deins le dit Countee, forspris de les Fees des chivalers qi sount en les mayns de le honurable Pier en Dieu l'Erchevesqe de Canterbirs, et de les Fees des Chivalers qi sont en les mayns de toutz autres Seignurs Espirituelx et Temporelx deins mesme le Countee, qi veignent as Parlementz, par auctorite des briefs nostre dit tres soverain Seignur le Roi.

Responsio. Soit l'estatuit ent fait mys en due execution.

Rot. Parl. IV, 49 (32)

(55) *The method of legislation* 1428

Item, le xxv jour de Marce, qe feust le darrein jour de cest present Parlement, une autre Petition feust baillez a nostre Seignur le Roi en mesme le Parlement par les Communes d'icell; le tenour de quell Petition cy ensuyt.

Please au Roi nostre soverain Seignur considerer, coment plusours Petitions ount estez baillez et exhibitez a vostre tres noble hautesse, par les Communes de cest present Parlement, pur ent avoir covenable remedie, et unquore nient determinees, d'ordeiner par advys des Seignurs Espirituelx et Temporelx, et assent dez Communes avauntditz, que les dites Petitions purront estre de-liverez a les Seignurs de vostre tres sage Conseill; les queux appellez a eux lez Justices, et autres gentz aprisez en vostre ley, si bosoigne y soit, aiaunt poair par auctorite du dit Parlement, parentre cy et la Feste del Nativite du Seint Johan Baptiste prou-chein a venir, d'oier et terminer lez ditz Petitions; et que ycelles ensi terminez de l'advys et assent suisditz, purront estre enactez, enrollez et mys de recorde, en le Rolle de mesme vostre Parlement.

Responsio. Le Roi le voet.

Rot. Parl. iv, 334 (45).

(56) *Election of knights of the shire by forty-shilling freeholders* 1429

Item come lez eleccions dez Chivalers des Countees esluz a venir as parlements du Roi en plusours Countees Dengleterre, ore tarde ount este faitz par trop graunde et excessive nombre dez gents demurrantz deinz mesmes les Countes, dount la greindre partie estoit par gentz sinon de petit avoir ou de null valu, dount ches-cun pretende davoir voice equivalent quant a tielx eleccions faire ove les pluis valantz chivalers ou esquiers demurrantz deins mesmes les Countes; dount homicides riotes bateries et devisions entre les gentiles et autres gentz de mesmes les Countees verisem-blablement sourdront et serront, si covenable remedie ne soit purveu en celle partie; Nostre seignur le Roy considerant les premisses ad purveu et ordene par auctorite de cest parlement qe les Chivalers des Countes deins le Roialme Dengleterre, a esliers a venir a les parlementz en apres atenirs, soient esluz en chescun Counte par gentz demurrantz et receantz en icelles, dount chescun ait frank tenement a le valu de xls. par an al meins outre les reprises...

S.R. ii, 243, 8 Hen. VI, c. 7.

(57) *Wages of burgesses* 1429

Item, priont les Communes de cest present Parleament, qe la ou Citezeins et Burgeis eslus de venir a vostre Parleament, par les elections dez Gentz des Citees et Burghs deinz vostre Roialme, ount ewe, et d'aunciene temps accustume de droit devoient avoir, pur lour gages et expenses, chescun jour durant vostre Parleament, iis.; c'est assavoir, chescun d'ieux iis. pur chescun jour duraunt vostre dit Parleament;...Que please a vostre Roial Mageste, le dit matere de considerer, et grauntier par auctorite de cest present Parleament, qe lez ditz Citezeins et Burgeis, et chescun d'eux, aient lour gages de iis. come devaunt est dit, pur chescun jour duraunt vostre Parlement, et a fyne de chescun Parleament, eient lour Brief a Viscount pur lever lez ditz deniers, si come les ditz Chivalers des Countees ount,...

Responsio. Le Roi s'advisera.

Item, priount les Communes, qe toutz les Citees, Burghs, Villes et Hamelettes, et les resceantz deinz iceux, forspris Seignurs Espirituelx et Temporelx veignauntz a Parlement, et gentz de Seint Esglise, et ceux Cittees et Burghs, qi trovent Citezeins ou Burgeis a Parlement, soient desore enavaunt contributoriez a toutz jours, as expenses des Chivalers eslus ou esliers a les Parlementz.

Responsio. Le Roi s'advisera.

Rot. Parl. iv, 350 (41); 352 (46).

(58) *Privilege of members; freedom of members' servants from arrest. Wm. Larke's case* 1429

Priount les Communes, qe la ou un William Larke, Servaunt a William Milrede, venant al vostre Court de icest Parlement, pur la Citee de Londrez,...par sotiell ymagination et conjecture de un Margerie Janyns, fuist arrestez en le Courte l'Abbe de Westmonstier de pipoudrez,...et d'illoeqes remoeve en vostre commune Bank, par Brief de corpus cum causa,...et par voz Justicez de vostre dit Bank commaundez a vostre prisone de Flete; et la en prison detenez a present,...sibien au cause qe le dit William Larke fuist condempne al suyte de dit Margerie, en vostre dit Bank, en un action de trespas, au cez damagez de ccviii li. vi s. viiid.,...Please a vostre Roial Majeste de considerer, coment le dit William Larke, al temps de dit areste, fuist en la service le dit William Milrede, supposant verraiment par la previlege de vostre Court de Parlement, d'estre quietez de toutz arestez, durant vostre

dit Courte, forprise pur treson, felonie, ou suerte de pees; d'ordeigner par auctorite de mesme vostre Parlement, qe le dit William
Larke purra estre deliverez hors de vostre dit prison de Flete, le
dit condempnation,...nient obstant. Salvant toutz foitz au dit
Margerie, et a cez Executours, lour execution hors de dit juggement envers le dit William Larke, apres le fyne de dit Parlement,
et auxi de grauntier par auctorite suisdite, qe null de voz ditz
Lieges, c'est assavoir, Seignurs, Chivalers pur voz Countees,
Citezeins, Burgeys, au voz Parlementz desore a venirs, lours
servauntz et familiers, ne soient ascunement arestez, ne en prison
deteynez, durant le temps de voz Parlementz, s'il ne soit pur
treson, felonie, ou suerte de pees, come desuis est dit.

Responsio. Le Roi, par advis des Seignurs Espirituelx et Temporelx, et a les especiales requestes des Communes,...et auxint
de l'assent du Counseill du Margerie Janyns...voet...qe
William Larke...soit deliverez au present hors de la prison de
Flete. Et qe la dit Margerie, apres le fyne de cest Parlement, ait
sa execution del juggement, q'ele aveit envers le dit William, en le
commune Bank...

Rot. Parl. iv, 357 (57).

(59) *Parliament and council* 1433

Memorandum, yat after yat ye Kyng, at ye request of his Communes, and be the avis and assent of ye Lordes Spirituell and
Temporell assembled in his Parlement, ye xxiiii day of Novembre,
ye xii yere of his reigne, had praied and desired my Lord of
Bedford' to abide in yis lond, in ye manere, and to yentent,
declared on ye behalve of the said Communes by ye mouth of
Roger Hunte, yeire Speker; and yat my said Lord of Bedford, had
answered to ye Kyngs said desire and praiere, as it appiered of all
yese yngs before reherced, be an Acte made yereupon in ye
Parlement rolle; my said Lord of Bedford, on ye Wednesday next
folwyng, yat was ye xxv day of the said November, repetyng his
foresaid answere to ye remenant of ye Lordes of ye Kyngs Counseil,
beyng assembled in ye Sterrid Chambre; remembrid also howe
yat afore yis, as wele hym self, for the tyme of his beyng in yis
lond chief of the Kyngs Counseil, as his brother of Gloucestre,
had some tyme, by yavis and ordinance of the Kyngs greet
Consail in Parlement, and at some tyme, by yavis and ordinance
of ye Kyngs Consail out of Parlement, oyerwhile ye somme of
viii m. marcs yerly for yeire service and intendance, oyerwhile

vi **m**. marcs, oyerwhile v **m**. marcs, and oyerwhile iiii **m**. marcs
yerly. Wherfore sith it lyked the Kyng to commaunde hym to
entende to his service and Consail in yis land, and to be as reson
will, Chief yereof, accordyng to his birth; he desired for to knowe,
what some he shuld yeerly have of the Kyng, for his said service
and entendance;...

Rot. Parl. IV, 424 (19).

(60) *Audit of accounts* 1433
Rauf Cromwell's Petition being Tresorer of England.

To the Kyng oure soverain Lord...also that hit be ordeined
and appointed, that no yift ne Graunte of lyfelod, Revenue or
good, balangyng to youre Hienesse, ne paiementes to be made of
youre good', be appointed or passed by youre Counseill, withoute
yat the Tresorier be called to yeve information in swich cas to
youre Counseill, and be first herde therappon:...Subsequenter-
que, idem Thesaurarius exhibuit tunc ibidem, dictos Libros de
Statu Regni, per Officiarios et Ministros Regis Scaccarii predicti
ut premittitur editos, et presenti Rotulo consutos, qui tunc ibidem
in eodem Parliamento, de mandato Domini Regis summarie per-
lecti fuerunt et auditi. Subsequenterque, preceptum fuit prefato
Thesaurario Anglie, de avisamento et assensu predictis, quod
dictum Statum Regni, Communibus ejusdem Parliamenti, in
eorum Domo communi, eodem modo in crastino ostenderet et
declararet, quod et factum fuit.

Rot. Parl. IV, 432.

(61) *Trial of peeresses* 1442
Item, priont les Communes,...

Que vous please, par advis et assent des Seignurs Espirituelx et
Temporelx en cest present Parlement assemblez, declarer, qe
tielx Dames issint enditez, ou en apres a enditierz, de ascun
Treson ou Felonie par eux faitz, ou en apres a fairez, coment qe
eles soient covertez de Baron, ou soulez; qe eles ent soient mesnez
en respoundre, et mys a rendre et adjuggez, devaunt tielx Juges
et Peres de le Roialme, si come autres Peres de le Roialme serroient, s'ils fuissent enditez ou empeschez de tielx Tresons ou
Felonies faitz, ou en apres a fairez, et en autiel manere et fourme,
et en null autre.

Responsio. Le Roi le voet.

Rot. Parl. V, 56 (28).

(62) *Statute regulating elections* 1445

[*Recital of statutes*, 1 Hen. V, c. 1, and 8 Hen. VI, c. 7.]

...par force de quele estatut eleccions dez Chivalerz a venir
a parlement ascun foitz ont estez duement faitz et loialment
retornez, tanqe a ore tarde qe diversez Viscontz dez Counteez...
pur lour singuler availl et lucre ne ont faitz due eleccions dez
Chivalers, ne en temps covenable, ne bons et verroiez retornez
et ascun foitz null retornez dez Chivalers Citizeins et Burgeisez
loialment esluz pur venir as parlementz, mez ont retornez tielx
Chivalers,...qe ne furent unquez duement eslieux,...Et ascun
foitz lez Viscontz ne ont retornez briefs qils avoient pur fair
eleccions dez Chivalers a venir as parlementz einz lez ditz briefs
ont embesillez, et oustre null precept as Mair et Bailifs...dez
Citees et Burghs pur eleccions des Citezeins et Burgeisez de venir
as parlementz firent par colour de cestz parolx contenuz en lez
ditz briefs, *quod in pleno Comitatu tuo eligi facias pro Comitatu tuo
duos milites, et pro qualibet civitate in Comitatu tuo duos Cives et pro
quolibet Burgo in Comitatu tuo, duos Burgenses*: Et auxint pur ceo qe
sufficeant peyne et covenable remedie pur la partie en tiel cas
greve ne sont pre ordeignez en lez ditz estatutz vers lez Viscontz
Mairs et Bailiffs qi facent encountre la forme dez ditz estatutz:
le Roi...ad ordeigne...qe lez ditz estatutz soient duement
gardez et observez en toutz pointz...Et qe chescune Viscont a
chescune foitz qil face le contrarie dicest estatut ou dascun autre
estatut pur eleccion dez Chivalers...de venir al parlement devant
sez hoeurez fait encorge la peyne contenu en le dit estatut fait le
dit an oeptisme; Et oustre ceo forface...a chescune persone en
apres eslieu Chivaler Citezein ou Burgeis en son Counte de venir
a ascun parlement, et nemye par luy duement retorne, ou a ascun
autre person qi en defaute de tiel Chivaler Citezein ou Burgeis
suer le voet C. livres dont chescun Chivaler Citezein et Burgeis
issint greve severalment ou ascun autre persone qi en lour defaulte
suer voet eit sa accion de dette envers le dit Viscont...a demaunder et aver lez ditz C. livres ove sez costagez en cest cas
despenduz...Et en mesme le manere a chescune foitz qe ascune
Mair et Baillifs,...retornent ou retorne autres qe ceux qi sont
esluz par lez Citezeins et Burgeisez...encorge et forface a Roi
xl livres et enoustre forface et paie a chescune persone enapres
eslieu Citezein ou Burgeis a venir al parlement...ou autre persone qi en defaulte de tiel Citezein ou Burgeis issint eslieu suer
voet, xl livres...Et qe chescune Viscont qi ne face due eleccion

dez Chivalers pur venir al parlement en temps covenable,...
parentre le houre de viij^e et le hoeur de xj^e devant le none, saunz
collusion en cest partie, et chescune Viscont qi ne face bon et
verray retorne dez tielx eleccions...forface envers le Roi C.
livres....Issint qe lez Chivalers dez Counteez pur le parlement en
apres a esliers soient notablez Chivalers dez mesmez lez Counteez
pur lez queux ils serront issint esluz, ou autrement tielx notablez
Esquiers gentils homez del Nativite dez mesmez lez Counteez
come soient ablez destre Chivalers; et null home destre tiel
Chivaler qi estoise en la degree de vadlet et desouth.

S.R. ii, 340, 23 Hen. VI, c. 14.

(63) *Impeachment of the Duke of Suffolk* 1450

Memorandum, quod septimo die Februarii, Cardinalis Eborum,
Cancellarius Anglie, ac quamplures alii Domini tam Spirituales
quam Temporales, in notabili numero, de mandato Regis missi
fuerunt ad Communes in presenti Parliamento existentes; et
iidem Communes, per Willielmum Tresham Prelocutorem suum,
coram prefatis Dominis accusaverunt et impetiti fuerunt Willielmum de la Pole Ducem Suffolkie, nuper de Ewelme in Comitatu
Oxonie, de quibusdam altis proditionibus, necnon offensis et
mesprisionibus per ipsum Ducem contra Regiam magestatem
factis et perpetratis, prout in quadam Billa certos Articulos con-
tinente magis evidenter apparebit; quam quidem Billam, iidem
Communes per prefatum Prelocutorem suum, prefato Cancellario
et Dominis deliberaverunt: supplicantes eisdem, ut pro eis prefate
Regie Magestati instarent, ut dicta Billa in presenti Parliamento
inactitaretur, quodque contra prefatum Ducem super Articulis
predictis in eodem Parliamento secundum legem et consuetudinem Regni Anglie procederetur: Cujus quidem Bille tenor
sequitur in hec verba:—

To the Kyng oure Soverayn Lord; Sheweth and piteously com-
pleyneth youre humble and true obeisauntes Commens of this
your noble Reame, in this your present Parlement by your high
auctorite assembled,...That William de la Pole Duke of Suffolk,
...falsely and traiterously hath ymagined, compassed, purposed,
forethought, doon and committed dyvers high, grete, heynous and
horrible treasons, ayenst your moost Roiall persone,...

[*Articles against Suffolk follow*]

Item, the xiii day of Marche than next folowyng, the seid Duke
of Suffolk was sent for, to come tofore the Kynges Highnes, and

his Lordes Spirituelx and Temporelx, for to answere to such
Articles concernyng dyvers grete and horrible treasons, uppon
which he is accused and empeched by the Commens of Englond,
assembled in this present Parlement, and to declare hymself
therin for his excuse...
...The seid Chaunceller, by the Kynges commaundement, seid
unto hym ageyne in this fourme.
   Sire, y conceyve you that ye not departyng from youre answers
and declarations in the maters aforeseid, not puttyng you uppon
youre Parage, submitte you hooly to the Kynges rule and governaunce. Wherfore the Kyng commaundeth me to sey you, that
as touchyng the grete and horrible thinges in the seid first Bille
comprised, the Kyng holdeth you neither declared nor charged.
And as touchyng the secund Bille putte ayenst you,...the Kyng,
by force of youre submission, by his owne advis, and not reportyng
hym to th'advis of his Lordes, nor by wey of Jugement, for he
is not in place of Jugement, putteth you to his rule and governaunce: That is to say, that ye, before the first day of May next
commyng, shull absente youre self oute of his Reame of Englond;...

Rot. Parl. v, 177 (18), 182 (49–51).

(64) *Attainder of John Cade* 1451

Prayen youre Communes of this present Parlement, where the
fals Traytour John Cade, namyng hym self John Mortymer, late
called Capteyn of Kent, the viii day of Jule, the yere of youre
reigne xxviii, atte Southwerke in the Shire of Surrey, and atte
ix day of Jule of the yere aforesaid, atte Dertford and Rouchestre
in the Shire of Kent, also atte Rouchestre aforesaid and elles
where, the x and xi day of Jule than next ensuyng, within this
youre noble Reame of Englond, falsely and traiterously ymagyned
your deth, destruction and subversion of this your seid Reame, in
gederyng and reryng grete nombre of your poeple,...And howe
be it thaugh he be dede..., yet by the lawe...not punyshed, to
consider the premisses, and to putte such Traytours in doubte
soo to doo in tyme commyng, and for savation of youre self and
youre said Reame, by advis of your Lordes Spirituelx and Temporelx in this your present Parlement assembled, to ordeyne
by auctorite of the seid Parlement, that he be atteynt of thees
Treasons, and by auctorite aforesaid forfeit to you all his Goodes,
Londes, Tenementes, Rentes and Possessions, which he hadde

the seid viii day of Jule or after, and his blode corrupted and disabled for ever, and to be called within youre seid Reame fals Traitour for evermore.

Responsio. Le Roy le voet.

Rot. Parl. v, 224 (19).

(65) *Attainder of the Duke of Suffolk* 1451

To the Kyng our Soverain Lord.

Prayen the Commons; that where in your Parlement last holden at Westminster, the Communalte of this your Roialme in the same Parlement assembled, accused and empeched William de la Pole thenne Duke of Suffolk, aswell of divers grete, heynous and detestable Treasons, as of many other fauxtees, deceites and other untrue mesprisions, by him doon and commytted: Unto whiche accusementes and empechementes he beyng put to answere therto, yave non answere sufficient after the Lawes of this youre Lande, as in the Actes and processe hadde upon the said accusement and empechement, the tenour wherof herto is annexed, more pleynly it appereth; by cause wherof, Jugement of Atteyndre of the seid Treasons ought to have ben yeven ayenst him, and he convict of the seid Mesprisions after the cours of youre seid Lawes; and forasmoche as suche Jugement ayenst him than was nought hadde, as Justice after his merites required. Please hit youre Highnesse to graunte, ordeyne and establissh, by the Avyse and Assent of the Lordes Spirituelx and Temporelx in this present Parlement assembled, that by Auctorite of this same Parlement, the seid William de la Pole be adjuged, demed, declared, published and reputed, as Traytour to you, ayenst youre Regalie, Dignitie, and youre Corones...

Rot. Parl. v, 226.

(66) *Fines for non-attendance* 1454

Memorandum, quod ultimo die Februarii, Anno regni dicti Domini Regis Tricesimo secundo, quedam alia Petitio exhibita fuit eidem Domino Regi, in presenti Parliamento, hanc seriem verborum continens:

Please it the Kyng our Soveraigne Lord, that for asmoche as dyvers and mony Lordes of this Lande, aswell Spirituell as Temporell, the which have be sommoned and commaunded by your Writtes directed unto everyche of theim severally, to have come and be at this your present Parlement, the whiche in no wyse be come, nor have be at your seid Parlement at your Paleys of Westminster, sith the xiiii day of Feverer last passed unto this day, that is to sey, the last day of Feverer the yere of your reigne xxxii[ti]; but have absented hem sith the seid xiiii day of Feverer of commyng to the seid Parlement, wherto they have be called, sommoned or warned; to ordeyne and establissh by auctorite of this present Parlement, that every of the seid Lordes so not comen, but beyng absent, be charged to yeve and paie unto you and to your use, such sommes of money and in suche manere as folowith. That is to sey, every Archebisshop, and every Duke, c li; every Bisshop, and every Erle, c marcs; every Abbot, and every Baron, xl li; to be leevede uppon ther Londes and godes...

Responsio. Le Roy le voet.

Rot. Parl. v, 248 (46).

(67) *Legislation by bill* 1454

Memorandum, that the Saturday the ix day of Marche, the yere of the reigne of Kyng Harry the vi[th]. xxxii[ti], Rauf Lord Cromwell asked sueerte of the peas of Herry Duke of Excestre, before Rychard Duke of York, the Kynges Lieutenaunt in this present Parlement, and John Cardynall Archebisshop of Caunterbury and Chaunceler of Englond, and other Lordes Spirituelx and Temporelx in the same Parlement assembled; wherof the seid Lord Cromwell put in a Bille to the Kyng, and to the seid Lordes, which was too tymes radde the same day; and it was thought by the seid Lordes, that sueerte ought to be had and founde; but as to the grete paynes conteigned in the seid Bille, the seid Lordes seyde they wolde be advised, and deliber theruppon unto Moneday or Tuesday then next commyng. And aftirward, the xx day of Marche then next ensuyng, the seid Bille was aggreed and assented unto by the seid Lordes; and so the xxii[ti] day of Marche next folowyng, the seid Lieutenaunt commaunded that the forseid Bille shuld be sent unto the Commons, and so hit was doon.

Rot. Parl. v, 264 (62).

(68) *Control of the executive* 1455

Memorandum, that the xiii day of the said moneth of November, it was shewed to the Duke of York, the Kynges Lieutenaunt in this present Parlement, and to the Lordes Spirituell and Temporell, by the mouthe of Burley, accompanyed with notable nombre of the Communes, in name of all the Communes. That howe it had liked the Kynges Highnesse for certayn causes hym moevyng, to assigne the said Duk of York to be his Lieutenaunt in this present Parlement, and to procede in matiers of Parliament, as in the Kynges letters theruppon made and late radde before the said Communes it is playnly conteyned, and that the said Duke of York had taken uppon hym so to procede. Wherfore it was thought by theym that were commen for the Communes of this lande, that if for suche causes the Kyng heraftre myght not entende to the protection and defence of this lande, that it shuld like the Kyng by th'advis of his said Lieutenaunt and the Lordes, to ordeigne and purvey suche an hable persone, as shuld mowe entende to the defence and protection of the said lande, and this to be doon as sone as it myght be,...

And there it was aggreed by all the Lordes Spirituelx and Temporelx, every Lord severally yevyng his voice and assent, considered the grete noblenesse, sadnesse and wysdome of the Duc of York, the sad governaunce and polletique rule had in this lande, the tyme that he was last Protectour... that he shuld nowe take the charge uppon hym ayen,...

Rot. Parl. v, 284 (31); 285 (33).

(69) *Privilege of members; claim for freedom of speech.*
Thomas Yong's case 1455

To the right wise and discreet Comons in this present Parlement assembled; Bisechen humbly Thomas Yong. That whereas he late beyng oon of the Knyghtes for the Shire and Towne of Bristowe, in dyvers Parlementes holden afore this, demened him in his saiyng in the same, as wele, faithfully, and with alle suche trewe diligent labour, as his symplenesse couthe or myght, for the wele of the Kyng oure Soverain Lorde, and this his noble Realme; and notwithstonding that by the olde liberte and fredom of the Comyns of this Lande had, enjoyed and prescribed, fro the tyme that no mynde is, alle suche persones as for the tyme been assembled in eny Parlement for the same Comyn', ought to have theire fredom to speke and sey in the Hous of their assemble, as to theym is thought convenyent or resonable, withoute eny maner chalange, charge or punycion therefore to be leyde to theym in eny wyse. Neverthelesse, by untrewe sinistre reportes made to the Kinges Highnesse of your said Bisecher, for matiers by him shewed in the Hous accustumed for the Comyns in the said Parlementes,

he was therefore taken, arrested, and rigorously in open wise led
to the Toure of London, and there grevously in grete duresse long
tyme emprisoned, ayenst the said fredom and liberte,...Please
hit your grete wisedoms tenderly to consider the premisses, and
therupon to pray the Kyng...to graunte and provide, by th'avice
of the Lordes Spirituell and Temporell in this present Parlement
assembled, that for the said losses, costes, damages and imprisone-
ment, your said Bisecher have...recompense...

Responsio. The Kyng wolle, that the Lordes of his Counseill do
and provyde in this partie for the seid Suppliant, as by theire
discrecions shal be thought...resonable.

Rot. Parl. v, 337.

(70) *Grant of taxation by the lords* 1472

9....To the pleasir of Almyghty God, and for suerte and defence
of this Reame of Englond, considered that the Kyng oure
Soverayn Lord, is disposed by the grace of God in his owne
persone to passe forth of this his seid Reame, with an Armee
Roiall, for the saufegarde of the same Reame, the subduyng of
the auncien ennemyes of hym and of his seid Reame; for the
assistence, furnysshyng, and settyng forth therof, the Lordes
Spirituell and Temporell of this Reame, beyng Lordes of Parlement, of their fre wille, toward, herty, and lovyng dispositions,
over and beside all other promyses made by any of the seid Lordes
Temporell to attende in their persones apon the Kyng oure said
Soverayn Lord in his seid Armee, graunte to oure seid Soverayn
Lord, the xth part of value of oon yere oonly, that yere to begyn
at the fest of Circumcision of oure Lord God last passed, of the
issues and profittes of all maner Honours, Castelles, Lordships,
Manoirs, Londes, Tenementes, Rentes, Fees, Annuiteez, Offices,
Corrodies, Pensions, and Fee fermes,...

Rot. Parl. vi, 6 (9).

(71) *Privilege of members; freedom from arrest.*
Wm. Hyde's case 1472–5

Prayen the Commens in this present Parlement assembled; that
for asmoche as William Hyde Squyer, Burges of the Toune and
Burgh of Chippenham in Wilteshire electe, came by your high
commaundement to this youre present Parlement, and attendyng
to the same in the Hous for the Commens accustumed, after his
said comyng, and duryng this your said Parlement, was arested

at Lambhith in the Counte of Surrey, by colour of a Capias ad
satisfaciendum, that was directed to the Shireff of Middlesex, and
so there by myschevous men, murtherers, unknowen for any
Officers, taken, and withoute the shewyng of any Warant, caried
hym to London, at the sute of John Marshall, Citezein and
Mercer of the same, for lxix li. supposed to be due to hym by
the said William, and for the same enprisoned in the Counter
there, and from thens had to Newegate, as and he had bee a
Traitour,...

It pleas your Highnes, by the advis and assent of the Lordes
Spirituelx and Temporelx in this present Parlement assembled,
and by auctorite of the same, to ordeyne and stablish, that your
Chaunceller of Englond have power, to direct your Writte or
Writtes to the Shirefs of London, commaundyng theym and
everych of theym by the same, to have the said William Hyde
afore hym withoute delay, and then to dismysse hym at large...so
that the said William Hyde may attende to this your Parlement
as his duetie is to doo...

Responsio. Le Roy le voet.

Rot. Parl. VI, 160 (55).

(72) *Redress of grievances before supply* 1484

Memorandum, quod Communes Regni Anglie in presenti Parliamento existentes, et coram Domino Rege in pleno Parliamento
predicto, Vicesimo die Februarii, Anno predicto, videlicet,
Ultimo die presentis Parliamenti, comparentes per Willelmum
Catesby Prelocutorem suum declarabant, qualiter ipsi, de assensu
Dominorum Spiritualium et Temporalium in Parliamento predicto existentium, concesserunt prefato Domino Regi certa Sub-
sidia,...sub certa forma in quadam Indentura inde confecta et
eidem Domino Regi ad tunc ibidem exhibita contenta levanda:...

Rot. Parl. VI, 238.

(73) *Attainder of Walter Roberd* 1484

Item, quedam alia Billa coram prefato Domino Rege in dicto
Parliamento exhibita fuit, hanc seriem verborum continens.

Forasmoche as oon Walter Roberd,...falsly and traiterously
levied Werre ayenst oure said Soveraigne Lorde. And afterwards,
the xth day of Fevrier,...herboured...othre the Kings Traitors
and Rebells,...Bee it therfor ordeigned, stablisshed and enacted,
by the Kyng oure Soveraigne Lorde, and the Lords Spirituall

and Temporell, and the Comens, in this present Parliament assembled, and by auctorite of the same, that the said Water Roberd be atteynted of high Treason, and forfaite to oure said Soveraign Lorde and his heires, all his Lands and Tenements, and other Hereditaments and Possessions, . . .

Cui quidem Bille Communibus dicti Parliamenti transportate iidem Communes assensum suum prebuerunt in hec verba.

A cest Bille les Communez sont assentuz.

Qua quidem Billa coram eodem Domino Rege in Parliamento predicto lecta et plenius intellecta, de assensu Dominorum Spiritualium et Temporalium, ac Communitatum predictarum in dicto Parliamento existentium, necnon auctoritate ejusdem, respondebatur eidem in forma sequenti.

Responsio. Le Roy le voet.

Rot. Parl. VI, 251 (7).

(74) *Repeal of benevolences* 1484

Item nostre seignur le Roy remembrant coment lez Comens de cest son Roialme par novelx et desloialx invencions et enordinate covetise, encountre la ley de cest Roialme ount este misez a graund servitude et enportablez charges et exaccions, et en especiall par une novell imposicion appelle Benevolence, paront diversez ans lez subgiettes et Comens de cest terre encountre leur volentees et libertie ount paiez graundz sommez de moneie a lour bien pres finall destruccion, qar diversez et plusours hommez honorables de cest Roialme par encheson dicell furent compellez del necessite a dessolver lour hostielx et vivre en graund penurie et miserie, lour dettes nonpaiez et leur enfantz nient preferrez et tielx memorialx quelx ils avoient ordeinez par la salue de lour aulmes furent anientisez a graund despleasure Dieu et la destruccion de cest Roialme: Pur qoi nostre dit seignur le Roi de ladvys et assent des ditz seignurs et Comens en le dit parlement assemblez et par auctorite dicell voet et ordeigne qe ses subgiettes et Cominalte de cest son Roialme de cy enavant en null manere soient chargez par null tiel charge ou imposicion appelle Benevolence, ne par tiel semblable chargee, et qe tielx exaccions appellez Benevolence devant cest temps prisez soient pris pur null example de faire tiel ou ascune semblable charge dascuns sez ditz subgiettes de cest Roialme enapres, mes soit il dampne et adnulle pur toutz jours.

S.R. II, 478, I Ric. III, c. 2.

CHAPTER V

THE CHANCERY

INTRODUCTION

In the thirteenth century the importance of the chancery lay in the vast secretarial and administrative work which the chancellor and his clerks carried out for the crown. The chancellor had possession of the great seal, and controlled the issue of all formal documents, which had already become distinctive and stereotyped, such as charters and letters patent and close. The practice of enrolling such documents had become usual; the great series of patent, close, charter, fine and liberate rolls, begins in the early years of the century. In addition, the judicial reforms of Henry II had greatly increased the sphere of the chancellor's work, since all original writs for judicial purposes were issued from chancery. There had been at first no separate department of chancery; the clerks had worked within the household, as also in the exchequer; but as the great seal became more public the chancery gradually emerged, while the other branches of the *curia* were developing their own secretariats, as, for example, that of the household, which was using the king's private seal.[1] Similarly, the chancellor himself was dissociated from the exchequer about 1230.

During the personal rule of Henry III the great seal was entrusted to men of subordinate position,[2] while the household was engrossing more powers; but differentiation went on, notably when a separate office of the hanaper was set up to deal with fees, which were no longer to be administered by the chancellor alone, but to be accounted for at the wardrobe.[3] After 1258 the barons wished to restore the office of chancellor to its former dignity and a salary was allotted to it. Under Edward I the chancellor continued to have great power, but the king was willing for his public and household departments to work in the closest co-

[1] See below, pp. 208 ff.
[2] L. B. Dibben, "Chancellor and keeper of the seal under Henry III", *E.H.R.* xxvii, 1912.
[3] B. Wilkinson, *The chancery under Edward III*, p. 59.

operation; promotion was usual from one to the other, and the
privy seal was increasingly used for official purposes. This was
directly counter to baronial policy, and the ordinances of 1311
provided that the privy seal should have its own keeper with a
defined sphere of control. In Edward II's reign the chancery
was finally freed from the supervision of the household, when
after 1324 the hanaper ceased to account to the wardrobe and
answered instead to the exchequer.[1] From this time the administrative and secretarial work of the chancery increased rapidly on
normal lines, and in this alone the chancellor's position was of
supreme importance. He was brought into close touch with the
courts of law which looked to his department for the writs under
which they acted; he had a part in the appointment of local
officials; he had an extensive clerical patronage, for by custom he
had the right to present to all livings in the king's gift under
twenty marks *per annum*.[2] The clerks of chancery had charge of
the records of parliament(3), and the chancellor was intimately
connected both with parliament and council throughout the
period. Similarly, the chancery and office of privy seal, which
was being frequently used for formal matters and especially for
conciliar business, were closely related, and at first it was not
uncommon to select the keeper of the privy seal from among the
chancery clerks. One change was indicated in the Walton
ordinance of 1338,[3] when warrants under the privy seal were
made compulsory for the issue of writs from chancery to exchequer authorising payments: it is not known how far the
ordinance was carried out, but it was becoming usual for the privy
seal to be used for such warrants.[4]

The chancellor was indeed first in dignity in the state, as
William of Wykeham later claimed(12). Usually he was a great
cleric, and normally a salaried official, though there was sometimes a reaction, as in Edward II's reign, to the early thirteenth-
century practice that the office should depend only on fees.[5]
The experience of appointing lay chancellors from 1341 to 1345,
after the quarrel between Edward III and Archbishop Stratford,
was not attended with great success, though they devoted much
care to their duties. After that time little is heard of anti-cleri-
calism; and the second period of lay ministers, from 1371 to 1377,

[1] See above, p. 107.
[2] W. S. Holdsworth, *A history of English law*, 1, 417.
[3] Tout, *Chapters*, III, 70; the document is given pp. 144–50.
[4] *Ibid.* III, 78; v, 12; and see below, p. 209.   [5] *Ibid.* II, 77, 310.

made little change.[1] Our knowledge of the organisation of chancery at this time is derived from a notable document which most probably refers to chancery in 12 Richard II(17), but it would seem that the careful system of grading the clerks was already in existence in the preceding reign.[2] Twelve clerks of the robe were associated with the chancellor, at first living in common with him, later, however, having their own households. Chief among them was the keeper of the rolls, who could have six clerks. Clerks of the second grade were twelve in number, and included the keeper of the hanaper. Below them were the twenty-four "cursitors" who produced writs *de cursu*, original writs which began actions in the royal courts and being of common form were issued on demand. The clerks had many privileges(15), and there was chance of promotion from the second to the first grade.

Apart from its administrative work, the most significant development of chancery was on the judicial side, whereby it became a great court of equity by the end of the medieval period. This can be accounted for in several ways. Already chancery had a common law jurisdiction;[3] and the issue of original writs gave the chancellor great authority, for not only had he to decide on the writ suitable for a case, but sometimes a new writ had to be devised, though this had been forbidden as early as 1258 and again by Edward I.[4] The fact that the chancery had enrolments of the most important series of documents meant that constant reference was being made to the chancellor for information, and it was an easy step for him to take over the hearing of a case. Moreover, there was a great increase in the number of petitions delegated or made directly to him: from Edward I's time he had been accustomed to deal with cases handed over to him by king and council, and later by parliament(2, 4); and the fact that the chancery was nearly always at Westminster made it more accessible to petitioners.[5]

The evolution of a court of chancery was necessarily slow, especially because of the close connection with the council, yet traces of such a court can be found in a statute of 1340; and in 1349, in a sheriff's proclamation, the king ordered that petitions

---

[1] Tout, *Chapters*, III, 266 ff.; and Wilkinson, *op. cit.* pp. 114 ff., 128 ff.

[2] Tout, *Chapters*, III, 210, 445 ff.; and his paper in *Essays...presented to R. L. Poole*, pp. 62 ff. Wilkinson, *op. cit.* pp. 214–23, gives the ordinances with a critical survey of the texts.

[3] Holdsworth, *op. cit.* I, 452–3.

[4] Baldwin, *The king's council*, pp. 238 ff.   [5] Wilkinson, *op. cit.* pp. 94 ff.

concerning the common law should be pleaded before the chancellor, and that he, or the keeper of the privy seal, should hear
cases concerning the royal favour (7). With the increase of business
more definite forms were being adopted; and a procedure closely
akin to that of the council gave the chancery a clear advantage
over the common law courts (cf. 27). It was always open to the
suitor, it used no jury, and its writs were adapted to the needs of
equity. These writs, in contrast to those of the common law, did
not include the cause of summons; and while they retained some
established formulas, certain penalties were added which increased
the efficiency and stringency of summons. In the writ *quibusdam
certis de causis* (23) a general inhibition was included, while in
premunire (p. 58) and *sub poena* (9) a definite penalty was stated.
The writ *sub poena* was most generally used, though common
law writs, such as *scire facias* (14), *venire facias* (24) and *corpus cum
causa* (16), might also be issued.[1]

By the mid-fourteenth century, then, the court of chancery was
emerging, and its equitable jurisdiction increased rapidly after
this time. The limitation of the judicial work of the exchequer
did away with one possible rival.[2] The chancellor had also to deal
with many cases which arose because of the rigid procedure of
the courts of common law; an appeal from a judgment given in a
court of common law could only be made on a point of error;[3] the
chancery went further and gave a new hearing to a disputed case,
thus satisfying a need that was expressed as early as 1315 (1). In
some cases the chancellor's interference was specially needed,
as for the enforcement of simple contracts, until by his action
here the judges were roused after the middle of the century to
offer an effective remedy at the common law.[4] Above all it was
in connection with uses and trusts that the chancery had its
opportunity. It had become a common practice for an owner
of land, *A*, to convey his land to another, *B*, who should hold it
to the use of *A*, or of a third party, *C*, who would thus have the
practical advantage of possession (13). In this way feudal incidents
might be avoided; and certain statutes, such as that of mortmain,
could be evaded, since *A* could transfer land to *B* to be held in
trust for a religious house (20). A landowner, again, who feared
that he would be convicted of treason, could evade the forfeiture
of his lands by transferring them to the use of his heirs. From
1377, however, there were several statutes against uses for the

[1] *Cases before the king's council*, pp. xxxviii–xxxix, and *Select cases in chancery*,
pp. xiv–xv.
[2] See below, p. 229.   [3] Holdsworth, *op. cit.* I, 214–15.   [4] *Ibid.* I, 455–7.

purposes of fraud, culminating in the statute of uses in 1535.[1] Meanwhile, many were the disputes arising from legal difficulties concerning uses; as when the recipient of a trust did not carry out the agreement that was involved (21, 28). The common law gave no remedy to the person or persons for whose benefit the land was conveyed, but the chancellor could in equity force the trustee to discharge his obligation. In the fifteenth century especially an enormous amount of business resulted, and jurisdiction over uses and trusts became the most important branch of chancery work.[2]

It is not until late in our period that we can begin to distinguish the work of the chancellor alone from his activities in the council. It was usual for him to have the assistance of councillors (2, 26). In petitions he had been associated with other officials, the treasurer, the keeper of the privy seal; then gradually he alone was addressed (5, 10, 11, 19, 25). In a number of documents a distinction between council and chancery can be traced (2), though it is dangerous to generalise on the change. Even in the mid-fifteenth century members of the council were attending chancery (29);[3] but in 1474 the chancellor was giving judgment alone (30), and at the end of the century it was admitted that he could judge *per se sine aliquo iusticiario*.[4] By that time he had an unrivalled position in the state. He figured in the government as one of the greatest officials; he opened and presided over parliament, which had been summoned by writs under the great seal; he was still regarded as judicial president of the council, and this is all the more interesting in view of the development of the office of privy seal. Above all, his independent jurisdiction was coming to surpass all other functions; it had been the object of frequent attack by the commons in parliament, who were jealous for the prestige of the common law (8, 18, 22); but the triumph of equity was assured in the fifteenth century, when political faction weakened the council, and when the law courts were themselves corrupt and inefficient.

BIBLIOGRAPHY

I. ORIGINAL SOURCES

P.R.O. Ancient petitions.

BAILDON, W. P. (ed.). *Select cases in chancery*, 1364–1471, S.S. vol. x, 1896.

---

[1] Holdsworth, *op. cit.* IV, 443 ff.   [2] *Ibid.* I, 454–5.
[3] *Select cases in chancery*, p. xiii.   [4] Baldwin, *op. cit.* p. 253.

Rotuli parliamentorum. London, 1783.
Proceedings in chancery in the reign of Queen Elizabeth (including proceedings from Richard II), vol. I. London, 1832.
SANDERS, G. W. (ed.). *Orders of the high court of chancery...*, vol. I, pts. 1, 2. London, 1845.

2. SECONDARY AUTHORITIES

BALDWIN, J. F. *The king's council in England during the middle ages.* Oxford, 1913.
LYTE, H. C. MAXWELL. *Historical notes on the use of the great seal of England.* London, 1926.
MAITLAND, F. W. *Equity, also the forms of action at common law.* Cambridge, 1909.
TOUT, T. F. *Chapters in the administrative history of medieval England.* Manchester, 1920–30.
WILKINSON, B. *The chancery under Edward III.* Manchester, 1929.

3. ESSAY

TOUT, T. F. "The household of the chancery and its disintegration", *Essays in history presented to R. Lane Poole* (ed. H. W. C. Davis). Oxford, 1927.

(1) *Early evidence of equitable jurisdiction* 1315

A Nostre Seignur le Roi prie Alianore qi fu la femme Henry de Percy, qe come le dit Henry son Baron puis q'il l'avoit espose chargea le Maner de Lekenfeld de dys livres de Rente, a paier par an a Monsire Emon Darel a tote la vie Monsire Emon, saunz assigner le nule certeine Terre ou Rente en le dit Maner, et la dite Alianore ne soit pas dowe des dites dis livres, q'il plese a nostre Seignur le Roy faire assigner a la dite Alianore seon resonable Dower pur meismes le dis livres des Terres et Tenementz qi furunt au dit Henry, et qi sont en la main le Roy par le noun age son heir; desicome ele ne put mie aver recovrir par Bref de Dower, pur ceo qe le dit Edmond n'est pas seisi de certeine parcele de Terre, ne de Rente, en le dit Manoir, mes prent les dites dis livres par an par les mains celi qi tient le Manoir.

Responsio. Sequatur in Cancellaria ubi Extente returnantur, et vocato Edmondo Darel, visisque literis de concessione illarum decem librarum; et fiat sibi ibidem justitia, quia non potest juvari per Communem Legem per Breve de Dote.

Rot. Parl. I, 340.

(2)   *Case of the Bishop of Durham's franchisal rights* 1315

...Et super hoc Dominus noster Rex per Litteras sub Privato Sigillo suo scripsit Dominis Johanni de Sandale, Cancellario, et Waltero de Norwico Thesaurario, suis, in hec verba:

Edward, etc. a Noz chers et foialx Johan de Sandale nostre Chancellier, et Monsire Wauter de Norwiz nostre Tresorier, Salutz. Nous vous mandoms qe, appellez a vous ceux de nostre Conseil qe vous verrez qe facent appeller, facez regarder les Petitions qe l'onurable Piere en Dieu l'Evesqe de Duresme fit liverer a nostre darrein Parlement a Nicole, et puis, sur aucunes busoignes touchantes lui et la Franchise de sa Eglise de Duresme, lesquieux ne sont mie encore respondues a ceo q'est dit, et eu plener avisement sur les choses contenues en meismes les Petitions, facez deliverer les dites busoignes si en haste comme vous porrez bonement, fesantz a lui droit et reson selonc la Lei et l'usage de nostre Roiaume, issint q'il n'en soit plus delaiez. Done souz nostre Prive Seal, a Mortelak, le xxi jour de Juyn, l'an de nostre Regne nevisme.

Rot. Parl. i, 362.

(3)   *The chancery and parliamentary records* 1319

[*The Abbot of St James outside Northampton was cited to parliament after Easter, 12 Ed. II, at York, and he appointed Hen. of Blithesworth as procurator.*]

Et quia nec idem Abbas nec prædecessores sui, unquam antea ad parlamentum fuerant citati, idem procurator quæsivit in Cancellaria, utrum per simplex breve vel per registrum fuerat citatus. Et scrutatis rotulis Cancellariæ invenit nomen Abbatis, inter citandos ad parlamentum, irrotulatum. Et per illud irrotulamentum semper ad quodlibet parlamentum esse inter alios vocaturum. Qui quidem procurator rogavit cum effectu Dominum Willielmum de Aermynne, tunc Custodem Rotulorum, ut nomen prædicti Abbatis deleretur; desicut nunquam antea irrotulatum fuit, et desicut idem Abbas nihil tenet de Rege in capite nec per baroniam, sed tantum in puram et perpetuam eleemosynam...Idemque Custos respondit, se aliquo modo non posse nec velle rotulos Cancellariæ in aliquo cancellare...

[*The abbot then appealed to Thomas, Earl of Lancaster, Steward of England.*]

Postea videbatur eidem procuratori, quod si hujusmodi billæ in communi concilio executionem fecisset, crimen scandali

Domino Cancellario et Custodi Rotulorum pro tali irrotulamento imposuisset, ac idem Cancellarius et cæteri pro parte sua fovenda et pro facto suo advocando dicerent quod idem Abbas juste citatus fuerat, et quod juste citandus esset, unde inquisitiones, dampna, et expensæ, et cætera multa pericula emergere possent. Hac de causa, dictus procurator non deliberavit billam prædictam: sed aliam billam Domino Cancellario et ejus Clericis ordinavit et tradidit, cujus billæ tenor talis est.

Abbas Sancti Jacobi extra Northampton irrotulatur de novo in Cancellaria Domini Regis inter citandos ad parlamentum, et non tenet per baroniam nec de Rege in capite, sed tantum in puram...eleemosynam: et nec ipse Abbas nec prædecessores sui unquam in Cancellaria irrotulati fuerunt, nec ad parlamentum citati huc-usque; unde idem Abbas petit remedium.

Ad cujus billæ executionem Dominus Cancellarius, cum suo consilio de Cancellaria ordinavit, quod nomen prædicti Abbatis a registro Cancellariæ deleretur, et ita pluribus circumspectis, idem Abbas est absolutus. Sed quia idem Abbas vel ejus successores ad stimulationem aliquorum malivorum possent alias, per casum, irrotulari et per consequens citari, prædictus procurator dictam exsecutionis formam propter evidentiam in scripturam redegit.

Facta est ista exsecutio per visum Domini Johannis de Otham Episcopi Eliensis, Cancellarii Domini Regis, Domini Willielmi d'Ayermynne tunc Custodis Rotulorum, Domini Roberti de Bardelby, [7 *others*] et aliorum Clericorum Cancellariæ et aliorum diversarum Curiarum Domini Regis ac Regni etc.

Parliamentary writs, vol. II, pt. ii, pp. 199–200.

(4) *Treatment of petitions to parliament* 1325

Et auxint, Sire, prient Voz liges gentz, qe par la ou il ount bote avant lour Petitions en diverses Parlementz des diverses grevances, et les unes sount ajournes devant le Roi, et les autres devant le Chauncellier, dount nul issue n'est fait, q'il pleise a vostre haute Seignurie comander remedie.

Responsio. Il plest au Roi.

Rot. Parl. I, 430 (5).

(5) *Petition to the chancellor* 1325

A Chaunceller nostre Seigneur le Roi Emma la femme Roger de Plat prie grace et deliveraunce, pur Dieu, qe Vous voillez regarder la Peticioun qe feust livere au commun Parlement a la Seint Johan, et respondu par Comun Conseil, et a Vous liveri; et Vous commaundastes de suyre Bref a Sire William de Herle, de faire venir le Record et le Proces devaunt Vous; lequel Record est ore venu, e livere en Chauncellerie par my la mayn Sire William de Herle, et la dite Peticion feust en la garde Syre William de Herlaston.

Rot. Parl. i, 437 (25).

(6) *Transference of the great seal* 1340

Memorandum de Magno Sigillo Archiepiscopo Cantuariensi liberato

Memorandum quod die Veneris...videlicet, vicesimo octavo die Mensis Aprilis,...Dominus Johannes de Sancto Paulo, Custos Rotulorum Cancellariæ ipsius Domini Regis, Magnum Sigillum...in quadam Bursa inclusum, et Sigillo præfati Johannis consignatum,

Quod in Custodia ipsius Johannis, de Mandato dicti Domini Regis, remansit, et quod idem Dominus Rex ad Se, per ipsum Johannem, in Cameram ejusdem Domini Regis, vocatam LA BLAUNCHE CHAUMBRE super Aquam Thamesis, in Palatio suo Westmonasteriensi, deportari fecit,

......

Qui quidem Dominus Rex idem Sigillum a dicto Johanne recepit,

Et in manu sua usque in parvam Cameram, dictæ Albæ Cameræ, ex parte Australi, conjunctam, deportavit,

Et illud, in eadem Parva Camera, Venerabili Patri, Johanni Archiepiscopo Cantuariensi, totius Angliæ Primati (quem dictus Dominus Rex ad Officium Cancellarii exercendum assumpsit) in præsentia prædictorum Comitum et Militum, liberavit:

Qui quidem Archiepiscopus (præstito Sacramento de eodem Officio fideliter exercendo) dictum Sigillum a præfato Domino Rege Manu propria recepit, et secum usque Manerium suum de Lambeheth deferri, et Cartas, Literas Patentes, et Brevia, in Crastino, in Camera ipsius Archiepiscopi, apud Lambeheth, consignari fecit.

Foedera, v, 180.

(7) *Edward III's proclamation to the sheriffs of London* 1349

volumus quod quilibet negocia tam communem legem regni nostri Anglie quam graciam nostram specialem concernencia penes nosmetipsos habens exnunc prosequenda, eadem negocia, videlicet, negocia ad communem legem penes venerabilem virum electum Cantuariensem confirmatum Cancellarium nostrum per ipsum expedienda, et alia negocia de gracia nostra concernenda penes eundem Cancellarium seu dilectum clericum nostrum Custodem sigilli nostri privati prosequantur [*sic*]; ita quod ipsi vel unus eorum peticiones negotiorum que per eos, nobis inconsultis, expediri non poterunt, una cum avisamentis suis inde, ad nos transmittant vel transmittat, absque alia prosecucione penes nos inde facienda, ut hiis inspectis ulterius prefato Cancellario seu Custodi inde significemus velle nostrum.

Printed in *Select cases in chancery* (S.S.), p. xvii, from Close roll.

(8) *Petition of the commons concerning writs* 1352

Item prie la Commune, qe come contenu soit en la Grande Chartre, 'Qe nostre Seignur le Roi ne vendra ne deleiera droit a nulli:' Et ceux qi vodroient purchacer Briefs en la Chauncellerie, queux Briefs sont la primere partie de sa Leie, quele Leie est soverein Droit de son Roialme et de sa Corone, ne poent aver Briefs sanz Fyn faire illoeqes pur yceux, issint qe plousours de son Roialme qi ne poent Fyns doner sont malement desheritez a touz jours par cele cause. Et d'autre part, nostre dit Seignur le Roi averoit molt plus del Fee de son Seal, ensemblement od issues et amerciementz queux lui deveroient acrestre par meismes les Briefs, q'il n'ad ore, s'ils fuissent grantez franchement sanz Fyn. Prie la dite Commune qe lui pleise,...granter, qe touz qi vodront Briefs avoir en sa Chancellerie les puissent avoir fraunchement sanz Fyn, paiaunt le Fee de Seal acustume.

Responsio. Homme ne poet toller le profit le Roi qe soleit estre donez pur Briefs de grace en auncien temps. Mes le Roi voet qe le Chanceller sur le granter des tieux Briefs soit si gracious come il poet estre bonement, en eise du poeple.

Rot. Parl. II, 241 (40).

(9) *Writ of* sub poena 1365

Edwardus, etc. dilecto sibi Ricardo Spynk de Norwyco, salutem. Quibusdam certis de causis tibi præcipimus firmiter injungentes quod sis coram consilio nostro apud Westmonasterium, die Mercurii proximo post quindenam nativitatis Sancti Johannis Baptistæ proximo futuram: ad respondendum super hiis que tibi objicientur ex parte nostra, et ad faciendum et recipiendum quod curia nostra consideraverit in hac parte. Et hoc sub pœna centum librarum nullatenus omittas. Teste meipso apud West-monasterium, tercio die Julii, anno regni nostri tricesimo sep-timo etc.

Palgrave, *The original authority of the king's council*, p. 41 n.

(10) *Petitions to the chancellor* 1376

Plese a chaunceller nostre seignour le Roi graunter al Admirall del South' et West' vne comission darester touz les Niefs del portage de xx tonelx ou plus et auxi touz les mariners qe nulle ne passe hors du roialme sanz conge du Roi ou del Admirall sur forfaiture de quant qil purra forfaire deuers le Roi.

Ancient petitions, F. 298, no. 14877. (Cf. *Cal. close roll*, Ed. III, xiv (1374-7), 302, for dating.)

Pleise au chaunceller nostre seignour le Roi granter a Johan Pykenham et a Raulyn Knyghton, marchaundz de Londres, brief directe as maire Baillifz et custumers el port de la ville de Neof Chastel sur Tyne, qe les ditz Johan et Raulyn poent charger des carbonnz en diuerses neofs pour lour custume ent duez paiant pour segler deuers (?) Sprus en Estlond pour remesner Bord' Tar' et autres maneres marchandises en Engleterre.

Ancient petitions, F. 298, no. 14861. (Uncertain date.)

(11) *A case in chancery; disputed election of a prior* 1377

A Chauncelere nostre seignur le Roy.

Monstre Johan Walyngfford, Priour del esglise de Seint Frise-wyth d'Oxenford, qe come il estoit eslieu par le Couuent de mesme l'esglise d'estre Priour par licence de sire Edward, nadgairs Roy d'Engleterre, aiel nostre seignur le Roy q'ore est, patron del esglise auauntdit, et conferme par l'Euesque diocesan de mesme le lieu, et en paisible possession come Priour par trois anz tanqe il fuist ouste par Johan Dodeford; Sour qei le dit Johan Walyng-ford est venuz a ceste presente parlement de pursuire son droit a nostre seignur le Roy et a son Conseil; et le dit John Dodeford luy ad fait prendre issi q'il est en gard de viscount de Londres: Par qei vous pleise de maundere breef a viscountz de Londres d'amesner le dit Johan Walyngford deuant vous issint q'il poet pursuir sez busoignes de la matiere auauntdit; et ensement de maunder breef al dit Johan Dodeford de vener cy a ceste presente parlement d'estree present affaire discussion de la matiere auauntdit selonc droit et reson.

Indorsed. Memorandum quod predictus Johannes Dodeford audiens de prosecucione per predictum Johannem de Walyngford sic facta, xxvj die Septembris anno regni regis Ricardi nunc primo, in Cancellaria Regis apud Westmonasterium, coram venerabili patre Episcopo Meneuense, Cancellario ipsius Regis, personaliter comparebat, prefato Johanne de Walyngford tunc comparere non curante, et audita materia in ista peticione contenta, protestabatur prosecucionem et suggestionem predicti Johannis de Walyngford minus veras existere, allegando ipsum Johannem Dodeford, vacante Prioratu Sancte Frideswide, per Conuentum dicte domus de eorum communi assensu de licencia regia in Priorem eiusdem domus mere electum, et super hoc, adhibito regio assensu auctoritate Ordinario, rite et legitime confirmatum fuisse, et ipsum sic Priorem et pastorem dicte domus existere; per quod petiit quod partes predicte et causa illa ipsorum Ordinario dimittantur ibidem discuciende;

Ac prefatus Cancellarius comperto per rotulos et memoranda Cancellarie Regis quod dicte electio et confirmacio in forma predicta facte fuerunt et iam resident in filaciis dicte Cancellarie, perpendens causam predictam ac cognicionem eiusdem ad forum ecclesiasticum et non ad Curiam regiam nec aliam Curiam laicalem mero iure pertinere, dimisit partes a dicta Curia ac causam et materiam supradictas, precipiens et iudicialiter discernens quod partes predicte causam illam coram Ordinario suo vel aliis iudicibus ecclesiasticis prosequantur si sibi viderint expedire.

Select cases in chancery (S.S.), pp. 104–5.

(12) *The Bishop of Winchester charged before the council* 1377

The third day after yᵉ bishop came to yᵉ counsaile through yᵉ haule at Westminster,...and some sixe serieantes of yᵉ lawe of his counsaile, and entered into yᵉ white chamber before yᵉ lordes;... and then by commandement a clarck began to reed yᵉ article how 80 *li.* were raced out of yᵉ chancerye and how 40 *li.* were redeliuered by yᵉ clarck of yᵉ hamper of yᵉ said chancery to Sʳ Jhon Gray of Rotherfield by reason of a bargayn...; and hearof yᵉ said bishop offered yᵉ first day to dischardge him self by his oath, which yᵉ lordes would not suffer, because he could not loyally be gainsayed; and therefore he had another day assigned him. And the third day agayne he came into ye counsaile and was questioned with about ye rasing of ye roules; and hearto he aunswered y^t ye said rasing was neuer made for his aduantage... but for almose, for it was euell enrouled and contrary to conscience; besides y^t to this matter he ought not by law to aunswear for at y^t tyme he was chanceler, ye secondary in England next to ye kinge, which office is of such auctority y^t he y^t is chanceler is not bound to accompt for his office ...Hearto among ye rest Sr William Skipwith justice said, "Sr Bishop, ye law is y^t euery of ye kinges officers, in what soeuer office he be...is bound to accompt for his office, as well ye Chanceler and Tresorer as any other..."

Appendix to Chron. Angliae (R.S.), fragment found among Stow's miscellaneous papers, pp. lxxviii–lxxix.

(13) *The will of Lord Latimer: instructions to feoffees* 1381

Testamentum domini Willielmi de Latymer.

......

Remembrance de nostre darrein volente fait le xiij jour de Avyll l'an le Roy Ricarde seconde puis le conquest quart; premerement que lez Manoirs ov touz lour appertenauncez de nostre heritage apres nostre piere, les queux nous avons done par chartre de fee symple a Henri evesque de Wircestre Ricarde Counte d'Aroundell et de Surrey et as autres come apiert par la dite chartre enroullee en la chaunceree, soient done apres nostre deces par les ditz Henri Ricarde et autres enfeffee par lour chartre al seigneure de Nevill et sez heyres mals ou femailes,[1] et q'ils portent noz armes, et a quel heure que le dit seigneur de Nevill est enfeffe il paira pur l'enfeffement des ditz terres a noz executours trois mill marcz, except le manoir de Wodeton ove l'avoweson del eglise et toutz autres appurtenancez en le Counte de Surr' done par la dite chartre as ditz Henri Ricarde et autres, le quele nous volloms que Thomas Canoys nostre cosyn eit apres nostre deces a lui et ses heirs mals,...Item nous volloms que si noz meobles ne purront suffire pour acquiter noz dettes et regarder noz servantz come devise est en nostre testament...que toutz les terres de nostre parchas soient venduz a eaux que plus voillent doner,... Item nous volloms que nostre houstell apelle le Erber ove les appurtenances en la paroche de Saint Marie de Bothawe en la

[1] Latimer's daughter and heir had married John, Lord Neville.

cite de Loundres soit vendu, si nous devions devaunt nostre
retourne, a eaux que plus veullent doner, et deux chapeleyns
covenables soient perpetuelement estables celebrer especialment
pour l'alme nostre seigneur le Roi Edward que Dieu assoile, et
pour nostre alme, en la esglise de Appelton entre quatre chapeleyns devaunt ordenez solonc la devise de nous et Robert de
Bolton' et chargeoms nos executours sur la paril de lour almes
q'ils soient ordenez soit il par esglise ou par terre si hastiment
come ils bonement purront...
Escrit a Preston en le Counte de Kent le jour et l'an susditz.

Testamenta Eboracensia, pt. 1 (Surtees Society, 1836), pp. 113–16.

(14) *Writ of* scire facias 1383

Ricardus, etc., vicecomiti Essex, salutem. Cum per inquisicionem
per Johannem Clerk de Ewell, nuper escaetorem nostrum in
comitatu predicto, de mandato nostro captam et in cancellariam
nostram retornatam sit compertum quod Henricus de la Newelonde tenuit die quo obiit in dominico suo ut de feodo manerium
de Newelonde...et quod manerium predictum tenetur de nobis
in capite ut de Honore Bolonie per seruicium unius feodi militis,
et quod predictus Henricus obiit..., quodque Ricardus, filius
ejusdem Henrici est heres ejus propinquior et infra etatem; jam-
que Willelmus de Clopton, miles, nobis supplicauerit ut cum
idem Henricus...predictum Willelmum et Willelmum Chamberleyn...de manerio predicto,...habendum sibi et heredibus suis
imperpetuum foffasset, qui quidem Willelmus Chamberleyn
postea...totum jus et clameum que habuit seu habere potuit in
eodem manerio predicto Willelmo de Clopton remisit,...ac idem
Willelmus de Clopton...in pacifica possessione et seisina ejusdem
manerii fuisset quousque tam colore inquisicionis predicte quam
litterarum nostrarum patencium per quas manerium predictum
...Willelmo de Wauton, militi, sub certa forma habendum nuper
commisimus ammotus fuisset minus juste absque hoc quod predictus Henricus aliquem statum habuit in eodem manerio predicto die quo obiit..., velimus litteras nostras predictas reuocari
et manerium predictum...in manum nostram resumi et illud
prefato Willelmo de Clopton una cum exitibus inde a tempore
mortis predicti Henrici perceptis restitui et liberari jubere: Nos
volentes in hac parte fieri quod est justum precipimus tibi...quod
scire facias prefato Willelmo de Wauton quod sit coram nobis in
cancellaria nostra a die Pasche proximo futuro in unum mensem

ubicumque tunc fuerit ad ostendendum si quid pro nobis aut se
ipso habeat vel dicere sciat quare littere nostre predicte reuocari
et manerium predictum...in manum nostram resumi et eidem
Willelmo de Clopton...restitui et liberari non debeant, et ad
faciendum ulterius et recipiendum quod curia nostra considerauerit in hac parte. Et habeas ibi nomina illorum per quos ei
scire feceris et hoc breue. Teste me ipso apud Westmonasterium
xx die Februarii anno regni nostri sexto. Burton'.
[*Endorsed*:] Scire feci Willelmo de Wauton militi infranominato
quod sit coram domino Rege in cancellaria sua ad diem infra
contentum...facturus et ostensurus quod istud breue requirit
per Robertum Rigge et Ricardum Johan.
    Galfridus Dersham, vicecomes...
Select cases before the king's council (S.S.), pp. 71–2.

(15) *Judgment over clerks of chancery* 1386

Pro clericis Cancellarie Regis de recordo etc. mittendis.

Rex dilecto et fideli suo Roberto Tresilian Capitali Justitiario
suo salutem Cum Ricardus Curteys civis et scissor Londonie nuper
in Curia nostra coram justitiariis nostris de Banco per breve
nostrum implacitasset Johannem de Leycestre unum Clericorum
Cancellarie nostre per nomen Johannes de Sleford de comitatu
Leycestrie de debito viginti et quatuor librarum et sexdecim
solidorum quod idem Ricardus a prefato Johanne exigit Et pro
eo quod clerici de Cancellaria nostra et Progenitorum nostrorum...vel eorum servientes ibidem ad respondendum coram
aliquibus justitiariis seu ministris nostris preterquam coram Cancellario nostro seu Custodibus sive Custode Magni Sigilli nostri
qui pro tempore fuerint super aliquibus placitis...que nos non
tangunt in locis illis ubi placea illa esse contigerit emergentibus
(placitis de libero tenemento feloniis et appellis duntaxat exceptis)
juxta consuetudinem hactenus usitatam et approbatam contra
voluntatem suam trahi vel compelli non debeant Mandaverimus
prefatis Justitiariis nostris de Banco per aliud breve nostrum quod
omnibus placitis et querelis versus ipsum Johannem per prefatum
Ricardum coram eis in Banco predicto motis vel movendis ulterius
tenendis supersederent omnino Prout in recordo et processu
loquele ejusdem plenius continetur Ac postmodum ad prosecu-
tionem prefati Johannis nobis suggerentis errorem in recordo et
processu predictis intervenisse mandaverimus dilecto et fideli
nostro Roberto Bealknap Capitali Justitiario nostro de Banco

predicto quod si judicium inde redditum esset tunc recordum et
processum predicta cum omnibus ea tangentibus et dictum breve
nostrum sibi inde directum nobis sub sigillo suo mitteret ita quod
ea haberemus a die Sancti Michaelis ultimo preterito in unum
mensem ubicunque tunc essemus in Anglia...
Nos pro eo quod principale placitum loquele prædicte ad cogni-
tionem Cancellarii nostri et nullius alterius juxta consuetudinem
predictam mere pertinet et ex consequenti ejus accessorium ad
eundem Cancellarium pertinere debet Volentes jurisdictionem...
hujusmodi a tam longo tempore obtenta et approbata illesa
firmiter observare Vobis Mandamus quod recordum et processum
predicta...in Cancellariam nostram...sine dilatione mittatis et
hoc breve...Teste Rege apud Westmonasterium viii die Novembris.

G. W. Sanders, *Orders of the high court of chancery*, vol. I, pt. 2,
p. 1027.

(16) *Writ of* corpus cum causa 1388

Ricardus [etc.] Vicecomitibus Londoniarum, salutem. Precipimus vobis firmiter iniungentes quod omnibus aliis pretermissis et
excusacione quacumque penitus cessante, Habeatis coram nobis
in Cancellaria nostra die lune proximo futuro vbicumque tunc
fuerit Johannem Milner de Takiley in Comitatu Essexie per vos
in prisona nostra de Neugate sub aresto detentum vt dicitur,
vnacum causa arestacionis et detencionis sue. Et hoc sub incumbenti periculo nullatenus omittatis, hoc breve vobiscum
deferentes. Teste me ipso apud Westmonasterium xix die Nouembris, anno regni nostri duodecimo.

Select cases in chancery (S.S.), p. 9.

(17) *Reform of chancery* (?) 1388–9

Ordinacio Cancellarie

Hic subscripte sunt Ordinaciones Cancellarie Domini Regis facte
anno XII. regni Regis Ricardi Secundi.

Ordinatum est per dominum Cancellarium Anglie Et per duodecim clericos de prima forma ad robas in Cancellaria domini
Regis concordatum Quod inter omnes clericos de Cancellaria tam
de numero quam de gestu ipsorum de cetero teneatur et obser-
vetur ordo subscriptus viz.

13-2

Custos Rotulorum sex clericos[1]

Imprimis cum ab antiquo ordinatum fuerit quod Custos Rotulorum Cancellarie predicte pro tempore existente haberet tres clericos scribentes in eisdem Rotulis et non plures Pro eo tamen quod negocia in dictis rotulis inserenda indies confluunt multo magis quam solebant Ordinatum est quod idem Custos jam habeat sex clericos et non plures scribentes in rotulis predictis ex causa supradicta Proviso quod nullus eorundem clericorum sic scribencium uxoratus existat.

Roba habeat tres clericos. Clerici duodecim clericorum ad robas

Item quilibet predictorum duodecim clericorum ad robas habeat tres clericos ad magis hujusmodi condicionis scilicet non uxoratos manibus suis propriis scribentes sub nomine magistri ad Sigillum domini Regis in Cancellaria predicta Et quod nullus eorundem duodecim plicet brevia communiter ad sigillum predictum preter prefatum Custodem Rotulorum et preceptores per Dominum Cancellarium nominandos et perficiendos Nisi et liberacione et precepto ipsius Domini Cancellarii vel ejusdem Custodis et presentes preceptores Johannes Hartipole clericus et Johannes Ffranke clericus.

Hospicium duodecim clericorum ad robas

Item quod iidem duodecim clerici ad robas in hospiciis propriis seu saltem conductis insimul per se vel divisim et non inter alios minoris gradus aut status hospitentur et conversentur propter honestatem honoris et gradus eorundem Sub pena expulcionis a Curia.

Custos hanaperii non inscribat ad sigillum

Item propter multiplices causas necessarias Curie satis notas custos hanaperii Cancellarie predicte cujusque status...sit vel fuerit in futurum nec clerici ejus nullo modo scribi faciat ad sigillum predictum nomine suo proprio...nisi hujusmodi custos de prima forma fuerit et ab antiquo eruditus sciverit cursum ejusdem Curie et cum quo Cancellarius...de consensu predictorum clericorum de prima forma gratiosius voluerit dispensare Et pro presenti dispensatum est cum Henrico Raye uno clericorum de prima forma jam custode hanaperii predicti qui ab antiquo eruditus scit cursum ejusdem Curie.

[1] The chapter headings are in the Hargrave MS. used by Sanders.

Hospicium clericorum de secunda forma

Item quod omnes clerici de secunda forma extra hospicium prefati Custodis Rotulorum seu alicujus alterius clerici de prima forma comorantes in hospiciis ipsorum clericorum de sua forma propriis seu aliis per ipsos conductis insimul per se vel divisim et non inter alios minoris gradus consimiliter morentur, . . . propter honestatem in gradus eorundem clericorum et Curie Sub pena supradicta scilicet amocionis a Curia Et quod quilibet ipsorum habeat sub nomine suo unum clericum duntaxat minime uxoratum scribentem ad sigillum predictum Exceptis duobus Clericis de Corona qui sunt de eadem forma Quorum uterque propter paria negocia dominum Regem tangencia que indies confluunt habeat cum necesse fuerit duos clericos tantum et non plures scribentes ad sigillum predictum nisi necessitatis articulo et hoc per dispensacionem prefati domini Cancellarii. . .

Pro plicacione brevium

Item quod nullus eorundem clericorum de secunda forma brevia sua de cursu nec aliquis cursista de Cancellaria predicta aliquas cartas litteras patentes seu brevia sua ponant ad manus Domini Cancellarii nec coram ipso [nisi] per unum dictorum clericorum de prima forma prius examinentur vel nisi per eundem Dominum Cancellarium super hoc mandatum habeat speciale Simul nec Clerici de Corona ponant brevia et commissiones que facient in manibus prefati Domini Cancellarii nisi ex certa causa eis per ipsum Dominum Cancellarium primitus insumatur.

Qui sedebunt extra barram

Item omnes predicti clerici de secunda forma exceptis clericis de parva baga cum uno clerico vel duobus clericis ac clerico pro scrutinio rotulorum Cancellarie predicte in Turri London et clerico pro lectura recordorum et placitorum dicte Cancellarie sedeant extra barram ejusdem Cancellarie tempore sigillacionis et placitorum tenendorum in locis eis assignatis prout ab antiquo fieri consuevit ac eciam extranei nisi certis de causis evocentur.

Pro sessione clericorum in Curia Regis

Item quod omnes predicti clerici tam de prima quam de secunda forma ordinem suum prout in rotulo inseruntur teneant in liberacionibus hospiciorum ad parliamenta et consilia eciam de sessionibus suis in mensa infra Curiam ac in Curia cum apud Westmonasterium vel alibi fuerit Et quod quilibet cedat alii in premissis ac eciam in honoribus et reverenciis juxta formam eleccionis et prefeccionis eorundem prout ab antiquo fieri consuevit.

Ne quis sedeat in hanaperio

Item quod aliquis de prima vel secunda forma non sedeat in hanaperio Cancellarie predicte nec in hanaperio de communi banco ad aliqua brevia ibidem legenda et ex partibus prosequentibus liberanda propter honestatem gradus et Curie...

xxiiij Cursiste

Item quod de cetero sint viginti et quatuor cursiste in Cancellaria predicta et non plures qui brevia per ipsos conficienda manibus suis propriis scribant nisi illi qui fuerint senes languidi aut impotentes cum quibus Curia graciose voluerit dispensare In quo casu habeat quilibet eorum sub nomine suo unum clericum sufficientem et non uxoratum duntaxat scribentem ad sigillum predictum...

Juramentum clericorum ad sigillum scribentium

Item quod nullus scribat ad sigillum predictum nisi sit juratus domino Regi et admissus pro cursista ad scribendum nomine suo proprio Exceptis clericis illorum de prima forma et secunda sub nominibus magistrorum suorum scribentibus ac eciam clericis illorum cursistarum qui ad hoc licenciati fuerint...

Quod clerici Curie jurentur

Item quod omnes predicti Clerici tam de prima quam de secunda forma ac eciam cursiste qui nunc sunt et eorum successores...jurentur ad premissa omnia et singula firmiter...tenenda et observanda prout ad quemlibet ipsorum pertinet in forma predicta...

G. W. Sanders, *Orders of the high court of chancery*, vol. 1, pt. 1, pp. 1 ff. (Mr B. Wilkinson has printed the document, collated from three MS. copies, in Appendix VI of his *Chancery under Edward III.*)

(18) *Writs of chancery and the common law* 1389

Item prient les Communes, qe al suite de partie, ne al suggestion, null des liges du Roy soit fait venir par Brief Quibusdam certis de causis, ne par null autre tiel Brief, devant le Chanceller, ou le Conseill le Roy, de respondre d'ascune manere dont recoverer est done par la commune Ley, s'il ne soit par Brief de Scire facias, la ou il est fonde par la commune Ley, ou autrement par Estatut, sur peyne a le Chanceller de cent livers, a lever a l'oeps le Roi; et le Clerc qi escrivera le Brief, de perdre son Office en la Chancellerie, sanz james estre restitutz a ascun Office en la Chancellerie suis dite.

Responsio. Le Roy voet sauver sa Regalie, come ses progenitours ont faitz devant luy.

Rot. Parl. III, 267 (33). (Cf. *Rot. Parl.* III, 474 (95) for a similar complaint in 1401.)

(19) *Petition to the chancellor* 1390

Al treshonurable Chaunceller le Roy Dengleterre monstrent... Johan Weston et Alice sa femme, qe come ils porteront vn bref dassise de nouel desseisme a Wynchestre deuaunt William Rykhyll et Johan Cassy Justices nostre seignur le Roy des assisez en le counte de Suthampton le lundy prochein auant la feste de seint Marie Maudeleyn lan nostre seignur le Roy qore est xij⁰, vers William Upton de lour franc tenement in Warblyngton,...a quel iour le dit William ne vient...vn Johan ? Haruy respondit come baillief du dit William et dit qe le dit William...fuit vtlage al suite Johan Steuenes en le Counte de Sussex en vn bref de conspiracie par cause de quelle vtlagie lez tenementz dont la pleinte fut fait furent seisis par leschetour nostre seignur le Roy...en lez maynes nostre seignur le Roy, par quoy les Justices auantditz ne voleyent aler auant a lassisse prendre issint mesme ceux Johan et Alice furent delayes de lour pursuite et droit, dont vous pleise de vostre graciouse pitie grantier bref as Justices auantditz daler auant a lassise prendre et feire ceo qe la ley voet et ceo en honure de charite.

Ancient petitions, F. 303, no. 15117. (Cf. *Cal. close roll*, Ric. II, IV (1389–92), 112, for dating.)

(20) *Restraints on uses by which the statute of mortmain*
could be evaded 1391

[*Reference to the statute of* 7 *Edward I* de Religiosis.]

...Et en outre accordez est...qe toutz ceux qi sont possessionez par feoffement ou par autre voie al oeps de gentz de religion ou autres persones espiritiels, des terres tenementz fees advoesons ou autres possessions qeconqes pur les amortiser, et dont les ditz religiouses et persones espiritiels preignent les profitz, qe parentre cy et le fest de Seint Michel proschein venant ils les facent estre amortisez par licence du Roi et des seignurs, ou autrement qils les vendent et alienent a autre oeps parentre cy et le dit fest, sur peine destre forfaitz au Roi et as seignurs solonc la forme de lestatut de religious come tenementz purchasez par gentz de religion; et qe de cest temps enavant null tiel purchace se face...; et mesme cest estatut sextende et soit tenuz de toutz terres...et autres possessions purchacez...al oeps des gildes et fraternitees. Et enoutre est assentuz pur ce qe Mairs Baillifs et Communes de Citees Burghs et autres villes qont commune perpetuel et autres qont offices perpetuels sont aussi perpetuels come gentz de religion, qe de cest temps enavant ils ne purchacent a eux et a lour commune ou office sur la peine contenue en le dit estatut de religiouses; et de ce qe autres sont possessionez ou serra purchacez en temps avenir a lour oeps et ils ent preignent...les profitz, soit semblablement fait come devant est dit de gentz de religion.

S.R. II, 79, 15 Ric. II, c. 5.

(21) *A case in chancery concerning a trust* 1393

A tresreuerent piere en Dieu et tres gracious seignur, l'Euesque d'Excestre, Chaunceller d'Engleterre.

Supplient tres humblement Thomas Godwyne et Johanne sa femme nadgairs femme a Piers atte More de Suthewerk, qe come en le feste de seint Michel en l'an du regne...le Roy Richard q'or'est xvij^e le suisdit Piers atte More en sa viuount enfeffa Thomas Profyt, parsone del eglise de seint George en Suthewerk, Richard Saundre et John Denewey en vn tenement oue sez appurtenantz assis en Suthwerk,...sur tiels condicions q'ensuient, c'estassauoir, qe lez suisditz trois feffetz, mayntenaunt apres la mort du dit Piers, duissent enfeffer la dite Johanne en touz les ditz terres et tenementz...a terme de vie du dite Johanne, la remeyndre apres soun decesse a vn Nichol atte More, frere a dit Piers, a auer a luy et a ses heirs de soun corps engendres, et pur defaute d'issue la remeyndre outre pur estre vendu par quatre bonnes gentz du dit parosche, et la monoye pur yceux receu, doner a seinte esglise pur s'alme; Sur quey le dit Piers murrust; apres qy mort deux des dites feffetz, Richard et Johan, pur procurement d'un Johan Solas, relesseront al dit Thomas Profyt tout lour estate...pur la graunt affiaunce q'ils auoient en le dit Thomas Profyt qi fuist lour confessour, et q'il voleit parfourmer la volunte du dit Piers en fourme desuisdite;...apres quelle reles ency faite, le dit Thomas Profyt...ad vendu a mesme le Johan Solas touz lez terres et tenementz auauntditz pur toutz iours; Et le dit Johan Solas est oblige al dit Thomas Profyt en cent liures

par vne obligacion a faire defence des ditz terres et tenementz par
brocage et maynteynaunce enuers chescuny; issint par lour fauce
interpretacion et conspiracion la dite Johanne Nichol et seinte
eglise sount en poynt d'estre disherites...Que plese a vostre
tresdroiturel seignurie pur comaunder lez ditz Thomas Profyt,
Richard Saundre et Johan Denewey venir deuaunt vous, et eux
examiner pur la dire de verite de toute la matere suisdit, issint qe
la dite Johanne, qi n'ad de quoy viuere, purra auoir soun droit
en lez ditz terres et tenementz, come par l'examinacion deuaunt
vous, tresgracious seignur, serra troue et proue; pur Dieu et en
oeure de seint charite.

Select cases in chancery (S.S.), pp. 48–9.

(22) *The jurisdiction of council and chancery* 1394

Item prie la Commune, qe par la ou plusours liges du Roialme,
par nient vraies suggestions faitz si bien a Conseill nostre Seignur
le Roi come en la Chancellarie nostre Seignur le Roi, sont envoiez
de comparer devant le dit Conseill, ou en la Chancellarie, sur
certeine peyne, a certein jour, par ont les loialx liges du Roialme
sont torcenousement travaillez et vexez, a grant damage de voz
ditz liges,...sanz recoverir ent avoir de lour damages et coustages: Qe plese ordeiner et establer en cest present Parlement, qe
le Chanceller d'Engleterre qi pur le temps serra eit plein poair de
faire les parties compleignantz en tielx Briefs, sub certa pena, de
trover sufficeantz plegges et seurete de faire gree a partie defendant,
en cas qe sa suggestion ne soit vraie. Et qe le dit Chanceller eit
plein poair d'assesser et taxer les costages et damages ensy avenuz
a les parties defendantz par la partie pleintif, et ent faire execution
pur les faux suggestions suis ditz. Purveuz tout foitz, qe null
frank tenement, n'autre action qeconqe, qi poet estre trie par la
commune Ley, ne soit tret n'amesne en la Chancellarie sus dite,
n'aillours, mes devaunt les Justices du Roi, come ad este usez
devant ces hures.

Responsio. Le Roy voet, qe le Chanceller pur le temps esteant
eit poair d'ent ordeiner, et agarder damages solonc sa discretion.
Rot. Parl. III, 323 (52). (Cf. *Rot. Parl.* IV, 156 (25) for a similar
complaint in 1421.)

(23) *Writ of* quibusdam certis de causis 1395

Ricardus...Rogero Tyce, nuper balliuo de Briggewater, salutem.
Quibusdam certis de causis nos specialiter monentibus tibi precipimus firmiter iniungentes quod omnibus aliis pretermissis et

excusacione quacumque cessante, in propria persona tua sis coram nobis et consilio nostro apud Westmonasterium in Octabis Sancti Martini...ad respondendum ibidem super hiis que tibi tunc obicientur ex parte nostra et ad faciendum vlterius et recipiendum quod per nos et dictum consilium nostrum de te tunc contigerit ordinari. Et hoc sub incumbenti periculo nullatenus omittas. Et habeas ibi hoc breue. Teste me ipso apud Westmonasterium quarto die Nouembris anno regni nostri decimo nono.

Gaunstede.

P.R.O. Early chancery proceedings, 3/27.

(24) Writ of venire facias 1396

Ricardus, [etc.] vicecomiti Cornubie, salutem. Quibusdam certis de causis coram nobis in Cancellaria nostra per Johannem Haule de Dertemuth seniorem propositis, tibi precipimus firmiter iniungentes quod venire facias coram nobis in dicta Cancellaria nostra in quindena Sancti Michaelis ubicumque tunc fuerit Johannem Tretherf [11 *other names follow*], ad respondendum super hiis que sibi ex parte nostra et predicti Johannis Haule plenius exponentur tunc ibidem, et ad faciendum ulterius et recipiendum quod curia nostra considerauerit in hac parte [etc.] 26 July, 20 Ric. II.

Indorsed. Manucaptores Johannis Tretherf [*and six others*]
  Andreas Borlas, Ricardus Respreua,
  Andreas Pensynton, Regle Tretherf.
  Thomas Derry [*and four others*] infra scripti nichil habent in balliua mea per quod eos coram vobis venire facere possum, nec sunt inventi in eadem.

Willelmus Talbot, vicecomes.

Select cases in chancery (S.S.), p. 18.

(25) Petition to the chancellor (?) 1396–7

A tres-reuerent pier en dieu le Chanceller Dengleterre supplie treshumblement Nichol de Wynyngton esquier, qe come le dit Nichol soit enditeez...maliciousement par vn enqueste de Westmonstier deuaunt les seneschall et marescall [del] hostiel nostre tresredoute seignur le Roy, de diuerses trespasses faitz et perpetreez deinz la verge de dit hostiel, queux trespasses ne sount conuz a dit Nichol, pleise a vostre hautesse enuoier pur toux les enditementz deuaunt nostre dit seignur le Roy en sa bank de quelconqes trespasses dont il est enditeez au fyn qil puisse respondre solonc ce qe la commune ley demand...deuaunt nostre dit seignur le Roy en le dit bank des trespasses desuisditz pur lamour de dieu et en oeuere de charitee.

Ancient petitions, F. 299, no. 14932.

(26) *A case in chancery. Petition of citizens of Waterford* 1398

A tres gracious seignur et tres reuerent pere en Dieu, l'Euesque d'Excestre, Chanceller d'Engleterre,

Supplie humblement William Foxhill, Mair et Citezein de la Cite de Waterford en Irland, qe come les progenitours nostre seignur le Roy par lour chartres eiont grauntez a lez Citezeins du dite Cite, qe de chescune niefe qe vindra a dite Cite oue vins chargez, qe les Baillifs de la dite Cite, en presence del Prouost de mesme la Cite, deussent eslire deux tonelles de vin de chescune nief, c'est assauoir, vne deuant la mast et l'autre aderere, paiant pur le tonel xx *s*; des queux tonelles les ditz Citezeins aueront vne en releuacion et eide de lour ferme du dite Cite, reseruant l'autre tonel al oeps nostre seignur le Roy;...les queux Citezeins... d'une nief appelle 'la Trinitee' de Bristuyt, de quele nief Markys Spaynoll et Johan Palmer sont possessours, charge oue les vins d'un Nichol Compayng et des autres Marchantz, pristrent et eslierent a Waterford deux tonelles de vin solonc les grauntz... auantditz; nientmains l'euantdit Nichol, ...et autres Marchantz,...firent arester vne nief du dit suppliant a Bristuyt...: Qe plese a vostre tres gracious seignurie considerer la matier auantdit, et graunter briefs directz a les Mair, Baillifs et Viscount de Bristuyt, pur faire le dit suppliant re-auoir et d'estre repaiez de ce qe il ad paie a les auantditz Nichol et Robert...: Pur Dieu et en oeuere de charite.

Indorsed. Le vintisme iour d'Auerille l'an, etc., vint et primer. Accordez est par le Counsail que briefs soient faitz desouz le grant seal sur la contenue de ceste peticion.

Presens Messeignurs les {
Chanceller,
Tresorer,
Gardein du priue seal,
Le Clerc des roules,
Messires Johan Bussy,
Henri Grene,
Johan Russell et
Robert Faryngton, clerc.
}

Select cases in chancery (S.S.), pp. 37–8.

(27) A case in chancery, Jasper, son of John de Dent, v. Philip Gernon 1408

Alias ad prosecucionem cuiusdam Jasper filii et attornati Johannis Dent, armigeri, commorantis in civitate Veron' in Lumbardia, preceptum fuit Philippo Gernon de Sancto Botulpho quod in propria persona sua esset coram domino Rege in Cancellaria sua in octabis Sancti Hillarii proximo preteriti...ad respondendum super hiis que sibi obicerentur tunc ibidem...; Ad quem diem tam predictus Philippus in propria persona sua,...quam predictus Jasper in propria persona sua in Cancellaria predicta comparuerunt; et super hoc predictus Philippus per venerabilem patrem, Thomam, Archiepiscopum Cantuariensem, Cancellarium Anglie, in eadem Cancellaria examinatus fuit super contentis in quadam petitione per prefatum Jasper ibidem exhibita et in filaciis dicte Cancellarie residente, et iuratus super sancta Dei euangelia de veritate dicenda in premissis; qua quidem examinacione sic facta, ac auditis rationibus, exceptionibus, allegationibus et responsionibus per consilium vtriusque partis ibidem propositis, captaque ad requisitionem earumdem parcium, pro pleniori informatione rei veritatis in premissis, testificatione Willelmi domini de Willughby tunc ibidem presentis in Curia, et noticiam materie illius vt asseruerunt habentis, de auisamento Justiciariorum et Seruientum domini Regis ad legem et aliorum peritorum de Consilio domini Regis in eadem Cancellaria ad tunc existentium; Consideratum fuit quod predictus Philippus dimittatur de Curia et exinde recedat quietus sine die, et quod prefatus Jasper prosequatur ad communem legem pro remedio in hac parte habendo si sibi viderit expedire.

Select cases in chancery (S.S.), pp. 89–90.

(28) Petition to the Duke of Gloucester; Early Henry VI

To the full hye, excellent and gracious Prince, the Duc of Gloucetre, Protectour of Englande,

Byseketh mekely your pouere bedwoman and Widowe, Maude Annors, graciously consider that throgh the vertu of your full gracious lettres the Rector of Assherige seced and left his maintenaunce agaynes your forseid widowe, Wherfore god quyte you in heuen euerlastyngly; & thervpon she entred in her land by a writ of the statute of Northampton, and enfeoffed on Adam Alford for trust and socour in the forseid land, the whiche Adam wolde compelle your forseid widowe to gif hym the same lande for xls. for euermore, ther it is worth xxli. clere, and halt her oute ther of: Wherfore like it to your gracious lordship to graunt your forseid bedwoman that she may haue of the Chaunceller of Englond a writ that is called *sub pena* direct to the forseid Adam, to be byfore the forseid Chaunceller the Trinite terme next comyng, to answere to the cause aforseid; for godesake and in the waye of Charite.

Select cases in chancery (S.S.), p. 129.

(29) *Decision in a case in chancery* 1456

Robert and Agnes Bale v. *Nicholas Marchall*

[*Indorsed on bill.*]

Memorandum quod quintodecimo die Nouembris anno regni Regis Henrici sexti post conquestum Angliae tricesimo sexto, tam materia in ista billa contenta et specificata ac responsione infrascripti Nicholai Marchall ad materiam illam, quam replicatione et reiunctione vtrarumque parcium infrascriptarum in Cancellaria predicti domini Regis apud Westmonasterium visis, lectis, pleniusque intellectis, Habitaque matura deliberacione cum Justiciariis ipsius domini Regis de vtroque Banco, aliisque de Consilio eiusdem domini Regis tunc ibidem presentibus, per aduisamentum eorundem Justiciariorum Consideratum est in eadem Curia quod infrascripti Robertus et Agnes recuperent versus predictum Nicholaum centum et quater viginti et quatuordecim marcas de bonis et catallis infrascripti Thome Haunsard defuncti, videlicet l marcas pro infrascriptis terris et tenementis per prefatum Thomam Haunsard venditis, situatis apud barras Sancti Georgii in Suthwerk, in dicta billa specificatis, ac Cxliiij marcas per prefatum Thomam Haunsard de exitibus ceterorum terrarum et tenementorum in parochia Sancte Marie Magdalene in Suthwerk predicta receptis, in eadem billa similiter specificatis.

Select cases in chancery (S.S.), pp. 149–50.

(30) *A case in chancery; judgment given by the chancellor alone* 1474

George Archbishop of York and Edmund Gower *v.* Richard Osborn.

To compel Defendant who is feoffee in trust of the manor of Henton Pipard, in the counties of Wilts. and Berks., to release the same to Plaintiffs.

To the right honorable and full nobill Lord th'erll of Essex, gardein of the grete seale of oure liege lord the Kynge.

Besechen humbly, George archbisshop of Yorke and Edward Gower, that where Alice Thorp, of Thorp in the counte of Surrey, was seased of the maner of Henton Pypard...with thappurtenancez in her demesne as of fee, and so therof seased of the same maner, to gedur with other maners, landes, and tenementez, infeffed John Bourghchier lord Barners, Thomas Kyrkby, Piers Ardern, knyght, Richard Ludlowe, William Skern, and Richard Osbern, to have to them, theire heirez and assignez, upon trust only, and to the behofe of the seid Alice; and after the seid Alice entred agayn into the seid maner, and put oute her seid ffeffeez, and the seid Lord Berners, maister Thomas Piers [sic], Richard Ludlowe, and William Skern, in the life of the seid Alice, and at her request, relessed into the possession of the seid Alice all their right and title in and of the seid maner of Henton, and in like wise the seid Alice required the seid Richard Osborn to relesse to hur all his right of the seid maner, and he so to do refused; and after the seid Alice bargeyned and sold unto the seid Edward the seid maner of Henton, and thereof enfeffed the seid archbisshop and Edward and other to the use and behofe of the same Edward, to have to theyme and to the heirez of the seid Edward; by force of which feffement they were therof seized; that is to say, Edward in his demesne as of fee, and the seid archbisshop and other in ther demesne as of freholde; after which feffement, and after the deces of the seid Alice, the seid George and Edward have oft tymez requyred the seid Richard Osborn to relesse his right...and the seid Richard that to do hath refused. Wherfore please it your good lordship to graunte a writte sub pena, to be directed unto the seid Richard Osborn, commaundyng hym to appere afore the Kyng in his chauncerie, at a certen day within this terme, to do that the court woll award in this behalf.

Plegii de prosecutione,
      Willelmus Curteis de London' gentilman, et
      Clemens Clerk de eadem, gentilman.

Indorsed. Coram domino Rege in Cancellaria sua die Veneris.

Dies datus est partibus infrascriptis ad producendos testes ad probandam materiam in hac billa contentam hincinde usque octabas sancti Martini...

Decree indorsed.

Memorandum quod quinto die Julij anno regni regis Edwardi quarti quartodecimo ista peticione...coram prefato domino Rege in Cancellaria sua exhibita necnon responsione et replicacione alijsqe examinacionibus et probacionibus in ea parte similiter factis et habitis et in eadem Cancellaria apud Westmonasterium visis lectis auditis plenius et intellectis habitaqe superinde matura et diligenti deliberacione in ea parte consideratum et adjudicatum existit per venerabilem patrem Thomam episcopum Lincolniensem Cancellarium prefati domini regis quod prefatus Ricardus Osborn facit sufficientem statum in lege predicto Edwardo Gower de et in manerio de Hynton Pippard cum pertinentiis infraspecificatis habendo eidem Edwardo Gower heredibus et assignatis suis imperpetuum.

Cal. of Proceedings in chancery in the reign of Queen Elizabeth (Rec. Com.), 1 (1827), xciv.

CHAPTER VI

THE SEALS

INTRODUCTION

The history of the different seals in the late medieval period
illustrates the way in which the crown made repeated efforts to
set up an independent administration distinct from the normal
channels of government; it is a history of repetitions, as one by
one the personal seals of the king were wrested from his control
and used for public and official work. First the great seal, then
the privy seal, and after it the signet became official in their scope,
while other fourteenth-century seals ceased in turn to exist. The
great seal of the chancery, and the duplicate great seal of the
exchequer, were, by the thirteenth century, limited to formal and
specialised business; and already there was emerging a small seal
for the king's personal needs, which might be used as a substitute
when the great seal followed the king abroad, as in Richard I's
time. In John's reign a small or privy seal was most probably
associated with the administration of the chamber. Its history is
not altogether clear for the greater part of Henry III's reign,
though it is known that careful arrangements for sealing were
made when the king was absent from the kingdom. After the
1258 crisis the privy seal was most likely being used to advance
royal interests; "one is almost forced to conclude that Henry was
consciously setting up the privy seal, which he controlled, against
the great seal, which had escaped from his hands".[1]

During Edward I's reign and later the privy seal came to play
an important part in the normal administration(1–3, 5). We know
that the wardrobe was responsible for the issue of writs of privy
seal, and it would seem that the controller of the wardrobe was
also keeper of the privy seal.[2] It is not surprising, therefore, that
one of the aims of the lords ordainers in the next reign was to
detach the privy seal from the wardrobe and to limit and
define its functions (p. 16); in the ordinance of 1318 this development can be seen, when the work of the clerk of the privy seal

[1] Tout, *Chapters*, I, 307. [2] *Ibid.* II, 36 ff.

was defined(3). Even after this Edward II again tried to restore the privy seal to the wardrobe, but in 1323 there was a definite separation. At the same time a secret seal was being used for the personal service of the crown, which in effect was to take the place of the privy seal for this purpose(4, 6).

During the first years of Edward III the privy seal was gaining in importance; in the Walton ordinances of 1338 it was given much responsibility, since without its authorisation no warrants of chancery were to be issued, nor payments made out of the exchequer.[1] These ordinances may not have been enforced, but they suggest a significant development actually taking place, whereby warrants of privy seal were used to signify royal decisions to the chancery and other places. In the same way writs under the privy seal were being issued for summons to the council,[2] and similar writs tended to replace liberate writs of chancery to the exchequer. In this way the keeper of the privy seal was rapidly taking his place with the chancellor and treasurer as a great officer of state, as is clear from a variety of documents.[3] He was still regarded as the king's secretary, until William of Wykeham, the last keeper to be thus known, became chancellor in 1367.[4] As in other departments, much depended on the character of the officials themselves and on the political issues of the time; in war, for example, the keeper and his staff usually accompanied the king abroad, and "during the war the keeper of the privy seal became the second chancellor".[5] In Richard II's reign the official position of the keeper is clear when we find the commons petitioning that he, as well as the chancellor and treasurer, should be nominated in parliament (p. 65). At least after 1360 the office had permanent quarters at Westminster.[6]

Letters under the privy seal were less formal than those of the chancery; they were normally in French(2) (later in English), and were not necessarily either written on parchment or enrolled. The secretarial work of the privy seal increased rapidly as a result of its connection with the council, which came to be as close as that between great seal and parliament. Further, the keeper was gradually acquiring some jurisdiction, as is indicated in a decree of 1349 (p. 188). By an ordinance of 1390 matters of "less

[1] Tout, *Chapters*, III, 143–50, and 69 ff. [2] See above, p. 54.
[3] References to the increasing authority of the keeper of the privy seal will be found especially in the sections on the Council and on Justice.
[4] F. M. G. Evans, *The principal secretary of state*, p. 13.
[5] Tout, *Chapters*, v, 55. [6] *Ibid.* v, 73.

charge" were reserved to him, as distinct from the jurisdiction of the chancellor (p. 68). Gradually, too, individual petitions were being made directly to him, and in this way his jurisdiction was being recognised. Nevertheless, the commons continued to view any such development as an encroachment on the sphere of common law,[1] though their petitions on the subject had little effect (7, 9–11), for the judicial powers of the keeper seem to have been steadily maintained (17). It is interesting to note that when the Court of Requests was established about 1493 as "the Court of Poor Men's Causes", it was presided over by the lord privy seal, although any exact continuity need not be traced from the earlier period.[2]

While the privy seal was thus becoming important, the crown was using a secret seal for a variety of purposes. Its origin can be traced in the thirteenth century, and although there was still some confusion in Edward II's reign between privy and secret seals, it would seem that the secret seal was being used for the king's personal communications, and that warrants under the secret seal were being issued to authorise writs of privy seal (6), which in turn could order the issue of a writ under the great seal. In this singularly cumbrous way the wheels of administration were set in motion during the period.

The secret seal underwent further development in Edward III's reign, when five separate seals can be traced (cf. 8),[3] and already with the emergence of the second secret seal in 1331 the word "signet" is being applied. By the end of the reign the secret seal had dropped out of use, the signet remaining. Other seals are known to have existed, and the Griffin was especially set up for the reserved lands of the chamber from 1335 to 1354.[4] The signet itself had an increasingly important position during Richard II's reign. Between 1383–6 its functions were considerably extended and it was superseding the privy seal for royal purposes; for this reason it was attacked by the commons as well as by the baronial opposition, and after the political crisis of 1386–8 its use was defined (12). Nevertheless it was of the greatest help to Richard II in his last years; many of his grants were made under the signet (13, 14), and on that account were revoked in the first parliament of Henry IV. After this time, however, the use of the signet came to be recognised as a normal part of the administration rather than as a weapon of the royal prerogative (16), and as the

---

[1] See below, p. 251.
[2] J. R. Tanner, *Tudor constitutional documents*, p. 299.
[3] Tout, *Chapters*, v, 171–8.   [4] See above, p. 96.

means of communication between the crown and the keeper of the privy seal. In the fifteenth century it became "another cog in the already complicated wheel of administrative machinery".[1] Most important in the development of the signet was the emergence of the secretary, who, at least from the early years of Richard II, was in charge of this seal, which had previously been in the hands of the clerk of the chamber. The organisation of the work of the signet was helped by the interchange of officials between departments; thus in 1402 John Prophet, a privy seal official, became secretary (15), when he apparently resigned from the council.[2] A secretary might be promoted and become keeper of the privy seal, or even chancellor or treasurer.[3] At first the secretary was not a member of the council and, though he might later attend its meetings, his presence there was not recognised until Tudor times. Conciliar business was still transacted by clerks of the privy seal; but during the century it is possible to trace the emergence of a special staff for the signet.[4] In Henry VI's reign there were two clerks, in Edward IV's time there were four writers of the king's signet, assistant to the secretary (23). At the same time we hear of other secretaries, one being employed for French affairs (19). When the French possessions were lost a secretary for the French language was appointed; John Prophet (to be distinguished from the earlier official of the same name), who held this office from 1468 to 1476, was succeeded by Oliver King as *primus et principalis Secretarius noster in lingua gallica* (22). While there was only one keeper in charge of the signet itself until Tudor times, there is every indication that the work of the office was increasing, and that some differentiation would be necessary in the future.

BIBLIOGRAPHY

1. ORIGINAL SOURCES

P.R.O. Chancery warrants.
Collection of ordinances and regulations for the government of the royal household (*Society of Antiquaries*). London, 1790.
Proceedings and ordinances of the privy council. London, 1834–7.
Rotuli parliamentorum. London, 1783.
RYMER, T. *Foedera, etc.* London, 1706.
Statutes of the realm. London, 1810–28.

---

[1] Tout, *Chapters*, v, 226. [2] Evans, *op. cit.* p. 16 n.
[3] *Ibid.* chap. I, *passim*; cf. Tout, *Chapters*, v, 225.
[4] Evans, *op. cit.* pp. 17 ff.

2. Secondary authorities

Baldwin, J. F. *The king's council in England during the middle ages.* Oxford, 1913.

Davies, J. C. *The baronial opposition to Edward II.* Cambridge, 1918.

Déprez, E. *Études de diplomatique anglaise, 1272–1485. Le sceau privé, le sceau secret, le signet.* Paris, 1908.

Evans, F. M. G. (Mrs Higham). *The principal secretary of state.* Manchester, 1923.

Lyte, H. C. Maxwell. *Historical notes on the use of the great seal of England.* London, 1926.

Tout, T. F. *Chapters in the administrative history of medieval England.* Manchester, 1920–30.

—— *The place of the reign of Edward II in English history.* Manchester, 1914.

3. Article

Dibben, L. B. "Secretaries in the thirteenth and fourteenth centuries", *E.H.R.* xxv, 1910.

(1) *Writ of privy seal for an appointment* 1307

De Officio Marescalciae Angliæ Commisso.

Rex omnibus ad quos, etc. salutem.

Sciatis quod commisimus dilecto et fideli nostro Roberto de Clifford Officium Marescalciæ Angliæ.

Habendum et custodiendum, cum omnibus ad officium illud spectantibus, quamdiu nobis placuerit.

In cujus, etc.

Teste Rege apud Carliolum, 3. die Septembris.

Per breve de privato Sigillo.

Et Mandatum est Thesaurario et Baronibus de Scaccario, quod ipsum, quem præfatus Robertus loco suo deputaverit ad faciendum ea quæ ad Officium illud pertinent, in eodem Scaccario, loco ipsius Roberti, recipiant in forma prædicta.

Teste ut supra.

Foedera, iii, 9.

(2) *Writs of privy seal*

(i) 1316

Edward par la grace de dieu Roy Dengleterre seignur Dirlaunde et Ducs Daquitaine A noz chers et foiaux Lonurable pere en dieu W. par meisme la grace Erceuesque de Canterbir' primat de tote

THE SEALS 213

Engleterre Johan de Sandale Eslyt de Wyncestre nostre Chauncellier et monsire Wauter de Norwiz nostre Tresorier saluz. Por
ce qe nostre cher marchaunt Manent ffrancisk de fflorence nous
fist cheuissaunce daucunes sommes de deniers...si come il vous
sauera monstrer des queux il nad vncore eu nul paiement par
quoi il est encoru grant damage, a ce qil dit. Vous mandoms qe
vous regardez de queles sommes et de combien il nous fist cheuissaunce a cele foiz et coment nous en porroms faire plus couenable-
ment son gre par paiement ou par assignement et de quoi et ou
et de quele somme nous lui puissoms faire regard pur ses ditz
damages issint qil ne soit perdaunt, et de ce qe entre vous serra
sur ce acordez nous voloms qe vous auantdit Chauncellier facez
faire au dit Manent lettres souz nostre grant seal en due forme.
Done souz nostre priue seal a Euerwyk le xxj iour Daugust Lan
de nostre regne disme.

Chancery warrant, F. 95, no. 3717.

(2) 1316

Edwardus...venerabili in Christo patri J. eadem gracia Electo
Wintoniensi confirmato Cancellario nostro, saluz. Mandamus
vobis quod ad ecclesiam de Whitbern' Dunelmensis diocese vacan-
tem et ad nostram donacionem spectantem ratione Episcopatus
Dunelmensis vacantis et in manu nostra existentis dilectum clericum nostrum Nicholaum de Welleburn' per litteras sub magno
sigillo nostro in forma debita presentetis. Datum sub priuato
sigillo nostro apud Neuburgh' xxiiij die Octobris anno regni nostri
decimo.

Chancery warrant, F. 95, no. 3751.

(3) 1318

Edward...Al honurable piere en dieu J. par la meisme grace
Euesque de Wyncestre nostre Chauncellier saluz. Nous vous mandoms qe vous facez faire lettres recommendatoires en si graciouse
forme come vous les sauerez deuiser par reson souz nostre grant
seal a nostre seint piere le pape et as Cardinalx et a noz autres
amys en court pur nostre cher clerc Richard de Elsefeld priauntz
eux par meismes noz lettres qe les peticions qe nostre dit clerc fera
bailler au dit pape des choses touchantes son auancement soient
graciousement ottroiees et esploitees pur amur de nous. Done
souz nostre priue seal a Westmonstier le xx iour de marz Lan de
nostre regne vnzisme.

Chancery warrant, F. 103, no. 4593.

*(3) Extract concerning the privy seal, from the household ordinance
of York* 1318

Le Clerk de la priue Seal

Item vn clerk suffissant gardein de priue seal, qi eit vn esquier mangeant en la sale. et prendra pour chambre demi sexte de vin, vj chaundelx, ij tortis, et vn torche, et litere par tout lan, et busche pour la soison diuer del vssher de la sale, et vn liuere pour soun chambirleyne: cestassauoir vn dare de payne, vn galoun de la seruoyse, et vn messe gros de la coisine, et robez en drap, ou viij marcs par an, al fest de Noell et Pentecost par ouelx portions. et sil soit seigne ou maladez, preigne sa liueree, cestassauoir ij d. de payn, vn piche de vin, ij messes de gros de la cuissine, et vn messe de rost. et sil soit agagez tant qil soit auancez. Item iiij clercz pour escriuer au prive seal, qi prendrount toutz ensemble pour lour chambre ij piche de vin, vj chaundelx, ij tortis, et litere pour tout lan, et bousche pour la soison dyuer de la vssher de la sale. Et sils dynent ou maungent al loustell par certeyn reasoun, deux vn liuere a dyner et chescun vn liuere a manger sicome lez clercz de la countee desuis nomez. Auxint si nulle soit seigne ou maladez, eit mesme la liuere. Et chescun agagez, a pluis ou ameyns, solonque ceo qil serroit destat, et al discrecion du seneschall et tresorer, tanque ils soient auancez par le roi; et ij robez par an ou deniers solonque lour gagez.

Additional MS. 32097, m. 47d–48. (Printed in Tout, *Edward II*, p. 273.)

(4) Writs under the secret seal

(1) 1321

Edward par la grace de dieu Roi Dengleterre Seignur Dirlaunde et Ducs Daquitaine as Gardeins de nostre grant seal salutz. Come nostre cher mariner Johan Rose de Grenewyz nous eit monstrez aucunes greuances qe nadgaires lui furent faites es parties de Gascoigne countre reson a ce qil dit vous mandoms qe escoutees les resons qil sur ce vous voudra monstrer lui facez droit ensemblement od tote la grace qe nous lui purroms faire par reson. Done souz nostre secre seal le xxx iour Daugust Lan de nostre regne xvme.

Chancery warrant, F. 1329, no. 35.

(2) 1322

Edward...a Lonurable piere en dieu J. par la meisme grace Euesque de Norwiz nostre Chauncellier salutz. Come nous eoms

donez et grauntez a nostre cher et foial Rauf Basset de Drayton'
les manoirs de Hameldon' et Market Ouerton' en le Counte de
Roteland qi furent a Bertholmeu de Badelesmere iadys nostre
traitre et rebel od feez auouesons et fraunchises y appendantz a
auer et tenir a terme de sa vie aussi entierement et fraunchement
come le dit Bertholmeu les tint vous mandoms qe sur ce facez
faire au dit Rauf chartres dessouz nostre grant seal en due fourme.
Done souz nostre secre seal a Hatheleseie le xvme. iour...de Juyn
Lan de nostre regne quinzisme.

Chancery warrant, F. 1329, no. 49.

(5) *Writ of privy seal to the council* 1324

Edward...a noz chers et foialx bones gentz de nostre conseil a
Londres saluz. Por ce qe nous auoms entenduz par clamour de
nostre poeple qe plusours mefesours...en diuerses parties de nostre
roialme fesauntz plusors roberies homicides arzons batenes de
gentz et autres diuerses felonies et trespacz contre nostre pees, et
en afrai de nostre dit poeple, de quoi nous sumes molt durement
ennoiez. Vous mandoms et chargeoms qe euz conseil et auisement entre vous ordenez sur ceste chose si bon et si couenable
remedie come vous porrez pur la meintenance de nostre pees et
lese de nostre poeple et qe les ditz mefesours soient puniz en tieu
manere qe autres se chastient par ensample de eux. Done souz
nostre priue seal a Berkhamstede le iiij iour de Decembre lan de
nostre regne oytisme.

P.R.O. Ancient correspondence, xlv/185.

(6) *Writ of secret seal* 1325

Edward...A noz chers clercs Mestre Robert de Baldok Ercedeakne
de Middlesex nostre Chaunceller et Mestre Henri de Clif gardein
de nostre priue seal saluz. Nous vous mandoms qe sanz nul delay
facez faire lettres souz nostre priue seal bones et chargeantes a
nostre cher et foial Robert de Kendale Conestable de nostre
Chastel de Doure et gardein de nostre passage illoeqes qil ne
soeffre messager quicumqe le quel qil veigne de nostre treschere
compaigne la Roine ou de Leuesqe de Norwiz et noz autres
messages ou de nul autre des noz qi soit es parties de dela en la
compaignie nostre dite compaigne bailler ne monstrier nulle lettre
ne counter nouelles a nuly du mounde tantqil veigne a nous et a
ceste chose faire face le messager jurer et iadumeins face enuoyer

aucun des soens de qi il se fie en la compaignie le dit messager pur lui conduyre tantqil veigne a nous et de prendre garde touz iours qe le dit messager ne face en autre manere et qe le dit nostre conestable face ceste chose si bien et si auisement qe les nouelles ne soient publiees auant qeles veignent a nous par qoi nostre poeple en puisse estre affraiez sicome il mesme se voille sauuer de damage et respondre ent a son peril. Et vous auantdit chaunceller sachez qe nous serroms y ce mardy au soir a Stonham et le Mekredy prechein suyant a Beaulieu, par qoi vous mandoms qe mesme ce mekredy soiez illoeqes a nous od nostre chauncellerie et... exploitez les busoignes qe sont a exploiter et deliuerez nostre poeple. Done souz nostre secre seal a le secund iour de Aueril Lan de nostre regne xviij^{me}.

Chancery warrant, F. 1329, no. 104.

(7) *Commands under the great and privy seals*
shall not delay justice 1328

Ensement acorde est et establi qe mande ne soit, par le grant seal ne par le petit seal, a destourber ou delayer commune droit; et mesqe tielx mandementz veignent qe par tant les Justices ne sursessent pas de faire droit en nul point.

S.R. i, 259, 2 Ed. III, c. 8. (Statute of Northampton.)

(8) *Writ under the secret seal* 1354
de par le Roi.

Reuerent piere en dieu Nous grantasmes naguers a nostre cher et foial Geffrai de Say la garde de nostre Chastel de Roucestre ensemblement od la ville de Roucestre a auoir et tenir a toute sa vie en meisme la manere qe le Counte de Huntyngdon' les tynt de nostre grant, et sur ce vous maundasmes de lui faire patente tielle come apartient et le dit Geffrai nous ad certefie qe sa patente ne parle forsque du chastel nyent fesaunt mencion de la ville si voloms qe vous facez renoeueler sa dite patente sibien de la ville come du chastel et nest pas nostre entencion qil paie plus pur le fee qil ne paia einz voloms qe le fee de la patente qe vous lui ferrez ore lui soit pardonez. Done souz nostre secre seal a Wodestoke le ix iour de Septembre.

Chancery warrant, F. 1334, no. 11, 28 Ed. III. (Cf. the writ printed in Tout, *Chapters*, v, 175, n. 4. This was the fourth secret seal of Edward III; cf. *ibid.* v, 175–6.)

(9) *The seals and the common law* 1377

Item, pur ceo qe la Ley de la Terre et commune Droit ont estez
sovent delaiez par Lettres issues si bien desouz Prive Seal le Roi
come de Secret Signet, a graunde grevaunce du people; Qe plese
a nostre Seignur qe desormes la Ley de la Terre ne commune
Droit ne soient delaiez ne destourbez par Lettres des ditz Sealx;
et si rien soit fait en nulle place de la Court nostre Seignur le Roi,
ou aillours, par tielx Lettres issues desouth les ditz Sealx encountre
droiture et Ley de la Terre, rien ne vaille, et pur nient soit tenuz.
Responsio. Se tiegnent les Estatutz ent faitz en touz pointz.
Rot. Parl. III, 23 (96).

(10) *Letter of privy seal* 1379

Item monstrent les Communes, coment ore tarde, puis la darrein
Conseil tenuz a Westmonstier, furent mandez diverses Lettres de
Credence dessouz le Prive Seal, par certains Chivalers et Esquiers
de la Courte le Roi, es diverses parties du Roialme, pur faire
chevance d'argent a l'oeps le Roi; queles Lettres avoient les cowes
blankes, et les ditz credensours de lour auctoritee demesne escri-
verent les Nouns des plusours gentz sur les cowes des Lettres suis
dites, et baillerent a eux les Lettres, affermantz qe le Roi les
maunda a eux, et demanderent de eux grandes sommes tielles
come lour pleust, et ceux qi se excuserent de les paier tielles
sommes les manacerent fortement de par le Roi, et les comande-
rent de par le Roi d'estre devant le Conseil le Roi, et assignerent
a eux jours a leur volentee; a grande damage et affraye des ditz
povres Communes, et ensclandre du Roi, et encontre la Loye de
la terre. Par quoy supplient les dites Communes, q'ordene soit,
qe coment q'il plese au Roi d'envoier Lettres pur apprompter
argent en temps a venir, et celui a qi la Lettre vient excuse
resonablement du dit apprompt, q'il soit a ce receu, sanz lui
mettre au travail, ou lui grever par sommons, ou par autre manere.
Responsio. Il plest au Roi.
Rot. Parl. III, 62 (30).

(11) *Letters under the signet shall not delay the law* 1388

Item ordeyne est et estably qe lettres de signet ne du secre seal
nostre seignur le Roy ne seient desormes envoiez en damage ne
prejudice de roialme nen destourbance de la loye.
S.R. II, 55, 11 Ric. II, c. 10.

(12) *Warrants of privy seal necessary for pardons*
for murder, etc. 1390

Nostre Seignour le Roy a son parlement tenuz a Westmonstier
Lundy prochein apres le fest de Seint Hiller lan de son regne
treszisme oie la grevouse compleint de sa commune en mesme
le parlement des outrageouses meschiefs et damages qi sont avenuz
a son dit roialme purceo qe tresones murdres et rapes des femmes
sont trop communement faitz et perpetrez et ceo le plus purceo
qe chartres de pardon ont este trop legerement grauntez en
tieux cases, la dite commune pria a nostre seignour le Roi qe
tieux chartres ne fuissent mes grauntez, a qoi nostre seignour le
Roi respondy qil vorroit salver sa libertee et regalie come ses
progenitours ont fait devant ces heures, mes pur la greindre quiete
et pees nurrer deinz son roialme, del assent des grantz et nobles
en mesme le parlement esteantz, ad grantee qe null chartre de
pardon desore soit alowe devant qiconqes Justices pur murdre
mort de homme occys par agayt assaut ou malice purpense
treson ou rape de femme, si mesme le murdre ou mort de homme
occys... treson ou rape de femme ne soient especifiez en mesme la
Chartre et si la chartre de mort de homme soit alegge devant
qiconqes Justices en quelle Chartre ne soit especifie qe celuy de qi
mort ascun tiel soit arreigne feust murdres ou occis par agait...,
enquergent les Justices par bone enquest del visne ou la mort
fuit occys sil fuist murdre ou occys par agait assaut ou malice
purpense et sils trovent qil fuist murdy ou occis par agait...soit
la Chartre disalowe et soit fait outre solonc ceo qe la ley demande.
Et si ascun prie au Roy pur Chartre de pardon pur murdre mort
de homme occys par agait...treson ou rape de femme si le
Chamberleyn endose tiel bille ou face endoser mette le noun de
celuy qi pria pur tiel Chartre sur mesme la bille sur peine de
M^l. marcz; et si le Southchamberlein endose tielle bille face
semblablement sur peyne de cynk Centz marcz; et qe null autre
qe Chamberleyn ou Southchamberlein endose ne face endoser
null tiele bille sur peyne de M^l. marcz; et qe tielle bille soit envoie
et directe al Gardeyn du prive seale et qe null garant du prive
seale soit fait pur tiel Chartre avoir sinoun qe le Gardein de
prive seale eit tielle bille endose ou signe par le Chamberleyn ou
Southchamberleyn come desuis est dist; et qe null Chartre de
pardon de treson ne dautre felonie passe la Chauncellarie sanz
garant du Prive Seale forsqe encas ou le Chaunceller le puisse
granter de son office sanz ent parler au Roi; et si celuy a qi

prier ascune Chartre de pardon pur murdre mort de homme tue par agait. . . treson ou rape de femme soit grante, soit Archevesqe ou Duc, paie au Roi M^l. livres. et sil soit Evesqe ou Count paie au Roy M^l. marcz, et sil soit Abbe Prior Baron ou Baneret, paie au Roi Cynk Centz marcz, et sil soit Clerc Bacheler ou autre de meyndre estat de quele condicion qil soit, paie ou [*sic*] Roi deux Centz marcz et eit lemprisonement dun an.

S.R. II, 68–9, 13 Ric. II, s. 2, c. 1. (Cf. Maxwell Lyte, *Great seal*, p. 23. He adds that Richard II was careful to reserve his prerogative, and that later in the reign some pardons were being issued "per ipsum Regem".)

(13) *Complaints against Richard II's interference in administration* 1399

Item, idem Rex, ut liberius adimpleri et sequi posset in singulis sue arbitrium voluntatis, illicite fecit et mandavit, quod Vicecomites per totum Regnum suum ultra antiquum et solitum Juramentum jurarent, Quod omnibus mandatis suis sub Magno et Privato Sigillis suis, ac etiam literis sub Signeto suo, quotienscumque eis directe fuerint, obedirent. Et in casu quo iidem Vicecomites scire poterunt aliquos de Ballivis suis, cujuscumque conditionis fuerint, aliquod malum dicere sive loqui publice vel occulte quod cedere possit in dedecus aut scandalum Persone Regis, ipsos arrestarent, vel facerent arrestari, et prisone mancipari, in eadem salvo custodiendos donec aliud a Rege habuerint in mandatis; prout reperiri poterit de recordo. Quod quidem factum posset verisimiliter tendere ad destructionem quorumcumque ligeorum dicti Regni.

Rot. Parl. III, 420 (37). (Cf. Crown section, pp 28–9.)

(14) *Use of the signet by Richard II* 1399

Item, priont les Communes pur Henry vostre fitz, Prince de Gales, Duc de Cornewaille, et Counte de Cestre; Qe come, de vostre grace et puissante Seignurie, il Vous ad plu a luy doner et graunter toutes les Debtes et arrerages de Debtes, Rentes, Fermes, et Issues quelconqes a Vous, tres redoute Seignur, duez et a derere devant cez heures, en les avant ditz Principaltee, Duchee, et Countee: Et ascuns du Counseill vostre dit fitz sont enformez, qe le darreinement Roy, quant il estoit darreignement en Gales, fesoit diverses Relessementz et Pardons, si bien especiales come gene-

rales, as plusours des parties sus dites, qi serroient a sa tres grant
damage si feurent effectueles, et esterroient en lour force; Plese a
vostre tres puissante Seignurie a revoker et adnuller touz les
Relessementz et Pardons semblables des Debtes et Arrerages sus
dites, faitez en contraire de vostre honorable Doun et Grant a luy
faitz en manere sus dite.

Responsio. Si ascun eit Pardon ou Relesse souz le Grant Seal,
estoisent en lour force. Et touz les Pardons et Relesses faitz desouz
le Signet, ou autres tielx petites Sealx, ou par bouche du dit nadgairs Roy, soient repellez tout outrement.

Rot. Parl. III, 442 (142).

(15) *A letter of the king's secretary (John Prophet to his nephew,
Thomas Felde, and William Plofelde) (?) 1403*

Treschiers et fiables amys. Je vous salve souvent de cuer Et pour
ce que au temps que je baillay au Tresorer Dengleterre deinz son
houstell a Londres lettres du prive seal pour moy faire avoir
paiement ou assignement de les cent livres a moi dues par nostre
Seignur le Roy pur mon service a lui fait au temps que jestoie un
de son conseil les quelles lettres furent de commandement du dit
tresorer mys en filace deinz la receite; Il me permetta que tost
apres la feste de Pasques darein passe javeroie sufficeant assignement de la dite somme...Si jay par tant escrit au dit tresorer lui
empriant de mottroier ycelle assignement sur les Viscontes de
Suthampton et de Wiltshire pres de mes benefices en celles parties
ou en autres lieux...Par quoi vous prie...que vous vuillez faire
instance envers le dit tresorer de ma part et ainsi pursuer devers
lui que je puisse avoir sufficeant assignement...
Et le benoit filz de Dieu vous ait en sa seinte garde.
Escrit a Wircestre le tierz jour de May.
        John Prophete Secretaire du Roy nostre souverain seignur.

In dorso...mes treschiers et fiables amys Thomas Felde mon
neveu et...William Plofelde.

A.P.C. II, 78.

(16) *A letter to Henry IV from the chancellor, treasurer and
keeper of the privy seal 1405*

Tresexcellent tresredoute et nostre tressoverein seignur, Le plus
humblement come nous savons ou poons nous nous recommen-
dons a vostre treshaute magestee roiale, a la quele plese savoir

qendroit des lettres desouz vostre prive seal a estre envoiees as
ercevesqes et evesqes de vostre roiaume pur exciter les chapelleins
stipendiairs et autres nient contributoirs ovec le clergie de vostre
roiaume pur vous granter aucun subside de lour stipendies et
salaries..., avons eu communicacion et parlance ovec li tresreverent pere en Dieu Lercevesqe de Cantirbirs et autres prelatz
de vostre grant consail...pur savoir sur ce lour bon avis et
deliberacion, li quel lour avis et le nostre ils envoiont presentement en escrit devers vostre roiale magnificence, Toutesvoies sil
plest a vostre hautesse qe en temps avenir aucuns lettres serront
depar vous en ce cas faites as susditz ercevesqes et evesqes, il nous
semble pur le mieux sauvant toutdis vostre tressage avis qe a quel
heure il vous plerra qe tieles lettres soient faites, qeles passent
desouz vostre signet. Car par ce serront sibien les prelatz come les
chapelleins stipendiairs et autres plus excitez daccomplir vostre
roial entencion et desir en cell partie qe ne serront par lettres
desouz voz grant ou prive sealx a ce qe nous pensons bien de
certein...

Plese a vostre excellence le reenvoier devers nous ovec vostre
gracious voluntee...sur ce et sur autres choses queles il vous
plerra nous commander...

Tresexcellent tresredoute etc.

Voz treshumbles et foialx liges les { Chanceller / Tresorer et / Gardein du prive seal.

A.P.C. II, 100.

(17) *Petition to the keeper of the privy seal* (?) 1428

A soun treshonurable seignur le Gardein de priue seal supplie
humblement soun chaplein le priour de Birkhened qe come Roger
de Diddesbury soun predecessour par noun de priour de Birkhened estoit coillour de la moite dune disme graunte a seignur
Richard le seconde nadgers Roi Dengleterre lan de soun regne
seszime en lercedeconye de Cestre en le countee de Cestre, dount
la somme amounte a xlix li. ix s. iiij d. ob. qᵃ. de quelle somme soun
dit predeccssour auoit vn escallement de treis ans appaier en
lescheqer du Cestre al oeps le dit nadgers Roi, par Johan Waltham
nadgers Euesqe de Salebirs adonqe Tresorer Dengleterre, la quelle
somme fut illeoqs paie en fourme suysdite [comme] appiert de
Record; et nyentmeyns mesme la somme courte en demande
deuers le dit suppliant hors de lescheqer cy a Westmonstier, a
cause qe soun dit predecessour nestoit mye illeoqs acquite de
record, qe pleise a soun dit treshonurable seignur de graunter

lettres du priue seal directez a chaumberleyn de Cestre ou a soun lieutenant dent certefier la plein verite et la circumstance dicell en loffice de priue seal perensi qe vous purrez faire montre pur le dit suppliant ceo qe droit et ley demande en la matere auauntdite pur dieu et en oeure de charite.

[*Added*] le vynt et sisme jour de may lan etc. sisme, a West-monstier lettre feut faite a le prince pur escrire a son chamberlain de Cestre pur sercher les roulles de lescheqer illoeqs du temps le Roy Richard et pur certifier au Conseil du Roy si la suisdite somme y feut paiee ou noun, au fin qe sur cell certificacion le Conseil purroit faire et ordener ce qe droit et reson demandoit en le cas.

P.R.O. Council and privy seal, F. 21, no. 161.

(18) *Writs of privy seal* 1432

vj^{to}. die Julii anno decimo apud Westmonasterium in camera consilii parliamenti concessum et concordatum est per dominos magni consilii Regis quod Petrus de Mera clericus ambassiator domini nostri Pape nuper per ipsum domino nostro Regi certis de causis missus habeat de dono Regis per viam regardi l. marcas habendo de thesaurario suo, et quod superinde fiant litere sub privato sigillo Regis Thesaurario et Camerariis ut in forma.

xij°. die Julii anno decimo apud Westmonasterium concessum et concordatum est per dominos consilii parliamenti quod fiat breve Custodibus portuum et passagiorum de Londoniis Dovorra Orewell' sive de Sandewico ac aliorum portuum et passagiorum de permittendo Petrum de Mera clericum ambassiatorem domini Pape libere et sine impedimento transire quocumqe sibi placuerit cum summa centum librarum in auro bagagio et aliis hernesiis suis ac servientium suorum et quod inde fiant litere sub privato sigillo Regis ut in forma.

A.P.C. iv, 120.

(19) *The king's secretary in France* 1434

Ultimo die Junii anno xij°. apud Gravesende concessum fuit quod fiat warantum sub privato sigillo Thesaurario et Camerariis de scaccario de solvendo Jacobo Lunayn secretario Regis de regno suo Francie nuper per Cancellarium et consilium suum ibidem pro negociis Regis penes Regem misso viginti marcas per viam regardi.

A.P.C. iv, 259.

THE SEALS

223

(20) *Royal warrants* 1444

Pro Cancellario Angliæ de et pro Warantis Regiis Allocandis.

Henry,... to our Chaunceller of England Gretyng.

All such Grauntes, as that, sith the tenth Yere of our Reigne unto this tyme, ye by force and vertue of Billes with our oun Hond, and by Letters undre our Signetes of the Egle and Armes, and also by Billes Endoced by our Chamberleyn's Hands and Clerk of our Counsail, have made our Lettres Patentes under our Grete Seel, We hold theym Ferme and Stable, and of as grete strength and valewe, and to yowe as sufficeant Warrant, as though ye had for theime our Letters of Prive Seel; any Statute, Charge, Restraint, Act, or Commaundement, to yowe made in to the contrarie, notwithstondyng.

Yeven undre our Prive Seel, at our Manoir within our Park of Wyndesore, the vii. Day of Novembre, the Yere of our Regne xxiii.

Foedera, XI, 75.

(21) *Warrants to the duchy of Lancaster* 1454

In the Sterred Chambre at Westminster the last day of May the yere etc. xxxij. it was ordeigned and advised by the lords of oure souverain lord's Counsail, that notwithstanding that in tyme passed the Chaunceller of the duchie of Lancastre of that part that is putte in feffement hadde in commaundement from oure said soverain lord not to receyve any letter for his warrant of any thing to be spedde by him under any seel saufe the signet of the Egle oonly, the prive seel shall from hensforth be sufficient warrant unto the said Chaunceller of the said part of the said duchie unto the time oure said souverain lord otherwise yeve him in commaundement, and that he receive nor obey any other lettre for his warrant but the prive seel.

[12 *names follow.*]

Exemplificatum fuit xxxᵐᵒ. die Maii anno xxxijᵈᵒ.

T. Kent.

A.P.C. VI, 188. (Cf. Introduction, p. cxlvii. The eagle signet was used in addition to the signet.)

(22) *The secretary for the French language* 1476

De officio principalis secretarii in lingua Gallica concesso.

Rex omnibus, ad quos, etc. salutem.

Sciatis quod nos, de gratia nostra speciali, ex certa scientia et

mero motu nostris dedimus et concessimus,...dilecto servienti
nostro Olivero Kyng, septem liberalium artium magistro, ac in
legibus licenciato, officium primi et principalis secretarii nostri
in lingua Gallica, ...cum tanto et consimili feodo legalis monetæ
Angliæ, sicut magister Gervasius, quondam in Anglia Secretarius
in eadem lingua, alias habuit, solvendo eidem servitori nostro,
durante vita sua, per æquales portiones, ad duos anni terminos,
per manus custumariorum nostrorum in portubus maris, aut per
manus aliorum officiariorum nostrorum infra regnum nostrum
prædictum, ubi eum commode assignari pro dicta summa contigerit.

Habendum...officium prædictum, cum memorato feodo, ad
terminum vitæ suæ, una cum omnimodis libertatibus, præ-
eminentiis, prærogativis, regardis, emolumentis, et proficuis quibuscumque, adeo libere...sicut dictus Gervasius...dictum
officium habuit...

Et insuper, de uberiori gratia nostra, damus...quod memora-
tus Oliverus poterit,...billas omnimodas manu nostra signatas
accipere, et quæcumque warranta, Cancellario nostro Angliæ vel
Privato nostro sigillo dirigenda, una cum literis nostris, tam in
Latino quam Anglico, conficere, atque regarda consueta pro
eisdem recipere, adeo libere et quiete, sicut aliquis Secretariorum
nostrorum qualiscumque; aliquo statuto, concessione, re, causa,
vel materia, in contrarium factis, non obstantibus.
In cujus etc.
Teste Rege apud Bukden, decimo octavo die Martii...
Foedera, xii, 26.

(23) *The office of secretary* temp. *Edward IV*

A Secretary, sitting in the King's chambre or hall, with a person
of like servyse; and he shall have eting in the hall, one gentilman.
Item, for his chambre for all day, iii loves, ii messes of grete mete,
dim' a picher wyne, ii gallons ale, one torche, one percher, ii
candells wax, iii candells peris', in wynter season, and iii tallwood,
ruyshes and litter, all the yere of the serjeaunt ussher of the hall and
chambyr, parchemynte and paper, sufficiaunt of the office of the
grete spycery, by oversyght of comptroller or his clerks, and that to
be allowed in the countyng-house, and also red wax; and whan he
hathe nede of muche writing, than he to have commaundment
from the seyd countyng-house for perchers of tallowe, or smaller
candells peris'. To this office are belonging iiii clerks, sufficiaunt

writers of the King's signet under the seide Secretary, eting dayly in the King's hall;...The Secretary and his clerks pay for theire carriage of harneys in courte, except a littell coffer in which the King's warraunts and billes assigned, and other lettres and remembraunces be kept upon a filace. This coffyr is carried at the King's cost, whereas the Countroller wull assigne. The Secretary he hath into this courte iii persones wayters on hym for all that office. The remanent of all other servaunts to be founden at his lyvery in the countrey deliverede by the herberger, sufficiauntly for hym and all the clerks; and whan hymself is oute of courte, he hath a yoman to kepe his chaumber, etyng at the Chaumberlayn's bourde in the hall: both he and his clerks take clothing of the King's warderober.

Ordinances and regulations for the government of the royal household (Society of Antiquaries), 1787–90, p. 35.

CHAPTER VII

THE EXCHEQUER

INTRODUCTION

Before the end of the twelfth century the administrative and financial work of the exchequer was already highly organised, and by the early fourteenth century a vastly complicated system had been built up upon the earlier, and comparatively simple, structure. This system involved primarily the use of credit instead of cash payments being made in the lower exchequer, a change due to the ever-increasing needs of government for which the royal revenue was becoming more and more insufficient. In the fourteenth century and especially in Edward III's reign it was usual for assignments to be made, whereby a creditor of the crown could obtain payment or part payment of the sum due to him from a royal official such as a sheriff or a collector of taxes, who would have been ordered by writ to have such a sum in readiness when the creditor showed his exchequer tally. When the official accounted to the exchequer allowance would be made for the tallies which he produced. Sometimes simply a writ of privy seal was sent to a local official to authorise payment. The wardrobe also issued, in return for cash, bills which could be presented to the exchequer. Such a varied system, while favouring the crown, had its drawbacks for the creditor, who might meet with many delays and frauds, while the assignments were often dishonoured. The records of the exchequer, such as the receipt rolls, indicate the delays and evasions which followed, and, while the exchequer still dealt with cash payments as well as assignments, yet it is impossible to use the records literally for financial calculations. The extract below(15) is given to show the connection between local officials and the exchequer. Further, it is clear that the financial control entailed much administrative work(4) for which writs of chancery were used(10).

The main constitutional interest of the history of the exchequer in this period lies in two problems—the relations between the exchequer and other departments, and the extent of the judicial

THE EXCHEQUER   227

authority of the exchequer itself. While financial business had
necessitated a separate and specialised administration, there was
still a close connection between council and exchequer. The
council met in the exchequer buildings to transact important
business, for which the secretariat of the exchequer was doubtless
used,[1] and in the later middle ages the exchequer still had miscellaneous duties; foreign treaties, for example, were there received
and stored, and crown jewels and plate(6), and it has been suggested that its officials were largely responsible, under royal direction, for the administration of foreign affairs.[2]

The early fourteenth century was a critical period for the
exchequer. We have seen that the king was trying to control
certain sources of revenue through his household departments
independent of the exchequer.[3] The opposition of the barons
to this policy can be seen especially in the ordinances of 1311
(pp. 12 ff.) and the struggle was a long one. Ultimately the exchequer was left with final control of revenue, and the other
departments had not only to look to the exchequer for their
income but had to account to it for their expenditure. With this
centralisation of accounts the whole system of accounting had to
be reorganised and developed, and this was begun in a remarkable
series of reforms, at the end of Edward II's reign.[4] The most
important changes were detailed in the Cowick ordinance of
1323(7): "foreign" accounts (including wardrobe accounts), as
well as all outstanding debts, were to be removed from the great
roll of the pipe, which was left as originally for the sheriffs' accounts. The work of the king's remembrancer, and the lord
treasurer's remembrancer, offices which had originated in
Edward I's reign, was carefully divided; the king's remembrancer
was to enrol writs directed to the barons, and to deal with the
casual revenue of the crown; while the lord treasurer's remembrancer had control of the fixed revenue, and dealt with writs
received by the treasurer. Both officials had their memoranda
rolls with the record of business in the exchequer during the legal
terms; the lord treasurer's remembrancer had also the originalia
rolls(10). Mention was also made in the ordinance of the accounts

[1] Baldwin, *King's council*, pp. 210 ff.
[2] *Ibid.* pp. 215–16; but cf. the review of this book by Tout, reprinted in his
Collected papers (1932), I, 193.
[3] See above, pp. 94–5.
[4] Hall, *Red book of the exchequer*, III, 848–907, gives the 1323 ordinance; and
cf. Tout, *Edward II*, pp. 187 ff.

15-2

rendered by local officials to the exchequer, and a somewhat premature attempt was made to restrict its judicial work. A special clerk was to administer lands of the chamber, and a fifth baron was to be chosen.[1] This ordinance was supplemented by two others in 1324 (cf. pp. 106 ff.) and 1326(8).

It would seem that the reforms were not all carried out immediately; we find, for example, that in Edward III's reign "foreign" accounts, such as those of the wardrobe, might still be enrolled in the great roll of the pipe, while a regular series of enrolled foreign accounts does not begin until 42 Edward III.[2] Yet we may say that the reforms altered the structure of administration and defined the inter-relations of the great departments. It was no longer possible for the chancellor to interfere at the exchequer in the interests of the crown,[3] and the exchequer was further secured from arbitrary interference on the part of the king by means of a routine which was hardening into constitutional law. In matters of finance the exchequer was indeed supreme, and it remained the final source of revenue. Even in Edward III's reign, when the wardrobe was ministering to the king's military and extra-financial needs, the exchequer had final control of supplies. In the same way it supervised the offshoots of the wardrobe, as in the case of the great wardrobe which, after 1324, was to be supplied independently by the exchequer and not by the wardrobe.[4] Similarly, just as the chamber lands had been transferred to the exchequer in 1322, so Edward III had to relinquish his plan of providing a large revenue from lands assigned to the chamber.[5]

With so extensive a sphere of action, the treasurer's position was one of the greatest importance. In his administrative duties he was closely associated with the chancellor; petitions might be made to him directly(5), and with the chancellor he had considerable control over local affairs. The duplicate great seal of the exchequer could indeed be used independently for most business. The work of the barons came to be confined to judicial matters and in time the chief baron came to preside in the court of the exchequer. From Edward II's reign the chief barons were mainly clerics.[6]

[1] Tout, *Chapters*, II, 343 ff.
[2] Tout, *Edward II*, pp. 203–4.
[3] Hall, *op. cit.* III, cccxxxiv.
[4] *Ibid.* III, 912; and Tout, *Chapters*, IV, 379.
[5] See above, pp. 96–7.   [6] Tout, *Chapters*, III, 208–9.

The judicial work of the exchequer had an early origin, since there were bound to be cases of difficulty necessitating the decision of the great officials, a fact commented on by the writer of the *Dialogus de Scaccario* (Bk. I, c. IV).[1] The plea rolls of the exchequer begin in 1236–7, and are almost continuous from the end of Henry III's reign. Nor did matters of revenue provide the only source of dispute(3); the fact that the exchequer retained conciliar procedure, and was not bound by the formal system of the common law,[2] for a time increased the number of petitions which needed equitable judgment. It is significant that in Edward I's reign, when a distinction can be made between legal and lay members of the court,[3] an attempt was made to legislate against such development, but the statutes were evaded and the exchequer at the beginning of the fourteenth century was extending its jurisdiction. Mercantile cases, for example, were heard before the treasurer, chancellor of the exchequer, and the barons. Common law writs were at first used, such as *scire facias* and *venire facias*, but later, writs utilised by council and chancery were adopted.[4]

Yet the exchequer had little hope of rivalling the jurisdiction of chancery. Already in 1311 its judicial powers had been checked (p. 15); later, faced by the opposition of chancellors, it gradually lost its equitable powers(9), and the barons were left with a common law jurisdiction over such matters as debt. The exchequer had one important dispute with the court of king's bench relating to the correction of error arising from judgment in the exchequer, concerning which there was a petition in parliament in 1347(11). On this matter there was no exact precedent. In 1308, for example, the treasurer with a number of councillors was dealing with a case of error(1); but the king's bench, because of a long association with the council, had a strong counter-claim. Final decision was given in a statute of 1357, whereby the chancellor and treasurer could hear appeals with the advice of the justices and others(12). Thus originated the statutory court of the exchequer, known later as the exchequer chamber;[5] a petition of 1378 asked for a reversal of this statute, but this was refused;

---

[1] Cf. pp. 67–8 of edition of A. Hughes, C. G. Crump, and C. Johnson (1902).
[2] See above, p. 51.
[3] Hall, *op. cit.* III, cccxxxiij.
[4] See above, p. 183.
[5] For other courts known as the exchequer chamber cf. introduction to *Select cases in the exchequer chamber* (S.S.), 1933.

other reforms of the period were of less fundamental importance, as they only defined further the work of the department(13, 14). The system of the exchequer continued with few changes as from Edward II's reign; but "it is sufficiently evident that that system proved more and more unequal to the increased financial strain and before the accession of Henry VII had completely broken down".[1]

BIBLIOGRAPHY

1. ORIGINAL SOURCES

P.R.O. Exchequer accounts. Memoranda rolls, K.R., L.T.R.
HALL, H. (ed.). *Red book of the exchequer*, pt. III, R.S. London, 1896.
PALGRAVE, F. (ed.). *The antient kalendars and inventories...of the exchequer*, 3 vols. London, 1836.
Rotuli parliamentorum. London, 1783.
Rotulorum originalium in curia scaccarii abbreviatio. Rec. Com. vol. II. London, 1810.
Statutes of the realm. London, 1810–28.

2. SECONDARY AUTHORITIES

BALDWIN, J. F. *The king's council in England during the middle ages.* Oxford, 1913.
MADOX, T. *The history and antiquities of the exchequer...*, 2nd edition. London, 1769.
MILLS, M. H. (ed.). *The pipe roll for 1295 Surrey membrane*, Surrey Record Society, no. 21. 1924.
TOUT, T. F. *Chapters in the administrative history of medieval England.* Manchester, 1920–30.
—— *The place of the reign of Edward II in English history.* Manchester, 1914.

3. ARTICLES AND ESSAYS

JENKINSON, H. "Medieval tallies, public and private", *Archaeologia*, LXXIV, 1925.
STEEL, A. "Some aspects of English finance in the fourteenth century", *History*, XII, Jan. 1928.
—— "The practice of assignment in the later fourteenth century", *E.H.R.* XLIII, 1928.
WILLARD, J. F. "The memoranda rolls and the remembrancers, 1282–1350", *Essays...presented to T. F. Tout.* Manchester, 1925.

[1] M. S. Giuseppi, *Guide to the MSS. preserved in the Public Record Office* (1923), I, 73.

(1) *Review of error in the exchequer* 1308

A Nostre Seignur le Roy e a son Conseil monstrent Nichol
Pike, et Niel Drury, nadgairs Vescuntz de Loundres, qe
come il ussent en comaundement a lever xxxii li. xviii s.
et x d. de la rent qe fust a Adam de Stratton, qe court en
pipe entre les autres dettes le Roy, et ceux deneers paer
au Priour de Merton, meismes ceux Nichol et Niel ount
levee cele Rent auxi avaunt com il poyent des tenementz
qe sont destreignables, mais il i ad une void place, qe
eynces fust edifie, e soloit rendre xxx s. et une seu de an
Chepe, qe fust a Sire Johan de Banquello, qe est ore voide,
qe soleit rendre iiii^or marcz et d'autre parte, a l'amoun-
taunce de iii s. et vii d. pur le queux home ne soit ou
destreindre, des queux deniers le Barons de L'escheker
volent condempner les ditz Viscountz e paer a l'avauntdit Priour, auxi avaunt com il fussent levable, dount il
prient remedie par charite, e qe le Priour soit assigne
aliers a recovre celes defautes...

Responsio. Mandetur per breve de Cancellario Thesaurario
Domini Regis, quod assumptis secum quibusdam Justiciariis et aliis de Concilio Regis, prout viderit expedire,
audiant omnes Peticiones et querelas tangentes processus habitos in Scaccario, in quibus asseritur error
intervenisse, ac injustas oneraciones factas ibidem, ut
dicitur, et eas ibi terminent, et faciant prosequentibus
Justiciam competentem.

Rot. Parl. I, 274 (7).

(2) *Audit of accounts of the exchequer* 1310

Dominus Rex mandauit breue suum de magno sigillo
quod est inter communia de hoc anno in hec uerba.
De clericis
deputatis
ad audien-
dum com-
potos in
scaccario.

Edwardus dei gratia etc. Thesaurario et Baronibus suis
de scaccario salutem. Quia intelleximus quod clericis ad
audiendum compotos forinsecos qui in eodem Scaccario
sunt reddendi quam plurimum indigetis, vobis mandamus
quod tres vel quatuor clericos quos ad hoc magis sufficientes et idoneos esse inuenietis eligatis et ipsos ad compotos predictos in eodem Scaccario audiendos deputetis.
Mandauimus enim vobis prefato Thesaurario et camerariis nostris quod cuilibet dictorum clericorum viginti

marcas per annum dum huiusmodi compotis audiendis intenderint pro expensis suis liberari faciatis. Teste me ipso apud Byger vj^{to} die Octobris anno regni nostri quarto per ipsum Regem apud Shene anno tercio.

Pretextu cuius mandati electis per dictos Thesaurarium et Barones Willelmo de Fulbourn', Willelmo de Corton', et Theobaldo de Bray, ad intendendum audicioni compotorum etc. in forma predicta, ijdem Willelmus, Willelmus, et Theobaldus presentes coram Thesaurario et Baronibus hic assidente eis H. de Lacy, comite Lincolnie tenente locum domini Regis in Anglia ipso Rege nunc agente in partibus Scocie et aliis de consilio etc. modo die martis tercio die mensis Nouembris deputati sunt ad intendendum audicioni compotorum etc. et prestiterunt sacramentum eodem die coram eodem consilio de bene et fideliter se habendo etc....

Memoranda roll, K.R., no. 84, 4 Ed. II, m. 54.

(3) *Judicial work of the exchequer* 1313

Adhuc. Communia de termino Sancti Hillarii anno regni Regis Edwardi filii Regis Edwardi sexto.
Adhuc Recorda.

Cornubia, De J. de Bedewynde occasionato de transgressione facta domino Regi ad sectam Antonij de Pissaigne pro Rege.

Presente coram Adomaro de Valencia comite Pembroch' J. de Sandale tenente locum Thesaurarii et Baronibus et aliis de consilio modo die veneris proxima post festum sancti Hillarii in scaccario, Johanne de Bedewynde clerico nuper vicecomite Cornubie, Antonius de Pessaigne mercator Regis presens, etc. dicit pro Rege contra eundem Johannem de Bedewynde quod idem Johannes nuper in pleno Comitatu suo tento apud Lostwythyel tempore quo fuit vicecomes Cornubie palam dicebat dominum Regem malos habuisse consiliarios et malum consultum fuisse quando ipse dominus Rex concessit eidem Antonio emptionem stagminis in Comitatu Cornubie ad opus Regis innuendo insufficienciam in ipso domino Rege et consilio suo etc. in contemptum ipsius domini Regis...

Item dicit quod postquam dominus Rex assignauit eidem Antonio emptionem stagminis etc. dictus Johannes iuit de loco in locum vbi stagminarii operabantur ad minam stagminis extrahabendam etc. et ipsos operarios induce-

bat et procurabat quod de operacionibus suis huiusmodi
cessassent etc. ad dampnum domini Regis et contemptum etc. Et petit pro domino Rege quod idem Johannes
super premissis responderet domino Regi.

Et prefatus Johannes de Bedewynde allocutus per Barones
super premissis dicit quod ipse non est culpabilis... et hoc
offert verificare qualitercumque Curia etc. Et prefatus
Antonius...petit pro Rege quod inde Inquiratur. Ideo
fiat inde Inquisicio. Et concordatum est quod Willelmus
Botereux miles et Thomas de la Hyde capiant inquisicionem inde in Comitatu Cornubie...

Memoranda roll, L.T.R. no. 83, 6 Ed. II.

(4) *Royal writs to the barons of the exchequer* 1313

Rex mandat Baronibus quod allocent Rogero de Welles- Baronibus
worth nuper escaetori suo citra Trentam in compoto suo pro Rogero
de exitibus balliue sue predicte ad scaccarium Regis de Welles-
worth.
iiij vij li. xs. qui ei a retro sunt de annuo feodo suo de
Lli. quod Rex ei concessit percipiendum in officio predicto, videlicet a xxvj die Aprilis anno regni sui iiij^to
vsque xxx Decembris anno regni sui sexto. Nisi prius
allocacionem inde habuit in toto vel in parte. Teste
Rege apud Westmonasterium xviij die Februarii anno
sexto.

Quia Henricus Dyue habuit seruicium suum cum Baronibus
domino Edwardo quondam Rege patre Regis nunc in pro Henrico Dyue.
exercitu suo Wallie anno regni sui quinto pro tercia
duorum feodorum militum quod tunc eidem patri Regis
nunc recognouit, sicut per inspeccionem rotulorum marescalcie dicti patris Regis nunc de eodem exercitu Regi
constat. Rex mandat Baronibus quod Henricum Dyue
consanguineum et heredem predicti Henrici de scutagio
quod ab eo per summonicionem scaccarii Regis ad opus
suum pro tercia parte predicta de exercitu predicto
quietum esse faciant. Et districcionem si quam ei ea
occasione fieri fecerint sine dilatione Relaxari faciant
eidem. Teste Rege apud Wyndesore, xiiij die Februarii, Anno sexto.

Memoranda roll, L.T.R. no. 83, 6 Ed. II, Hilary term.

(5) *Petition to the treasurer and council circ.* 1316

Al Tresorer et al cunsail nostre seignur le Roy monstre Willame le Duyn chaumbrelein de Norgales qe par laon (cer)teins maners ount este tous iours en meyns des Justices et des ascuns autres ministres a respoundre al Escheqer de Caernaruan...(*MS. torn*) le Roy de vne certeine ferme a tenir en lour meyns ou a lesser a plus haute ferme a lour oeps demeisme. E dount le manor de Neuyn oue les apurtenaunces ad tut temps issi este a ky qe fuist Chaumbreleyn de Caernaruan emparnaunt le auauntage en eyde de son fe outre le certeyn du au Roi xxxiiijli. par an Griffin ap Howel ny ad guers al dirrein parlement de Nichol purchascea vn comaundement du Roy a la Justice de auoir cel manoir pur la ferme qil rendy plus haut a tenir a la volente le Roy dount le dit Chaumbrelein prie qe le dit manoir lui demoerge pur lestat del office qe auaunt ad este et il durra au Roi chescun an pur son temps xls. outre le ferme auauntdite. Estre ceo le dit Griffyn est trop mauueys dettour e deit au Roy plus de xlli. de vn temps quil fuise south viscounte de Monmuth et autres dettes oueqe les queus deners hom ne poet leuer pur nul maundement del escheqer...

Ancient petitions, F. 322, E. 545. (Cf. *Cal. fine rolls*, II, 271, referring to grant of Nevyn to G. ap Howel, dated at Lincoln, Feb. 1316.)

(6) *Varied activities of the exchequer* 1321 *etc.*
Judicial rolls kept in the Exchequer 1321

Memorandum quod vicesimo primo die Novembris anno regni Regis Edwardi filii Regis Edwardi quintodecimo, Dominus Johannes de Mutford liberavit Thesaurario et Camerariis dicti Regis de Scaccario per breve Domini Regis, tresdecim rotulos de deliberacionibus Gaolarum Huntyngdone Cantie Aylesbury Okham Leycestrie Waltham et Bedefordie, et unum rotulum de audiendo et terminando de morte Willelmi filii Rogeri de Ormesby in Comitatu Norffolkie. Scilicet de annis dicti Domini Regis secundo tercio quarto quinto et sexto. In cuius rei testimonium sigilla Scaccarii Recepte et predicti Domini Johannis huic indenture alternatim sunt appensa. Datum apud Westmonasterium, die et anno supradictis.

Royal plate stored at the Exchequer 1327

Edward par la grace de Dieu Roi d Engleterre, Seignur d Irlaunde et Ducs d Aquitaine, as Tresorier et Chambreleins de nostre Escheqier saluz. Nous vous mandoms qe la vessele d argent et les jueux l onurable Piere en Dieu lEvesqe de Nicole qe feurent pris de lui, en temps nostre trescher Seignur et Piere, et liverez a nostre cher clerc Thomas de Usflete...et puis sont devenuz en vostre garde, et auxint les tentes et pavillons le dit Evesqe qe vous avez en garde facez liverer a mesme lEvesqe ou a son attournez par endenture.

Done souz nostre prive seal a Estaunford le xxvi jour d Averil l an de nostre regne primer.

Palgrave, *Antient kalendars and inventories*, III, 122, 143.

Memoranda of the Exchequer 1360

Memorandum quod xvii die Februarii anno xxxiiij Regis Edwardi tercii post conquestum, apponetur in cista in Camera computatorum ultra et supra Receptam Scaccarii, quedam Indentura sub sigillo Comitisse Surrie per quam dimisit Domino Regi omnia Castra terras et tenementa sua que tenuit in dotem ex assignacione dicti Domini Regis post mortem J. Comitis Surrie quondam viri sui in Comitatu Eborum. De Castris et aliis terris Domino Regi dimissis per Johannam de Bares Comitissam Surrie in Comitatu Eborum.

Memorandum quod quedam indentura facta inter Thesaurarium et Camerarios et Willelmum Makeuat, Vicecomitem Kancie de diversis vessalamentis argenteis Domini Regis liberatis predictis Thesaurario et Camerariis per Nicholaum Espilion Majorem Sandwyci que quidem indentura imponitur in quadam cista existente in Camera computatorum...

Memorandum quod xxiij° die Augusti anno xxxiiii° libcratum fuit Venerabili Patri Wyntoniensi Episcopo Cancellario Anglie, sigillum de Cancellaria Domini Regis usitatum in Cancellaria Anglie, tempore quo Rex fuerat in partibus Francie... Magnum Sigillum de Cancellaria.

Memorandum quod xxiiij^{to} die Augusti anno xxxiiii^{to}. liberatum fuit in Receptam Scaccarii per Dominum Johannem Episcopum Roffensem Thesaurarium Anglie, Privatum Sigillum Domini Regis sub nomine Thome de Privatum Sigillum Regis sub nomine Thome de Wodestoke.

Wodestoke filii Regis Custodis Anglie, ipso Domino Rege in partibus Francie existente, quod quidem sigillum "in custodia" Johannis de Bukyngham Clerici ad passagium Domini Regis versus partes predictas, per ipsum Dominum Regem et consilium fuit liberatum. Et remanet in quodam coffino pixide ad tale signum.

Palgrave, *Antient kalendars and inventories*, 1, 189–90.

(7) *Extracts from the ordinance of the exchequer* 1323

Ceux sount les articles ordinez et purveues sus le arraiement des choses en l'Escheqier le Roi, terme de la Trinité, l'an du regne le Roi Edward fiuz le Roi Edward seszime, a tenir, faire, et garder en l'Escheqier avant dit.

1. Qe les Barouns nentendont nul jour a plee tenir, tant que Viscounte acountant soit appose de la Pipe; ne nul plee teignont si noun, etc.

Por ce qe les acomptes des viscountes et baillifs des fraunchises acomptanz al Escheqier,...ne poent estre suffisaument renduz, oyz, ne espleites, saunz grant diligence et bone quiete; se soient desore les Barons entendantz nul jour, apres lour venue en Court, en nul manere a plee ne querele oyr ne tenir tantque viscountes et baillifs presentz en Court a acompter soient par bon examinement et bone diligence appose devant le Tresorier et eux mesme, de taunt come devera suffire pur la journe de escrivre en grant roule. Et se avisent les Barons qe nul plee desore soit tenuz en l'Escheqier saunz especial maundement du Roi, ou qe les pleez soient touchantz le Roi en chose qi appent a la place, ou ses ministres illoeques; et celes choses se facent en manere qe lesploit des acomptes ne soit delaie ne destourbe.

6. Des dettes remuables hors de Foreyns Acomptes remuer, et les mettre en Somonses.

Et quant as autres acomptes qi ount este avant ces houres renduz al Escheqier,...et appellez illoeques foreyns acomptes, come les acomptes de la Garderobe le Roi, acomptes de Gascoyne, Dirlaunde, et de Gales, des custumes des leynes des eschetries, des voidaunces des Evescheez, Abbathies, Prioritez, et autres dignitez quant escheiront, des eides des clercs et lays, et autres maneres des eides sovent grantez, et ensement acomptes des chasteux, honors, forestes, manoirs, villes, hundredz, et des autres plusours choses le Roi qi nestoient poynt baillez a ferme, eynz a garder et a respoundre des issues de yceles al Escheqier; soient touz tieux acomptes peniblement serchez et les dettes queles qe eles soient contenues en meismes les acomptes...soient pleynement saunz nul entrelesser remuez en roule annal ou en autre a ce ordine, issint qe nule tiele dette peusse cesser saunz estre mise en somonse et demaunde et levee al oeps le Roi, tant qe il en soit de ce respondu en due manere.

Et por ce qe cela busoigne requert grant occupation de temps et diligence graunde, et conoissance a le faire, soit le clerk qi est appelle Grosser en l'Escheqier en qi garde les roules sont, et qi mieuz en ce se conust, charge de par le Roi a ce faire, prenant a lui a les custages le Roi tantz par queux il puisse plus en haste la chose parfaire covenablement.

Item, face meisme cesti clerk, desore, si tost come il avera les acomptes foreyns engrosse, tutes les dettes qu'en meismes les acomptes demoeront, sur qi queles demoergent, meintenaunt remuer en roule annal, ou aillours la ou eles soient demaundez par somonses al oeps le Roi tant qil en soit de ce respondu en due manere, come estre doit. Et ceste manere estoise por temps avenir com chose establie, a faire et tenir par celui qi le dit Office de Grosser avera et tendra al Escheqier.

9. Qe le Remembrauncer le Roi remembre devers lui soulement tutz les briefs du Grant Seal et de Prive, envoiez, etc. Et remembre ou et quant il soient allowez.

Por ce qe le office de deux Remembrauncers en le Escheqier ad este molt entremelle par grant temps passe, et est uncore, issint qe li un ne li autre ad este en certain qi de eux primes dcvoit remembrer plusurs choses remembrables en la place,...; par quoi la Court ad este sovent en awer, et est, de qi de eux demaunder les choses avantdites; acordee est por les dites doutes ouster...qe les choses qi se ensuent touchantes le dit office soient desore par lun, lautre et ceux qi meisme le office sont a tenir, garde et tenuz por temps avenir; cest assavoir, qe par la ou lun et lautre ad cea en arere enroule en lour

roules de remembraunces tutes maneres des briefs le Roi
et lettres qi ont este envoiez por le Roi ou par autre au
Tresorier, ou as Barons, ou a tutz deux; desore, nient
contreesteant cel usage, le Remembrauncer le Roi soulement face enrouler tutz tieux mandementz devers lui,
saunz estre remembre devers l'autre; et puys les baille au
mareschal a garder come avant soleit estre fait. Car il y
ont este fete a chescun an et sont a temps de ore plus des
tieux brefs et lettres liverez al Escheqier qe estre ne
soloient en dys aunz ou plus, en temps devant; et par
ceste manere la escripture qe ad este annuelement de ce
faite dune part serra abrege, et autres choses plus busoign-
ables mieuz esploitez...

46. De purveer suffisaunt eide pur deliverer les acomptes qi sont a rendre du temps passe, et des terres ia de
novel forfaites.

Et pur ce qe plusurs acomptes demoeront a prendre,
auxibien de la Garderobe come dautres, par diverses
enchesons, et auxi les acomptes des issues des terres forfaites de ceux qi ne sount pas apparuz devant les Auditours en pays, devers queux la Court fait execution,
queux acomptes ne purront estre parfaites saunz y
mettre plus des ministres qi ore ne sont en la place a ce
faire; acorde est par le Roi qe estre Tresorier et les
quatre Barons qi sont en meisme la place ordine soit le
qint Baron, et estre les Clerks qi leynz sont eidantz a les
acomptes deliverer, et ceux qi sont remembrez en les
articles pardevant en ce roule, soient a meyns esluz par
Tresorier et Barons selonc lour discretion quatre hommes
suffisantz ove lour clerks qi soient entendantz peniblement a oyr les ditz acomptes par la survewe et la tesmoignaunce de un des Barons, qi adessement soit entendant les jours a surveer et tesmoigner lesploit de ceux
quatre assignez, issint qe tutes les choses qi charge portent
ou difficulte soit trove en les acomptes avantditz,...soit
cel reporte au Tresorier et as autres Barons, a les deliverer
par acord.

47. De un clerk assigner de garder et suyre les choses
tochauntes les terres forfaites.

Et pur ce qe il y ad tres grantement a faire a mettre en
due execution les choses qi sont a deliverer en lEscheqier

des terres et chateux forfaitz au Roi qi furent as countes de Lancastre et de Hereford, et plusurs Barons et chivalers et autres et lour aerdantz nadgers enemyablement contrariantz au Roi,... Acorde est qe un Clerk suffisant soit purveu par Tresorier et Barons de par le Roi a les coustages le Roi a demoerer en l'Escheqier, especialement jure a bien et loiaument garder estentes tutes les remembraunces qi leynz sont liverez, ou a liverer, qi touchent les terres et les chateux avantditz, et de faire la suyte devers tutez ceux qi de ce deyvent respondre par acompte ou en autre manere, tantqe le Roi en soit de ce respondu et servi,...

Red book of the exchequer, pt. III, pp. 848–904.

(8) *Extract from the ordinance of the exchequer* 1326

Qe lEscheqier des acountes soit un, come dauncien temps fut establi, et qe touz les acountes des viscountes qi se fount des fermes du Countee, ou des issues, ou des dettes le Roi queles qe eles soient, demaundez par somonses del Escheqier, et ensement les acountes des escuages et des taillages, assises en les demeynes le Roi, soient renduz et oiz en plein Escheqier et de coste en une meisme meson. Car sur tieux acomptes serront touz jours plusurs allouances demandez a faire par briefs et par diverses fraunchises donez et grantez a plusurs par le Roi qore est, ou ses auncestres, et plusurs dettes de lour temps a trier et purer, et assez dautres choses a sercher qi sount en les grantz roules du temps passe, qi ne pount covenablement estre severez. Et touz les autres acountes, qi sount nomez foreins acomptes, soient oiz et renduz en autre meson, joignant de coste, a ceo purveue, cest assaver: les acountes de Garderobe, et du clerk de la grant Garderobe, du Botiller, des purveours, resceivours, et gardeins des vitailles, des gardcins des chivals le Roi sojornantz hors del houstiel, et ensement des harez, des issues du seal de la Chauncellerie par le clerk gardeyn del Hanaper, des cuillours del anciene custume et de la novele. Item, des gauges des vins, des Escheteries de cea Trente et de la, des Eschaunges de Loundres et de Canterburs, des chasteux, manoirs, et autres terres le Roi nient mises a ferme, des forestz le Roi, de Gales, de Gascoigne, Dir-

launde, des eides grantez par clerks ou lays, des gardes
des erceveschees, eveschees, abbeies, et autres digniteez
quant eles escheent, et des mynes dargent et desteymerie
de Deveneshire et de Cornewaille, et de office del aunage
de draps et tutz autres tieux acomptes, soient renduz en
une place de lEscheqier par eux, ou nul ny vigne forsque
ceux qi averont les acountes a rendre et lour clerks, et les
auditours qi serront assignez a les oir et exploiter, ou
autres qi sur meismes les acountes averont especialement
a faire. Et certeins Barons soient assignez a surveer et
examiner les faitz et lexploit des auditours de tieux
acontes. Et les allowances a faire par brefs et tailles a la
fyn de tieux acomptes se facent en plein Escheqier....

Red book of the exchequer, pt. III, pp. 930–2.

(9) *Restraint on the issue of writs from the exchequer* 1327

...pro
Roberto de
Hastang.

Rex Thesaurario et Baronibus suis de scaccario salutem.
Cum dominus Edwardus Rex Anglie pater noster per
literas suas patentes concessisset dilecto et fideli suo
Roberto de Hastang custodiam ville nostre super Hull' et
manerii de Myton cum pertinentiis habendam ad totam
vitam suam prout in literis predictis plenius continetur,
ac iam ex parte ipsius Roberti nobis sit ostensum quod
vos pretendentes ipsam dictam villam propter debilitatem
et impotenciam suam custodire non posse eidem per
breue nostrum de scaccario sub vestro testimonio prefate
Thesaurie demandastis quod esset coram vobis ac aliis
de consilio nostro apud Eboracum sub ea celeritate qua
posset ad audiendum et recipiendum super custodiam
predictam quod per consilium nostrum inde contigerit
ordinari, de quo miramur plurimum et mouemur presertim cum huiusmodi breue absque consciencia nostra
de dicto scaccario emanare non debuisset nec idem
Robertus de libero tenemento suo quod inde habet iuxta
concessionem predictam absque breue nostro ad communem legem respondere teneatur. Nolentes igitur eundem Robertum in hac parte indebite pregrauari, vobis
mandamus firmiter iniungentes quod ipsum Robertum
custodiam predictam habere et tenere permittatis iuxta
tenorem literarum ipsius patris nostri predictarum ipsum
contra tenorem earundem nobis inconsultis nullatenus

molestando. Teste Rege apud Wygorniam xxviij die Decembris.

Close roll, 1 Ed. III, pt. II, m. 2.

(10) *Chancery writs for the exchequer* 1331

In Originalibus de anno Regni Regis Edwardi tercii post conquestum v^{to}.

Rex assignavit Johannem Perebroun et Edmundum Jerberge ad custumam lane, etc. in portu ville de Magna Jernemuth colligendam et levandam, etc. Norff.

Rex commisit Hugoni le Makelyn ballivam hundredi R. de Mounselawe in comitatu Salop' habendam quamdiu etc. reddendo, etc. Salop.

Mandatum est Willelmo Trussel escaetori citra Trentam quod capiat in manus Regis omnes terras et tenementa de quibus Ardulphus Hager qui etc. obiit seisitus... Citra Trent'.

Rex commisit Ricardo Symound officium senescalcie comitatus Pembr' cum pertinentiis habendum quamdiu etc. Ita quod, etc.

Rex concessit Johanni de Shardelowe et Agneti uxori ejus quod ipsi habeant visum franci plegii de hominibus et tenentibus suis in manerio de Fulbourne in comitatu Cant' ac emendas assise panis et cervisie per eosdem homines et tenentes ibidem fracte cum omnibus ad hujusmodi visum et emendas spectantibus ad totam vitam eorundem, reddendo inde per annum duodecim solidos. p. 48 b. Cant'.

Rex assignavit Johannem Filiol et Willelmum de Northon ad scutagia in comitatibus Surr' et Sussex' levanda et colligenda, etc. p. 49 a. Surr' et Sussex.

Rex cepit fidelitatem Thome de Wedon filii et heredis Thome de Wedon defuncti de duobus mesuagiis, tribus partibus unius virgate terre et quarta parte unius virgate terre cum pertinentiis in Chesham que de Rege tenentur in capite per servicium quinque solidorum et duorum denariorum per annum. Et ideo, etc. p. 49 b. Buk'.

Rex commisit Johanni de Sutton officium ulnagii pannorum ultra marinorum in terra Regis Hibernie habendum quamdiu, etc. Ita quod, etc. p. 50 a. Hib'n.

Rex constituit Willelmum de Botereaux senescallum et custodem castrorum maneriorum burgorum villarum etc. Regis in comitatu Cornub' quamdiu etc.... p. 50 b.

242 CENTRAL GOVERNMENT

p. 51 a.
Cornub'. Rex commisit Johanni de Carmynou custodiam forestarum parcorum boscorum et warennarum Regis tam viridi quam de venacione necnon deductus Regis in comitatu Cornub' habendam quamdiu, etc. Ita quod idem Johannes Regi de proficuis pannagii et herbagii infra forestas, etc. ad Regem pertinencium, etc. respondeat, etc.

p. 55 b. Mandatum est Galfrido le Scrop' et sociis suis justiciariis ad placita coram Rege tenenda, quod visis recordo et processu placiti habiti, etc. super quodam clameo facto per Robertum Pugeys de visu franci plegii in manerio ipsius Roberti de Stoke in comitatu Buk' de omnibus tenentibus suis, etc. si comperiatus, etc. tunc Johanni de Molyns et Egidie uxori ejus nunc dominis ejusdem manerii libertatem illam per rationabilem finem faciendum restitui faciant.

Rotulorum originalium in curia scaccarii abbreviatio, ii, 48 ff. (These rolls contain copies of writs issuing from chancery whereby the exchequer could collect fines through the sheriffs, etc.)

(11) *Petition of the commons concerning
judgments in the exchequer* 1347

Item prie la dite Commune, Qe les juggementz renduz en l'Escheqier soient redressez et reversez, si Errour y soit, en Baunk le Roi, auxi bien come les juggementz renduz en la Commune Place; et ne mye devant eux mesmes qi renderent le juggement: Car il n'est mye semblable a verite homme doit avoir bone conceite contre sa opinion demesne.

Responsio. Il plest a nostre Seignur le Roi, qe a quele heure qe homme se pleint de tiel Errour faite en l'Escheqier, qe les Chanceller et Tresorer qi pur temps serront, et deux Justiz, soient assignez par Commission de faire venir devant eux en l'Escheqier le Record et Process du plee, ou Errour est suppose, et de les corriger solonc ce qe appent.

Rot. Parl. ii, 168 (26).

(12) *Errors in the exchequer* 1357

Item, acorde est et establi qe en touz cas touchauntz le Roi ou autres persones, ou homme se pleinte derrour fait en proces en Lescheqier, les Chaunceller et Tresorer facent venir devant eux, en ascune chambre du conseil joust Lescheqier, le record du proces hors de Lescheqier, et prises a eux Justices et autres sages tieux come lour semblera...et facent auxint appeller devant eux les Barons de Lescheqier pur oier lour informacions et les causes de lour juggement, et sur ceo facent duement examiner la busoigne; et si ascun errour ysoit trove, le facent corriger, et amendre les roules, et puis reenvoier les en lescheqier pur faire ent execucion sicome appartient.

S.R. i, 351, 31 Ed. III, s. i, c. 12.

(13) *Ordinance for reform in the exchequer* 1363

Item, pur ce qe pluseurs Gentz acquitez par Juggement en l'Escheker en une Place, sont grandement grevez et endamagez en autres Offices et Places du dit Escheqer de mesmes les choses dont ils sont issint acquitez, a grant meschief du Poeple; est ordeine, qe un Clerc de la Rembrancie soit title de seer amont le Clerc de la Pipe, de veer les Descharges faites en la Pipe, et les enbrever en la Rembrancie, pur faire cesser toute manere de proces sur ce faite. Et aussint qe la sommons de la Pipe soit retrete solonc ce qe parties sont deschargez. Et en cas qe defaute volentrivement soit trove, le Tresorer par commandement le Roi le ferra duement punir.

Rot. Parl. ii, 280 (b).

(14) *Officials of the exchequer and the discharge of writs* 1381

Item est accordez et assentuz qc lc Clerc de Pipe et les Remenbrancers del Escheqier soient jurrez qe de terme en terme ils verront tant come le dit Escheqier serra overt toutz les briefs de grant Seal et lettres de Prive Seal, qe serront mandez al dit Escheqir mesme le terme pur final descharge daucune persone du Roialme daucun demande currant al dit Escheqier, et qe chescun de eux a qi il appartient ferra due execucion du dit mandement. Et est

auxint ordenez et assentuz qe les ditz deux Remenbrancers soient jurrez de lour part qe chescun terme de
cy en avant ils ferront une cedule de toutes les persones qi
serront deschargez en lour office par juggement...en
mesme le terme daucunes demandes en dit Escheqier,
contenante la manere de mesmes les descharges, et de
faire liverer celle cedule al dit Clerc du Pipe mesme le
terme...et auxint soit le dit Clerc du Pipe jurrez qe il de
terme en terme demandera les ditz cedules et...il des-
chargera les dites parties en manere suisdite; et...face le
Clerc du Pipe pur sa partie certifier en escrit as ditz
Remembrancers de touz tielx descharges...

S.R. II, 22, 5 Ric. II, s. 1, c. 14. (Cf. *Rot. Parl.* III, 118
(97).)

(15)   *The exchequer and local administration* 1426[1]

margin">m. 1.</p>

Writ to a sheriff to hold an inquisition

margin">Bed'.
Buk'.</p>

Rex, etc. vicecomiti, salutem. Quia Edmundus nuper
Comes Marchie qui diem suum clausit extremum vt
accepimus tenebatur nobis die quo objit in vj^{ml} xlvj li.
xiij s. iiij d. de remanentia de x^{ml} marcis de quodam fine
per ipsum facto cum domino Henrico nuper Rege
Anglie patre nostro anno regni sui tercio, quod possit se
maritare ad voluntatem suam vbicumque voluerit absque
aliqua impeticione dicti patris nostri seu heredum suorum, tibi precipimus etc. et per sacramentum proborum
et legalium hominum de balliua tua diligenter inquiras
quibus die et anno predictus Edmundus objit, et que et
cuiusmodi bona et catalla et cuius precium predictus
Edmundus habuit in dicta balliua tua dicto die quo
objit, et ad cuius vel quorum manus post mortem ipsius
Edmundi deuenerunt, et in cuius vel quorum manibus
nunc existant, et ea omnia in quorumcumque manibus in
dicta balliua tua capias in manum nostram ad valenciam
debiti predicti, et inde fieri facias debitum illud. Ita quod

---

[1] We are greatly indebted to Miss M. H. Mills for this reference.
There are three loose membranes in a vellum bag; m. 1 gives the
writ and local inquisition; m. 2 gives the particulars of the profits
from the manors concerned; this membrane is not quoted, as its two
extracts are repeated on m. 3, which gives the final account forwarded
to the exchequer to be entered upon the pipe roll.

denarios illos habeas ad scaccarium nostrum apud Westmonasterium in Octabis Sancte Trinitatis nobis ibidem
soluendos. Et si forte bona et catalla predicta ad solu-
cionem debiti predicti non sufficiant, tunc per sacramentum eorundem proborum et legalium hominum de
dicta balliua tua diligenter inquiras quas terras et que
tenementa et cuius annui valoris predictus Edmundus
habuit in dicta balliua tua aliquo tempore dicto anno
tercio seu vnquam postea et in cuius vel quorum manibus
eadem terre et tenementa nunc existant. Et ea omnia in
quorumcumque manibus nunc existant in dicta balliua
tua exceptis illis que per mortem ipsius nuper comitis ad
manus nostras deuenerunt, capias in manum nostram.
Et ea saluo custodias. Ita quod de exitibus eorundem
terrarum et tenementorum nobis respondeas quousque
nobis de debito predicto plenarie fuerit satisfactum. vel
aliud inde tibi preceperimus. Et constare facias Baronibus
de dicto scaccario nostro ad diem et locum predictos que
et cuiusmodi bona et catalla et cuius precium necnon
quas terras et que tenementa et cuius annui valoris
ceperis in manum nostram accione premissa, et vbi etc.
Teste J. etc. x° die maij anno regni nostri quarto per
magnum rotulum de anno secundo Regis nunc in Itinere
Norff' quoad debitum. Et quendam actum parliamenti
anno regni domini Regis nunc secundo tenti ad scaccarium hic missum et irrotulatum in memorandis de
eodem anno secundo inter Recorda de termino Pasche
ex parte Rememoratoris Regis in quo quidem acto inter
cetera continetur quod predictus Edmundus nuper Comes
Marchie fecit finem predictum predicto anno tercio
predicti Regis Henrici quinti.

Inquisitio capta apud Wedon' in comitatu Buk'. die
lune proxima post festum Sancte Trinitatis anno regni
Regis Henrici sexti post conquestum quarto, coram
Johanne Cheyne, armigero, vicecomite comitatus predicti, virtute breuis predicti eidem vicecomiti directi,
et dicte inquisitioni consuti per sacramentum Johannis
Arches et aliorum juratorum, Qui dicunt super sacramentum suum quod Edmundus nuper Comes Marchie in
breui predicto nominatus obijt die veneris xix° die Januarii anno regni Regis Henrici sexti post conquestum
tercio. Et quod idem comes nulla bona seu catalla in

comitatu predicto die obitus sui habuit. Et eciam dicunt quod predictus Edmundus nuper Comes Marchie fuit seisitus in dominico suo vt de feodo anno tercio Regis Henrici quinti de manerio de Whadon' Nassh' et Beerton' cum pertinentiis in Comitatu Buk'. Et de manerio de Stepylclaydon' cum pertinentiis in eodem comitatu. Et quod quedam finis leuata in curia domini Regis apud Westmonasterium in crastino Sancti Johannis Baptiste anno tercio predicti Regis Henrici quinti patris domini Regis nunc coram Ricardo Norton et socijs suis tunc Justiciariis ipsius Regis Henrici quinti de Banco et alijs domini Regis fidelibus tunc ibidem presentibus inter Ricardum Comitem Warruici Johannam que fuit uxor Willelmi Beauchamp de Bergevenny, Walterum Lucy iam miltem [*sic*] Thomam Chaucers et alios prout in fine predicta plenius apparet querentes, et prefatum Edmundum nuper Comitem Marchie deforciantem, de manerio de Whaddon' Nassh' et Beerton' cum pertinentiis et de manerio de Stepylclaydon' cum pertinentiis in comitatu predicto per quem quidem finem de licencia predicta domini Regis Henrici quinti per litteras suas patentes quarum datum est xviij° die Junij dicto anno tercio prefatis Juratis in euidencia monstratur de maneriis de Whaddon' et Stepylclaydon' cum pertinentiis in dictis finibus inter alia contentis predictus Edmundus...recognouit predicta maneria cum suis pertinentiis in comitatu predicto inter alia esse Jus ipsorum comitis Warruici Johanne Willelmi Walteri Thome Chauceres et aliorum prout in fine apparet, Et sic Jurati predicti dicunt quod virtute finis predicti ijdem Comes Warruici...et alij feoffatores de eisdem maneriis cum suis pertinentiis...a tempore leuacionis finis predicti ac tempore mortis predicti nuper Comitis Marchie et in presenti in dominico suo vt de feodo seisiti fuerunt et adhuc existunt, et exitus et proficua inde per idem tempus prouenientes perceperunt et habuerunt. Et eciam dicunt quod manerium de Whaddon' se extendit in villis de Whaddon' et Nassh' et Beerton' cum pertinentiis valet per annum vltra reprisam quinquaginta marcas et dictum manerium de Stepylclaydon' cum pertinentiis valet per annum vltra reprisam sexdecim libros. Et vlterius dicunt quod predictus Edmundus...nulla alia siue plurima maneria terras

siue tenementa habuit in comitatu predicto quam modo
et forma superius specificantur. In cuius rei etc.

Auditores. Thomas Banestre, Baro.   m. 3.
Johannes Geryn, clericus.

Compotus Johannis Cheyne de Isnampstede armigeri   Buk'.
nuper vicecomitis comitatus Buk'. de exitibus manerii
de Whaddon' cum pertinentiis...ac manerii de Stepilclaydon' vnacum omnibus terris et tenementis vocatis
Bentleys in Amondesham cum pertinentiis in comitatu
predicto in quibus Edmundus nuper Comes Marchie fuit
seisitus in dominico suo vt de feodo, anno tercio Regis
Henrici quinti nuper Regis Anglie in manus Regis nunc
Henrici sexti seisitis pro eo quod idem nuper comes
tenebatur die quo obijt eidem Regi nunc in vj^{ml} xlvj li.
xiij s. iiij d. [*here repeating the preceding writ*] sicut continetur
in duobus breuibus huius scaccarij eidem nuper vicecomiti directis remanentibus in ligula breuium executis
pro Rege de termino Sancte Trinitatis anno quarto Regis
nunc Henrici sexti ex parte Rememoratoris Thesaurarii,
videlicet de exitibus maneriorum ac omnium terrarum et
tenementorum predictorum a diuersis diebus subscriptis
quibus dictus nuper vicecomes causa predicta eadem
maneria terras et tenementa cum pertinentiis seisiuit in
manus Regis vsque festum Sancti Michelis proximum
sequens, scilicet anno quinto eiusdem Regis nunc Henrici
sexti a quo quidem festo sancti Michelis dicto anno quinto
Willelmus Massy nunc vicecomes ibidem de exitibus
maneriorum terrarum et tenementorum...est computa-
turus.

Idem reddit compotum de xvij li. xvj d. de exitibus   Recepta
dictorum maneriorum de Whaddon' et Stepilclaydon' cum   denariorum.
pertinentiis in comitatu predicto que fuerunt predicti
Edmundi nuper comitis Marchie dicto anno tercio Regis
Henrici quinti causa predicta in manus Regis nunc
seisita et que ad xlix li. vj s. viij d. seperatim extendunt per   amercietur
annum sicut continetur in quadam Inquisitione coram   vicecomes
  quia
prefato nuper vicecomite virtute vnius breuis breuium   declarauit
predictorum capta, et eidem breui consuta,...scilicet per   statum
  quorundam
vnum quarterium anni et xxxv dies iuxta ratam extente   feoffatorum
  in inquisi-
predicte per idem tempus, sicut continetur in quadam   tione vltra
  mandatum
cedula de particulis hic in thesauro liberata. Et remanet.   Regis.

Et de xj s. iij d. de exitibus omnium maneriorum terrarum et tenementorum predictorum vocatorum Bentleys
in Amondesham predicta cum pertinentiis in comitatu
predicto que fuerunt predicti Edmundi...in manus predicti Regis nunc causa predicta seisita et que ad xl s.
extendunt per annum, sicut continetur in quadam alia
Inquisitione coram prefato nuper vicecomite virtute
alterius breuis breuium predictorum capta et eidem breui
consuta,...scilicet per vnum quarterium anni et xj dies,
iuxta ratam extente predicte per idem tempus sicut continetur ibidem. Et remanet.

Bed'. Summa recepte. xvij li. xij s. vij d.

Sheriff's account, 2/11.

Entry on the pipe roll, 4 Hen. VI.

Bed'. Buk'.   Johannes Cheyne de Jsnamstede armiger nuper vicecomes comitatus Buk. reddit compotum de xvij li. xij s.
vij d. de exitibus manerii de Whaddon' cum pertinentiis
quod se extendit in villis de Waddon' Nassh' et Berton' ac
manerii de Stepilclaydon' vnacum omnibus terris et tenementis vocatis Bentleys in Amondesham cum pertinentiis in comitatu predicto in quibus Edmundus nuper
Comes Marchie fuit seisitus in dominico suo vt de feodo
videlicet tam a die lune proximo post festum Sancte
Trinitatis accidente xxvij° die maij anno quarto quam a
die Jouis proximo ante festum Sancti Johannis Baptiste
accidente xx° die Junij anno quarto vsque festum Sancti
Michelis anno quinto sicut continetur in compoto suo
inde rotulo quarto rotulo compotorum in thesauro
xvij li. xij s. xj d. quinto die decembris anno quinto. Et
habeat.

CHAPTER VIII

JUSTICE

INTRODUCTION

The origins of the system of common law are to be found in
Henry II's reforms, in his institution of the writ process, in his
organisation of circuits for the visitation of itinerant justices as
begun by Henry I, and in his decision to set aside five justices *de
familia sua* who should hear suits apart from the king. From this
time royal justice steadily encroached on private franchise; suitors
were encouraged to apply to the royal courts for remedy, and
with the increased business which resulted there was bound to be
differentiation within the *curia*, though at first we can only distinguish between cases heard by the justices *in banco* and the more
difficult matters reserved for the justices *coram rege*.

Clause 17 in Magna Carta had stated that common pleas should
not follow the king but be held in a fixed place; from this time
we can trace the growth of a court of common pleas, which was
developing its procedure at a time when the great lawyers, Bracton
and then the anonymous author of the book called *Britton*, were
stating the law. Its procedure was formularised in accordance
with the writs issued out of chancery, of which there were over a
hundred in Henry III's time.[1] The essoin[2] rolls of this court exist
from 11 Henry III, and the plea rolls from 1 Edward I. In 1272
there was appointed a separate chief justice of the common pleas;
after 1316 only once was there chosen a clerical judge,[3] and it
became usual to recruit the bench from the order of serjeants
at law. The court of common pleas was held normally at Westminster, but it was at York from 1333 to 1339, where the chancery
had its headquarters from 1332 to 1336, and the exchequer from
1333 to 1338.[4] The king's bench moved more frequently, and

[1] Baldwin, *King's council*, p. 49.
[2] essoin = excuse for non-attendance.
[3] Tout, *Edward II*, p. 368.
[4] Tout, *Chapters*, III, 57–8. Cf. D. M. Broome, "Exchequer migrations to
York in the thirteenth and fourteenth centuries", in *Essays...presented to T. F.
Tout.*

the commons more than once petitioned that the benches should have permanent quarters (2, 11).

In the early fourteenth century the court of common pleas had considerably more business than the king's bench. The most important jurisdiction of common pleas was that concerning real actions, over which it had a monopoly during the medieval period.[1] It could moreover supervise the local courts, both communal and seignorial; by the writ *pone* it could transfer cases from such courts to itself, and by writs of false judgment it could interfere in the jurisdiction of inferior courts.[2] Yet such a power was bound to decline as the local courts became unimportant; further, cases might be taken from the common pleas to the king's bench by means of a writ of error.

The king's *curia* had from Norman times heard great causes and matters concerning the crown, and it had become usual to refer difficulties to the justices *coram rege*. On this basis the king's bench was developing its jurisdiction during the thirteenth century by writ procedure. By the time of Edward I it had its own records, a chief justice, a court of professional justices, and already it could interfere in the jurisdiction of the court of common pleas. Nevertheless, the king's bench remained very closely connected with the king and his council. Its records, for example, continued to include much conciliar business which was administrative as well as judicial.[3] The nature of its jurisdiction kept it in close connection with the crown, and it still often accompanied the king on his journeys. That it became more independent was due partly to the existence of the court of the marshalsea, which was in close contact with the royal court,[4] and partly to the strength of the common law procedure which, by the end of the fourteenth century, completely differentiated king's bench from the equitable jurisdiction of the council.

It is remarkable that the king's bench managed to build up a civil jurisdiction in addition to its criminal work. It had cognisance of all pleas of the crown, though in practice most criminal cases were heard in the counties by the itinerant justices. Most important was the power to hear appeals on matters of error in cases tried in other courts; the process here was by writ of error, which could be used for civil as well as criminal causes. Further, by writ of *certiorari* (24), issued either out of chancery or king's bench, the

---

[1] Holdsworth, *A history of English law*, 1, 198.
[2] *Ibid.* 1, 51 ff.; the writs are given on pp. 653, 654.
[3] Baldwin, *op. cit.* p. 64.   [4] See below, pp. 253–4.

JUSTICE251

king could demand to see the record of any case tried in an
inferior court, and in this way the case could be transferred to the
king's bench.[1] Before the end of the period it was also encroaching
on the original civil jurisdiction of common pleas by means of
legal fictions,[2] though the result of this was not effectively felt
until later.

In this way the king's bench was developing its common law
jurisdiction, and while it was drawing away from the council there
was a closer connection with parliament. After the middle of the
fourteenth century parliament and not the council was hearing
appeals on matters of error in the courts of common law.[3] We can
also understand why the king's bench was claiming to hear
appeals from the exchequer, and why the barons were resisting.[4]

The common law was itself being extended and defined through
the work of the justices. That it was being distinguished from
equity is seen in a Year Book entry for 1343 which does not lend
itself to full quotation: in the opinion of a chief justice the writ
of *Audita Querela*[5] was given *plus dequite qe de commune ley*.[6] Petitions
were continually being presented in parliament on behalf of the
common law and against the encroachments of the prerogative
courts(32) and of chancery(12–14). A few changes were made by
statutes: in 1340 presentment of Englishry was abolished(5); a
later law provided that English should be used in the courts(10),
but this was not observed, and an effective enactment was not
made until the eighteenth century.[7] It is interesting to notice that
more attention was being given to the keeping of court records(17).

In Edward III's reign new seals were adopted for the benches.
The king was in financial difficulties in the early stages of the
French war, and, following the practice of allowing grants from
the issues of the great seal in return for loans, in 1344 he pledged
to a foreign merchant the issues from the judicial writs of both
benches. At the same time two new royal seals were made, one
for each bench, which made it possible for the writs required in
the course of procedure to be obtained without recourse to
chancery(7); later the fees were paid to a separate hanaper of the

---

[1] Holdsworth, *op. cit.* I, 228, 658–9; and Baldwin, *op. cit.* p. 531.
[2] Holdsworth, *op. cit.* I, 198.   [3] Baldwin, *op. cit.* p. 335.
[4] See above, p. 229.
[5] Holdsworth, *op. cit.* I, 224, quotes Blackstone on this writ, by which "a
defendant against whom judgment is recovered...may be relieved upon good
matter of discharge which has happened since the judgment".
[6] *Year Book*, R.S. 17 Ed. III, p. 371.
[7] C. Grant Robertson, *Select statutes, cases and documents*, p. 209.

benches.[1] The change led to an increase in the charge of writs, and the commons were soon petitioning against this (8). Professor Tout suggested that the duplication of the great seal for judicial purposes may have been due to the lay chancellors.[2]

The extracts which are given below to illustrate the work of the courts of common law (1, 3, 4) indicate the slowness of their judicial processes, and also the dependence of the central courts on the local administration. It was here that the itinerant justices could do valuable work. At the beginning of the fourteenth century there were two systems of local judicial and administrative commissions. Most unpopular were the general eyres, instituted at irregular intervals by a commission, and given wide and indeed almost unlimited powers. To meet these justices the sheriff was ordered to summon the most important men of the county, and all present and past officials; and the justices could hear any pleas that had arisen since the last eyre. The proceedings of all other courts in the county were stopped for the time being, and the eyre was clearly used for fiscal and administrative, as well as judicial purposes. In the early fourteenth century a list of new articles (22) was added to the already lengthy list of old articles upon which presentment might be made.[3]

There seem to have been only a few eyres during the century, and these were often incomplete: there was a Kentish eyre in 1313 (19, 20),[4] and one in London in 1321. In 1329 commissions for a general eyre were issued for Northamptonshire and Nottinghamshire, which had had no such visitation since 1285 and 1280 respectively, but this was probably due to Mortimer's policy. There is no evidence that the eyre was at all general, and later in the reign an eyre for Kent had to be abandoned in 1333, and similarly in the case of London in 1341. In 1348 the commons were demanding that these eyres should cease, and actually no others were held.[5]

This decline is partly accounted for by the success of the regular judicial assizes of the itinerant justices in serving the judicial needs of the county, partly by the changing sources of revenue. The justices were responsible for the criminal and civil processes which had been instituted by Henry II, and which had since

---

[1] Article by B. Wilkinson in *E.H.R.* 1927; and Tout, *Chapters*, III, 154–5.
[2] Tout, *op. cit.* III, 154.
[3] Article by H. M. Cam, *E. H. R.* 1924; and her *Studies in the hundred rolls.*
[4] *Eyre of Kent* (S.S.).
[5] Holdsworth, *op. cit* I, 272.

developed. Magna Carta (cc. 18, 19) and the 1217 reissue of the charter (cc. 13–15) had provided that the petty assizes should be taken in the county courts by royal commissioners.[1] In Edward I's reign other commissions were given to the justices, though not regularly at first. By the *nisi prius* system civil actions could be heard locally which would otherwise have originated in the central courts; the sheriff was charged by writ to summon jurors in such cases to Westminster *nisi prius* the assize justices visited the county. The commission of *oyer and terminer* (21) gave the right to hear and determine all criminal pleas pending in the counties, while that of gaol delivery authorised the justices to inspect gaols and to try charges against prisoners. In the early fourteenth century these commissions were granted regularly to the justices of assize on each new circuit (23). In 1318 the *nisi prius* system was extended to all pleas of land and further developed later.[2] In 1329 the commission of trailbaston was revived, with wider functions than those of keeping the peace:[3] and when the commission of the peace was organised, the justices of assize were included.[4] With the increase in judicial business it was necessary to have frequent sessions, and the counties were normally visited three times a year (24). It was found necessary, also, for the justices to be men trained in the law, and their number always included justices of the two benches and barons of the exchequer. Thus while the assize justices were acting on temporary commissions on circuit, in practice their permanence was assured; with the vast extension of their work they came to represent the king's bench and common pleas in the counties, and later statutes throw some light on their office (25–27).

Lastly, there were the prerogative courts, of which the commons were continually complaining on account of their encroachment upon the courts of common law.

The court of the king's household, known as the marshalsea, has been mentioned as affecting the development of the king's bench. The steward and marshal had a general jurisdiction "within the verge" (i.e. within a twelve-mile radius of the court), acting as deputies of the chief justice of the king's bench unless he was himself itinerating with the court. This jurisdiction was in fact taken over by the king's bench: but the steward and marshal could also sit as judges of the court of the marshalsea, and there

[1] Stubbs, *S.C.* pp. 295, 342.   [2] Holdsworth, *op. cit.* 1, 278 ff.
[3] *Ibid.* 1, 273–4.   [4] See below, pp. 325–6.

had cognisance of the pleas of the crown, and three common pleas, of debt, covenant and trespass, within the verge, limited to the members of the royal household (28–30).[1]

The court of chivalry of the constable and marshal was in origin a military court for the enforcement of martial law in war time, and it dealt with various matters relating to war; it also came to deal with heraldry.[2] Then it began to encroach upon the common law by hearing cases of treason and felony, and it was attacked in parliament (32). In 1390 the sphere of the constable's jurisdiction was more narrowly defined (33); yet he continued to hear cases pleadable at the common law (34), and in his court resort might be made to the *duellum* if there was not sufficient evidence by witness (36). A statute of 1399 provided that criminal appeals concerning matters done outside the realm should be determined by this court instead of by parliament, but that the courts of common law should have cognisance of all such matters within the kingdom (35). A remonstrance against this jurisdiction failed in 1429, and the court progressed on these lines during the fifteenth century. There seems to be no reason to assert that in Edward IV's reign exceptional powers were given to the constable, save in one instance when Earl Rivers was appointed constable in 1467; he remained in office only for a short time, and the patents of appointment for John Tiptoft, Earl of Worcester, were normal. The jurisdiction of the constable was further developed in Tudor times, but the limitation of Richard II's statute was never disregarded.[3]

The development of the court of admiralty has less constitutional importance. At first maritime cases, such as those connected with shipping, piracy, evasions of customs, etc., were dealt with by the council, while some were delegated to chancery in Edward II's time. The number of appeals to the king and council about such matters increased so considerably, however, that a part of the work was delegated to the admirals.[4] The first reference to an admiral's court has been found for 1357,[5] but in the fourteenth century there were several admirals for the different coasts, and several courts, and it was not until the next century that there was one admiral for the whole country. Before this time the courts of

[1] Holdsworth, *op. cit.* I, 208–9.
[2] *Ibid.* I, 573 ff.
[3] Cf. L. W. V. Harcourt, *His grace the steward*, pp. 390–9. He quotes letters patent conferring appointments.
[4] Baldwin, *op. cit.* pp. 272–5.
[5] *Select pleas of the admiralty* (S.S.), pp. xli, xlii.

admiralty had been encroaching upon the jurisdiction of coastal towns in civil and criminal matters; this was forbidden by statute in 1389(38) and 1391, after which time the admiral's court was strictly limited to maritime cases.[1] Actually it was never popular and remained closely supervised by the council, which, with the chancery, continued to deal with matters that were closely concerned with commerce and foreign relations: and it was not until Tudor times that there was any significant change in the jurisdiction of the admiralty court.

BIBLIOGRAPHY

1. ORIGINAL SOURCES

P.R.O. Ancient indictments.
—— Plea rolls, court of common pleas.
—— Plea rolls, court of king's bench.
Abbreviatio placitorum, Richard I–Edward II. London, 1811.
BOLLAND, W. C. (ed.). *The eyre of Kent*, vol. I, S.S. vol. XXIV. 1909.
MARSDEN, R. G. (ed.). *Select pleas in the court of admiralty*, vol. I, S.S. vol. VI. 1892.
Proceedings and ordinances of the privy council. London, 1834–7.
Rotuli parliamentorum. London, 1783.
Statutes of the realm. London, 1810–28.

2. SECONDARY AUTHORITIES

BALDWIN, J. F. *The king's council in England during the middle ages.* Oxford, 1913.
BOLLAND, W. C. *The general eyre.* Cambridge, 1922.
CAM, H. M. *Studies in the hundred rolls. Oxford studies in social and legal history*, vol. VI. Oxford, 1921.
HARCOURT, L. W. V. *His grace the steward and trial of peers.* London, 1907.
HOLDSWORTH, W. S. *A history oᶠ English law*, vol. I, 3rd edition. London, 1922.
TOUT, T. F. *Chapters in the administrative history of medieval England.* Manchester, 1920–30.
—— *The place of the reign of Edward II in English history.* Manchester, 1914.
TWISS, T. (ed.). *Monumenta Juridica, The black book of the admiralty*, R.S. (Introduction). London, 1871.

---

[1] Holdsworth, *op. cit.* I, 544 ff.

3. ARTICLES

CAM, H. M. "The general eyres of 1329–30", *E.H.R.* xxxix, 1924.

GELDART, W. M. "The year books of Edward II", *E.H.R.* xxvi, 1911.

PUTNAM, B. H. "The ancient indictments in the Public Record Office", *E.H.R.* xxix, 1914.

RICHARDSON, H. G. "Year books and plea rolls as sources of historical information", *Trans. R.H.S.* 4th series, v, 1922.

VINOGRADOV, P. "Constitutional history and the Year Books", *Collected Papers*, vol. i, *Historical*. Oxford, 1928.

WILKINSON, B. "The seals of the two benches under Edward III", *E.H.R.* xlii, 1927.

(1) THE COURTS OF COMMON LAW

(1) *Abstracts of pleas in the king's court* 1317–19

Placita coram Domino Rege apud Westmonasterium de termino Pasche anno regni Regis Edwardi filii Regis Edwardi decimo.

Suff'. Johannes Giffard recuperat ccccc lib. pro dampnis versus Hugonem Giffard personam ecclesie de Barewe pro bonis et catallis suis captis.

Berk'. Johannes filius Thome de Mulward implacitat Willelmum Ascelyn et xj alios pro depastione bladorum et herbe sue apud Upledecombe, etc. Qui dicit quod clamat habere communem suam ibidem, etc....

Sutht' Preceptum est vicecomiti quod plenariam seisinam habere faceret Ricardo Hurum de manerio de Shaldeflet et de j messuagio et ij carucatis terre in Chesthull juxta finem inde levatum inter predictum Ricardum querentem et Henricum Trenchard deforciantem anno quinto Edwardi patris Regis nunc, eo quod dictus Henricus et Alionara uxor ejus et Thomas de Grimsted summoniti per breve de scire facias non venerunt.

......

Kanc'. Judicium redditum tam per monstracionem cartarum regum et recordorum quam per breve Regis contra vicecomitem Kancie qui distrinxit homines et tenentes abbatis Sancti Augustini Cantuariensis de maneriis suis de Menstre Chistlet Stury Littlebourn Northbourn Lenham et

Plumsted ad sectam faciendam ad turnum vicecomitis et
levavit de eis diversas pecuniarum summas pro hutesio et
aliis forisfactis in dictis maneriis per turnum predictum
presentatis...

Allocatur majori et civibus Eboraci cognicionem placiti Ebor'.
transgressionis etc. super monstracionem cartarum suarum
quas proferunt, et hic narratur in uno rotulo et dimidio...

Placita coram Domino Rege apud Eboracum de termino Sancti Michelis anno regni Regis Edwardi filii
Regis Edwardi duodecim.

Ballivus domini Regis de hundredo de Hurstingston Hunt'.
recuperat xx lib. pro dampnis versus Rogerum de Hyrst
et iij alios pro rescusso facto de catellis captis pro wither-
namio apud Woldhurst nomine districcionis...

Cassatur jurata in placito transgressionis eo quod Ebor'.
querens est excommunicatus.

Duo brevia Regis ad attachiandos vicecomites qui Dors'.
levaverunt diversas pecuniarum summas de communitate
patrie pro expensis militum apud parliamentum Regis et
dictos denarios dictis militibus non solverunt...

Walterus episcopus Exoniensis attachiatur per vice- Cornub'.
comitem eo quod contra inhibicionem Regis exercuit
jurisdiccionem ordinariam super capellam Sancte Beriane
liberam fundatam per predecessores Regis et excom-
municacionis sentenciam promulgavit durante causa predicta indiscussa.

Placitorum...abbreviatio, pp. 326–32.

(2) *The common bench shall not be moved
without warning* 1328

Et pur ce qe par remuement du commune Bank les pleez
bien sovent ont demore saunz jour, a grantz damage, et
en peril de desheritance des pluseurs; acorde est et establi
qe desore en avant les Justices, avant ce qe le Bank se
remuera, soient garniz par temps, issint queux peussent
ajorner les parties si par temps queles ne perdent mie lour
proces.

S.R. I, 259, 2 Ed. III, c. 11. (Statute of Northampton.)

(3)   *Extracts from the plea rolls of the court of common
pleas.*[1]   *Michaelmas term, 7 Ed. III* 1333

Placita apud Eboracum coram Willelmo de Herle et
socijs Justiciariis domini Regis de Banco in Octabis Sancti
Michelis anno regni Regis Edwardi tercij a conquestu,
septimo.

m. 3.
Surr'.

Johannes filius Johannis le Mareschal de Guldeford per
Henricum Rocer attornatum suum petit versus Johannem
Brocas et Margaretam vxorem eius decem et octo acras
terre cum pertinentiis in Guldeford vt Jus per breue de
ingressu etc. Et Johannes et Margareta per Ricardum
ffry attornatum suum veniunt. Et petunt inde visum
habeant, dies datus est eis hic in Octabis Sancti Hillarii,
etc...

m. 4.
Dors'.

Johannes le Botiler de Haydon' per Johannem de
Coliford attornatum suum optulit se iiij^{to} die versus
Ricardum le fforester de Bokland Dynham, de placito
quod reddat ei rationabilem compotum suum de tempore
quo fuit receptor denariorum ipsius Johannis etc. Et ipse
non venit. Et preceptum fuit vicecomiti quod caperet
eum, etc. Et vicecomes modo mandat quod non est
inuentus, nec aliquid habet, etc. Ideo sicut prius preceptum est vicecomiti quod capiat eum...

m. 4.
Som's.

Johannes le Botiler de Haydon Junior, per Johannem
de Coliford, attornatum suum, optulit se iiij^{to} die versus
Ricardum le fforester de Bokland Dynham, de placito
quod reddat ei centum et tres solidos et sex denarios quos
ei debet et iniuste detinet, etc. Et ipse non venit. Et
sicut pluries districtus per catalla ad valenciam duodecim denariorum...Et sicut pluries preceptum est vicecomiti quod distringat eum per omnes terras, etc...Et
quod habeat corpus eius hic in octabis Sancti Hillarii,
etc....

m. 5 d.
Hertf'.

Preceptum fuit vicecomiti quod venire faceret hic ad
hunc diem xij etc. de visneto de la Dene in parochia de
Bekenesfeld, per quos, etc. Et qui nec Willelmum atte
Lee et Elenam vxorem eius nec Johannem atte ffelde de
Maydenhethe et Ricardum fratrem eius executores testa-

---

[1]   P.R.O. roll 296. There are 460 membranes in all, each about
2½ feet in length and about 9 inches wide. An attempt has been made
to take typical entries.

menti Stephani atte ffelde aliqua, etc. si quoddam scriptum obligatorium quod ijdem Willelmus et Elena in Curia Regis apud Westmonasterium proferunt sub nomine predicti Stephani de duobus bobus, duabus vaccis.

Jurata inter Willelmum atte Lee et Elenam vxorem Hertf'. eius querentes, et Johannem atte ffelde de Maydenhethe et Ricardum fratrem eius executores testamenti Stephani atte ffelde de placito debiti, ponitur in respectum hic vsque in Octabis Sancti Hillarij pro defectu Juratorum quia nullus venit. Ideo vicecomes habeat corpora, etc.

Jurata inter Johannem de Sancto Paulo clericum m. 7. London'. querentem, et Thomam Cully de London', Armurer, de placito compoti, ponitur in respectum hic vsque in Octabis Sancti Hillarij pro defectu Juratorum, quia nullus venit. Ideo vicecomes habeat corpora Juratorum, etc.

Johannes de Hecham optulit se iiij die versus Johan- Cant'. nem Chanyn capellanum, executorem testamenti Ricardi de Hecham, nuper persone ecclesie de Weston Coleuill' de placito quod reddat ei nouem marcas quas ei iniuste detinet, etc. Et ipse non venit...

Robertus de Wykham optulit se iiij versus Thomam m. 7 d. Oxon'. Wale et Nicholaam vxorem eius et Egidium de Arderne de placito quod permittant ipsum presentare idoneam personam ad ecclesiam de Swalclyne que vacat, et ad suam spectat donacionem, etc. Et ipsi non venerunt. Et habuerunt inde diem hic ad hunc diem per essoniatores suos postquam summonitionem, etc...

Ricardus de Bercheston per Willelmum de Northwyk m. 12. Warr'. attornatum suum, optulit se iiij die versus Robertum Aleyn de Sibbeford, capellanum, Ricardum ffelice de Bercheston, Johannem Wyberd de Sibbeford, Ricardum atte Clyne de Tiddelinynton, et Aliciam vxorem eius et Johannem filium eorundem Ricardi et Alicie, de placito quare ipsi simul cum Ricardo filio Thome Aleyn de Sibbeford vi et armis domum ipsius Ricardi de Bercheston apud Bercheston fregerunt et bona et catalla sua ad valenciam centum librarum ibidem inuenta maliciose combusserunt, et alia enormia ei intulerunt ad graue dampnum ipsius Ricardi de Bercheston et contra pacem etc. Et ipsi non venerunt. Et preceptum fuit vicecomiti sicut pluries quod caperet eos, etc. Et vicecomes modo mandat quod predicti Robertus Aleyn de Sibbeford,

Ricardus ffelice et Johannes Wyberd non sunt inuenti,
etc...Et de predictis Ricardo atte Clyne et Alicia vxore
eius et Johanne filio eorundem Ricardi et Alicie mandat
vicecomes quod mortui sunt,...

m. 15.
Deuon'.
Essoniator Abbatis de Boklond optulit se iiij die versus
Bonum Abbatem de Tauystok et fratrem Alexandrum
de Legh' commonachum eiusdem Abbatis de Tauystok,
et Johannem Dauy, de placito quare ceperunt catalla
ipsius Abbatis de Boklond et ea iniuste detinuerunt contra
vadium et plegium etc. Et ipsi non venerunt. Et habuerunt diem hic ad hunc diem...

m. 15.
Deuon'.
Jurata vtrum vnum mesuagium et viginti acrae terre
cum pertinentiis in Southlegh sint libera elemosina per-
tinens ad ecclesiam de Southlegh vnde Philippus de Norwico est persona ecclesie de Southlegh...an laicum feodum Johannis Walramed et Johanne vxoris eius, ponitur
in respectum vsque in Octabis Sancti Hillarij hic pro
defectu Juratorum quia nullus venit...

m. 17.
Suff'.
Stephanus de Ampton et Alicia vxor eius dant quadraginta solidos pro licencia concordandi cum Willelmo
de Ingham persona ecclesie de Ampton et Edwardo de
Rysby capellano, de placito conuencionis de manerio
de Ampton cum pertinentiis et aduocacione ecclesie eiusdem ville, per plegium Johannis de Ingham de eodem
comitatu. Et habent cyrographum per pacem admissam,
coram J. de Shardlow...

m. 21.
Ebor'.
Jurata inter Idoneam que fuit vxor Ade de Buryngham
de Saltmersh petentem, et Robertum filium Ricardi de
Buryngham de Saltmersh tenentem, de placito dotis,
ponitur in respectum hic vsque in crastino Animarum,
pro defectu Juratorum, quia nullus venit. Ideo vicecomes
habeat corpora, etc.

m. 21 d.
Ebor'.
Essoniator Johannis de Kelm de Neuwerk optulit se
iiij^{to} die versus Matillam que fuit vxor Johannis Campion
de Neuwerk et Johannem Dant, de placito quare secuti
sunt placitum in Curia Christianitatis de catallis et
debitis que non sunt de testamento vel matrimonio
contra prohibicionem, etc. Et ipsi non venerunt. Et preceptum fuit vicecomiti quod attachiaret eos. Et vicecomes
mandat quod nichil habent, etc...

m. 23 d.
Ebor'.
Richerus de Ledes, capellanus, qui tulit assisam noue
disseisine versus Thomam filium Willelmi Graa et alios in

breui de tenemento in Sandhoton, non est prosecutus.
Ideo ipse et plegij sui de prosecutione, scilicet Johannes
del Mylnehous et Adam del Chapell in misericordia, etc.
Willelmus de Whale dat viginti solidos pro licencia m. 48.
Westml'.
concordandi cum Willelmo de Sandford de placito con-
uencionis de manerio de Whale cum pertinentiis. Et
habent cyrographum, per J. de Anlaghby...

(4) *Extracts from the plea rolls of the court of king's
bench.*[1] *Michaelmas term, 7 Ed. III 1333*

Placita coram domino Rege apud Eboracum et Lincolniam
de termino sancti Michelis anno Regni Regis Edwardi
tercij post conquestum septimo.

Adhuc de Octabis Sancti Michelis. Wilughby. m. 8.
Norff'.
Johannes othe Hill', Barbour, in propria persona sua
optulit se iiij^{to} die versus Nicholaum de Rokhagh',
Bakestere, [7 *others*] de roberia et pace Regis fracta vnde
eos appellat. Et ipsi non venerunt. Et preceptum fuit
vicecomiti quod attachiaret eos. Et vicecomes retornat
quod predicti Nicholaus et alij non sunt inuenti, etc.
Ideo preceptum est vicecomiti quod capiat eos si etc...
Ita quod habeat corpora eorum coram Rege in Octabis
sancti Martini vbicumque etc...

Rogerus de Dicleburgh per Johannem de Dicleburgh m.8
Norff'.
attornatum suum optulit se iiij^{to} die versus Edmundum
de Bacunsthorp nuper vicecomitem Regis comitatus predicti de placito contemptus et transgressionis. Et ipse non
venit. Et preceptum fuit vicecomiti quod distringeret
eum. Et vicecomes retornat quod predictus Edmundus
districtus est per catalla vnde exitus ijs. et manucaptus
per Johannem Sewale, Willelmum Parlet, Johannem
Stace et Henricum Styward. Ideo ipsi in misericordia.
Et preceptum est vicecomiti sicut prius quod distringat
predictum Edmundum per omnes terras, etc...

Preceptum fuit vicecomiti sicut pluries quod venire m. 10.
Bed'.
faceret coram Rege ad hunc diem scilicet in Octabis
Sancti Michelis vbicumque etc. xxiiij tam milites etc. de

[1] P.R.O. no. 294. There are 167 very long membranes for this
period. Then comes the roll of fines, extending over 2½ membranes.
Then 34 membranes for the cases of Michaelmas term and the
delivery of the gaol at York and at Lincoln.

visneto de fflute per quos etc. Et qui nec Abbatem de
Wobourn nec Willelmum Waleys aliqua affinitate attin-
gerent, ad recognicionem etc. si predictus Willelmus simul
cum Willelmo Inge et Adam atte Halle de fflute die
Jouis in festo Sancti Petri ad vincula anno regni domini
Regis nunc quinto vi et armis herbam ipsius Abbatis in
prato suo apud fflute nuper crescencem necnon herbam
suam ibidem falcatam ad valenciam centum solidorum
cum quibusdam auerijs videlicet bobus vaccis bouiculis
bidentibus et equis depastus fuit conculcauit et consump-
sit contra pacem etc. sicut predictus Abbas dicit vel non
sicut predictus Willelmus Waleys dicit. Et vicecomes
retornat quod breue adeo tarde, etc... Idem dies datus
est partibus predictis coram Rege vbicumque. [*Added*]
Ad quem diem vicecomes non misit breue. Ideo sicut
pluries preceptum est vicecomiti quod venire faciat coram
Rege a die Pasche in xv dies vbicumque xxiiij^or tam
milites...

m. 18.
Cant'.   Johannes de Hildeburworth venit hic in Curia die
Mercurii in xv Sancti Michelis hoc anno et cognovit se
debere Ade de ffyncham quadraginta solidos vnde soluet
eidem Ade vnam medietatem in crastino Animarum... et
aliam medietatem ad festum Natalis domini... et nisi
fecerit concedit quod vicecomes fieri faciat de terris et
catallis suis etc.

m. 21.
Suff'.   Willelmus filius Johannis de la Howe per attornatum
suum optulit se iiij^to die versus Walterum filium Walteri
ffaucoun et Willelmum of the Grene de Suddon de placito
conspiracionis et transgressionis. Et ipsi non venerunt.
Et preceptum fuit vicecomiti quod attachiaret eos. Et
vicecomes retornat quod predictus Walterus attachiatus
est per Johannem ffaucoun et Thomam de Pesenhale. Et
predictus Willelmus of the Grene per Walterum de
Langedon et Walterum del Lyng. Ideo ipsi in misericordia. Et preceptum est vicecomiti quod distringat predictos Walterum et Willelmum of the Grene per omnes
terras, etc. Et de exitibus, etc. Ita quod habeat corpora
eorum coram Rege in Octabis Sancti Hillarii vbicumque,
etc.

m. 25.
Kanc'.   Stephanus de Cobham, Chiualer, per Johannem de
Whatton, attornatum suum, optulit se iiij^to die versus
Henricum atte Lee et Willelmum filium eius de placito

quare vi et armis bona et catalla ipsius Stephani ad
valenciam centum solidorum apud Wythyhamme inuenta
ceperunt, et asportauerunt et alia enormia etc. et contra
pacem, etc. Et ipsi non venerunt. Et preceptum fuit
vicecomiti quod attachiaret eos, etc...

Jurata inter Godefridum de Watford de London' per   Sussex.
Loth'. de Saumpford attornatum suum querentem et
Johannem Heury de Stanmere, de placito transgressionis,
ponitur in respectum vsque a die Sancti Hillarij in xv dies
vbicumque, etc. pro defectu Juratorum, quia nullus etc.
Ideo vicecomes habeat corpora Juratorum coram Rege,
ad prefatum terminum, etc.

Thomas atte Appelgarth de Clathorp in misericordia   m. 74.
pro pluribus defaltis. Idem Thomas attachiatus fuit ad   Linc'.
respondendum Willelmo Sturmy persone ecclesie de Helhowe, de placito quare vi et armis bona et catalla ipsius
Willelmi ad valenciam viginti marcarum apud Helhowe
et Clathorp inuenta cepit et asportauit et alia enormia ei
intulit, ad graue dampnum ipsius Willelmi, et contra
pacem Regis, etc. Et vnde idem Willelmus per Robertum
de Gayton attornatum suum queritur quod predictus
Thomas die veneris in crastino Assumpcionis beate marie
virginis anno regni domini Regis nunc quinto vi et
armis...bona et catalla ipsius Willelmi...ad valenciam
viginti marcarum apud Helhowe et Clathorp inuenta
cepit et asportauit et alia enormia etc. contra pacem, etc.
vnde dicit quod deterioratus est et dampnum habet ad
valenciam Centum librarum. Et inde producit sectam,
etc.

Et predictus Thomas per Johannem de Totel attornatum suum venit, et defendit...Et dicit quod in nullo
est culpabilis de transgressione predicta sibi inposita, et
de hoc ponit se super patriam. Et predictus Willelmus
similiter. Ideo veniat inde Jurata coram Rege a die
Sancti Hillarij in xv dies vbicumque, etc...

Assisa venit recognoscere si Willelmus filius Roberti de   m. 87
ffarford et Willelmus filius Ricardi de ffarford iniuste etc.   Linc'.
disseisiuerunt Ricardum de ffarford de libero tenemento
suo in Luda post primam etc. Et vnde queritur quod
disseisit eum de vno mesuagio et tercia parte vnius mesua-
gii medietate vnius tofti et tercia parte vnius tofti cum
pertinentiis, etc.

Et Willelmus filius Roberti venit et Willelmus filius Ricardi non venit set predictus Willelmus filius Roberti respondet pro predicto Willelmo filio Ricardi tamquam eius balliuus, et pro eo dicit quod ipse nullam ei inde fecit iniuriam seu disseisinam. Et de hoc ponitur se super assisam.

Et Willelmus filius Roberti respondet vt tenens etc. Et dicit quod assisa inde inter eos fieri non debet quia dicit quod tenementa predicta et alia terre et tenementa fuerunt in seisina cuiusdam Juliane que fuit vxor Ricardi de ffarford de Luda, matris predicti Ricardi qui nunc queritur, etc. cuius heres ipse est, que quidem Juliana de seisina sua feoffauit quendam Robertum de ffarford patrem ipsius Willelmi cuius heres ipse est de tenementis predictis, et aliis terris et tenementis, tenendis prefato Roberto et heredibus suis imperpetuum, et obligauit se et heredes suos ad warantizare tenementa predicta prefato Roberto et heredibus et assignatis suis, et profert inde cartam que hoc testat, etc. Et dicit quod si ipse ab aliquo alio extraneo de tenementis illis implacitaretur, predictus Ricardus vt filius et heres predicte Juliane eidem Willelmo vt filio et heredi predicti Roberti tenementa predicta teneretur warantizare. Et petit iudicium si assisa inde inter eos fieri debeat, etc.

Roll of fines

Rotulus finium coram domino Rege de termino Sancti Michelis anno regni Regis Edwardi tercij post conquestum septimo.

e.g.
Linc'.   De Theobaldo Pyte de fine pro diuersis transgressionibus super ipsum presentatis coram Radulpho de Neuill et sociis suis Justiciariis domini Regis in Comitatu predicto assignatis, per plegium Andree de Apthorp et Johannis de Eyworth de comitatu Norht'. x s. . . .

Leicestr'.   De Johanne de Lynlegh vno manucaptorum Johannis Baillolf de fine quia non habuit in curia domini Regis coram ipso domino Rege. . . 1 marca. . .

Ebor'.   De Johanne filio Johannis de Grantham de fine pro disseisina facta vi et armis Elene filie Thome Stibayn de tenemento in Colthorp per plegium Thome de Grantham et Willelmi de Grantham de Eboraco. xl d.

Adhuc de termino Sancti Michelis.

Jurati ad sectam domini Regis ad recognicionem etc. m. 30.
simul cum quibusdam Juratis de comitatu Norht'. si Bedf'.
Alexander filius Willelmi Elis, Robertus de Sheuesby,
senior, Robertus de Sheuesby Junior, Willelmus le Garlekmongere, Adam le Garlekmongere, Ricardus de Cor-
tenhale, Philippus Malesouers, Johannes de Sheuesby, et
Johannes le Bakere culpabiles sint de morte Roberti le
fferrour de Hertford apud Norht'. nocte diei lune in
vigilia Sancti Martini in hieme anno regni domini Regis
nunc quinto, felonice vulnerati qui postmodum apud
Harewold in comitatu Bedef' predicto die lune proxima
post festum concepcionis beate Marie proximum sequentem ex vulneracione predicta obiit, unde Sarra que
fuit vxor predicti Roberti le fferrour in curia Regis coram
Rege eos appellauit et postmodum etc. non fuit prosecuta
nec ne ponitur in respectum vsque a die Pasche in xv dies
vbicumque etc. pro defectu Juratorum quia nullus, etc.
Ideo vicecomes habeat corpora omnium juratorum coram
Rege ad prefatum terminum, etc...

(5) *Presentment of Englishry abolished* 1340

Item pur ce qe moultz des meschefs sont avenuz en divers
pays Dengleterre, qils navoient mye conisance de presentement denglescherie, par quoi les communes des
Countees estoient sovent devant les Justices errantz
amerciez, a grant meschief du poeple; si est assentuz qe
desore en avant nul Justice errant ne mette en article,
nen opposicion, presentemente denglescherie, devers les
communes des Countees ne devers nul de eux; mes de
tut soit lenglescherie et le presentement dycel pur touz
jours ouste, si qe nul par celle cause soit desore empeche.
S.R. 1, 282, 14 Ed. III, s. 1, c. 4.

(6) *To avoid delays in justice* 1340

Item pur ce qe moultz des meschiefs sont avenuz de
ceo, qe en diverses places, aussibien en la Chauncellerie,
en le Bank le Roi, le commune Bank, et Lescheqer, les
Justices assignez et autres Justices a oyer et terminer
deputez, les jugementz si ount este delaiez,...; si est
assentuz...qe desore en avant a chescun parlement
soient esluz un prelat, deux Contees, et deux Barons, qi

eient commission et poair du Roi, doier, par peticion a eux
liveree, les pleintes de touz ceux qi pleindre se vorront de tieux
delaies, ou grevances faites a eux; et eient poair a faire venir devant eux a Westmonstier, ou aillours,...les tenours des recordz
et proces de tieux jugementz ensi delaiez, et facent venir devant
eux meismes les Justices qi serront adonqes presentz, pur oyer
lour cause...queux cause et reson ensi oiez, par bon avis de eux
meismes, des Chancellier, Tresorer, Justices del un Bank et del
autre, et autres de counseil le Roi, taunz et tieux come ils verront
qe busoignable serront, aillent avant apprendre bon accord, et
bon juggement faire;
...Et en cas qe lour semble qe la difficulte soit si grande, qele ne
poet pas bonement estre termine sanz assent du parlement, soit la
dit tenour...portez...a proschein parlement, et illoeqes soit
pris final acord;...

[*A commission was then chosen.*]

Et coment qe les ministres eient fait serement avant ces hures, ne
pur quant pur eux rementiner de mesme le serement, si est assen-
tuz qe aussibien Chancellier, Tresorer, Gardein du privee Seal,
Justices del un Bank et del autre, Chancellier et Barons del
Escheqer, come Justices assignez, et touz ceux qi se medlent es
dites places desoutz eux, selonc lavisement des ditz Ercevesqe,
Contes, et Barons, facent serment de bien et loialment servir au
Roi et au poeple; et par avisement des avantditz Prelat, Contes, et
Barons, soit ordene dencrestre le nombre des ministres, par la ou
il ia busoigne, et de le amenuser en mesme la manere; et issint de
temps en temps, quant officers serront novelement mys en les ditz
offices, soient en la manere avantdite serementez.

S.R. i, 282, 14 Ed. III, s. i, c. 5.

(7) *The seals of the two benches* 1347

Item monstre la Commune de sa terre, qe come nostre dit Seignur
le Roi ad ordeignez deux Grantz Seals, pur ensealer les Briefs
judiciels en Commune Baunk, et en Baunk le Roi, et issint chescun
de la dite Commune paie pur chescun Judiciel viid. et pur un
Original vid. Qe lui pleise ordener un petit Seal pur Briefs
judiciels; c'est assaver, pur chescun Brief judiciel ne paie fors qe
iiid. en tout pur le Seal, a grant eese de la dite Commune. Et
donqes serront plusours Briefs purchacez, en grant avantage de
nostre Seignur le Roi; qar la suite est si dure et chiere, qe les
Simples de la Commune ne purront suffire lour droitz a pursuire.

Responsio. As povres homme donne pur Dieu: et ceux qi sont suffisantz reson voet q'ils paient selonc ce q'ad este usez en temps avant.

Rot. Parl. II, 170 (45).

(8) *Petition against excessive charges for writs* 1350

Item prie la Commune qe plese a nostre Seignur le Roi granter, qe le Fee de Grantz Seals en Commune Baunk et en Baunk le Roi, c'est assavoir de chescun Brief de Juggement vid. soit oste et pardone. Et qe tiels Briefs de Juggementz puissent estre resceus par Viscontes et lour Ministres, soutz le Seal de Justice Chief de la place dount ils isseront, come homme fait en eire, trelsbastons, en assise, et en oier et terminer. Qar le paiement est ore si grevous pur les Briefs de Juggement, c'est assavoir pur le meyndre Brief qe soit vid. pur le Grant Seal, et id. pur le Seal de Justice, et iiid. pur l'escripture, en destruction de povere poeple, et a grant arreriscement de profit le Roi.

Responsio. Il semble au Roi qe ceste Petition est noun resonable, et overtement countre l'Estatut; Par quoi il ne fet mie de l'ottreire.

Rot. Parl. II, 229 (25).

(9) *Petition for judicial reform* 1352

Item, Pur ceo qe les Leys, si bien la Commune Ley come les Estatutz ordinez par nostre Seignur le Roi et ses Progeniturs cea en arere, n'ont pas este tenuz...pur ceo qe les Justices as queux les Leys ount este commises a faire, qi a le foitz par lour noun leiser pur trop occupation des diverses Sessions; ascun foitz pur ceo qe en lour Commissions des pointz qi a eux attient a faire expresse mention n'ad este faite; et ascun foitz, pur ceo q'ils n'ount pas estee eseez pur grande meintenance a lour office faire: Prie la Commune, qe les Grantz de la terre, Contes, et Barons, chescun en sa Marche, od les plus loialx et sages de la Ley en celles parties, noun pas trop grant noumbre, esluz en cest present Parlement par avis des Grantz et autres de la dite Commune, qi sont sermentez, soient assignez en eide de poevre poeple, a oier et terminer aussi bien a la suyte de partie come a la suyte le Roi, si bien deinz Fraunchises come dehors, d'an en an, des totes maneres de felonies et trespas, et des totes maneres des extorsions,...faites au poeple par Officers, et Vitaillers, si bien de l'Hostiel le Roi, come des autres Officers et Ministres quecunqes, des Laborers, artificers,...et des totes choses comprises en l'Estatut...Et qe les ditz Justices, et touz autres assignez a oier et terminer felonies et trespas, facent covenable garnissement au meyns de xv jours de lour Sessions, si qe le poeple ne soit subdust d'estre mys en perde de lour issues, n'en exigende, ne suppris a la suyte de partie ne a la suyte le Roi, sanz covenable garnissement et proces faire.

Responsio. Le Roi envoiera son Baunk la ou il verra qe plus de mestier serra; et totes les foitz qe mestier serra, il assignera autres Justices covenables d'oier et terminer trespas et felonies par aillours la ou bosoigne serra. Mes il voet qe les Commissions des Laborers estoisent en lour force.

Rot. Parl. ii, 238 (13).

(10) *English to be used in the lawcourts* 1362

Item pur ce qe monstre est soventfoitz au Roi, par Prelatz, Ducs Counts Barons et tout la commune, les grantz meschiefs qe sont advenuz as plusours du realme de ce qe les leyes custumes et estatutz du dit realme ne sont pas conuz communement...par cause qils sont pledez monstrez et juggez en la lange Franceis, qest trop desconue en dit realme; issint qe les gentz qi pledent ou sont empledez en les Courtz le Roi et les Courtz dautres, nont entendement ne conissance de ce qest dit pur eulx ne contre eulx par lour Sergeantz et autres pledours...et en diverses regions et paiis, ou le Roi les nobles et autres du dit realme ont este, est bon governement et plein droit fait a chescun par cause qe lour leyes et custumes sont apris et usez en la lange du paiis: Le Roi desirant le bon governement et tranqillite de son poeple...ad pur les causes susdites ordeigne et establi del assent avantdit qe toutes plees...devant ses Justices queconqes ou en ses autres places ou devant ses autres Ministres qeconqes ou en les Courtz et places des autres Seignurs qeconqes deinz le realme, soient pledez...en la lange engleise; et qils soient...enroullez en latin; et qe les leyes et custumes du dit Realme, termes et processes, soient tenuz et gardez come ils sont et ont este avant ces heures;...

S.R. i, 375, 36 Ed. III, s. 1, c. 15.

(11) *Petition of the commons for a permanent fixed bench* 1365

Item, Pur ce qe Bank nostre Seignur le Roi est errant de Countee en Countee par tout le Roialme, et es Countees ou le dit Bank demura toutes les Communes de Countees sont faitz venir et

demorer devant les Justices du dit Bank par une cause ou par
autre, a grant destruction et coustages de les dites Communes, de
qoi le Roi ne prent qe poy des avantages. Et aussint pluseurs
gentz sont susduit de feet et anientiz pur defaute de sage Conseil,
q'ils ne poent nul trover en celle place, et pur la noun-certeinete de
lieu. Prie la Commune, qe le dit Banc demoerge en certein a
Westminster ou a Everwyk, la ou le commune Bank demoert, qe
home puisse avoir sage Conseil de l'une place ou de l'autre, issint
qe nul homme soit susduit pur defaute de sage Conseil, et pur la
noun-certeinete de lieu.

Responsio. Le Roi ne voet ne ne poet desporter de mander son
Bank ou lui plerra, mes sur ce ordeinera en manere qe mieltz
serra en ese et quiete de son Poeple.

Rot. Parl. II, 286 (12).

(12) *Petition concerning the common law* 1371

...Item priont les Comunes, qe come en les Estatuz faitz en
darrein Parlement fuist ordene, Qe nul homme soit mys a respoundre sanz presentement devant Justice, ou chose de Record
ou due Proces par Brief original, solonc l'auncienes Leys de la
Terre; nientmains pluseurs gentz depuis les ditz Estatuz faitz en
diverses Places du Roi ont este mys et constreintz par diverses
maneres de respoundre a singulers persones autrement qe par
cours de Commune Ley, countre la fourme del ditz Estatuz. Par
qoi prie la dite Commune, qe le dit article soit recitee et confermee
en cest present Parlement, et comande q'il soit pleinerment tenuz
desoreenavant en toutes les Places le Roi, et riens fait ou attempte
a l'encountre.

Responsio. Celui qi se sente greve veigne et monstre sa grevance en
especial, et droit lui serra fait en manere q'ad este ordeine avant
ces heures.

Rot. Parl. II, 308 (41).

(13) *Petition for better justice* 1378

Item, supplient les Communes, qe depuis la volentee le Roi est,
qe les meschiefs du Roialme et de commune Loy de la terre soient
amendez ou defaut y est, et qe la Loy de la terre soit fermement
tenuz, et ordene est par Estatut devant ces heures, Qe nul Justice
du Roi lesse de faire son office pur lettre du Prive Seal ne de
Grant Seal, lequel Estatut n'est pas pleinement tenuz au present:

Qe plese, qe le dit Estatut soit afferme, adjoustant a ycel, qe pur nulle lettre d'autre Seignur du Roialme ne lesse de faire son office, en manere come est dit en l'autre Estatut suisdit.

Responsio. Le Roi ne voet mye qe pur Brief, ou lettre de Grant ou Prive Seal, ou del Secret Seal, ou autre mandement quelconque issant contre la Loy, ou les Estatutz avant ces heures faitz, les Justices ne surseent de faire la Loy, ne pur priere de nully.

Rot. Parl. III, 44 (51).

(14) *Royal commissions and the common law* 1383

Item prient les Communes, qe desormes nule Comission soit directe hors de la Chancellerie, ne Lettre de Prive Seal, pur destourber la possession d'aucun liege le Roy, sanz due proces et respons du partie, et especialment quant la partie est prest de faire ce qe la Loy demande: Et qe toutes tieles Commissions faites devaunt ces heures, et directes encontre la Loy de la Terre, soient en ce Parlement repellez. Et q'en ce present Parlement, et chescun qi serra, soient toutes les Billes responduz et endossez des toutes les liges qi ne poent avoir autre remede qe par Petition, eiantz consideration de les grantz diseases et damages qe les lieges q'ont longement pursuiz avoient et ont de jour en autre tan qe due remede ent soit ordenez.

Responsio. Ceux qi se sentent grevez monstrent lour grevance en especial a Chanceller, qi lour purvoiera de remede. Et quant as ditz Petitions et Billes, le Roy voet qe celles qi ne purront estre esploitez sanz Parlement soient esploitez en Parlement, et celles qi purront estre esploitez par le Conseil du Roy soient mis devaunt le Conseil, et celles Billes qi sont de grace soient baillez au Roy mesmes.

Rot. Parl. III, 162 (50).

(15) *Commission of enquiry on miscarriage of justice.* *Riot Act* 1414

...Mesme nostre Seignur le Roy...ad ordeigne et establie, qe si defaute soit trovee en les ditz deux Justices de la Pees ou Justices dassises et le Viscount ou Soutzviscount del Countee ou tiele riote assemble ou route se ferra,...qadonqes al instance de la partie grevee, issera Commission le Roy desouz son graunt seal, denquerer sibien de la veritee del cas...come de la defaute...des ditz Justices Viscount ou Soutzviscount..., a adresser as suffi-

ceantz persones indifferentz a la nominacion et advis du Chaunceller Dengleterre; et qe les ditz Commissioners meintenant envoient en la Chauncellerie les enquestes et matiers devant eux
celle partie prisez et trovez: Et outre ceo qe les Coroners de mesme
le Countee...ferront les panelles sur la dice commission retourn-
ables, pur le temps qe le Viscount issint en defaute supposee
estoise en son office; les quelles Coroners retourneront nulles
persones mes tielx qi ont terres tenementz ou rent a le value
de xli. par an a meyns;...

S.R. II, 184, 2 Hen. V, s. 1, c. 8.

(16) *Writs and the common law* 1421

Item priount les Communes, qe come il soit contenuz en diverses
Estatuts faitz en temps de les nobles Progenitours nostre soveraigne
Seignur le Roi, qe null de ses Lieges serra amesnuz en respounse,
sinon par Brief Original et due Proces selonc la Leie de la Terre;
et ensi soit, qe diverses des Lieges de nostre dit soveraigne Seignur
sont faitz venir devaunt son Conseil et son Chanceller, par lettres
de Priveez Seales, et briefs Sub Pena, encountre les purveaunces
...avauntditz: qe nulles tieles lettres ne briefs soient grauntez
desore en avaunt; et si ascuns tiels lettres ou briefs soient grauntez,
et puisse apparer par la declaration del Pleintif, qe sa action est a
la commune Leie, qe le Defendant soit admiz de prendre exception al jurisdiction de court, et dire qe le Pleintif ad remedie
sufficeant pur luy a la commune leie en son cas, et qe cell exception soit a ly aloue, et sur cell dimissez hors de court,...; et qe
toutz tielx Lettres et Briefs ore pendantz devant les ditz Conseill
ou le Chanceller, soient voidez et tenuz pur nulles; et ceux vers
queux tieles lettres et briefs sont pursuez, soient dimissez hors des
Courtes suisditez, par auctorite de ceste present Parlement; fors-
priz ceux qi sont en les Courts avauntditz par auctoritee du
Parlement: et ceo pur Dieu et en oevere de charitee.

Responsio. Soit il advisee par le Roi. Et dureront tres toutz les
ordinances suisditz tanqe a le Parlement proschcinement a tenir.

Rot. Parl. IV, 156 (25).

(17) *Judicial records* 1439

Praieth the Comyns of this present Parliament. That where the
Rolles, Reconisauncez, Suertees of pees, Enditementes, Presenta-
mentes, Writtes, and al other maner of Recordes and Processes of

youre Bynche,...out of tyme that no mynde is, have be kept in youre Tresory therto accustumyd and ordeyned with in the Abbey of Westmynstre, under the kepyng of youre Chief Justice of youre Bynche...and in lyke wyse al the Rolles, Recordes and Processes, hadde afore youre Justices of youre commyn Bynche, have remayned in the kepyng of the Chief Justice of the same Bynche, ...tyl all the maters in the said Rolles...were fynally...determyned...and now late by vertu and colour of a Writte directed unto Sir William Cheyney, late Chief Justice of youre said Bynche, and by another Writte directed unto Sir John Juyn, late Justice of youre saide comyn Bynche, thaym severally commaundyng, that the said Sir William, al the Recordes of youre saide Bynche, and the said Sir John, all the Recordes of youre saide commyn Bynche,...schold delyvere unto the Chamberleynes of youre receyte, the saide Justices,...haveth delyvered al the Recordes...unto youre saide Chamberleyns; by the whiche delyverance...youre Clerkes and Felicers may nought make processe,...

Please hit unto youre noble Grace to considere thes premisses, and by the assent of youre Lordis Spirituelx and Temporelx, and by auctorite of this present Parliament, to ordeyne, that the saide Rolles...be remaundid and send ayeine unto the said Places of the whiche thei were remeved...

Responsio. Le Roy s'advisera.

Rot. Parl. v, 29 (53).

(18) *The oath of the justices (fifteenth century)*
Sacramentum Justiciariorum.

Le serment des Justices est qe bien et leaument serviront le Roi en Office de la Justicerie et dreiture a lour pouer frount a touz auxi bien as poures come as riches et qe pur hautesce ne pur richesce ne pur amour ne pur haour ne pur estat de nuly persone ne pur bienfait doun ne premesse de nuly qi fait lour seit ou lour purra estre fait autri dreiture ne destourberont. ne respiterount countre reson et countre les leis de la terre mes saunz resgard de nuly estat ne de persone leaument frount faire dreiture a chescun solonc les leys usees et qe riens ne prendrount de nuly saunz conge le Roi et puis graunta le Roi qils puissent prendre mangier et beyvre quant a la journee Item puis ajousta le Roi ces poyntz au serment Cest assavoir qils jurrount qe a nule malice de nul de lour compaignouns ne assenterount mes cels destourberont en quanqils purrount et sils nel poent faire ils le monstrent a ceux du Conseil le Roi et sils ne le amendent ils le monstrent au Roi meismes.

First report on public records (1800), p. 236; and cf. *Red book of the exchequer*, p. lxx.

(2) THE EYRE AND ITINERANT JUSTICES

(19) *The eyre of Kent; commission of the justices appointed to hold the eyre* 1313

Edwardus etc. archiepiscopis, episcopis, abbatibus, prioribus, comitibus, baronibus, militibus et omnibus aliis de comitatu Cancie salutem. Sciatis quod constituimus dilectos et fideles nostros Hervicum de Stantone, Willelmum de Ormesby, Henricum Spigurnel, Johannem de Mutford, et Willelmum de Goldingtone Justiciarios nostros ad itinerandum ad omnia placita hac vice in comitatu predicto attaminata terminandum; Constituimus eciam eosdem H. etc. Justiciarios nostros ad omnia placita deliberandum, audiendum et terminandum juxta provisiones et ordinaciones per nos inde factas et ad querelas et transgressiones omnium querencium seu conqueri volencium, tam de ballivis et ministris nostris quibuscumque quam de ballivis et ministris aliorum et aliis quibuscumque et ad querimonias quorumcumque amerciendum et competentes emendaciones inde faciendum secundum legem et consuetudinem regni nostri...Et ideo vobis mandamus quod eisdem H. etc. tanquam Justiciariis nostris itinerantibus ad ea que ad placita illa pertinent intendentes sitis et respondentes sicut predictum est. In cujus rei testimonium etc.

Et peus sire H. de Stauntone chief justice moustra la volunte nostre seignour le roi et la cause de lour venue qe feust tiele, qe le roi voleit qe les trespasours feusent puniz solom lour desert et qe owel droit feust fait as povres et as riches, en priaunt la comunalte del countee qil meisent tiel eide qe par lour venues bone et certeyne pees pout estre estably al honour del roialme et a lour profit demesne. E peus comaunda al vicounte de countee de rendre son bref de la somons del eyre, et le vicounte enci fist, le qel bref fust tiel.

[*The writ of general summons is then given.*]

Eyre of Kent (S.S.), I, I.

(20) *The eyre of Kent; writ of general summons* 1313

Rex vicecomiti Kancie salutem. Summone per bonos summonitores archiepiscopos, episcopos, abbates, priores, comites, barones, milites, et omnes liberos tenentes de comitatu tuo, et de quibuscumque villis iiij legales homines et prepositum, de quolibet burgo xij legales burgenses per totam ballivam tuam et omnes alios qui coram justiciariis itinerantibus venire solent et debent, quod sint apud Cantuariam in octabis nativitatis sancti Johannis Baptiste proximo futuris coram dilectis et fidelibus nostris Hervico de Stauntone, Henrico Spigurnel, etc....quos tunc missuri sumus ibidem audituros et facturos preceptum nostrum. Fac etiam venire coram eisdem fidelibus nostris omnia placita corone nostre que placitata non sunt, vel que emerserunt postquam justiciarii ultimo itineraverunt in partibus illis, et omnia placita et omnia attachiamenta ad placita illa pertinencia, et omnes assisas et omnia placita que posita sunt ad primam assisam coram justiciariis nostris cum brevibus assisarum illarum et placitorum, ita quod assise ille et placita pro defectu tui vel summonicionis tue non remaneant. Fac etiam clamari et sciri per totam ballivam tuam quod omnes assise et omnia placita que fuerunt atterminata et non finita vel que fuerunt summonite coram justiciariis nostris apud Westmonasterium vel coram justiciariis nostris qui ultimo itineraverunt in comitatu predicto ad omnia placita vel coram justiciariis nostris illuc missis ad assisas nove disseisine capiendas vel ad gaolas deliberandas, quod tunc sint coram prefatis fidelibus nostris apud Cantuariam in eodem statu in quo remanserunt per preceptum nostrum vel justiciariorum itinerantium vel justiciariorum nostrorum de banco. Summone etiam per bonos summonitores omnes illos qui vicecomites fuerunt post ultimam itineracionem justiciariorum in partibus illis, quod tunc sint ibidem coram prefatis fidelibus nostris cum brevibus de assisis et placitis que tempore suo receperint ad respondendum de tempore suo sicut respondere debent coram justiciariis. Precipimus etiam tibi quod per totam ballivam tuam, videlicet tam in civitatibus burgis quam in villis mercatoriis et alibi, publice proclamari facias quod omnes illi qui libertates aliquas assignatas per cartas predecessorum nostrorum regum Anglie vel alio modo habere clamant sint coram prefatis fidelibus nostris ad diem predictam ad respondendum cujusmodi libertates habere clamant et quo waranto, et tu ipse tunc sis ibi paratus una cum ballivis et ministris tuis ad certiorandum ipsos fideles nostros super hiis et aliis nego-

ciis illud tangentibus. Precipimus etiam tibi quod publice proclamari facias quod omnes conquerentes seu conqueri volentes tam
de ballivis et ministris nostris quibuscumque quam de ballivis et
ministris aliorum et aliis quibuscumque veniant coram dilectis et
fidelibus nostris ad predictos diem et locum ad quascumque
querimonias ibidem ostendendum et ad competentem emendam
inde recipiendum secundum legem et consuetudinem regni nostri
et secundum ordinacionem per nos inde factam... et prout iidem
fideles nostri tibi sciri facient ex parte nostra, et habeas ibi summonitores et hoc breve. Teste, etc.

[*Then follows an account of the sheriff's oath; sheriffs who did not attend
on the first day, and coroners who had not brought their rolls, were
punished. Those who held by barony attended in person or by attorney.*]

Et peus les justices fesoient iiij cries.

La primer Crie.

La primer qe touz ceus qi furent ateintz de conspiracies ou de
meyntenaunces de fauce querele en le dreyn eyre, ou peus devant
sire Rogger Brabasoun et ses compaignouns justices assignez en
le dit countee de trailbaston, qil se aloinassent hors de la ville de
Caunterbirs a xii lewes durant leyre sanz returner, sils ne feussent
en ple, et qe adonqes venisent as justices et se mustracent ensuit
qils peusent meyntenaunt estre deliveres et returner mesme le
jour, et ceo al peril qe apendoit.

La seconde Crie.

La seconde crye qe nul marchee ne feire ne feust tenuz en le dit
countee durant leyre sinoun en la ville de Caunterbirs.

La terce Crie.

La terce crie qe nule court ne counte ne fust tenuz en le dit
countee durant leyre sinoun par resoun de plee de terre, et ceo
par bref de droit patent ou de apels en countee.

La quarte Crie.

La quarte qe nul home ne fust si hardy de lower mesouns a
nules gentz qi furent venuz par resoun del eyre duraunt leyre en
la ville de Caunterbirs[1]...

...... *Proclamation of the justices*[2]

Item qe nul court de baron fut tenu neo nul plee plede en la
Counte de Kente ne ayllours en le counte durant le Eyre, forpris
breve de droit ouert et appels en Counte...

---

[1] *Eyre of Kent* (S.S.), I, 2–7.
[2] *Ibid.* I, 25, as given in another version of the court business.

(21) *Commission of oyer et terminer* 1328

Et quant au punissement de felonies, roberies, homicides, trespas
et oppressions du poeple, faitz en temps passe; acorde est qe
nostre Seignur le Roi assigne Justices en divers lieux de sa terre,
ove le Baunk le Roi par aillours, come estoit faite en temps de son
dit ael, des grantz de la terre qi sont de grant poair, ovesqes
ascuns des Justices de lun Baunk ou de lautre, ou autres sages de
la lei, denquere, auxibien a seute de partie, come a la seute le
Roi, et doier et terminer totes maneres des felonies...countre la
lei, Les estatuz et la custume de la terre, auxibien par ministres
le Roi come par autres qi qils soient, et ce auxibien dedeinz
fraunchises come dehors. Et auxint denquere des Viscontes,
Coroners, Southeschetours, Hundreders, Baillifs, Conestables, et
touz autres Ministres deinz franchise et dehors, et lour south-
ministres, et doier et terminer a la seute le Roi et de partie. Et
nostre Seignur le Roi et touz les grantz du Roialme en plein
parlement ont empris de meintenir la pees, garder et sauver les
Justices le Roi...qe les juggementz et les execucions ne soient
pas arestuz, mes executz...Mes nest pas lentencion du Roi ne
de son conseil qe par ceste acord prejudice aveigne a les grantz de
la terre, eantz franchises, ne a la Citee de Loundres, ne as autres
Citees ne Burghs, ne a les Cynkportz en droit de lour fraunchises.

S.R. 1, 259, 2 Ed. III, c. 7. (Statute of Northampton.)

(22) *New articles of the general eyres* 1329–30

Noui Articuli.

De ministris Regis qui ratione officij sui custodire debent
assisam de vinis et victualibus qui marchandizauerunt de vinis
et victualibus illis in grosso vel ad retallium dum ad officium illud
fuerint intendentes post statutum inde editum apud Eboracum in
tribus septimanis Sancti Michelis anno regni Regis Edwardi filii
Regis Edwardi xij°.

De hiis qui fuerunt armati et cesserunt de nocte vel de die in
feriis vel mercatis in presencia Justiciariorum vel aliorum ministrorum domini Regis officia sua facientium vel alibi in terrorem
populi vel inperturbacionem pacis post statutum apud Northampton' inde editum anno regni Regis Edwardi tercii a conquestu
secundo. Et qui huiusmodi armatos ceperint quos et quando et
quas armaturas et quantum valuerunt.

De vicecomitibus et aliis ministris Regis et dominis libertatum et eorum balliuis et maioribus [et] balliuis Ciuitatum Burgorum Constabulariis et Custodibus pacis infra custodias suas qui huiusmodi armatos non ceperint iuxta inde idem statutum.

De pannis qui ponuntur ad terram qui non sunt vlnerati per vlnatorem Regis inpresencia maiorum et balliuorum vbi maior est et balliuorum vbi maior non est per mensuram contentam in eodem statuto.

De maioribus et balliuis vbi maior aut balliuis vbi maior non est in villis aut locis vbi huiusmodi panni venerunt qui non fuerunt parati ad examinacionem facere de huiusmodi pannis temporibus quibus requisiti fuerunt per voluntatem Regis absque aliquo capiente de mercatoribus pro examinacione predicta etc.

Expliciunt articuli de itinere anno Regni Regis etc.

Egerton MS. 2811, f. 227; and printed in article by H.M. Cam, *E.H.R.* xxxix. For the standard version of the articles before 1321 see her *Studies in the hundred rolls* (1921).

(23) *Justices of assize, gaol-delivery, and keepers of the peace* 1330

Ensement est acorde qe bones gentz et sages, autres qe des places si homme les puisse trover suffisantz, soient assignez en touz les Counteez Dengleterre apprendre les assises, jurees, et certificacions, et a deliverer les gaoles; et qe les ditz Justices preignent les assises, jurees, et certificacions, et deliverent les gaoles, au meyns troiz foitz par an, et plus sovent si mestier serra, et soient auxint assignez bones gentz et loialx, en chescun Countee, a garder la pees; et soit fait mencion es ditz assignementz, qe ceux qi serront enditez ou pris par les ditz gardeins, ne soient pas lessez au meynprise par les Viscountes...sils ne soyent meynpernables par la lei, ne qe tieux enditez ne soient deliverez forqe a la commune lei. Et eient les Justices...poair a deliverer les gaoles de ceux qi serront enditez devant les gardeins de la pees; et qe les ditz gardeins mandent devant les ditz Justices lour enditementz, et eient les ditz Justices poair denquere sur viscountes, gaolers,...sils facent deliverance ou lessent a meynprise nulles issint enditez, qi ne sont mie meynpernables, et de punir les ditz viscountes, gaolers et autres sils facent riens contre cest acord.

S.R. i, 261, 4 Ed. III, c. 2.

(24) The itinerant justices in Shropshire 1374

m. 1.   *Writ of certiorari*

Edwardus...dilecto et fideli suo Nicholao Burnel salutem. Volentes cercis de causis cerciorari super quibuscumque indictamentis factis coram vobis et sociis vestris custodibus pacis nostre et Justiciariis nostris ad diuersas felonias et transgressiones in Comitatu Salop' audiendas et terminandas assignatis de quibuscumque feloniis et transgressionibus vnde Willelmus Longnorle [7 *names follow*] indictati sunt vt dicitur, vobis mandamus quod omnia indictamenta predicta cum omnibus ea tangentibus nobis in cancellariam nostram sub sigillo vestro distincte et aperte sine dilatione mittatis et hoc breue; vt vlterius inde fieri faciamus quod de iure et secundum legem et consuetudinem regni nostri Anglie fuerit faciendum. Teste me ipso apud Westmonasterium xij die Octobris anno regni nostri Anglie quadragesimo octauo regni vero nostri ffrancie tricesimo quinto.   Martyn.

m. 2.   *Presentments of jurors*

xij iuratores presentant quod Willelmus de Longenorle die Lune proxima ante festum Sancti Petri ad uincula anno regni regis nunc xlij felonice interfecit Willelmum de Wirley Taylour apud Salopiam in alto vico.

Item presentant quod Philippus le Tiler die Jouis proxima post festum Ramis Palmarum anno regni regis nunc xxxviij felonice interfecit Johannem Ondrewe apud Salopiam. Et Willelmus de Longenorle eodem tempore balliuus ville predicte cepit de predicto Philippo centum solidos postquam idem Philippus commissus fuit in custodia sua occasione predicta. et ipsum Philippum a custodia sua euadere permisit pro predictis centum solidis die Lune proxima post festum Pentecoste anno supradicto apud Salopiam.

Item presentant [quod] Philippus Godberd die martis proxima ante festum Sancti Michelis anno regni regis nunc xliij felonice fregit domum Ricardi Pigot apud Salopiam et ibidem felonice furatus fuit sex cartas et alia munimenta sub custodia ipsius Ricardi existencia que quidem carte et munimenta exteterunt Thome de Lodelawe et aliorum ingnotorum [*sic*].

m. 3.   *Writ of certiorari*

JUSTICE 279

m. 4. *Letters patent to the justices*

Edwardus dei gratia Rex Anglie...dilectis et fidelibus suis
Nicholao Burnell, Johanni Kayme et Rogero Partrich salutem.
Sciatis quod assignauimus vos et duos vestrum quorum vos prefate
Nicholae vnum esse volumus ad inquirendum per sacramentum
proborum et legalium hominum de Comitatu Salop' tam infra
libertates quam extra per quos rei veritas melius sciri poterit de
quibuscumque felonijs transgressionibus oppressionibus extor-
sionibus conspiracionibus confederacionibus cambipartiis ambi-
dextriis forstallariis regratariis dampnis et grauaminibus et excessibus nobis et populo nostro in Comitatu predicto infra libertates vel extra per quoscumque et qualitercumque factis siue
perpetratis et de premissis omnibus et singulis...plenius veritatem
et ideo vobis mandamus quod ad cercos dies et loca quos vos vel
duo vestrum...ad hoc prouideritis inquisiciones super premissis
factis et eas distincte et aperte factas nobis in Cancellariam
nostram sub sigillis vestris vel duorum vestrum...et sigillis
eorum per quos facte fuerint sine dilatione mittatis et hoc breue.
mandauimus enim vicecomiti nostro comitatus predicti quod ad
cercos dies et loca quos vos vel duo vestrum...ei scire faciatis
venire faciat coram vobis vel duobus vestrum...tot et tales probos
et legales homines de balliua sua tam infra libertates quam extra
per quos rei veritas in premissis melius sciri poterit et inquiri. In
cuius rei testimonium has litteras nostras fieri fecimus patentes.
Teste me ipso apud Westmonasterium vj die Julij anno regni
nostri Anglie quadragesimo octauo regni vero nostri ffrancie
tricesimo quinto.   Martyn.

m. 5.
Inquisicio capta apud Salopiam coram Nicholao Burnel,
Johanne Kayme et Rogero Partrich Justiciariis domini Regis die
mercurii proxima post festum Sancti Petri ad uincula anno regni
regis nunc xl octauo, virtute commissionis domini Regis huic
inquisicioni consute per sacramentum Johannis de Leynthale [11
names follow] Qui dicunt super sacramentum suum quod Willelmus
de Staunton de Bruggenorth' die dominica in festo Pentecoste
anno regni regis nunc xlviij in Aliciam vxorem Walteri le Glouare
apud Bruggenorth insultum fecit et ipsam verberauit et male
tractauit et eam ad terram proiecit violenter et super eam tri-
pidauit contra pacem Regis. Item presentant quod Thomas
Carpenter de Brugge die Lune proxima post festum Sancti

Nichomedis anno regni regis nunc xlv^to apud Bruggenorth felonice furatus fecit vnam patellam eneam et vnum caminum ferreum... In cuius rei testimonium huic inquisicioni Juratores predicti sigilla sua apposuerunt datum die loco et anno predictis...

m. 6.   *Extracts from presentments*

Inquisicio capta apud Biriton coram Nicholao Burnell Johanne Kayme et Rogero Partrich Justiciariis domini Regis die sabbati proxima post festum Sancti Jacobi apostoli anno regni regis Edwardi tercij post conquestum Anglie quadragesimo octauo virtute commissionis ipsius Regis huic inquisicioni consute per sacramentum Philippi de Rodyngton [11 *names follow*] qui dicunt super sacramentum suum quod Matilla Petynger indictata fuit pro feloniis et bona et catalla sua videlicet vnum chetel ollas eneas patella lectos et alia bona ad valenciam decem librarum arestata per Willelmum Dounton balliuum Abbatis de Salopia de Monkeforyate et tunc venit Willelmus de Longenorle die dominica proxima post festum Sancti Barnabe apostoli anno...quadragesimo, quandam domum ipsius Abbatis apud Monkeforyate felonice fregit et bona et catalla predicta a domo predicta felonice furatus fuit contra pacem domini Regis...

Item presentant quod Willelmus atte Waterhous et Willelmus Meke de Drayton sunt communes forstallatores ferri in Comitatu Salop' et totum ferrum quod factum fuit apud Rounhay iuxta Drayton per duos annos...in grosso emerunt et ferrum illud forstallauerunt et postea per regratarios vendiderunt ad voluntatem eorum per quod ferrum in Comitatu predicto carius est quam solebat in Triplo ad dampnum tocius patrie viginti librarum....

Item presentant quod Johannes de Dodynton [*and 4 others*] nolunt permittere aliquos extraneos vendere aliquem pannum venientem de Wallia in villa Salop' nisi voluerint vendere integrum pannum. Set ita per oppressionem emunt per regratarios omnes pannos...et illos postea vendunt per vnam vlnam vel duas vlnas ad voluntatem eorum per regratarios multo carius quam alij extranei vendere voluissent in depauperacionem tocius communitatis patrie et sic fecerunt per tres annos proximos elapsos...

Item presentant quod Thomas de Cherleton de Appeley die sabbati proxima post festum Sancti Barnabe apostoli anno regni regis nunc xlvj vi et armis in separali piscario Johannis de Cherleton de Appeley piscatus fuit apud Hadeley et transgressionem illam per vices continuauit per duos annos proximos sequentes et piscem inde ad valenciam x solidorum cepit et asportauit contra pacem Regis. In cuius rei testimonium huic inquisicioni Juratores predicti sigilla sua apposuerunt. Datum die loco et anno supradictis.

Ancient indictment, King's Bench, 102; compared with the Assize Roll, no. 749, which gives in addition letters patent to Burnell and three others, anno 37 Ed. III. (Cf. the articles by B. H. Putnam, *E.H.R.* 1914, 1915.)

(25) *Justices of assize* 1384

Item prient les Communes, qe par la ou Justices des Assises sont en lour propre pays, qi sont as fees et robes des pleusours Seignurs en mesmes les pays, et ont grandes alliances et autres affinitees illoeqes, dont grantz malx et grevances aviegnent diversement au poeple, desqueux n'est my honest de parler en especial: einz entre autres ils lour covient de faire, et font, trop grant favour as unes, et reddour as autres. Qe plese a nostre Seignur le Roi en ce present Parlement ordeigner par Estatut, qe nul homme de Loi desore en avant soit Justice des Assises en son propre pais, pur grant ease et relevement de sa dite Commune; ne qe le Chief Justice de l'un Bank ne de l'autre ne soit my Justice des nulles Assises, a cause qe s'ils font errour ce serroit redresse devant eux mesmes; Et entendable chose est, q'ils serroient trop favorables en lour Juggementz demesne.

Responsio. Quant al primer point de ceste Petition, le Roy le voet. Et quant al seconde poynt tochant le Chief Justice de Commune Bank, le Roi voet q'il soit assigne Justice d'Assises entre autres. Mes quant al Chief Justice de Bank le Roy, le Roy voet q'il soit fait come ad este fait et use pur la greindre partie de centz ans darrein passez.

Rot. Parl. III, 200 (17).

(26) *No lawyer shall be a judge in his own county* 1384

Item concordatum est et statutum quod nullus homo de lege sit decetero Justiciarius assisarum vel communis deliberacionis gaolarum in propria patria sua et quod capitalis Justiciarius de communi Banco assignetur inter alios ad huiusmodi assisas capiendas et ad gaolas deliberandas set quoad capitalem Justiciarium de

Banco Regis fiat sicut pro majori parte Centum annorum proximorum preteritorum fieri consuevit.

S.R. II, 36, 8 Ric. II, c. 2.

(27) *Justices of assize* 1410

Item, priont les Communes, qe soit ordine en cest present Parlement, qe Justices des Assises par commission nostre Seignur le Roy en Countees du Roialme a prendre assignez, et assigners, desorenavaunt facent deliverer pleinement a vostre Tresorie toutz les Recordes de les Assises de novel disseysen, de mort-d'auncetre, et de certifications, ove toutz les appurtenauntz, et appendantz devaunt eux determinez, chescun second an apres qe le plee ent soit determine et juggement rendue, sanz pluis delaye. Et qe les Recordes et Processe des Plees realx et personelx, et d'Assises...ne soient en ascun manere amendez, n'enpeirez, par novel entre des Clercs, ou par record ou chose certifie ou tesmoigne, ou commaundement d'aucun Justice queconqe;...Et en outre, qe toutz les ditz Justices des Assises soient ferment chargez a tenir les Assises en le chief Ville du Countee.

Responsio. Le Roy le voet.

Rot. Parl. III, 642 (62).

(3) THE PREROGATIVE COURTS
(a) THE MARSHALSEA
(28) *Judicial work of the steward and marshal* 1309

Del estat du Seneschal, et des Mareschaux, et des pledz qe eux deivent tenir et coment, ordene est qil ne tiegnent plai de frank tenement, ne de dette, ne de covenant, ne de contract des gentz du poeple fors tantsolement des trespas del hostel, et autres trespas fetz deinz la verge, e des contractz, et covenanz, qe aucun del hostel le Roi avera fet, a autre de meisme lostel, et en meisme lostel, et nemie aillours. Et nul plai de trespas ne pledront, autre qe ne soit attache par eux avant ceo qe le Roi isse hors de la verge, ou le trespas serra fait, et les pledra hastiement de jour en jour, Issint qil soient parpledez et terminez, avant ceo qe le Roi isse hors des boundes de cele verge, ou le trespas fust feit. Et si par cas dedeinz les bundes de cele verge ne poent estre terminez, cessent ceux pledz devant le Seneschal, et soient les pleintifs a la commune ley...

S.R. I, 155, 3 Ed. II. (Statute of Stamford.)

(29) *Definition of the marshal's jurisdiction and of the verge* 1344

Item prie la dite Commune, qe la place de la Mareschalcie determine les Pledz de trespas faitz dedeinz la verge, et ne mye autres
Pledz qi attiegnent as autres places, et qe la verge soit tenuz xii
lieux environ, come auncienement soleit.

Rot. Parl. ii, 149 (12).

(30) *The jurisdiction of the steward and marshal defined* 1376

Item prie la dite Commune, qe come ils sont grevousement et
sovent travaillez et tariez par diverses Plees devaunt les Seneschal
et Mareschall de l'Hostel nostre Seignur le Roi: Pleise a sa tresexcellent Seignurie ordeigner, qe le dit Seneschal ou Mareschall
ne tiegne ne se melle de nul autre Plee mes tiel come est ordeigne
en l'Estatut appelle Articuli super Cartas. Et qe touz ceux qi
voillent autrement suir eient lour suites a la Commune Ley. Et
qe l'espace combien des Leukes la Verge s'extendra soit limite en
certein; et ou il s'extendra, ou de la presence nostre Seignur le
Roi, ou del lieu de son Hostell, et non pas de l'un et de l'autre a
un foith, s'ils ne soient ensemble. Item, qe les Seneschall face sa
Session deinz la bounde des trois Leukes environ de la presence
nostre dit Seignur le Roy, ou de son Hostell, sicome soleit estre en
auncien temps: Et hors de cell bounde nul ne soit tenuz a respondre en la dite Court, issint qe le poeple ne soit travaillez
outrageousement. Et qe les ditz Seneschal et Mareschall ne se
medlent d'enquere des Articles quex deyvent estre enquis devaunt
Justices en Eyre, et Justices del Bank le Roi. Et qe certeigne peine
soit ordeignie s'ils ailent ou empreignent encontre ascuns des
Articles avaunt ditz; laquele peine soit levable a la suite le ou a
la suite ceux qi soi sentont grevez.

Responsio. Eient lour Jurisdiction de la place ou le Roi mesmes est,
ou del lieu ou le Tynell se tient, par xii lieux entour chescune part
tant soulement, et nemye de l'une et de l'autre a une foitz. Et en
oultre les Estatuz ent faites se tiegnent.

Rot. Parl. ii, 336 (91).

(31) *The office of steward of the household temp.* Edward IV

Styward of housholde, receyveth his charge of the King's highe
and propyr person, and the staffe of houshold, by these wordes
following; "Seneschall tenez la baton du notre hostiell;" by

whiche he is also forthwith Steward of the whoole courte of Marchalcye, that is, the courte of houshold, in whiche he is judge of lyfe and lymme; and except thoes causes, the Thesaurer. Countroller, Coffyrrer, two Clerkes of the Greene Clothe, and the Chiefe Clerk of the Countrollment, for any matters elles done within the houshold, or apperteynyng thereto; they sitte with hym at the bourd of doome within the houshold, that is, at the greene clothe in the countyng-house as recorders and witnessers to the trouthe. The secundary estate and rule under the Kinge, of all his excellent houshold, is wholly committed to be ruled and guyded by his reason, and his commaundmentes principally to be obeyed and observed for the Kinge...

Ordinances and regulations for the government of the royal household, Society of Antiquaries, 1787–90, p. 55.

(b) COURT OF THE CONSTABLE AND MARSHAL

(32) *Petition concerning the jurisdiction of the constable and marshal* 1379

Item supplient les Communes, pur ce qe nous veons novelx faitz moevez devant le Conestable et Mareschal, de ce qe certaines persones des liges le Roi sont appellez par Bille devant les ditz Conestable et Mareschall, des tresons et felonies supposes estre faitz deinz le Roialme d'Engleterre, et illoeqes demesnez et emprisonez, contre la Loy du Roialme, et contre la forme del Grande Chartre, qi voet, Qe nul Homme serra n'emprisone,...sinoun par loial jugement des ses Piers, et la Loy de la terre. Quelle chose s'il soit suffert serroit tresmal ensample, et anientisement de la Loy de Roialme: Par quoi Vous pleise ent ordeiner remede, qe les dites Conestable et Mareschall cessent des tielx plees tenir: Et touz tieux plees des choses supposez estre faite deinz le Roialme d'Engleterre soient triez et terminez devaunt Justice, par commune Loy du Roialme, et la forme del Grande Chartre susdite; eantz regard, qe touz les gentz du Roialme, de quel estat...q'ils soient, purront estre issint empeschez et destruitz par fauxe compassement de lour enemys.

Responsio. Pur ce qe les heirs qi cleiment l'Office de Conestable sont de tendre age, et en la garde nostre Seignur le Roi; et la chose demande grant deliberation, et tuche si haute matire, et l'estat de la Corone nostre Seignur le Roi, et le Parlement est pres a fyn; les Seignurs du Parlement ne poent, ne ne oesent, ent faire finale discution quant au present. Mais quant a la querele q'est novelement attame devaunt les ditz Conestable et Mareschall, tuchant un Appell de Treson faite en Cornewaill, a ce q'est dit; nostre Seignur le Roi prendra la dite querele en sa main, et en outre ferra assigner des tieux Commissioners come luy plerra, pur oier et terminer la dite querele, selonc les Loys et Usages de la terre, sauvant chescuny droit.

Rot. Parl. III, 65 (47). (Cf. *S.R.* II, 37, forbidding the constable and marshal to deal with matters of common law, 1384.)

(33) *The jurisdiction of constable and marshal defined* 1390

Item pur ce qe la commune fest grevousement compleint qe la Court del Conestable et Mareschall ad accroche a luy...con-tractz covenances trespasses dettes et detenues...pledables par la commune ley...; nostre seignur le Roy...ad declare en cest parlement par advys et assent des seignurs espritueles et temporeles le poair et jurisdiccion du dit Conestable en la fourme qensuit; Al Conestable appartient davoir conissance des contractz tochantz faitz darmes et de guerre hors du roialme, et auxint des choses qi touchent armes ou guerre deinz le roialme queux ne poent estre terminez ne discus par la commune ley...Et si ascun soi voet pleindre qascun plee soit comence devant le Conestable et Mareschall qe purroit estre trie par la commune ley de la terre eit cell pleintif brief de prive seal du Roi sanz difficulte direct as ditz Conestables et Mareschall de surseer en celle plee tanqil soit discus par le Conseil du Roi si celle matire doit de droit appartie-gner a celle Courte ou autrement estre triez par la commune ley du Roialme et qils surseent en la mesne temps.

S.R. II, 61, 13 Ric. II, s. 1, c. 2.

(34) *A case before the court of constable and marshal* 1397

A nostre tresexcellent treredoute et tresgracious seignur le Roi.

Supplie treshumblement vostre poevere liege Johan Cavendissh de Loundres qe come le xxvij^e jour de Marcz lan de vostre regne xviij^e un Richard Piryman appela le dit Johan de tresoun a Westmonstier devaunt vostre tressage counseill lui quel Richard ad estee devaunt certeins seignurs trois foitz a respounse et le dit Johan ne poet venir a null respounse pur null seute qil sache faire par deux ansz et pluys les queux Johan et Richard sount en le prisoun de vostre banc pur lappel avauntdit. Qe plese vostre treshautisme seignurie charger Sire Richard Waldegrave, Chevalier, et Laurence Drew, Esquier, denvoier desouth les honurables lettres de vostre prive seal touz les matiers et processe queux le dit Richard ad mys sur le dit Johan devaunt eux pendauntz direct al Court de Conestable et Mareschal illoesqes pur estre determinez qar tresredoute Seignur, si la matier et processe de lappel avauntdit serroit determine a la commune ley le dit John neusse qe mort par une enqueste de dousze homes deins la fraunchise du dite citee par procurement et brocage des certeins persones les queux persones ne vorroient pur cynk mill livres qe la verite du dite appel fusse overtement conuz.   Le Duc Dexcestre.

A.P.C. I, 77. (Petition to the king referred to the council after September, 1397. "Le Roy voet qe droyt ly soyt fet par avys de consayl.")

(35) *Appeals of things done out of the realm to be tried by constable and marshal* 1399

Item pur plusours graundes inconveniences et meschiefs qe plusours foitz ont avenuz par voie des plusours appelles faites deinz le Roialme Dengleterre devant ces heures, ordeinez est et establiz qe desore enavant toutz les appelles affairs des choses faites deinz le roialme soient triez et terminez par les bones leys du Roialme, faites et usez en temps des tres nobles progenitours nostre dit seignur le Roi; et qe toutz les appelles affairs des choses faites hors de Roialme soient triez et terminez devant les Conestable et Mareschall Dengleterre pur le temps esteantz. Et outre ceo accordez est et assentuz qe nulles appellez soient desores faitz ou pursuez en parlement aucunement en null temps avenir.

S.R. II, 116, I Hen. IV, c. 14.

(36) *Treason appeal before the constable* 1453

Memorandum that on the xj. day of May in the xxxj. yer of the reign of owr soverayn lord Kyng Henry the Sext at a court holden thene in the Whit Halle at Westminster by John Hanford knyght, lieutenante unto the ryght noble Prince, sir Edmond duc of Somerset and constable of Englond, John Lyalton appelled Robert Norres of high treson the which he surmitted to have been don unto owr seid souverayn lord by the seid Robert, and the said Robert denyed that appelle to be true, wheropon the seid parties joyned battaill to be don betwix theym and [the] xxv. day fro thene next suyng thay wer assigned and limitted ther, and by

the seid Lieutenant to do the seid bataill in Smythfeld, and after
that in the seid White Halle at a court holden byfor the seid
Lieutenante at the speciall request of both the seid parties it was
assigned and lymitted that ayther of the seid parties shuld do that
bataill with certen weppens, that is to say, with gleyve, short
sword, dagger and with axe, instede of longe sword, and at the
request of the seid John Lyalton ther was assigned John Astley
knyght... [and 5 others]... and Thomas Parker, armorer, for to
be of counsell with the seid John Lyalton for the premissez, and
Thomas Bee, peyntour, for thynges concernyng the premissez...
[and similarly for Norres.]... wherfor ther ough to be made a prive
seall to the Chaunceller of Englond for to directe a writte to the
Shirefs of London that they make redy in all thyng the place
in Smythfeld ayenst the seid xxv. day, that is to say, in gravelyng
and sandyng the seid place and in makyng a scaffold for the Kyng
and barrers and lystez covenably and sufficiantly for bataill ther
to be hadde; also ther aght to be severall lettres under the prive
seall directe unto every person assigned or lymitted for ayther
of the seid parties for to do as it is above rehersed, also ther aght
a prive seall directe to the Sergeant of the Kynges armory... commaundyng hym for to ordeigne and purvey sufficiaunt and convenient armor and weppen for performyng of the seid bataill.
By the seid John Hanford, knyght.

A.P.C. vi, 129.

(37)   *The office of the conestable and mareschalle* 15th century

In the time of werre is to punysh all manner of men that breken
the statutes and ordonnaunce by the kynge made to be keped in
the oost in the said tyme, and to punysh the same accordyng to
the peynes provided in the said statutes. The conestable and
mareschall hath knowleche upon all maner crymes, contracts,
pleets, querelle, trespas, injuries, and offenses don beyonde the
see in tyme of werre betwene souldeour and souldeour, bytwene
merchaunts, vytelers, leches, barbours, launders, corvesers, laborers,
and artificers necessary to the oost, and yf any of the personnes be
oone, and the other personne be a straunger, the conestable and
mareschalle shall have knowlech in the said matere done in the
werre beyonde the see, and of all maner dedes of armes here
within the londe doone he hath congnoissaunce, and of the offenses
doon beyonde the see he hath knowleche of here in the londe.

Blacke booke of the admiralty, R.S. i, 281 (cf. p. lxxix).

(c) COURT OF THE ADMIRAL

(38)   The admirals' jurisdiction defined 1389

Item prient les Communes, qe come les Admiralx et lour Deputees tiegnent lour Sessions en diverses places deinz le Roialme,
si bien deinz Franchise come dehors, acrochantz a eux pluis grant
poair qe a lour Office n'appartient, en prejudice de nostre Seignur
le Roy, et la Commune Ley du Roialme, et grant emblemissement de plusours diverses Franchises, en destruction et empoverissement del commune Poeple: Qe plese ordeiner et establir lour
Poair en cest present Parlement, q'ils ne soi mellent n'empreignent
sur eux conissances de nulles Contracts, Covenances, Regra-
teries, . . . lesqueux deivent et purront estre terminez devant autres
Jugges nostre Seignur le Roy, deinz les Quatre Miers d'Engleterre,
deinz Franchise et dehors; et qe les Justices de la Pees eient poair
d'enquerre de ceux qe riens font al contraire: Et qe si ascuns des
Admiralx, ou lour Deputees, soient de ce duement convictz, les
Admiralx de perdre lour office, et cynk centz marcz au Roy, et
lour Deputees de perdre lour office, et cent marcz au Roy.

Responsio. Le Roy voet, qe les Admiralx et lour Deputees ne soi
mellent desoreenavant de null chose faite deinz le Roialme; mes
soulement de chose faite sur le Meer, solonc ce q'ad este duement
use en temps du noble Roy Edward, aiel nostre Seignur le Roy
q'or est.

Rot. Parl. III, 269 (41).

PART II

THE CHURCH[1]

INTRODUCTION

The chief interest of church history in the fourteenth and fifteenth centuries lies in the adjustment of relations between church and state, church and papacy, and ecclesiastical and lay jurisdiction. The old trouble over the relations of clergy to the civil courts, and over the conflicting authority of canon and common law, was not yet satisfactorily overcome, and now difficulties were arising over the attitude of the clergy to parliament and to the developing system of taxation.

Parliament in the early fourteenth century was an established institution, although its form was not yet defined; since 1295 it had been usual for a summons to be sent out demanding attendance of the prelates and representatives of the lower clergy. It is fairly clear that the prelates sat as lords of parliament, and that they shared in privileges as such(18), although their baronial status was not certain;[2] but a difficulty arose when judicial matters were under consideration. They certainly took part in trials, but if the sentence involved life or limb the prelates had to withdraw, according to their own regulation(19, 24). They shared fully in any discussions upon legislation, but had no special power allowed them as a spiritual body. Thus the protests of the clergy against some of the laws enacted were quite in vain, although important enough to be noted in the rolls of parliament(15, 20). The lower clergy, however, were not at all ready to take advantage of representation, and, despite special attempts made from time to time to enforce attendance(1), the clerical proctors gradually dropped out of parliament, the king came at last to acquiesce in their absence, and the clergy were left to do their own work in convocation.[3]

When taxes were voted in parliament, the grant was clearly intended to include clergy as well as laity, but the clergy were

[1] This section has been purposely left slight, in view of the work which is now being done on this period of church history, and the forthcoming revised edition of Wilkins' *Concilia*. It has been thought better to include no documents from the old edition.

[2] H. M. Chew, *The English ecclesiastical tenants-in-chief*, pp. 172 ff.

[3] Cf. the evidence given by E. C. Lowry, *E.H.R.* 1933, from records of certain manors in the diocese of Ely, to show that clerical proctors attended parliament at times during the thirty years after 1341.

loath to yield power in this respect, and insisted on bringing the question before convocation and legalising grants made in parliament, until the king recognised the right of the clergy to tax themselves, and asked them directly for subsidies (3, 4, 5, 16).

In regard to justice, though the thirteenth century had seen some problems settled, difficulties still remained. The temporalities of the church, including advowson, were definitely under the jurisdiction of the lay courts, but land in frankalmoign, claimed by the clergy to be subject to church jurisdiction only, was liable to be treated as lay fee.[1] For breaches of forest law, high treason and misdemeanours, clergy were brought for trial before lay courts, and civil actions were outside the sphere of ecclesiastical privilege.[2] The right of benefit of clergy in cases of lesser treasons and greater felonies was, however, recognised and more exactly defined, especially in 1352 (6, 8, 11); in that year an already existing practice was legalised, by which clergy could be convicted in the lay court, where the reading test was applied, before being delivered to the bishop.[3] The jurisdiction of spiritual courts over laymen was generally allowed in certain matters—testaments, marriage, immorality, heresy, slander, and breach of contract where damages were not sought (6, 30)—but any encroachment into the sphere of common law was strictly forbidden.

A vital question at the close of the fourteenth century, and one in which both church and state were concerned, was the growth of heresy. This was primarily a matter for the church courts, but they failed to check the evil, and appealed to the state, which stepped in to assist them. Acts were passed against heretical preaching (17); and by the statute *de haeretico comburendo* offenders convicted before a spiritual court were to be handed over for punishment to the secular authority (25). The rising of Sir John Oldcastle in 1414 increased the dread felt by the state, and a new statute put the initiative against the heretics into the hands of civil justices (26).

The relation of the English church to the papacy affects constitutional history, since papal claims interfered with the normal working of ecclesiastical organisation, and involved questions of taxation, causing the promulgation of certain statutes. The claims made by the pope, beyond those for money, were chiefly concerned with the hearing of appeals, and the filling of episcopal

---

[1] Pollock and Maitland, *History of English law*, I, 250–1.
[2] *Ibid.* I, 130.
[3] L. C. Gabel, *Benefit of clergy*, pp. 35–6, 58–9.

sees and benefices, to the exclusion of the right of chapters and patrons (2, 7, 9). In the early fourteenth century John XXII extended papal rights considerably in this latter respect. He claimed the right to fill benefices the previous holders of which had been appointed by the pope or who had died in Rome, and others which were vacated by pluralists. Even when direct appointment was prevented, the pope could do a great deal by making provision for a coming vacancy, or by translating from one see to another. He could also interfere with the authority of the archbishop as *legatus natus* by sending an occasional *legatus a latere*, and his demands for revenue were very heavy, in addition to the tribute due on account of John's submission. There are frequent examples of the increasing opposition to the papacy (14, 21), the clergy themselves resisting the heavy demands, and John's tribute was definitely refused in 1366 (13). The king backed up clergy or pope according to his need for support from one side or the other; but whatever the royal attitude there was increasing objection in the country to foreign interference, and to sending money out of England. The statutes of provisors, 1351 and 1390 (10, 22), were an attempt to check papal interference with episcopal appointments; and the statutes of praemunire, 1353 and 1393 (12, 23), did something to reduce the practice of appeals. The exact intention of these latter statutes, however, is a matter of considerable dispute, and it would appear that in no case was the complete suppression of papal authority contemplated: the later opposition of the clergy to the statute of 1393 was partly caused by its use as a restraint on the spiritual courts. In the fifteenth century the dislike of foreigners was shown by the confiscation of the alien priories (27); and Gloucester made use of the statute of praemunire in his struggle with Beaufort. The effort to keep Beaufort out of the council on account of his acceptance of the dignity of cardinal illustrates the fear of Rome and Roman influence (28).

BIBLIOGRAPHY

I. ORIGINAL SOURCES

GIBSON, EDMUND. *Codex juris ecclesiastici Anglicani*, 2 vols. London, 1713; Oxford, 1761.

HALE, Archdeacon W. H. *A series of precedents...extracted from act-books of ecclesiastical courts in the diocese of London*, 1475–1640. London, 1847.

LYNDWOOD, W. *Provinciale*. Oxford, 1679.

Rotuli parliamentorum. London, 1783.

Statutes of the realm. London, 1810–28.

WILKINS, DAVID. *Concilia Magnae Britanniae et Hiberniae*, A.D. 446–1718, 4 vols. London, 1737. (A new edition of this work is in preparation; the documents of the present edition are not wholly trustworthy.)

2. SECONDARY AUTHORITIES

CHURCHILL, I. J. *Canterbury administration. The administrative machinery of the archbishopric of Canterbury...*, 2 vols. S.P.C.K. 1933.

GABEL, L. C. *Benefit of clergy in England in the later middle ages.* Northampton, Mass. 1928.

HODY, HUMPHREY. *A history of English councils and convocations and of the clergy's sitting in parliament.* London, 1701.

JOYCE, J. W. *England's sacred synods....* London, 1855.

KENNET, WHITE. *Ecclesiastical synods and parliamentary convocations in the church of England.* London, 1701.

LATHBURY, THOMAS. *A history of the convocation of the church of England,* 2nd edition. London, 1853.

MAKOWER, FELIX. *Die Verfassung der Kirche von England.* Berlin, 1894. (Translation) *The constitutional history and constitution of the church of England.* London, 1895.

PERROY, E. *L'Angleterre et le Grand Schisme.* Paris, 1934.

Report of the commissioners appointed to inquire into the constitution and working of the ecclesiastical courts. London, 1883.

WAKE, WILLIAM. *The state of the church and clergy of England,....* London, 1703. (Appendix contains records.)

3. ARTICLES AND ESSAYS

DEELEY, A. "Papal provision and royal rights of patronage in the early fourteenth century", *E.H.R.* XLIII, 1928.

GRAVES, E. B. "The legal significance of the statute of Praemunire", *Anniversary essays...by students of C. H. Haskins.* New York, 1929.

LOWRY, E. CLARK. "Clerical proctors in parliament and knights of the shire, 1280–1374", *E.H.R.* XLVIII, 1933.

ROBINSON, J. ARMITAGE. "Convocation of Canterbury: its early history", *Church Quarterly Review*, LXXXI, Oct. 1915.

WAUGH, W. T. "The great statute of Praemunire, 1393", *E.H.R.* XXXVII, 1922.

(1) *Special writ to enforce attendance of clergy in parliament* 1314

Mandatum de parliamento...

Edwardus *etc.* venerabili in Christo patri Waltero eadem gracia Archiepiscopo Cantuariensi, totius Anglie Primati salutem. Crescente malicia Roberti de Brous etc....

Quo circa vobis tenore presencium injungimus et mandamus,

quatinus prefatos Suffraganeos nostros Decanos Priores Abbates
Archidiacanos Clerumque predictum nostre provincie Cantuariensis peremptorie premuniri et citari faciatis quod dictis die et
loco sint et compereant juxta formam ejusdem brevis una nobis-
cum tractaturi et ordinaturi super premissis prout utilitati ecclesie et animarum saluti visum fuerit expedire, et hiis que,
Domino disponente, ibidem salubriter contigerit ordinari, suum
prout decet consensum adhabituri ad quem diem vestram ibidem
presenciam exhabieatis personalem: et qualiter hoc presens mandatum nostrum fueritis exsecuti nos eisdem die et loco cum tenore
presencium legitime certificetis. Datum apud Otteford v° idus
April' anno Domini M°CCC^mo quarto decimo.

Parliamentary writs, II, ii, pt. 1, 123.

(2) *Papal provisions* 1322

Ad Papam, super Præbenda, de non molestando.
Papæ Rex devota pedum oscula beatorum.
Sic, dilecti Clerici nostri, Magistri Roberti de Baldok, Archi-
diaconi Middlesexiæ, fructuosa obsequia, nobis indies impensa
(quibus etiam carere commode non possumus) Nos alliciunt ad
ipsius Honores procurandum, quod pro eisdem vestri Apostolatus
apicem interpellare non cessamus.
Vestræ Sanctitati, quanto devotius poterimus, supplicantes,
quatinus de Episcopatu, infra Regnum nostrum, proximo vaca-
turo, et ad vestram Provisionem seu Dispositionem spectante,
eidem Clerico nostro, nostris precibus, dignemini providere:
Et de Briga, contra ipsum mota in vestra Sacra Curia, de Præbenda de Aylesbury, in Ecclesia Lincolniensi, quam habet, ex
Collatione nostra, Jure nostro Regio (in quo quidem Negotio Jus
nostrum specialiter versatur) quietem sibi, Juxta rogamina nostra,
vestræ Beatitudini alias vobis inde facta, præparare:
Ac super hiis, quæ, dilectus nobis in Christo, Frater Robertus
de Wirksop, de Ordine Sancti Augustini, Sacræ Theologiæ
Doctor, in præmissis, vobis ex parte nostra exposuerit viva voce,
fidem sibi credulam adhibere.
Conservet, etc.
Teste Rege apud Pontem fractum, 19. die Martii.

Foedera, III, 935.

(3) *Clerical taxation* 1322

Rex dilecto sibi in Christo Abbati de Waltham Sancte Crucis,
salutem. Quanta mala strages hominum destrucciones eccle-

siarium et populi regni nostri Scoti inimici et rebelles nostri in eodem regno hactenus perpetrarunt, vobis et ceteris fidelibus nostris ignotum esse non credimus et quod gravius est rei evidencia satis manifestat. Cum itaque ad obstinatam maliciam dictorum inimicorum et rebellium nostrorum cum Dei adjutorio reprimendam in instanti seisona estivali manu potenti ad partes Scocie ordinaverimus proficisci ad quod necnon pro custodia marchie regni nostri contra hostiles aggressus dictorum inimicorum nostrorum interim facienda pecuniam quasi infinitam nos effundere oportebit, ac in subvencionem expensarum hujusmodi Prelati, Comites, Barones et Proceres, necnon Communitates dicti regni apud Eboracum ad tractandum super dictis negociis et aliis nos et statum dicti regni tangentibus nuper convocati, decimam de bonis de Communitate ejusdem regni et sextam de Civitatibus, Burgis et antiquis Dominicis nostris nobis liberaliter concesserunt et gratanter. Nos considerantes mala predicta tam in sacra ecclesia quam in locis aliis per dictos inimicos nostros illata fuisse, volentesqe precipue salvacioni sancte ecclesie contra dictorum inimicorum jacula pro viribus providere, ad quod vos speramus ut tenemini manus velle apponere adjutrices, vobis mandamus in fide et dileccione quibus nobis tenemini firmiter injungentes, quatinus ad concilium provinciale quod venerabilis pater Walterus Cantuariensis Archiepiscopus apud Lincolniam in proximo convocabit ad tractandum cum Prelatis et Clero dicte provincie de competenti subsidio nobis in tam urgente necessitate de bonis suis ecclesiasticis et aliis ecclesiaticis annexis concedendo vos personaliter transferatis, et tale ac tam competens auxilium pensatis necessitatibus supradictis, una cum Clero predicto concedatis et concedi ab aliis pro viribus procuretis quod benivolenciam quam ad honorem nostrum regium et salvacionem regni nostri optinetis possimus effectualiter experiri, et vos et eundem Clerum debeamus exinde habere in oportunitatibus specialius commendatos. Teste ut supra.   Per ipsum Regem.

Parliamentary writs, II, ii, 280.

(4) *The clergy taxed in convocation* 1339

Item, Acordez est et assentuz en dit Parlement par touz les Grauntz et Communes illoeqes assemblez, qe Lettres soient faites, souz les Sealx l'Ercevesqe de Canterburs, et des autres Prelatz, Countes, et Barouns esteantz en cel Parlement a Westmonstier, a...l'Ercevesqe d'Everwyk et a la Clergie de sa Provynce, de les exciter de faire un covenable Aide pur la Garde de la Marche d'Escoce, et pur les autres busoignes du Roi celes parties; fesauntes mention, qe il lour covendra a fyn force de faire le pur la defense de Seinte Esglise du Roialme, et de eux meismes, et coment la Clergie de la Provynce de Canterburs ount fait covenable Aide par la cause susdite...

Item, De faire Brief de faire Convocation de la Clergie de la Provynce de Canterburs a l'Esglise de Seint Poul, a la Quynzeyne de Seynt Hiller; et autre Brief de faire autiele Convocation de la Clergie de la Provynce d'Everwyk, a trois semaygnes de Seynt Hiller.

Item, Fait a remembrer de somoundre le Parlement as oytaves de Seint Hiller susdit.

Rot. Parl. II, 105 (16); 106 (24, 25).

(5) *Exemption from the ninth for alien priors, etc.* 1340

A Queu Samady, apres grant Trete et Parlance eue entre les Grantz et les ditz Chivalers, et autres des Communes, esteantz au dit Parlement, si est acordez et assentuz par touz les Grantz et Communes, qi vindrent en dit Parlement, Qe les trois choses grantees a nostre Seignur le Roi en son darrein Parlement, c'est assavoir les Neofismes garbes, toisons, et aigneux, soient venduz par les assignez a ceo faire, et par les surveours a ce deputez, solonc ce q'est contenuz en les Commissiones ent faites; ensi q'ils passent la Taxe si les choses valent plus ou al meyns au Taxe...

Item acordez est et assentuz, qe les Priours Aliens, et autres qi ont lour Maisons et Possessions a ferme par Commissions de nostre Seignur le Roi, et qi paient lour ferme, soient quites del neofisme garbe, neofisme toyson, et neofisme aignel, tant come lour dites Maisons et autres Possessions demurreront en la mayn du Roi.

Item acordez est, qe Abbes et Priours, et autres gentz de Religion qi paient lour Dismes, et qi ne sont pas somons de venir au Parlement, eient Briefs de surseer de lever le Neofisme de eux tan qe a la quinzeyne de Seint Michel proschein a venir.

Item, qe les Hospitalx qi sont founduz pur Pours ou Malades, et qi ne soleint estre taxez eynz ces houres, soient fait quites de Neofisme.

Rot. Parl. II, 117 (5); 119 (17).

(6) *Judicial privileges of the church* 1341

Item acorde et assentuz est qe le Roi et ses heires eient la conisaunce des usereres mortz; et qe les Ordinares de seinte esglise eient la conisaunce des usureres vifs, desicome a eux attient, faire compulsioun par censures de seint esglise pur le pecche, de faire restitucion des usures prises contre la lei de seinte esglise.

Item acorde est qe les Ministres de seinte esglise pur diners prises pur redempcion de corporele penaunce, ne pur proeve et acompte des testamentz, ou pur travaille entour ceo mys, ne pur solempnete des esposailles, ne pur autre cause touchaunte la jurisdiction de seinte esglise, ne soient apeschez ne aresonez ne chacez a respoundre devant les Justices le Roi ne ses autres ministres. Et sour ceo eient les Ministres de seinte esglise briefs en la Chauncellerie, a les Justicez et autres ministres, totes les foiths qils les demanderunt.

S.R. i, 296, 15 Ed. III, s. i, cc. 5, 6.

(7) *Petition against papal provisions* 1344

Item fait a remembrer, qe puis fu mys avant en Parlement une autre Petition par les Communes avant dites, dont la tenour s'ensuit:

Por ce qe avant ces heures ne feust pas ordeignez certeyne penance ne punissement contre ceux qi pursuent en la Court de Rome, pur anientir et adnuller les Juggementz renduz par dues Processes en la Court le Roi, sur Presentementz des Esglises, Provendes, et autres Benefices, ou autre quecumqe Juggement renduz illoeqes; si ont les uns este esbaudez le plus de faire tieles Seutes et Processes, queu chose est prejudicele au Roi et en defesance de la Ley de sa terre, et desheriteson de sa Corone. Par qoi prie la Communaltee du Roialme, qe acordez soit et establi, qe si nul mes face tieles Seutes en la Court de Rome, ou autre Court Cristiene, en enervation ou destourbance des Juggementz renduz par dues Proces en la Court le Roi, ou de l'effect ou execution de meismes les Juggementz, de quecumqe condition q'il soit, Provisour, ou Procuratour, Promotour, Executour, ou Notaire, ou autre quecumqe, et de ce soit atteint, eit perpetuele prisone, ou forsjure le Roialme; et en cas q'il soit mye trovez, soit mys en Exigende et utlagez, et qe sur ce soit fait Briefs forme en la Chancellerie de les attacher par lour corps. Et si la partie grevez voudra avoir Brief hors des Roules des Justices devant queux

tieux Juggementz sont renduz, pur les attacher, come desus est
dit, lui soit grantez, si bien a la suite le Roi come d'autres qi
pleindre se voudront. Et nientmeyns Justices as assises prendre
assignez et a gaoles deliverer, et Justices assignez d'oier et terminer
felonies et trespas par les Countees, eient poair par cest Estatut
d'enquer, oier, et terminer sur cest Article, aussi bien a la suite
le Roi come de partie; et Viscontes aussint en lour tourns enquergent estreitement sur ce point, et ceux qi serront duement enditez
devant eux facent prendre, et mettre en la gaole, saunz estre
lessez a meynprise tan qe a prochein deliverance de la gaole: Et
en cas ou tieux enditez ne sont pas trovez, soient les Enditementz
faitz venir par Briefs en l'un Baunk ou en l'autre, et illoeqes
terminez par les processes susditz: Et meisme la Ley soit fait vers
touz Provisours q'ont ascun Benefice acceptez ou occupez puis le
darrein Parlement, tenuz a Westmonstier l'an du Regne nostre
Seignur le Roi xviime, encontre l'Ordinance et acorde faites en
meisme le Parlement, et lour Procuratours, Promotours, Executours, Notairs, ou autres quecumqes q'averont portez nulles bulles,
proces, ou instrumentz, deinz le dit Roialme, prejudiciels au Roi
ou a son people, ou rien attemptez contre les Ordinances et
acordes susdites, et jadumeyns soient Justices assignez especialment par Commissions d'enquere, oier et terminer sur ces pointz
a totes les foitz qe mestier serra.

Item, Qe les Provisions, Ordinances, et Acordes faites en le
dit Parlement, le dit an xviime, des tieles Provisions et Reservations
de la dite Court de Rome, soient affermez par Estatut perpetuelment a durer.

Item, Pleise a nostre Seignur le Roi establer, qe si nul Ercevesqe,
Evesqe, Abbe, Priour, ou autre Patron espirituel des Benefices,
apres la voidance des tieux Benefices acceptez par Provisours et
occupez, ou par la Court de Rome reservez, ne presentent ou
facent collation deinz les quatre mois, qe adonqes au Roi a cel
foitz, si tiel Patronage de lui soit tenuz, ou a autre de qi il soit
tenuz, accresce action et title de presenter. Et tut soit il qe
defaute ne soit trovez en tielx Ercevesqes,...ou autres Patrons
espirituels, par tant q'ils presentent ou font collations deinz les
quatre mois a tiels Benefices, jadumeyns, s'ils soient destourbez
par Provisions ou Reservations de la Court de Rome, enqore
nientcontresteant q'ils font ce q'en eux est d'aver tieux presentementz ou collations, qe droit de presenter accresce au Roi, ou as
autres, come desus est dit, a cel foitz. Sauve as Ercevesqes,...ou
autres Patrons espirituels, lour droit de presenter ou faire col-

lation a lour voidances qe cherront en tout temps apres. Et en
cas qe Seignurs desqueux tieux Avowesons sont tenuz soient
negligentz ou remys, par qoi ils ne presentent pas ou font collation deinz les trois moys apres ce qe tieux presentementz ou
collations a eux soient devolutz par le passer des quatre moys,
come desus est dit, q'adonqes au Roi a cel foitz accresce droit de
presenter, ou faire collation, par lour defaute...

Rot. Parl. ii, 153 (32–4).

(8) *Ecclesiastical privileges* 1344
La Chartre pur la Clergie

Edward *etc.*...a touz ceux qi cestes Lettres verront ou orront,
Saluz. Sachez, qe a nostre Parlement tenuz a Westmonstier le
Lundy prochein apres les oytasves de la Trinite prochein passez,
entre autres choses monstrees,...en dit Parlement si furent monstrees,...les choses souzescrites. Primerement, coment plousours
choses furent attemptees par la partie nostre Adversaire de France
contre la Trewe prise nadgairs en Bretaigne entre Nous et lui, et
coment il s'afforce tant come il poet a destruire Nouz, noz Alliez
et Suggitz, Terres et Lieux, et la Lange d'Engleterre; et sur ce fu
priez de par Nous, as Prelatz, Grantz, et Communes, q'il Nous
donassent tieu Conseil et Eide come busoigneroit en si grande
necessite; et les ditz Prelatz, Grantz, et Communes eu ent bone
deliberation et avis,...si conseillerent joyntement et severalment,
et supplierent od grande instance a Nous, qe en asseurance de
l'eide de Dieu et de nostre bone querele, Nous Nous afforceons par
totes les bones voies qe Nous purrons, de faire fyn a ceste foitz
de nostre Guerre; et qe pur Lettres ne paroles ne beaux premesses
Nous ne lessons nostre passage, si Nous ne veons effect de la
Busoigne. Et par ceste cause les ditz Grantz granterent de passer
et lour aventeurer ovesqe Nous. Et les ditz Prelatz et Procuratours de la Clergie Nous granterent par meisme la cause une
Disme triennale, a paier as certeyns jours;...Et Nous par ceste
cause en meyntenance de l'Estat de Seinte Esglise, et en eese des
ditz Prelatz et de tote la Clergie d'Engleterre, par Assent des
Grantz et des Communes si grantasmes de nostre bone grace les
choses souzescrites: C'est assaver, Qe nul Ercevesqe ne Evesqe
ne soit empeschez devant noz Justices par cause de cryme, si
Nous ne le comandons especialment, tan qe autre remedie ent soit
ordeignez.

Item, Qe si nul Clerc soit aresnez devant noz Justices a nostre

THE CHURCH 299

seute ou a la seute de partie, et le Clerc se tiegne a sa Clergie,
alleggeant, q'il ne doit devant eux sur ce respondre; et si homme
lui surmette pur Nous ou pur la partie, q'il eit esposez deux
femmes, ou une veve, qe sur ce les Justices n'eient conissance ne
poair de trier par Enquest ou en autre manere la Bigamie, einz
soit mandez a la Court Christiene come ad este fait en cas de
Bastardie. Et tan qe la Certification soit mandez par l'Ordinaire,
demoerge la persone en quele Bigamie est alleggez par les paroles
susditz, ou en autre manere, en garde s'il ne soit meynpernable.

Item, Qe si Prelatz, Clers beneficez, ou gentz de Religion, q'ont
purchacez terres et les ont mys a mortmayn soient empeschez ou
aresonez sur ce devant noz Justices, et ils monstrent noz Chartres
de Licence et Proces sur ce fait, par Enquest Ad quod Dampnum,
ou de nostre grace, ou par fyn, q'ils soient lessez franchement en
Pees saunz estre outre empeschez pur le dit purchace. Et en cas
q'ils ne purront sufficeaument monstrer q'ils soient entrez par due
processe apres la Licence a eux grantez en general ou en especial,
q'ils soient bonement resceuz a faire covenable fyn, et qe l'enquerre de cest Article cesse de tut selonc l'acorde ent prise en ceo
Parlement.

Item, Qe les Estatutz touchantz Purveances de Nous et des
Noz faitz en temps passez par Nous et par noz Progenitours pur
gentz de Seinte Esglise soient tenuz en touz pointz, et qe les
Commissions a faire sur tieux Purveances soient, forspris les fedz
de Seinte Esglise et biens des Gentz de Seinte Esglise en quecumqe
lieu q'ils soient trovez.

Item, Qe nulle Prohibition isse desormes hors de la Chancellerie,
sinoun en cas qe Nous averons la Conissance et devons avoir de
droit.

Item, Qe par la ou Commissions sont faites de novelle as divers
Justices, q'ils facent Enquestes sur Juges de Seinte Esglise,...en
blemissement de la Franchise de Seinte Esglise; qe tieles Commissions soient repellez, et desormes defenduz, sauvez l'article de
Eire tiel come il doit estre.

Item, Qe par la ou Briefs de Scire facias eient este grantez, a
garnir Prelatz, Religious, et autres Clers a respondre des Dismes
en nostre Chancellerie, et a monstrer s'ils eient rien pur eux, ou
sachent riens dire pur quoi tieux Dismes a les demandantz ne
deyvent estre restitutes, et a respondre auxi bien a Nous come a
partie des tieux Dismes; Qe tieux Briefs desoreenavant ne soient
grantez, et qe les processes pendantz sur tieux Briefs soient any-
entez et repellez; et qe les parties soient dimisses devant seculers

Juges des tieux maneres des Pledz: Sauvez a Nous nostre Droit tiel come Nous et noz Auncestres avons eu, et soleions avoir de reson;

Et tesmoignance desqueux choses, a la Requeste des ditz Prelatz, a cestes presentes Lettres avons fait mettre nostre Seal. Done a Loundres le viii jour de Juyl, l'an de nostre Regne d'Engleterre dysoytisme, et de France quint.

Rot. Parl. II, 152 (24–31).

(9) *Opposition to papal reservations* 1347

Item prie la Commune, qe come Seinte Esglise doit estre fraunche et franche Election avoir; Et ore de novel le Pape comence a doner Abbeies et Priories par Reservation faite, qe unqes mes ne feust veuz. Et issint desore serront les Abbeies et Priories par tieles Collations donez as Aliens et persones meyns covenables, et en cas as Cardinals; en destruction et anientissement des Religious d'Engleterre, a tant des Avoweries nostre Seignur le Roi come des autres Seignurs de la terre, en desheritance nostre Seignur le Roi et autres Seignurs, et blemissement de les Franchises de Seinte Esglise: Qe lui pleise sur ce remeide ordeigner par avisement de son Conseil.

Responsio Nostre Seignur le Roi s'avisera ove son bon Conseil qe mieltz serra a faire en tiel cas.

Rot. Parl. II, 171 (50).

(10) *Statute of provisors* 1351

Come jadis, en le parlement de bone memoire Sire Edward Roi Dengleterre, Ael nostre Seignur le Roi qore est, lan de son regne trentisme quint a Kardoil tenuz, oie la peticion mise devant le dit Ael et son conseil en le dit parlement par la communalte de son Roialme, contenant qe come seinte eglise Dengleterre estoit founde en estat de prelacie, deins le Roialme Dengleterre, par le dit Ael et ses progenitours, et Countes Barons et Nobles de son Roialme et lour ancestres, pur eux et le poeple enfourmer de la lei Dieu, et pur faire hospitalites aumoignes et autres oeveres de charite es lieux ou les eglises feurent foundes pur les almes de foundours et de lour heirs et de touz Cristiens; et certeins possessions, tant en feez terres et rentes come en avowesons qe se extendent a grande value, par les ditz foundours feurent assignez as prelatz et autres gentz de seinte eglise du dit Roialme, pur cele charge sustenir, et nomement des possessions qi feurent assignes as Ercevesqes, Evesqes, Abbes, Priours, Religious et autres gentz de seint eglise...Et ja monstre soit a nostre Seignur le Roi, en cest parlement tenuz a Westmonstier a les Oetaves de la Purificacion de nostre Dame, lan de son regne Dengleterre vintisme quint, et de France duszisme, par la greveuse pleinte de toute la commune de son Roialme qe les grevances et meschiefs susditz sabondent de temps en temps, a plus grant damage et destruccion de tut le Roialme, plus qe unqes ne firent; cest assaver qore de novel nostre seint piere le Pape, par procurement des clercs et autrement ad reservee et reserve de jour en autre a sa collacion, generalment et especialment, sibien Ercevesches, Eveschees, Abbeies, et Priories, come totes dignetes et autres benefices dengleterre, qi sont del avowerie de gentz de seinte eglise, et les donne auxibien as aliens come as denzeins, et prent de touz tiels benefices les primeres fruitz et autres profitz plusours; et grande partie du tresor del Roialme si est emporte et despendu hors du Roialme, par les purchaceours de tieles graces; et auxint par tieles reservacions prives, plusours clercs avances en ceste Roialme par lour verroies patrons, qi ont tenuz lour avancementz par long temps pesiblement, sont sodeinement ostes; sur quoi la dite Commune ad prie a nostre Seignur le Roi qe desicome le droit de la Corone Dengleterre et la loi du dite Roialme sont tieles, qe sur meschiefs et damages qi si aviegnont a son Roialme il doit et est tenuz par son serement, del acord de son poeple en son parlement, faire ent remede et lei, en ostant les meschiefs et damages qensi avignont, qe lui pleise de ce ordiner remede; Nostre Seignur le Roi, veiant les meschiefs et damages susnomes et eant regard al dit estatut fait en temps son dit Ael...par assent de touz les grantz et la Communalte de son dit Roialme, Al honur de Dieu et profit de la dite eglise Dengleterre et de tut son Roialme, ad ordine et establi, qe les franches eleccions des Erceveschees, Eveschees et tutes autres dignites et benefices electifs en Engleterre, se tiegnent desore, en manere come eles feurent grantes par les progenitours nostre dit seignur le Roi, et par les auncestres dautres Seignurs foundes. Et qe touz prelatz, et autres gentz de seinte eglise qi ont avowesons de quecomqes benefices des douns nostre Seignur le Roi et de ses progenitours, ou dautres Seignurs et donours, pur faire divines services et autres charges ent ordines, eient lour collacions et presentementz franchement en manere come ils estoient feffes par lour donours. Et en cas qe dascune Erceveschee, Eveschee, dignite ou autre quecumqe benefice, soit reservacion, collacion, ou provision faite par la court de Rome, en desturbance des eleccions, collacions ou presentacions susnomes, qe a meisme les temps des voidances, qe tieles reservacions, collacions et provisions deusent prendre effect, qe a meisme la voidance nostre Seignur le Roi et ses heirs eient et enjoicent pur cele foitz les collacions, as Erceveschees, Eveschees, et autres dignites electives, qe sont de savowerie, autieles come ses progenitours avoient avant qe franche eleccion feust graunte, desicome les eleccions feurent primes grantez, par les progenitours le Roi, sur certeines forme et condicion, come a demander du Roi conge de eslir, et puis apres la eleccion daver son assent roial, et nemye en autre manere;...

S.R. i, 316, 25 Ed. III.

(11) *An ordinance for the clergy* 1352
Ordinacio pro Clero

Nostre Seignour le Roi, veues et examinez par bone deliberacion les peticions et articles a lui bailliez en son parlement, tenuz a Westmonster en la feste de seint Hillary lan de son regne Dengleterre vintisme quint, et de France duszisme, par Lonurable piere en Dieu Simon Ercevesqe de Canterbirs et autres Evesqes de sa province, sur et pur certeines grevances queles ils disoient estre faites a seinte eglise et a la clergie, encontre les privileges de seinte eglise, et dunk ils prierent qe covenable remedie ent fuist ordene, al reverence de Dieu et de seinte eglise, et de lassent de son dit parlement, pur lui et ses heirs voet et grant les pointz southescriptz.

Confirmation of privileges

Primerement qe toutz les franchises et privileges grantez par devant a la dite clergie soient confermez et tenuz en toutz pointz.

Clerks convicted of felony or treason to be delivered to the Ordinaries

...Item come les ditz Prelatz eient grevousement pleint enpriant ent remedie, de ce qe clercs seculers, auxi bien Chapelleins come autres, Moignes et autres gentz de religion, eient este treinez et penduz par agard des Justices seculers, en prejudice des franchises, et depression de jurisdiccion de seinte eglise; si est acorde et grante par le Roi, en son dit parlement, qe touz maneres des clercs, auxibien seculers come religiouses, qi serront desore convictz devant les Justices seculers pur qecomqes felonies ou tresons touchantes autres persones qe le Roi meismes ou sa roiale majeste, eient et enjoient franchement desore privilege de seinte eglise, et soient saunz nule empeschement ou delai liverez a les Ordinaries eux demandantz. Et pur ce grant le dit Ercevesqe promist au Roi, qe sur le punissement et sauve gard de tieux clercs meffesours, qi serront ency as Ordenares liverez, il enferroit ordenance covenable, par la quelle tieux clercs enserroient salvement gardez et duement puniz, ensi qe nul clerc emprendreit mes baudure de ensi meffaire par defaute de chastiement...

S.R. 1, 324, 25 Ed. III, s. 6, cc. 1, 4.

(12) *Statute of praemunire* 1353

Statutum contra adnullatores judiciorum Curiae Regis, factum anno xxvij.

Nostre Seignur le Roi...ad ordene et establi les choses souzescriptes.

Primerement purce qe monstree est a nostre dit Seignur le Roi, par grevous et clamous pleintes des Grantz et communes avantditz, coment plusours gentz sont et ount este traites hors du roialme, a respondre des choses dount la conissance appartient a la Court nostre Seignur le Roi; et aussint qe les juggementz, renduz en meisme la Court, sont empeschez en autri Court, en prejudice et desheritson nostre Seignur le Roi et de sa corone, et de tout le poeple de son dit roialme, et en defesance et anientissement de la commune lei de meisme le roialme usee de tout temps: Sur quoi eue bone deliberacion od les grantz et autres du dit conseil, assentu est et acorde, par nostre dit Seignur le Roi et les grantz et communes susditz, qe totes gentz de la ligeance le Roi, de quele condicion qils soient qi trehent nulli hors du Roialme, en plee dount la conissance appartient a la Court le Roi, ou des choses dount juggementz sont renduz en la Court le Roi, ou qi suent en autri Court a deffaire ou empescher les juggementz renduz en la Court le Roi, eient jour contenant lespace de deux mois, par garnissement affaire a eux en le lieu ou les possessions sont qi sont en debat, ou aillours ou ils averont terres ou autres possessions, par le viscont ou autre ministre du Roi, destre devant le Roi et son conseil, ou en sa Chancellerie, ou devant les Justices le Roi en ses places del un Baunk ou del autre, ou devant autres Justices le Roi qi serront a ce deputez, a respondre en lour propre persones au Roi du contempt fait en celle partie; et sils ne veignent mie au dit jour en propre persone de esteer a la lei, soient ils, lour procuratours, attournez, executours, Notairs, et meintenours, de cel jour enavant mis hors de la proteccion le Roi, et lour terres, biens et chateux forfaitz au Roi, et soient lour corps ou qils soient trovez, pris et emprisonez et reintz a la volunte le Roi; et sur ce soit brief fait de les prendre par lour corps, et de seisir lour terres biens et possessions en la main le Roi; et si retourne soit quils ne sont mie trovez, soient mis en exigend et utlaghez...

S.R. I, 329, 27 Ed. III, s. 1, c. 1.

(13) *The end of papal tribute* 1366

En ce present Parlement tenuz a Westmonstier, Lundy preschein apres la Invention de la Seint Croice, l'an du Regne le Roy Edward quarantisme, tant sur l'estat de Seint Esglise, quant des droits de son Roialme et de sa Corone meinteinir, entre autres choses estoient monstrez, Coment ad este parlee et dit, qe le Pape, par force d'une fait quele il dit qe le Roi Johan jadys Roi d'Engleterre fesoit au Pape au perpetuite de lui faire Homage pur le Roialme d'Engleterre et la Terre de Irlande, et par cause du dite Homage de lui rendre un annuel Cens, ad este en volunte de fair Proces devers le Roi pur les ditz Services et Cens recoverir: laquele chose monstree as Prelatz, Ducs, Countes, Barons, et la Commune, pur ent avoir lour Avys et bon Conseil, et demandee de eux ce qe le Roi en fera en cas qe le Pape vorroit proceder ou rien attempter devers lui ou son Roialme pur cele cause. Queux Prelatz, Ducs, Countes, Barons, et Communes, eu sur ce plein deliberation, responderent et disoient d'une accorde, Qe le dit Roi Johan ne nul autre purra mettre lui ne son Roialme ne son Poeple en tiele subjection saunz Assent de eux, et come piert par plusours Evidences qe si ce feust fait ce feust fait saunz lour Assent, et encontre son Serement en sa Coronation.

Rot. Parl. II, 290 (8).

(14) *Growing opposition to papal taxation* 1376

Fait a remembrer pur commune Profit, qe le Collectour du Pape, q'est Aliene, et de l'obeisance de France, et auxint plusours autres appertez Enemys et Espies de privetes du Roialme d'Engleterre, demurent continuelement en la Cite de Loundres, et ont lours Procuratours et Exploratours Engleys et Lumbardz, et autres parmy le Roialme, pur espier la vacation des grandes Benefices et Dignites de Seint Esglise, et envoient continuelement par lettres et credences a la Courte de Rome, as Cardinalx, et autres gentz

la demurrantz, desqueux la greindre partie sont Enemys, pur
purchacer du Pape mesmes les Benefices et Dignites: Et auxint
envoient la la certeigniete des secres du Roialme, en grant prejudice du Roialme.

Rot. Parl. II, 338 (104).

(15) *The clergy resist legislation in vain* 1380

Item, soient adjoustez a la Commission de Justices de Pees les
pointz ensuiantz: [*Fresh powers granted to them*]...Et fait a remembrer, qe les Prelats et la Clergie firent lour Protestation en ce
Parlement expressement sur cest novel Grant, d'oier et terminer
Extorsions, qe ce ne passast unqes ne ne passeroit jammais de lour
assent ou voluntee, en emblemissement del Libertee de Seinte
Esglise, si par cas l'en vorroit par vertu de mesme le parole,
Extorsion, proceder trop largement avant envers les Ordeinairs et
autres gentz de Seinte Esglise, n'autrement ils ent durroient lour
assent, sinoun qe feust fait en temps a venir come ad este duement
fait et usee devaunt ceste heure. A quoi y feust repliez pur nostre
Seignur le Roi, Qe le Roi pur lour dice Protestation, n'autres
lours paroles en celle partie, ne lerroit de faire ses Justices en ce
cas, et en touz autres come il soleit faire de temps passe, et est
tenuz de faire par vertu del serement fait a son Coronement.

Rot. Parl. III, 83 (38).

...... (16) *Clerical taxation in convocation* 1380

Item, quant les Communes s'avoient autre foitz avisez, et longement tretez de le manere del dit levee, Ils vindrent en Parlement,
faisantz lour Protestation, q'ils ne vindrent illoeqes quant a cel
jour pur rienz grantir; mais ils pensoient bien a ce q'ils disoient, qe
si la Clergie vousist supporter le Tierce denier de la charge, ils
vorroient granter C M. livres a lever une certaine quantitee des
Grotes de chescune singulere persone masle et femmele parmy le
Roialme, issint qe les Lays feussent mys a C M. marcz, et le Clergie
qi occupie la tierce partie del Roialme feust mys a cynquante
M. marz: Em priantz a nostre Seignur le Roi, et as Seignurs
Temporelx, q'ils vousissent prier le Clergie q'ils vousissent hastier
le terme de lour conseil et assemble, et emprendre sur eux la dite
charge de L M. marz a cest foitz. A quoy feust reppliez par le
Clergie, qe lour Grant ne feust unqes fait en Parlement, ne ne
doit estre, ne les Laies gentz devroient ne ne purroient constreindre

le Clergie, ne ne poet ne doit en celle partie constreindre les Layes gentz; mais leur semble, qe si aucun deust estre frank ce serroit pluis tost la Clergie qe les Lays gentz.

Rot. Parl. III, 90 (13).

(17) *Law against heresy* 1382

Item purceo qe notorie chose est coment ya plusours malurees, persones deinz le dit Roialme alantz de Countee en Countee et de ville en ville en certains habitz souz dissimulacion de grant saintee, et sanz licence de Seint piere le pape ou des ordinairs des lieux ou autre auctorite suffisante, prechent de jour en autre, nemye soulement es esglises et cimitoirs einz es Marches feires et autres lieux publiques ou greindre congregacion du poeple y est, diverses predicacions conteignantes heresyes et errours notoires a grant emblemessement de la foy et destruccion de loies et de lestat de Seinte Esglise a grand peril des almes du poeple et de tout le roialme Dengleterre, come plus pleinement est trovez et suffisantement provez devant le reverent pere en dieu Lercevesqe de Canterbirs et les Evesqes et autres prelatz et Maistres de Divinite et Doctours de Canoun et de Civile et grant partie del Clergie del dit roialme especialment pur celle cause assemblez; et les queles persones prechent auxint diverses matiers desclaundre pur discord et dissencion faire entre diverses estatz du dit roialme sibien temporelx come espiritelx en commocion du poeple a grand peril de tout le roialme; lesqueles prechantz citez ou somonez devant les ordinaires des lieux pur y respondre dont ils sont empeschez, ne veullent obeire a lours somonce et mandementz, ne lours monicions ne les censures de Seinte Esglise chargent point einz les despisent expressement; et enoultre par lours subtiles paroles attreent et engynont le poeple doier lours sarmons et de les maintenir en lours errours par forte main et par grantz routes; ordene est en cest parlement qe commissions du Roi soient directz as Viscontz et autres Ministres du Roi ou as autres suffisantes persones apres et solonc les certificacions de prelatz ent affaires en la Chancellarie de temps en temps darester toutz tieux precheours et lours fautours maintenours et abettours et de les tenir en arest et forte prisone tanqe ils se veullent justifier selonc reson et la ley de Seinte Esglise; et le Roi voet et commande qe le Chanceller face tieles commissions a touz les foitz qil serra par les prelatz ou ascun de eux certifie et ent requis come dessuis est dit.

S.R. II, 25, 5 Ric. II, s. 2, c. 5.

THE CHURCH

(18) *Claim of the Archbishop of Canterbury for the prelates as peers* 1388

[*Appeal in parliament against the Archbishop of York, etc.*]

...Et sur ce l'Ercevesqe de Canterbirs, pur luy et touz autres... Seignurs Espirituels du Parlement de sa Province, fist une Protestation, et la livera en mesme le Parlement en escript, dont le tenour cy ensuyt:

In Dei nomine, Amen, Cum de jure et consuetudine Regni Anglie ad Archiepiscopum Cantuariensem...necnon ceteros suos suffraganeos, Confratres, et Coepiscopos, Abbates, et Priores, aliosque Prelatos quoscumque per Baroniam de Domino nostro Rege tenentes, pertineat in Parliamentis regiis quibuscumque ut Pares Regni predicti personaliter interesse, ibidemque de Regni negotiis et aliis ibi tractari consuetis, cum ceteris dicti Regni Paribus, et aliis ibidem jus interessendi habentibus, consulere et tractare,...ac cetera facere que Parliamenti tempore ibidem iminent facienda; In quibus omnibus...Nos Willielmus Cantuariensis Archiepiscopus,...pro nobis nostrisque suffraganeis Coepiscopis et Confratribus,...protestamur, et eorum quilibet protestatur qui per se vel procuratorem hic fuerit modo presens, publice et expresse, quod intendimus et intendit,...in hoc presenti Parliamento, et aliis ut Pares Regni predicti more solito interesse, consulere, tractare,...cum ceteris jus interessendi habentibus in eisdem, statu et ordine nostris et eorum cujuslibet in omnibus semper salvis. Verum quia in presenti Parliamento agitur de nonnullis Materiis in quibus non licet nobis, aut alicui eorum, juxta sacrorum Canonum instituta, quomodolibet personaliter interesse; Ea propter, pro nobis et eorum quolibet protestamur,...quod non intendimus,...sicuti de jure non possumus nec debemus,...in presenti Parliamento dum de hujusmodi Materiis agitur vel agetur quomodolibet interesse, set nos et eorum quemlibet in ea parte penitus absentare: jure Paritatis nostre, et cujuslibet eorum interessendi in dicto Parliamento, quoad omnia et singula inibi excercenda nostris et eorum cujuslibet statui et ordini congruentia in omnibus semper salvo. Ad hec insuper protestamur, et eorum quilibet protestatur, quod propter hujusmodi absentiam non intendimus...nec eorum aliquis intendit...quod processus habiti et habendi in presenti Parliamento super materiis antedictis, in quibus non possumus nec debemus, ut premittitur, interesse, quantum ad nos et eorum

20-2

quemlibet attinet, futuris temporibus quomodolibet impugnentur, infirmentur, seu etiam revocentur.

Quelle Protestation lieu en plein Parlement, a l'instance et priere du dit Ercevesqe et les autres Prelatz susditz est enroullez ycy en Roulle du Parlement, par comandement du Roy, et assent des Seignurs Temporels et Communes.

Rot. Parl. III, 236.

(19) *The commons ask that judgments in parliament shall have force despite the absence of the clergy* 1388

Item, qe les Apelles, pursuites, acusementz, processe, jugementz, et execution, faitz et renduz en cest present Parlement soient approvez, affermez, et establiz, come chose faite duement, pur le bien et profit du Roi nostre dit Seignur et de tout son Roialme nientcontresteant qe les Seignurs Espiritels, et Procuratours des Seignurs Espirituels, soi absenteront hors du Parlement a temps des ditz Juggementz renduz, pur l'oneste et salvation de lour estat, come contenu est en une Protestation pur mesmes les Seignurs Espiritels et Procuratours livere en cest present Parlement...

Rot. Parl. III, 250 (38).

(20) *Protests of the clergy in parliament* 1389

L'Ercevesqe de Canterbirs et l'Ercevesqe d'Everwyk firent une Protestation en plein Parlement, en la forme q'ensuit: In Dei nomine, Amen. Nos Willelmus permissione divina Cantuariensis Archiepiscopus, totius Anglie Primas, et Apostolice sedis Legatus, et Nos Thomas eadem permissione Eboracensis Archiepiscopus Anglie Primas, et Apostolice sedis Legatus, protestamur publice et expresse pro Nobis et Suffraganeis nostris ac toto Clero nostrarum Cantuariensis et Eboracensis Provinciarum, quod nolumus nec intendimus alicui Statuto in presenti Parliamento nunc noviter edito, nec antiquo pretenso innovato, quatenus Statuta hujusmodi seu eorum aliquod, in restrictionem Potestatis Apostolice, aut in subversionem, enervationem, seu derogationem Ecclesiastice Libertatis tendere dinoscuntur, quomodolibet consentire, set eisdem dissentire,...et contradicimus in hiis scriptis, prout semper dissensimus,...temporibus retroactis. Et petimus quod hii nostri dissensus, protestatio, reclamatio, et contradictio per Clericum Parliamenti irrotulentur, in fidem et testimonium eorumdem. Laquelle Protestation fuist lieu overtement par comandement du Roy en plein Parlement, et a l'instance et priere des ditz Erceves-

qes, et des autres Prelatz y esteantz, est enroullez ycy en Roulle de
Parlement par comandement de nostre Seignur le Roy.

Rot. Parl. III, 264 (24).

(21) *Resistance to papal taxation* 1389
Contra Novitates et Imposiciones Papales

Rex Venerabili in Christo Patri W. eadem gratia Archiepiscopo
Cantuariensi, tocius Anglie Primati, Salutem. Licet vos non lateat
qualiter ad conservacionem Jurium et Consuetudinum Regni
nostri Anglie, ac Indempnitatis et recte Gubernacionis populi
nostri ejusdem vinculo Juramenti sumus astricti, ac de jure et
consuetudine predictis Imposicio aliqua eidem populo nostro
absque comuni Consilio et assensu ejusdem Regni fieri seu levari
non debeat ab eodem quovis modo; Supplicante insuper Nobis, in
Parliamento nostro apud Westmonasterium nuper tento, Communitate ejusdem Regni contra hujusmodi Imposiciones Clero
Regni nostri predicti per Summum Pontificem eo tempore
publicatas et exactas remedium apponere; Et quod qui extunc
ligeorum nostrorum, vel alius, aliquas Bullas Papales pro hujusmodi Imposicionibus levandis,...deferret, vel si quis de hujusmodi Imposicione...sine assensu nostri et Regni nostri predicti
colligi vel levari seu solvi fecerit, tanquam proditor Nobis in Regno
nostro predicto adjudicatur, et execucionem habet; de assensu
ejusdem Parliamenti per Nos concessum fuisset ibidem, quod
nichil foret levatum vel solutum quod in oneracionem vel dampnum
num Regni nostri predicti, vel ligeorum nostrorum ejusdem,
cedere posset: Nichilominus, jam de novo, ut accepimus, quedam
Imposicio Clero ejusdem Regni nostri, ad quoddam Subsidium
denariorum eidem Summo Pontifici ad imposicionem suam solvendum, et auctoritate vestra sive suffraganeorum vestrorum ad
mandatum vestrum levanda, absque hujusmodi comuni Consilio
et assensu Regni nostri predicti, facta existit...Vobis in fide qua
Nobis tenemini,...injungimus et mandamus, quod ab hujusmodi
novis Imposicionibus et exaccionibus Clero nostro predicto
faciendis omnino desistentes, ea omnia et singula, per vos, seu ad
mandatum vestrum, pro levacione et exaccione hujusmodi Sub-
sidii sive Imposicionis facta vel attemptata, sine dilacione et
difficultate quacumqe revocetis, et revocari faciatis, ac summas
denariorum quascumqe,...personis a quibus levate fuerunt integre et sine dilacione restitui et resolvi faciatis...Teste Rege apud
Westmonasterium, x die Octobris.

Rot. Parl. III, 405.

(22) *Statute of provisors* 1390

Item come le noble Roi Edward Aiel nostre seignur le Roi qorest a
son parlement tenuz a Westmonstier al oeutaves del Purificacion
nostre dame lan de son regne vynt et quynt, fist reciter lestatut
fait a Kardoile en temps son Aiel le Roi Edward fitz au Roi Henri
tochant lestat de Seint Esglise Dengleterre, le dit Aiel nostre
seignur le Roi qore est, del assent des grantz de son roialme en
mesme le parlement tenuz le dit an vynt et quynt esteantz, al
honour de dieu et de seint esglise et de tout son roialme ordeigna
et establist qe franks eleccions des Ercheveschies Eveschies et touz
autres dignitees et benefices electives en Engleterre se tendroient
delors en manere come eles furent grauntez par ses progenitours
et par les auncestres des autres seignurs foundours et toutz prelates
et autres gentz de seint esglise qi avoient avowesons...de done le
Roi...ou dautres seignurs et donours eussent franchement lour
collacions et presentementz: et surceo certein punyssement estoit
ordeigne en mesme lestatut pur ceux qi acceptont ascun dignite
ou benefice au contraire du dit estatut fait a Westmonstier le dit
an xxv. come devant est dit; le quele estatut nostre seignur le Roi
ad fait recitier en cest present parlement al request de sa commune en mesme le parlement; la tenure de quele estatut est tiel
come sy ensuyt:

[*Recital of the statute of* 25 *Edward III*]

Et outre ce nostre dit seignur le Roi qore est de lassent des
grantz...ad ordeigne et establi, qe de toutz Erceveschees Eveschees et autres dignites et benefices electives et autres benefices de
Seint Esglise qeconqes, qi comencerent destre voidez de fait le vint
et noefisme jour de Januer lan du regne nostre dit seignur le Roi
Richard treszime ou puis, ou qe se voidront en temps avenir deinz
le roialme Dengleterre, le dit estatut fait le dit an xxv. soit
fermement tenuz pur touz jours et mys en due execucion de temps
en temps en toutz pointz: et si ascun face ascun acceptacion dascun benefice...a contrarie de cest estatut et ce duement prove et
soit depar de la demurge exile et banny hors du roialme pur toutz
jours...et sil soit deinz le roialme soit il auxi...banny...issint
qil soit hors du roialme deinz sys semaignes procheins apres tiel
acceptacion; et si ascun recette ascun tiel banny venant depar de
la ou esteantz deinz le roialme apres les sys semaignes avantditz
conisant de ce soit auxint exile et banny...Purveu nepurqant qe
toutz yceux as queux nostre seint pier le Pape ou ses predecessours
ont purveu ascun Ercevesches (*etc.*)...del patronage des gentz

de Seint Esglise, acause de voidance devant le dit xxix. jour de Januer...eient et enjoient lour ditz Erceveschees...pur lour vies...Et si le Roi envoie par lettre ou en autre manere a la Courte de Rome al excitacion dascune persone, ou si ascun autre envoie ou prie a mesme la Courte, parount qe la contrarie de cest estatut soit fait touchant ascun Erceveschee (*etc.*)...si cely qi fait tiel excitacion ou tiel prier soit prelate de Seinte Esglise paie au Roi le value de ses temperaltees dun an, et sil soit seignur temporel paie au Roi le value de ses terres et possessions nient moebles dun an, Et sil soit autre persone destate pluis bas paie au Roi la value du benefice pur quel tiel prier soit fait et eit la prisone dun an...

Item ordeigne est et establi qe si ascun port ou envoie deinz le roialme ou le poair nostre dit seignur le Roy ascun somonces sentences ou escomengementz envers ascun persone de quel condicion qil soit a cause de la mocion...fesance assent ou execucion du dit estatut des provisours, soit il pris et arestuz et mys en prisone et forface toutz ses terres et tenementz bien et chateux pur touz jours et outre encourge la peyne de vie et de membre. Et si ascun Prelat face execucion des tieux somonces sentences ou escomengementz qe ses temperaltes soient prises et demurgent es mayns nostre dit seignur le Roy tanqe due redresse et correccion ent soit fait. Et si ascun person de meyndre estate qe prelat de quel condicion qil soit face tiel execucion soit pris et arestuz et mys en prison et eit emprisonement et face fyn et raunceon solonc la discrecion du conseill nostre dit seignur le Roy...

S.R. II, 69, 73–4, 13 Ric. II, s. 2, cc. 2, 3.

(23) *Statute of praemunire* 1393

Item come les Communes du Roialme en cest present parlement eient monstrez a nostre tresredoute seignur le Roi grevousement compleignantz, qe parla ou mesme nostre seignur le Roy et toutz ses liges deivent de droit et soloient de tout temps purseuer en la Courte mesmc nostre seignur le Roi, pur recoverer lour presentementz as Esglises prebendes et autres benefices de seinte Esglise as queux ils ount droit a presenter, la conisance de plee de quelle purseute appartient soulement a Courte mesme nostre seignur le Roy, daunciene droit de sa coronne...et qant juggement soit rendu en mesme sa Courte sur tiel plee et purseute, les Ercevesques Evesques et autres persones spiritueles qount institucion de tiele benefice deinz lour jurisdiccion sont tenuz et ont fait execucion des tieux juggementz par mandement des Rois, de tout le temps avantdit sanz interrupcion, qare autre lay persone ne poet tiele execucion faire...; Mes ore tarde diverses processes sont faitz par le seint piere le Pape et sensures descomengement sur certeins Evesques Dengleterre purceo qils ount fait execucion des tieux mandementz en overte desheritance de la dite corone et destruccion de regalie nostre dit seignur le Roi, sa Lay et tout son Roialme, si remede ne soit mys: et auxint dit est...qe le dit seint piere le Pape ad ordeigne et purpose de translater aucuns prelates de mesme le Roialme, ascuns hors du Roialme et aucuns de un Eveschee a autre deinz mesme le Roialme, saunz assent et conisance nostre seignur le Roy et saunz assent du prelat...queux prelatz sont moult profitables et necessaires a nostre dit seignur le Roi et tout son Roialme; par queux translacions sils fusent sufertz les estatutz du Roiaume serront defaitz;...et ensi mesme le Roiaume destitut sibien de counseill come davoir a final destruccion de mesme le Roialme; et ensy la Corone Dengleterre qad este si frank de tout temps qele nad hieu null terrien soveraigne, mes immediate subgit a Dieu en toutes choses tuchantz la regalie de mesme la Corone et a null autre, serroit submuys a Pape et les leys et estatutz du Roialme par luy defaitz...a sa volente,...; et disoient outre les Communes avantdites qe les dites choses ensi attemptez sount overtement encountre la corone...; Par quoy ils et touz les lieges communes...veullent estere ovec nostre dit seignur le Roi et sa dice corone...; et prierent outre a nostre seignur le Roy...qil vorroit examiner touz les seignurs en parlement sibien spiritueles come temporeles severalment et touz les estatz du parlement, coment lour semble des cases avantditz...et coment ils voillent estre en mesmes les cases...Sur quoy les seignurs temporelx ensi demandez ount respondu checun par soy, qe mesmes les cases avantdites sont overtement en derogacion de la Corone nostre seignur le Roy...et qe ils veullent estre ovec mesmes les Corone et regalie en mesmes cestes cases en especial et en touz autres cases qe serront attemptez encountre mesmes les Corone et regalie...: et outre ce demandez estoit des seignurs espirituels et illeqes esteantz et des procuratours des autres absentz de lour estre avys...queux seignurs cestassavoir Ercevesques Evesques et autres prelates...fesantz protestacions qil nest pas lour entencion de dire ne affermer qe nostre Seint Piere le Pape ne poet excomenger Evesques ne quil poet faire translacions des prelatz solonc la ley de Seinte Esglise, respoignent et diount qe si aucunes execucions des processes faitz en la Courte

du Roi come devant soient faitz par ascuny, et censures de escomengementz soient faitz encountre ascun Evesque Dengleterre
ou ascun autre liege du Roi purce qils ount fait execucion des
tieux maundementz, et qe si aucuns execucions des tieux translacions soient faitz dascuns prelatz de mesme le Roialme...siqe
lavoir et tresor du Roialme purroit estre destruit, qe ce est
encountre le Roy et sa Corone sicome est continuz en la peticion
avant nome: et semblablement les ditz procuratours...ount respondu et dit en noun et pur lour seignurs come les ditz Evesqs
ount dit et respondu...Sur quoy nostre dit seignur le Roy del
assent avantdit et a la priere de sa dit commune ad ordeigne et
establie, qe si ascun purchace ou pursue ou face purchacer ou
pursuer en la Courte de Rome ou aillours ascuns tieux translacions processes et sentences de escomengementz bulles instrumentz ou autre chose qeconqe qi touche le Roi nostre seignur
encountre luy sa corone et regalie...et ceux qi les porte deinz le
Roialme ou les resceive ou face ent notificacion ou autre execucion
qeconqe deinz mesme le Roialme ou dehors, soient ils lour
notairs procuratours meintenours abbettours fautours et con-
seillours mys hors de la proteccion nostre dit seignur le Roy, et
lours terres et tenementz biens et chatieux forfaitz au Roy nostre
seignur; et qils soient attachez par lour corps sils purront estre
trovez et amesnez devant le Roy et son Conseil pur y respondre es
cases avantditz, ou qe processe soit fait devers eux par premunire
facias en manere come est ordeigne en autres estatutz des provisours et autres qui seuent en autry Courte en derogacion de la
regalie nostre seignur le Roy.

S.R. II, 84–6, 16 Ric. II, c. 5.

(24) *The commons ask that the clergy shall have a lay proctor* 1397

Item, mesme le Marsdy les Communes monstrerent au Roy,
Coment devant ces heures pluseurs Juggementz, Ordenances,
faitz en temps des progenitours nostre Seignur le Roy en Parlement, ount este repellez et adnullez, pur ceo qe l'Estat de Clergie
ne feust present en Parlement a la faisaunce des ditz Juggementz
et Ordenances. Et pur ceo prierent au Roi, qe pur seurte a sa
persone, et salvation de son Roialme, les Prelatz et le Clergie
ferroient un Procuratour, ovec poair sufficeant pur consenter en
leur noun as toutz choses et ordenances a justifiers en cest present
Parlement; et qe sur ceo chescun Seignur Espirituel dirroit pleinement son advis. Sur qoi les ditz Seignurs Espirituelx severalment

examinez se consenterent de commetter leur plein poair generalment a une Lay persone, et nomerent en especiale Monsire
Thomas Percy, Chivaler...

Rot. Parl. III, 348 (9).

(25) *Act against Lollards. De haeretico comburendo* 1401

Item cum domino nostro Regi ex parte Prelatorum et Cleri Regni
sui Anglie in presenti parliamento sit ostensum, quod licet fides
catholica super Christum fundata et per apostolos suos et ecclesiam
sacrosanctam sufficienter determinata declarata et approbata,
hactenus per bonos ac sanctos et nobilissimos progenitores et
antecessores dicti Domini Regis in dicto Regno inter omnia Regna
mundi extiterit devocius observata, et ecclesia Anglicana per predictos inclitissimos progenitores...ad honorem Dei et tocius Regni
predicti laudabiliter dotata et in suis juribus et libertatibus susten-
tata, absque hoc quod ipsa fides seu dicta ecclesia per aliquas
doctrinas perversas vel opiniones iniquas hereticas vel erroneas
lesa fuerat vel graviter oppressa seu eciam perturbata; nichilominus tamen diversi perfidi et perversi cujusdam nove Secte, de
dicta fide sacramentis ecclesie et auctoritate ejusdem dampna-
biliter sencientes, et contra legem divinam et ecclesiasticam pre-
dicacionis officium temere usurpantes, diversas novas doctrinas et
opiniones iniquas hereticas et erroneas, eidem fidei ac sanctis
determinacionibus ecclesie sacrosancte contrarias, perverse et maliciose infra dictum Regnum in diversis locis sub simulate sanctitatis
colore predicant et docent hiis diebus publice et occulte, ac de
hujusmodi secta nephandisqe doctrinis et oppinionibus...con-
federaciones illicitas faciunt, scolas tenent et excercent, libros
conficiunt atque scribunt, populum nequiter instruunt et infor-
mant, et ad sedicionem seu insurreccionem excitant quantum
possunt, et magnas dissenciones et divisiones in populo faciunt ac
alia diversa enormia auditui horrenda indies perpetrant et com-
mittunt, in dicte fidei catholice et doctrine Ecclesie sacrosancte
subversionem diviniqe cultus diminucionem, ac eciam in destruc-
cionem status jurium et libertatum dicte ecclesie Anglicane; per
quas quidem sectam falsasqe et nephandas predicaciones doctrinas
et opiniones dictorum perfidorum et perversorum nedum maxi-
mum periculum animarum, verum eciam quam plura alia dampna
scandala et pericula eidem Regno quod absit poterunt evenire,
nisi in hac parte per regiam Magestatem uberius et celerius
succurratur; Presertim cum Diocesani dicti Regni per suam juris-

diccionem spiritualem dictos perfidos et perversos absque auxilio
dicte Regie Magestatis sufficienter corrigere nequeant nec ipsorum
maliciam refrenare, pro eo quod dicti perfidi et perversi de diocesi
in diocesim se transferunt et coram dictis diocesanis comparere
diffigiunt, ipsosque Diocesanos et suam jurisdiccionem spiritualem
ac claves Ecclesie et censuras ecclesiasticas despiciunt penitus et
contempnunt; et sic suas nephandas predicaciones et doctrinas
indies continuant et excercent, ad odium juris et racionis ordinem
atque regimen penitus destruendum: Super quibus quidem novita-
tibus et excessibus superius recitatis prelati et Clerus supradicti, ac
eciam Communitates dicti Regni in eodem parliamento existentes,
dicto Domino Regi supplicarunt ut sua dignaretur Regia celsitudo
in dicto parliamento providere de remedio oportuno; qui quidem
Dominus Rex premissa...considerans, pro conservacione dicte
fidei catholice et sustentacione dicti cultus divini, aceciam pro
salvacione status jurium et libertatum dicte ecclesie Anglicane, ad
Dei laudem ipsiusque Domini Regis meritum ac tocius Regni sui
predicti prosperitatem et honorem, et pro hujusmodi dissen-
cionibus...evitandis et ut hujusmode nephande secta...cessent
decetero et penitus destruantur, ex assensu magnatum et aliorum
procerum ejusdem Regni in dicto parliamento existencium, concessit...quod nullus infra dictum Regnum seu alia Dominia sue
regie Magestati subjecta predicare presumat publice vel occulte
absque licencia loci Diocesani petita primitus et obtenta, curatis
in suis propriis ecclesiis et personis hactenus privilegiatis, ac aliis a
jure canonico concessis dumtaxat exceptis; nec quod aliquis decetero aliquid predicet teneat doceat vel informet clam vel palam,
aut aliquem librum conficiat seu scribat contrarium fidei Catholice
seu determinacioni ecclesie sacrosancte, nec de hujusmodi secta
nephandisque doctrinis et opinionibus conventiculas aliquas faciat
vel scolas teneat vel excerceat quovismodo; aceciam quod nullus
imposterum alicui sic predicanti aut tales vel consimiles conventiculas facienti, seu scolas tenenti vel excercenti, aut talem
librum facienti seu scribenti, vel populum sic docenti informanti
vel excitanti quomodolibet faveat, nec ipsorum aliquem manu-
teneat aliqualiter vel sustentet; et quod omnes et singuli aliquos
libros seu aliquas scripturas de hujusmodi nephandis doctrinis et
opinionibus habentes, omnes hujusmodi libros et scripturas loci
Diocesano infra quadraginta dies a tempore proclamacionis istius
ordinacionis et statuti liberent seu liberari faciant realiter cum
effectu. Et si que persona vel persone cujuscumque sexus status
vel condicionis existat vel existant, decetero contra dictam ordina-

cionem regiam et Statutum predictum in premissis vel aliquo premissorum fecerit vel attemptaverit fecerint vel attemptaverint, vel hujusmodi libros in forma predicta non liberaverit vel liberaverint, tunc loci Diocesanus in sua Diocesi ipsam personam in hac parte diffamatam vel evidenter suspectam, seu ipsas personas diffamatas vel suspectas et ipsarum quamlibet, possit auctoritate dictorum ordinacionis et statuti facere arestari et sub salva custodia in suis carceribus detineri, quousque de articulis ei vel eis impositis in hac parte canonice se purgaverit seu purgaverint, vel hujusmodi nephandas sectam predicaciones doctrinas et opiniones hereticas et erroneas abjuraverit vel abjuraverint prout jura ecclesiastica exigunt et requirunt. Ita quod dictus Diocesanus per se vel Commissarios suos contra hujusmodi personas sic arestatas...procedat, et negocium hujusmodi infra tres menses post dictam arestacionem, impedimento legitimo cessante, terminet juxta canonicas sancciones. Et si aliqua persona in aliquo casu superius expressato coram loci Diocesano seu Commissariis suis canonice fuerit convicta, tunc idem Diocesanus dictam personam sic convictam pro modo culpe et secundum qualitatem delicti possit in suis carceribus facere custodiri prout et quamdiu discrecioni sue videbitur expedire; ac ulterius eandem personam preterquam in casibus quibus secundum canonicas sancciones relinqui debeat Curie seculari, ad finem pecuniarium Domino Regi solvendum ponere, prout hujusmodi finis eidem Diocesano pro modo et qualitate delicti competens videatur; In quo Casu idem Diocesanus per litteras suas patentes ipsius sigillo sigillatas de hujusmodi fine ipsum Regem in Scaccario suo cerciorare tenebitur, ad effectum quod hujusmodi finis de bonis ejusdem persone sic convicte auctoritate Regis ad opus suum exigi poterit et levari. Et si aliqua persona infra dicta Regnum et Dominia, super dictis nephandis predicacionibus *etc*....senialiter coram loci Diocesano vel Commissariis suis convicta fuerit, et hujusmodi nephandas sectam predicaciones *etc*. debite abjurare recusaverit, aut per loci Diocesanum vel Commissarios suos post abjuracionem per eandem personam factam pronunciata fuerit relapsa, ita quod secundum canonicas sancciones relinqui debeat Curie seculari, super quo credatur loci Diocesano seu Commissariis suis in hac parte, tunc Vicecomes Comitatus illius loci, et Major et Vicecomites seu Vicecomes aut Major et Ballivi Civitatis Ville vel Burgi ejusdem Comitatus, dicto Diocesano seu dictis Commissariis magis propinqui in Sentenciis per dictum Diocesanum aut Commissarios suos contra personas hujusmodi et ipsarum quamlibet proferendis,

cum ad hoc per dictum Diocesanum aut Commissarios ejusdem
fuerint requisite, personaliter sint presentes: et personas illas et
quamlibet earundem post hujusmodi sentencias prolatas recipiant,
et easdem coram populo in eminenti loco comburi faciant, ut
hujusmodi punicio metum incuciat mentibus aliorum; ne hujusmodi nephande doctrine et opiniones heretice et erronee vel
ipsarum auctores et fautores in dictis Regno et Dominiis, contra
fidem catholicam religionem Christianiam et determinacionem
Ecclesie sacrosancte quod absit, sustententur seu quomodolibet
tollerentur: In quibus omnibus et singulis premissis dicta Ordinacionem et Statutum concernentibus Vicecomes Majores et Ballivi
dictorum Comitatuum Civitatum Villarum et Burgorum dictis
Diocesanis et eorum Commissariis sint intendentes auxiliantes
eciam et faventes.

S.R. II, 125–8, 2 Hen. IV, c. 15.

(26) *Statute against heresy* 1414

Item pur ceo qe grandes rumours congregacions et insurreccions
cy en Engleterre par diverses lieges le Roy, sibien par ceux qi
furent del secte de heresie appelle Lollardrie come par autres de
lour confederacie excitacion et abbettement, se firent jatard al
entent de adnuller et subverter la foy chretiene et la leie Dieu
dedeins mesme le Roialme et auxi a destruer nostre tressovain
Seignur le Roy...Mesme nostre seignur le Roy...del advis et
assent suisditz et a la priere des ditz Communes ad ordeigne et
establie, qen primes soient les Chaunceller Tresorer Justices de
lun Banc et de lautre Justices dassises Justices du Pees Viscontz
Mairs et Baillifs des Citees et Villes et toutz autres Officers eiantz
governance du poeple qore sont et qi pur le temps serront facent
serement, en prises de lour charges et occupacions, de mettre lour
entiere peine et diligence doustier et faire oustier cesser et destruir
toutz maners heresiez et errours appellez vulgairement Lollardries,
deinz les lieux es queux ils excercent lour offices et occupacions...
Et pur tant qe la conusance des Heresies errours ou Lollardries
apparteignent as Juges de Seinte Esglise et nemye as Juges
seculers, soient tieux enditeez liveres as Ordinaries des lieux ou a
lour Commissaries par endentures entre eux affairez dedeinz x.
jours apres lour arest ou pluis tost si ceo purra estre fait pur ent
estre acquitez ou convictz par les leies de Seinte Esglise...

S.R. II, 181–2, 2 Hen. V, s. 1, c. 7.

(27) *Confiscation of the alien priories* 1414

Item prient les Communes, qe en cas qe final Pees soit pris par
entre Vous nostre soverein Seignur, et vostre Adversarie de
France, en temps a venir, et sur ceo toutz les possessions des
Priories Aliens en Engleterre esteantz, as chiefs Maisons de Reli-
geouses de par dela, as queux tieux possessions sont regardantz,
serront restitutz, damage et perde aviendroient a vostre dit
Roialme, et a vostre people de mesme le Roialme, par les graundes
fermes et apportz de Monoye quel d'an en an toutz jours apres
serroient renduz de mesmes les possessions a les chiefs Maisons
avaunt ditz, a tres graunde empoverissement de mesme vostre
Roialme en cell partie, qe Dieu defende; Plese a vostre tres
noble et tres gracious Seignurie, par consideration, qe a la commencement de la Guerre commencee par entre les ditz Roialmes,
de toutz les possessions queux voz lieges alors avoient des douns de
voz nobles progenitours en les parties de par dela deinz la jurisdiction de France, par juggement renduz en mesme le Roialme de
France, sont pur toutz jours oustez et desheritez. Et sur ceo
graciousement ordeiner en cest present Parlement, par assent de
voz Seignurs Espirituelx et Temporelx, qe toutz les possessions des
Priories Aliens en Engleterre esteantz purront demurrer en voz
mains, a Vous, et a voz heirs pur toutz jours; a l'entent, qe divines
services en les lieux avaunt ditz purront pluis duement estre faitz
par gentz Englois en temps a venir, qe n'ont este faitz avaunt ces
heures en ycelles par gentz Frraunceys. Forspris les possessions de
Priories Aliens Conventuelx, et des Priours qe sont inductz et
institutz. Et forspris qe toutz les possessions Aliens donez par le
tres gracious Seignur le Roi vostre piere, qi Dieu assoille, a le
Mestre et College de Fodrynghay, et a ses successours, de la
fundation de nostre dit Seignur le Roi vostre piere, et la fundation
de Edward Duc de York, non obstant la Pees a faire si ascun y
serra, ovesqe toutz maners franchises et libertees par nostre dit
Seignur le Roi vostre piere grauntez as ditz Mestre et College, et
a ses successours, et par Vous confermez, demurgent perpetuelment par auctorite d'icest present Parlement as ditz Mestre et
College et a ses successours, a l'oeps et entent, selonc le tenure et
purport de les Lettres patentz de nostre dit Seignur le Roi vostre
piere de la fundation du dit College, saunz ascun charge ou apport
a Vous, tres soverain Seignur, et voz heirs, ou a ascuny autres
persones ou persone apportierz. Savaunt les services duez a les
Seignurs de fees Engloys, si ascuns y soient, non obstant qe mesme

la graunte fait par nostre suis dit Seignur le Roi vostre piere as ditz Mestre et College, et a ses successours ne soy extende forsqe durant la Guerre par entre Vous, tres soverain Seignur, et vostre Adversarie de France: Et savant auxi a chescun de voz lieges, si bien Espirituelx come Temporelx, l'estat et possession q'ils ount a present en ascuns de tieux possessions Aliens, soit il purchacez ou a purchacerz, en perpetuite, ou a terme de vie, ou a terme d'ans, de les chiefs Maisons de par dela, par licence de nostre Seignur le Roi vostre tres noble piere, qi Dieu assoile, ou de Roi Edward le Tierce vostre besaiel, ou de Roi Richard le Second puis le Conquest, ou de vostre gracious doun, graunt, confirmation, ou licence euz a present en cell partie. Paiantz et supportantz toutz les charges, pensions, annuitees, et corrodies grauntez a ascuny de voz lieges par Vous, ou ascun de voz nobles progenitours, a prendre de les possessions ou Priories Aliens suis ditz.

Responsio. Le Roi le voet: Et auxi qe les ditz Mestre et College de Fodrynghay eient exemplification du Roi desoutz son graunde Seal d'iceste Petition, pur lour greindre seurete ceste partie; et ceo de l'assent des Seignurs Espirituelx et Temporelx en ceste present Parlement esteantz.

Rot. Parl. IV, 22 (21).

(28) *Failure of the attempt to exclude Beaufort from the council* 1429

Memorandum, quod licet transactis temporibus in Regno Anglie visum non fuerit ut speratur, quod aliqui Anglice nationis ad statum et dignitatem Cardinalis per sedem Apostolicam sublimati, post susceptam hujusmodi dignitatem, ad interessendum Consiliis Regiis, veluti Regis et Regni Consiliarii, hactenus admissi extiterunt: Considerata tamen Consanguinitatis propinquitate, qua reverendissimus in Cristo Pater Henricus, tituli Sancti Eusebii Presbiter Cardinalis de Anglia vulgariter nuncupatus, metuendissimi Domini nostri Regis Avunculus carissimus, ipsum Dominum nostrum Regem attingit; Industria etiam et discretione, ac fidelitate et circumspectione, quibus ipsum Cardinalem Altissimus insignivit non immerito ponderatis;...de avisamento et assensu Dominorum Spiritualium et Temporalium, in presenti Parliamento existentium concordatum fuit et unanimiter avisatum; quod prefatus Cardinalis, ad interessendum Consiliis Regis ut unus Consiliariorum suorum nedum admitti, set etiam ad intendendum eisdem Consiliis, ex parte ejusdem Domini Regis

320 THE CHURCH

requiri deberet specialiter et hortari: sub Protestatione tamen sub-
sequente, videlicet, quod quotiens aliqua materie, cause, vel
negotia, ipsum Dominum Regem, aut Regna seu Dominia sua ex
parte una, ac sedem Apostolicam ex parte altera concernentia, in
hujusmodi Consiliis Regiis communicanda et tractanda fuerint,
idem Cardinalis se ab hujusmodi Consilio absentet, ac communi-
cationi eorumdem causarum, materiarum et negotiorum non
intersit quovis modo...

Rot. Parl. IV, 338 (17).

(29) *Freedom from arrest for members of convocation* 1429

In primis quia prelati et Clerus regni Anglie ad convocacionem
evocati, eorumque servientes et familiares qui cum eisdem ad convocacionem hujusmodi veniunt, sepius ac frequenter arestantur
molestantur et inquietantur: Volens igitur dictus dominus noster
Rex pro securitate et quiete dictorum prelatorum et Cleri in hac
parte prospicere graciose, ad supplicacionem eorundem Prelatorum
et Cleri et de assensu procerum Magnatum et Communitatis predictorum, ordinavit et statuit quod vocandi in futurum ad Convocacionem Cleri pretextu brevis regii, eorumque servientes et
familiares eadem libertate sive immunitate veniendo expectando
et redeundo plene gaudeant et utantur perpetuis futuris temporibus, qua gaudent et gaudere consueverunt sive gaudere debent in
futurum proceres sive Magnates et Communitas regni Anglie ad
parliamentum domini Regis vocati sive vocandi.

S.R. II, 238, 8 Hen. VI, c. 1.

(30) *Cases before the court of the Commissary of London* 1475–89

Acta habita coram Magistro W. Wylde, Commissario reverendi in
Christo Patris Domini Thomae Kempe Londoniensis episcopi qui
onus commissionis suscepit xxix die Marcii anno domini mccccclxv.

1475

XLI. *Matfellon.* Johanna Talbot peperit absque matrimonio,
et recessit a loco ubi peperit non purificata; comparuit xvi die
Novembris, et habet 3 dominicis precedere processionem nudis
pedibus, in Kirtela capite flammiola nodata cooperto, in parochia
Sancti Dionisii.

1476

LIV. *Marie Muntar.* Rector ecclesie Sancte Marie Muntaur
communiter jurat per corpus et membra Christi, exercendo ludum

alearum temporibus illicitis, contra prohibicionem juris, et super hoc laborat fama per totam parochiam, et ad exhibendam pluralitatem; citatus fuit rector ad quartum diem Septembris; dimittitur.

LXIV. *Martini in Vynteria.* Nicholaus Haukyns non audit divina, set jacet in lecto in tempore matutinarum et misse de die dominica in dominicam, citatus fuit Nicholaus ad viii diem Marcii, quia non comparuit, ideo suspensus. (Non fiat processus.)

1480

I. *Petri Pore.* Ambrosius de Borazeos contempnit Deum dicendo, quod non est custus parcialis, et quod unum diligit melius quam alium; et contempnit beatam Mariam Katerinam et Margaretam vocando eas meretrices, ad instanciam Petri de Epecyys de eadem. xxiii die Junii Ambrosius comparuit, negavit articulum,... Ambrosius...die Julii præstitit juramentum de implendo penitentiam sibi injunctam, quod offerret ceream ponderis ii llb. apud Salvatorem, et quod solveret ecclesie sue parochiali x libras cerae, si amplius fuerit convictus super detectione.

VIII. *Botulphi Algat.* Petrus Cornelus recusat solvere clerico parochiali ibidem pro solempnisacione matrimonii...

X. *Alphegi.* Johannes Stokys utitur incantacionibus sortilegiae pro febribus.

XI. *Andr. Hol.* Johannes Pynner injecit manus violentas in dominum Petrum Gilbert in ecclesia, et fregit brachium suum, quod non potuit celebrare, et spoliasset eum in ecclesia. Vir citatur ad xxviii diem Novembris...xiiii die Decembris partes comparuerunt et compromiserunt in Mr. Lety et Bell, ita quod ferant laudum citra crastinum Hillarii.

1481

XVI. *Michaelis Cornhille, Petri Chepe.* Johannes Hungerforde et Willielmus Rowse executores testamenti Georgii Rowse recusant exhibere unum capellanum, in ecclesia sancti Petri per annum, et recusant solvere vis. viii d. legatos Willielmo Burwell...xxv die Maii partes comparuerunt, et executores habent ad crastinum corporis Christi, ad exhibendum Inventarium.

XVII. *Petri Pore.* Auicia Shrewysbury fregit fidem, in non parendo certo laudo et arbitrio inter eam et Johannem Cole coriatorem et Willielmum Standon, arbitratorios per eam juratos et electos per eam et Ricardum Bursell...

XIX. *Omnium Sanctorum Honylane.* Thomas Potynger comparuit

coram commissario in domo officii xxiii die Augusti, et prestitit juramentum, quod numquam contraxhit matrimonialiter cum Margareta Hudson...

XX. *Alphegi.* Johannes Mongoy non accedit ad ecclesiam parochialem diebus festivis ad divina audienda, et dicit, quod non vult accedere ad ecclesiam suam nisi ad placitum suum; comparuit 5 die Septembris, nescit contradicere. Continuatur ad crastinum, vi die Septembris dimittitur.

1482

XXXIV. *Omnium Sanctorum Stanyng.* Thomas Wassyngborn ipse est hereticus; dicit quod sacramentum altaris est panis materialis; xii die Septembris comparuit, negavit articulum et comparebit die Lune proximo...

XL. *Botulphi Algate.* Godfrey Speryng cum familia non audit divina in ecclesia parochiali, subtrahit decimas et jura ecclesiastica. Vir citatus ad vi diem Februarii, et presertim purificacionis Beate Marie ultimo preterito, oblaciones suas Deo et ecclesie debitas subtrahendo, sententiam excommunicationis in hac parte latae incurrendo; quia non comparuit, ideo suspensus; quia non comparuit, excommunicatus.

1489

LXXI. *Christophori.* Lodwicus Ambrose adulteravit cum Elisabetha Reynold: citatus ad xi diem Januarii, illo die non comparuit, ideo suspensus; xxii die comparuit et fatebatur crimen, et solvit pro redempcione penitencie iiis. iiiid.; unde apparitor habuit pro feodo suo xd. pro dimissione vid. et sic restat pro domino iis., et habet ad solvendum iiis. et iiiid. infra mensem.

Hale, *A series of precedents...extracted from act-books of ecclesiastical courts...*, pp. 1–17.

PART III

LOCAL GOVERNMENT

BIBLIOGRAPHY
(Chapters I–VI)

1. ORIGINAL SOURCES

P.R.O. Court rolls.

AULT, W. O. (ed.). *Court rolls of the abbey of Ramsey and of the honor of Clare.* New Haven, Yale University Press, 1928.

FOWLER, G. H. (ed.). *Rolls from the office of the sheriff of Beds. and Bucks.* 1332–4. Beds. Historical Record Society, 1929.

GROSS, C. (ed.). *Select cases from the coroners' rolls,* 1265–1413, S.S. vol. IX. 1895.

MAITLAND, F. W. (ed.). *The court baron,* S.S. vol. IV. 1890.

—— *Select pleas in manorial...courts,* vol. I, S.S. vol. II. 1888.

Parliamentary writs, vol. II, div. ii. London, 1830–4.

Proceedings and ordinances of the privy council. London, 1834–7.

Rotuli parliamentorum. London, 1783.

Statutes of the realm. London, 1810–28.

TURNER, G. J. (ed.). *Select pleas of the forest,* S.S. vol. XIII. 1899.

2. SECONDARY AUTHORITIES

BEARD, C. A. *The office of justice of the peace in England.* New York, Columbia University Press, 1904.

CAM, H. M. *The hundred and the hundred rolls.* London, 1930.

HEARNSHAW, F. J. C. *Leet jurisdiction in England....* Southampton, 1908.

HOLDSWORTH, W. S. *A history of English law,* vol. I, 3rd edition. 1922.

MORRIS, W. A. *The early English county court, in University of California publications in history,* vol. XIV, no. 2. 1926.

—— *The frankpledge system, in Harvard historical studies,* vol. XIV. New York, 1910.

—— *The medieval English sheriff to 1300.* Manchester, 1927.

PUTNAM, B. H. *The enforcement of the statutes of labourers.* New York, Columbia University Press, 1908.

STEWART-BROWN, R. *Calendar of county court, city court and eyre rolls of Chester,* 1259–97. Chetham Society, 1925.

TOUT, T. F. *Chapters in the administrative history of medieval England.* Manchester, 1920–30.

324 LOCAL GOVERNMENT

3. ARTICLES

CAM, H. M. "Some early inquests before 'Custodes pacis'", *E.H.R.* XL, 1925.

—— "The Quo Warranto proceedings under Edward I", *History*, XI, July, 1926.

CRUMP, C. G. and JOHNSON, C. "The powers of justices of the peace", *E.H.R.* XXVII, 1912.

GIBSON, S. T. "The escheatries, 1327–41", *E.H.R.* XXXVI, 1921.

JENKINSON, H. "Plea rolls of the medieval county courts", *Cambridge Historical Journal*, I, no. I, 1923.

JENKINSON, H. and MILLS, M. H. "Rolls from a sheriff's office in the fourteenth century", *E.H.R.* XLIII, 1928.

PLUCKNETT, T. F. T. "New light on the old county court", *Harvard Law Review*, XLII, 1928–9.

PUTNAM, B. H. "The justices of labourers in the fourteenth century", *E.H.R.* XXI, 1906.

—— "Early records of the justices of the peace", *E.H.R.* XXVIII, 1913.

—— "The transformation of the keepers of the peace into justices of the peace, 1327–80", *Trans. R.H.S.* 4th series, XII, 1929.

SILLEM, R. "Commissions of the peace, 1380–1485", *Bulletin of the Institute of Historical Research*, X, no. 29, 1932.

WOODBINE, G. E. "County court rolls and county court records", *Harvard Law Review*, XLIII, 1929–30, and answer of T. F. T. Plucknett with reference to his article quoted above.

WRIGHT, E. C. "Common law in the thirteenth-century English royal forest", *Speculum*, III, 1928.

CHAPTER I

THE JUSTICES OF THE PEACE

INTRODUCTION

The chief interest in the history of local government in the fourteenth and fifteenth centuries is in the emergence and amazing development of the office of the justice of the peace. The origin of the office is to be found in the appointment of keepers of the peace, and after a long transitional period these officials were involved in administrative and judicial work which increased in importance. As justices of the peace, after the middle of the fourteenth century, they had manifold duties and extensive powers, some of which were transferred from older officials, such as the sheriffs; before the end of the middle ages the justices had in fact superseded nearly all the older machinery of local government, and it is not surprising that the Tudors made great use of the office.

We first hear of the appointment of knights as keepers of the peace in 1195, when they were to assist the sheriff to maintain order. This practice continued during the thirteenth century, when knights were chosen at different times to carry out administrative as well as judicial work. This was especially the policy of Edward I, and in 1285 justices were also set up to help in the enforcement of the statute of Winchester.[1] At first there was no regular system (1), but at the end of Edward II's reign a general commission was issued, instituting keepers of the peace in each county; this was followed in 1327 (2) and later, and in 1328 they were given authority to punish offenders (3). Their powers were extended during the following years; they began to work in concert with the justices of assize, and they could punish local officials for certain matters. Their judicial powers were further defined in 1332 (4), and in 1344 when they, together with men learned in the law, were to hear and determine felonies and trespasses (5).

The most interesting phase, however, is the transitional period after the middle of the century, when the keepers of the peace were charged with the administration of the labour legislation

[1] Miss Cam, in her article in *E.H.R.* 1925, gives documents illustrating the attempts made in 1277 and 1308 to enforce the statute of Winchester by inquests held before the *custodes pacis*.

which attempted to deal with the economic troubles of the time. In 1349 and 1351 the ordinance and then the statute of labourers were issued, and the next years saw various methods for enforcing their administration.[1] From March, 1351, until December, 1352, joint commissions for peace and labour were issued, but these were followed by separate commissions which lasted until November, 1359; during these seven years, however, the same people might be serving on both commissions in any county. A change was made in 1359,[2] when the plan of having separate justices of labour was given up and the work transferred to the keepers of the peace. The statutes of 1361(7) and 1368(9) gave permanent standing to the justices of the peace, as they came to be called, three or four of whom were assigned in each county with one lord to keep the peace and to hear and determine felonies and trespasses; after 1363 they were holding their sessions four times a year(8); and they received four shillings a day during sessions.[3]

From this time the position of the justices was assured. There was at first some uncertainty and dispute over the form of appointment; the opposition in parliament wished the office to be elective, but the king was determined to retain the right of nomination in council, as seen in Edward III's answer to a petition of the commons in 1376(10). In 1380, after renewed complaints, a commission was drawn up by the great council(11), defining clearly the powers of the justices, and the sheriff was ordered to take their oath(12). Ten years later it was provided by statute that in addition to the justices of assize there should be six justices of the peace in each county(13), and the number was increased to eight in 1390. In the next century the status and position of the justices were further defined: among other orders, they were to be resident in their counties(18), and to be in possession of landed property to the annual value of twenty pounds(19).

During this century the duties of the justices were extended along the lines already laid down in fourteenth-century legislation (14–16, 20).[4] They had the supervision of many economic tasks, as in the enforcement of labour regulations(17), control of industry, and regulation of prices. They had the increasingly onerous task

[1] B. H. Putnam, *The enforcement of the statutes of labourers*, pp. 10–17.
[2] *Ibid.* Appendix, pp. 31–2.
[3] Cf. Tout, *Chapters*, III, 183–4.
[4] C. A. Beard, *The office of justice of the peace in England*, pp. 58–71.

of maintaining good order in the country, and were partly responsible for the administration of laws against heresy. In judicial matters the justices were gradually taking over the powers of the sheriffs, and were more and more being made responsible for the misdeeds of local officials.[1] At the same time the frequent complaints against the justices themselves suggest that they were not always able or willing to carry out the work entrusted to them; and it is here that there was the greatest change in Tudor times. The fifteenth-century legislation was a precedent for the extensive use of the office of justice of the peace later; in the next period the office was itself reformed and brought into line with the strong centralising policy of the Tudors.

(1) *The keepers of the peace* 1307

De custodibus pacis per Angliam constitutis.

Rex dilectis et fidelibus suis Ricardo de Wyndesore Willelmo de Brok et Vicecomiti Middlesex', salutem. Cum pro quibusdam arduis negociis nos et regnum nostrum tangentibus ad partes transmarinas simus cum Dei auxilio in proximo profecturi, per quod ea affectuosius desideramus quod pax nostra maxime dum extra regnum fuerimus firmiter manuteneatur...assignamus vos custodes pacis nostre in Comitatu predicto vobis firmiter injungendo mandantes ne vos extra Comitatum predictum in nostra absencia transferatis, set personaliter in eodem moram faciatis, eundo de loco in locum per Comitatum predictum, tam infra libertates quam extra quociens necesse fuerit pro pace nostra ibidem firmiter conservanda. Ita videlicet quod in singulis Civitatibus, Burgis, Villis Mercatoriis, Hundredis, Wapenthaciis, et aliis locis ubi videritis expedire publice proclamari faciatis, quod pax nostra et statutum Wyntonie in singulis articulis et similiter ea que continentur in brevibus et mandatis celebris memorie Domini Edwardi quondam Regis Anglie patris nostri nuper singulis Vicecomitibus regni Anglie inde directis firmiter...observetur, et si forte aliquod periculum turbacionis pacis nostre alicubi in Comitatu predicto de novo emergere quod absit vel aliquos contrarios aut rebelles, qui huic mandato nostro pererere contempserint, inveniri contigerit, tunc assumpto vobiscum si necesse fuerit posse Comitatus predicti periculo hujusmodi caute et viriliter resistatis et tales contrarios et rebelles per eorum corpora arestetis et salvo

[1] See below, pp. 343–4.

et secure custodiatis, donec aliud a nobis inde habueritis in mandatis, volumus eciam...quod in singulis locis predictis publice distincte et aperte scire faciatis omnibus et singulis ex parte nostra quod nos monetam nostram tanti ponderis tantique valoris in omnibus nunc existere quanti moneta dicti patris nostri fuit, quodque in eadem moneta nominis nostri superscripcio existit veraciter attendentes, nolumus monetam illam mutare seu cambire...

Et ut hec in singulis Civitatibus, Burgis, et Villis mercatoriis in Comitatu predicto firmiter...observentur, ad eligendos et assignandos nomine nostro de qualibet Civitate duos Cives, et de quolibet Burgo duos Burgenses, necnon de qualibet Villa mercatoria...duos probos et legales homines qui prestito juramento coram vobis premissa omnia et singula in Civitatibus, Burgis, et Villis predictis districte et firmiter faciatis observari, vobis tenore presencium committimus potestatem, volumus insuper quod si quos huic ordinacioni nostre contrarios aut rebelles, aut eciam forestallarios aliquos...inveneritis eos per eorum corpora attachiari et salvo custodiri faciatis, donec aliud inde preceperimus. Et ideo vobis mandamus firmiter injungentes quod ad premissa omnia et singula facienda...in forma predicta cum diligencia qua poteritis intendatis, Taliter super hiis vos habentes quod per vestram diligenciam..., premissa in omnibus et singulis suis articulis in Comitatu predicto firmiter observentur. In cujus etc. Teste Rege apud Westmonasterium xxiiii. die Decembris, etc.

Parliamentary writs, ii, ii, pt. 2, p. 8.

(2) *The keepers of the peace* 1327

Item pur la pees meultz garder et meyntener, le Roi veot qen chescun Countee qe bones gentz et loialx, queux ne sont mye meyntenours de malveis baretz en pays, soient assignez a la garde de la pees.

S.R. i, 257, i Ed. III, s. 2, c. 16.

(3) *Powers of justices assigned to keep the peace* 1328

Et quant a la garde de la pees en temps avenir, acorde est et establi qe les estatuz faites en temps passez, ovesqe lestatut de Wyncestre, soient tenuz et gardez en touz pointz; ajouste au dit estatut de Wyncestre, la ou contenuz est en la fin, qe Justices assignez eient poair denquere des defautes et des reporter au Roi en parlement dont home nad pas veu issue, qe les ditz Justices assignez eient poair de punir les desobeissantz et contrevenantz.

S.R. i, 259, 2 Ed. III, c. 6.

(4) *Judicial powers given to keepers of the peace* 1332

Cestes choses issint pronunciez par les ditz Ercevesqe et Evesqe, si pronuncia Monsire Geffrei le Scrope, par le comandement nostre Seignur le Roi, et en sa presence et des touz les autres Prelatz, Countes, Barons, et autres Grantz, Coment le Roi avoit entendu, et si feust ce chose conue as touz, qe divers Gentz, diffuantz la Lei, feurent levez en grant Compaignies en destruantz les liges Gentz nostre Seignur le Roi, auxi bien les Gentz de Seinte Esglise, les Justices le Roi, come autres; Prenantz acuns de eux et detenauntz en prisone, tant q'ils avoient receu pur lur vies sauver greves Fyns et Raunceouns a la volunte des ditz Mesfesours, et acuns mettantz a la mort, acuns desrobeaunz de lur biens et chatelx, et fesant plusours autres malx et felonies, en despit du Roi et en affrai de sa pees, et destructioun de son poeple. Et sur ce chargea le dit Monsire Geffrei de par nostre Seignur le Roi touz les ditz Prelatz, Countes, Barouns, et autres Grantz, en les fois et ligeaunces queux ils devoient a nostre Seignur le Roi, de lui conseiller, auxi bien de son aler devers la Terre Seinte, quel il desira sovereynement a faire par lur bons consealx, come coment sa pees poet mielz estre garde,...

Et pur ce qe avis feust a les ditz Prelatz, q'il ne atteneit pas proprement a eux de conseiler du garde de la pees,...si alerent mesmes les Prelatz et les Procuratours de la Clergie par eux mesmes a conseiler des choses susdites; et les ditz Countes, Barouns, et autres Grantz, par eux mesmes. Lesqueux Countes, Barouns, et autres Grantz puis revindrent, et respondirent touz au Roi par la bouche Monsire Henri de Beaumount, Qe totes autres choses lessez, homme ordinast a de primes de la garde de la pees, et qe l'empeschement des ditz malveis feust ouste par lei, par force, et par totes les autres bones voies qe avis serroit a nostre Seignur le Roi, et a son bon Conseil. Et ordinerent les ditz Countes...en ceste manere, Q'en chescun Counte d'Engleterre soient des plus Grantz de mesme le Counte assignez Gardeins de mesme le Counte par Commission le Roi, et qe les Gardeins de la pees einz ces houres assignez, Viscountes, et touz les gentz des Countez ou ils en serrount assignez, soient entendauntz a les ditz Grantz pur la dite pees garder, auxi avant come au corps nostre

Seignur le Roi mesmes s'il y feust. Et qe les ditz Grantz facent venir devant eux quatre hommes, et le Provost de chescune Ville, et facent arraier les gentz de mesmes les Villes, issint qe si gentz armez, ou autres de qi homme eit suspecioun de mal, passent par mesmes les Villes en compaignies, ou autrement; qe les ditz gentz des Villes facent lever Hu et Crie, et les pursuent de Ville en Ville, de Hundred' en Hundred', et de Counte en Counte, et les arestetent, preignent, et sauvement gardent; Et de lur fait ent certifient les ditz Grantz. Et s'il aveigne qe les gentz des dites Villes ne puissent arester tielx passantz, qe adonqes meyntenant certifient les ditz Grantz ou ils serront trovez; Et mesmes les Grantz, od tot le poer du Counte, les pursuent du Counte en Counte, tant q'ils soient pris. Et eient les ditz Grantz poer d'oier et terminer auxi bien felonies faites par ceux qi sont issint a arester et prendre, come par ceux qi serront enditez devant eux: Et auxint de punir ceux q'ils troveront desobeisantz a eux,...Et qe nostre Seignur le Roi chivauche en sa terre du Counte en Counte, et doigne es tout coment les ditz Grantz et autres se portent entour le chastiement des tielx Mesfesours, et face punir ceux q'il en trovera coupables ou desobeisantz. Et s'il busoigne qe les ditz Grantz nulle part soient afforcez, qe nostre Seignur le Roi mande des soens dont il s'affie de les afforcer, ou autrement ordeyne, issint totefoiz qe les ditz malveys soient chastiez. Lesqueles choses issint ordinez par les ditz Countes, Barouns, et autres Grantz, luez devant nostre Seignur le Roi, et les Prelatz, Chivalers des Countez, et les Gentz du Commun, furent pleisantz a eux touz, et par nostre Seignur le Roi, Prelatz, Countes, Barouns et autres Grantz, et auxint par les Chivalers des Countez, et Gentz du Commun, furent pleynement assentuz et acordez. Et auxint feust acorde et assentu par nostre Seignur le Roi, *etc.*...qe une Sentence ordine par les Prelatz et la Clergie feust pronuncie en l'Eglise de Seint Poul de Loundres, et mande en totes les Evesches d'Engleterre a pronuncier, la fourme de quele Sentence a pronuncier s'ensuyt.

Rot. Parl. II, 64 (5).

(5) *Keepers of the peace* 1344

Et aussint, qe deux ou trois des mieultz vauetz des Countees, soient assignez gardeins de la pees par commissions le Roi; et quele heure qe mestier serra, mesmes ceux ovesqes autres sages et apris de la leye soient assignez par commission le Roi doier et terminer felonies et trespas faites contre la pees en mesmes les Countees, et punissement faire resonablement, solonc la manere du fait.

S.R. I, 301, 18 Ed. III, s. 2, c. 2.

(6) *Appointment of keepers of the peace and justices of labour* 1354

A Nostre Seignur le Roi prie la Commune, Qe les Gardeyns de la Pees soient des plus loialx, sages, et sufficeantz des Countees, demorantz en meisme le Countee et nient foreins lieux. Et des Justices de Laborers en meisme le manere. Et qe nul Justice soit assigne par commission s'il ne soit sufficeant d'estat et condition a respoundre au Roi et au poeple. Et qe les Nouns des Justices des Laborers soient veues et examinez par le Chaunceller, et Tresorer, et Justices de l'un Baunk ou de l'autre, et en presence des Chivalers du Countee; et ceux qi sont covenables demoergent pur tiel noumbre come busoigne solonc la graundure du pais. Et en lieu de ceux qi serront oustez soient autres nomez par les ditz Chivalers, queux ne soient mye oustez sanz especial commandement nostre Seignur le Roi, ou resonable cause tesmoignee par lour compaignons. Et qe les ditz Justices soient chargez a seer a meyns quarant jours en l'an, ou plus s'il bosoigne. Et q'ils facent bone execution de l'Estatut et Ordinances ent faitz. Et qe les Gardeyns de la Pees et les Justices des Laborers soient uns la ou bonement poet estre fait.

Responsio. Quant a la primere Petition, ele est resonable, et par tant nostre Seignur le Roi voet q'ele soit ottroie.

Rot. Parl. II, 257 (17).

(7) *Powers of the justices of the peace* 1361

Statutum factum in parliamento tento apud Westmonasterium anno xxxiiij[to].

Ces sont les choses queles nostre Seignur le Roy Prelatz Seignours et la commune ont ordinez en ceste present parlement tenuz a Westmustier le dymenge preschein devant la feste de la Conversion de Seint Poul a tenir et publier overtement parmy le Roialme. Cestassavoir. Primerement que en chescun Countee Dengleterre soient assignez pur la garde de la pees un Seignur et ovesque lui trois ou quatre des meultz vauez du Countee ensemblement ove ascuns sages de la ley, et eient poer de restreindre les meffesours, riotours, et touz auters barettours et de les pursuir, arester, prendre, chastier selonc leur trespas ou mesprision et de faire emprisoner et duement punir selonc la ley et custumes du roialme et selonc ce qils verront mieltz affaire par lour discrescions et bon avisement, et auxint de eux enformer et denquere de touz ceux qi ont este pilours et robeours es parties de dela, et sont ore revenuz et vont vagantz et ne voillent travailler come ils soleient avant ces hours, et de prendre et arester touz ceux qils purront trover par enditement ou par suspecion et les mettre en prisone, et de prendre de touz ceux qi sont de bone fame ou ils serront trovez souffisant seurete et meinprise de lour bon port devers le Roi et son poeple, et les auters duement punir au fin que le poeple ne soit par tieux riotours troble nendamage ne la pees enblemy ne marchantz nauters passantz par les hautes chemyns du roialme destourbez ne abaiez du peril que purra avenir de tieux meffesours. et auxint etc.

Printed in *E.H.R.* xxvii, 1912, 234, from Statute roll; article by C. G. Crump and C. Johnson.

(8) *Times of sessions of the justices of the peace* 1362

Item qe en les commissions des Justices de la pees et des laborers, soit faite expresse mencion qe mesmes les Justices facent lour Sessions quaterfoitz par an; cestassavoir une session deinz les Oetaves de la Tiphaine, la secunde deinz la secunde simaigne de demy Quaresme, le tierce entre les festes de Pentecoste, et de Seint Johan Baptistre, le quart deinz les oet jours de Seint Michel.

S.R. i, 374, 36 Ed. III, c. 12.

(9) *Enforcement of the statute of labourers* 1368

Item, est accorde et assentu, qe lestatut et ordenance faitz de laborers et artificers, soient tenuz et gardez et duement executz; et sur ycels soient commissions faites as Justices de la pees en chescun Contee, doier et terminer les pointz du dit estatut, et de agarder damages al suite de partie, solonc la quantite de trespas.

S.R. i, 388, 42 Ed. III, c. 6.

(10) *The appointment of justices of the peace* 1376

Item, prie la Commune, qe come les Justices de la Pees sont souvent assignez par brocage des Meyntenours du pays qi font grande outrage par leur mayntenance as povres gentz du pays, et sont communement mayntenours de les mesfesours; Supplie la Commune, qe les ditz Justicz soient nomez en chescun Countee par les Seignurs, Chivalers des Countees en Parlement; et q'ils soient sermentez devant le Conseil le Roi en mesme la manere come autres gentz sont, et q'ils ne soient remuez saunz assent du Parlement; quele chose tournera a grande profit du Roi: Et qe Gages y soient assignez as ditz Justicz pur leur Sessions faire covenables; qar saunz Gage ils n'ont cure de faire leur Sessions, q'est grande perde au Roi.

Responsio. Ils serront nomez par le Roi et son continuel Conseil; et quant as Gaiges, le Roi s'advisera.

Rot. Parl. ii, 333 (67). (Cf. *Rot. Parl.* iii, 44 (50); 1378.)

(11) *Commission of the justices of the peace* 1380

Et fait a remembrer, qe en Terme de Pasqe proschein apres le fyn de cest Parlement, les Seignurs Temporelx assemblez a West-monstier a un grant Conseil illoeqes tenuz, si firent autre foitz lire devant eulx l'enroullement de l'Ordinance faite en cest Parle-ment touchant la poair des Justices de la Paix, en presence de Monsire d'Espaigne, Chanceller, Tresorier, et de touz les Justices, et illoeqes mesmes les Seignurs Temporelx firent Declaration de poair des Justices de la Paix avant ditz. Qar ils y disoient, qe lour entente estoit en dit Parlement coment ce n'estoit clerement enroullez a celle foitz, Qe entre autres articles et pointz, mesmes les Justices de la Paix auroient poair d'oier et terminer toutes maneres d'Extorsions si bien a la suite le Roi, come de partie, et de certaines autres articles comprises en dit poair. Ils y firent auxint declaration, et sur ce estoit une certaine note faite de la Commission, par l'advis de touz les Justices nostre Seignur le Roy si bien de l'un Bank come de l'autre lors presentz illoeqes: Et celle note lue en dit Conseil devant eulx touz, assentirent a ycelle note, et lour pleust bien qe ce passast le Seal le Roy souz celle forme. Et issint furent les Commissions faites enseales et envoiez a chescun Countee d'Engleterre, ensemble avec un Brief direct al Viscont de chescun Countee, del prendre les serementz des Commissioners de bien et loialment user lour Commission, et droit faire a chescune persone, si bien as povres come as riches,...Desqueux Brief et Cedule, qe furent auxint faites par l'advis du Conseil le Roi, et de la note de la Commission avant dite, les tenours ou copies s'ensuent de mot a mot:

Rex Dilectis et Fidelibus suis A.B.C.D. etc. Salutem. Sciatis, quod assignavimus vos conjunctim et divisim ad Pacem nostram, necnon Statuta apud Wyntoniam, Norhamtunam, et Westmonasterium, pro conservatione Pacis ejusdem edita, in omnibus et singulis suis articulis in Comitatu H. tam infra Libertates quam extra, custodiendam et custodiri faciendam: et ad omnes illos quos contra formam Statutorum predictorum delinquentes inveneritis castigandos et puniendos prout secundum formam Statutorum eorundem fuerit faciendum. Et ad omnes illos qui aliquibus de populo nostro de corporibus suis vel de incendio Domorum suarum minas fecerint, ad sufficientem securitatem de pace et bono gestu suo erga Nos et populum nostrum inveniendos coram vobis venire, et si hujusmodi securitatem invenire recusaverint, tunc eos in prisonis nostris quousque hujusmodi securitatem invenerint salvo custodiri faciendos. Assignavimus etiam vos quinque, quatuor, tres et duos vestrum, Justiciarios nostros ad inquirendum per sacramentum proborum et legalium hominum in Comitatu predicto,...per quos rei veritas melius sciri poterit, de quibuscumqe latrociniis notorie vel aperte, ac mahemiis, et hominum interfectionibus per insidias vel maliciam precogitatam, ac murdris, et aliis feloniis,...in Comitatu predicto per quoscumque et qualitercumque factis sive perpetratis, et que exnunc ibidem fieri contingat. Et etiam de omnibus illis qui in conventiculis contra pacem nostram et in perturbacionem populi nostri seu vi armata ierint vel equitaverint, seu exnunc ire vel equitare presumpserint...Et etiam de hiis qui capiciis, et alia liberata de unica secta, per confederationem et pro manutenentia, contra defensionem ac formam Ordinationum et Statutorum inde ante hec tempora factorum, usi fuerint, ac aliis hujusmodi liberata imposterum utentibus. Ac etiam de Hostellariis, et aliis qui in abusu Mensurarum et Ponderum ac in venditione Victualium; et etiam de quibuscumqe Operariis, Artificibus, et Servitoribus, et aliis qui contra formam Ordinationum et Statutorum...inde factorum delinquerint, vel attemptaverint, in Comitatu predicto, vel exnunc delinquere vel attemptare presumpserint. Et ad processus versus omnes quos de Feloniis hujusmodi contigerit indictari quousque capiantur,...faciendo...Ac extorsiones et regratarias predictas, et omnia alia que per hujusmodi Hostellarios et

alios...in aliquo presumpta vel attemptata fuerint, tam ad
sectam nostram quam aliorum quorumcumque, coram vobis pro
Nobis vel pro seipsis conqueri vel prosequi volentium, audiendas
et terminandas; et ad eosdem Operarios...per fines, redemp-
tiones, et amerciamenta, et alio modo, pro delictis suis,...casti-
gandos et puniendos, secundum legem et consuetudinem Regni
nostri Anglie, ac formam Ordinationum et Statutorum predictorum. Proviso semper, quod si casus difficultatis super deter-
minatione Extorsionum hujusmodi coram vobis evenire contigerit,
quod ad judicium inde nisi in presentia unius Justiciariorum
nostrorum de uno vel de altero Banco, aut Justiciariorum nostrorum ad Assisas in Comitatu predicto capiendas assignatorum,
coram vobis minime procedatur...
Et ideo vobis et cuilibet vestrum mandamus, quod circa Custodiam Pacis et Statutorum predictorum diligenter intendatis, et
ad certos dies et loca, quos vos quinque, quatuor, tres, vel duo
vestrum ad hoc provideritis, inquisiciones super premissis factas,
et premissa omnia et singula audiatis et terminetis, ac modo
debito et effectualiter expleatis, in forma supradicta: Facturi inde
quod ad Justiciam pertinet, secundum legem et consuetudinem
Regni nostri Anglie. Salvis Nobis amerciamentis et aliis ad Nos
inde spectantibus. Mandavimus enim Vicecomiti nostro Comitatus predicti, quod ad certos dies et loca, quos vos quinque
etc. vel duo vestrum ei scire faciatis, venire faciat coram vobis
quinque etc. et duobus vestrum, tot et tales probos et legales
homines de Balliva sua, tam infra Libertates quam extra, per quos
rei veritas in premissis melius sciri poterit et inquiri. Et insuper
vobis et cuilibet vestrum super salva Custodia Pacis et Statutorum
predictorum pareat et intendat, quando et prout per vos vel
aliquem vestrum fuerit super hoc ex parte nostra rationabiliter
premunitus.
...In cujus etc.
Teste Rege apud Westmonasterium, xxvi die Maii.
Per ipsum Regem et Consilium.
Rot. Parl. III, 84–5 (40).

[*The royal letter to the sheriff was sent on 27 May, followed by
the form of oath to be taken by the justices.*]

(12) *The oath of the justices of the peace* 1380

Vous jurrez, qe bien et loialment servirez le Roy en l'office de
Gardein de la Paix, et de Justicierie des Artificers, Laborers, Pois

et Mesures, et d'oier et terminer les tortz et grevances faitz au Roi et a son poeple, et des autres choses quelconqes comprises pluis pleinement en la Commission a vous et autres voz compaignons ent fait; selonc voz seu et poair ent ferrez avoir plein droit as touz, si bien as povres come as riches, si qe pur hayour, favour, amistee, ou estat de nulluy persone, ne pur bienfait, doun, ou promesse qe vous soit ou serra fait en temps a venir, n'autrement par art ou engyn quelconqe, Droiture nient respiterez ne delaierez a nulluy, contre reson, ne contre les Loies, Estatutz, Ordinances, et Custumes del Roialme. Mes sanz regard avoir de persone quelconqe, loialment ent frez droit a touz, selonc les Lois. . . Et conseil le Roi touchant ceux qi serront enditez devant vous, celerez, et auxint compellerez les Jurrez en Enquestes de le celer de lour part loialment, et touz les Recordz et Proces qe serront faitz devant vous ferrez mettre en bone et seure garde, et les Extretes des fins et amerciementz, et d'autres profitz ent au Roi appurtenantz, ferrez entierment mettre en escript endentee, de temps en temps, dont l'une partie ferrez deliverer a Viscount del Countee, et l'autre partie ent ferrez envoier seurement en l'Escheqier le Roi, pur y charger le Viscount sur son accompt. Et touz les Briefs qe vous vendront souz le Grant Seal le Roi loialment servirez, et ferrez executer sanz delaie. Et qe vous ne prendrez ne resceiverez nul Clerc devers vous pur faire escrire ou garder les Recordes et Proces avant dices, s'il ne soit primerement jurez devant vous de celer le conseil le Roi, et de faire et perfournir bien et loialment de sa part qant qe a son office et degree apent en celle partie, si Dieu vous aide, et ses Seintz.

Rot. Parl. III, 85 (41).

(13) *Six justices of the peace in each county* 1388

Item ordeinez est et assentuz qen chescun commission des Justices de la Paix ne soient assignez qe sys Justices, outre les Justices dassises; et qe les ditz sys Justices tiegnent lour sessions en chescun quarter del an au meyns, et ce par trois jours si mestier soit sur peyne destre puniz solonc ladvys du conseil le Roy a suyte de chescun qi soy vorra pleindre; et enquergent diligealment entre autres choses touchantz lour offices si les ditz Meirs Baillifs Seneschalx et Conestables et auxint gaolers ont duement faitz execucion des ditz ordenances et estatuts des servantz et laborers mendinantz et vagerantz, et punissent ceux qi sont punissables par la dice peyne de C s. par mesme la peyne; . . . et pregne chescun des ditz Justices pur lour gages iiijs. le jour pur le temps de lour ditz sessions et lour clerc, deux s. le jour des fyns et amerciementz surdantz et provenantz de mesmes les sessions, par mayns des Viscontz; et qe les seignurs des franchises soient contributoirs as ditz gages solonc lafferant de lour part des fyns et amercimentz susditz; et qe null Seneschall de seignur soit assigne en null des ditz commissions et qe null associacion soit faite as Justices de la paix apres lour primer commission. Et nest pas lentencion de cest estatut qe les Justices de lun bank et de lautre ne les sergeantz de ley en cas qils soient nomez en les ditz commissions soient tenuz par force de cest estatut de tenir les ditz sessions quatre foitz par an come sont les autres Commissioners qi sont continuelment demurrantz en paiis mes qils le facent qant ils a ce poent bonement entendre.

S.R. ii, 58–9, 12 Ric. II, c. 10.

(14) *Powers of the justices of the peace; forcible entries and riots* 1391

Item accordez est et assentuz qe lestatuz et ordeinances faitz et nient repellez de ceux qi font entrees a forte mayn en terres et tenementz ou autres possessions qeconqes et lour teignent einz ove force, et auxint de ceux qi font insurreccions ou grantz chivaches rioutes routes ou assemblees en destourbance de la pees ou de la commune ley ou en affray du poeple, soient tenuz et gardez et pleynement executz; ajouste a ycelles qe a toutz les foitz qe tielx forcibles entrees soient faitz, et pleint en veigne a Justices de la pees ou a ascun de eux qe mesmes les Justices ou Justice preignent ou preigne poair sufficeant du Counte, et voisent ou voise al lieu ou tiel force soit fait, et sils troevent ou troeve ascuns qi teignent tiel lieu forciblement apres tiel entree faitz, soient pris et mys en proscheine gaole a y demurer convict par record de mesmes les Justices ou Justice tanqils eient fait fyn et ranceon au Roy; et qe toutz gentz du Counte sibien Viscont come autres soient entendantz as ditz Justices pur aler et enforcier mesmes les Justices pur arester tielx malfesours sur peine demprisonement et de faire fyn au Roy. Et en mesme le manere soit fait de ceux qi font tielx forcibles entrees en benefices ou offices de seinte Esglise.

S.R. ii, 78, 15 Ric. II, c. 2. (This law was extended in the statute 13 Hen. IV, c. 7 (see below); and again, at great length, in the statute 2 Hen. V, s. 1, c. 8; and statute 8 Hen. VI, c. 9.)

(15) *Justices of the peace; gaol delivery* 1394

Item pur ceo qe larons notoirement diffamez et autres prisez ove mainoeure pur long demure en prisone apres ceo qils sont arestuz sont deliverez par chartres et favorables enquestes procurez a grant anientissement du poeple: Accordez est et assentuz qen chescune commission de la pees parmy le roialme ou y bosoignera soient assignez deux hommes de ley de mesme le Counte ou tiel commission se fra, daler et proceder a deliverance des tielx larons et felons tant et si sovent come bon lour semblera.

S.R. ii, 90, 17 Ric. II, c. 10.

(16) *Powers of the justices of the peace; the suppression of riots* 1411

Item ordeignez est et establiz, qe si aucun riot assemblee ou rout des gentz encontre la loie se face en aucune partie de Roialme, qe les Justices de paix, trois ou deux de eux a meyns, et le Viscont ou Southviscont du Counte ou tiel riote...se ferra enapres, veignent ove le poair de Counte si bosoigne serra pur eux arester et eux arestent; et aient mesmes les Justices et Viscont ou Southviscont poair de recorder ceo qils troevent ensi fait en leur presence encontre la ley; et qe par le record de mesmes les Justices et Viscont ou Southviscont soient tielx trespassours...convictz en manere et fourme come il est contenuz en lestatut de forcibles entrees. Et sil adviegne qe tielx trespassours...soient departiz devant la venue des ditz Justices et Viscont ou Southviscont, qe mesmes les Justices, trois ou deux de eux enquergent diligealment deinz un moys apres tiel riote..., et ent oient et terminent solonc la loye de la terre. Et si la veritee ne poet estre trove en manere come dessuis est dit, adonqes deinz un moys lors proschein ensuiant certifient les ditz Justices...et le Viscont ou Southviscont suisditz devant le Roy et son Counseil tout le fait et les circumstances dicell, quell certificat soit dautiel force come le presentement de xij: Sur quel certificat soient les ditz trespassours...mys a responce, et ceux qi serront trovez coupables soient puniz solonc la discrecion du Roy et de son dit Consail. Et si tielx trespassours...traversent la matire ensy certifie, soient celles certificat et travers mandez en banc le Roy pur y estre triez et terminez come la ley demande: Et si mesmes les trespassours...ne viegnent my devant le Roy et son consail, ou en Bank le Roy, a primer mandement, adonqes soit fait autre mandement direct a Viscount de Countee, de prendre les ditz trespassours...

sils purront estre trovez et eux amesner a certein jour devant le
Roy et son dit Consail, ou en bank le Roy, et sils ne purront estre
trovez qe le Viscont ou Southviscont face proclamacion, en pleine
Countee proschein ensuiant la liveree du seconde mandement, qils
viegnent devant le Roy et son dit Counsail, ou en bank le Roy, ou
en la Chauncellarie en temps de vacacion deinz trois semaignes
lors proschins ensuiantz. Et en cas qe mesmes les trespassours...
ne viegnent...soient ils convictz et atteintz de les riote, assemble
ou route dessuisditz, non obstant aucun estatut ou ordinance fait
a contraire. Et en outre qe les Justices de la paix demurrantz les
pluis proscheins en chescun Counte ou tiel riote...se ferra en
apres, ensemblement ove le Viscont ou Southviscont de mesme le
Counte, et auxi les Justices dassises pur le temps qils serront
illeoqes en lour Sessions, en cas qe aucun tiel riote...se ferra en
lour presence, facent execucion de cest estatut chescun sur peine
de C. livres a paiers au Roy atant des foitz qils serront trovez en
defaut del execucion de mesme lestatut.

S.R. ii, 169, 13 Hen. IV, c. 7.

(17) *Administration of the statutes of labourers; and the powers
of justices of the peace* 1414

Et auxi qe toutz les Estatutz et Ordeignances des Laborers
servantz et artificers...soient exemplifiez desoutz le graunt seal
et mandez a chescun Viscont Dengleterre dent faire proclamacion
en pleine Countee, et puis celle proclamacion fait qe chescun
Viscount face deliverer la dice exemplificacion a luy direct as
Justices de la Pees en son Countee nomez en la Quorum ou a
un de eux...
Et qe les Justices de la Pees en chescun Countee nommez en la
Quorum receantz deinz mesme le Counte exceptz seignurs nom-
mez en la Commission de Pees, et auxi exceptz les Justices de lun
Banc et de lautre Chief Baron de lescheqer sergeantz de la leie et
Attournes du Roy, pur le temps qe mesmes les Justices Chief
Baron sergeantz et Attournez sont entendantz et occupiez en les
Courtz du Roy ou aillours occupiez en service le Roy, facent lour
Sessions quatre foitz par an;...
[*The times of the sessions are then given.*]
Et qe mesmes les Justices teignent lour Sessions parmy tout
Engleterre en mesmes les semaignes chescun an desore enavant.
Et auxi qe les Justices de la Pees desormes eient poair dexaminer

sibien toutz maners laborers servantz et lour mestres come
artificers par lour serementz, de toutz maters et choses par eux
faitz a contraire des estatutz et ordinances avantditz, et sur ceo de
les punir sur lour conisance, selonc leffect de les estatutz...sicome
ils furent convictz par enquest: Et qe le Viscount de chescun
Countee en Engleterre face bien et duement son Office celles
parties sur peyn de perdre au Roy xx livres.

S.R. II, 177, 2 Hen. V, s. 1, c. 4.

(18) *Justices of the peace to be resident in the counties* 1414

Primerment, qe les Justices de la pees desore enavant affaires
deinz les Countees Dengleterre, soient faitz de les pluis sufficeantz
persones demurrantz en mesmes les Countees, par advis du
Chanceller et Conseyll le Roy, sanz prendre autres persones
demurantz en foreins Countees a tiel office occupier, forspris les
seignurs et les Justices dassises ore nomez et anomerz par le Roy
et son Conseil; et forspris auxi les Chiefs Seneschalx du Roy des
terres et seignuries del Duchee de Lancastre en le North et le
South pur le temps esteantz.

S.R. II, 187, 2 Hen. V, s. 2, c. 1.

(19) *Qualifications of justices of the peace* 1439

Item, priount les Communes, qe come par l'Estatutz faitz en
temps du voz nobles Progenitours ordeigne soit, qe en chescun
Counte d'Engleterre, soient assignez Justices du la pluis vailauntz
du mesme les Countes, pur gardier la peas et aultres choses
affaire,...les qeux Estatuitz nient obstantz, en plusours Countees
d'Engliterre ore tarde ount este deputez et assignez, pluis graunde
noumbre qe ne soloit avaunt ces hures, dount ascunz sont du
petite avoir, par qeux les gentz ne voilent estre governez ne
demeosnes, et ascunz pur lour necessite fount graunde extortion
et appression sur le people,...

Please a vostre noble grace d'ordeigner et establier par auctorite
de cest present Parlement, qe nul Justice du Peas deins le Roialme
d'Engliterre, en nul Counte soit assigne ou depute, s'il n'eit
Terrez et Tenementz a la value du xx li. par an. Et si ascun soit
ordeigne en apres Justice du Peas en ascun Counte, qi n'ad
Terrez et Tenementz a le value suisdit, qe il de ceo notifie le
Chaunceller d'Engliterre...le quel mette un aultre suffisaunt en
son lieux,...

[*Penalty for disobedience should be xx li.*]

purveu toutz foitz, qe cest Ordenaunce ne se extende as Citees,
Viles, ou Burghs, qeux sount Countees encorporates de eux mesmes,
ne as Citees, Viles ou Burghs, qi ount Justice du Peas du gentz
demurantz en icels, par commission ou grauntz du Roy, ou de
sez Progenitours.
Responsio. Le Roy le voet. Purveu toutz foitz, qe s'ils ne soient
gentz suffisantz, eiantz Terres et Tenementz a le value suisdit,
apris en la ley et de bon governaunce, deinz ascun tiel Counte, qe
le Chaunceller d'Engleterre...eit poair de mettre autres discretz,
apris en la ley, en tielx Commissions,...
Rot. Parl. v, 28 (47).

(20) *Powers of the justices of the peace; arrests and bail* 1484

Item pur ceo qe diversez personez de jour en autre sont arestuz et
emprisonez pur suspecion de felonie, ascun foitz de malice et
ascun foitz de legier suspecion, et ensi gardez en prison saunz
baille ou mainprice a leur graund vexacion et trouble, Il est
ordeigne et establie par auctorite de cest present parlement, qe
chescune Justice del peas en chescune Countee Citee ou Ville aiet
auctorite et poiar par sa ou leur discrecion de lesser tielx prisoners
et persones ensi arestuz en baille ou mainprice en semblable forme
si come mesmes lez prisoners et persones ent furent enditez de
recorde devant mesmes les Justices en lour Session; Et qe Justices
de peas aient auctorite denquerrer en leur Sessions de toutz
maners eschapez de chescune persone arestuz et enprisonez pur
felonie; et qe null Viscount ne Eschetour Baillif de Fraunchise ne
ascune autre persone preigne ou sease lez biens dascune persone
arestuz devant qe mesme la persone ensi arestuz et enprisonez
soit convict ou atteint dautiel felonie accordaunt a la leie, ou
autrement mesmes les biens autre maner lealment forfaitz, sur
peine de forfeire le double value de les biens ensi prisez a celluy
qi est issint endamagez en cell partie par accion de dette en cell
partie destre pursue par semblable processe Jugement et execucion
come est usuelment usee en autres accions de dette pursuez al
communen leye; et qe null essoin ou proteccion soit allouez en
ascun tiel accion, Ne qe le defendaunt en ascune tiel accion soit
admis de gager...sa leye.

S.R. II, 478–9, 1 Ric. III, c. 3.

CHAPTER II

THE SHERIFFS

INTRODUCTION

At the beginning of the fourteenth century the sheriff had already lost many of the powers which had made the office so significant from Norman times.[1] The appointment of new officials, such as the coroner, and still more the justices of the peace, was to deprive the sheriff of much administrative and judicial work, though he retained many responsibilities. He still had to account to the exchequer for the revenue of the shire, and frequently complained that it was impossible to meet the full ferm. He presided over the county court, and transacted there a considerable amount of business, including the return of knights of the shire to parliament. Outlawry was still proclaimed there, but the civil jurisdiction of county and hundred only covered cases involving less than forty shillings value.[2] There was fuller representation when the county met the itinerant justices, but otherwise both at the monthly court and the six-monthly *curia generalis* attendance was limited, and the cumbrous machinery of a law based on archaic custom forced cases to take a lengthy course, even when a new procedure based on royal writs had been superimposed. The sheriff's tourn, the full hundred court held twice yearly, had petty criminal jurisdiction, but hundreds were often in private hands, in which case a leet had superseded the tourn.[3]

Yet while the jurisdiction of the sheriff was of diminishing importance, he had a vast field of administrative work, and in recent years interesting records have been discovered which throw light on his activities.[4] It is clear, indeed, from MSS. recently published,[5] that the amount of work demanded from the sheriff and his subordinates was enormous; writs received from

[1] W. A. Morris, *The medieval English sheriff to* 1300.

[2] Cf. W. A. Morris, *The early English county court* (for the thirteenth century); and G. H. Fowler on the fourteenth-century court in *Rolls from the office of the sheriff of Beds. and Bucks.* pp. 48 ff.

[3] See below, pp. 363–4.

[4] Article by H. Jenkinson and M. H. Mills, "Rolls from a sheriff's office in the fourteenth century", *E.H.R.* 1928.

[5] Fowler, *op. cit.*

central courts(4) were entered in the sheriff's roll, orders were given to the bailiff or other official for their execution(10), the bailiff's reply was again enrolled and return made to the central authority. In this system there had to be a careful organisation of messengers for the delivery and return of writs, both locally and to the central court, whether the chancery, exchequer, or one of the courts of common law, wheresoever they might be. From the records of king's bench and common pleas[1] it is clear that the sheriffs and their subordinates were sometimes negligent, and that often they were unable to make returns; these records also show the extent of the administrative work at that time.

Our knowledge of the work of the sheriff and his subordinates in the later medieval period is largely derived from the complaints constantly presented by the commons about local maladministration, and there were several statutes for the reform of abuses(6–8). By the statute of Lincoln, in 1316(2), the appointment of the sheriff was declared to lie with the chancellor, treasurer and chief justices; this avoided the danger of seignorial control; moreover, the sheriff was to be a landowner, and as such was thought to be in a better position to answer for the misdeeds of his servants and any deficiencies in their work. It was continually demanded that the office of sheriff should be an annual one, as was the case after 1340(5); from 1377 no sheriff was to be re-appointed until after a three years' interval(9). Later it was enacted that sheriffs should be resident in their bailiwicks(11).

The form of the sheriff's oath suggests in itself some of the difficulties of the office.[2] Moreover, the bailiffs in some cases were difficult to control, since they might have the hundreds at farm(3), until this was forbidden in 1445(15). At the end of the fourteenth and still more in the fifteenth century, complaints were levelled against the sheriff and his subordinates(12, 13), especially with reference to the tourns(14). The frankpledge system had long since failed as an attempt to keep the peace, but jurors still made presentment and the articles of presentment were widely interpreted. A statute passed in 1461 had the effect of depriving the sheriff of the police jurisdiction he had hitherto exercised in the tourn. He could no longer arrest or levy fines, but could only transfer indictments to a neighbouring justice of the peace(16).

---

[1] See above, pp. 258 ff.
[2] Cf. Fowler, *op. cit.* p. 1. The fifteenth-century escheator's oath given below, p. 357, is exactly similar to the sheriff's oath, fourteenth century, as quoted in the *First report on public records*, Rec. Com. pp. 236–7.

A still later statute attempted to secure more responsible jurors (17). In the abuses thus revealed we can trace at least some of the causes of the general disorder and restlessness of the fifteenth century; and it is significant that in all the attempted reforms the sheriff was consistently degraded while the justice of the peace was given a position of greater trust.

(1) *Royal nomination of a sheriff* 1314

Edward par la grace de dieu Roi Dengleterre, Seignur Dirland et Ducs Daquitaine, as Tresorer et Barons de nostre Escheqier, Salutz. Por ce qe nous voloms qe nostre cher et foial monsire Johan de Brakenbergh soit Viscounte de Nicole, qi a ce qe nous auoms entendu par gentz dignes de foi est homme de bones condicions et suffisant dauoir le dit office, Vous mandoms qe vous receuez le dit monsire Johan al office auantdit et lui ent facez auoir sa commission sanz delai en due forme.

Done souz nostre priue seal a Knaresbourgh le v. iour de Aueril Lan de nostre regne septisme.

Ancient Correspondence, XLV, 223.

(2) *The appointment of sheriffs and orders for the hundreds* 1316

Por ce qe nostre Seignur le Roi Edward,...a son parlement a Nicole...entendi grantz damages estre faitz a lui, et trop griefs oppressions et desheritaunces a son poeple, par la reson qe meins suffisantz Viscontes et Gardeins des Hundredz ont este avant ces houres, et uncore sont en dit Roiaume; nostre seignur le Roi... establi qe Viscontes desoremes soient mis par le Chancellier, le Tresorier, et les Barons del lescheqer, et par les Justices;...et qe nul ne soit visconte sil neit terre suffisaument, en meisme le Contee ou il serra Visconte, por respondre au Roi et au poeple; et qe nul qe soit seneschal ou Baillif de grant seignur seit fait Visconte, sil ne oste de autre servise,...

En meisme la manere est accorde..., qe les Hundredz le quel qil soient au Roi ou as autres, soient gardez par gentz covenables eantz terre suffisaument en meisme le Hundred, ou en le Countee ou le Hundred serra: et si ascuns Viscountes ou Hundreders soient a ceo meins suffisantz, soient tantost remuetz, et autres covenables mis en la forme avantdite; et qe les hundredz soient lessez et bailletz a tieux gentz a renable ferme issint qil ne coveigne pas qil facent extorsion sur le poeple, pur trop utrageouse ferme; et qe nul Visconte, ne Hundredor, ne baille a autre son office a garder a ferme, ne en autre manere; et qe les execucions des briefs, qi vendroint as viscontes, soient faites par les hundredors conus et juretz en plein Contee, et nemie par autres...

[*A letter to the sheriffs follows.*]

Et fait a remembrer, qe meisme lestatut fu seale souz le grant seal et maunde as Tresorer et Barons del Eschekier, et auxint as Justices de lun Bank et de lautre, de fermement garder en tuz ses pointz.

S.R. i, 174, 9 Ed. II, s. 2. (Statute of Lincoln.)

(3) *Hundreds let to farm* 1330

Item purceo qe les viscountes ount avant ces houres lessez les Hundredz et Wapentaks, en lour baillies a si haute ferme, qe les baillifs ne poient cele ferme lever, forqe par extorsion, et duresce, a faire au poeple; Si est acorde qe les viscountes lessent desore les Hundredz et Wapentaks a launciene ferme, et ne mye outre; et qe les Justices assignez eient poair denquere sur les viscountes, et de punir ceux qils troveront fesauntz le contraire.

S.R. i, 265, 4 Ed. III, c. 15.

(4) *Sealed writs to the sheriffs* 1338

A Nostre Seignur le Roy et a son Conseill monstrent Johan de Hildesle, Chaunceller de l'Escheqer nostre dit Seignur le Roy, Johan de Wodehous, Clerk de l'Hanaper de la Chauncellerie...qe come contenu soit en le serement de chescun Viscount, q'il ne soeffra le profitt le Roy estre soutret ou amenuse a son poair, et q'il ne receivera nul Brief de Jugement si noun enseale d'un des Seales de la Chauncellerie ou de l'Escheqer, et ensi eit este comaunde par les Roys d'Engleterre, et auxint use...en temps passe..., les Viscounts avantdits, nul regard eu a lour dit serment, ne a les choses avandites comandes..., receivent de jour en autre Brefs de jugement ensealles des Seales as Justices, ou par lour negligence par lour Ministres soeffrent estre receus, par ount les fees des ditz Seales...sont amenuses et destruez trop graundement, a gref damage nostre dit Seignur le Roy. Dount le dit Chaunceller de l'Escheqer, et le Clerc de l'Hanaper, prient a nostre dit Seignur le Roy, qe lui pleise a les choses suisdites avoir regard,...

Responsio. Soit Bref maundie a Justice de Comune Baunk, contenaunt le effect de la Peticion, qe ils pur lui avisement facent tel remedie en lour place,...

Rot. Parl. ii, 99 (6).

(5) *Annual appointment of sheriffs* 1340

Item, pur ce qe ascuns viscontes ont lour baillies a terme des ans, du grant le Roi, et ascuns se fient tant de lour long demoere en lour baillie par procurement, qils sont esbaudiz de faire moultz des oppressions au poeple, et de mal servir au Roi et a son poeple; si est assentuz...qe nul viscount demoerge en sa baillie outre un an, et adonqes soit autre covenable ordene en son lieu, qad terre suffisante en sa baillie, par les Chauncellier, Tresorer, et chief Baron de Lescheqer, pris a eux les chiefs Justices del un Bank et del autre, sils soient presentz; et ce soit fait chescun an lendemein des Almes a Lescheqer.

S.R. 1, 283, 14 Ed. III, s. 1, c. 7.

(6) *Justices of assize to inquire into misdemeanours of local officials* 1346

Item voloms et avoms ordenez qe les Justices as assises prendre assignez, eient sufficiante commission denquerre en lour sessions, des Viscontz, Echetours, Baillifs des Fraunchises et lour souz Ministres, et aussint des Meintenours, communs assissours et jurours en pais, cestassavoir, des douns, regardz et autres profitz qe les ditz ministres parnent du poeple pur faire lour offices...et pur faire larrai des paneles, mettantz en ycelles jurours suspectz et de male fame;...Et sur ceo avoms charge noz Chaunceller et Tresorer, doier les pleintes de touz ceux qi pleindre se voudrent, et dordeiner qe hastif droit et remede ensoit fait. Par quoi vous mandoms qe les pointz et ordinances susdites facez overtement monstrer et publier en nostre dite Citee...

    Done a Westmonstier le xxviij Davril.
        per ipsum Regem et Consilium.
Consimilia brevia diriguntur singulis Vicecomitibus per Angliam.

S.R. 1, 305, 20 Ed. III, c. 6.

(7) *Panels of jurors* 1361

Item porce qe viscontes et autres ministres sovent arraient lour panels en tote manere denquestes des gentz procurez et pluis lointifs du Countee, qi nont conissance du fet dount lenqueste serra prise; Acorde est, qe tieu paneles soient faites des plus prescheins gentz, qi ne sont pas suspectes, ne procurez; et qe les viscontes, Coroners et autres ministres qi font alencontre soient puniz devant les Justices qi la dite enqueste prendra, selonc la quantite de leur trespas, sibien devers le Roi come devers la partie, pur la quantite du damage qil ad suffert en tieu manere.

S.R. 1, 365, 34 Ed. III, c. 4.

(8) *Proceedings against corrupt jurors* 1361

Item, qe en chescun plee dount lenqueste ou lassise passe si aucun des parties voudra suir vers ascuns des Jurrours qil ad pris de son adverser ou de lui, pur dire son verdit, soit oy; et eit sa pleinte meintenant par bille devant les Justices devant queux ils jurrerunt, et qe le jurrour soit mis a respoundre saunz nul delai; et sils pledent au paiis, qe enqueste soit pris maintenant: et si nul homme autre qe la partie vodra suyr pur le Roi vers le jurrour, soit oy et termine come dissus est dit; et si le jurrour soit atteint a suite dautre qe la partie et face fin, qe la partie qi seust eit la moite du fin; et qe les parties au plee recoverent lour damages,... et qe le Jurrour issint atteint eit la prisone dun an quel emprisonement le Roi grante qe ne soit pardone pur nul fin...

S.R. 1, 366, 34 Ed. III, c. 8.

Further penalties 1364

...est assentu...qe si nuls Jurours en assises, jurees,...soient atteint,...paie chescun des ditz Jurrours dis foitz a tant come il avera pris; et eit celuy qi ferra la suite lun moite, et le Roi lautre moite:...

S.R. 1, 384, 38 Ed. III, s. 1, c. 12.

(9) *No sheriff to be re-elected within three years* 1377

Item ordeigne est qe nully Qad este Viscont dune conte par un an entier, ne soit deinz les trois anz proscheins ensuantz reesluz ou remys en dite office de Viscont; si y soit autre suffisant en dite Contee des possessions et biens pur respondre a Roi et a poeple.

S.R. 11, 4, 1 Ric. II, c. 11.

(10) *Writs of a sheriff to local bailiffs* 1378

Edmundus de Stonore, vicecomes Oxon', dilecto suo Johanni Pentere, ballivo hundredi de Dorchestre, hac vice ballivo itineranti in comitatu predicto, salutem. Ex parte domini Regis tibi mando quod non omittas propter aliquam libertatem in comitatu predicto, quin capias Johannem Barayte de Bradhinton commorantem apud Brydecote in parochia de Dorchestre, ubicunque

inventus fuerit in comitatu predicto, et eum usque Castrum Oxon'
duci facias: ita quod habere possim corpus ejus coram Gilberto
Wace et sociis suis, justiciariis domini Regis de pace in comitatu
predicto, apud Watlyngton die Lune proximo post festum Sancti
Luce Evangeliste ad respondendum tam domino Regi quam
Willelmo Gryme de Dorchestre de placito transgressionis contra
formam statuti.

Edmundus de Stonore, vicecomes Oxon', ballivo hundredi de
Chadlyngton salutem. Summone per bonos summonitores xxiiij
legales homines de balliva tua de visneto de Keyngham, quod sint
coram justiciariis domini Regis ad assisas in comitatu Oxon'
capiendas assignatis apud Oxoniam, die Jovis proximo ante festum
Convercionis Sancti Pauli, ad recognoscendum super sacramentum
suum si Willelmus de Wyndesore, chivaler, et Alicia, uxor ejus,
Johannes Nouwer, chivaler, [7 *other names*] injuste et sine judicio
disseisiverunt Johannem atte Halle...de libero tenemento suo in
Keyngham post primam, etc. Et interim habeant visum, et
nomina juratorum imbreviari facias. Et pone per vadium et
salvos plegios predictos Willelmum, Aliciam, Johannem Nowers
...vel ballivos suos si ipsi inventi non fuerint, quod tunc sint
ibi audituri illam recognicionem. Et habeas ibi summonitores,
nomina plegiorum, et hoc preceptum.

Endorsed are the names of the sureties of John de Nouwers and
Hervy, and of Hankyn and Carter. "De omnibus aliis non habeo
plegios, quia nil habent in balliva mea."

Edmundus de Stonore, vicecomes Oxon', ballivo libertatis
hundredi de Dorchestre salutem. Mandatum domini Regis in hec
verba [recepi: Ricardus],...vicecomiti Oxon' salutem. Pre-
cepimus tibi quod distringas Hugonem Chastillom et Matilldim,
uxorem ejus, per omnes terras et tenementa in balliva tua. Et
quod de exitibus eorundem nobis respondeas. Et quod habeas
corpora eorum coram justiciariis nostris apud Westmonasterium,
in Octabis sancti Michaelis ad respondendum Thome Camoys et
Elizabethe, uxori sue, de placito vasti de tenemento in Chesel-
hampton cum pertinenciis etc. Et ad audiendum judicium suum
de pluribus defaltis. Et habeas ibi hoc breve. T. R. Bealknapp
apud Westmonasterium x° die Julii anno regni nostri secundo.
Quare tibi mando quod mandatum istud diligenter executaris et
de execucione michi respondeas in Castro Oxon' inde etc. cum hoc
mandato.

Stonor letters and papers (Camden 3rd Series), xxix, 6, 9, 15.

(11) *Every sheriff to be resident, etc.* 1402

Item ordeignez est et assentuz qe chescun Viscont Dengleterre soit demurrant en propre persone deinz sa baillie pur le temps qil serra tiel Officer; et qil ne lesse sa dice baillie a ferme a nully par le temps qil occupiera cel office. Et qa ce faire soit tiel Viscont jurrez de temps en temps en especiale entre les autres articles comprises en le serement de Viscont.

S.R. II, 134, 4 Hen. IV, c. 5.

(12) *Restraints on sheriffs' officers* 1413

Item pur ceo qe les lieges nostre seignur le Roy nosent my pursuir ne compleindre des extorsions et oppressions a eux faitz par les Ministres des Viscountees, cestassavoir par Southviscountz Clerks des Viscountes Resceyvours et Baillifs des Viscountes, a cause qe les ditz Southviscountes...sount sy continuelment de an en an demurrauntz ovesqe les Viscountes enterchaungeablement en un office ou en autre: Nostre seignur le Roy...ad ordeignez et establiz, qe ceux qi sount Baillifs des Viscountz par un an ne soient en nul tiel office par les trois ans proschein ensuantz, forspris les Baillifs des Viscountes queux sont enheriteez en lour Viscountees: et qe nul Southviscount ne Clerk de Viscount, Resceivour ne Baillif de Viscount soit attourne en aucun Court de Roy pur le temps qil est en office ou aucun tiel Viscount.

S.R. II, 171, 1 Hen. V, c. 4.

(13) *Misdeeds of sheriffs* 1425

To our soverain Lord ye Kyng, and to all ye Lordes Spirituell and Temporell of yis present Parlement. Bisecheth humbely ye Commens of yis present Parlement, that where diverses Writtes at ye suite of partie, ben severally directe to Shirrefs of yis lond, to take diverses persones by ther bodys, the said Sherefs...taken gret sommes of money of ye parties yat buth so sued, by duresse for yer meyinpris. And over yat yei taken grete sommes of money for ye embesillyng of Writtes in diverses cases, to grete lettyng and hyndryng of ye parties yat suyth...And where Writtes ben directe to ye said Sherefs, to enpanell diverses persones to passe in enquestes bytwene parties, and her names to retourne and to certifie into the Kynges Court, ye said Sherefs...yei retourne and certifie diverse mennys names enpanellud, with oute any warnyng of hem at any tyme, to her grete losse and enporisshyng.

Wherfore plese hit our said soverain Lord ye Kyng, to graunte
and ordeine by auctoritie of yis present Parlement; that every
Sheref for ye tyme beyng, retourne his Writtes into ye Kynges
Court, at such daies as yei buth retournable; and yat he take
sufficeant seurtee of suche persones, as he hath auctorite by ye
Kyngis Writte to areste, yat yei shall kepe her day in ye Kynges
Court,...And yat ye Sherefs warne in resonable tyme, all such
persones as buth enpanelled to passe in enquestes...And zif any
Sheref do ye contrarie of any of yese articles above seide, that
yenne ye partie yat fynde hym greved, may sue be Bille or Writte
upon his cas, ayeins ye Sherefs, as well in ye Escheqer, as in any
oyer Court of the Kyngs;...Alweyus be hit for sey, yat yis
Petition extende not so ferre, but yat ye said Sherefs by auctorite
of ye Kynges Writtes, may take and areste...menne by yere bodis
for execution of dette or dammages recovered, and for felonie and
treson,...And that ye Justice of ye Peas, Stuardus of Letus and
Hundredis, may have power to enquerre of suche misprisions and
defautes of ye said Sherefs,...
And yat yis ordinance shall endure to next Parlement.

Responsio. Ceste Petition est graunte, toutz les Estatutz faitz par
devaunt, et nient repellez, esteantz en lour force.

Rot. Parl. IV, 306 (32).

(14)   *The sheriff's tourn in Cornwall* 1432

To the right wyse and discrete Commens of this present Parlement
assembled, prayen mekely all the Communes of the Shire of
Cornewaill, yat there as is conteyned in ye Statut of the grete
Chartre,...yat there should no man ben amerced bote after the
quantite of his trespas, and yat non amercementes be sett ne put
apon no person, but by the othes of worthy and lawefull persones,
as in the saide Statut more pleynly apereth; and with ynne the
saide Shire, by cause the Decennare and Decennes, oder wyse
called Thethyngman and Thethyngs, comen noght hole and full
unto the Sherrefes tourn, they ben amerced, and ye amercement
affred byfore ye Sherref, and among oder issues and profites
of the saide Shire, in estretes written and delivered unto the
Baillifs of every Hundred withine ye Shire, to make leve therof,
and to accompte there for, yn discharge of ye Shiref for the tyme
beyng, before ye Auditours of ye Duche of Cornewaill, atte
Eschequer ther at Loftwythyell...and noght withstondyng any
Statut yerof made noue late, the Auditours of ye seide Duchee han

put, and yut fro yere to yere putten for suche manere defautes, apon the saide Decennes or Thethynges, grete fynes and sommes at hure aune will, and chargen ye saide Bailifs ther with apon theire accomptes, and committen hem to prison,...Wherefore please hit unto youre worthy and noble wisdoms...to pray oure soveraigne Lord ye Kyng, and all the Lordes Espirituell and Temporell, that the saide Estatut, and all other yerof made, stonde in theire strenght;...

Responsio. Soit la commune leye tenuz et gardez.

Rot. Parl. iv, 403 (36).

(15) *The farm of counties, etc.* 1445

Item le Roi considerant lez graundez perjure extorcion et oppression queux sont et ont esteez en cest Roialme par sez Viscountz, Southviscountz et lour Clerks Coroners Seneschalls dez fraunchisez, Baillifs et Gardeinz dez prisons,...ad ordeigne par lauctorite suisdit, en eschuyng dez toutz tielx extorcions...qe null Viscount lesse a ferme en ascun manere son Counte, ne ascun de sez Baillifwiks, Hundredez ne Wapentakez; ne qe lez ditz Viscountz, Southviscountz [*etc.*]...retourne sur ascun bref ou precept a eux direct de retourner ascuns enquestez en ascun panell sur ceo destre fait, ascuns Baillifs, Officers ou Servauntz a ascun de lez Officers suisditz en ascun panell par eux issint affair;...

S.R. ii, 334, 23 Hen. VI, c. 9.

(16) *Limitation of powers of the sheriff* 1461

...Nostre dit Soverayn seignur le Roi les premissez considerez, par ladvis assent des seignurs espirituelx et temporelx et a la request dez Communes en la dit parlement assemblez...ad ordeigne...qe toutz manerez denditementez et presentementz, quelx serront prisez en apres devaunt ascun de ses Viscountez de sez Counteez,...lour Suthviscountz, Clerkes, Baillifs ou Ministres a lour Turnez ou Lawedaies..., naient ne null de ceux ait poair ne auctorite darester attacher ou mettre en prison ou lever ascuns fines ou amerciamentz dascun persone ou persones issint enditez ou presentez...; Ne de faire ou prendre dascun tiel persone ou persones issint enditez...ascun fine ou raunsome; mes qe les Viscountez suisditz, lour Suthviscountz [*etc.*]...toutz autielx enditementz et presentementz prisez devaunt eux..., amesnent, presentent, et deliverent a les Justicez du peax au leur proschein

cession de peax qi serra tenuz en le Counte...lou autielx enditementz et presentementz serront prisez...[*penalty, officials to forfeit*
*£*40]. Et qe les ditz Justices de peas aient poair et auctorite
dagarder processe, sur toutz tielx enditementz et presentementz,
come la ley requiert, et en fourme semblable, si come les ditz
enditementz et presentementz feussent prisez devaunt lez ditz
Justicez de peax en le dit Counte...Et auxi darrainer et deliverer
toutz tielx persones ou persone, issint enditez...et...de faire
oveqs eux et chescun deux tiel fine, come loialment par leurs
discrecions semblera, et les estretez de lez ditz fines et amerciamentz
soient enrollez, et par endentur destre deliverez a lez ditz Viscountz...al oeps et prouffit celuy qi fuist Viscount en ascun
Countee, au temps de les ditz enditementz et presentementz
prisez...

S.R. II, 390, 1 Ed. IV, c. 2.

(17) *Jurors and sheriffs' tourns* 1484

Item pur ceo qe divers graundez enconviencez et perjuries de jour
en autre aveignent en diversez Countees Dengleterre par faulx
verdites donez es enquisicions...devaunt Viscountes en lour
Tournes par persones de null substance...En eschuer de qoi Il est
ordeignez par nostre dit Seignur le Roy...qe null Baillif ne autre
Officer decy enavaunt retourne ou enpanelle ascune tiel persone
en ascune Countie Dengleterre destre prise ou mys en ou sur
ascune tiel enquerre en ascun de les ditz Tournes mez tielx quelx
sount de bon noune et fame et aiantz terres et tenementes de
fraunk tenure deinz mesmes lez Countees al annuel value de xxs.
au meyns ou autrement terres et tenementes tenuz par Custume
de maner vulgarment appellez Copihold deinz les ditz Countees
al annuell value de xxvj s. viij d. oustre toutz charges au meyns...

S.R. II, 479, 1 Ric. III, c. 4.

CHAPTER III

THE CORONERS

INTRODUCTION

In 1194 the justices itinerant were directed to cause two persons to be elected in every county to keep the pleas of the crown,[1] and the office of coroner was much developed during the next two centuries, when there came to be four coroners in each county, whose duty it was to safeguard royal interests in every sphere. They were elected in the county court(3), and received no salaries until Henry VII's reign. Their duties varied very much: they dealt, for example, with cases of wreck and treasure trove; they dealt with appeals (accusations of crime made by an individual) and declared the outlawry of those who for persistent failure to appear or for some other reason had incurred that penalty(1); they heard the confessions of felons who had fled to sanctuary.

The coroners had to be present in manorial courts when the seignorial right of infangthief was used; they had to hold an inquest on the bodies of those who had died by supposed violence, and this was to become the function usually associated with the office; they also heard cases of presentment of Englishry even after this was abolished by statute.[2] The coroners had to produce their rolls for the justices in eyre, and it was natural that they should come to act as deputies of the sheriff in both judicial and administrative matters.

The coroner's jury normally consisted of twelve men, probably representing the hundred, together with men from the township concerned and the three neighbouring vills(2), each vill being usually represented by the reeve and four men.[3] A presenting jury, whatever its form,[4] dealt not only with cases of sudden death but also with felonies. In this way the coroner, whose duties were increasing, was fast coming to act as a check upon the sheriff. In the fourteenth century, statutes concerning the appointment and status of the coroner were enacted in very similar terms to those regulating the office of sheriff, and the oaths of coroner and sheriff were practically the same.

[1] Stubbs, *S.C.* p. 254. [2] *Select coroners' rolls*, p. xliii; and see above, p. 265.
[3] *Select coroners' rolls*, pp. xxx ff. [4] *Ibid.* p. xlii.

(1) *Northamptonshire, coroners' rolls; case of outlawry* 1313

Ad comitatum Norht' tentum die Jovis in crastino Sancti Petri ad Vincula anno regni regis Edwardi vij. venit breve domini regis in hec verba.

Edwardus dei gracia rex Anglie, dominus Hybernie et dux Aquitanie vicecomiti Norht' salutem. Precipimus tibi quod exigi facias Johannem Dotyne Du Boys de comitatu in comitatum quousque secundum legem et consuetudinem regni nostri utlagetur si non comparuerit. Et si comparuerit tunc eum capias et salvo in prisona nostra custodias, ita quod habeas corpus ejus coram nobis in Octabis S. Hillarii ubicumque tunc fuerimus in Anglia ad respondendum Alexandro de Bowdone de placito quare vi et armis in ipsum Alexandrum apud Brykelesworthe insultum fecit et ipsum verberavit, vulneravit et male tractavit et alia enormia ei intulit ad grave dampnum ipsius Alexandri et contra pacem nostram ut dicit, et unde tu ipse nobis retornasti in crastino Sancti Johannis Baptiste quod predictus Johannes non est inventus nec aliquid habet in balliva tua per quod potest atachiari. Et habeas ibi hoc breve. Teste R. le Brabazone apud Westmonasterium xxv. die Junii anno regni nostri sexto.

. . . . . .

Ad comitatum Norht' tentum die Jovis in vigilia Sancti Clementis Pape anno predicto predictus Johannes Dotyne Du Boys quinto interrogatus est et non venit. Ideo per judicium et consideracionem tocius comitatus utlagatus est.

Select cases from the coroners' rolls (S.S.), pp. 62–3.

(2) *Cambridgeshire, coroners' rolls* 1338

Accidit in villa de Westone Colville die Jovis in festo Ascencionis Domini anno regni regis Edwardi tercii post conquestum duodecimo quod Johannes filius Radulphi de Mareys de Westone Colville etatis trium annorum inventus fuit submersus. Et Emma Siger de Westone primo invenit eum. Plegii ejusdem Emme Radulphus Leverer et Robertus Colt. Et super hoc Johannes Fitz-Jon coronator domini regis in comitatu Cant' accessit ibidem die Sabbati proximo sequenti et habuit visum corporis predicti Johannis filii Radulphi et diligenter inquisivit de morte ipsius per quatuor villatas propinquiores videlicet Westwratting, Brinkele, Wylingham, Carleton' et per villatam de Westone Colville et per xij. scilicet . . .

Qui dicunt super sacramentum suum quod predicto die Jovis in festo Ascencionis Domini anno supradicto predictus Johannes filius Radulphi ivit ludendo juxta quendam communem puteum vocatum Tonewalle in quadam virida [*sic*] placea in Westone Coleville, et cespitavit et per infortunium cecidit in predictum puteum et ibidem submersit. Ideo preceptum est obstupare predictum puteum, etc.

Et sunt quatuor vicini propinquiores scilicet:

Vicini {
Radulphus Alfrich, plegii ejusdem Henricus Factour et Willelmus Elianor.
Johannes Factouressone, plegii ejusdem Willelmus Factour et Willelmus Alfrich.
Johannes Rote, plegii ejusdem Bartholomeus Bad et Johannes Bad.
Thomas Godwyne, plegii ejusdem Hugo Swyn et Philippus Waleman.

Select cases from the coroners' rolls (S.S.), p. 41.

(3) *The appointment of coroners* 1354

A Nostre Seignur le Roi et a son Conseil prie la Commune, qe come les Coroners soleient estre esluz par les Grantz et meuth vanes de chescun Countee et du pais ou ils demoeront, ore viegnent ascuns procurantz cel office a lour profit demesne, donant largement de lour pur avoir l'office; disauntz au poeple, q'ils donent grante ferme pur ycel, la ou nostre Seignur le Roi soleit doner le soen pur le dit office bien garder: Et aussint vont en pais, et par colour de cel office feynent enditementz estre faitz devant eux, attachent ou pernont diverses gentz en diverses parties de lour Baillies, et les detiegnent en prison tant q'ils eient faitz Fyn a eux a lour volunte, a grante damage et empoverissement de tut le poeple. Prie la dite Commune, qe tieux Coroners soient esluz des meuth vanez du pais, solonc ceo qu'ad este usee avant ces heures, et qils soient sermentez en plein Countee de faire lour office come est ordine par l'Estatut de Westmonstier primer.

Responsio. Soient les Coroners esluz es pleins Countees par la Commune de mesmes les Countees, des plus covenables et plus loiax a faire le dit office; sauve l'estat de ceux qi par reson de lour Seigneurie deivent faire Coroners. Et si nul Coroner face attachementz ou enditementz noun duement, soit desclare qe ceo soit, et le Roi ent fra mettre covenable remede.

Rot. Parl. II, 260 (38).

CHAPTER IV

THE ESCHEATORS

INTRODUCTION

Of the other royal officials we need only mention the escheators. Their duty was to administer the lands which had reverted to the crown either for want of an heir or through forfeiture. In 1258 two escheatries were already in existence for the lands north and south of the Trent, and this was still the case until 1323. The history of the office during the next years is more complicated, since it became involved in the royal and baronial struggle. The barons favoured the old system of two escheatries, but in 1323 eight officials were appointed with smaller areas of administration. During the early part of Edward III's reign a return was made to the old scheme, but in 1332 the eight escheatries were restored until 1335, when escheators were appointed for the south, and north, with a third for the south-west. The evils of the system, however, provided cause for baronial complaint during the political crisis of 1340–1, when the smaller escheatries were again revived(1); the office of escheator was then brought into line with that of the sheriff, and there was no return to the great escheatries. By the fifteenth century the office had been subjected to legislation similar to that regulating the work and status of other officials(2), and the escheator's oath is similar to that taken by his fellow-workers in the county(3).[1]

(1) *The appointment of escheators* 1340

Et come en ascuns temps avant ces heures il navoit forsqe deux Eschetours en Engleterre, cest assavoir un Eschetour de cea Trente, et un autre de dela, pur quoi le Roi et le poeple furent meins bien serviz qe avant ces houres nestoient, quant il y aveit plus des Eschetours et de meindre estat; si est assentuz...qe desore en avant soient tauntz des Eschetours assignez, come estoient en le temps quant le Roi quore est prist le governement de son Roialme Dengleterre; et qe mesmes les Eschetours soient

Cf. article by S. T. Gibson, *E.H.R.* xxxvi; and Tout, *Chapters*, iii, 49 ff.

esluz par les Chauncellier, Tresorer, et chief Baron de Lescheqer, pris a eux les chiefs Justices del un Bank et del autre, sils soient presentz, en manere come est susdit des viscountes; et qe nul eschetour demoerge en son office outre un an; et qe nul Coroner soit esluz sil neit terre en fee suffisauntment, en mesme le Contee, dont il purra respondre a tote manere des gentz.

S.R. I, 283, 14 Ed. III, s. 1, c. 8.

(2) *Property qualification for escheators* 1368

Item come contenue soit et en les estatuz ordenez, pur commune profit des Eschetours, qe nul Eschetour soit, sil neit sufficeantie de terre, dont il poet respondre au Roi et a son poeple; est assentu, qe nul Eschetour soit fait sil neit vint liverees de terre au meinz ou plus en fee; et qils facent leur office en propre persone, et si autre soit, soit ouste.

S.R. I, 388, 42 Ed. III, c. 5.

1472

...Si est ordeigne par lauctorite de cest present parlement qe null Eschetour affair apres la Nativite nostre seignur qe serra en lan nostre seignur Dieu M̕CCCClxxiij preigne sur luy loffice deschetour,...sinon le dit Eschetour...ait...terrez tenementz ou rent en fee simple fee taill ou terme de vie annuel value de xxli. gisauntz et esteauntz deinz mesme le Counte ou Counteez dunt il serra fait Eschetour; ne qe ascune tiel Eschetour...vende ne mette a ferme la dit office descheterie en ascune maner, ne face ascun deputee ou deputez forsqe tiel ou tielx pur qe ou queux il voet respondre a son perill, le noun ou nouns du dit depute ou deputez destre certefie par mesme leschetour, par sez lettrez patentz, au Tresorer et Barouns del Eschequer nostre seignur le Roy...deinz xx. jours apres tiel deputacion affair;...
Et si ascune persone ou personez apres mesme la feste face ou facent contrarie de lez premissez ou ascune de eux, forface ou forfacent a chascune default xlli....Et qe lez Justices du peas... aient poiar, denquerer oier et terminer chascune autiel forfaiture, sur presentement ent devant eux en lour sessions;...

S.R. II, 443-4, 12 Ed. IV, c. 9.

(3) *The oath of the escheator* 15th century

Ye shall Swere That ye shall serue the Kyng wele and trewly in the Office of the Eschetour...and do the Kynges Profit in all that longeth to you to do be Wey of your Office after youre Witte and youre Power and His Rightes and all that longeth to His Corone ye shall trewly keepe ye shall not assent to decresce ne to concele the Kyngis Rightes nor of His Fraunchises and where-somever that ye haue Knowledge of the Kyng's Rightes or of his Corone be it in Landes Rentes Franchises or Sutes that be con-celed or wythdrawn ye shall do youre trewe Peyne and Diligence to withstand it. And if ye may not do it ye shall say it to the Kyng or to some of His Councell such as ye knowe for certeyne will sey it to the Kyng. Ye shall trewly and right wisly trete the Pepull of your Baillewyke and do Right to every Man as well to Pore as to Ryche in that that longeth to you to doo be Wey of youre Office Ye shall do no Wronge to eny Man nother for Gifte Promyse ne Hate ne no Mannys Right ye shall disturble Ye shall take no Thyng whereby that Right may be disturbled letted or delayed. Ye shall treuly and right wisly retorne and serve all the Kynges Writtes Ye shall in youre propre Persone make the Extentes of Landys after the veray Value and Enquestis to retorne hem as ofte as they betake afore you and that within a Moneth after they betake. Ye shall take no Baillie in to youre Seruice but suche as ye will answer for. And ye shall do your Baillifs to make suche Othe as it longith to theym. Ye shall trewly and rightwisly yelde Accompt at the Kyngis Exchequier here of all the Issues of youre seide Baillewyke. Ye shall take your Enquestes in Open Places and that by Endenture after the Effect of the Statut thereof made as God keep you and his Saintes.

Printed in the *First report on the public records* (1800), pp. 234–5.

CHAPTER V

THE FORESTS

INTRODUCTION

After the issue of the Forest Charter in 1217 the crown was never again able to increase its forest and hunting rights, and although the strictly organised forest laws were maintained,[1] in practice the amount of forest land was steadily diminishing. Edward I ordered a forest inquisition to be taken, and tried in some way to safeguard the people from unscrupulous forest officials, but even then complaints of such oppression were among the grievances which led up to the confirmation of the Charters in 1297, when the barons made a serious attempt to disafforest the land, while the king on his side was determined to retain intact so important a source of his revenue. The forest ordinances of 1305 and 1306 made little advance. There were later attempts to limit the extent of the forests; in 1327 it was ordered that the perambulations initiated by Edward I should be completed, and there was some settlement in 1330. During the fourteenth century petitions against the evil practices of foresters continued, but after that time the system was so much weakened that it ceased to be the object of political attack.

Extracts from forest eyre rolls 1334

Placita foreste de Shirewod' tenta apud Notingham die lune proxima post festum Sancti Georgii anno regni regis Edwardi tercii post conquestum octauo coram Radulpho de Neuill', Ricardo de Aldeburgh' et Petro de Middleton' Iusticiariis domini regis itinerantibus ad placita foreste per mandatum domini regis in hec verba:—
[Copy of letters patent is given.]
Presentatum est et conuictum per eosdem quod Hugo de Wotehalc dc Wodeburgh', Willclmus Hycnd', Wilkock' quondam seruiens persone de Clifton' et Stephanus Flemyng' de Notingham die Iouis proxima post festum sancti Willelmi archiepiscopi anno regni regis Edwardi filii regis Edwardi decimo octauo fuerunt in bosco de Arnale in loco qui dicitur Throwys cum arcubus et sagittis; et bersauerunt vnum ceruum, vnde habuit mortem; et carnes inuente fuerunt putride et per vermes deuorate in loco qui

---

[1] G. J. Turner, *Select pleas of the forest* (S.S.), Introduction, *passim*.

dicitur Thweycehilli; et sagitta inuenta fuit in dicto ceruo vnde fuit bersatus. Et predictus Hugo venit coram iusticiariis et liberatur prisone. Et predicti Willelmus et Wilkock' non sunt inuenti, nec aliquid habent per quod etc., nec prius etc., nec scitur etc., ideo exigantur. Et predictus Stephanus Flemyng' mortuus est; ideo de eo nichil. Et postea predictus Hugo eductus est a prisona, et condonatur quia pauper. Et predicti Willelmus et Wilkoc exacti fuerunt in comitatu et non comparuerunt; ideo vtlagati sunt.

. . . . . .

Quesitum est ab omnibus ministris foreste super sacramentum suum a quo vel quibus forestarii domini regis debent et solebant capere et habere sustentacionem suam; qui dicunt quod Edwardus rex auus domini regis nunc inter alia hoc fecit inquirere per breue suum missum Willelmo de Vescy tunc iusticiario foreste, cuius transcriptum ostenderunt hic in hec verba:—

[Copy of the writ follows.]

Vnde fuit facta inquisicio apud Notingham coram prefato Willelmo de Vescy die Martis proxima ante Pentecosten anno regni regis Edwardi decimo septimo per...viridarios foreste de Shirwode...regardatores eiusdem foreste...agistatores eiusdem foreste et per duodecim iuratores predictis ministris adiunctos, videlicet,...

Qui dicunt super sacramentum suum quod Robertus de Eueringham racione balliue sue debuit fugare leporem, vulpem, scurellum et catum in foresta.

Item dicunt quod debuit habere corticem et couporones quercuum quas dominus rex dederat de dominicis boscis suis per breue suum.

Item dicunt quod debet habere retropannagium quociens contigerit.

Item dicunt quod debuit habere expeditacionem canum non expeditatorum, videlicet de quolibet cane non expeditato tres solidos de tribus annis in tres annos quando breue domini regis venit ad regardum faciendum.

. . . . . .

Item dicunt quod tenuit decem feoda militum de domino rege in capite de quorum seruicio exoneratus fuit propter custodiam foreste et ad inueniendos forestarios suos sumptibus suis propriis.

Item dicunt quod omnes terre sue quas habuit in foresta sunt extra regardum racione balliue sue et omnes canes de feodo suo non erunt expeditati.

Item dicunt quod balliua predicti Roberti abiudicata fuit de se et heredibus suis imperpetuum in vltimo itinere Willelmi de Vescy et sociorum suorum iusticiariorum domini regis ad placita foreste apud Notingham itinerancium pro pluribus defaltis de quibus fuit conuictus in eodem itinere; per quod dominus rex balliuam forestarii feodi de Shirewode potest conferre cuicunque sibi placuerit.

In cuius rei testimonium predicti ministri et alii jurati presenti inquisicioni sigilla sua apposuerunt.

Et dicunt quod nesciunt aliud dicere nisi quod predicti iurati dicebant. Et sic ponitur in respectu.

. . . . . .

Rotulus de amerciamentis de conuictis in attachiamentis de transgressionibus viridis vltra precium quatuor denariorum et que non potuerunt amerciari nisi in itinere.

De Radulfo filio Reginaldi de Edenestowe pro vna quercu decem denariorum, vnde viridarii sunt onerati in rotulo de precio viridis. Et pro transgressione in misericordia nunc in itinere. Plegii Ricardus de Normanton' et Ricardus Godard' de Thouresby. ijs.

. . . . . .

De Radulfo Molendinario de Sutton' pro trescentum lattarum, precii duodecim denariorum, vnde viridarii etc.   xviijd.

De Iohanne super moram de Warsepe pro vna carectata maeremie, precii sex denariorum, vnde viridarii, etc.   xviijd.

. . . . . .

De Gilberto Fadir et Gileberto Gilling' pro melle asportato de bosco, precii sex denariorum, vnde viridarii, etc.   xijd.

De Thoma Sheth de Mamesfeld' pro vna domo vendita.   ijs.

De precio viridis; et amerciamenta viridariorum quia non habuerunt rotulos de tempore suo.

De viridariis anno regis Edwardi aui domini regis nunc quinto decimo de precio viridis de attachiamentis de Maunnesfeld' de eodem anno.   vjs. vd.

De eisdem viridariis quia non habuerunt rotulos de attachiamentis de Lindeby, Bulwell', Caluerton et Eden' de eodem anno; in misericordia.   xs.

. . . . . .

De viridariis de anno eiusdem regis septimo decimo de precio viridis de attachiamentis de eodem anno.   lxxiijs. vijd.

Select pleas of the forest (S.S.), pp. 65–9.

CHAPTER VI

SEIGNORIAL JURISDICTION

INTRODUCTION

From Norman times manorial courts for economic purposes were held by every lord by unquestioned right: as seen in the laws of Henry I, the great tenants-in-chief had also their honor courts,[1] in which they could hear civil cases between their vassals,[2] and by means of which their estates could be administered. Even if a lord possessed more than one honor, each was treated as a unit, with a specialised organisation, the complexity of which can best be seen in later records. At the same time seignorial lords had been encroaching on royal franchise: many hundreds were in private hands at the end of the Anglo-Saxon period, and there was an increasing tendency for the private courts to assume jurisdiction in petty criminal matters, whether obtained by royal grant or not. By the thirteenth century, indeed, most lords had in their court leet a jurisdiction equivalent to that of the sheriff in his tourn.

The fourteenth and fifteenth centuries are of far less importance in the history of private franchise and jurisdiction than the period after the Norman Conquest, but court records become abundant from the late thirteenth century, and a few extracts are given below to show something of the survivals of feudal justice. It is clear that the extension of royal justice was weakening the private as well as the communal courts. From Henry II's time it had been possible for any freeholder to avail himself of royal writs and assizes for the defence of his tenement or seisin. The king had cognisance of all cases of error, and only the older procedure of *duellum* and wager of law was left to the seignorial courts, unless both parties agreed to use a jury. Further, the judicial interpretation of the statute of Gloucester (1278) deprived these courts, as it had already deprived the communal courts, of personal actions involving cases of more than forty shillings value.[3]

[1] Stubbs, *S.C.* p. 126, cap. LV.
[2] *Ibid.* p. 122: "Order for the holding of courts...".
[3] W. S. Holdsworth, *A history of English law*, I, 72–3.

Yet the enquiries of Edward I which resulted in the Quo Warranto proceedings[1] brought to light the extreme claims and assumptions of lords, and the hundred rolls further give a very intimate picture of local jurisdiction and conditions.[2] While Edward's reign saw so remarkable an advance in royal justice and administration, it is a mistake to assume that the king had won an unqualified triumph over the barons. His victory consisted in the recognition of the principle that all such jurisdiction could only be held by delegation. In practice the barons retained many of their franchises intact, and by supplementary statutes of 1290 their privileges were confirmed if they could show possession from the coronation of Richard I. In fact, considerable profits were derived by lords from their jurisdictions, and especially from courts such as those of honors. The lay or ecclesiastic lord of an honor still held regular three-weekly courts for his suitors from one or more counties. It is difficult to generalise on such matters as the status of the suitors, but the extracts from one honor court(2) show that the business entailed a carefully organised and specialised administration.[3] A late fourteenth-century statute suggests that the honor court continued to encroach upon royal preserves(4).

The chief problem for the holder of an honor court was to enforce attendance; some of the more important tenants were regularly fined for non-appearance, and there were delays in justice for the same reason. Most of the profits came from fines for the transfer of land and tenements, and this seems to have been the real reason for the continuance of these courts, as it was for the continuance of manorial courts dealing with copyhold tenure. A number of writs are quoted(3) to show the connection of the honor court with royal justice and to indicate the relations between the lord and important tenants.

Apart from the great honorial holdings, many lords were in possession of royal franchises such as the return of writs, the right to hold fairs, to hold the assize of bread and ale, or to hold a hundred court. This last was most important, since the sheriff could be excluded and the private leet would then take the place of the sheriff's tourn. In the leet franchises could be easily administered, and of these the view of frankpledge had become

[1] Cf. Stubbs, *S.C.* pp. 449–50.
[2] Cf. H. M. Cam, *The hundred and the hundred rolls*, and her historical revision in *History*, 1926.
[3] W. O. Ault, *Court rolls of the abbey of Ramsey and of the honor of Clare.*

the most important. In earlier times the frankpledge system had been instituted for the better keeping of the peace; it was necessary for every male over twelve years to be in a tithing (which was either a group of men, or a geographical area), with the tithing-man or chief pledge in charge.[1] At least from Henry II's time the view of frankpledge had come to be associated with the tourn, as later with the leet. He had instituted a presenting jury to make final presentment on various articles after the preliminary pre-sentment from localities, and in process of time a more simplified procedure had grown up in the private leets, where it had come to be usual for a single presentment of all offences to be made to the lord's steward by the chief pledges, whatever their number.[2] Extracts are given below(1) to show the great variety of cases in a court leet, and the administration of a group of leets within an honor; and it is easy to understand why petty criminal matters continued to be dealt with in private courts, in some cases until modern times.[3] A small profit made it worth while to hold the courts in addition to the manorial courts serving economic needs.

In the boroughs leet jurisdiction was capable of much develop-ment, and in fact existed in some towns for centuries.[4] In the counties, however, it was natural that the twice-yearly leet, like the sheriff's tourn, proved ineffective; the officials were unpaid, and a fine was the only form of punishment. As in the case of the sheriff's jurisdiction, the private courts lost all effective powers, which were assumed by the justices of the peace.

[1] W. A. Morris, *The frankpledge system, passim.*
[2] *Ibid.* Cf. F. W. Maitland, *Select pleas in manorial...courts,* pp. xxvii ff.
[3] Cf. Holdsworth, *op. cit.* I, 136–8.
[4] F. J. C. Hearnshaw, *Leet jurisdiction in England...,* pp. 247 ff.

(1) *Extracts from court rolls of leets within the honor*
of Clare 1321

Leta ibidem tenta Die Martis in festo Sancti Dunstani *Arnyngton.*
anno regni regis Edwardi xiiij⁰.

Ricardus [op.]² Maryote de communi³ per Robertum *Essonie.*
Gory j⁰ aff:⁴ Johannes Waryn [op.] de eodem per
Thomam Wauencys, j⁰. Thomas Koc de eodem per
Johannem Koc...

Philippus Cosselyn, Petrus Pons, Galfridus Wodekoc, *Arnyngton.*
capitales plegii de Aryngton presentant quod dant de *communis*
finis
cerco fine dimidiam marcam.⁵ *di. mr.*

Item presentant quod Thomas Pogeys [xij d.] Johannes *mie.*
de Wauton [iij d.] Ricardus Camel [vj d.] liberi tenentes *xxj d.*
non veniunt ideo etc....

Item presentant quod Agnes fferour [vj d.] est pistor *mie.*
et vendit contra assisam. Et est regrator ceruisie ideo etc. *xij d.*

Item presentant quod tastatores ceruisie bene fecerunt *mie.*
officium et postea dicunt contrarie... *ij s.*

De omnibus braciatricibus quia non portauerunt men- *mia.*
suras ideo ipsi in misericordia. *xd.*

De Johanne Barlych [vj d.] et Johanne Saap [vj d.] *mia.*
tastatores ceruisie contradixerunt Capitalibus plegiis di- *xij d.*
cendo quod false presentauerunt quod Braciatrices vendiderunt contra assisam ideo ipsi in misericordia, plegii alter
alterius.

De Petro Puffe quia non habuit Adam Selwyn decen- *mia.*
narium suum, ideo ipse in misericordia. *iij d.*

Et quia capitales plegii non presentauerunt predictum *mia.*
Adam Selwyne ideo ipsi pro concelamento in miseri- *xij d.*
cordia.   Summa, xvij s. iij d.

¹ Court roll, 214/5, m. 1. These leets are in Cambridgeshire,
? Arrington, Harlton and Toft. Interlineated passages are given
within square brackets. The Feast of St Dunstan is May 19.
² op.=optulit se.
³ de communi summonitione. This is an essoin of one of the regular
suitors.
⁴ j⁰ aff:=primo affidavit. The essoiner pledged his faith for the
first time that the excuse would be made good.
⁵ A common fine of varying amount was paid in every leet;
possibly it was originally a payment whereby inhabitants were saved
from appearing at the sheriff's tourn. Cf. article in *E.H.R.* xix,
715–19, giving tithing lists of chief pledges and their tithing-men,
each paying 1d. for the common fine.   ⁶ Misericordie.

Harlton.
finis.
iiijs.
Thomas Hokedych, Adam Secke, Thomas atte hil, Thomas West, Rogerus le Palmere, Willelmus Weelt, capitales plegii presentant quod dant de cerco fine, iiijs.

mie.
xvd.
Item presentant quod Rogerus de Huntyngfeld [vjd.] Johannes de la Lude [vjd.] Willelmus Amys [iijd.] liberi tenentes faciunt defaltam ideo etc.

mia.
vs.
Et quia capitales plegii concellauerunt predictum Willelmum Amis, ideo ipsi in misericordia...

finis
xijd.
Item presentant quod Thomas le Bray vendidit Willelmo de Taleworth vnum messuagium et vnam acram terre. Et postea predictus Willelmus vendidit dicta tenementa predicto Thome, ideo preceptum est, etc. Postea venit dictus Thomas et finem fecit pro ingressu habendo, per plegium Nicholai atte Well...

finis
iiijd.
Item presentant quod Johanna filia Nicholai Hobekyn adquisiuit de feodo domini vnam dimidiam acram terre de Matilla Gerard que venit et finem fecit pro ingressu habendo, per plegium Ballivi...

mie.
ijs. iiijd.
Item presentant quod Mabilla Wayte, [ixd.] Alecia Seck, [vjd.] Agnes Weld, [vjd.] Matilla atte Well, [vjd.] sunt braciatrices et vendunt contra assisam.

mie.
xijd.
Item presentant quod Thomas Hokedych [iijd.] et Thomas West [ixd.] sunt tastatores ceruisie non fecerunt officium ideo etc.

mia.
iijd.
De Thoma Hokedych quia non habet Alanum de Chastreton decennarium suum ideo ipse in misericordia...

Summa, xxjs. vijd.

Toft.
finis.
ijs. vjd.
Willelmus Machoun, Galfridus Nosse et Henricus Basely presentant quod dant de cerco fine ijs. vjd.

mie.
xviijd.
Item presentant quod Prior de Bernewell [Breue] Thomas Tolyn [vjd.] Bartholomeus Custe [vjd.] Sayer Hough [iijd.] Nicholaus Lauman [iijd.] sunt liberi tenentes et faciunt defaltam. ideo etc.

mia.
xijd.
Item presentant quod Prior de Bernewell non mundauit fossatam suam per quod communis via emerguntur [sic] ad dampnum et nocumentum vicinorum, ideo etc.

mia.
vjd.
Item presentant quod Willelmus le Soutere percussit Matillam Hykedoun per quod dicta Matilla leuauit hutesium iuste.

Et quia capitales plegii simul cum constabulario non fecerunt officium attachiare partes, ideo ipsi in misericordia. Summa, xiij s. *mia. vj d.*

Leta ibidem tenta Die Mercurii proxima post festum Sancti Dunstani anno regni regis Edwardi xiiij^mo. *Lytlington.*[1]

Omnes capitales plegii de Lytlington presentant quod dant de cerco fine, xiij s. iiij d. [*sic*]. *communis finis. x s.*

Item presentant quod Priorissa sancte Radegund [vj d.] Johannes Howel [iij d.] liberi tenentes faciunt defaltam, ideo etc.... *mia. ix d.*

Item presentant quod Johannes Staleworth fecit rescussum super Rogerum filium Hugonis, ideo ipse in misericordia. *mia. vj d.*

Item presentant quod predictus Johannes traxit sanguinem de predicto Rogero filio Hugonis ideo ipse in misericordia, per plegium predictum. *mia. vj d.*

Et quia predicti capitales plegii dictam presentatam concelauerunt ideo ipsi in misericordia... *mia. ij s.*

Adhuc leta de Lytlington vt patet inferius... *m. 1 d.*

Item presentant quod Johannes Gay insultum fecit Willelmo de Lecheffeld per quod predictus Willelmus iuste leuauit hutesium super dictum Johannem. Et quia constabularii pacis non fecerunt officium attachiare partes ideo ipsi in misericordia... *mia. vj d.*

Item presentant quod Johannes person fecit purpresturam super regale cheminum de longitudine et latitudine xvj pedium, ideo etc. Et irrigatur. Et quia capitales plegii variauerunt in dicta presentacione, in misericordia. *mia. vj d. mia. xij d.*

Item presentant quod Johannes le Meleward assportauit duas garbas de Eustachio Dansy,...ideo in misericordia. Et quia variunt in dicta presentacione dicendo postea quod asportauit iiij garbas [*sic*]. *mia. vj d. mia. xij d.*

Item presentant quod Warinus Howayn [vj d.] Ricardus Surpleft, Junior, [vj d.] Walterus le Weche, [vj d.] vendiderunt carnes non sanos, ideo ipsi in misericordia. per plegium Ricardi Surplet, Roberti le Erl... *mie. xviij d.*

Item presentant quod Margeria le Somenour [10 *names follow*] braciatrices, et vendiderunt contra assisam, ideo ipse in misericordia... Summa, xxxij s. *mie. vs. iij d.*

[1] Litlington, Morden and Tadlow are to the west of Royston, and Abington south-east of Cambridge.

Mordon.
finis,
communis.
xs.

Item quod omnes capitales plegii de Mordon dant de cerco fine, xs.

mie.
iiijs. xd.

Item presentant quod Abbas de Wardon [breue] Prior de Bernewell [xld.] Johannes de Maydenebery [vjd.] Johannes Kok, [vjd.] Ricardus Caus, [vjd.] liberi tenentes...non venerunt, ideo etc....

mia. iijd.

De Alano Gyn capitale plegio quia non habuit Petrum Lukke decennarium suum, ideo etc...

Summa, xxxijs. vijd.

Tadelowe.
finis.
di. mr.

Omnes capitales plegii presentant quod dant de cerco fine dimidiam marcam.

mia. vjd.

Item presentant quod Johannes le Neweman fecit rescussum super Willelmum Russh de vno bidencio ideo etc.

mia. iijd.

Item presentant quod predictus Willelmus iuste leuauit hutesium super dictum Johannem per plegium Johannis Bercarii, Johannis atte Pond...

mia. ijs.

Item presentant quod Prior de Chikesond, [xijd.] tenentes tenementi Willelmi Sancti Georgij, [vjd.] Ricardus de Colne, [vid.] qui debent sectam non venerunt, ideo ipsi in misericordia...

Summa, xvjs. vd.

Auynton.
finis, ijs.

Omnes capitales plegii de Abynton presentant quod dant de cerco fine, ijs.

mie.
xviijd.

Item presentant quod Ricardus Byboys [vjd.] [3 *others*] sectatores Lete faciunt defaltam, ideo etc.

mia. vjd.

Item presentant quod Ricardus le Wodeman braciator vendiderat contra assisam, ideo etc.

Summa, iiijs.

m. 2.

1321. *Royal writ*

Edwardus dei gratia Rex Anglie, Dominus Hibernie, et Dux Aquitanie, Balliuis Rogeri Damory honoris de Clare in Comitatu Essex, salutem. Cum de communi consilio regni nostri prouisum sit quod si qui in diuersis hundredis habeant tenementa non habeant necesse venire ad visum franci plegii nisi in balliuis vbi fuerint conuersantes, vobis precipimus quod non distringatis Imbertum de Scoteneye ad veniendum ad visum franci plegii in Curia predicti domini vestri honoris predicti in Comitatu predicto contra formam prouisionis predicte. Et discriccionem si quam ei ea occasione feceritis, sine dilacione relaxetis eidem. Teste me ipso apud Westmonasterium, primo die Junii, anno regni nostri quarto decimo.

[*Membranes* 4–10 *give leets for Denston* (*Suffolk*), *Wollee* (? *Woolley, Hunts.*), *Great Gransden* (*Hunts.*), *Harlton, Toft, etc.* (*as above*) *for the years* 15–19 *Edward II, but not so complete as above. Attached to the bottom of m.* 10 *is the following writ:*]

1326

Edwardus dei gratia *etc.* Balliuis Elizabeth de Burgo de Arnyngton, salutem. Cum de communi consilio regni nostri prouisum sit quod viri religiosi non habeant necesse venire ad visum ffranci plegii nisi eorum presencia ob aliam causam specialiter exigatur. Vobis precipimus quod non distringatis Priorem Hospitalis Sancti Johannis Jerusalem in Anglia ad veniendum ad visum ffranci plegii in Curia predicte domine vestre de Arnyngton contra formam prouisionis predicte. Et districcionem si quam ei ea occasione feceritis sine dilacione relaxetis eidem. Teste me ipso apud Portestr' v^to die Septembris anno regni nostri vicesimo.

(2) *Extracts from a court roll of Clare honor* 1324

Curia Honoris ibidem tenta die Mercurii proxima post *Clare.*[1] festum Sancti Griggorii pape,[2] anno Edwardi xvij°.

......

Preceptum est attachiare Evorard le Vernon ad re- *Northf.* spondendum Willelmo de cauenedisch in placito debiti. *preceptum est.*

Preceptum est retinere vnum equum captum de Radulpho Lessete et plus etc. pro homagio et feodelitate et pro ingressu in tenementis perquisitis de Oliuero Wych ... qui illa tenementa prius tenuit de honore de Clare in capite.

Herincus Lessete et Rogerus Edrich fecerunt homagium et fidelitatem pro tenementis perquisitis de dicto Oliuero. Et habent diem de gratia Domine ad ostendendum

---

[1] There is a very complete series of rolls for Clare honor in Norfolk, Suffolk and Essex, after 1308. (Cf. W. O. Ault, *Court rolls of the abbey of Ramsey and the honor of Clare.*) These extracts are taken from Court roll 212/40, m. 8. The business of each court is very lengthy, and covers one side, and sometimes part of the dorse, of a large membrane.
[2] March 12.

transcriptas...de finibus factis pro ingressu in dictis tenementis prius in curia de Clare in proximum adventum
senescalli in partibus de Walsingham.

*Suff.
finis, iijd.* Johannes le Bakester finem facit pro ingressu habendo
in vno cotagio adquisito de Roberto de Cloptone in
Kenteford.

Ricardus de Euefeld attachiatus fuit ad respondendum
Thome de Redeswell, persone ecclesie de ffordham de
placito debiti vnde idem Thomas queritur quod in
octabis Sancti Andree anno regni regis Edwardi patris
domini regis Edwardi nunc x°, apud ffordham dictus
Ricardus obligauit se teneri dicto Thome in viginti solidis
soluendis eidem Thome apud Pentelowe in crastino die
Pasche proximo sequente. Ad quem diem nihil ei soluit
sed adhuc detinet ad dampnum dicti Thome xld. et inde
producit sectam, etc. Et super hoc predictus Thomas
profert scriptum predicti Ricardi quod hec testatur. Et
predictus Ricardus presens in Curia predictum debitum
*Essex
cognicio,
preceptum
est.* nunc scriptum non potuit dedicere, ideo consideratum
est quod dictus Thomas recuperet predictum debitum
viginti solidorum simul cum dampno, et dictus Ricardus in misericordia...Et postea ad instanciam dicti
Ricardi predictus Thomas per atturnatum suum concessit eidem Ricardo dies solucionis predicti debiti, scilicet
medietatem ad festum Pentecoste...et aliam medietatem
ad festum Sancti Michelis...

*Norff.
mia. xijd.* De Thoma Deakne et plegiis suis de prosecutione quia
non est presens uersus fratrem Paulum, Abbatem de Der-
ham et alios in querela. Et predicti Abbas et alii inde
sine die.

*Norff.
finis, iijd.* De Thoma Cole ut possit recedere de querelis suis
motis uersus Willelmum Roteney eo quod testatum est
per balliuum quod dictus Willelmus nichil tenet per quod
potest attachiari...

mie. iijd. De primis plegiis Johannis Cotere et Cristiane vxoris
eius quia non habent eos ad respondendum Johanni atte
Bek in placito transgressionis. Et preceptum est ponere
ipsos per melios...

*Norff.
finis, vjd.* De Roberto Carpenter pro licencia concordandi cum
Emma Haukyn in placito transgressionis.

finis, iijd. De Benedicto Dauy pro licencia concordandi cum
Matilla Dauy in placito debiti...

Henricus Brond finem facit pro ingressu in j acra terre perquisita de feodo domine in parua Saunfford... *Essex. finis ixd.*

Nicholaus Blendhare finem facit pro respectu homagii sui domine faciendi usque proximam curiam tentam post Pascham pro viij acris terre quas tenet de domina in capite... *Essex. finis iijd.*

Memorandum quod ad istam curiam Benedictus le Schipwrighte, Willelmus Cach' et Jacobus de Cheddeston receperunt de Domina Elizabeth de Burgh Domina de Clare manerium suum de Sothewold vna cum wrecco maris finibus amerciamentis letarum et curiarum eiusdem ville a festo sancti Michelis vltimo preter vsque finem quinque annorum... soluendum annuatim pro predicto manerio quatuordecim libros bone et legalis monete apud castrum de Clare, ad festa Pasche, centum solidos, Natiuitatis Sancti Johannis Baptiste quatuor libros, et Sancti Michelis centum solidos sine vlteria dilacione. Et si contingat quod predicti Benedictus, Willelmus, et Jacobus, in parte vel in toto predictum (?) pecunium ad terminos supradictos deficere, quod absit, quod predicta Domina possit predictum manerium cum omnibus proficuis suis supradictis ingredi et retinere, et per balliuos suos ministrare. In cuius rei testimonium transcripto huius rotulamenti Robertus de Cheddeworth senescallus honoris de Clare sigillum suum apposuit. *Suff. m^d. Suthwold*

Ricardus de Brecham Neuton capellanus queritur de Priorissa de Blakebergh et eiusdem loci conuentu de placito conciencie, plegii de prosecutione Willelmus ffaber de Brecham et balliuus. Et preceptum est attachiare predictam priorissam et conuentum ad respondendum dicto Ricardo in placito predicto. Et predictus Ricardus ponit loco suo Johannem de Bosco vel Willelmum atte hil, plegii dicte priorisse et conuentus, Thomas Hokk' et Willelmus Motte. *Norff. Querela. preceptum est.*

Johannes de Haukedon et Johannes le Breton exsecutores testamenti Stephani de Haukedon queruntur de Waltero filio Humfridi de placito debiti, per plegium Johannis de Borough... *Essex. preceptum est.*

Summa xjs. ixd. vnde Norff. vjs. vjd. *m. 8 d.*

Suff.   xxjd.

Essex. iijs. vjd.

(3) *Writs sent to an honor court* 1326 *etc.*

1326. *The writ of right*[1]

Curia[2] honoris de Clare tenta die mercurii proxima post festum Sancti Dunstani anno regni regis Edwardi filii Regis Edwardi, xix°.

Essex.
Queritur
per breue
de recto.

Thomas filius Walteri de Yerdele queritur de Willelmo de Wauton de placito terre prout per breue domini Regis plenius continetur. Edwardus dei gratia Rex Anglie Dominus Hibernie et Dux Aquitanie, Elizabeth de Burgo de Clare, salutem. Precipimus tibi quod sine dilatione plenum rectum teneas Thome filio Walteri de Yerdelee de quatuor acris terre cum pertinentiis in Thaxsted quas clamat tenere de te per liberum seruicium vnius denarii per annum pro omni seruicio quas Willelmus de Wauton ei deforciat. Et nisi feceris vicecomes Suff' faciat ne amplius inde clamorem audiendum pro defectu recti. Teste me ipso apud Hailes primo die maij anno regni nostri decimo nono. Et dictus Thomas inuenit plegios de prosecutione Johannes filius Roberti et Robertus Andreu. Virtute cuius breuis consideratum est quod dictus Willelmus summoneatur quod sit ad proximam curiam ad respondendum predicto Thome de placito predicto.

Curia[3] Honoris de Clare tenta ibidem die mercurii in festo Sancti Barnabe apostoli, anno xix°.

Essex preceptum est.

Willelmus de Wauton summonitus fuit per Willelmum Sauser et Stephanum Bateman ad respondendum Thome filio Walteri de Yerdele de placito quod ei reddat quatuor acras terre cum pertinentiis in Thaxsted, et non venit, ideo preceptum est capere predictam terram in manus domine quovsque etc. Et summonere predictum Willelmum quod sit ad proximam etc.

Curia[4] Honoris de Clare tenta die mercurii post festum apostolorum Petri et Pauli, anno xix°.

Essex. lex.

Quia Willelmus de Wauton summonitus fuit veniendum ad vltimam curiam ad respondendum Thome filio Walteri de Yerdelee de placito terre vt patet, etc., ad

[1] Cf. Pollock and Maitland, *History of English law*, II, 62. Extracts have been taken from the Court roll, 212/42.
[2] m. 11 d.   [3] m. 12.   [4] m. 13.

quem diem non venit, per quod terra capta fuit, etc. et replegiatus fuit infra quindenam, Et ad istam curiam predicte partes optulerunt se et predictus Willelmus respondit ad defaltam curie precedentis et dicit quod non fuit summonitus secundum legem Anglie et inde vadiauit legem, plegii de lege Ricardus Grigges et Ricardus de Spaldyng, et habent diem vsque ad proximam.[1]

1335. *Writ to the steward*[2]

Elizabeth de Bourg, Dame de Clare, a nostre cher vallet Johan de Hertford nostre Seneschal de Clare, salutz. Purce qe monsire Johan Haward...vous ad fait feaute pur terres et tenementz qil tient de nous de leritage sa cumpaigne et sur ceo ly auoms respite son relief tanqe a la quinzeyne de la Purificacion prescheyn auenyr. Vous mandoms qe vous ly suffrez en pees tanqe au dit temps sanz nulle duresse a ly faire ou destresse prendre...Et ce ne lessez A dieu Escript a Berdefeld le xviij iour Doctobre.

1340. *Writ to the steward*[3]

Elizabeth de Bourg dame de Clare a nostre cher vallet Johan de Hertford nostre seneschal de Clare, salutz. Purce qe Lore de Henham et Johan son fitz ount suy a nous par vne peticion pur quinze acres de terre en la ville de Bumstede queux furent mys en morgage a Johan de Ruly qi fust bastard et morust saunz heir de son corps, et la terre en sa seisine. Apres qi mort la dite terre feut seisie en nostre meyn come nostre eschete, et nous de nostre grace especiale et par oeure de charite auoms graunte as ditz Lore et Johan la dite terre A auoir et tenir a touz iours en mesme lestat come ils le tiendrent auantceo qils le mistrent en morgage. Vous maundoms qe as auantditz Lore et Johan la dite terre par garant de cestes facet deliuerer. Et qe ceste lettre soit enroule en nostre court de Clare. A dieu qe vous gard. Escript a Angleseye le xxvij^me iour de marcz Lan du regne le Roi Edward tierz puis le conquest quatorzisme.

---

[1] There is no trace of the case in the next courts.
[2] Court roll, 212/50, m. 2, 9 Ed. III.
[3] Court roll, 213/3, m. 7.

(4) *Private courts and cases of freehold* 1391

...accordez est et assentuz qe null lige du Roi desore
enavant soit artez compellez ne constreint par nulle voie
de venir ne dapparoir devant le conseill dascun seignur
ou dame pur y respondre de son frank tenement ne de
chose qi touche frank tenement ne de null autre chose
reale ou personele qappartient a la ley de la terre en
ascune manere. Et si ascun se sent grevez en temps avenir
encontre ceste ordeinance et accorde, sue al Chaunceller
qi serra pur le temps et il en ferra remede.

S.R. II, 82, 15 Ric. II, c. 12.

CHAPTER VII

THE TOWNS

INTRODUCTION

At the close of the thirteenth century the more important of the English towns had acquired a considerable amount of self-government, although they had never become communes in the foreign sense of the word. London, however, and other boroughs had bought charters of privilege, which gave them the right to pay annually the *firma burgi* (a lump sum in lieu of various payments which would otherwise have been collected by royal officials), to have their own court of justice, and to elect their own officials, and in the highest stage of development their own mayor. There were, however, some towns which had not yet reached this form of municipal government; those on the lands of ecclesiastical or lay lords (*Reading, Leicester*) were slower in acquiring independence than those on the royal demesne. During this period royal towns were still receiving grants of *firma burgi*, and of the right to elect a mayor (*Norwich*). Despite this progress it cannot be said that the corporate character of the towns was yet completely recognised. The community had developed considerably. A town might have its own seal and its own property, but formal charters of incorporation are not found before the fourteenth century, and in many cases the idea of the community as a collective personality is only actually defined in the next century (*Southampton*). The chief interest of the period lies in the advance of those towns which had not yet obtained self-government, the development of the formal idea of an urban corporation, and the formation of a more or less regular system of town government. Some towns, following the example of London, acquired the rights of a county (*Bristol, Norwich, Southampton*).

The development of the towns was due to their growth in wealth and industry, and the trading element was, therefore, of great importance in their history. The exact part played by the gild merchant in the history of the towns is less significant in this than in the earlier period; the fourteenth century saw for the most part the amalgamation of gild and borough until only one governing body was supreme in the towns, in some cases the gild element being predominant, in others the municipal organisation superseding that of the gild (*Reading*). At this period also the various craft gilds or mysteries were coming to the fore as each trade became increasingly important, and there were frequent struggles between crafts and municipality as to where the chief authority should reside. Were members of the crafts to gain control over town government, or should the trades be subject to the control of the municipality? (*London*).

The main interest of the period, however, is in the development of the common council, whereby a more democratic influence over town government was obtained, at least for a time. In some cases an already existing assembly was adapted, and an elected common council was added to the governing body (*London, Norwich*). In other towns a common council might be created by the most influential burgesses in the name of the rest to act as a check on the excessive powers exercised by the chief officials (*Bristol*). The effort to form a more popular body, however, was not generally successful. Even the claim to have elected representatives was often suppressed, and the town constitutions tended to become more and more narrow in character. The governing bodies became smaller, and in many cases self-chosen; the choice of officials was in the hands of a limited number of electors; and the member of parliament might be representative of a small body only. The oligarchical character of the towns and the power of the rich merchants became increasingly marked during the fifteenth century, although in some cases the final defeat of the democracy was delayed until Tudor times.

BIBLIOGRAPHY

1. GENERAL

BATESON, M. *Borough customs*, S.S. vols. XVIII, XXI. 1904–6.
GREEN, A. STOPFORD. *Town life in the fifteenth century*, 2 vols. London, 1894.
GROSS, C. *A bibliography of British municipal history, in Harvard historical studies*, vol. v. New York, 1897.
—— *The gild merchant*, 2 vols. Oxford, 1890.
HEMMEON, M. DE W. *Burgage tenure in mediaeval England, in Harvard historical studies*, vol. xx. 1914.
HIBBERT, F. AIDAN. *The influence and development of English gilds,....* Cambridge, 1891.

2. ARTICLES

TAIT, J. "The origin of town-councils in England", *E.H.R.* XLIV, 1929.
—— "The borough community in England", *E.H.R.* XLV, 1930.
—— "The common council of the borough", *E.H.R.* XLVI, 1931.

3. MUNICIPAL HISTORIES

BRISTOL

BICKLEY, F. B. (ed.). *The little red book of Bristol*, 2 vols. Bristol and London, 1900.
HARDING, N. D. (ed.). *Bristol charters*, 1155–1373, vol. I. Bristol Record Society, 1930.
SEYER, S. (ed.). *The charters and letters patent...of Bristol*. Bristol, 1812.

LEICESTER

BATESON, M. (ed.). *Records of the borough of Leicester*, vol. II, 1327–1509. London, 1901.

LONDON

MS. authority, Guildhall, Records office, Letter books, A–L.
RILEY, H. T. *Memorials of London*, 1276–1419. London, 1868.
—— *Munimenta gildhallae Londoniensis: Liber Albus, R.S.* London, 1859.
SHARPE, R. R. (ed.). *Calendar of Letter books, A–L.* London, 1899–1912.
THOMAS, A. H. (ed.). *Calendar of plea and memoranda rolls of London*, 1323–1412, 3 vols. London, 1926–32.

NORWICH

HUDSON, W. and TINGEY, J. C. (eds.). *The records of the city of Norwich*, vol. I. Norwich, 1906.

OXFORD

OGLE, O. (ed.). *Royal letters addressed to Oxford*. Oxford, 1892.
SALTER, H. E. (ed.). *Munimenta civitatis Oxonie*. Devizes, 1920.

READING

GUILDING, J. M. (ed.). *Diary of the corporation of Reading*, vol. I, 1431–1602. London, 1892.

SOUTHAMPTON

CHAPMAN, A. B. W. (ed.). *The black book of Southampton*, vols. I, II. Southampton Record Society, 1912.
GIDDEN, H. W. (ed.). *The charters of the borough of Southampton*, vol. I, 1199–1480. Southampton Record Society, 1909.
STUDER, P. (ed.). *The oak book of Southampton*, vol. I. Southampton Record Society, 1910.

BRISTOL

BRISTOL is an example of a town in which many disputes took place between the leading men who acquired the chief power and the community of townsmen. In 1344 a common council was established to assist the mayor(1), and this council, originally forty-eight "of the chiefest and discreetest burgesses", was reduced in number in the fifteenth century. In 1499, however, this body ceased to have much popular character, as it was to be elected by the mayor and two aldermen chosen by him with the assent of the commonalty(9).

In 1373 Bristol had been made into a county(4), with its own sheriff(5). The craft gilds, though wealthy and numerous, seem to have been under the control of the municipality(8).

(1) *Ordinances* 1344

...Anno regni regis Edwardi tercii post conquestum decimo octauo ordinaciones, consuetudines ac libertates subscriptas pro communitate ville predicte factas recordari feci...Et licet pro conseruacione premissorum in villa predicta Maior pro gubernatore efficiter, ad requisicionem tamen Stephani le Spicer in maiorem anno supradicto ibidem electum ad statum suum et villam in melius gubernandum electi sunt sibi pro consultoribus ac sessoribus et ad negocia ville auxilianda et expedienda de communi assensu quadraginta octo de potencioribus et discrecioribus ville predicte videlicet:—

Little red book of Bristol, 1, 25.

(2) *The keeping of the peace* 1347

Edwardus *etc*....Omnibus ad quos presentes littere peruenerint; salutem. Quia vt accepimus quamplures malefactores et pacis nostre perturbatores in villa Bristollie diebus et noctibus vagantur et discurrunt, dampna maleficia et excessus hominibus parcium illarum diuersimodo perpetrantes in populi nostri ibidem terrorem non modicum ac dicte pacis nostre lesionem manifestam. Nos desiderantes pacem nostram in villa predicta, sicut in ceteris locis regni nostri Anglie firmiter obseruari, ac volentes perturbatores, et violatores eiusdem pacis nostre debite puniri prout decet; concessimus pro nobis et heredibus nostris dilectis nobis; Maiori Balliuis et probis hominibus dicte ville Bristollie, quod ipsi vnum dolium pro prisonibus infra villam predictam de nouo facere et illud habere possint et tenere sibi et successoribus suis imperpetuum, ad imprisonandum in eodem huiusmodi malefactores,...si quos ibidem de nocte vagantes inueniri contigerit eodem modo et prout in Ciuitate nostra Londonie est vsitatum. Concessimus eciam...eisdem Maiori, Balliuis et probis hominibus, quod ipsi et successores sui predicti pro meliori custodia assise panis in villa predicta faciende decetero facere possint talem punicionem de Pistoribus assisam illam ibidem frangentibus, videlicet ad trahendum huiusmodi Pistores contra assisam illam delinquentes super cleias per vicos ville predicte, et ad ipsos alio modo castigandos, prout in dicta Ciuitate nostra Londonie de huiusmodi pistoribus similiter est vsitatum...Teste Leonello filio nostro carissimo, Custode Anglie apud Redyngam vicesimo quarto die Aprilis. Anno regni nostri Anglie vicesimo primo, regni vero nostri Francie octauo. per breue de priuato sigillo. Sewenh'.

Bristol charters (ed. Harding), p. 108.

(3) *Admission to the freedom of the town* 1366–7

Item accordee est et assentuz qe nully soit receu deynz notre fraunchise de Bristuyt sil ne soit marchaund conu homme de bone fame et honeste conuersacion. Et a quele houre qil soit receu paiera la fyn a la communalte de x. liures au meynz saunz rien diceo estre pardonee par ascun manere colour...

Ordinee est et assentuz qe touz yceux qe ne sount pas burgeys et voillent marchaunder ou art vser deynz la ville et ne ount de quei ou ne voillent paier la dite summe de x. liures pur estre enfraunchiz qilz soient receu portmen et facent fyn al communalte solonc la descrecion du mair et seneschals qe pur le temps serrount et solomc lour estat pur leur profist ent faire.

Little red book of Bristol, II, 47, 48.

(4) *Bristol formed into a county* 1373

Edwardus *etc.*....Venerabilibus in christo patribus Iohanni Episcopo Bathoniensi et wellensi willelmo Episcopo wygorniensi et dilectis sibi in christo waltero Abbati Glastonie et Nicholao Abbati Cirencestrie ac dilectis et fidelibus suis Edmundo Clyuedon' Ricardo de Acton' Theobaldo Gorges henrico Percehay waltero Clopton' et Iohanni Seriaunt salutem. Sciatis quod cum octauo die Augusti proximo preterito concesserimus...dilectis nobis Burgensibus ville nostre Bristollie et eorum heredibus et successoribus

suis, imperpetuum quod predicta villa Bristollie cum suburbiis
suis et procinctu eorundem; de Comitatibus Gloucestrie et
Somersete decetero separata sit pariter et in omnibus exempta tam
per terram quam per aquam et quod sit Comitatus per se et
Comitatus Bristollie nuncupatus imperpetuum et quod dicti Burgenses et eorum heredes et successores imperpetuum habeant infra
dictam villam Bristollie et suburbia eiusdem et eorum procinctum
certas libertates et quietancias et eis plene gaudeant et Vtantur
prout in carta predicta plenius continetur. Nos volentes certiorari
super metis et bundis ville et suburbiorum predictorum ac procinctus eorundem et quod inter eadem villam suburbia et procinctum iam Comitatum Bristollie sic existencia et nuncupata et
Comitatus Gloucestrie et Somersete diuise perpetue per certas
metas et bundas fiant et decetero per metas et bundas illas tam
diuise predicte quam procinctus dictorum Comitatuum Bristollie,
Gloucestrie et Somersete in certo ponantur, ne super metis et
diuisis dictorum trium Comitatuum Ambiguitas imposterum
habeatur. Assignauimus vos nouem octo septem et sex vestrum
Iusticiarios nostros ad perambulacionem inter dictum Comitatum
Bristollie et procinctum, eiusdem tam per terram quam per
aquam et dictos Comitatus Gloucestrie et Somersete, extra procinctum eiusdem Comitatus Bristollie per sacramentum tam
Militum quam aliorum proborum et legalium hominum tam de
dictis Comitatibus Gloucestrie et Somersete quam de dicto Comitatu Bristollie tam infra libertates quam extra per quos rei veritas
melius sciri poterit fideliter faciendam et ad certa signa et metas
et diuisas que imperpetuum cognosci valeant inter dictum procinctum Comitatus Bristollie et dictos Comitatus Gloucestrie et
Somersete in perambulacione illa ponenda. Et ideo vobis mandamus quod ad certos dies et loca quos vos...ad hoc prouideritis
circa premissa intendatis et perambulacionem faciatis in forma
predicta. Mandauimus enim vicecomitibus nostris dictorum Comitatuum Gloucestrie et Somersete ac Maiori dicte ville Bristollie
quod ad certos dies et loca quos vos...eis scire faciatis venire
faciant coram vobis nouem...tot et tales tam Milites quam alios
probos et legales homines de tribus Comitatibus predictis tam
infra libertates quam extra per quos rei veritas in premissis melius
sciri poterit et inquiri. Et scire faciatis nobis in Cancellaria nostra
ad cicius quo commode poteritis vbicumque tunc fuerit sub sigillis
vestris...et sigillis quatuor legalium Militum ex illis qui perambu-
lacioni illi interfuerint per que signa metas et diuisas perambulacio
illa facta fuerit: In cuius rei testimonium has litteras nostras fieri

fecimus patentes. Teste me ipso apud westmonasterium primo die
Septembris Anno regni nostri Anglie quadragesimo septimo regni
vero nostri Francie tricesimo quarto.

Bristol charters (ed. Harding), p. 142.

(5) *Appointment of sheriff* 1373

Edwardus...Maiori Burgensibus liberis hominibus et toti Communitati ville Bristollie ac suburbiorum et procinctus eorundem;
salutem. Cum commiserimus dilecto nobis Iohanni Viel Comitatum nostrum Bristollie custodiendum per vnum annum iuxta
libertates dilectis nobis Burgensibus ville predicte per cartam
nostram concessas et confirmatas. Ita quod firmas debitas nobis
reddat annuatim et de debitis nostris ac omnibus aliis ad officium
vicecomitis dicti Comitatus Bristollie spectantibus nobis respondeat ad scaccarium nostrum prout in litteris nostris patentibus
inde confectis plenius continetur. Vobis mandamus quod eidem
Iohanni tanquam vicecomiti Comitatus Bristollie in omnibus que
ad officium vicecomitis eiusdem Comitatus pertinent intendentes
sitis et respondentes. In cuius rei testimonium has litteras nostras
fieri fecimus patentes. Teste me ipso apud westmonasterium primo
die Octobris Anno regni nostri Anglie quadragesimo septimo
regni vero nostri Francie tricesimo quarto.

per ipsum Regem
Faryngton.

Bristol charters (ed. Harding), p. 166.

(6) *Bond of mayor and commonalty concerning the lease of the farm* 1408

Hec indentura facta inter dominam Johannam Dei gracia Reginam Anglie ex una parte et Johannem Fyssher, Maiorem ville
Bristollie, et Communitatem eiusdem ville ex parte altera, testatur,
cum predicta domina Regina per alias litteras suas indentatas de
dato de vicesimo die Novembris anno regni regis Henrici quarti
post conquestum decimo [1408] concessit, et ad totam vitam suam
ad firmam dimisit prefato Johanni Fyssher, Maiori ville predicte
et Communitati eiusdem ville et eorum successoribus, villam
Bristollie et suburbia eiusdem cum omnibus terris et tenementis,
redditibus, curtilagiis, celdis, toftis, gardinis, molendinis, scabellis
vocatis fflesshameles et aliis scabellis, stagnis, tyna Castri, redditi-

bus, langabulis, theoloniis, placitis, perquisicionibus, reversionibus, Curiis, feriis de mercatis, feodis et aliis juribus, consuetudinibus et comoditatibus ad villam predictam...pertinentibus, exceptis in dictis aliis indenturis exceptis, unacum libertate, privilegiis et franchesiis in predictis indenturis contentis, et eisdem Maiori et Communitati...concessis, et per metuendissimum dominum nostrum Regem eidem domine Regine ad terminum vite sue concessis...Reddendo proinde annuatim prefate domine Regine ad terminum vite sue ad receptam suam apud Westmonasterium centum, octoginta et duas libras, septem solidos et decem denarios, ad festa Pasche et Sancti Michaelis...Datum apud Westmonasterium vicesimo octavo die Novembris, Anno regni Regis Henrici quarti post conquestum decimo.

Little red book of Bristol, I, 171–3.

(7) *The staple* 1436

Memorandum quod Johannes Milton, nuper Major ville Bristollie ac Stapule Bristollie dum in illis officiis steterat, diem suum clausit extremum...

...scire dignetur vestra dominacio reuerenda nos prefatos Constabularios ac communitatem mercatorum, tam indigenarum quam alienigenarum, Stapule predicte de communi assensu nostro eligisse Nicholaum Devenyssche in majorem Stapule predicte pro residuo anni predicti...Datum in Stapula Bristollie die veneris in crastino Purificacionis beate Marie Virginis, anno regni Regis Henrici Sexti post conquestum Anglie quarto decimo.

Little red book of Bristol, I, 178, 181.

(8) *The crafts and the borough* 1452–3

Carta domini Henrici quarti facta tinctoribus Bristollie de diuersis ordinacionibus pro misteria tinctorum, etc. Henricus *etc*....Inspeximus quoddam scriptum certarum ordinacionum pro saniori gubernacione mistere tinctorum ville Bristollie per Johannem Drois nuper Majorem dicte ville, Johannem Fissher nuper Vicecomitem, Jacobum Cokkes et Dauid Dudbroke nuper Balliuos ejusdem ville per auisamentum et assensum tocius communis consilii ville predicte et de assensu proborum hominum dicte mistere editum, sigillo majoratus ville predicte consignatum in hec verba:—

Little red book of Bristol, II, 89.

(9) *Charter of Henry VII* 1499

Henricus Dei gratia *etc.* Sciatis quod nos ob singularem affec-
tionem et dilectionem quas penes nunc majorem et communitatem villæ nostræ Bristollie gerimus..., concessimus...præfatis
nunc majori et communitati ejusdem villæ, hæredibus et successoribus suis, quod de cætero sint in dicta villa Bristollie de
tempore in tempus in perpetuum sex aldermanni modo et forma
sequente nominandi...viz. quod recordator prædictæ villæ
Bristollie..., ac quilibet alius recordator villæ illius pro tempore
existens...erit unus dictorum sex aldermannorum; et quod re-
sidui quinque aldermanni eorundem sex aldermannorum per
majorem et communeconcilium villæ illius...ad eorum libitum
infra unum annum a data præsentium sequentem eligantur...
[p. 152] Ulterius concessimus...præfatis majori et communitati...quod major dictæ villæ Bristollie...ac duo aldermanni...
per majorem ejusdem villæ...nominandi et assignandi de assensu
communitatis villæ prædictæ eligere poterunt successive in perpetuum de tempore in tempus quadraginta homines de melioribus
et probioribus hominibus villæ,...quoties opus fuerit; quod si in
aliquibus custumis sive consuetudinibus...in dicta villa Bristollie...habitis et usitatis aut de novo emergentibus difficultates vel
defectus fuerint, in quibus remedium nondum est appositum,
in casibus antedictis iidem major et duo aldermanni ad hoc nominandi...et quadraginta homines villæ illius...potestatem habeant ordinandi et stabiliendi competens remedium sive competentia
remedia, quod consentaneum fuerit vel quæ consentanea fuerint
rationi,...et quod dictus major et duo aldermanni...et quadraginta homines...pro necessitate et proficuo dictæ villæ Bristollie...de communi assensu suo super bonis omnium hominum
et personarum villæ prædictæ...de qualibet persona juxta
statum suum tam super redditibus suis, quam pro mysteriis et
merchandizis suis et aliter, prout melius faciendum viderint,
tallagia assidere poterunt, et ea levare absque impetitione nostri,
...justiciariorum aut aliorum ministrorum nostrorum...quo-
rumcunque;...

Charters of Bristol (ed. Seyer), pp 123–53.

LEICESTER

LEICESTER is an interesting example of a town in the hands of a great lord, which in consequence had a comparatively late development; it only obtained a lease of the bailiwick from John of Gaunt in 1375(1), and then only on a short term lease, later renewed. With the accession of Henry IV, the borough as part of the Lancastrian inheritance came into direct relation with the crown, but it still seems to have been treated as a seignorial and not a royal borough.

Another feature of importance is the coalescence of the government of port and gild. In the thirteenth century the powerful gild merchant controlled the revenues of the town; but it was distinct from the borough, which possessed judicial authority in its borough court. The Mayor's Sessions or Common Hall was formed by the union of gild-hall and port-moot, which had completely coalesced by the fifteenth century.

The government of Leicester was never very democratic; the twenty-four "fellows of the mayor" or "brethren of the bench" were not elected, though there was at one time the possibility of a common meeting. This was limited in 1466, when the unenfranchised (non-gildsmen) were excluded from the common-hall meetings(3); already in 1464, when justices of the peace had been granted for the town, the choice of justices and coroners was put into the hands of the mayor and twenty-four(2). In 1489 the community was ordered to hand over its rights to forty-eight of their number, to be chosen in the same way(4).

(1) Charter from John of Gaunt leasing the farm of the borough 1375

Ceste endenture faite parentre le tres noble seigneur Johan Roy de Castille...dune part et le Maire, burgeises et la communalte de la ville de Leycestre daultre part tesmoigne que le dit Duc ad graunte et a ferme lesse as dites Maire, burgeises et communalte, la baillie de la ville susdite et des suburbes dicell, oue toutes manere des execuciones deinz ycell affaire par lours baillifs par eaux deputeez si auant des briefs nostre seigneur le Roy come des aultres execuciones qecomqes..., ensemblement oue toutes manere profites des portmotes, courtes de la feyre et du marchee de dite ville et suburbes, et des aultres courtes qeconques deinz la dite ville et suburbes par eaux ou lours deputeez ateners, oue toutes manere des rentes, fermes et profites deinz la dite ville et suburbes, oue chatealx des futifs et des felones, wayf et extray, fynes et

amercementz qecomques faites deuant eaux...forsprises rentes et
fermes des fornes, molynes et de leawe, et les rentes qe sont leu-
ables par le porter du chastel come auant cestes heures soleient
estre leuez, et saluant au dit Duc et a ses heirs escheteez des
franches tenementz et sa court a tener en le chastel de Leycestre
de trois simaignes en trois, somonces, attachementz, et destresses
et toutes aultres manere execuciones en la dite court...Ensement
le dit Duc ad graunte as dites Maire, burgeises et communalte...
la garde des toutes manere des prisones prises en la dite ville et
suburbes, si auant pour felonie come pour trespasses agarder
solonc la ley et come auant cestes heures attient as baillifs de dit
Duc, a auoir et tener as dites Maire, burgeises et communalte...
toutes les choses et profites auantdites, forsprises les forsprises
auantnomeez et saluez a terme des dys ans,...: Rendant ent par
an a dit Duc et a ses heirs par les mains son Resceuour de Leycestre...quatre vintz liures de bone monee as festes de la purificacion nostre Dame, Pentecoste, et la seint Michel,...En tes-
moigniance de quele chose a lune part de ceste endenture le dit
Duc ad mys son seal et a laultre part des dites endentures les
auantdites Maire, burgeises et communalte ount mys lour commune seal. Done a Leycestre le lundy proschein apres le feste de
lasumpcion nostre Dame lan du regne le Roi Edward tierce puis
le conqueste quarante neofisme.

Records of...Leicester (ed. Bateson), II, 149–52.

(2) *Growth of oligarchy. Letters patent of Edward IV* 1464

Edwardus, [*etc.*]...omnibus ad quos presentes litere pervenerint, salutem. Sciatis quod nos, volentes securitati et quieti di-
lectorum ligeorum nostrorum majoris et burgensium ville sive
burgi nostre Leycestrie, concessimus...Johanni Yoman nunc
majori ejusdem ville sive burgi et burgensibus ejusdem, ac successoribus suis...quod hujusmodi major et quatuor de discre-
scioribus comburgensibus ville sive burgi illius,...eligendi et
nominandi, quamdiu in hujusmodi officiis majoratus aut burgensium fuerint, cum uno legisperito imperpetuo nominando recordator Leycestrie, sint justiciarii nostri et heredum nostrorum
ad pacem infra villam sive burgum predictum, procinctum et
limites ejusdem ville sive burgi, necnon ad statuta et ordinaciones
de artificibus et laboratoribus edita conservanda et custodiri
facienda imperpetuum; et quod iidem major et quatuor comburgenses...tres vel duo eorum, cum dicto recordatore, plenam

habeant coreccionem...et auctoritatem cognoscendi, inquirendi, audiendi, et terminandi omnes res et materias, tam de omnibus feloniis, transgressionibus, mesprisionibus, et extortionibus, quam de omnimodis aliis causis, querelis, malefactis quibuscumque, infra eandem villam sive burgum, procinctum et limites ejusdem, qualitercumque contingent..., adeo plene et integre sicut custodes pacis nostre et justiciarii ad felonias, transgressiones, et alia malefacta audienda et terminanda assignati et assignandi ac justiciarii servientium, laboratorum et artificium in comitatu Leycestrie extra villam sive burgum ac procinctum predictum habent, seu in futuris qualitercumque habebunt; terminacionibus de omnimodis feloniis, ac de contrafactura, tonsura, et alia falsitate monete regni nostri Anglie duntaxat exceptis. Et quod nullus custos pacis, justiciarius aut commissionarius nostri, vel heredum nostrorum, ad premissa sive aliquod premissorum in comitatu predicto audienda et terminanda assignati, in aliquo intromittat infra villam sive burgum predictum, aut procinctum...ejusdem...Et insuper concessimus,...quod iidem major et viginti quatuor comburgenses ...de anno in annum in festo Sancti Mathei Evangeliste eligere possunt de ipsis viginti quatuor comburgensibus predictos quatuor discreciores comburgenses essendi justiciarii nostri...ac de eisdem viginti quatuor comburgensibus duos coronatores qui officium coronatorum infra villam sive burgum predictum...faciant et exequentur...Concessimus eciam...prefatis majori et burgensibus...quod nec ipsi nec eorum aliquis ponatur neque ponantur, impanellentur neque impanelletur in aliquibus assisis, juratis, inquisicionibus, seu recognicionibus, licet tanget nos vel heredes nostros...nec jurentur nec onerentur, nec ullus eorum juretur seu oneretur super triacione arraiamenti alicujus assise sive panelli coram aliquibus justiciariis seu commissionariis nostris...In cujus rei testimonium has literas nostras fieri fecimus patentes. Teste meipso apud Wodestoke, vicesimo quarto die Augusti, anno regni nostri quarto.

J. Throsby, *The history and antiquities of...Leicester* (1791), p. 70 (translation in Bateson, *op. cit.* II, 280).

(3) Order excluding from the Common Halls all who are not franchised 1466

Hit was ordeyned and agreed at a comen hall holden at Leycestre the xxv day of Octobre the 6ᵗᵉ yere of the regne of the Kyng oure souereyne lord Edward the IIIIᵗᵉ, in the time of mairaltie of

Roger Wygston than beyng Maire of the seyd towne of Leycestre,
by a generall assent and agrement as wele of the same Maire, his
brethern and all the comens of the same toune...that from that
tyme forth no man presume to entre into the Gilde hall otherwise
cald the Maires hall at eny comen hall ther holden...but oonly
thoes and siche as ben fraunchest, that is to say men entred into
the Marchaundes Gild, on payne of inprisonment as long as the
Maire lykes forthwith doon vpon euery suche persone doing the
contrary at eny comen Hall.

Bateson, *op. cit.* II, 285.

(4) *Order from Henry VII on town government* 1489

Herry by the grace of God...to our trusty and welbeloved the
Mayr, baillief, comburges and burges of our toun of Leycestre...
greting. And for as much as we bee enfourmed that at euery
eleccioun of the Mayr ther, or burges of the parliamentes, or at
assessyng of eny lauful imposicions, the commonaltie of oure said
towne, as well pore as riche, have alway assembled at youre comen
hall, wher as such persones as bee of lytyll substaunce or reason
and not contributories, or ellys full lytill, to the charges susteyned
in such behalue, and haue had interest thorugh theyr exclamacions
and hedynes to the subuersion not oonly of the gode polyce of
oure seid town but lykly to the often breche of the peax...for
reformacion wherof,...we woll and straitly charge you...the said
Mayr, bailief, and xxiiii comburgeses of our seid toun,...that at
all comen halles...aswel for the eleccioun of the Mayr, of the
Justicez of the peax, and burgesses of our parliamentes, as also at
assessyng of eny lauful imposiciouns or othrewise, ye ioyntely
chese and call unto yov our baillief of our seid toun...and oonly
xlviii of the most wise and sad comyners inhabitants pere after
your discrecions of the same cominaltie and no mo. And ye than
to ordre and direct all maters...as by your reasons and consciens
shalbe thoughte lieful and moost expedient. Yeven at our palays
of Westmynster vnder our seale of our said Duchie the secound
day of Juyll the iiii^te yere of our reigne.

Per consilium ducatus predicti.

Bateson, *op. cit.* II, 324–5.

LONDON

LONDON was exceptional in retaining the possession of an elective common council, although the choice of members was eventually confined to a small body of electors. In Edward I's reign the city had for a time fallen under royal displeasure, and from 1285 to 1298 was under the rule of a warden nominated by the king, instead of an elected mayor. In 1298 the old liberties were restored and a mayor was elected by the aldermen and twelve men from each of the wards into which the city was divided; the mayor thus chosen had to be presented to the king and receive his confirmation. The city was again deprived of its liberties for a time under Edward II(4).

The Londoners evidently took great interest in the election of the mayor, and the townsmen endeavoured to assert their right to join in the choice, with the result that there was frequent disturbance. This was met by a royal proclamation stating that only good folk of the better sort, especially summoned, should be present(3). The elections, however, were still stated to take place before "a very great commonalty", and in 1346 the number of men to be sent from each ward was reduced, according to its size. In 1351 an effort was made by the crafts to secure authority(5), and in 1376 each elected its representatives to attend the common council, the greater crafts sending six, the lesser four or two(8). In 1384 it was decided to return to election by the wards(11); in the choice of the mayor two names were to be sent up by the electors, leaving the final decision with the outgoing mayor and aldermen. London suffered at Richard II's hands in 1392, when the city was placed under a commissioner instead of the mayor and sheriffs, but its liberties were soon restored and the fines remitted(12, 13). In the fifteenth century the electors were limited in number(14), and in 1467 it was decreed that the mayor and sheriffs should be chosen by the common council, by the masters and wardens of each mystery coming in their livery and by good men specially summoned(15), while in 1475 the commoners summoned from the wards were to be livery men.

(1) *Election of mayor* 1309

Thomas Romayn electus est in maiorem ciuitatis Lon- Eleccio
donie die martis in festo Apostolorum Simonis et Jude Thome Romayn
anno regni Regis Edwardi filij Regis Edwardi tercio per in maiorem
Nicholaum de Farndone prius maiorem Johannem de Londonie.
Wengraue, Willelmum de Leire, Johannem de Wynde-
sore, Simonem de Paris, Johannis [*sic*] le Coroner,
Nicholaum Pikot, Henricum de Dureme, Willelmum
Trente, Johannem de Gisorcio, Galfridum de Conductu,
Simonem Bolet, Ricardum de Wirhale, Willelmum
Seruad, et Ricardum de Refham aldermannos et Roge-
rum le Paumer et Jacobum filium ffulconis de Sancto
Edmundo vicecomites et xij homines de singulis Wardis
ad hoc summonitos etc.

Et die Mercurii proxima sequente predictus Thomas
per predictos Aldermannos et communitatem fuit presentatus coram Baronibus de Scaccario apud Westmonasterium et ibidem admissus et iuratus.

Postea die Lune in festo Concepcionis beate Marie Virginis predictus Thomas Romayn presentatus fuit coram
domino Edwardo Rege apud Westmonasterium et tanquam maior fuit a dicto domino Rege admissus etc.

Letter book D, f. ii.

(2) *Election of sheriffs* 1313

Die veneris in vigilia Sancti Michelis anno regni Regis Eleccio
Edwardi filij Regis Edwardi vij°, per Johannem de vicecomi-
Gisorcio tunc maiorem, Nicholaum de ffarendon', [11 vij°.
others], aldermannos, Johannem Lambyn et Adam
Ludekyn vicecomites et per communitatem hic sum-
monitam pro vicecomitibus suis eligendis electi sunt in
vicecomites videlicet, Robertus Burdeyn aurifaber et
Hugo de Garton mercer et Jurati ad officium predictum
etc. Et sciendum est quod ordinatum fuit eodem die et
concordatum per predictos maiorem aldermannos et
communitatem pro quibusdam periculis que in huiusmodi eleccione vicecomitum iminere possent in euentu
euitandis quod de cetero singulis annis summoniantur de
qualibet Warda probiores homines essendi hic in festo
Sancti Mathei apostoli et euangeliste pro eleccione vice-

Nota de
ordinacione
facta ad
summonien-
dam com-
munitatem
pro
eleccione
facienda.
comitum facienda vna cum maiore et aldermannis qui pro tempore fuerint. Ita quod illi quos eligere continget ad predictum officium recipiendum melius possint prouideri etc.

Letter book D, f. iii b.

(3) *Royal proclamation on elections* 1315

Breue Regis
de modo
et forma
eleccionis
maioris e
viceco-
mitum.

proclama-
cio facta
per pre-
dictum
breue.
Dominus Rex mandauit breue suum maiori et vicecomitibus Londonie in hec verba...Virtute cuius breuis facta fuit quedam proclamacio que subsequitur.

Purceo qe nostre Seignur le Roi ad entendu qe ascune gent du poeple de sa vice de Loundres eynz ces heures sount venuz a la Gyhale a les elecciouns du maire et des viscountes la ou vnques somons ne furent, ne illoeqes riens ne ount en afaire et vnt desturbe les elecciouns du maire et des viscountes issint qil ne poeyent estre faites en due forme ne en bone manere auxi come il soleyent, et souentefoiz par manaces et par cries tiels maneres des elecciouns vnt troblez en despit du Roi, et emblemissement de sa coronne, en defesaunce dil estat de sa dite citee, Comaunde qe nul ne soit si ose ne si hardi qe viegne al eleccioun des viscountes qe ore de nouel sount a eslire, ne al eleccioun du maire, qe en temps auenir serra esleu sil ne soit meire, viscountes, Audermans, et autres bones gentz des meillours de la dite cite qi per ministres de meisme la cite illoqes auenir especiaument sount somons, ou qe a eux afiert de y estre sur peyne de enprisonement de lour corps hors de quele prisoun nostre Seignour le Roi voet qe tiels si nuls soient trouez ne soient deliuerez sanz especial comandement de lui.

Letter book D, f. iv b.

(4) *Restoration of city liberties* 1326

Breue Regis
de maioratu
Londonie
restituto.
Edwardus...dilectis suis aldermannis vicecomitibus et toti comunitati Ciuitatis Londonie salutem. Actendentes laudabilia obsequia que vos et progenitores vestri nobis et progenitoribus nostris multipliciter impendistis et adhuc impendere non desistitis hiis diebus, Considerantes etiam comoda magna que in futurum contingere poterunt si maioris liberam eleccionem habueritis prout alias

habere consueuistis. Volentes que vobis hiis de causis gratiam facere specialem officium maioritatis nuper coram Justiciariis nostris vltime itinerantibus ad communia placita apud turrim nostram Londonie in manum nostram captum vobis duximus restituendum habendum et excercendum eodem modo quo illud habuistis ante capcionem predictam in manum nostram. Ideo vobis mandamus quod infra octo dies a tempore recepcionis presentium maiorem de vobis eligatis et eum presentetis et omnia alia in negocio illo facienda faciatis prout in negocio predicto ante capcionem predictam in manum nostram fieri consueuit. Teste Edwardo filio nostro primogenito custode regni nostri apud Hereford vj^{to} die Nouembris anno regni nostri vicesimo.

Ista litera irrotulatur ad scaccarium in memorando anno xx. Regis Edwardi filij Regis Edwardi inter recorda de termino Sancti Michelis.

Letter book E, f. clxxi.

(5) *Election of the common council by the mysteries* 1351

Die lune proxima ante festum Sancti Martini anno regni regis Edwardi tercij post conquestum xxv^{to} Quedam Billa missa fuit per Andream Aubrey maiorem vnam billam duobus hominibus de mesteris subscriptis vt patet inferius in hec verba.

Willelmo Welde et Drapers, per maiorem;
Johanni de Bures,

Assembletz les bones gentz du dit mestier et facetz eslire par commune assent iiij bones gentz du dit mestier les pluis sachantz et suffisauntz decreter ou les meire audermans et viscountes des ascunes grosses busoignes tochantes lestat de la dite citee. Et ceo ne lessetz en la fey qe vous deuetz a nostre Seignur le Roy Et eietz les nouns et les persones des ceux issint esluz a la Gyhale iceo July en la veille de Seint Martyn.

[*The names are given of two men from each mystery.*]

Letter book F, f. ccvj.

(6) *Penalty for non-attendance at the common council* 1354

Congregacio maioris aldermannorum vicecomitum et immense communitatis ciuitatis die sabbati proxima post
festum Sancti Dunstani anno regni Regis Edwardi tercij
post conquestum vicesimo octauo. Et fuerunt presentes
Adam ffraunceys maior, [19 *others*], Aldermanni ffuerunt
eciam presentes in eadem congregacione sapienciores et
diciores omnium Wardarum Ciuitatis predicte.

quod
quilibet
qui facit
defaltam
soluet
communi-
tati ijs.

In ista congregacione ordinatum fuit et concessum
quod cum decetero aldermanni et alij ciues ciuitatis
Londonie summoniti fuerint essendi apud Gyhaldam Londonie pro arduis negocijs communitatem ciuitatis predicte tangentibus et non venerint ibidem hora prima apud
Sanctum Paulum pulsata amercientur ad ijs. ad opus
communitatis leuandos.

Letter book G, f. xix.

(7) *Levy of one and a half fifteenths on the wards* 1370

ordinacio
et con-
cessio facte
pro exen-
niis domino
principi et
principisse
factis. etc.

Memorandum quod in congregacione maioris et aldermannorum ac immense communitatis coram eis summonite xxvijⁿ die Januarij anno regni regis Edwardi tercij
post conquestum xliiijᵗᵒ ex eorum vnanimi assensu et
voluntate ordinatum fuit concordatum et concessum per
eosdem quod in singulis Wardis ciuitatis predicte leuare-
tur de hominibus Wardarum illarum xvᵗᵒ et dimidia xvᵉ
pro duobus exenniis inde faciendis vno videlicet domino
Edwardo principi Wallie et altero principisse consorti sue
in aduentu suo Londoniis post reditum suum in Anglia de
partibus Vasconie.

Letter book G, f. cclxij b.

(8) *Royal letter on the form of elections* 1376

Litera
domini
Regis missa
maiori
Recorda-
tori, vice-
comitibus,
alderman-
nis et com-
munitati
Londonie.

Edward...A noz bien amez maire recordour viscontes
aldermans citeins et communs de nostre citee de Londres
saluz. Donez nous est entendre coment vous estes en
dissension et diuerses opinions sur les eleccions des mair
viscontes et aldermans et autres ordenances afaire en
nostre dite citee pur le bon gouuernement dycelle, et la
sauuetee et conseruacion de nostre pees illeoqes cestassauoir les vns de vous veullantz qe les dites eleccions et

ordenances feussent faites par certeines persones eslieuz
par les communs de les gardes et les autres veullantz les
dites eleccions et ordenances estre faites par certeines
persones des mesteres eslieuz par gentz de mesmes les
mesteres, dont graunt riot damage et meschief purroient
sourder...Et porce qe nous auons ordenez destre en
nostre persone a nostre Paleys de Westmonster en la feste
de Seint Michel prochein venant et dauor delez nous a
mesme le temps illoeqes le prelatz et seignurs de nostre
grant conseil pur certeines grosses busoignes touchantes
lestat de nous et de nostre roialme auant dit deuant quex
nous volons qe la matire sur quele vous estez ensi en
dissension et diuerses opinions come dessus soit declaree
et debatue et les resons monstrees et oyees dune part et
dautre siqe vne fyn couenable ent puisse lors estre fait...
vous mandons et chargeons fermement et vous defendons
sur peine de forfaiture sibien de voz franchises et priui-
leges come de voz terres et tenementz biens et chateux
et de tout de quanqe vous purrez forfaire deuers nous qe
vous surseez outrement de proceder attanier debater plus
auant ou ordener sur la dite matire par qiconque voie
parentre cy et la dite feste...
Done souz nostre priue seal a nostre Chastel de Haddele
le xxix iour de Juyl lan de nostre regne dengleterre
cynquantisme et de ffrance trente septisme.

[A letter in reply denied the above charge.]

f. xlv b. (*The matter was raised of complaints against the city
in the last parliament, concerning the misdoings of certain
individuals: also about the evil practice of some city officials
granting lands, etc. without the consent of the commonalty.*)

f. xlvj.
...Et quant al seconde pleinte le maire et aldermans et
la commune auysez qentre autres soit compris en lur
chartre des franchises qils poent as touz temps qe lur
busoigne par comun assent amender les difficultes et
defautes trouez en lur vsages...Et come ils furent auisez
qe bone foy et reson demandoient qe les suffisantz communes deussent estre presentz et priuez al fesance de
chescune ordenance touchante la citee en commun...Si
ount les ditz maire et aldermans par assent de toute la
commune ordeignez...Qe chescun an encontre le iour

qe le nouel maire serra chargez par serement de son office, qe les surueours de chescun suffisant mestier de la citee deiuent assembler les mesteres chescun par soi ou lur mieltz plerra et esliront certeines persones en queux ils se tendront content de quanqe serra par le maire les aldermans et ceux esleutz assentuz et ordeignez en la Guyhall et qe ceux esleutz et nuls autres soient sommons as eleccions des maires et viscontes et auxint as toutes heures qe ascune matire serra touche a la Guyhalle pur quel couendra assembler et prendre conseil de la commune. Et qe chescun mestier retourne les nouns des issint eslieutz al nouel maire le primer iour de sa charge, issint toute foith qe le greindre mestier ne eslire plus qe vj persones, les moyenes iiij et les meyndres ij queux demorreront pur lan ensuiant en cele office du conseil sanz eschange si mort ou autre verroie et resonable cause ne les excuse. Et si rien soit ordeigne par maire et aldermans qi touche la commune sanz assent de ceux eslieutz, ou la greindre partie de enaux, ou au meynz de xij les plus suffisantz mesteres, qil soit tenuz pur nul Et qe toutz ceux issint eslieuz soient chargez par serement qils vendront prescement a chescune sommonse sils neient verroie essoyne...

Letter book H, f. xliv ff.

(9) *Royal charters, temp. Edward III*

Charta Regis Edwardi Tertii.

Quod cives Londoniarum habeant libertates suas, secundum formam Magnæ Chartæ,...

Item, quod Major Londoniarum qui pro tempore fuerit sit unus Justiciariorum ad Gaolam de Neugate.

Item, quod cives Londoniarum habeant Infangthef, et Outfangthef, et catalla felonum de omnibus illis qui adjudicati fuerint coram eis infra libertatem civitatis prædictæ.

Item, cum cives Londoniarum onerati fuissent per Vicecomitatum Londoniarum et Middelsexiæ ad Scaccarium Domini Regis de cccc libris, quod ipsi cives in posterum essent de c libris quieti.

Item, quod cives Londoniarum tenementa sua infra

libertatem existentia legare possunt tam ad manum mortuam quam alio modo.

. . . . . .

Item, quod Major, . . ., officium Escaetriæ infra civitatem prædictam exerceat.

Item, quod cives Londoniarum non distringantur ad proficiscendum seu mittendum in guerram extra civitatem prædictam.

Item, quod Constabularius Turris Londoniarum non faciat prisas, per terram nec per aquam, de victualibus aut aliis rebus quibuscunque.

. . . . . .

Item, quod Vicecomites. . . non distringantur ad faciendum sacramentum ad Scaccarium nostrum, nisi super redditione compotorum eorundem.

. . . . . .

Item, quod cives Londoniarum, in auxiliis, concessionibus, et contributionibus, taxentur et contribuant cum communitate regni, sicut homines comitatuum et non sicut homines civitatum et burgorum; et quod de omnibus aliis tallagiis sint quieti.

. . . . . .

Item, quod nullus civis implicitetur seu occasionetur ad Scaccarium nec alibi per billam; nisi de hiis quæ tangunt Dominum Regem vel hæredes suos.

. . . . . .

Alia Charta Regis Edwardi Tertii.

Item, de Vicecomitatu Londoniarum et Middelsexiæ civibus Londoniarum dimisso ad firmam, pro trecentis libris sterlingorum.

Quod cives de seipsis faciant Vicecomites, quos voluerint.

. . . . . .

Item, si Vicecomites fecerint delictum per quod debent incurrere periculum vitæ vel membrorum, judicentur, sicut judicari debent, per legem civitatis.

. . . . . .

Alia Charta Regis Edwardi Tertii.

Quod Major et cives habeant et teneant omnes libertates suas et liberas consuetudines, quas habuerunt tempore Regis Henrici, avi Regis Henrici, etc.

Item, quod Major, absente Rege et hæredibus, præsentetur Baronibus de Scaccario.

. . . . . .

Item, quod nullus Justiciarius assignabitur infra civitatem, nisi Justiciarii Itinerantes apud Turrim, Justiciarii pro Gaola de Neugate et erroribus apud Sanctum Martinum Magnum etc.

Item, quod Major et Vicecomites civitatis prædictæ juxta tenorem Chartarum progenitorum Domini Regis eligantur, et non alio modo.

. . . . . .

Item, quod tallagia et auxilia, in civitate ad opus Regis assidenda per Majorem et Aldermannos, non augmententur seu exaltentur nisi de communi consensu civitatis.

Item, quod denarii de hujusmodi tallagiis provenientes sint in custodia quatuor proborum hominum, Communiariorum civitatis prædictæ.

. . . . . .

Item, quod Commune Sigillum civitatis sit in custodia duorum Aldermannorum et duorum Communiariorum.

. . . . . .

Item, quod Camerarius, Communis Clericus, et Communis Serviens per Communitatem civitatis eligantur et amoveantur.

. . . . . .

Item, quod licet cives libertatibus seu liberis consuetudinibus hactenus plene usi non fuerunt etc., ipsi tamen eis et eorum quolibet de cætero plene gaudeant et utantur.

. . . . . .

Liber Albus, pp. 144–53. (The charters of Richard II and Henry IV and V are mainly repetitions.)

(10) *Writ sent to the aldermen* 1380

Billa missa cuilibet Aldermanno pro vj d. de qualibet libra redditus et vna quintadecima in ciuitate Londonie leuanda.

...Vous chargeantz outre qe vous facez assembler touz les gentz de vostre garde deuant vous parentre cy et lundi ore proschein, pur auoir lour auys sil soit pur le meux de tenir le commune consail par mestiers soulement si come y ad este tenuz deuant ces houres ou par les plus suffisantz gentz des gardes pur icelle par les dites gardes eslieux eyantz plein poer de treter consailler et ordeigner pur

diuerses chargeantz busoignes du dite cite ou autrement
par partie des gardes et partie des mestiers et si soit acorde
entre vous qil serra tenuz par les bones gentz des gardes
adonqe eyez prest ala Guyhall le marsdi ore proschein les
nouns de vj bones gentz de vostre garde et plus suffisantz
eyantz poair come dessus est dit aient eyantz regard sils
ount este en office de auderman ou de viscounte ou
nemye. Escript dessouz le dit seal le tierce iour de
Nouembre lan quart du regne nostre seignur le Roi
Richard second.

Letter book H, f. cxxvj b.

(11) *Election of the common council by wards* 1384

De Communi Consilio per Wardas.

Die Veneris proximo ante festum Purificationis Beatæ
Mariæ Virginis, anno regni Regis Ricardi Secundi septimo, in præsentia Majoris, Aldermannorum, et im-
mensæ Communitatis proborum et discretorum virorum
dictæ civitatis, in Guihalda Londoniarum...iidem probi
homines dictas ordinationes subscriptas, quas cum plena
ordinatione ordinaverunt in dicta congregatione, et legi
fecerunt, in forma quæ sequitur:

Par cause qui compleint dez plusours bonez genz de la
ville fait au Maire, qui ore est, coment divers foitz en le
Counsel use dedeins la Sale et Chambres de la Guihalle
graunt rumour et perile ad estee sentuz, sibien par
grauntez assemblez, et trop sovent come par noun-
sufficeauntz personez deputes as ditz Counsels, sovent
foitz view lez jugementz dez dites counseils, plus par
clamour qui par resoun: a graunt destourbe du pees et
quiete entre le poeple pur temps passe, et plus assetz
semblable en temps a venire, si remedi ne fuisse purveu.
Sur quoy, le Maire, ove sez Aldermans et la bone Comune,
eslirent certeins persones, pur ent, par deliberacioun,
lour avisere coment tiel rumour et perile purroit meultz
estre escheux et remediez; lez queux persones,...ount
par loure avys ordeygnez...lez articles apres escriptz;...
Primes, pur Comune Counsel de la ville continuere par
sufficieauntz gens, sibien davoire come de sen, soit ordeignez qe chescun an, apres le jour Seint Gregory, quaunt
lez Aldermans soient establis, qe lez Aldermans establis

pur lan ensuaunt soient fermement charges, quinse jours apres le dit jour, pur aler assemblere lour Gardes par bone deliberacoun, lour charger deslire quatre des plus suffi-ciauntz persones qi sount en lour Garde, lessaunt pur nulle estate qils ount porte paravaunt, pur estre de Comune Counsel lan ensuaunt, et lez nouns dez ditz quatre presentere a Maire...; lez queux persones ser-rount acceptez par le Maire, et maundez pur prendre lour seurment, come est compris par escript pardevaunt ces heures.

Purveu toutefoitz, qui le Maire,...ne receive en toute la ville de nulle mestiere, pur Comune Counsel, outre eopt persones dun mestiere, saunz plus; tout soit il quil aveigne, qe plusours qui eopt persones dun mestier soient presentes et eslieux; en quel caas, quaunt le Maire, par avys de sys Aldermans, serrount acceptes eopt persones de lez plus sufficeantz, et lez autrez retournes a lour Garde, pur eslyre en loure lieu autrez sufficeauntz qi ne soient de tiel mistiere.

Et par cause qe de chescune Garde parmy la ville, ne serra trove toutdis quatre persones, et sufficience, pur estre del Counsel avaundit, soit estably qui de lez Gardes qi sount grauntz et sufficeauntz dez heritantz, dascuns sys, dascuns quatre, et des ascuns deux, solonc qui les Gardez puissent de suffisantie porter...qi amountent en toute quatre-vintz sesse persones; et ceo est le nombre de chescune Garde, un parmy autre quatre persones.

Liber Albus, pp. 461–3.

(12) *The mayor replaced by a royal official* 1392

Commissio Edwardi Dalyngregge ad essen-dum custos Londonie. Ricardus...Omnibus ad quos presentes littere peruene-rint, salutem. Sciatis quod nos attendentes notabiles et euidentes defectus quos in minus discreta et insufficiente gubernacione et regimine ciuitatis nostre Londonie tem-pore Johannis Hende maioris ac Johannis Shadeworth et Henrici Vanner vicecomitum eiusdem ciuitatis notorie reperimus et aperte necnon dampna et pericula intole-rabilia que exinde nisi manus nostras adiutrices in hac parte celerius apponamus...de assensu et auisamento consilii nostri ipsos Johannem, Johannem et Henricum de officiis suis predictis duximus penitus amouendos...

constituimus dilectum et fidelem militem nostrum Edwardum Dalyngrugge de cuius fidelitate et circumspeccione plenam fiduciam reportamus custodem ciuitatis predicte quamdiu nostre placuerit voluntati dantes ei tenore presencium plenam et sufficientem auctoritatem et potestatem populum nostrum dicte ciuitatis regendi et gubernandi ac omnia alia et singula que ad bonum regimen et sanam gubernacionem eiusdem ciuitatis pertinent faciendi....Teste me ipso apud castrum de Notyngham xxv die Junij anno regni nostri sextodecimo.

Letter book H, f. cclxx b.

(13) Restoration of city liberties 1392

Ricardus...Omnibus ad quos presentes littere peruenerint, salutem. Sciatis quod cum nuper per litteras nostras patentes assignauerimus carissimos auunculos nostros Edmundum ducem Eboraci et Thomam ducem Gloucestrie ac quosdam alios Justiciarios nostros ad inquirendum de omnibus et singulis erroribus...in ciuitate nostra Londonie pro defectu bone gubernacionis maiorum vicecomitum et aldermannorum eiusdem ciuitatis...et ad premissa omnia et singula tam ad sectam nostram quam aliorum quoruncumque coram prefatis Justiciariis nostris conqueri volencium secundum legem et consuetudinem regni nostri Anglie audiendum et terminandum...iuxta formam cuiusdam statuti tempore carissimi domini et aui nostri Regis Edwardi defuncti inde editi et prouisi prout in litteris predictis plenius continetur. Coram quibus quidem Justiciariis nostris Willelmus Venour nuper maior, Johannes Loney et Johannes Walcote nuper vicecomites, Willelmus Baret [21 *names follow*] nuper Aldermanni ciuitatis nostre predicte iudicati fuerunt de eo quod ipsi diuersos mesprisiones et defectus factos in ciuitate nostra predicta pro defectu gubernacionis sue in eadem ciuitate non correxerunt neque punierunt ac processus versus eos coram prefatis Justiciariis nostris factus fuerit quousque ipsi inde conuicti fuissent Super quo consideratum fuit per predictos Justiciarios nostros quod nos haberemus de prefatis nuper maiore vicecomitibus et aldermannis pro primo defectu suo mille marcas et pro secundo defectu suo duo milia marcarum et pro eorum tercio defectu quod

Pardonacio et restitucio libertatis.

libertas ciuitatis nostre predicte caperetur in manum
nostram que quidem libertas in manum nostram sic capta
in dicta manu nostra adhuc remanet ex causa supradicta.
Nos de gracia nostra speciali ex cerca sciencia nostra et ad
supplicacionem carissime consortis nostre Regine, concessimus vicecomitibus et aldermannis ac omnibus ciuibus ciuitatis nostre predicte quod habeant omnes libertates et franchesias sic seisitas in manum nostram ac eis
gaudeant et vtantur modo et forma quibus illas habuerunt
et eis gaudebant et vtebantur ante iudicium de dicta
libertate in manum nostram sic capiendam redditum
quousque aliter ordinauerimus pro eisdem. In cuius rei
testimonium has litteras nostras fieri fecimus patentes.
Teste me ipso apud Wodestoke decimo nono die Septembris anno regni nostri sexto decimo.

per breue de priuato sigillo.

Letter book H, f. cclxxij.

(14) *Method of choosing the common council; and the oath
taken by those elected, early fifteenth century*

Modus tenendi Commune Consilium talis est.—Quod
pridie ante celebrationem ejusdem, Major et Aldermanni
per servientes Cameræ summoneri facient de veniendo
ad Guyhaldam in crastino de singulis Wardis civitatis
xvi, xii, viii, vel iiii, secundum quod Warda fuerit magna
vel parva, de sapientioribus et ditioribus singularum
Wardarum; et quod nulli, nisi fuerint summoniti, veniant,
nec hujusmodi Consilio interesse præsumant, sub pœna
imprisonamenti, ex antiquo et de novo, sub certa pœna
et castigatione in quadam ordinatione, tempore Nicholai
Wottone Majoris facta,... Et amercietur ac solvet quilibet
dictorum summonitorum non venientium ii solidos ad
quodlibet tempus, etc.

Sacramentum autem hominum ad Commune Consilium
electorum est tale—"Tu jurabis quod eris fidelis Domino
nostro Regi N et hæredibus suis; et præsto venies, cum
summonitus fueris, pro Communi Consilio civitatis, si non
fueris rationabiliter excusandus; et bonum et fidele consilium dabis, secundum sensum et scire tuum; et pro
nullius favore manutenebis proficium singulare contra
proficium publicum vel commune dictæ civitatis; et

postquam veneris ad Commune Consilium, sine causa rationabili vel Majoris licentia non recedes priusquam Major et socii sui recesserint; et quod dictum fuerit in Communi Consilio celabis, sicut Deus te adjuvet et Sancta Dei Evangelia "...

Liber Albus, pp. 40–1, cap. xiii. (Nicholas Wottone was mayor in 1415, cf. *Cal. Letter Book*, i, p. 144.)

(15) *Ordinances of the common council* 1467

Commune consilium tentum die Mercurie vicesimo tercio die Septembris anno regni regis Edwardi quarti post conquestum septimo Concordatum fuit per Johannem Yong maiorem Johannem Norman [15 *names follow*] aldermannos ac communitatem ciuitatis Londonie quod nullus liber homo aut officiarius ciuitatis predicte capiat aut vtatur liberatura alicuius domini seu cuiuscumque alterius magnatis sub pena libertatis et officij perdendi pro perpetuo, etc. Ordinacio quod officiarij non vtantur liberatura magnatis.

Item in eodem communi consilio concordatum fuit per dictos maiorem et aldermannos quod de cetero eleccio maioris et vicecomitum tantummodo fiat per commune consilium, magistros et gardianos cuiuslibet mistere istius ciuitatis, venientes in liberatura sua, et per alios probos homines ad hoc specialiter summonitos. Ordinacio pro eleccione maioris et vicecomitum.

Item in eodem communi consilio concordatum fuit per dictos maiorem aldermannos et communitatem quod nullus officiarius ciuitatis Londonie aut alter quiscumque qui gaudet libertate ciuitatis predicte tantum ex officio, officio suo finito gaudeat libertatem ciuitatis predicte. Ordinacio pro admittendo in libertatem ex officio.

Letter book L, f. 53.

NORWICH

Norwich occupied an important position in the fourteenth and fifteenth centuries as an industrial and trading town, especially in connection with the woollen industry. The chief officials were the four bailiffs, aided by a body of twenty-four, who were elected by the community. The common assembly was not in any way democratic, as its members were normally chosen by the officials from the four leets of the town; a body of twenty-four, possibly the same as the assistants to the bailiffs, was taking over more powers, though this was resisted by the democratic element. In 1380 the bailiffs and twenty-four were allowed to make ordinances for municipal government(1), and the clause "by the consent of the commonalty" was omitted, though this was apparently not discovered by the commons until Henry V's reign. In 1404 by royal charter Norwich became a shire, with mayor and two sheriffs instead of the bailiffs(2). An attempt seems to have been made to set up a common council of eighty citizens; and a long quarrel followed between the commons and the twenty-four over the right of election of the mayor. In 1415 a compromise was arranged(3), and two years later a charter was given(4); aldermen, chosen for life, were to act with a common council of sixty, elected by the four wards, and resident citizens could be present with the aldermen and common council at the election of mayor and sheriffs. This constitution, modelled on that of London, suffered little change, save that in 1447 the presence of freemen at the election of officials was forbidden.

(1) *Charter of Richard II* 1380

Concessimus insuper eisdem ciuibus Norwici...quod ipsi et eorum successores Ciues Ciuitatis predicte et nullus alius extraneus a libertate sua Norwici emat vel vendat victualia seu mercandisas aliquas ad retalliam vel per parcellas infra libertates Ciuitatis predicte nisi secundum formam et tenorem statuti nostri in parliamento nostro apud Gloucestriam...Preterea concessimus...prefatis ciuibus nostris quod si fortassis alique consuetudines in dicta ciuitate hactenus obtente et usitate in aliqua sui parte difficiles siue defectiue fuerint sic quod propter aliqua in eadem ciuitate de nouo emergencia ubi remedium prius clare non extitit ordinatum emendacione indigeant, Balliui dicte Ciuitatis pro tempore existentes de assensu viginti et quatuor conciuium suorum pro communitate dicte ciuitatis singulis annis eligendorum vel maioris partis eorundem viginti et quatuor...potestatem habeant et auctoritatem remedium congruum bone fidei et consonum rationi pro communi utilitate ciuium dicte Ciuitatis et aliorum fidelium nostrorum ad eandem confluentium apponendi et ordinandi ac ordinaciones huiusmodi execucioni debite demandandi quotiens et quando opus fuerit et eis videbitur expedire...

Records of...Norwich (ed. Hudson and Tingey), 1, 30; cf. lv.

(2) *Charter of Henry IV* 1404

Concessimus quod...dicta Ciuitas ac tota terra infra dictam Ciuitatem et Libertatem eiusdem cum suburbiis et hamelettis suis ac procinctu eorundem et tota terra in circuitu eiusdem Ciuitatis infra Libertatem dicte Ciuitatis Norwici (Castro et le Shirehous exceptis que infra corpus Comitatus Norfolc' iam existunt) ab eodem Comitatu separata sint ex nunc penitus et in omnibus exempta tam per terram quam per aquam et quod dicta Ciuitas ac suburbia...(exceptis preexceptis) sint de cetero Comitatus per se et Comitatus Ciuitatis Norwici nuncupatus in perpetuum.

Volumus eciam...quod predicti Ciues et Communitas[1]... eligere possint singulis annis successiuis unum Maiorem de se ipsis et quod quilibet Maior...quam citius in Maiorem electus fuerit et prefectus sit Escaetor noster et heredum nostrorum in Ciuitate, suburbiis etc. Et quod dicti Ciues et Communitas...loco quatuor Balliuorum ab antiquo usitatorum (quos et quorum nomina... omnino deleri volumus)...eligere possint singulis annis suc-cessiuis duos Vicecomites de se ipsis...Et quod iidem Escaetor et Vicecomites...easdem habeant potestatem jurisdiccionem et libertatem...in Ciuitate etc...quas ceteri Escaetores et Vice-comites alibi infra regnum nostrum Anglie habent...Et quod predicti Vicecomites Ciuitatis...comitatum suum ibidem per diem lune de mense in mensem teneant eodem modo et prout alii Vicecomites nostri...Et quod...curiam suam ibidem similiter teneant et proficua inde percipiant prout Balliui Ciuitatis antea facere...consueverunt...

Et ulterius concessimus eisdem Ciuibus et Communitati quod ipsi...habeant cognicionem omnimodorum placitorum assisarum noue disseisine et mortis antecessorum de terris etc...infra Ciuitatem etc...coram Maiore et Vicecomitibus...in le Gild-halle Ciuitatis...Et quod Escaetor et Vicecomites...quolibet anno profra sua ad Scaccarium nostrum...facere et computare

---

[1] Note the difference here expressed: Cives=select body of aldermen.

possint per attornatum suum...per literas patentes sub sigillo communi Ciuitatis signatas...absque hoc quod Escaetor et Vice-comites...personaliter venire compellantur...

Hudson and Tingey, *op. cit.* i, 33 ff.; cf. lviii.

(3) *Tripartite indenture with seals of the mayor, sheriffs and the commonalty* 1415

In ye name of ye Trinite fader sone and Holy gost, thre persones and on god in Mageste, principal and special avowe of Norwich Cite and of alle ye Commonaunte...The Meir of ye Cite of Norwich ȝerly shal be chosen uppon ye day of apostles Phillipp and Jacob in ye Gyldhalle, to wiche eleccion ye Meir and xxiiij^ti Conciteȝeyns of ye same Cite and iche of hem shal come, but he yat hath resonable cause of excusacion, uppon peyne of ijs. to ye use of ye Comonalte be ye Comone Sergeant to be arered and payed. And also alle tho persones for ye Comon counseil for ye ȝer chosen un to ye same eleccion shullen come and iche of hem shalle come uppon peyne of xijd. but he yat hath cause of resonable excusacion. And also alle ye Citezeyns Dwellers wit inne ye same Cite...shul frely come as they arn beholden, and ye doores of ye Halle to all Citeȝeinis ther wollyng entren and comen inne shulle ben oopen, and not kept ne none from thens forbarred ne avoyded but foreyns...the Comone Speker shal standen up thus seyand to alle ye Commons ther generaly assembled, "Sires and frendes for ye loue of god Ihu Crist in procedynge of this present eleccion behaue ȝow and rewle ȝow goodly and honestly and leeveth not for loue haate ne dreed yat ȝe chesen and nemelen two suffisant persones for ye Office of Meir sweche as ben honourable and profitable for ye Cite of wiche iche of hem haþ ben Meir or Shreve of ye Cite and of wiche nouther hath ben Meir thre ȝer aforn"...And ye same two so ther chosen her names in a bille shuln ben entred and writen and be ye Comone Speker and sexse of ye Comon Counseil[1] shuln be notified to ye Meir and ye xxiiij^ti beand in the Chambr of ye Halle...And than ye Comone Clerk be ouersight of ye Recordour and ye Comon Speker shalle haue ye forseid bille in kepynge. Unto wiche thre persones ye Meir aloone in propre persone shalle come to apart of ye same Chambr and to hem shal nemele seueraly and secretly oon of ye forseid two persones whom he wille haue to ye office of Meir and up ye same fourme iche of ye nombre of ye

---

[1] The sixty as distinct from the twenty-four.

xxiiij^{ti} ther beande unto ye forseid thre persones shal comen and shal name seueraly and secretly oon of ye forseid two persones weche of hem he wil haue to ye office of Meir and he of ye forseid two yat hath most voyce be ye forseyd serche and Scrutinie shal be prefixed and admitted in Meir for ye ʒer yan next folwyng...

2. And also it is acorded yat ye Shreves of ye Cite of Norwych iche ʒer shuln be chosen in ye day of Nativity of oure Lady uppe this fourme, yat is for to seyne the Meir Shireves xxiiij^{ti} and ye lx^{ti} persones of ye comon counseil shuln comen to ye same eleccion uppon ye peyne ther uppon in ye eleccion of Maire ordeyned, but he yat hath cause resonable of excusacion. And alle other Citeʒeyns unto ye same eleccion shullen frely comen in the same manere and fourme as it is ordeigned for to come to ye eleccion of Maire. And þan ye Meir Shireves [and] ye xxiiij^{ti} shuln gon up in to ye Meires chambr and ther ye Meir and ye xxiiij^{ti} of his counseil be ye avis and assent of hem or of ye more part shuln chese on Shireve, comptynge ye Meir for two voyces ʒif trauers falle, swiche as they wiln answer for...And uppe that ye Meir shall ʒive in commaundement to ye Comonaunte for to gon to gidder and chesen a Conciteʒeyn dwellyng wit inne ye Cite in to another Shireve swiche on for whom thay wiln answeren for ye ʒer than nexste suyng...And ʒif ony variance falle amonge ye poeple and ye Commons uppon ye eleccion of a Shreve that þan yis manere of variaunce shall be tried be ye lx^{ti} persones of ye comon counseil as uppon ye variance of ye eleccion of Meir is ordeyned...

3. The eleccion of the xxiiij^{ti} shalle ʒerly be chosen on ye same foure days yat ye comone counseil shalle be chosen euery Warde be hemself uppon this fourme...Sexse Suffisaunt men for Conesford ʒif yere ben so manye suffisant in ye same Warde...vj for Mancroft Warde vj for Wymer Warde and vj for ye Warde over ye Water shuln frely be chosen uppon ye iiij dayes whan ye common counseil is chosen as more pleynly here after is specified...

4. Also it is acorded yat ye eleccion of ye lx Citeʒenis for ye comone counseil shul be chosen ʒerly be ye iiij Wardes...And thise persones þus chosen for ye Common counseil in Norwich shuln haue poer as swiche persones chosen for ye common counseil in London han poer in ye Cite of London....

10. Also it is ordeigned yat whan ye newe elyt in Meir hath þus chosen his officers forth wit the same day in ye assemble ye hool assemble shal chese ye Recordour, Belleman, and Dykkepere, and þan ye Meir and ye xxiiij^{ti} shuln chese be hemself a Comone

Clerk, oon Crouner, two Clauers and viij Constables. And þan
ye lxᵗⁱ persones of ye Commone counseil shul witinne hemself
chese a Common Speker, oon Crouner, two Clauers and viij
Constables. And on seynt Mathu day next after in assemble
assigned be ye Meir ȝerly shuln be chosen for ye ȝer folwynge be ye
Meir and ye xxiiijᵗⁱ oon Chamberleyn, oon Tresorer, two Auditours yat arn not acomptable of ye Comon good¹ and thre Comoners for to be of counseil wit ye Chamberleyns for ye ȝer. And
ye lxᵗⁱ persones of the comone counseil chosen for ye ȝer shuln
witinne hemself for hemself and be hemself chesen also oon
Chamberleyn, oon Tresorer, on Comone Sergeant, two Auditours,
weche be not acomptable of ye comone good¹ and thre Comoners
for to be of Counseil wit ye Chamberleyns of the Cite....
    In to witnesse of all thynge aforseid ye Mair Shreves and the
Comonalte be ye hool assent of alle ye Cite han in tookne of
ful acord for to be duely kept do sette to her Comone seel and
ye Meir and ye Shreves her seils. Maade atte Norwich on seynt
Valentyns day ye ȝer of Kinge Henry afornseid.

Hudson and Tingey, *op. cit.* I, 93 ff.; cf. lxviii.

(4) *Charter of Henry V* 1417

De gracia nostra...concedimus pro nobis...prefatis Ciuibus et
Communitati quod ipsi et successores sui in perpetuum viginti et
quatuor Conciues suos Ciuitatis predicte in Aldermannos necnon
sexaginta alios Ciues eiusdem Ciuitatis pro Communi Consilio
Ciuitatis illius modo et forma inferius contentis eligere facere et
creare possint qui quidem viginti et quatuor Conciues sic electi
nomen Aldermannorum Ciuitatis Norwici habeant et gerant in
perpetuum. Et quod predicti Maior et Vicecomites in forma
subscripta annuatim eligantur et preficiantur Videlicet omnes
Ciues Ciuitatis illius in eadem commorantes...
    Preterea concessimus...quod si fortassis alique consuetudines
...emendacione indigeant quod tunc Maior Ciuitatis predicte pro
tempore existens ac Aldermanni sive major pars eorum pro tempore existens plenam potestatem...habeant ad nouum remedium
congruum fidei...de assensu predictorum sexaginta Conciuium
pro Communi Consilio Ciuitatis predicte in forma precedenti
annuatim eligendorum sive majoris partis eorundem apponendum
et ordinandum etc.

Hudson and Tingey, *op. cit.* I, 37; cf. lxix.

¹ I.e. not accomptable to the community for any obligations.

OXFORD

Municipal development at Oxford was closely affected by the presence of the University. With two self-governing communities existing in the same place a certain amount of friction was inevitable, and this led to a series of royal letters and grants of privilege(1).

The borough constitution was closely connected with the gild merchant, which had control over the rising craft-gilds. Burgesses or freemen of Oxford were members of the gild,[1] from whose ranks all the officials were chosen. Other townsmen might own free-holds and could be suitors at the Husting, but were not eligible for election to municipal offices(2). Oxford was one of the towns which looked to London as its model.

(1) *Charter of Edward III* 1327

Edvardus Dei gratia Rex Anglie etc.

[Recital of charters of Henry II, John and Edward I.]

Nos autem concessiones...predictas ratas habentes et gratas eas pro nobis et heredibus nostris, quantum in nobis est, predictis Burgensibus ejusdem Ville concedimus et confirmamus, sicut carte predicte rationabiliter testantur. Preterea volentes iisdem Burgensibus gratiam facere ampliorem Concessimus iis...quod, licet ipsi vel eorum predecessores libertatibus vel quietantiis pre-dictis vel earum aliqua, aliquo casu emergente, hactenus usi non fuerint, ipsi tamen et eorum heredes...libertatibus....de cetero nihilominus plene gaudeant et utantur sine occasione vel impedi-mento nostri vel heredum nostrorum seu ministrorum nostrorum quorumcunque. Insuper cum in predicta carta predicti Domini Henrici...contineatur, quod Cives Oxon et Cives London sint de una et eadem consuetudine lege et libertate, et quod habeant omnes libertates..., sicut eas unquam melius habuerunt, et sicut Cives London eas habuerunt, nulla specificatione facta in cartis predictis quibus libertatibus...dicti Cives London utantur. Nos pro securitate et utilitate dictorum Burgensium Oxon,...quasdam libertates...quas dicti Cives London habent prefatis Burgensibus nostris Oxon in forma que sequitur duximus specificandas et con-cedendas. Videlicet, quod nullus eorum placitet vel implacitetur coram nobis vel heredibus nostris aut aliquibus Justiciariis seu ministris nostris vel heredum nostrorum extra predictum Burgum

[1] Cf. *Munimenta Civitatis Oxonie* (ed. Salter), p. xxvii.

Oxon de terris aut tenementis que sunt in Burgo illo aut suburbiis ejusdem nec de transgressionibus...in iisdem Burgo et suburbiis factis vel aliis quibuscunque ibidem emergentibus, sed omnia hujusmodi placita que coram nobis...vel aliquibus Justiciariis nostris...sumoneri contigerit...coram majore et ballivis Burgi illius qui pro tempore fuerint et non aliis infra eundem Burgum placitentur et terminentur, nisi placita illa tangant nos vel heredes nostros vel comunitatem dicti Burgi...

Et quod major et ballivi Burgi predicti...executiones facere possint infra Burgum et suburbia predicta de omnibus coram eis recuperatis et recognitis et dampnis coram eis adiudicatis eodem modo quo faciunt Cives nostri London.

Et quod exnunc scribatur in cancellaria nostra et heredum nostrorum per brevia nostra de recto patentia majori et ballivis Burgi predicti prout scribitur majori et vicecomitibus London. Et quod iidem Burgenses in omnibus actionibus tenementa redditus et tenuras suas predicta tangentibus placitare possint per idem breve nostrum de recto patens certa protestatione inde facienda iuxta formam et naturam cuiuscunque brevis nostri ad eorum electionem placitandi...

Et quod iidem Burgenses...per totam [*sic*] regnum et potestatem nostram tam per terram quam per aquam tam infra London quam extra in omnibus locis libere possint omnimodo mercimonia et victualia tam de alienigenis quam de indigenis emere et ea eis vendere sine impedimento alicuius, sicut Cives nostri London, et prout supra in carta domini Henrici...continetur...

Et quod dicti Burgenses...in perpetuum sint quieti per totum regnum et potestatem nostram de theleonio, muragio pavagio pontagio passagio stallagio lastagio caragio picagio...rivagio ancoragio strandagio chiminagio terragio et de omni alia huiusmodi consuetudine de omnibus rebus bonis et mercandizis suis...

Et quod nullus qui non sit de eorum gilda vina aliqua seu mercimonia aut quecunque alia bona venalia infra dictam villam Oxon vel eius suburbia ad retalliam vendat.

Et quod ipsi heredes et successores sui predicti sint quieti de pecunia danda pro murdro infra Burgum...

Et quod nullus eorum faciat duellum.

Et quod de placitis ad coronam pertinentibus se possint disrationare secundum legem et consuetudinem London.

Et quod Hustengum semel tantum in hebdomada infra Burgum illum teneatur.

Et quod Aldermanni Burgi illius in Aldermannis suis bis in anno tenere possint visum franci plegii, et omnia ea facere que ad visum illum et custodiam pacis nostre pertinent et poterint pertinere. Ita tamen quod cancellario magistris et scolaribus universitatis Oxon super libertatibus...per nos...concessis preiudicium aliquod pretextu concessionis nostre predicte nullatenus generetur...

Datum per manum meam apud Notyngham decimo die maii anno regni nostri primo.

Royal letters addressed to Oxford (ed. Ogle), pp. 36–40.

(2) *Town officers and suitors of the court* 1469

Electio officiariorum die Lune viz. nono die Octobris anno regni regis Edwardi quarti post conquestum nono coram Iohanne Dobbus maiore ville Oxonie, Stephano Havell et Iohanne Atkyns de novo electis pro anno proximo sequente

Aldermanni,	[4 *names*]
Constabularii,	4
Supervisores nocumentorum,	4
Taxatores domorum,	2
Custodes quinque clavium,	5
Custodes clavium ciste communis,	2
Scrutatores carnium,	2
Scrutatores piscium,	2
Serviens maioris,	1
Subballivi,	2
Clamator,	1
Clericus ville,	1
Receptores redditus de le Swyngilstok,	2
Camerarii,	2
Consilium Maioris,	28

Sectatores curie[1] husteng a festo sancti Michaelis anno regni regis Edward IV nono usque idem festum extunc proximo sequens coram Iohanne Dobbus maiore, Stephano Havell et Iohanne Atkyns ballivis de novo electis. 52.

Munimenta Civitatis Oxonie (ed. Salter), pp. 229–31.

[1] Mr Salter, *op. cit.* p. xxvii, says that the burgesses were members of the gild; and the sectatores were owners of freehold who were not burgesses but could be suitors at the Husting.

READING

READING had been on the royal demesne, but in 1125 it was granted by Henry I to the Abbey which he had founded there, and the town came to be so closely supervised by the abbot that it was in danger of losing its independent burghal status. Its only chance of free development was in the gild merchant, which had come to be identified with the borough community. In 1253 an especially fierce quarrel broke out between the abbot and burgesses, and in the final concord of the next year the abbot retained many powers. The extracts given below are taken from the diary of the acts of mayors and burgesses (1431–1602), and they show that the abbot continued to have much authority during the rest of the medieval period. A part of the fines for entrance into the gild was paid to him, and he chose the mayor from a list of three burgesses nominated in the gild. In the later period the municipal government became more aristocratic, the number of burgesses in the gild never reaching fifty. As a result of the prolonged struggle with the abbey the communal rights of the town were gradually recognised, and by the sixteenth century the mayor was holding a weekly court, though the abbot still controlled the port-moot. The town was not free, however, until the abbey was dissolved, after which a royal charter was obtained in 1542.[1]

Extracts from the diary of the corporation of Reading 1432–1507

p. 1

(1432) Die Sabbati [Apr. 12] proximo ante festum Ramis Palmarum electi sunt xxiiij^or Burgenses pro communi Consilio ad tenendum diem cum Abbate Radyngie, videlicet, Thomas Lavyngton [23 *names follow*].

p. 37

(1451) *Tempore Simonis Porter, tunc Majoris ville de Redyngia, die Veneris [Jun. 25] proximo post festum Corporis Christi*, . . .

Ad istam diem fuit facta j billa ad ostendendum consilium Abbatis de Redyngia de articulis Gilde per concensum Majoris et tocius burgi Gilde Merchaunt.

p. 43

(1454) In þe tyme of William Rede, Meyre, and alle þat have be Meyrys, with all þe Bourgeys of þe Geld Halle, byndyth them selfe by þer feyth to abyde a rule as in expence for materys þe

[1] Cf. *Victoria County History, Berkshire*, III, 342–54.

wheche be betwyxt my lord of Redynge and þe same Meyres and
Bourgeys of þe same Gyld.

p. 46

(1456) *Anno regni Regis Henrici sexti xxxv^{to}, Willelmus Rede, Major.*
Tempore Willelmi Rede, tunc Majoris. Ad istam diem Veneris
[Sep. 24] proximo ante festum Sancti Michaelis Archangeli, anno
regni Regis Henrici Sexti post conquestum tricesimo quinto, venit
Gylbertus Sayere et dat de fine ad intrandum Gildam Aulam
Mercatoriam ibidem vjs. et viijd. de qua summa xld. ad pro-
ficuum ejusdem Aule et xld. in Abbathiam, et vjs. et viijd. pro
jantaculo pro Majore et fratribus suis. Plegii Johannes Sayere et
Thomas Beke, et habet diem usque festum Sancti Michaelis
proximum futurum.

p. 49

(1459, May 25)
Willelmus Hunte,
Willelmus Rede, } electi sunt in officium Majoris ville de
Willelmus Pernecote, } Redyngia per omnes Burgenses.
. . . . . .

Willelmus Pernecote die Sancti Michaelis [Sept. 29], anno regni
Regis Henrici Sexti tricesimo octavo, curatus est in officium
Majoratus ville de Redyngia per dominum Johannem Thorne,
abbatem Monasterii Radyngie predicte, cum concensu omnium
Burgensium.
Custodes Alti Vici, Ricardus Goldsmyth et Willelmus Wylcokes.
Custodes Novi Vici, Robertus Carpentere et Herre Barton.
Custodes Vici London, Robertus Cotelere et Johannes Nicholl.
Custodes Veteris Vici, Johannes Nayssche et Harre Aleweke.
Custodes de Mynsterward, Johannes Alaw et Thomas Colver-
howse.

Willelmus Rede, } electi sunt Burgenses Parliamenti domini
Willelmus Lynacre, } Regis, anno regni regis Henrici Sexti
} xxxviij°.
. . . . . .

Sectatores pecuniarum Willelmi Rede et Willelmi Lynacre,
Burgensium Parliamenti tenti apud Coventre, vicesimo die Novem-
bris, anno regni Regis Henrici Sexti xxxviij°.
Collectores earundem pecuniarum Thomas Tanner et Johannes
Hastyng.
. . . . . .

Johannes Walker electus est in officium constabularii cum Roberto Stapper existente in officio predicto.

p. 98

(1499) The seid day and yere [Dec. 10] the seid Richard Cleche, Mayor, discharged Robert Benett and John Tornour of the office of the Constabulles, which were elected and chosen by the Abbott and not by the eleccion of the seid Mayor, ne bi his predecessours, ne yit of the Comburgensis of the seid Gilde.

p. 105

(1507) *The decree.*

It is to be had in mynde...that in the yere of oure Lord God M^{l}ccccvij,...in the tyme of Cristyn Nicolas, then being Mayre of the Gilde Merchaunte of the burghe of Redyng, certayne variauncez...were dependyng betwene abbot John Thorne, lorde of Redynge forseid, and the Mayre and Burgesses of the same, by the space of xix yeres before the date above writen, for approving of the Corporacion of the seid Gilde Merchaunte, for ordering of Constables and Wardens, with other articles, which grevons...the foreseid Mayre with Richard Cleche and Thomas Carpenter, burgessez and late Mayres of the seid Gylde,...shewyd unto Doctour Fox, Lord Prive Seale, Bysshoppe of Wynchestre, and to Lorde Daubeney, Chamberlayn to our saide Soverayne Lorde, for the whiche the same Lordes wyllinge and desyringe the seid Maire, Richard and Thomas, Burgessez,...t'abyde the dyrection of Robert Rede, knyght, Cheif Justice of the Comen Benche at Westmynstere, and John Kyngesmylle, Justice of the same Benche, wherupon the seid Justicez...gave sentence and affermyd the seid Maire and Burgessez of the seid Gilde Merchaunte to be Corporat, ande concernyng alle other the premissis, for a fulle conclusioun and a contynualle peace betwene the parties aforeseid for evir to be had...it is advysed by the seid Lorde and Justices that the Burgeses of the seide Gylde shalle name and present iij^e good and able Burgeses of the seid Gylde to the seid Abbot yerely...and in the same Monastery desyer and pray the same Abbot...to chose and admytt one of the same iij^e persones to be Keper of the seid Gylde...And also that alle other thynges and articles comprised in the same fyne shalbe bytwene the seide Abbot and the forseid Keper of the seid Gylde and Burgeses therof fermely observed and kept according to th'effecte and purporte of the same fyne.

...And for election of ij° Constables and x Wardmen of v Wardes,...it is moved by the seide Lorde and Justices that the seid Abbot shalle suffer the Keper of the seide Gylde and the Commenalte, howseholders of the seide towne...to chose one able and dyscrete persone of the Burgeses of the seide Gylde to be one Constable, and v honest Burgeses to be v of the Wardmene... and also the seide Keper, Burgeses, and Comynnalte,...to chose an other able persone of the same Comynnalte at large, beyng no Burges of the seide Gylde, to be the other Constable,...and other v able persones...and no Burgeses therof to be th'other v Wardmen...and alle the same electiouns to be made in the Lete and Lawday of the seid Abbot of his seid towne, and also bothe the seid Constables and x Wardmene to be admytted and solemply sworne onely in the same Lete and Lawday, before the Stewarde of the seide Abbot...

And as to makyng of Burgeses of the seide Gylde it is dyrected... that whensoever any persone shalbe abled and named by the Keper and Burgeses of the seide Gylde to be a Burges of the same, that then the Keper...shalle shew the seid Abbot therof by the space of fortenyghte next before the same persone shalbe made Burges, and requyre the same Abbot,...to assigne a monke of the same Monastery to surveie and be present at cessyng of the fyne...the one halfe of every suche fyne to be leveid to the use of the seide Abbot...and the other halfe therof to the use of the seid Keper and Burgeses of the seide Gylde...

Diary of the corporation of Reading (ed. Guilding), vol. i.

SOUTHAMPTON

The great importance of Southampton was due to its trade, especially with foreign parts. It was also a town on the royal demesne, and the king's officials long exercised considerable control over municipal affairs. This was especially the case with the constable of the castle, who retained his authority much longer than did the other constables and seriously diminished the importance of the mayor. Another striking characteristic is the great strength of the gild merchant, and the amalgamation of gild and borough as early as at the beginning of the fourteenth century. Before that time the gildsmen held all the principal offices in the town; eventually the gild alderman became the mayor, the burgesses were those townsmen who were members of the gild, and the gild book became known as the "burgess book" (1). Other townsmen might be "franchisers", who were burgesses of old standing not belonging to the gild, or "strangers", who had no privileges though they might be allowed to reside in the town.

The town government was in no sense democratic, although the community as distinct from the burgesses is occasionally mentioned as giving consent and sharing in elections. The mayor was not chosen by the community, but only selected from two candidates nominated to the meeting by the outgoing mayor.

In 1445 the town received formal incorporation (4), and in 1447 was made into a county (5). The government, however, became increasingly oligarchical, and only a few of the gildsmen came to the council. This body, known as "the bench", took the place of all the burgesses, and the share of the community was diminished, although efforts were made to prevent this by the ordinances of 1491 (7).

(1) *Proceedings of the borough court* 1392–1414

I, p. 4. *Ordinance concerning strangers.* Sept. 25, 1392.

Die mercurii proximo ante festum Sancti Michaelis Archangeli anno regni regis Ricardi II[di] xvi[mo] ordinatum est et concordatum per maiorem et communitatem quod quilibet burgensis et alius commorans infra libertatem ville Suthamptone seu commoraturus et respondebit versus alienigenos et extraneos in placito pedis pulverosi, non obstante aliqua libertate per prius habita seu possessa, in placitis debiti pro aliquibus rebus vel mercimoniis venditis seu emptis infra libertatem predictam. Et quod per inter indigenos seu infra libertatem ville commorantes ac burgenses, placita terminentur in curia Regis ville secundum consuetudinem antehac usitatum.

I, p. 26. *Enrolment of a will.* Sept. 24, 1392.

Approbatio sive inbreviatio testamenti Ricardi Mey senioris burgensis ville predicte facta coram Johanne Polymond tunc maiore, Johanne Flete tunc Ballivo, sectatoribus curie et scabinis[1] in communi advocacione et associatione burgensium die martii proximo ante festum Sancti Michaelis Archangeli anno regni regis Ricardi secundi sextodecimo...

[1] Officials of the gild, and at Southampton specially connected with finance.

I, p. 64. *Assembly.* 1402.

Suthamptona. Curia ibidem tenta coram Thoma Middelyngton tunc ibidem maiore, Henrico Holewey et Willielmo Nicholl tunc ibidem Ballivis, die martis proximo post festum Sancti Valentini Martyris anno Regni Regis Henrici quarti post conquestum tercio.

I, p. 96. *Assembly.* 1406.

Suthamptona. Congregacio facta sive assemblement burgensium tenta ibidem coram Willielmo Overey tunc ibidem maiore, W. Ravenston, R. Bradewey et H. Holewey aldremannis, J. Beneyt, W. Nicholl et T. Welles de probioribus hominibus ville Suthamptone, J. Cosyn et T. Armorer Ballivis, die martis in vigilia concepcionis beate Marie virginis Anno regni regis Henrici quarti octavo.

I, p. 120. *Changes in the title of the court.* Oct. 15, 1409.

Suthamptona. Curia Domini Regis tenta apud Suthamptonam...coram Johanne Beneyt maiore, Johanne Maschall et Thoma Armorer ballivis ville predicte anno regni regis Henrici quarti undecimo.

I, p. 146. March 13, 1414.

Suthampton. Ad curiam communem domini Regis tentam apud Suthamptonam coram Johanne Beneyt tunc ibidem maiore et Thoma Regald alias dicto Thoma Belle et Thoma Armorer Ballivis, etc., die martis proximo post festum Sancti Gregorii pape Anno regni regis Henrici quinti post conquestum primo.

I, p. 152. April 15, 1414.

Suthamptona curia communis domini Regis tenta apud Suthamptonam coram Johanne Beneyt tunc ibidem maiore ville Suthamptone, Thoma Armorer et Thoma Regald ibidem tunc Ballivis, Petro Jamys ad tunc ibidem Senescallo, die martis proximo post quintumdecimum diem mensis Aprilis anno regni regis Henrici quinti post conquestum Anglie secundo.

[*The inclusion of the steward is exceptional.*]

II, p. 2. Nov. 10, 1414.

Suthamptona. Congregatione facta sive Assemblement Burgensium tenta coram Johanne Mascall tunc ibidem Maiore Johanne Beneyt, Willielmo Nycoll et Johanne Renawd eiusdem ville tunc Aldremannis Waltero Fetplace tunc ibidem Ballivo ac aliis de probioribus hominibus ville Suthamptone predicte Die

Sabbati decimo die Novembris, Anno regni regis Henrici quinti post conquestum secundo.

Southampton Black Book.

(2) *Charter of Henry V* 1415

Henricus, dei gracia Rex Angliae et Franciae et Dominus Hiberniae omnibus ad quos presentes litterae pervenerint salutem.

Sciatis quod nos debilitati et depauperationi villae nostrae Southampton, compatientes volentesque pro relevatione eiusdem providere, de gratia nostra speciali concessimus et licentiam dedimus pro nobis et heredibus nostris quantum in nobis est, Maiori et Burgensibus villae predictae quod ipsi et successores sui Maiores et Burgenses ibidem terras tenementa et redditus infra procinctum villae predictae cuiuscumque feodi existentis ad valorem Centum librarum per annum iuxta verum valorem eorundem adquirere possint habenda et tenenda sibi et successoribus suis predictis in auxilium supportationis onerum villae predictae incumbencium imperpetuum, statuto de terris et tenementis ad manum mortuam non ponendis edito non obstante. Dumtamen per inquisiciones inde in forma debita capiendas et in Cancellaria nostra vel heredum nostrorum rite retornandas compertum sit quod id fieri possit absque dampno seu preiudicio nostro vel heredum nostrorum aut aliorum quorumcumque. In cuius rei testimonium has litteras nostras fieri fecimus patentes. Teste me ipso apud Westmonasterium, duodecimo die Februarii, anno regni nostri secundo.

Charters of...Southampton (ed. Gidden), i, 38.

(3) *Charter of Henry VI* 1426

Henricus dei gratia *etc....*

(*Inspeximus of charter of Henry IV 1401*)

......

Concessimus pro nobis et haeredibus nostris quantum in nobis est eisdem Burgensibus et eorum haeredibus et successoribus Burgensibus villae predictae imperpetuum quod Maior[1] et Ballivi villae predictae pro tempore existentes habeant cogniciones omnium placitorum realium et personalium ac mixtorum tam assisarum et certificacionum quam aliorum quorumcumque de omnibus tenementis et tenuris infra villam et libertatem predictas

---

[1] In 1249 the town had received a curious grant that it should never be governed by a mayor.

existentibus, necnon de omnimodis transgressionibus debitis, compotis, convencionibus et aliis contractibus quibuscumque infra
easdem villam et libertatem tam in terra quam in aqua emergendis
seu faciendis videlicet in Guyhalda villae predictae coram eis
tenendis et per eosdem maiorem et ballivos ibidem plenarie et
finaliter terminandis...
Teste me ipso apud Westmonasterium, vicessimo quarto die
Octobris, anno regni nostri quarto.

Gidden, *op. cit.* I, 40 ff.

(4) *Charter of Henry VI* 1445

Henricus dei gratia etc...de gratia nostra speciali et ex mero
motu et certa scientia nostris concessimus et hac presenti carta
nostra confirmavimus...prefatis Burgensibus ac eorum haeredibus
et successoribus Burgensibus villae predictae imperpetuum libertates, franchesias, quietantias et immunitates subscriptas, videlicet quod villa de uno maiore duobus Ballivis et Burgensibus sit
imperpetuum corporata, et quod iidem Maior, Ballivi et Burgenses
et successores sui maiores, Ballivi et Burgenses villae illius sic
corporatae sint una communitas perpetua corporata in re et
nomine per nomen Maioris, Ballivorum et Burgensium villae
illius habeantque successionem perpetuam, et quod iidem Maior,
Ballivi et Burgenses et successores sui predicti per idem nomen
sint personae habiles in lege ad omnimoda placita, sectas, querelas
et demandas...prosequenda et defendenda...
p. 68. Datum per manum nostram apud Westmonasterium
vicessimo nono die Julij, anno regni nostri vicessimo tertio.

Gidden, *op. cit.* I, 54 ff.

(5) *Charter of Henry VI* 1452

p. 86. Henricus dei gratia *etc*...concessimus et per presentes
concedimus prefatis Maiori, Ballivis et Burgensibus et successoribus
suis quod villa nostra predicta cum suburbiis, procinctu et locis
predictis sit unus integer comitatus corporatus in re et nomine ac
distinctus et penitus separatus a comitatu Suthampton imperpetuum, et quod idem comitatus villae Suthampton sic corporatus,
distinctus et separatus a comitatu Suthampton comitatus noster
villae Suthampton pro perpetuo nominetur, nuncupetur et appel-
letur. Et quod Maior, Ballivi et Burgenses predicti et successores
sui habeant in eadem villa unum vicecomitem in forma subscripta

eligendum, videlicet, quod Burgenses eiusdem villae et successores sui quolibet anno, videlicet dicto die Veneris in loco supradicto unum de comburgensibus suis discretum, habilem et idoneum in vicecomitem eiusdem villae eligere valeant, et ipsum in vice-comitem eiusdem villae perficere et creare...

p. 96. Data per manum nostram apud Westmonasterium, duo-decimo die Septembris anno regni nostri tricesimo.

Per breve de privato sigillo et de data predicta auctoritate Parliamenti.

Gidden, *op. cit.* 1, 82 ff.

(6) *Ordinances; growth of oligarchy* (?) late fifteenth century

p. 120. No man oughte to come or enter, when the Counsell of the Towne setteth, excepte he be of the sayde counsell, vnlesse he be called thervnto by Mr. Mayor and his bretheren.

p. 126. Every yere...in the common assemblie, ther shalbe chosen by all the consente of Burgesses, in the gilde hall, or some other decent place...xij. of the Burgeasses with the Bailifes, to be assistante for the yere followinge to the mayor...And besides the saide xij., their shalbe chosen, the same daie, the Shryve, Bailiffes, Constables and all other officers of the discretiste and moste metest Burgesses, to serue the Kinges majestie and the Towne for the yere followinge...

p. 147. Noe man, not being free of this Corporacion, eyther by byrth or seruice, shall hereafter be admitted to be sworne a Burgesse, without the Consent of the greater part of the sayd Corporacion. And that noe man hereafter be made Burgesse, but that he shall be sworne at his admittance.

The oak book, 1, Appendix B, 120, 126, 147.

(7) *Ordinances* 1491

Item, first that the Gilde be holde and kept duly and truly at ij. tymes of the yere, lik as it is in the paxbrede[1] plainly specified. And at the holding of euery such Gilde, All the Articles, pointes, Statutes, constitucions, ordinaunces, and prouisions of the seid Gilde and of the ffranchies of this towne shalbe openly shewed and declared.

5. Item, that the xij Juries, that shalbe prouided at eny assemble of eleccion of Meires of this towne, to chese other Officers as

---

[1] Oak book.

Shirves, Bailives, Stuardys and other, be chose and electe by comune vois of the hole Assemble, and not be empanelled, not electe by eleccion of the bench only, as is ordeyned in con- stitucions of king Henry, Son of King John. And that the seid xij. Juries be helping to the Maire, Shrive, and Bailyves, supporting and strenghthing theym to execute the lawe in all that yere folowing after suche eleccion of the Maire...

The oak book, I, Appendix C, 151, 152.

GLOSSARY

afferer, to carry, attach, fasten.
affier, to swear, promise, trust.
afforter, to help, sustain.
agaite (*ageyt*), ambush.
agarder, to examine, award.
aignel, lamb.
aketon (*acton, haqueton*), a padded jacket.
aresoner, to question, summon.
arrerissement, violation, damage.
asparte, violence.
assoiler, to shrive.
avouerie, advowson, the right of nominating a clerk to a benefice.

bacinet, a small metal headpiece.
barettour, quarreller.
baterie, unlawful attack.
berbitz, sheep.
brief, writ.
brocage, corrupt farming of offices.

chandellure, feast of the Purification of the B. V. Mary.
chivache (*chevache*), expedition on horseback; a raid.
coillour, collector.
collacion, collation, bestowal by a cleric of a benefice on another, or appointment to a living.
corouce, despiteful, angry.
covyne, following, condition, situation.
custages, expense.
custumers, officials of the customs.

defesaunce, destruction, damage.

eire, circuit.

emblemissement, violation, injury.
encheson, reason, cause.
engyner, to invent, deceive.
esbaudir, to rejoice, encourage.
esclaundre, to slander.
escomengement, excommunication.
escuage, scutage.
espernir, to spare, save.
esteintz, abolished, extinguished.
esteym, tin.
estore, flock, fleet.
estrete, estreat, a true copy, payment.
Everwyk, York.
exigende, writ ordering the sheriff to summon defendant to appear in court on pain of outlawry.

ferme, fixed yearly rent.
fesance, making, action.
filace, file.
forspris, except.
forsque, except.

gaignerie, trade of sheath-making.
garbe, sheaf.
garnir, to defend, warn.
gaster, to save.
gasteyns, wastes.
gisantz, lying.
grosser, to engross.
guiement, guidance.

hanaper, department of chancery into which fees were paid for the sealing and enrolling of documents.

harez, stud.
hobeller, light horseman.
hostiel, household.
hundreder, chief official of the hundred.

Kardoil, Carlisle.

maheymes, mayhem, maim.
malveistes, evil deeds.
meffaire, to do wrong.
meffesour (*mefesour*), offender.
meintenour, supporter.
meneng (*mesneng*), servant, household official.
mesprision, offence.
mestier (*mistier*), trade, craft, gild.
mestier, need, necessity.
meynpernables, capable of being mainprised.
meynprise, action of procuring release of a prisoner by becoming surety for his appearance.
mustracer, to present.

Nichol (*Nicole*), Lincoln.

od, with.
oeps, use.
oytaves (*octaves*), period of eight days after and including a festival.

panelle, list of jurymen; jury.
pealx lanutz, wool-fells.
pilour, disturber of the peace.
plum, lead.

procuratour, proctor.
proveaunces, provisions.
provendre, provision of food, prebend.
purveour, purveyor, official who made purveyance for royal journeys, etc.

quir, leather.

rembrancie, office of the remembrancer.
resceant, resident.
rounceoun (*ranceon*), ransom.

sustretz, subtracted.
suturez, suitors, those who attend court.

Tiphaine, la, festival of the Epiphany.
tonell, cask, barrel.
trelsbastons, trailbastons, violent disturbers of the peace, against whom special commissions of justices were set up.
tuzon (*toison*), fleece.

utlager, to outlaw.

vadlet, servant.
verge, an area subject to the jurisdiction of the Lord Steward, within a 12-mile radius of the court.
viscont (*viscount*), sheriff.
voidance, vacancy.

LATIN TERMS

advocacio (*advocatio*), advowson.
affidare, to pledge faith.
agistator, agister, an official who assigns pasturage in a forest, collects fees, etc.

amerciare, to fine.
ancoragium, anchor dues.
appellare, to appeal; (special sense) when an individual brought a criminal charge against another.

GLOSSARY

assartum, see *essartum*.
attachiamentum, attachment, seizure of a person or of goods.
attachiare, to arrest, seize goods, to take in pursuance of a writ.
attornatus, a substitute.
averia, cattle.

balliva, bailiwick.
bersare, to hunt, shoot.
braciator, brewer.
breve, writ.
butillaria, buttery.

cambipartio, champerty; illegal proceeding whereby a party helps one of the litigants in a suit, on condition of receiving part of the property if successful.
camerarius, chamberlain.
cancellarius, chancellor.
capitales plegii, chief pledges, in charge of the tithings.
Carniprivium, Lent.
certiorare, to inform.
cheminagium (*chiminagium*), toll paid for the use of roads, repair of roads.
cista, chest.
cleiae, hurdles.
cognicio (*cognitio*), cognisance.
comitatus, county.
comitiva, a company.
communia (pl.), ordinary business of a court.
compotus, account.
contrafactura, counterfeiting.
contra-rotulus, counter-roll.
coquina, kitchen.
coronator, coroner.
custuma, custom, tax.
cyrographum (*chirographum*), chirograph, an indenture, a legal document written in duplicate or triplicate.

dampnum (*damnum*), damage.
decennarius, tithingman.
deforcians, defendant.
defortiare, to deforce, dispossess by violence.
dispensaria, steward's room.
disseisire (*dissaisire*), to dispossess.
districcio (*districtio*), distress, the action of distraining, legal seizure of a chattel.
distringere, to distrain, force.

elemosina pura, libera, frankalmoign, free alms, tenure freed from secular services.
elongare, eloign.
escaetor (*excaetor*), escheator.
essartum, a clearing in a wood.
essoniator, essoiner, one who excuses another for non-attendance at a court.
exigenda, writ of exigent; see French glossary.
exitus, issue.
expeditare, to law a dog, to cut the ball of the foot or three claws of a dog to prevent it from being used in hunting.

feodelitas, fealty.
feodum, fee, fief.
feoffare, to enfeoff.
filacium, a file.
finis, fine, a payment made to procure the end of a lawsuit or a royal favour, i.e. a composition, rather than an arbitrary fine; cf. *finali sconcordia*, final concord.
firma, a fixed payment, farm, yearly rent.
forisfactum, forfeiture.
forstallare, to forestall; to buy goods in advance.
forstallatores, forestallers.

garderoba, wardrobe.

hamsoca, attack upon a man's house.
hanaperium, hanaper, a department of chancery; *see* French glossary.
hustengum, hustings, a court in some towns.
hutesium, hue, calling for pursuit of a felon.

implacitare, to sue.
irrotulare, to enrol.

jurata, jury.

langabulum, land-gafol, rent from land.
lastagium, customary payment for goods sold by the last (measure).
leta, leet, a criminal court.
liberatura (*liberata*), livery.
ligantia, allegiance, liege, homage.
ligula, a file.

mahemium, mayhem, the crime of maiming a person.
manucapere, to mainprise, to become surety for a person.
manucaptor, a mainpernor, one who stands surety for another's appearance at court.
marescalcia, office of marshal, the marshalsea.
mesprisio (*misprisio*), misprision, misdemeanour, concealment of a crime.
minagium, toll on corn, wine, sold by the *mina* (measure).
misericordia, mercy, a fine at the discretion of king or overlord, etc.
mistera, craft.
muragium, toll for the repair of town wall.

namium, distress, seizure.

ordinarius, an ecclesiastical officer connected with justice.

passagium, toll for passage.
pavagium, payment for paving roads.
picagium, payment to owner of land for setting up booths.
pistor, baker.
placitum, plea.
plegium, a pledge.
plegius, a person pledging himself for another's appearance.
pontagium, payment of toll on a bridge; tax for repair of bridges.
prestitum, advance of money.
procurator, proctor.
purprestura, encroachment in a forest.

querens, complainant, plaintiff.
quindena, a period of fifteen days.

recognicio (*recognitio*), recognizance, a legal obligation.
regardator, regarder; see *regardum.*
regardum, regard, inspection, view; inspection of forests every three years by 12 knights (regarders).
regratarius, regrator, retailer, one who buys goods to sell at a profit.
rememorator, remembrancer.
rescussus, rescue.
respectus, respite.
retropannagium, money paid for pasturing pigs after normal season is over.

scabella, measure of land; small stool.
scabinus, town official.

scaccarium, exchequer.

secta, suit.

sectator, suitor.

seisina, possession as of freehold.

serura, lock.

sessor, assessor.

stallagium, right to have a stall in the market.

strandagium, payment to beach a boat, etc.

tallia, tally, a notched stick given as a receipt.

tastator cervisiae, aletaster.

terragium, land tax.

thelonium (*theolonium*), toll.

turnum, tourn, the royal leet; court held by the sheriff twice a year.

ulnagium, duty on cloth.

ulnator, ulnager, official who examined the quality of woollen goods, etc.

utlagare, to outlaw.

utlagaria, outlawry.

vadium, pledge (an object, not a person).

venacio (*venatio*), right of hunting.

vicecomes, sheriff.

virgata, virgate, the quarter of a hide.

viridarius, verderer, an official of the forest.

visus franci plegii, view of frank-pledge.

warantizare, to warrant, to confirm title, authorise.

withernamium, carrying off goods already distrained by an official.

INDEX